DELINQUENCY IN SOCIETY

Youth Crime in the 21st Century

Seventh Edition

Robert M. Regoli
University of Colorado

John D. Hewitt
Grand Valley State University

Matt DeLisi
Iowa State University

Mc
Graw
Hill

Boston   Burr Ridge, IL   Dubuque, IA   Madison, WI   New York
San Francisco   St. Louis   Bangkok   Bogotá   Caracas   Kuala Lumpur
Lisbon   London   Madrid   Mexico City   Milan   Montreal   New Delhi
Santiago   Seoul   Singapore   Sydney   Taipei   Toronto

Published by McGraw-Hill, an imprint of The McGraw-Hill Companies, Inc., 1221 Avenue of the Americas, New York, NY 10020. Copyright © 2008, 2006, 2003, 2000, 1997, 1994, 1991. All rights reserved. No part of this publication may be reproduced or distributed in any form or by any means, or stored in a database or retrieval system, without the prior written consent of The McGraw-Hill Companies, Inc., including, but not limited to, in any network or other electronic storage or transmission, or broadcast for distance learning.

This book is printed on acid-free paper.

1 2 3 4 5 6 7 8 9 0 WCK/WCK 0 9 8 7

ISBN: 978-0-07-340154-6
MHID: 0-07-340154-4

Editor in Chief: *Michael Ryan*
Publisher: *Frank Mortimer*
Sponsoring Editor: *Katie Stevens*
Marketing Manager: *Leslie Oberhuber*
Developmental Editor: *Teresa Treacy*
Project Manager: *Paul Wells*
Production Service: *Newgen*
Manuscript Editor: *Newgen–Austin*
Design Manager: *Margarite Reynolds*
Cover Designer: *Margarite Reynolds*
Photo Research: *Inge King*
Production Supervisor: *Dennis Fitzgerald*
Composition: *10/12 Sabon by Newgen*
Printing: *PMS 484, 45# New Era Matte, Quebecor World, Inc.*

Cover: ©1996 Digital Stock

Credits: The credits section for this book begins on page **591** and is considered an extension of the copyright page.

Library of Congress Cataloging-in-Publication Data

Regoli, Robert M.
    Delinquency in society / Robert Regoli, John Hewitt, Matt DeLisi.
        p. cm.
    Includes bibliographical references and indexes.
    ISBN-13: 978-0-07-340154-6 (alk. paper)
    ISBN-10: 0-07-340154-4 (alk. paper)
    1. Juvenile delinquency—United States.   2. Juvenile justice, Administration of—United States.
    I. Hewitt, John D., 1945–   II. DeLisi, Matt.   III. Title.
HV9104.R43 2008
364.360973—dc22

2007025203

The Internet addresses listed in the text were accurate at the time of publication. The inclusion of a Web site does not indicate an endorsement by the authors or McGraw-Hill, and McGraw-Hill does not guarantee the accuracy of the information presented at these sites.

www.mhhe.com

To those who, through the kindness of their hearts, give
blood. You have helped to save my child's life. I am so very
thankful to each and every one of you.
RMR

To my children, Eben Mann Hewitt and Sara Grey Lachman,
who taught me much about adolescence and growing up.
JDH

To autistic children and their families.
MD

Robert M. Regoli is professor of sociology at the University of Colorado. He received his Ph.D. in sociology from Washington State University. Dr. Regoli is a member of Phi Beta Kappa, the author of more than 100 scholarly articles, numerous chapters in scholarly collections, and several books, a former president and Fellow of the Academy of Criminal Justice Sciences, and the recipient of two William J. Fulbright Foundation Awards. His most recent book, coauthored with Professor John D. Hewitt, *Exploring Criminal Justice,* is available from Jones and Bartlett Publishers.

John D. Hewitt is professor of criminal justice at Grand Valley State University in Grand Rapids, Michigan. He received his Ph.D. in sociology from Washington State University. Professor Hewitt is the author or coauthor of four books, including *Exploring Criminal Justice* with Professor Regoli, and more than 50 scholarly articles. His writings have been published in journals such as *Crime & Delinquency, Journal of Social Research, Justice Quarterly, Law and Human Behavior, Law and Policy Quarterly,* and *Social Forces.*

Matt DeLisi is associate professor of sociology and coordinator of the Criminal Justice Studies program at Iowa State University. He received his Ph.D. in sociology from the University of Colorado, having previously worked for five years in a correctional institution. Professor DeLisi is the author of two books, *Career Criminals in Society* and *Criminal Justice: Balancing Crime Control and Due Process,* and more than 50 scholarly articles and chapters.

If it is true that in teaching we learn, we have had the good fortune to do quite a bit of both since the first edition of *Delinquency in Society* was published in 1991. Its continued success is a reflection of what we learn from the comments and suggestions of our students, our colleagues, and their students around the country who read the book. We do enjoy hearing compliments, but we pay very careful attention to the suggestions for improvements. Such suggestions have resulted in a number of changes to the seventh edition, which we have detailed below.

This edition continues to provide a comprehensive theoretical framework for understanding the evolving phenomenon of delinquency and society's response to it. Perhaps more exciting, this edition reflects the major innovations within the discipline that have enhanced the understanding of delinquency. While retaining its sociological core, criminology has become more interdisciplinary, adopted a life course perspective that links childhood misconduct to juvenile delinquency to adult crime, and focuses on the most serious, chronic, and violent offenders. This edition incorporates these themes, especially in Chapters 2, 3, 5, and 8. The most notable change in this edition is the addition of a third author, Matt DeLisi, who brings a new, exciting, and refreshing perspective to our discussion of juvenile crime.

THE SEVENTH EDITION

The seventh edition of *Delinquency in Society* has been thoroughly updated to reflect the most current literature, trends, and developments in criminology, including discussions of the history, institutional context, societal reactions to delinquency, and emerging social policies to prevent adolescent crime. Perhaps the most significant singular change has been the expansion of the theories of delinquency and associated policy implications not only from the fields of sociology, criminology, and criminal justice, but also psychology, human development, neuropsychology, and behavioral genetics. A few examples of changes made in each chapter are presented below:

- Chapter 1, "Defining Delinquency," has been fully updated with an expanded discussion of the relationship between violent video games and juvenile crime.
- Chapter 2, "Measuring Delinquency," has been completely updated with a new section on the overlap between official and victimization measures of crime, a new discussion of the importance of concentrated disadvantage to delinquency, and a new *Window on Delinquency* box providing a profile on juvenile delinquents behind bars. In addition, the section on serious, violent, and chronic juvenile offenders has been greatly expanded.
- Chapter 3, "Violent Youth Crime," has been entirely updated with new sections on juvenile psychopathy, theoretical causes of psychopathy, and

treatment of psychopathic delinquents. There is a greatly revised section on family- and community-based delinquency prevention programs. In addition, there is a new *Window on Delinquency* box about psychopaths and violence.

- Chapter 4, "Illegal Drug Use and Delinquency," has been totally updated and includes a new *Window on Delinquency* box on the science of ecstasy/MDMA. There is also a new section on the delinquency-drugs link based on Terrie Moffitt's developmental taxonomy and an improved and reorganized section on responding to adolescent drug use.

- Chapter 5, "Individual Theories of Delinquency: Choice and Trait Explanations," has been overhauled with new sections on autonomic hypoactivity/ADHD, frontal lobes and executive functioning, hormones and puberty, maternal cigarette smoking, and the interplay between nature and nurture in producing delinquency. There is also a new *Window on Delinquency* box on the dark history of biological criminology.

- Chapter 6, "Sociological Theory: Cultural Deviance, Strain, and Social Control," has an expanded discussion of these major sociological theories and new discussion of the work of Steven Messner and Richard Rosenfeld.

- Chapter 7, "Sociological Theory: Labeling and Conflict Explanations," has been updated from top to bottom with a new section on Frank Cullen's social support theory and its integration with Colvin's coercion theory. There is also a greatly expanded discussion of our own theory of differential oppression, which is becoming more widely accepted by criminologists worldwide. A new *Window on Delinquency* box describes the current status of America's children.

- Chapter 8, "Developmental Theories," has been completely updated and provides an expanded discussion of some of the most contemporary thinking about the causes of juvenile delinquency from a developmental or life course perspective. New additions include discussion of risk and protective factors, and new *Window on Delinquency* boxes on developmental risk factors for delinquency and the effects of child rearing on delinquency.

- Chapter 9, "Female Delinquency Theories," has been fully updated with new sections on gendered pathways into delinquency and recent biological and developmental explanations of delinquency. In addition, there are new *Window on Delinquency* boxes on improving programming for girls and the relationship between attractiveness and delinquency.

- Chapter 10, "The Family and Delinquency," has been updated with three new *Window on Delinquency* boxes that discuss family violence, prisoner parents, and child maltreatment. In addition, the family literature has been recast to reflect the life course perspective of contemporary research.

- Chapter 11, "Schools and Delinquency," has been updated and reorganized with an increased emphasis on bullying. New concepts, such as schools as a source of self-control, communal school organization, and school resource officer programs, as well as new *Window on Delinquency* boxes on school crime statistics and student deaths in American schools have been added.

- Chapter 12, "Peer Group and Gang Delinquency," has been updated and includes an expanded section on gangs and juvenile justice, and new concepts, such as the selection, facilitation, and enhancement models of gang formation. In addition, the chapter contains four new *Window on Delinquency* boxes on why people are group-oriented, MS-13, gang homicides, and the National Gang Threat Assessment.

- Chapter 13, "Police and Delinquency," has a new discussion of sealing and expunging juvenile police records. There is also expanded discussion of the role of legal and extralegal factors and their influence on police discretionary arrest decisions.

- Chapter 14, "The Juvenile Court," has been totally updated and includes new sections on youth courts, juvenile drug courts, the sentencing of juveniles convicted in criminal court, and the use of blended sentences. In addition, there is expanded discussion of restorative justice and the effects of race and sex in detention decisions.

- Chapter 15, "Juvenile Corrections," has expanded discussions of wraparound programs, HIV/AIDS in juvenile institutions, and Intensive Aftercare Programs. There is also new discussion of the use of GPS systems in monitoring juveniles on probation and a new box on the deadly brutality found in a Florida boot camp for juveniles.

OVERVIEW OF CONTENTS

- **Section 1,** "Nature and Extent of Delinquency," introduces students to historical and contemporary perceptions of children and how their misbehaviors have been defined as delinquent. It examines the major sources of data on delinquency and problems with measuring the extent of delinquency. Students are also given in-depth coverage of two of the most critical areas of contemporary delinquency in the chapters on youth violence and illegal drug use.

- **Section 2,** "Explaining Delinquency," provides students with an easy-to-understand discussion of all the major theoretical approaches to explaining juvenile delinquency. Students will be able to examine the substantial contributions of individualistic theories focusing on biological and psychological explanations and the dominant sociological theories ranging from social disorganization, strain, and social control to labeling, conflict, and developmental theories, as well as specialized explanations of female delinquency.

- **Section 3,** "The Social Context of Delinquency," contextualizes delinquency within three major social settings: the family, the school, and peer groups and the gang. Students will be introduced to provocative discussions dealing with the relationship of family structure and process on delinquency, the nature of delinquency within schools and how schools may contribute to the problem of delinquency, and the extensive problems related to peer-group relations and juvenile gangs.

- **Section 4,** "The Juvenile Justice System," examines the formal societal response to delinquency within the context of the police, the courts, and corrections. Each chapter provides extensive, cutting-edge coverage of procedures and issues critical in the juvenile justice system's attempt to prevent and control delinquency.

LEARNING AIDS

The seventh edition of *Delinquency in Society* contains many of the outstanding pedagogical features introduced in previous editions.

- **Chapter Outlines.** Each chapter begins with an easy-to-follow outline of the major topics that will be discussed. These outlines immediately alert students to the central issues of the chapter as well as to the order in which they are presented.

- **Think about It Questions.** Each chapter contains a wealth of provocative questions focusing on important issues. The questions are located in the margins next to the topics they explore further and are designed to stimulate discussion in class and sharpen student critical thinking.

- **Critical Thinking Questions for Photographs.** The variety of new photographs in the book are accompanied by intriguing questions or extended narratives designed to encourage critical thinking.

- **Theory in a Nutshell Asides.** Many students have difficulty grasping the differences among the various theories of behavior. To make theories more manageable and understandable, each of the more important theories is presented in brief encapsulated form.

- **Key Terms and Subject Glossary.** Students are provided with succinct definitions of commonly used terms and descriptions of important concepts found in bold type throughout the text. For easy reference when students are preparing for exams, each chapter's key terms are defined at the end of the chapter in addition to being included in the Glossary.

- **Name and Subject Indexes.** Separate name and subject indexes are provided at the end of the book to help students in their search for particular issues or concerns.

- **Unique and Exciting Boxes.** To make the text more relevant and interesting for students, we have created four different thematic boxes and inserted them where appropriate within the text:

  - **A Window on Delinquency.** A series of boxes discussing various facets of delinquency personalize the story of delinquency and bring into focus the different life situations of victims and offenders.

  - **Delinquency Around the Globe.** Thematic boxes providing students with brief glimpses into the nature of delinquency in other countries allow students to consider the similarities and differences among nations.

  - **From the Bench.** These boxes focus on the critical judicial decisions in the area of juvenile justice and help students to better understand the impact of legal rulings on the behavior and rights of children.

  - **Delinquency Prevention.** These thematic boxes focus on issues related to the prevention, reduction, or control of delinquency. Some of the programs discussed are well established and appear to most criminologists to be effective in achieving their goals. Other programs discussed hold great promise but are relatively new and untested.

SUPPLEMENTS

Visit our Online Learning Center Web site at www.mhhe.com/Regoli7.

For the Student

- On the student side of this open-access, book-specific Web site is content organized by chapter for ease of use in studying for exams or writing papers. This content includes quizzes with instant feedback so students can prepare for exams; flashcards, for studying key terms; and a link to *Theoretical Developments in Juvenile Delinquency* featuring brief descriptive essays and suggested reading.

For the Instructor

On the password-protected instructor side of the Web site, supplements include:

- *Instructor's Manual/Test Bank*. Chapter outlines, key terms, overviews, lecture notes, discussion questions, a complete test bank, and more.
- *Computerized Test Bank*. Easy-to-use computerized testing program for both Windows and Macintosh computers.
- *PowerPoint Slides*. Complete chapter-by-chapter slide shows featuring text, tables, and illustrations.
- *Course Management Systems Cartridges*. Available with our OLC content for professors who choose to teach the course online.

We would like to thank our team at McGraw-Hill for their continued support of *Delinquency in Society*. Our Publisher, Frank Mortimer, and Senior Editor Katie Stevens provided us with encouragement and guidance throughout the project. We thank our Developmental Editor Teresa Treacy, who was always available to answer our many questions, and for her active role in developing the outstanding supplement program that accompanies the seventh edition for students and professors. We also greatly appreciate the hard work on the project by Paul Wells, senior production editor, Shirley Michels, production coordinator for Newgen, and Inge King, our photo editor, who directed the spectacular photo program that is presented in the seventh edition of the text.

We also thank our colleagues and students for their solicited and unsolicited insights, guidance, criticism, and assistance, with special thanks to Rosalie Arndt, Rachel Bandy, Gregg Barak, Allison Bayless, Kevin Beaver, Joanne Belknap, Janet Behrens, Ingrid Bennett, Mark Berg, Dennis Blewitt, Bob Bohm, Phil Butcher, Lisa Campione, Sue Caulfield, Todd Clear, Mark Colvin, Sarah Corcoran, Frank Cullen, Brendan Dooley, John Fuller, Sarah Getman, Michelle Goetz, Lindsey Grall, Mark Hamm, Laura Hettinger, Andy Hochstetler, Lou Holscher, Charles Hou, James Houston, Peter Iadicola, Christopher Kierkus, Beverly Kingston, Paul Lasley, Richard Lawrence, Jean McGloin, Gloria Mendoza, Tiare Moorman, Bill Miller, Katie Murphy, Hal Pepinsky, Alex Piquero, Nicole Piquero, Eric Primm, Beverly Quist, Mike Radelet, Tom Reed, Adam Regoli, George Rivera, Rick Rogers, Eric Schwartz, Madison Serdinak, Chad Simcox, Vic Streib, Terry Thornberry, Laura VanderDrift, Amanda VanHoose, Michael Vaughn, Regina Verna, Lisa Hutchinson Wallace, Jules Wanderer, Ralph Weisheit, Tom Winfree, and John Wright.

Other colleagues who were selected by McGraw-Hill to review the text helped improve this seventh edition in innumerable ways. We extend our sincere gratitude to

L. Ann Butzin, *Owens Community College*

Geoffrey Grant, *South Dakota State University*

Howard Kurtz, *Oklahoma City University*

Elena Natalizia, *Mount Wachusett Community College*

Jay Watterworth, *Metro State College of Denver*

Karen Weston, *Gannon University–Erie*

Roy L. Austin, *Pennsylvania State University*

Alan S. Bruce, *Quinnipiac University*

James J. Chriss, *Cleveland State University*

Timothy Hart, *College of the Sequoias*

Mary Jackson, *East Carolina University*

David F. Machell, *Western Connecticut State University*

David Mackey, *Framingham State College*

John Quicker, *California State University, Dominguez Hills*

Todd Schroer, *University of Southern Indiana*

Theresa A. Severance, *Eastern Connecticut State*

Stanley L. Swart, *University of North Florida*

Kevin Thompson, *North Dakota State University*

Major writing projects always take their toll on those people closest to the authors; for us, those people are our wives. We would like to give very special thanks to Debbie, Avis, and Melissa, who have stood beside us as we worked on this project, providing encouragement, love, and both solicited and unsolicited insights that strengthened the final product.

Robert M. Regoli
robertregoli@comcast.net

John D. Hewitt
hewittj@gvsu.edu

Matt DeLisi
delisi@iastate.edu

As is true of most people, we are interested in the plight of young people. We are curious about their likes and dislikes, their choices of music, fashion, and hobbies, as well as their selection of friends. It is fascinating to try to understand their reactions to others and the reactions of others to them. As criminologists, we are particularly interested in their behaviors, both normative and deviant, and the choices they make. Sometimes their choices will tempt them and lead them astray while at other times it will keep them on the straight and narrow.

Reading through this edition of *Delinquency in Society,* we were reminded of the key readings of our graduate educations, and it became clear that no topic in criminology has been as central as the study of juvenile delinquency and juvenile justice. Whether you are a student of criminal career research or of white-collar crime, the origins of such subfields would not be completely understood without an understanding of juveniles and their delinquency. As a result of its history and prominence in criminology, much has been written, argued, and summarized about juveniles and crime; however, this line of research has not been effectively and efficiently summarized from both a 35,000-foot view and a 500-foot view. That is, until now.

Since the first edition in 1991, and continuing with this seventh edition, Regoli and his colleagues have done the field a wonderful service. Not only have they produced a masterfully written text, but as prominent scholars and teachers they have translated their passion for the topic of juvenile delinquency into a comprehensive text that provides students, both traditional and lifelong learners, with a glimpse into the world of juveniles, focusing not only on their deviant and criminal behaviors but also looking to help us understand the causes and correlates of delinquency. The study of the journey of the delinquent is not complete without a firm appreciation of how the justice system handles and deals with these young deviants. In this regard, *Delinquency in Society* represents the field's best inter- and multi-disciplinary thinking with regard to issues surrounding juvenile delinquency and juvenile justice.

We both have been quite impressed with the coverage, comprehensiveness, and readability of this text. Not only did it allow us to reflect upon our own introductions to criminology and its core components, it also taught us a great deal more about delinquency and juvenile justice and how central this strand of research is to all key components of criminological inquiry. As such, we believe that we have become better communicators of this literature, which, in turn, will make our students better consumers—and ultimately users—of such information.

We are especially honored and privileged to have been asked to write this foreword for such esteemed colleagues and to be associated with this book. We are convinced that in short order, you will find yourself in agreement with us that this book will challenge and expand your thinking on issues related to juvenile delinquency and juvenile justice, and that it will do the same for your students. As simultaneous teachers and students, we could ask for nothing more, and Regoli and colleagues give us nothing less.

Alex R. Piquero & Nicole Leeper Piquero
John Jay College of Criminal Justice / City University
of New York Graduate Center

section 1

Nature and Extent of Delinquency

outline

SECTION 1 INTRODUCES you to the problem of defining and measuring juvenile delinquency. Delinquency is not a simple problem easily described or measured, and experts have struggled to do so for more than 100 years. This opening section will also introduce two specific problem areas of delinquency: youth violence and illegal drug use.

Chapter 1 reports on the status of children in American society. We also review past and present definitions of delinquency, and discuss legal definitions of delinquency that regulated behavior of children in the American colonies, legal reforms of the child-saving movement at the end of the 19th century, status offenses, and recent changes in state and federal laws.

Chapter 2 examines the extent and nature of delinquency to understand how much delinquency there is. Knowing how much and what kind of delinquency juveniles commit, the characteristics of these acts, the neighborhoods these children live in, the kinds of social networks that are available, and the kinds of lives they lead is vital to understanding where the problem of juvenile crime exists in U.S. society. Such knowledge also helps us to understand the problem more completely. Is delinquency only a problem of lower-class males who live in the inner city? Does it also include females, middle-class children who attend quality schools, troubled children from good families, and "nice" children experimenting with drugs, alcohol, and sex? Chapter 2 reports on the prevalence and incidence of delinquency, groups of delinquents, such as chronic offenders, and what measures of delinquency tell us about the nature and extent of the problem.

(continued)

Chapter 3 and Chapter 4 examine the issues of youth violence and illegal drug use, respectively. Chapter 3 reports on the nature and extent of violent crimes committed by adolescents, juvenile psychopathy, serious and violent juvenile offenders, the rise and decline in violence, the role of firearms, and approaches to preventing juvenile violence. Chapter 4 probes into illegal drug use by juveniles, examines the role of drug use within the larger framework of antisocial behavior, and identifies several factors that help to explain why many adults believe a drug crisis exists in America. The chapter concludes with a discussion of the relationship between drugs and delinquency. ●

Defining Delinquency

Juvenile delinquency is a complex phenomenon that is difficult to understand and explain. Part of the reason why is that it shares a relationship with many other social institutions, including law enforcement agencies, juvenile and adult courts, media, families, and schools. One of the biggest mistakes anyone can make is to believe juvenile delinquency exists in a vacuum, stands alone, has no connection to other components of society, or is easily solved. It is a fact that delinquency is but one small piece of the lives of American children. There are many others that we are not able to dwell on here, but we will briefly identify a few of them so you can put the study of juvenile delinquency into context.

One in six children in the United States lives in poverty. One in eight or nearly 10 million children have no health insurance. On a regular basis, someone other than their parents cares for three out of five children under age 6. Only 31 percent of fourth-graders read at or above grade level. Three million children are reported abused or neglected every year. Almost 1 in every 10 teenagers drops out of school. Eight children die from gunfire in the United States each day; one child dies every three hours. Our children face a wide range of problems in today's world. None of the problems they confront exist in isolation: they are interconnected and related in often puzzling ways.[1]

Juvenile delinquency is but one of the many serious societal problems some children confront on a regular basis. It changes the lives forever of both offenders and their victims. In recent years, juveniles in the United States and around the world have committed innumerable serious and violent offenses that have affected how people think about crime, its causes, and solutions. For example, 13-year-old Alex King, who with his brother, Derek, age 14, murdered their sleeping father. Derek bashed his head with a baseball bat as Alex urged him on. To conceal the crime, the boys set fire to the house. After pleading guilty to third-degree murder, they were sentenced to 7 and 8 years in state prison, respectively. Another young offender, Michael Hernandez, age 14, slit the throat of a middle school classmate, Jaime Rodrigo Gough, in a school bathroom, and then calmly returned to class with blood-stained clothing. Hernandez was charged with first-degree murder, will be tried as an adult, and faces life in prison without parole.

A third juvenile whose crimes captured worldwide attention is John Malvo, age 17, who, with his 41-year-old companion, John Allen Muhammad, terrorized the Washington, DC, area, murdering 13 people and injuring many others. Malvo admitted to killing several of the victims and was charged and convicted of first-degree murder, receiving a sentence of life in prison without parole. He did not receive the death penalty because of his age at the time of the crime; however, his accomplice, Muhammad, was sentenced to death.[2] In Tokyo 12-year-old Satomi Mitarai was lured into an empty classroom during her school lunch hour where an 11-year-old classmate, "Girl A," cut her throat and slashed her arms with a box knife and left her to bleed to death. Several months earlier, a 12-year-old boy in Nagasaki (Japan) kidnapped, molested, and murdered a 4-year-old by shoving him off the roof of a car garage.

As shown in Box 1-1, juveniles worldwide commit heinous crimes. But juvenile delinquency is much more than the sensational crimes that are widely reported in newspapers and on television. Serious juvenile crime constitutes only a small fraction of the offenses youths commit. Most adolescent crimes involve minor transgressions, such as larceny–theft, liquor law violations, and drug offenses. Recently, for example, a teenager posing as a banker duped an Ohio car

6

box 1-1   DELINQUENCY AROUND THE GLOBE

Children and Crime

Juvenile crime is not the domain of children living in any particular country. Children commit crimes worldwide. Sometimes their crimes are violent; other times they are not. The excerpts below involve crimes committed for a variety of reasons ranging from needing shopping money, to retaliation, to racism. The first excerpt reports a crime committed in Canada. As you read it and then read crimes committed by children representing many different regions of the world, you will see that juvenile crime is not restricted to any race, sex, age, or location.

- In **Montreal, Canada,** seven young men were arrested in connection with a series of attacks and robberies that often targeted elderly women. The young men would surround and rob women walking alone. The youths, who range in age from 14 to 17, were part of an emerging street gang trying to prove themselves.

- In **St. Petersburg, Russia,** a group of 10 to 12 drunken teenagers beat and stabbed a 9-year-old Tajik girl to death, and severely wounded her father and 11-year-old cousin. The attackers were armed with knives, brass knuckles, chains, and bats, and assaulted the three Central Asians in a courtyard in the city center. Many Tajiks come to Russia in hopes of making a living and are often targeted in such attacks.

- In **Darwin, Australia,** two teenage boys murdered two female Thai prostitutes. The boys tied up the women and tossed them alive into a crocodile-infested river. They were convicted on March 19, 2005, and given sentences of life imprisonment, with nonparole periods set at 25 years. One of the boys during the police interview stated that he killed the prostitutes because "just suddenly something really irritated me, can't remember (what) but it just ticked me off really bad."

- In **London, England,** police arrested four teenagers in connection with the killing of a 10-year-old immigrant from Nigeria. The stabbing death, on the stairwell of a housing project, caused revulsion because of evidence that showed passers-by had let the boy bleed to death. The boy, Damilola Taylor, was attacked in the early evening as he returned from an after-school computer class. Stabbed in the leg, he dragged himself to the open stairwell, where he died from loss of blood.

- In **Ahmedabad, India,** a 15-year-old Indian boy died after setting himself ablaze upon hearing his parents were infected with HIV. Reports claimed that the boy was worried about his future and being ostracized from society. In India even schools turn children away whose parents have HIV.

- In **Accra, Ghana,** hundreds of youths returning from a funeral for Muslims killed in Africa's worst soccer disaster vented their anger, attacking a police station and destroying kiosks in a working-class neighborhood. The youths had come from a funeral service for 30 people killed in a mass stampede at the Accra sports stadium. A total of 126 people died in the crush.

Unfortunately, there are no reliable comparative data on juvenile crime across countries, which makes it impossible to make accurate cross-cultural comparisons on the amount of delinquency committed and the number of juveniles who are committing it.

Sources: Spiro Doukas, "Crowd Management: Past and Contemporary Issues," *The Sports Journal,* online at http://www.thesportjournal.org/2006Journal/Vol9-No2/Doukas.asp, accessed April 20, 2007; "New Damilola Trial is Considered," *BBC News,* online at http://www.212.58.240.37/1/hi/england/london/4874872.stm, accessed April 20, 2007; "Indian Boy Kills Self on Hearing Parents Have HIV," *Khaleej Times,* online at http://www.khaleejtimes.com/DisplayArticleNew.asp?col=&section=subcontinent&xfile=data/subcontinent/2006/July/subcontinent_July96.xml, accessed April 20, 2007; "Prostitutes Thrown to Crocs," *News 24, Breaking News, Fast,* online at http://www.news24.com/News24/HomeLite/, accessed April 20, 2007; "Racist Violence on the Rise," *World Press,* online at http://www.worldpress.org/Europe/2375.cfm, accessed April 20, 2007; "Teens Arrested in Rash of Robberies," *CBC News,* online at http://www.cbc.ca/canada/montreal/story/2006/06/30/qc-arrests.html, accessed April 20, 2007.

Delinquency is the culmination of a process that begins at conception; not at an arbitrary point established by criminologists. The life of the fetus in the womb might have a deleterious effect on a child throughout his or her life.

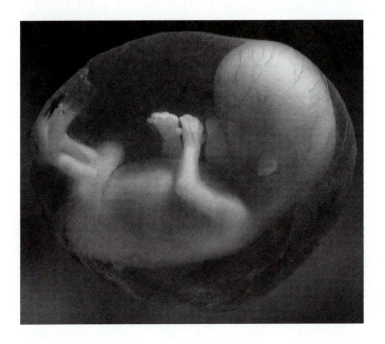

dealership into delivering a $123,000 BMW to him at his high school. After completing the paperwork that was mailed to him at his home, the youth called the auto dealer pretending to be a banker confirming a wire transfer, and the dealership in turn delivered the BMW to the high school.[3]

Regardless of the seriousness of their offenses, when children commit crimes, people ask questions, such as: Why do they do it? and What can be done to prevent it? These questions invite others: What is the child's family like? Does the mother work outside the home? Where is the father? Who are the child's friends? Did the child watch too much television? How should society react to serious juvenile crime? Should offenders be rehabilitated? Punished severely? How should we punish or treat juvenile offenders?

Our approach to juvenile delinquency is different than what is often articulated by other criminologists. We believe that delinquents *do not* parachute onto Earth when they are 10, 11, or 12 years old. In others words, whereas most criminologists ignore the first decade of a child's life in their explanations of delinquency, we, on the other hand, consider the first years of life to be the most critical. We also think that children who are called delinquents are produced by a society that practices the benign neglect of *all* children. In our view, juvenile delinquency represents the *culmination of a process that begins at conception and evolves through adolescence*. It "begins in the beginning" of life, and not at some arbitrary point identified by criminologists. *The womb after all is an environment*. One in which the unborn child develops more rapidly than at any other stage of his or her life. What occurs in the womb might adversely affect a child throughout life, including his or her life chances and opportunities. An ever-growing body of scientific research continues to affirm these claims. Scientists, for example, at the Harvard School of Public Health, have discovered that mercury in seafood may cause heart damage and irreversible impairment to brain function in children, both in the womb and as they grow.[4] Researchers at Washington University in St. Louis found that just two cocktails consumed by a pregnant woman may be enough to kill developing brain cells in an unborn child, leading to neurological problems that can haunt the youngster for a lifetime. Debilitations, such as low birth weight and brain damage have been found to be precursors to delinquency.[5]

STATUS OF CHILDREN

think about it

Should children have the right to vote? If so, what should the voting age be? If not, why not?

Status refers to a *socially defined position in a group characterized by certain rights, expectations, and duties.* Who someone is in relation to others affects how he or she interacts with them and how others interact with him or her. There are two types of statuses: achieved status and ascribed status. **Achieved status** is a position in a group based on merit, achievement, or accomplishments, such as being a college student or being a juvenile delinquent. **Ascribed status** is a position based on who you are, not on what you do; some examples include being born an Asian American or female. However, status involves a mixture of ascription and achievement: *Ascribed status influences achieved status.* It is no coincidence that children who live in poverty score lower on standardized tests, and it is also no coincidence they are more likely than children who grow up in stable middle- and upper-class homes to become delinquent.[6]

Of all statuses, the status of child is one of the least privileged. The systematic denial of privilege leads to oppression. *All* children are oppressed to one degree or another, but some are oppressed more than others. The personal and social cruelty children experience falls on a continuum ranging from straightforward demands for obedience to being yelled at constantly, which may be as damaging as physical abuse.[7] Some people believe unborn children are the least privileged of all, since they possess *no* constitutional rights, and, once born, the Constitution "does not . . . provide [them] with any protective rights,"[8] nor does the Constitution provide children with the opportunity to affect their status, for instance, by allowing them to vote. Thus, children often suffer grievously at the hands of adult caretakers. Two early incidents of child abuse concerning Emily Thompson and Mary Ellen Wilson, which produced very different outcomes, may better illustrate this.

Emily Thompson

In June 1871 Henry Bergh, who founded in 1866 the American Society for the Prevention of Cruelty to Animals was presented with his first case of child abuse. A woman entered Bergh's office and asked that he intervene on behalf of 8-year-old Emily Thompson. At the time, Emily was in the care of Mary Ann Larkin, who, according to neighbors, beat her almost daily in her backyard. Mary Ann Larkin claimed Emily's parents and grandparents were deceased. Emily was removed from the home and taken to the courts, which agreed she was abused after seeing her bruised and battered body, but then returned her to her abuser because she had no other living relatives. Within that same week, a woman named Violet Bickom showed up on Bergh's doorstep. Violet lived in New Jersey and had read about Emily's case in the newspaper. Surprisingly enough, Violet was Emily's allegedly dead grandmother. When Emily's parents died, her grandmother had felt she was too old to raise a child and turned her over to Mary Ann's care under the condition she be raised and treated as one of her own. Mary Ann took the child in and, a short time later, told Violet that Emily had died; she also told Emily that Violet had died. Emily went to live with her grandmother after this lie was discovered.[9]

Mary Ellen Wilson

Most criminologists consider the first case of child abuse in the United States to be that of Mary Ellen Wilson in 1874. It is more accurate, however, to say that Mary Ellen's case was the first child abuse case where a child was removed from an abusive home. (Emily Thompson had been returned to her abusive caretaker.)

In September 1874, Mrs. Etta Angell Wheeler heard about the abuse of a 10-year-old girl named Mary Ellen Wilson. Mary Ellen's father died at war, and her mother placed her in the temporary care of a babysitter. Mary Ellen's mother did not return for several months and did not provide her any support. Then one day she showed up drunk and newly married, wanting to take Mary Ellen home. The babysitter could see that this new marriage had changed Mary Ellen's mother, and she did not want to put Mary Ellen back with her, so she told her that Mary Ellen had died. Later, she could no longer care for Mary Ellen, so she took her to an orphanage claiming her mother had abandoned her.

A man who had lost all of his own children to illness later adopted Mary Ellen. He told his wife that Mary Ellen was his illegitimate daughter, and she

Mary Ellen Wilson was the victim in the first recorded child abuse case in the United States. Laws preventing cruelty to animals were used to remove her from the home of her abusive foster parents. This photo shows Mary Ellen, age 9, at her court appearance.

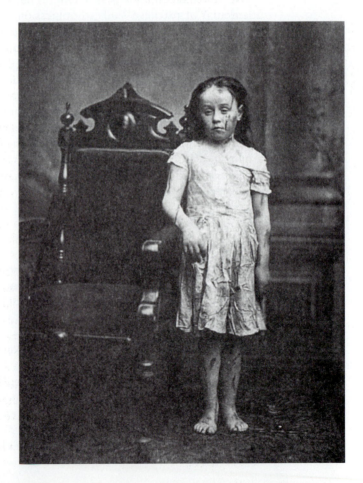

agreed to accept Mary Ellen but hated her every day she knew her. Mary Ellen was treated as though she were a slave. She was only allowed to wear one set of clothes and was rarely bathed. She slept on a piece of rug under a window in the living room and was locked in a closet whenever her mother left the house. Mary Ellen had no toys and was never allowed outside to play with the other children. When a police officer who lived in her building found her locked in a closet in her home, he gave her some candy, which she had never before tasted. Though he treated her well, the police officer never did anything to save Mary Ellen from her abuser.

Sadly, many people knew of the abuse Mary Ellen was suffering, including the police officer. Her suffering went on for years, until Etta Wheeler and Henry Bergh entered her life. Etta Wheeler first visited Mary Ellen's home in September 1874 and found her covered in bruises and scars. Mary Ellen had a gash in her forehead inflicted by the caretaker with a pair of scissors. She made several return visits to check on Mary Ellen. At the time, there were *no laws* in effect to protect children, so Wheeler persuaded Henry Bergh from the American Society for the Prevention of Cruelty to Animals, to go to court on Mary Ellen's behalf. Mary Ellen's "foster" mother, Mary Connolly, was convicted of assault and battery and sentenced to a year of hard labor in the city penitentiary. Mary Ellen stated to the court: "Mamma has been in the habit of whipping and beating me almost every day. She used to whip me with a twisted whip, a raw hide. I have no recollection of ever having been kissed and have never been kissed by Mamma."[10]

After the trial, Mary Ellen went to live with Etta Wheeler's sister. In 1888, at age 24, she married Lewis Schutt, and had two daughters who both became schoolteachers. Mary Ellen died October 30, 1956, at age 92.[11] Not until eight months after Mary Ellen's case, in April 1875, was the New York Society for the Prevention of Cruelty to Children created. Soon thereafter, other states began to form child protection agencies.

Like Emily and Mary Ellen, children today are often regarded as mere chattel or the property of their parents. Adults often act toward children in ways they are prohibited from behaving toward other adults. As Bill Cosby has said, "I brought you into this world, and I can take you out." For instance, in 2007, 17-year-old high school senior, Nicole Beecroft, stabbed her newborn baby 135 times then put her in a garbage can outside her home.[12] Debra Liberman beat her 7-year-old adopted daughter with a dog chain and keys, burned her wrists on a stove, doused her naked body with bleach, then locked the girl inside a closet in a coal cellar with a burning furnace filter.[13] And, since 1950, no fewer than 4,450 Catholic priests have been accused of molesting more than 11,000 minors.[14] Every year, nearly three million cases of *child maltreatment*, which includes abuse and neglect, are reported to child protection agencies, and roughly one million of the reported cases are confirmed.[15]

There is strong evidence that child maltreatment adversely affects the lives of children. In a now classic study by Cathy Widom and Michael Maxfield, which was conducted over a 25-year period, 908 children whose cases of victimization and child maltreatment had been substantiated were matched by sex, age, race, and family socioeconomic status with a comparison group of 667 children not officially recorded as being abused or neglected. They reported sobering results:

- Being abused or neglected increased the likelihood of arrest as a juvenile by 59 percent.

- Maltreated children were younger at the time of their first arrest, committing nearly twice as many offenses, and were arrested more frequently.
- Physically abused and neglected (versus sexually abused children) were the most likely to be arrested for a violent crime.
- Abused and neglected girls were also at increased risk of arrests for violence as juveniles and adults.

Childhood maltreatment represents a serious social problem. Child abuse and neglect increase the likelihood of delinquency, adult criminality, and violent criminal behavior. Victims of child maltreatment also are characterized by poor performance in school, mental health problems, and generally low levels of achievement.[16]

EARLY PROHIBITIONS OF JUVENILE BEHAVIOR

The systematic denial of privileges and subsequent oppression of children is not new. Throughout history it has been common for children to be viewed as different from and inferior to adults. In the process, many different human societies have constructed legal prohibitions aimed at regulating the behavior of juveniles.

The Code of Hammurabi

The Code of Hammurabi is one of the oldest known sets of written laws. Hammurabi ruled Babylon from 1792 to 1750 B.C. He created 282 rules for the kingdom, each accompanied by exact punishments. Many of the rules prescribed severe penalties, applying the dictum "an eye for an eye, a tooth for a tooth." Rule 195 was specifically aimed at children who disobeyed their parents: "If a son strikes his father, his hands shall be cut off." The Code also established a special set of rules for adopted children. For instance, Rule 192 stated: "If an adopted child says to his father or mother 'You are not my father or my mother,' his tongue shall be cut off." Rule 193 added that if an adopted son returned to his biological parents, then his eyes would be plucked out.[17]

The Greek Empire

The Greek Empire covered the years between the sixth and third centuries B.C., and juvenile misbehavior was considered to be a serious problem. The Greeks responded to delinquency by passing laws that held parents responsible for the behavior of their children. These are likely the first parent liability laws (see Box 1-2).

If today's definition of *assault* were applied to the behavior of ancient Greek children, Greek society would be said to have been filled with children who were "psychopathic delinquents." In fact, many Greek children were so bad that a law was passed specifically prohibiting them from beating up their parents. Some historians blame the aggressive behavior on the values of the larger society. Young Greeks were exposed to violence from an early age. Their heads were filled with stories of psychopathic gods and humans, such as Kronos, who castrated his father, and Hephaestus, who chained up his mother, and reprobate

---

box 1-2   **A WINDOW ON DELINQUENCY**

The House of Prayer

One shocking incident of child abuse took place several years ago in Atlanta at the *House of Prayer*. The event captured attention worldwide because it raised many questions. For instance: Under what circumstances is it acceptable to physically punish children? Is it acceptable to whip children in public? Should the law interfere with the religious beliefs of parents to rear their children?

Atlanta police recently arrested Pastor Arthur Allen, age 70, and five members of his 130-member church, who whipped children as a form of discipline. The *House of Prayer* leader and the church members were charged with cruelty to children. Even though they have been arrested, church members said they would continue to whip unruly children. They believe parents have an absolute right to discipline their children however they see fit. What parents do to their children is no business of the state. The beatings were done at the church, executed by parents and other adults with belts and switches under the supervision of Pastor Allen, who advised them on how severe the beatings should be. Allen based his decision on the seriousness of the infraction, the child's age, and whether the child had expressed remorse. For instance, teenage girls who had sex were whipped during church services, after having their skirts or dresses removed. Children who misbehaved at public school were later beaten at church. Three adults held one 7-year-old boy in the air while his uncle whipped him with a switch, as Allen stood by giving instructions. A 16-year-old girl was beaten with belts for 30 minutes. Police photographs showed 3-inch-long welts on some children, and a 10-year-old boy had open wounds on his stomach and side.

On October 18, 2002, Allen was found guilty of cruelty to children and sentenced to 10 years with 90 days in jail and the rest on probation. Allen violated his probation and eluded authorities for five months before being found by National Park Service rangers in a parked car. He was arrested, and is now out of jail after serving a two-year prison sentence. Four other church members were also convicted three years ago in connection with the beatings of children at the church and served time in jail.

Sources: Beth Warren, "County Won't Call Minister 'Indigent,'" *The Atlanta Journal-Constitution,* December 2, 2003:B2; Steve Visser, "Minister Sentenced to 2 Years," *The Atlanta Journal-Constitution,* August 26, 2003:B3; Jill Young Miller, "Judge Pleads for Compliance from Subdued Allen," *The Atlanta Journal-Constitution,* October 18, 2002: A18; "Pastor in Cruelty Case Out of Prison," online at http://www.rickross.com/reference/house/house46.html, accessed April 20, 2007.

---

humans, such as Oedipus, who killed his father and married his mother, and, Orestes, who killed his mother. They were also taught what parents might do to children:

- Heracles slaughtered his children in a fit of madness.
- Agave killed and dismembered her son, Pentheus.
- Tantalus chopped up his son, Pelops, for a banquet held in honor of the gods.
- Laius nailed together the ankles of his infant son, Oedipus, before leaving the child to perish on a mountain.
- Medea murdered her children to avenge herself upon her husband because he had abandoned her for another woman.

These and other related teachings created a society in which (1) violent and destructive relations between children and adults were not uncommon and (2) the propensity toward delinquency was in part rooted in one's relationship with one's parents.[18]

The Middle Ages

There is very little documentation describing adult–child relations in the Middle Ages (A.D. 500–1500). What writings there are suggest that children were treated poorly. In fact, it was not uncommon for mothers to suffocate their children and leave their dead bodies on the streets. However, despite their poor treatment, children in the Middle Ages were viewed more like miniature adults than they are today. Children were permitted to curse, openly engage in sex, drink (in taverns and at home), and wear firearms, and they were not required to attend school.[19] Laws regulating the problematic behavior of children began to emerge in the 10th century, when King Aethelstand (924–939) pronounced that a thief over age 12 should receive the death penalty if he or she stole more than eight pence (a considerably small amount of money). However, this declaration was later modified to provide that a person under age 16 could not be put to death unless he or she resisted or ran away.[20] These laws recognized that a child under a certain minimum age—12 years—was exempt from prosecution and punishment; they provided little distinction between older juveniles and adults.

The 16th and 17th Centuries

One of the best accounts of juvenile delinquency in the 1500s and 1600s is found in Mary Perry's *Crime and Society in Early Modern Seville*. The youths of Seville, Spain, committed many unlawful acts, including theft, gambling, prostitution, and homosexual solicitation. As Perry noted, boys and girls alike were arrested:

> Prostitution also offered a livelihood for boys. Some became pimps for their sisters or girl friends, but others became prostitutes themselves. Some boys involved in homosexual acts in Seville were as young as eight years, but it is likely that the younger boys were victims rather than working prostitutes. Children growing up in the streets learned the tricks of gambling very early. . . . They learned to mark cards with pin pricks, scratches, and watermarks.[21]

Most of the juveniles who were arrested were street children. Usually they were part of the underworld organization of Seville, and as such received protection for a price and were required to share their goods with the organization.

The legal regulation of juveniles in Seville came through secular law (a body of legal statutes developed separately from church or canon law). All children had a legal identity and were taken care of by their parents or another member of the community. Unfortunately, the law did not provide for dependent and neglected children as it does today. In early Seville, children had to fend for themselves, and since no law prohibited adults from beating them, their best defense was a pair of fast legs and a place to hide.[22]

The 18th and 19th Centuries

By the end of the 17th century concern about juvenile delinquency had become widespread throughout England. While most juvenile crime involved theft, violent crime was also common. Wiley Sanders has reported on some of the children's cases that were tried in the Old Baily (the primary criminal court in London) between 1681 and 1758:

- On January 17, 1684, John Atkins, a little boy, was indicted for stealing a silver tankard valued at 10 pounds. He was found guilty, sentenced, and sent out of the country.

- On April 16, 1735, John Smith, a young boy, was indicted for stealing 4 yards of printed linen valued at 5 shillings. He was found guilty and exiled from the country.

- On December 7, 1758, Thomas Lyon, age 12, was sentenced to be transported for 7 years for stealing a watch.[23]

At a time when juveniles were commonly being sentenced to prison or transported for theft, the penalties they received could be much more severe. In 1733, for example, Elizabeth Ran, a little girl, was sentenced to death for stealing from Stephen Freeman—to whom she was apprenticed. Prison, however, was the usual punishment for delinquency at this time. Between 1813 and 1815, 208 boys and 40 girls under age 15 were committed to Newgate prison in London. The next year, 429 boys and 85 girls were incarcerated.[24]

As an alternative to prison, many English children were banished along with adults. Two ships, the *Leviathan* and the *Retribution,* each held between 30 and 40 juveniles on their trips to Australia. And in 1829, of 4,000 convicts placed on board the *Euryalus,* nearly 300 were juveniles, 72 of them under age 13.[25]

By the mid-1800s juvenile delinquency had become a serious problem in England. In London, the greatly feared criminal class, with its large numbers of children, was being coupled with the related problems of poverty, internal migration, and population growth. John Wade, in his book *A Treatise on the Police and Crimes of the Metropolis,* reported on a theory of delinquency that was popularly subscribed to:

> There are, probably, 70,000 persons in the Metropolis [London] who regularly live by theft and fraud; most of these have women, with whom they cohabit, and their offspring, as a matter of course, follow the example of their parents, and recruit the general mass of mendicancy, prostitution, and delinquency. This is the chief source of juvenile delinquents, who are also augmented by children, abandoned by the profligate among the working classes, by those of poor debtors confined, of paupers without settlement, and by a few wayward spirits from reputable families, who leave their homes without cause, either from the neglect or misfortune of their natural protectors. Children of this description are found in every part of the metropolis, especially in the vicinity of the theaters, the marketplace, the parks, fields, and outskirts of the town. Many of them belong to organized gangs of predators, and are in the regular employ and training of older thieves; others obtain a precarious subsistence by begging, running errands, selling playbills, picking pockets, and pilfering from shops and stalls. Some of them never knew what it is to be in a bed, taking refuge in sheds, under stalls, piazzas, and about brick-kilns; they have no homes;

others have homes, either with their parents, or in obscure lodging-houses, but to which they cannot return unless the day's industry of crime has produced a stipulated sum.[26]

As reported in the writings of Wade and others, juvenile delinquents were seen as thieves or prostitutes, frequently employed by older criminals, living in urban poverty, often orphaned or deserted, and likely to end up in prison.[27]

Under the existing law, children under age 7 were presumed incapable of harboring criminal intent. Therefore, they were exempt from criminal penalties. Children between the ages of 7 and 14 were also presumed to be lacking criminal intent. However, the law did not always limit prosecutors, and historical records reveal that in the early 1800s a child of 13 was hanged for the theft of a spoon, and a 9-year-old boy was executed for minor theft from a printer.[28]

AMERICAN DELINQUENCY

Children in the American colonies were often treated badly by both adults and the law. How they were treated was a sign of how children generally were cared for in the Colonial era, which was very similar to the treatment they received years earlier in England. The English who settled the colonies saw children as a source of labor, service, and little more. As such, until about 1880, child labor was widespread in America. The apprenticeship system was widely practiced. It was customary for the poor to give their children to farmers or craftsmen who would teach them a trade. Orphaned children were sold into apprenticeship, where they were often poorly treated. Corporal punishment was the rule, not the exception.[29]

American Colonies

It was not just apprenticed children who faced strict regulations on their behaviors: all children did. In 1641 the General Court of Massachusetts Bay Colony passed the **Stubborn Child Law,** which stated that children who disobeyed their parents would be put to death.[30] The text of the statute was drawn almost verbatim from the Book of Deuteronomy (21:18–21). The Stubborn Child Law descended from the Puritans' belief that unacknowledged social evils would bring the wrath of God down upon the entire colony. The Puritans believed they had no choice but to react to juvenile misbehavior in a severe and calculated manner. However, not all colonies adopted the Stubborn Child Law. Outside Massachusetts, children found guilty of a serious crime frequently were whipped, and caning was commonly practiced.[31]

It was more than just the activity of children that concerned the colonists; children's *inactivity* bothered them as well. In 1646 the Virginia General Assembly passed legislation to prevent "slouth and idleness where young children are easily corrupted,"[32] and in 1672, the General Court of Massachusetts Bay Colony prohibited an adult from luring a young person from his or her studies or work. In addition, "rude, stubborn, and unruly" children were to be separated from their parents and placed with masters who would "correct" the misbehavior of boys until they were 21 and girls until age 18. Children over 14 who were found guilty of lying would be punished with a monetary fine for the first offense and higher fines thereafter.[33]

The Puritans were ambivalent toward children. While they believed children were born in sin and should submit to adult authority and hard labor, they also thought children required separate legal provisions. For instance, in 1660 the laws of the Massachusetts Bay Colony provided that

> for sodomy . . . children under fourteen were to be "severely punished" but not executed; for cursing and smiting parents, . . . only those "above sixteen years old, and of sufficient understanding" could be put to death; for being stubborn or rebellious sons . . . only those "of sufficient years and understanding [sixteen years of age]" were liable; for arson, . . . the law also applied only to those "of the age of sixteen years and upward" for "denying the Scriptures to be the infallible word of God," again the minimum age was sixteen for those who were liable to the death penalty.[34]

The Puritans made no distinction between delinquency and sin. The laws of the colony were the laws of God, and children who misbehaved violated God's law.

The Puritans were not the only people concerned about children. By the 18th century childhood was considered a special period of life during which children needed thoughtful guidance and discipline. Children were seen as "fragile, innocent, and sacred, on one hand, but corruptible, trying, and arrogant on the other hand."[35] This perspective of children was widely held by the upper class, which demanded the close supervision of children, the need for discipline rather than coddling, the importance of modesty, and strict obedience to authority.

Postcolonial Patterns of Delinquency

While humanitarian control motivated early interest in children, the actual purpose of reforms, such as compulsory or required education (see Chapter 11), was to *control* the children of poor immigrants. Their swarming, ragged presence on city streets made them highly visible to a worried and fearful public. For the first time, Americans were forced to confront large numbers of children who had no home or lived an undisciplined existence. Thus, the new concern for children was paradoxically tied to the fear that many of them threatened the well-being of society.[36]

This fear of children was based on personal experiences. In the early 19th century, America was in the midst of a massive economic depression. Crime soared. Lawlessness spread like wildfire. Particularly worrisome was the harassing and assaultive behavior of juvenile gangs (see Chapter 12). An editorial in a Philadelphia newspaper expressed both fear and outrage over the "new" street gangs:

> A few nights ago, a number of boys assembled on Fifth-street, between Market and Chestnut-streets to divert themselves with firing squibs. A gentleman and a servant driving a carriage, with a pair of horses had broken loose. The boys (saw this as) a fine opportunity for sport and mischief, and eagerly seized the moment, to light a squib, and fling it towards the horses. Luckily . . . the beasts were in good hands, and, though frightened, were prevented from (running off). Had not this been the case, the newspapers might (be reporting) a list of five or six persons killed or wounded.[37]

By the early 1800s juvenile gangs had become an unwanted fixture in big cities. They would hang out on street corners, verbally abuse pedestrians, and pelt citizens with rocks and snowballs; these were among the least threatening of their behaviors. The more serious behaviors of these violent gangs of juveniles included robbing innocent citizens.[38] Something needed to be done, but what?

The Child Savers

In the first quarter of the 19th century, America underwent rapid social change in response to the Industrial Revolution. Meanwhile, leisure time increased for wealthy people, public education burgeoned, and communal life in the cities began to break down. While simultaneously fearful and worried about the changes occurring around them, affluent people needed something to fill their lives. They turned their attention to saving other people's children, reasoning that in the long run they in turn would be saving themselves. Those who joined this movement formed a group called the Child Savers.

Like other Americans, the **Child Savers** believed in the goodness of children, seeing them as being born good and becoming bad. Juvenile crime was blamed on exposure to poverty, overcrowding, immigration, and lack of parental guidance. Therefore, the solution to youth crime was to remove problem children from bad homes and place them in good, rehabilitating environments.[39]

Early History of Institutional Control   Child Savers actively pursued the passage of legislation that would permit placing children in reformatories, especially juvenile paupers. The goal of removing children from extreme poverty was admirable, but resulted in transforming children into nonpersons (or people without legal rights). Children were shunted into factories, poorhouses, orphanages, and houses of refuge, where they were poorly treated with almost no attention given to their individual needs. All too often, the legal system hid these problems from public view, taking away children's freedoms and occasionally their lives in the process.

Under the guise of providing children with better preparation for life, the new institutions sometimes did children more harm than good. A case involving the Children's Aid Society clearly illustrates this point: The society originally sought to place "unwanted" children in good homes in the countryside where they would learn to value hard work and love nature, but what evolved was a profit-making organization that drafted nearly 250,000 children into indentured servitude until age 18 (see Box 1-3).[40]

Some of the first recorded attempts to formally control delinquency in the United States took place in the 1800s. By this time childhood was regarded as a period of life that deserved the care and attention its innocent nature demanded.[41] In cities, such as New York, Philadelphia, and Boston, conflicting aspects of juvenile behavior gained public notice. In big cities, the young delinquent stood in sharp contrast to the purity of childhood. Child Savers launched interventionist efforts to save delinquents, relieve the circumstances of their development, and guide them firmly toward the path of righteousness. This path, however, was often a winding one due to the anxieties of these well-meaning reformers. To them, delinquents were not just innocent children gone wrong; they were "bad seeds" capable of causing much harm and wreaking havoc on society. They had to be restrained from activities that violated social norms, and these restraints sometimes reached astonishing dimensions. As for their parents, some interventionists felt they should be sterilized to prevent further members of the "dangerous class" from being born.

think
about it

Were the orphan trains a viable solution for preventing delinquency? How does society today manage orphaned and unwanted children?

box 1-3 DELINQUENCY PREVENTION
The Orphan Trains

In the mid-19th century thousands of children who were orphans, runaways, and throwaways filled the streets of New York City. Many of them were incarcerated or put in poorhouses. Reverend Charles Loring Brace, who in 1853 established the Children's Aid Society to provide homeless children with shelter and education, took a more daring tact. Between 1854 and 1929, the society ran "orphan trains" that carried approximately 250,000 abandoned children from New York to locations in the West where they were adopted by Christian farm families.

The process of finding new homes for the children was haphazard. At town meetings across the country, farming families took their pick of the orphan train riders. Children who were not selected got back on board the train and continued to the next town. The children who were selected and those who adopted them had one year to decide whether they would stay together. If either decided not to, the child would be returned to the Society, board the next train out of town, and be offered to another family.

Although approximately 39 percent of the orphan train riders were female, Brace referred to his passengers almost exclusively as "lads." Female orphan train riders were treated decidedly different than the boys. Brace felt that street-girls were less salvage-able and "hopeless" after the age of 14 because he perceived them to be "weak in flesh" and prematurely "womanly." The Children's Aid Society did, however, continue to send girls to the undeveloped West, as it was in dire need of relief for the overworked farm wife. Orphan train girls were often treated harshly by their host families; considered cheap domestic help as opposed to new family members. It was thought that the best that could be expected of the female orphans was that they would eventually get married.

The impact of Brace's efforts on children's lives was variable. Some children thrived. Two boys became governors, one became a Supreme Court justice, and others became mayors, congressmen, or local representatives. Thousands of others did not fare so well. Many became drifters and thieves; at least one became a murderer. The vast majority of the children, however, led ordinary and unaccomplished lives.

Sources: D. Bruce Ayler, *The Orphan Train Collection,* online at http://www.orphantrainriders.com/, accessed April 20, 2007; Rachel Bandy, Robert Regoli, and John Hewitt, "Farmed-Out: A Case Study of Differential Oppression Theory and Female Child Farm Labor in the Early 20th Century," *Free Inquiry in Creative Sociology* 33:3–19 (2005); Stephen O'Connor, *Orphan Trains* (Boston: Houghton Mifflin Company, 2001); Marilyn Irvin Holt, *The Orphan Trains: Placing out in America* (Lincoln: University of Nebraska Press, 1992).

In this political climate, the doctrine of *parens patriae* emerged from English common law. This doctrine defined the state as a kind and caring parent, and as "the ultimate guardian of every child." As a "super-parent," the state enjoyed wide latitude in its efforts to redeem delinquent children. One of the earliest judicial expressions of *parens patriae* was fought vigorously in 1838 by a distraught father whose child had fallen victim to the "compassion" of the Philadelphia House of Refuge. Mary Ann Crouse was committed to the house of refuge by her mother, who alleged she was *incorrigible*, meaning her mother thought she was hopeless.[42] Mary Ann's father disagreed, arguing that the commitment procedures were unfair, and that she was only accused of committing what later became known as a **status offense** (see Chapter 2), an act only illegal for children.

In the early nineteenth century, children of any age could be brought before the court. Here, a three-year-old boy is being accused by his mother of terrorizing the home.

The child herself was allowed neither defense nor trial. The court accepted the mother's charge and committed Mary Ann to the state for guidance.

New York House of Refuge   The first house of refuge opened in 1825 in New York State; it represents another example of the mixture of concerns underlying the philosophy of *parens patriae*. In 1824 nearly 10,000 children under age 14 were living in poverty in New York City. Many were concerned not only for their welfare, but also "that this mass of pauperism [would] form a fruitful nursery of crime, unless prevented by the watchful superintendence of the legislature."[43] The New York House of Refuge served as one of the main instruments to remedy this problem. Designed to save children from a life of crime, the house soon revealed an orientation toward saving society from children.

The reformers' attitudes toward delinquency were rooted in their beliefs about poverty and delinquency. Poverty was linked with idleness, which was seen as a reprehensible moral quality that led to crime. The managers of the New York House of Refuge translated this equation into a severely regimented boot camp type of existence for house inmates where "children were marched from one activity to the next, were put on a rigid time schedule . . . and were corporally punished for being uncooperative."[44] Children suffered terribly at the hands of adults whose mixture of hostility and kindness produced a peculiar atmosphere. There was an emphasis on remorse and punishment, which was common to most houses of refuge. Not only were children accused of crimes persuaded to see the error of their ways, but they were also made to suffer for their crimes. Retribution in the form of punishment provided the most convenient method of conversion.

Juvenile Court   Progressive reformers continued looking for new solutions to the growing problem of juvenile delinquency. Their most significant remedy was the creation of the juvenile court in Cook County (Chicago), Illinois, in 1899.[45] Like the earlier houses of refuge, the juvenile court attempted to supervise problem children closely, but unlike the houses of refuge, this new form of supervision was to more often occur within the child's own home and community; not in institutions.

The Child Savers, who were outraged by the plight and the potential threat of so many needy children, joined hands with lawyers and penologists to establish the juvenile court. It began with an 1899 Illinois legislative act "to regulate the treatment and control of *dependent, neglected,* and *delinquent* children." This Act defined a delinquent child as someone "under the age of 16 years who violates any law of the State or any City or Village ordinance." A *dependent* or *neglected* child was one:

> Who for any reason is destitute or homeless or abandoned; or dependent upon the public for support; or has not proper parental care or guardianship; or who habitually begs or receives alms; or who is found living in any house of ill fame or with any vicious or disreputable person; or whose home . . . is an unfit place for such a child; or [one] under the age of 8 years who is found peddling or selling any article or singing or playing any musical instrument upon the street or giving any public entertainment.[46]

Procedures were *civil,* not criminal, perhaps because social workers spearheaded the court movement. They thought that children had to be *treated,* not punished, and the judge was to be a wise and kind parent. The new court would segregate juvenile offenders from adult offenders at all procedural stages. Furthermore, the court would hire probation officers to exercise friendly supervision over children involved in informal court proceedings.[47]

The juvenile court reaffirmed and extended the doctrine of *parens patriae.*[48] The paternalistic philosophy meant that reformers gave more attention to the "needs" of children than to their rights. In their campaign to meet the needs of children, the Child Savers enlarged the role of the state to include the handling of children in the judicial system. Because of its innovative approach, the juvenile court movement spread quickly. Less than a decade after Illinois established its juvenile court, 10 more states and the District of Columbia followed suit. By 1925 all but two states passed juvenile codes. When Wyoming established its juvenile court in 1945, the list was complete.[49]

In spite of its speedy reception by jurists and legislatures, "the legal sensibility of the country proved far more tractable than reality";[50] creating the juvenile court proved much easier than making it work. The promise of the all-encompassing child-caring role envisaged by court personnel crumbled as municipal officials who rushed to establish their own juvenile courts quickly discovered that the new institution frequently failed to live up to its goals. In many cities, juvenile courts simply did not function in their prescribed tasks. In virtually all states, reformatories and penal institutions were still filled with hundreds of children, and in many jurisdictions where detention homes had not been provided for court use, children were still confined in jails, often with adult criminals, to await hearings.[51] Responses to a 1918 Children's Bureau questionnaire that sought information on the workings of the new court system indicated that in most jurisdictions special provisions were not yet made to handle children coming before the courts. A report on punishments dealt out to children by one court provided commentary on the blending of old ways and new: "65 were sent to jail; 40 were placed in a chain gang; 12 were sent to a reformatory and 1 to an orphanage; 156 were placed on probation."[52] This report was not atypical; many judges still clung to their old attitudes and dealt out the old punishments. Moreover, this Children's Bureau study reported numerous other deficits in the court's operation: inadequate probation service, general unavailability of treatment facilities, inept record keeping and a failure to use the data that did exist, and unqualified judges who lacked either proper legal training or an understanding of children.

These problems became more acute by staffing and financial deficits. Ideally court officers were to be trained, experienced, and sympathetic; in practice the courts neither attracted nor retained highly qualified people. Top-flight judges increasingly avoided the juvenile court bench, and as time passed, enthusiasm for the court waned.[53] In many jurisdictions, particularly in large cities, a system of rotation was put in place where judges sat in a specific court no longer than three months at a time. However, this system hindered the ability of judges to thoroughly grasp individual cases and ensured that the fate of a child was often passed from one judge at the court to another—a situation that paralleled the outside world where the child was shunted from an inadequate home to a foster home, then perhaps to another, and finally to an institution before the cycle began anew. Part of the dilemma facing the early juvenile court had to do with who its clients should be; that is, which children and what behavior constituted juvenile delinquency?

DEFINITIONS OF JUVENILE DELINQUENCY

Delinquency is not an easy concept to define. Over the years, criminologists, policy makers, and social reformers all have struggled to describe what behaviors constitute delinquency and who is a delinquent. Legally, what delinquency is and who is the delinquent might be very different from how delinquency and the delinquent are defined by the general public. In the next section, we will review some definitions of delinquency and the delinquent that have emerged at different periods of time from legal scholars, criminologists, the public, and the media.

Legal Definitions

Through the first six decades of the 20th century, the juvenile court failed to make clear distinctions between dependent and neglected children, status offenders, and delinquents. In 1949 Paul Tappan provided a "legalistic" definition of juvenile delinquency, which underscores the blurring of these concepts:

> Delinquency is any act, course or conduct, or situation which might be brought before court and adjudicated whether in fact it comes to be treated there or by some other resource or indeed remains untreated. . . . The juvenile delinquent is a person who has been adjudicated as such by a court of proper jurisdiction though he [or she] may be no different, up until the time of court contact and adjudication, at any rate, from masses of children who are not delinquent.[54]

For people who accepted this definition, any child adjudicated by the juvenile court was a delinquent, and any child not adjudicated was not a delinquent.

For the most part, the period between the 1930s and the early 1960s was marked by little change in how juvenile delinquency was defined or in which activities constituted delinquent conduct. As the decades wore on, however, juveniles became increasingly involved in more serious crimes: for example, motor vehicle theft, vandalism, and gang-related incidents. In addition, research was beginning to show that more middle- and upper-class juveniles were also engaging in crime.[55]

In the 1960s legal and public concern with juvenile delinquency took a sharp turn. With **baby boomers** (people born between 1946 and 1964) reaching their teenage years in the first part of the decade, delinquency rates soared to alarming levels. Not only were juveniles being arrested for traditional minor property crimes, mischief, and status offenses, but also many young people were now being arrested for murder, forcible rape, aggravated assault, and robbery. Alarming statistics helped foster increased fear of juveniles among adults.

Some states responded with new policies whereby juveniles who posed a serious threat to the community would be treated as adults. New York, for example, is one of several states where juveniles between the ages of 16 and 18 are presumed to be adults for the purpose of criminal prosecution. However, New York's Youthful Offender Statute permits judges to grant youthful-offender status to "worthy" children between the ages of 16 and 18. This statute enables the court to legally process such youths as juveniles and consequently spare them from the stigma and severity of a criminal conviction.[56] Youths convicted of certain offenses, such as murder, arson, and kidnapping, are not eligible for the more lenient classification.

By the early 1970s many states had adopted legislation that redefined the noncriminal behavior of juveniles. New statutes were written to alter the previous vague distinctions among *status offenses, dependency,* and *neglect.* In 1976 the National Advisory Committee on Criminal Justice Standards and Goals recommended that *status offenses* be limited to only five specific categories:

1. *School truancy.* This is defined as a pattern of repeated or habitual unauthorized absence from school by any juvenile subject to compulsory education laws (see Chapter 11). The court's power to intervene in cases of truancy should be limited to situations where the child's continued absence from school clearly indicates the need for services.

2. *Repeated disregard for or misuses of lawful parental authority.* Family court jurisdiction under this category should be narrowly restricted to circumstances where a pattern of repeated disobedient behavior on the part of the juvenile or a pattern of repeated unreasonable demands on the part of the parents creates a situation of family conflict clearly evidencing a need for services.

3. *Repeated running away from home.* Running away is defined as a juvenile's unauthorized absence from home for more than 24 hours. Family court

Status offenses are acts that are only illegal for juveniles, such as drinking alcohol, running away, curfew, and smoking cigarettes. Few juveniles who only commit status offenses are adjudicated delinquent by the juvenile court.

jurisdiction in this category should be the last resort for dealing with the juvenile who repeatedly runs away from home, refuses or has not benefited from voluntary services, and is incapable of self-support.

4. *Repeated use of intoxicating beverages.* This is defined as the repeated possession and/or consumption of intoxicating beverages by a juvenile. In this category, the family court should have the power to intervene and provide services where a juvenile's serious, repeated use of alcohol clearly indicates a need for these services.

think about it

Why do we have status offenses? Should chronic status offenders be punished or treated? What should their punishment or treatment be?

5. *Delinquent acts committed by a juvenile younger than 10 years of age.* A delinquent act is defined as an act that would be a violation of federal or state criminal law or of local ordinance if committed by an adult. Family court delinquency jurisdiction covers juveniles ages 10 and above. This category is intended to cover the situation where a juvenile younger than 10 years repeatedly commits acts that would support a delinquency for an older child, or where the "delinquent acts" committed are of a serious nature[57]

Similarly, the International Association of Chiefs of Police (IACP) held that the term "juvenile delinquent" should be reserved for children who commit criminal offenses and who are in need of supervision or treatment. On the other hand, the IACP suggested that the term "unruly child" be applied to children who commit status offenses, are ungovernable or habitually truant from school, and are in need of treatment for those problems.[58]

The idea that noncriminal juvenile delinquents are in need of special treatment and supervision by the state—whether they are status offenders, neglected youths, or dependent youths—has spawned a variety of legal designations. While Georgia, Ohio, and North Dakota joined the IACP in using the term "unruly child," many other states adopted one or more of the following categorizations:

- MINS: minor in need of supervision
- CHINS: child in need of supervision
- PINS: person in need of supervision
- JINS: juvenile in need of supervision
- YINS: youth in need of supervision
- CHINA: children in need of assistance

In the 1980s many status offenders were unfortunately still being sent to institutions. One report found that of the more than 25,000 juveniles being held in long-term, state-operated correctional institutions, slightly more than 2 percent were in custody for status offenses, such as truancy, running away, and incorrigible behavior.[59] However, it would be misleading to conclude that the remaining 98 percent were in custody for serious criminal offenses. Many of these juveniles were **chronic status offenders** or children who continued to commit status offenses despite repeated interventions by family, school, or social service or law enforcement agencies. Chronic status offenders typically commit new status offenses while on probation and are consequently charged with the criminal offense of violating a valid court order specifying the particular conditions of their probation, a process known as *bootstrapping* (see Chapter 14).[60]

Social Definitions

As legal definitions of juvenile delinquency have varied, so too have its social definitions. As Norval Morris and Gordon Hawkins so aptly put it:

> Juvenile delinquency is not a simple term. It means different things to different individuals, and it means different things to different groups. It has meant different things in the same group at different times. . . . In popular usage, the term juvenile delinquency is used to describe a large number of disapproved behaviors of children and youth. In this sense, almost anything the youth does that others do not like is called juvenile delinquency.[61]

For example, a juvenile's parents, siblings, or relatives may call a certain behavior delinquent even though no law was violated. The youngster who refuses to do household chores, fights with siblings, associates with "bad" friends, talks back, and/or listens to the "wrong" music may well be called delinquent by parents, although the juvenile court would likely ignore the problem.

It is not unusual for parents to complain to their local probation department that their child is a juvenile delinquent and beyond their control. Once parents discuss the matter in detail with a probation officer, they may redefine their youngster as a problem child, or a person in need of supervision (PINS), but not as a delinquent. They may also find family counseling more appropriate than the juvenile court for many adolescent problems.

In the public's mind, a few juveniles hanging out together on a street corner elicits the image of a delinquent gang. While these juveniles may not belong to any formal gang, it is their appearance that determines a person's view. When juveniles use obscene language, pose in "threatening" ways, listen to explicit music, or wear clothing to set them apart from the adults observing them, it is not surprising they are labeled delinquent. However, their actual behavior need not be legally defined as delinquent for the public definition to be applied.

In each of the above settings, juvenile misbehaviors provoke public reactions. On some occasions and in some settings their misbehaviors may be tolerated, while in others they may not. When the legal definition of delinquency applies to a juvenile's behavior, it suggests that what he or she did exceeds the limits of public tolerance, and further suggests that behavior would be considered inappropriate for adults as well as for children.

Media Representations

The variety of legal and nonlegal definitions of juvenile delinquency suggests the there is much subjectivity in definitions and images of delinquency. These images frequently originate in literature, film, television, music, and video games. When art accurately reflects society, there is little doubt that some degree of reality is being represented. From the youthful pickpockets of Dickens's 19th-century London to the neglected and tormented youth in *Rebel without a Cause,* novels and films have been known to catch aspects of juvenile delinquency. However, these images of delinquency leave no room for the more subtle shadings of behavior, and they overemphasize the more dramatic. Unfortunately, for much of society, juvenile delinquency and the delinquent exist exactly as portrayed by text, film, or, more recently, in video games.

Literature   In *Oliver Twist,* Charles Dickens describes urban slum life and the corrupting effects of adults like Fagin on innocent youths.[62] Stephen Crane depicts the tribulations of children with his portrayal of a young girl forced into prostitution in *Maggie: A Girl of the Streets.*[63] Little doubt exists that their descriptions are reasonably reflective of the times. Similarly, Mark Twain's *The Adventures of Tom Sawyer* and *The Adventures of Huckleberry Finn* seemingly reflect youthful adventure and misbehavior in the rural Midwest during the late 1800s.[64] Indeed, Twain may have been among the first to identify a link between child maltreatment and delinquency (see Chapter 10) when he wrote about Huck running away after being beaten by Pap.[65] For Dickens, Crane, and Twain, juvenile delinquents are led astray by either corrupt adults or their own benign failures.

Portrayals of juvenile delinquency in early 20th-century American literature often focus on the immortalizing effects of the pursuit of wealth, as in Theodore Dreiser's *An American Tragedy.*[66] In addition, the teenage drinking, gang fighting, and sexual pursuits of Studs Lonigan in a trilogy of novels written by James Farrell in the 1930s suggests juvenile delinquency is largely a product of ethnic and lower-class socialization. In the novels, such activities are considered a normal part of life for a young boy growing up on the South Side of Chicago.

Another book written in the 1920s emphasizes the contribution of poverty and racial discrimination in the creation of juvenile delinquency. Richard Wright's *Black Boy,* an autobiographical account of Wright's childhood in the South, suggests that lying, drinking, torturing and killing animals, and stealing are all adaptive mechanisms used to distract one from the painful conditions imposed by the formal and informal rules of the Jim Crow South.[67]

The images of juvenile delinquency in literature of the 1940s and 1950s also reflect public concerns of the period. Novels such as *The Amboy Dukes, The Golden Spike,* and *The Cool World,* represent a new concern over urban gangs and youthful drug addiction.[68] Evan Hunter's *The Blackboard Jungle* describes a growing loss of control in inner city high schools,[69] while middle-class delinquency was introduced in J.D. Salinger's *The Catcher in the Rye.*[70] The novels of these two decades suggest an increased concern with the problems of youth in general, not just with the social and economic conditions that foster delinquency.[71] As time passed, not only did literature paint a picture of delinquency that reflected the beliefs of the public at large, it was also instrumental in molding, shaping, and creating those beliefs.

Movies   Film is perhaps even more important than the novel in reflecting 20th-century concerns about juvenile delinquency, and it continues to shape our attitudes today. By the early 1930s movies reached audiences of millions. Delinquency and adult crime were frequent film subjects. As in the early novels, films, such as *The Dead End Kids* and *Boys' Town,* emphasized the influence of slum life and urban poverty on juvenile delinquency. The juvenile delinquent is portrayed as a good boy gone bad; a "misunderstood victim of official ignorance, indifference, or corruption."[72]

In the 1930s and 1940s audiences were given two or three alternative portrayals of adolescents. On the one hand, there was Andy Hardy, an innocent, middle-class, Midwestern child with an understanding father and a wonderful mother and sister. Any misbehavior on Andy's part was always viewed as a youthful prank or a consequence of some misunderstanding. On the other hand, movies such as *Wild Boys of the Road, Mayor of Hell, Angels with Dirty Faces, Where Are Your Children, Youth Run Wild,* and *I Accuse My Parents,* were essentially indictments on parental neglect.

Films produced between 1955 and 1970 emphasize the many faces of juvenile delinquency. Rebellion, dropping out of school, terrorizing innocents, and teenage alienation are all messages in films of this period. Society was presented with such films as *The Wild Ones, High School Confidential,* and *The Bad Seed.* James Dean became a teenage idol representing the ambiguity and alienation of youths unable to bridge the gap to their "uncaring and materialistic" parents. Unlike films of previous decades, delinquency is portrayed as much more violent and threatening to community stability. Ranging from gangs and drugs in schools to rock and roll music, hot rods, and drag strips, these films show adults an image of adolescence very alien to their own.

In the 1960s youths were variously seen as good-hearted and fun-loving in numerous beach movies; as romantically involved gang members in *West Side Story;* as subjects of adult misunderstanding in Dick Clark's *Because They're Young;* and as drug-using, motorcycle-riding adolescents looking for thrills in *Easy Rider, The Wild Angels, The Trip,* and *The Love-In.* In the 1970s many films focused on "the good old days," exemplified by *American Graffiti, The Lords of Flatbush,* and *Grease,* where the delinquent was just "one of the guys" and not a "real" threat to anyone. The characters in these films would smoke, drink, experiment with sex (and often get caught), and drive souped-up cars. These activities produce an image of nice adolescents misbehaving, not juveniles bound for reform school. On the other hand, films of the 1980s and 1990s, such as *The River's Edge, The Outsiders, Bad Boys, Close Range, Colors, Over the*

Edge, The Lost Boys, Menace II Society, Boys N' the Hood, New Jack City, and *Juice,* portray alienated, defiant, and ultimately violent juveniles, willing—even anxious—to challenge the established order. Several more recent movies continue to help define delinquency, including Larry Clark's *Kids* and *Bully,* which paint a world of children divorced from adults. The "rave" scene is portrayed in *Go, Heavy Traffic,* and *Groove,* illustrating teenagers in their own element, parent free. One of the more recent films on the topic is *Thirteen,* which focuses on a girl who lives a life without parental input. By the movie's end, she ultimately succumbs to peer pressure and a variety of problem behaviors, including delinquency.

Television   Perhaps because television brings the same characters to audiences week after week, individual roles (and their actors) need to elicit more sympathy. Weekly shows aim to establish attractive and interesting characters. A juvenile who uses drugs, steals, or assaults vulnerable strangers will unlikely generate the desired audience reaction. Consequently, very few television serials hint at serious juvenile delinquency, the exception perhaps being *South Park* or *Jackass.* The standard portrayal of delinquency is one of "innocent" rebellion or youthful pranks, such as those in shows like *That 70s Show, Eight Simple Rules for Dating My Daughter, Quintuplets,* and *Still Standing.* In addition, television also shows movie reruns or made-for-TV movies. While reruns contain the images of delinquency already discussed, television film specials often focus on more controversial material. For example, *Born Innocent,* about the ordeal of a 14-year-old girl in a juvenile detention center, raises the issue of uncaring parents again but also describes how the brutality of the detention center staff and the other inmates destroys the girl's innocence. Ultimately, the audience is asked to judge a juvenile justice system that degrades even the most minor offender. In a very different vein, *Go Ask Alice* portrays a middle-class teenage drug abuser who, after running away from home, falls into prostitution and eventually dies of a drug overdose.

Music   One of the oldest elements of popular culture is music. By the Middle Ages, songs and ballads were used to comment on life situations. Popular music today, however, finds itself in a relatively unique position. It appears as though no other medium is as generational, compartmentalized, or specific as that of music. In other words, specific genres of music are produced and consumed by particular audiences, and the *age* of the consumer is an important factor in determining one's tastes. Rock music and rap songs portray perhaps the widest sharing of images of juvenile delinquency. Not coincidentally, these styles of music are largely youth oriented. Young people not only constitute the vast majority of consumers, but they make up a large number of the acts and artists producing the music as well. Robert Pielke suggests "rock music expresses anarchistic beliefs about the possibilities of a social life free from external authority," from Bob Marley's *I Shot the Sheriff* and Bobby Fuller's *I Fought the Law and the Law Won* to songs that reflect acceptance of illegal drugs, such as *Legalize It* (Peter Tosh), *In da Club* (50 Cent), *My Fault* and *Drug Ballad* (Eminem), and *Cocaine* (Eric Clapton), the challenge to conventional morality and law through music is extensive. Punk rock and heavy metal music are widely associated with delinquency and youth gangs. Gangsta rap music may present an even greater challenge to authority. Songs of sexual exploitation, rape, murder, robbery, and drugs are interspersed with songs attacking the police and politicians, such as *Mission Murder; Execution of a Chump; Street Killer; Famous When You're Dead; Nobody Move, Nobody Get Hurt; and G Code,* which reflect an acceptance of interpersonal violence. Meanwhile songs such as *F_ _ _ the Police* and *Cop Killer* express serious threats to law enforcement.

To what extent does gangsta rap music reflect widely held values in conflict with conventional society? Do the images of criminal and delinquent acts portrayed in gangsta rap reflect real social conditions, or is the delinquency greatly exaggerated for the "benefit" of the larger society? Does this musical genre influence the attitudes and behaviors of youths? To the extent that artistic expressions generally reveal something about the culture in which they exist, gangsta rap music may present some of the most disturbing images of adolescence in the popular culture to white society. Furthermore, regardless of the accuracy of the depictions, the music is instrumental in the formation of beliefs about delinquency in the minds of the public and even law enforcement officials.[73]

Video Games   A large body of research is beginning to identify a connection between violent video games, such as *25 to Life, Grand Theft Auto, Doom, True Crime, Mortal Kombat, Resident Evil,* and *Super Columbine,* and *Massacre RPG,* and aggressive behavior in children.[74] Because video games are interactive, the players often identify with and model the behavior of specific characters. What may be harmful for children is twofold: (1) what they see in video games shapes their definition of what constitutes delinquent and criminal behavior and (2) more directly related to the game itself, what the child often sees in the game is a violent world, where he or she is required to shoot, harm, and kill people, including prostitutes and police, to be successful. In addition, in many of the video games manufactured in the 21st century, the sound effects are frightfully similar to reality; the shotgun reloads, the car swerves, and bodies fall.

Craig Anderson and his colleagues have conducted a series of studies on this topic and have concluded that when children play violent video games, it increases their physiological arousal, including higher systolic blood pressure; aggressive cognitions; aggressive emotions, perhaps causing intense frustration in children; and aggressive behavior, including aggressive play with objects and with peers.[75] There are several reasons why violent video games affect children in these ways:

- *Identification with an aggressor increases imitation.* In these games, children must take on the role of an aggressive character. This transition of the child most often occurs in "first-person shooter" games, where players "see" what their character would see if they were inside the video game themselves. The games force children to identify with a violent character, which may increase the likelihood of their imitating aggressive acts in the future.

- *Active participation also increases learning.* When children are enthusiastically involved in an activity, they learn more than when they are passively drawn in (e.g., watching television). By their nature, violent video games force children to engage in committing violent acts.

- *Practicing an entire behavioral sequence is more effective than practicing only a portion of it.* There are many steps to learn to complete a task successfully. To be successful in a violent video game, the child must decide to kill someone; choose the weapon to use; decide how to obtain the weapon; if the weapon is a gun, determine how to obtain ammunition and load the weapon; stalk the victim; aim the weapon; and ultimately use the weapon. In these games, children continuously repeat these steps. This sequence of events teaches some children the technique(s) for attempting to commit crime.

- *Violence is continuous.* The impact of violence on children is greater when the violence is unrelieved and uninterrupted. In video games the violence is reoccurring. Children must constantly be on alert for hostile enemies and select and execute aggressive behaviors.

- *Repetition increases learning.* The most effective way to learn any behavior is to repeat it (i.e., "practice makes perfect"). If you want to learn a new telephone number, you should constantly repeat it to yourself to place it in your memory. Some children play video games many hours during the day, and thus they are repeating violent acts over and over. Doing so increases the likelihood that children will learn from the games, some of what they learn becoming habitual to the point of being automatic.

In the end, parents and guardians play an important role in supervising the games children play. Unfortunately, however, while many parents lay down ground rules for how long their children may play video games, they often are shocked when they witness the content of the game. Even though manufacturers have been forced to produce a rating system to guide parents in their purchases, the rating system does not always accurately reflect the true content of the games. Some games rated by the industry as appropriate for "Everyone" contain harmful content; many games designed for teens contain violent content. As an example, cartoons are rarely looked at as dangerous, yet young children may still be affected by their violent nature. Extremely violent video games have been forced to include labels stating they are for mature audiences only. While the effect of playing violent video games is likely to vary among children, those most likely to be adversely affected are young children who have lax supervision and a history of aggression and violence.

about it

Should violent video games be made illegal? Is it a person's choice whether to play them?

Regardless of the impact of violent video games on some children, the courts have consistently ruled in favor of the video game industry. In 2006, for example, Federal District Court Judge James Brady overruled Louisiana's violent video game law, stating that video games are protected under the First Amendment; whether the games are violent or not, they are protected by free speech.[76]

WHAT IS DELINQUENCY? WHO IS DELINQUENT?

It is difficult to decide just which behaviors constitute juvenile delinquency and who juvenile delinquents are. The reason is because how society views children changes over time and from place to place. In fact, little uniformity exists among the 50 states regarding a definition of delinquency, beyond defining **juvenile delinquency** as behavior committed by a minor that violates the state's penal code. Some states clearly spell out, in legal statutes, what constitutes delinquent be-

figure 1-1   Continua of Delinquency

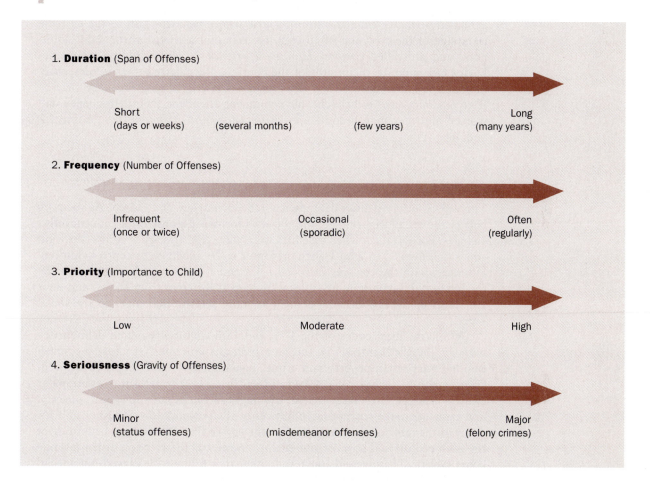

1. **Duration** (Span of Offenses)

Short
(days or weeks)   (several months)   (few years)   Long
(many years)

2. **Frequency** (Number of Offenses)

Infrequent
(once or twice)   Occasional
(sporadic)   Often
(regularly)

3. **Priority** (Importance to Child)

Low   Moderate   High

4. **Seriousness** (Gravity of Offenses)

Minor
(status offenses)   (misdemeanor offenses)   Major
(felony crimes)

think
about it

Do police select children to arrest based on their race, sex, or age? Might "official" delinquents be less intelligent than children who are not caught?

havior, while other states provide only a vague and imprecise definition of delinquency. The age of the offender is what distinguishes crime and delinquency. Delinquency refers to criminal acts committed by **juveniles** (in most states, people under age 18). When deciding who is a delinquent, criminologists often do not adopt a strict legal definition because nearly all children have broken the law and, had they been caught and prosecuted, could have been institutionalized for one or more years (see Chapter 2). However, differences in the behavior of children are measurable, and it is not instructive to argue all children are delinquent. Most children only sporadically act delinquent, while others are chronic offenders (see Chapter 2).

One way to characterize juvenile delinquency is to locate the behavior of children on a series of four continua that represent the (1) duration, (2) frequency, (3) priority, and (4) seriousness of the behavior. As shown in Figure 1-1, each factor forms its own continuum, with children falling at different points on each one. A **juvenile delinquent** is a child with a long and problematic history of involvement in crime.

Delinquent children are deeply committed (*priority*) to problem behavior and have committed many (*frequency*) serious offenses (*seriousness*) over an extended period of time (*duration*). Those whose behavior falls to the extreme right side of the continua often continue criminal activities throughout adulthood and are called *chronic delinquent offenders,* while children whose behavior falls more to the middle of the continua are referred to as *adolescence-limited offenders* because their delinquency is restricted to the teenage years.[77] If no one intervenes to help chronic delinquent offenders, their delinquency will worsen and they may become *life-course persistent offenders* (see Chapters 2 and 3).

conclusions

The way a society defines delinquency reflects its view of children. As society's beliefs about children change, the society's formal response to delinquency also changes. For instance, when juveniles were viewed as miniature adults, the legal codes that applied to adults were presumed to be adequate to control children. However, with the changes in social roles and relationships brought about by the Industrial Revolution, juveniles were seen as different from adults, and their violations of the law became defined as more serious challenges to the social order.

While the legal codes of the 17th and 18th centuries equated delinquency with sin, the 19th century saw this view replaced with one that forged a connection between urban poverty and crime. Juveniles were increasingly involved in crimes (mainly thefts) that resulted in their being sent to reform institutions or houses of refuge. To a large extent, the plight of the urban adolescent, poverty, and exposure to the corrupting influences of adult criminals were responsible for many of the reforms that took place at the end of the 19th and the beginning of the 20th centuries. The most significant reform was the creation of the juvenile court system. The juvenile court and codes that followed it carved out special areas of misbehavior and special conditions that permitted court intervention and the designation of a child as delinquent.

How delinquency is defined determines how criminologists measure and explain it. In the next chapter, measures of delinquency are discussed, with special attention given to what they tell us about the nature and the extent of the problem in modern society.

key terms

Achieved status   A status that is earned.

Ascribed status   A status that is received at birth.

Baby boomers   Persons born between 1946 and 1964.

Child Savers   The 19th-century reformers who believed children were basically good and blamed delinquency on a bad environment.

Chronic status offender   Children who continue to commit status offenses in spite of repeated interventions by family, school, social service, or law enforcement agencies.

Juvenile delinquency   Behavior committed by a minor that violates a state's penal code.

Juvenile delinquent   A child with a long and problematic history of involvement in crime.

Juveniles   In most states, people under age 18.

Parens patriae   The doctrine that defines the state as the ultimate guardian of every child.

Status   A socially defined position in a group.

Status offense   Acts illegal only for children, such as truancy.

Stubborn Child Law   This law passed in 1641 stated that children who disobeyed their parents might be put to death.

Measuring Delinquency

Historically, it has been difficult to measure juvenile delinquency. Years ago, the economist Sir Josiah Stamp said about crime statistics that they "come in the first instance from the village watchman, who just puts down what he damn pleases."[1] Criminologists have drawn the same conclusion. In 1947 Edwin Sutherland wrote that "the statistics of crime and criminals are the most unreliable of all statistics."[2] Twenty years later, Albert Biderman and Albert Reiss concluded that crime statistics involve "institutional processing of people's reports . . . the data are not some objectively observable universe of 'criminal acts,' but rather those events defined, captured, and processed by some institutional mechanism."[3]

There are other reasons why crime data are problematic. For example, crime is both *context* and *time* specific. Behavior is evaluated differently depending upon where and when it occurs. For instance, sexual promiscuity was judged differently in the Victorian period of the 19th century than today.[4] Additionally, some adolescents may commit crimes at relatively high levels but are never "caught" for their misdeeds, whereas others are arrested on their first offense. Thus, arrest records do not necessarily reflect actual delinquent behavior. Today, to ease these problems criminologists measure delinquency using multiple yardsticks, and when they are taken together, they provide a respectable approximation of the extent and nature of delinquency. The most popular sources of data for estimating delinquency are the *Uniform Crime Reports*, victimization surveys, and self-report studies.

UNIFORM CRIME REPORTS

The *Uniform Crime Reporting Program* is a nationwide, cooperative effort of more than 16,000 city, county, and state law enforcement agencies who voluntarily report to the Federal Bureau of Investigation (FBI) data on crimes brought to their attention. The data are published in an annual report titled, *Crime in the United States,* which is also called the **Uniform Crime Reports (UCR)**. The UCR contains data on:

1. *Crimes known to the police.* These are crimes police know about. They may be crimes reported to police or crimes police discovered on their own.

2. *Number of arrests.* The UCR reports the number of arrests police made in the past calendar year. The number of arrests is not the same as the number of people arrested because some people are arrested more than once during the year. Nor does the number of arrests indicate how many crimes the people who were arrested committed because multiple crimes committed by one person may produce a single arrest, or a single crime may result in the arrest of multiple persons.

3. *Persons arrested.* The third section of the UCR reports the number of persons arrested, the crimes for which they were arrested, and the age, sex, and race of those arrested.

A large number of the nations' law enforcement agencies participate in the UCR Program, and they represent more than 93 percent of the total U.S. population.

Since 1930 the FBI has administered the UCR Program. The Program's primary objective is to generate reliable information for use in law enforcement administration, operation, and management; however, over the years its data have become one of the country's leading social indicators. The American public looks to the *UCR* for information on fluctuations in the level of crime, and criminologists, legislators, municipal planners, the media, and other students of criminal justice use the statistics for varied research and planning purposes.

Historical Background

Recognizing a need for national crime statistics, the International Association of Chiefs of Police (IACP) formed the Committee on Uniform Crime Records in 1927 to develop a system of uniform crime statistics. Establishing offenses known to law enforcement as the appropriate measure, the committee evaluated various crimes on the basis of their seriousness, frequency of occurrence, pervasiveness in all geographic areas of the country, and likelihood of being reported to law enforcement. After studying state criminal codes and making an evaluation of the record keeping practices in use, the committee completed a plan for crime reporting that became the foundation of the UCR Program in 1929.

Beginning in 1991, the *UCR* has published data on the number of crimes motivated by hate reported by law enforcement. From 1991 to 2006, roughly 100,000 hate crimes have been reported. How do children learn to hate others and to commit crimes against them?

Seven main offense classifications, called **Part I crimes,** were selected to gauge the state of crime in the United States. These seven offense classifications eventually became known as the **Crime Index** and included the violent crimes of murder and nonnegligent-manslaughter, forcible rape, robbery, aggravated assault, and the property crimes of burglary, larceny, and motor vehicle theft. By congressional mandate in 1979, arson was added as the eighth Index offense. Data on an additional 21 less serious offenses were classified as **Part II crimes,** and included such offenses as simple assault, fraud, and liquor law violations.

During the early planning of the *UCR* Program, it was recognized that the differences among criminal codes in the various states precluded a mere aggregation of state statistics to arrive at a national total. Further, because of variances in punishment for the same offenses in different state codes, no distinction between felony and misdemeanor crimes was possible. To avoid these problems and to provide nationwide uniformity in crime reporting, standardized offense definitions by which law enforcement agencies were to submit data without regard for local statutes were formulated.

In January 1930, 400 cities representing 20 million persons in 43 states began participating in the *UCR* Program. For more than 75 years, the *UCR* Program has relied on police agencies to forward information to the FBI either directly or through a state-level crime-recording program. Police tabulate the number of offenses committed each month based on records of all reports of crime received from victims, from officers who discover violations, and from other sources. The data are forwarded to the FBI regardless of whether anyone was arrested, property was recovered, or prosecution was undertaken.[5] The FBI audits each agency report for arithmetical accuracy and for deviations from previous submissions. An agency's monthly report is compared with its earlier submissions to identify unusual fluctuations. Large variations from one month to the next might indicate changes in the volume of crime being committed or be due to changes in an agency's recording practices, incomplete reporting, or changes in the jurisdiction's geopolitical structure (land might have been annexed).

Recent Developments

Although *UCR* data collection had originally been conceived as a tool for law enforcement administration, by the 1980s, the data were widely used by other entities involved in various forms of social planning. Recognizing the need for more detailed crime statistics, law enforcement called for a thorough evaluative analysis that would modernize the *UCR* Program. These studies led to the creation and implementation of the *National Incident-Based Reporting System* (*NIBRS*) in 1989.

The *NIBRS* collects data on each single incident and arrest. For each offense known to the police within these categories, incident, victim, property, offender, and arrestee information are gathered. In total, 53 data elements on crimes in 22 categories are recorded. The detailed, accurate, and meaningful data produced by *NIBRS* benefit local agencies. Armed with comprehensive crime data, local agencies can better make their case to acquire and effectively allocate the resources needed to fight crime. Currently, almost 6,000 law enforcement agencies contribute *NIBRS* data to the national *UCR* Program. The data submitted by the agencies represent 20 percent of the U.S. population and 16 percent of the crime statistics collected by the *UCR* Program. The current timetable calls for all U.S. law enforcement agencies to be participating in the *NIBRS* Program by 2010.[6]

Three other reforms that have improved the quality of *UCR* data are also noteworthy. First, in 1988, to increase participation in the *UCR* Program, Congress passed the *Uniform Federal Reporting Act,* which mandates that all federal law enforcement agencies will submit crime data to the *UCR* Program. Second, in 1990, to facilitate the collection of data on a wider range of crimes, Congress passed the *Hate Crime Statistics Act.* The FBI in the annual *Hate Crime Statistics* report publishes these data—reporting the number of crimes motivated by religious, ethnic, racial, or sexual-orientation prejudice. Third, in 1990, in response to increasing crime on college and university campuses across the nation, Congress passed the *Crime Awareness and Campus Security Act.* This law, which requires colleges to tally and report campus crime data to the *UCR* Program, was passed after Jeanne Clery, a 19-year-old freshman at Lehigh University (Pennsylvania), was raped and murdered while asleep in her residence hall on April 5, 1986. When Jeanne's parents investigated the crime, they discovered that Lehigh University had not told students about 38 violent crimes on the Lehigh campus in the 3 years before Jeanne's murder. The Clerys joined with other campus crime victims and persuaded Congress to pass this law.[7] Today, every college in its annual campus security report publishes crime data that are available to all students, parents, and the public.

The most important change to the *UCR* Program was implemented in 2004 when it was decided that the Crime Index would be discontinued. However, the FBI will continue to publish in the *UCR* a serious *violent* crime total and a serious *property* crime total, until a more viable index is developed. The serious violent crime total includes the offenses of murder and nonnegligent manslaughter, forcible rape, robbery, and aggravated assault; the crimes included in the serious property crime total are burglary, larceny-theft, motor vehicle theft, and arson (see Box 2-1).

The Crime Index was first published in 1960. However, in recent years the Crime Index has not been a true indicator of the degree of criminality. The Crime Index was simply the title used for an aggregation of offense classifications, known as Part I crimes, for which data have been collected since the *UCR* Program's implementation. The Crime Index was driven upward by the offense with the highest number, in this case larceny-thefts, creating a bias against a jurisdiction with a high number of larceny-thefts, but a low number of other serious crimes such as murder and forcible rape. Currently, larceny-theft makes up nearly 60 percent of reported crime, and thus the sheer volume of those offenses overshadow more serious, but less frequently committed offenses.

Criticisms of *UCR* Data

In addition to a concern over the sometimes false perception that was created in the minds of criminologists, social planners, and the public by the now defunct Crime Index, criminologists disagree on whether the *UCR* generally is a valid measure of crime. Walter Gove and his associates think it is "a valid indicator of crime as defined by the citizenry."[8] Other criminologists contend that because the *UCR* only reports "crime known to the police," it grossly underestimates

box 2-1 THE FACE OF DELINQUENCY
Uniform Crime Report *Offenses*

The *UCR* is divided into eight *serious* violent and property crimes and 21 "other" offenses. Law enforcement agencies report data on the number of serious violent and property offenses known to them and the number of people arrested monthly to the FBI.

SERIOUS VIOLENT AND PROPERTY OFFENSES

1. *Murder and nonnegligent manslaughter:* The willful killing of one human being by another.
2. *Forcible rape:* The carnal knowledge of a female forcibly and against her will.
3. *Robbery:* The taking or attempting to take anything of value from the care, custody, or control of a person or persons by force or threat of force or violence and/or by putting the victim in fear.
4. *Aggravated assault:* The unlawful attack by one person upon another for the purpose of inflicting severe or aggravated bodily injury.
5. *Burglary:* The unlawful entry of a structure to commit a felony or theft.
6. *Larceny-theft:* The unlawful taking, carrying, leading, or riding away of property from the possession or constructive possession of others. Examples are thefts of bicycles or automobile accessories, shoplifting, and pocket-picking.
7. *Motor vehicle theft:* The theft or attempted theft of a motor vehicle.
8. *Arson:* Any willful or malicious burning or attempt to burn, with or without intent to defraud, a dwelling house, public building, motor vehicle or aircraft, or the personal property of another.

OTHER OFFENSES

1. Other assaults
2. Forgery and counterfeiting
3. Fraud
4. Embezzlement
5. Stolen property; buying, receiving, possessing
6. Vandalism
7. Weapons; carrying, possessing
8. Prostitution and commercialized vice
9. Sex offenses (except forcible rape and prostitution)
10. Drug abuse violations
11. Gambling
12. Offenses against the family and children
13. Driving under the influence
14. Liquor laws
15. Drunkenness
16. Disorderly conduct
17. Vagrancy
18. All other offenses (except traffic)
19. Suspicion
20. Curfew and loitering violations
21. Runaways

Source: Federal Bureau of Investigation, *Crime in the United States, 2006* (Washington, DC: U.S. Department of Justice, 2007).

the number of delinquent acts committed (**incidence**) and the number of juveniles committing delinquency (**prevalence**). Many crimes go unreported to the police. A report published in 2006 by the U.S. Department of Justice found that 62 percent of aggravated assaults, 42 percent of simple assaults, 56 percent of burglaries, 83 percent of auto thefts, and just 32 percent of thefts were reported to police. Victims did not report crime for a variety of reasons, including that they considered the crime to be a private or personal matter, that it was not important enough, or that they feared reprisal.[9] But because most crime is not reported, there exists an extremely large **dark figure of crime,** which is the gap between the actual amount of crime committed and crime reported to the police. One early criminologist who had observed the dark figure was the 19th-century scholar Adolphe Quetelet who wrote, "All we possess of statistics of crime and misdemeanors would have no utility at all if we did not tacitly assume that there is a nearly invariable relationship between offenses known and adjudicated and the total unknown sum of offenses committed.[10] A century later, Edwin Sutherland suggested that the *UCR* was invalid because it did not include data on "white-collar criminals."[11] In his work on female criminality, Otto Pollak reported that females were underrepresented in *UCR* because police treated them more leniently.[12] It is a fair conclusion to draw that the *UCR* might have more to say about police behavior than it does about criminality.

Another major limitation of the *UCR* is its reliance on the **hierarchy rule,** whereby in a multiple-offense situation police record only the most serious crime incident. If someone is robbed at gunpoint, forcibly rapes the victim, and steals the victim's car, only the forcible rape is reported in the *UCR* totals. The less serious offenses of robbery and motor vehicle theft are not counted. The hierarchy rule does not apply to arson, which is reported in all situations.

Its limitations aside, the *UCR* are widely used. It is one of only two sources of data that provides a *national* estimate of the nature and extent of delinquency. Criminologists who use *UCR* data assume the inaccuracies are consistent over time, and, therefore, the data accurately depict delinquency trends. In other words, while *UCR* data might be flawed, they yet may be stable enough to show year-to-year changes. Research supports the validity of the *UCR* and official crime data generally. Ramona Rantala and Thomas Edwards recently compared the *UCR* and *NIBRS* to determine if they produced similar estimates of crime. They do. Rantala and Edward found that when comparing data from the same year for the jurisdictions in this study, *NIBRS* rates differed only slightly from summary *UCR* rates. Murder rates were the same. Rape, robbery, and aggravated assault rates were about 1 percent higher in *NIBRS* than *UCR*. The *NIBRS* burglary rate was a mere 0.5 percent lower than the *UCR* rate. Differences in theft were slightly more than 3 percent, and motor vehicle thefts were just 4 percent. The convergence of *NIBRS* and *UCR* data suggests that both programs are worthwhile estimates of crime in the nation.[13]

think
about it

Should police exercise discretion when deciding how to report a crime? Is there any way to limit police discretion in crime reporting?

VICTIMIZATION SURVEYS

Surveys of crime victims were developed in the late 1960s in response to the weaknesses of the *UCR*, particularly the dark figure of crime. One popular measure is the **victimization survey.** Instead of asking police about delinquency, victimization surveys ask people about their experiences as crime victims. National crime surveys have several advantages over the *UCR*. They are a more direct measure of criminal behavior, and victim surveys provide more detailed information about situational factors surrounding a crime, for example, the physical location of the crime event, the time of day it occurred, whether a weapon was used, and the relationship between the victim and offender.[14]

National Opinion Research Center Survey

In 1967 the **National Opinion Research Center** completed the first nationwide victimization survey. Interviews were conducted with 10,000 households with 33,000 people. In each household, a knowledgeable person was asked a few short "screening" questions, such as "Were you or was anyone in the household in a fist fight or attacked in any way by another person—including another household member—within the past 12 months?" If the respondent answered, "yes" to the question, the victim was interviewed. What director Philip Ennis found was that the victimization rate for Crime Index offenses was more than double the rate reported in the *UCR*.[15] This finding triggered both surprise and alarm, and interest in victimization surveys soared, prompting the development of a much larger effort, the *National Crime Victimization Survey*, a few years later.

National Crime Victimization Survey

In 1972 the Bureau of Justice Statistics launched the *National Crime Survey,* which, in 1990, was renamed the **National Crime Victimization Survey** (*NCVS*), to emphasize more clearly the measurement of victimizations experienced by American citizens. The *NCVS* was redesigned in 1992, and it is thus problematic to compare results from surveys conducted in 1992 and later with those conducted from 1972 to 1991.[16]

The *NCVS* is the most comprehensive and systematic survey of victims in the United States, producing data on both *personal* and *household* crimes. The personal crimes are divided into two categories: crimes of violence (rape, robbery, and assault) and crimes of theft (larceny with or without contact). Murder is *not* measured by the *NCVS* because the victim cannot be interviewed. Household crimes tapped by the survey are burglary, household larceny, and motor vehicle theft. These eight offenses are the **crimes of interest.** They were selected because victims are likely to report them to police, and victims are typically able to recall them when Census Bureau interviewers question them.

NCVS data are obtained from interviews with more than 134,000 people who represent nearly 77,200 households. Only people age 13 and older are interviewed. (Information on people age 12 and under is obtained from older household members.) Each interviewee is asked a few screening questions to determine whether he or she was a victim of one or more of the *crimes of interest* (see Box 2-2). Respondents who answer *yes* to any of the screening questions are asked additional questions that probe the nature of the crime incident. On the basis of the responses received, the interviewer classifies the crime incident as falling into one of the crimes of interest categories.

Households are selected for inclusion using a rotated panel design. Every household—whether urban or rural, whether living in a detached single-family house or an efficiency apartment, whether consisting of a family or unrelated people—has the same chance of being selected. Once chosen for inclusion, the household remains in the survey for 3 years. If members of the household move during this period, that address remains part of the survey and the new occupants enter the sample. No attempt is made to follow past occupants who move to new addresses. After 3 years, a participating household is replaced with a new one, so new households are always entering the sample.

The National Crime Victimization Survey asks juveniles directly about crimes committed against them during a specific time period. The questions asked of children are similar to the following questions:

1. Did you have your pocket picked/purse snatched?

2. Did anyone try to rob you by using force or threatening to harm you?

3. Did anyone beat you up, attack you, or hit you with something, such as a rock or bottle?

4. Were you knifed, shot at, or attacked with some other weapon by anyone at all?

5. Did anyone steal things that belonged to you from inside any car or truck, such as packages or clothing?

6. Was anything stolen from you while you were away from home, for instance at work, in a theater or restaurant, or while traveling?

7. Did you call the police during the last six months to report something that happened to you that you thought was a crime? If yes, how many times?

Source: Bureau of Justice Statistics, *Criminal Victimization in the United States, 2006* (Washington, DC: U.S. Department of Justice, 2007).

NCVS data are a very useful source of information, particularly increasing our understanding of the dark figure of crime. To paraphrase L. Edward Wells and Joseph Rankin, *NCVS* data:

1. Confirm that a considerable amount of delinquency is unknown to police.

2. Have uncovered some reasons why victims do not report crime incidents to police.

3. Demonstrate that the amount of variation in the official reporting of delinquency changes across type of offenses, victim–offender relationships, situational factors, and characteristics.

4. Have drawn theoretical attention to delinquency often being the result of social interaction between a victim and offender.[17]

Like any measuring tool, the *NCVS* has flaws. Obviously the small number of crimes of interest is problematic. Even though it is important to collect data on the crimes of interest, they represent only a small fraction of all crimes committed. Most arrests are for crimes involving alcohol and illegal drugs, and many robberies, burglaries, and larcenies are committed against businesses and not individuals.[18] By excluding these and other crimes, the *NCVS* provides data on merely a small subset of crime incidents.

The *NCVS* is based on answers people give to questions regarding past and sometimes troublesome events. Thus, at least five known problems might affect the reliability of data:

1. *Memory errors.* People might have difficulty recalling when or how many times an event occurred.

2. *Telescoping.* Interviewees might "remember" a crime of interest as occurring more recently than it did because the event remains vivid in their memories.

3. *Errors of deception.* It may be difficult for victims to report events that are embarrassing or otherwise unpleasant to talk about or events that might incriminate them. It is also possible that people will fabricate crime incidents.

4. *Juvenile victimizations.* Adolescents might be less likely to discuss their victimizations with an adult stranger, particularly if their victimizations involve peers or a family member. Another difficulty when interviewing juveniles and people living in different cultures and belonging to different groups is they might define crime differently than an *NCVS* interviewer.

5. *Sampling error.* When samples are used to represent populations, there always is the possibility of a discrepancy between sample estimates of behavior and the actual amount of behavior. For instance, since the sampling unit in the *NCVS* is households, homeless children, who are at greater risk of victimization, are excluded from the sample.

To improve the likelihood that respondents will recall events accurately, recent changes have been made to the survey's methodology. The newly revised survey includes questions and cues that help to refresh the memories of victims. In addition, interviewers ask more explicit questions about sexual victimizations. For instance, today, interviewees are asked:

> Have you been forced or coerced to engage in unwanted sexual activity by: (a) someone you didn't know before, (b) a casual acquaintance, or (c) someone you know well.

Findings from the redesigned survey were first published in 1992. One of the most significant findings from the redesigned survey was that victims recalled and reported more types of crime incidents, particularly more incidents of rape, aggravated and simple assaults.

Consensus of Official and Victimization Data

To what degree do official and victimization data paint the same picture about the extent of crime in the United States? This is an important question. If official and victimization reports conflict widely, then we should have little confidence in our understanding about the true magnitude of crime. If official and victimization data converge, then we are likely measuring the crime problem with confidence, validity, and reliability.

Fortunately, official and victimization data generally match. Janet Lauritsen and Robin Schaum recently compared *UCR* and *NCVS* data for robbery, burglary, and aggravated assault in Chicago, Los Angeles, and New York from 1980 to 1998. As the three largest cities in the country, this sampling method represents the bulk of crime that is committed in the United States. They found that for burglary and robbery, *UCR* crime rates were generally similar to *NCVS* estimates over the study period. Police and victim survey data were more likely to show discrepancies in levels and trends of aggravated assault. Lauritsen and Schaum also found that even when *UCR* and *NCVS* data were different, the differences were not statistically significant.[19] Substantively, the *UCR* and *NCVS* tell the same story about the extent of these three serious crimes in the nation's three biggest metropolitan areas. Indeed, for over 30 years, criminologists have found that official and victimization data generally tell the same story about the incidence of crime and delinquency in the United States.[20]

SELF-REPORT STUDIES

think about it

Would you tell strangers the truth about crimes you committed? If so, would you embellish or minimize your involvement? Why might people lie?

A third source of information on the nature and extent of delinquency comes from **self-report studies,** which ask juveniles directly about their law-violating behavior (see Box 2-3). The advantage of self-report studies is the information that criminologists receive from juveniles regarding their involvement in crime has not been filtered through the police or through any other criminal or juvenile justice officials. It is raw data.

This strength, however, is also the principal weakness of self-reports. The crimes adolescents say they have committed may or may not be accurate for some of the same reasons victimization surveys are flawed, for example, memory errors, telescoping, and lying.

---

box 2-3   THE FACE OF DELINQUENCY
Self-Report Delinquency Survey

A self-report survey asks juveniles directly about their participation in delinquent and criminal behavior during a specific time period. For the following list of items please indicate in the past 12 months how many times you committed each one. Check the best answer.

OFFENSE	NEVER DID ACT	1 TIME	2–5 TIMES	6–9 TIMES	10 OR MORE TIMES
1. Petty theft	_____	_____	_____	_____	_____
2. Forgery	_____	_____	_____	_____	_____
3. Used cocaine	_____	_____	_____	_____	_____
4. Used marijuana	_____	_____	_____	_____	_____
5. Gambling	_____	_____	_____	_____	_____
6. Weapon violation	_____	_____	_____	_____	_____
7. Burglary	_____	_____	_____	_____	_____
8. Fighting	_____	_____	_____	_____	_____
9. Used fake ID	_____	_____	_____	_____	_____
10. Vandalism	_____	_____	_____	_____	_____
11. Truancy	_____	_____	_____	_____	_____
12. Runaway	_____	_____	_____	_____	_____
13. Curfew	_____	_____	_____	_____	_____
14. Liquor violation	_____	_____	_____	_____	_____
15. Drunk driving	_____	_____	_____	_____	_____

Historical Background

In 1946 Austin Porterfield published the first self-report study of delinquent behavior. He compared the self-reported delinquency of 337 college students with that of 2,049 youths who had appeared before the juvenile court. Porterfield found that over 90 percent of the college students surveyed admitted to at least one felony.[21] The next year James Wallerstein and J. C. Wyle conducted a survey of self-reported delinquent behavior using a sample of 1,698 adult men and women focusing on behavior they had committed when they were juveniles. They discovered that 99 percent of the sample admitted to committing at least one offense they could have been arrested for had they been caught.[22] In 1954 James F. Short Jr. reported findings from the first self-report study to include institutionalized juvenile delinquents.[23] In 1958 Short and F. Ivan Nye published a study of (1) juveniles in three Washington State communities, (2) students in three Midwestern towns, and (3) a sample of delinquents in training schools. They found that delinquency was widespread across these social groups.[24]

These findings inspired more systematic research. In 1963 Maynard Erickson and LaMar Empey interviewed boys between the ages of 15 to 17 and included four subsamples: (1) 50 boys who had not appeared in court, (2) 30 boys who had one court appearance, (3) 50 boys who were on probation, and (4) 50 boys who were incarcerated. They found that there was a tremendous amount of hidden or undetected delinquency, and those who had been officially labeled "delinquent" admitted to committing many more offenses than those who had not been so labeled (see Chapter 7).[25] Jay Williams and Martin Gold conducted the first nationwide self-report study of delinquency in 1967. Using interviews and official records of 847, 13- to 16-year-old boys and girls, they discovered that 88 percent of the teenagers admitted to committing at least one chargeable offense in the past 3 years.[26]

The most comprehensive and systematic self-report study to date is the **National Youth Survey** (*NYS*), started in 1976 by Delbert Elliott. The *NYS* is a nationwide survey of more than 1,700 youths who were between the ages of 11 and 17 at the time of the first interview. From more than 100 cities and towns, the respondents represented every socioeconomic, racial, and ethnic group. For more than 30 years this original group of respondents (now 30 to 40 years old) has reported to Elliott how often during the past 12 months (from one Christmas to the next) they have committed certain criminal acts, ranging from felony assaults to minor thefts.[27]

Strengths and Weaknesses

Criminologists have learned a great deal about delinquency from self-report surveys. It is now widely accepted that over 90 percent of juveniles have committed an act that, if they had been caught and prosecuted to the full extent of the law, could have had them incarcerated. Self-report studies have also made criminologists more aware of how large the dark figure of crime might actually be. The amount of delinquency hidden from criminal justice officials is between 4 and 10 times greater than what is reported in the *UCR*. Finally, self-report research has produced consistent evidence that is suggestive of a racial and ethnic bias in the processing of juveniles who enter the juvenile justice system.[28]

The criticisms of the self-report method are similar to the ones leveled at survey methodology generally. One complaint focuses on how the data are collected. Another concern is whether it is reasonable to expect that juveniles would admit their illegal acts to strangers. Why should they? Other problems critics of the self-report method point to are the same concerns that are raised regarding victimization surveys. When juveniles are asked about their involvement in delinquency, they may forget, misunderstand, distort, or lie about what happened. Some teenagers exaggerate their crimes while others minimize theirs.

These concerns have caused criminologists to design methods to validate the findings from self-report studies. One technique used is to compare the youth's responses with official police records. Studies using this technique have found a high correlation between reported delinquency and official delinquency.[29] Other techniques criminologists have used to validate self-reports include having friends verify the honesty of the juvenile's answers, testing subjects more than once to see if their answers remain the same, and asking subjects to submit to a polygraph test.[30]

Findings from studies implementing one or more of the validity checks have provided general support of the self-report method. In a comprehensive review of the reliability and validity of self-reports, Michael Hindelang and his colleagues concluded:

> The difficulties in self-report instruments currently in use would appear to be surmountable; the method of self-reports does not appear from these studies to be fundamentally flawed. Reliability measures are impressive and the majority of studies produce validity coefficients in the moderate to strong range.[31]

Despite the strong support of the self-report method, it has one glaring weakness, namely the worst delinquents usually do not participate. Stephen Cernkovich and his colleagues believe self-report studies might exclude the most serious chronic offenders and therefore provide a gauge of delinquency for only the less serious, occasional offenders. They reached this conclusion after comparing the self-reported behavior of incarcerated and nonincarcerated youths. The researchers detected significant differences in the offending patterns of the two groups, leading them to conclude: "Institutionalized youth are not only more delinquent than the 'average kid' in the general population, but also considerably more delinquent than the most delinquent youth identified in the typical self-report."[32]

The potential omission of the most serious and chronic delinquents is critical in two ways. First, surveys that lack the most active delinquent offenders are, by definition, not producing valid estimates of delinquency. Second, this results in a mischaracterization of delinquency trends because the behavior of chronic delinquents is significantly different than "normal" delinquents (see Box 2-4). The importance of chronic delinquents is discussed later in this chapter.

DELINQUENCY TRENDS

Of the more than 300 million people who live in the United States, 26 percent (78 million) are under age 18.[33] A violent crime is committed every 23 seconds, a forcible rape every 6 minutes, and a murder roughly every 32 minutes. Who is primarily responsible for this crime? Are the offenders more likely to be adults or juveniles? Are offenders more often males or females? Wealthy or poor? African American? White? Hispanic? When the offender is a child, adults ask a lot of questions. Are more children committing crime today than 10 years ago? Is the criminal behavior of girls becoming more like that of boys? Do African

box 2-4   A WINDOW OF DELINQUENCY
Juvenile Delinquents Behind Bars

Twice each year, the Office of Juvenile Justice and Delinquency Prevention conducts a census of juvenile residential facilities to produce information on the more than 100,000 youths that are detained in facilities in the United States. By taking a look at the characteristics of the children and adolescents who are behind bars, one can more clearly understand the diversity of the delinquent population. Although delinquency is normative during adolescence, the following profile illustrates the multiple problems that incarcerated youth face.

The typical detained delinquent has a substance abuse problem and has abused multiple types of drugs, including alcohol, marijuana, cocaine, and inhalants, among others. Many youths suffer from one or more psychiatric problems for depression, anxiety, and affective disorders. Among detained youth, the prevalence of conduct disorder, oppositional-defiant disorder, attention deficit/hyperactivity disorder (ADHD), and even psychopathy are dramatically higher than among youths in the general population. Youths behind bars are also significantly more likely to have been abused, neglected, and maltreated. In addition to higher rates of victimization, these young people overwhelmingly come from severely impoverished backgrounds. According to the most recent census, 26 youths died while in custody. The leading cause of death was suicide.

Today, only the most at-risk juvenile offenders are committed to state and private institutions. As this profile indicates, much treatment, counseling, and education is needed to aid in their rehabilitation. However, prior research indicates that rehabilitation of the most high-risk delinquents is well worth the investment. Mark Cohen found that high-risk youths create correctional and victimization costs between $1.3 million and 1.5 million per delinquent! Matt DeLisi and Jewel Gatling replicated Cohen's finding and also found that the most chronic offenders can create costs to society in excess of $12 million per offender. Recently, Michael Caldwell and his colleagues found that intensive treatment programs for unmanageable delinquent males yielded a cost–benefit ratio of 7 to 1. For every dollar invested in helping a high-risk youth, seven dollars and untold victimization and negativity is prevented.

Sources: Linda Teplin, Karen Abram, Gary McClelland, Amy Mericle, Mina Dulcan, and Jason Washburn, *Psychiatric Disorders of Youth in Detention* (Washington, DC: U.S. Department of Justice, 2006); Jill Gordon and Page Moore, "ADHD Among Incarcerated Youth: An Investigation on the Congruency with ADHD Prevalence and Correlates Among the General Population," *American Journal of Criminal Justice* 30:87–97 (2005); Dustin Pardini, John Lochman, and Paul Frick, "Callous/Unemotional Traits and Social-Cognitive Process in Adjudicated Youths," *Journal of the American Academy of Child and Adolescent Psychiatry* 42:364–371 (2003); Mark Cohen, "The Monetary Value of Saving a High-Risk Youth," *Journal of Quantitative Criminology* 14:5–56 (1988); Matt DeLisi and Jewel Gatling, "Who Pays for a Life of Crime?" *Criminal Justice Studies* 16:28–293 (2003); Michael Caldwell, Michael Vitacco, and Gregory Van Rybroek, "Are Violent Delinquents Worth Treating? A Cost–Benefit Analysis," *Journal of Research in Crime and Delinquency* 43:1148–168 (2006).

Americans commit more crime than whites? Are age and delinquency related? How does social class impact involvement in delinquency? These and other important questions are answered in this section.

In 2005 police made more than 14 million arrests, 15.3 percent (1.58 million) of *all* persons arrested were juveniles. For both adults and juveniles, most persons had been arrested for relatively minor crimes. For instance, juveniles were most commonly arrested for larceny-theft. The most recent data indicate that young people were arrested for 15 percent of *all* crimes and for 16 and 26 percent of serious *violent* and *property* offenses, respectively. Juveniles were most likely to be arrested for **status offenses,** a behavior that is unlawful only for children (see Chapter 1). In 2005 the *UCR* reported 92,556 juvenile arrests for liquor law violations, 104,054 arrests for curfew violators, and 81,222 arrests for running away. (Arrests for truancy, incorrigibility, and other status offenses are not reported in the *UCR*.) The juvenile proportion of arrests reported in the *UCR* for all offenses appears in Table 2-1.[34]

table 2-1 Percentage of All Crimes Resulting in a Juvenile Arrest, 2005

OFFENSE CHARGED	JUVENILE ARRESTS (%)
Murder and nonnegligent manslaughter	9.0%
Forcible rape	15.4
Robbery	25.2
Aggravated assault	13.6
Burglary	26.1
Larceny-theft	25.7
Motor vehicle theft	25.5
Arson	48.6
Violent crime	**15.8**
Property crime	**26.0**
Other assaults	19.0
Forgery and counterfeiting	3.5
Fraud	2.5
Embezzlement	6.1
Stolen property	16.6
Vandalism	37.2
Weapon violation	23.1
Prostitution	1.9
Other sex offenses	18.2
Drug abuse violations	10.4
Gambling	18.1
Offenses against family	4.2
Driving under the influence	1.3
Liquor laws	21.1
Drunkenness	2.9
Disorderly conduct	29.7
Vagrancy	14.0
All other offenses (except traffic)	9.4
Suspicion	14.6
Curfew and loitering violations	100.0
Runaways	100.0
TOTAL	**15.3**

Source: Federal Bureau of Investigation, *Crime in the United States, 2005* (Washington, DC: U.S. Department of Justice, 2006).

Is Delinquency Decreasing or Increasing?

Less delinquency is committed today than in earlier years. As shown in Figure 2-1, current violent victimizations with juvenile offenders are approximately 40 to 60 percent *below* the average over the past quarter century. From the peak of violent victimizations with juvenile offenders in 1993, the current levels are down approximately 120 percent. Juvenile violent Crime Index arrests tell a similar story. Current data indicate that adolescents are arrested for murder, rape, robbery, and aggravated assault at nearly 20 percent *below* the historical average. From the peak juvenile violent Crime Index arrest rate in 1993–1994, the current levels are down nearly 80 percent.[35]

According to the *NCVS,* from 1993 to 2005 the violent crime rate was down 58 percent from 50 to 21 victimizations per 1,000 persons age 12 or older. Property crime declined 52 percent from 319 to 154 per 1,000 households. The greatest recent declines in victimization occurred among persons ages 16 to 19 whose victimization rates dropped 19 percent. Overall, in the early 21st century, crime and victimization rates are at their lowest point in several decades.[36] Although the overall forecast is promising, violent crime increased 2 percent into 2006 and homicides were up about 5 percent.[37] While this is cause for public concern, crime analysts suggest that it is too soon to tell if very recent trends in violent crime are the beginning of a larger surge like the one that occurred in the early 1990s.[38]

figure 2-1   Juvenile Violent Crime, 1981–2003

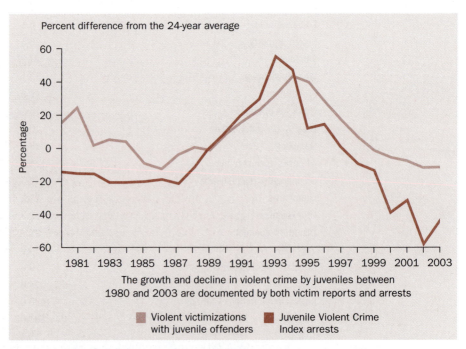

The growth and decline in violent crime by juveniles between 1980 and 2003 are documented by both victim reports and arrests

Source: Howard Snyder and Melissa Sickmund, *Juvenile Offenders and Victims: 2006 National Report* (Washington, DC: Office of Juvenile Justice and Delinquency Prevention, 2006).

The explanations most often given for the decline in crime are the economy, increased use of prisons, better policing, an aging population, and a decline in youth involvement in the crack market and gang involvement in crack distribution, and legalized abortion (see Box 2-5).[39] These different reasons are briefly explained below.

1. *Economy.* Reductions in delinquency have been attributed to the economy regardless of whether it is in recession or expansion. In "bad times," the economy may lead to fewer crimes because unemployed parents are more likely to be home supervising their children (see Chapter 10). In "good times," the economy provides young people with more legitimate opportunities to earn money, making it less likely that they will see crime as a necessary or desirable option.[40]

2. *Prisons.* Incarcerating more offenders for a longer period of time and with greater certainty reduces the crime rate. In fact, renowned criminologist James Q. Wilson believes that putting offenders in prison is the single most important thing society can do to decrease crime. Since 1985 the U.S. incarceration rate has increased fivefold. During this era, the amount of time served behind bars increased dramatically as most states adopted the 85 percent federal truth-in-sentencing standard. The impact of these policies and practices was that more active and chronic offenders were being sentenced to prison and they were staying there for longer periods of time. Criminologists have feverishly studied the effects of prison expansion on crime, and the bottom line is that the prison boom explains between 13 and 54 percent of the recent crime decline.[41]

3. *Policing.* Better policing is also sometimes cited as a reason for the drop in crime. One effective strategy is based on the "broken windows" thesis, which argues that just as a broken window left unattended is a sign nobody cares and will lead to more broken windows, so ignoring small crimes such as vandalism and public urination will lead to more serious crimes being committed if they go unpunished.[42]

4. *Age.* Crime rates also change in response to changes in the age distribution of the population. The most likely people to commit crime are young males, ages 15 to 24. When there is a smaller percentage of the population in the "crime-prone years," the overall crime rate naturally decreases.[43]

5. *Crack.* The United States experienced a crack cocaine epidemic in the 1980s and early 1990s. About the same time, violent juvenile crime skyrocketed. The increase in violent delinquency was blamed on factors related to crack, such as gang turf wars and street-corner crack markets. For many reasons, such as the younger brother syndrome, where today's teens witnessed the ravaging effect of crack addiction on an older sibling, crack cocaine has become less popular.[44]

6. *Abortion.* A recent and controversial argument is that the legalization of abortion in 1973 has reduced the number of children who would have been at greater risk for delinquency. Since millions of unwanted children never reached crime-prone years, a crime decline would be expected in the early to middle 1990s—precisely when it did occur. (For more on the abortion–crime decline thesis, see Box 2-5.)

t h i n k
about it

What do you think about the reported link between abortion and delinquency reduction? Proponents might suggest abortion is the merciful salvation from a life of delinquency. Do you agree?

box 2-5   DELINQUENCY PREVENTION

The Criminal Unborn

Between 1993 and 2005 the percentage of juveniles arrested for Crime Index offenses declined by almost 30 percent. Many explanations for the decline have been offered, including the economy, population changes, aggressive police practices, and increased incarceration of chronic offenders. However, no explanation is more controversial than the one offered by John Donohue III of Yale Law School and Steven Levitt, an economist at the University of Chicago. They attribute the decrease in crime to the 1973 *Roe v. Wade* decision that legalized abortion.

Donohue and Levitt offer evidence that legalized abortion has contributed significantly to recent crime reductions. The relationship between legalized abortion and crime is straightforward: A steep rise in abortions after 1973 has meant that many persons prone to criminal activity in the 1990s when crime began to decline were never born. There are two reasons for this:

1. Abortion shrinks the number of people who reach the age where they are most prone to commit crimes.
2. Abortion is not random. Teenagers, unmarried women, the poor, and African Americans are more likely than others to have abortions; they are also more likely to have children who are "at risk" for committing crimes later in life.

Similarly, women with unwanted pregnancies are less likely to be good parents and may harm their fetus during pregnancy by drinking alcohol and taking drugs that increase the likelihood of future criminality. Donohue and Levitt present three strands of evidence in support of their claim:

1. The precipitous drop in crime across the United States coincides with the period in which the generation affected by *Roe v. Wade* would have reached the peak of its criminal activity.
2. The five states that legalized abortion in 1970, three years before *Roe v. Wade,* were the first to experience the drop in crime.

3. States with high abortion rates from 1973 to 1976 have seen the largest decrease in crime since 1985, even after controlling for incarceration rates, racial composition, and income.

Donohue and Levitt conclude that current crime rates would be 10 to 20 percent higher if abortion had not been legalized. They estimate that legalized abortion may account for as much as 50 percent of the recent drop in crime. Furthermore, in terms of costs of crime, they believe that legalized abortion has saved Americans more than $30 billion annually.

Although the abortion–crime reduction hypothesis generated a great amount of controversy, criminologists have only recently attempted to replicate Donohue and Levitt's research. Carter Hay and Michelle Evans, for instance, used data from the National Survey of Children, which is a national panel study of American children to explore the abortion hypothesis. Hay and Evans found that being born of an unwanted pregnancy did increase the risk for status offending, general delinquency, substance abuse, and serious delinquency. However, these effects only occurred for very young mothers. Despite the fact that their findings lend empirical support to Donohue and Levitt's thesis, Hay and Evans called for more research. The controversy surrounding the impact of abortion on crime rates is far from settled.

Sources: Federal Bureau of Investigation, *Crime in the United States, 2006* (Washington, DC: U.S. Department of Justice, 2007); Steven Levitt and Stephen Dubner, *Freakonomics,* revised edition (New York: Harper, 2006); John Donohue and Steven Levitt, "The Impact of Legalized Abortion on Crime," *Quarterly Journal of Economics* 116:379–420 (2001); Carter Hay and Michelle Evans, "Has *Roe v. Wade* Reduced U.S. Crime Rates? Examining the Link Between Mothers' Pregnancy Intentions and Children's Later Involvement in Law-Violating Behavior," *Journal of Research in Crime and Delinquency* 43:36–66 (2006); John Donohue and Steven Levitt, "Further Evidence that Legalized Abortion Lowered Crime: A Reply to Joyce," *Journal of Human Resources* 39:29–49 (2004); Steven Levitt, "Understanding Why Crime Fell in the 1990s: Four Factors that Explain the Decline and Six that Do Not," *Journal of Economic Perspectives* 18:163–190 (2004).

Telephones that can film video and take photographs can capture delinquent acts that previously were never discovered, such as these girls fighting. Is this type of technology a way for criminologists and law enforcement to more accurately measure delinquency? (*Note:* The photograph is blurred because of the poor video resolution.)

There is no single reason why juvenile crime is less violent today than it was in the immediate past, but these are likely the most important factors.

Is Sex Related to Delinquency?

Delinquency is primarily a male phenomenon. Boys are arrested more often than girls for *all* crimes with the exception of prostitution and running away. Nine out of every 10 persons arrested for murder, forcible rape, robbery, carrying and possessing weapons, sex offenses (except prostitution and forcible rape), and gambling are boys. However, the arrest gap between the sexes is closing. On the surface, girls seem to be catching up. Since 1960 the difference in the sex–arrest ratios for serious violent and property offenses has steadily declined. In 1960 the sex–arrest ratio for violent offenses was 14 to 1; that is, 14 boys were arrested for each female arrested. By 1970 the ratio declined to 10 to 1, and by 1980 it dropped to 9 to 1. In the past decade, from 1996 to 2005, the sex–arrest ratio for serious violent offenses has declined to 4 to 1, one-third of what it was in 1960.

The trends shown in Table 2-2 indicate mostly dramatic reductions in juvenile arrests among males but a different story among females. From 1996 to 2005, female juvenile arrests increased for other assaults, weapons violations, prostitution, other sex offenses, drug abuse violations, driving under the influence, and disorderly conduct.

Self-report studies confirm *UCR* arrest data. Boys admit to committing more delinquency, and more boys commit delinquency than girls. Research also reports a higher sex–arrest ratio (in favor of boys) for serious rather than less serious crimes.[45] Data from the *NYS* also reveal that the gap in juvenile male–female behavior is closing. According to James F. Short, Jr.:

> Research demonstrates that the decline in gender ratios for most crimes has been especially pronounced for persons under age 18. That is, arrests of young females—compared to young males—have experienced greater increases than is the case for gender comparisons of older persons, and they have been greater for property crimes than for violent crimes.[46]

A similar pattern of convergence has been reported by Roy Austin who compared the arrest ratios of male rates to female rates based on juvenile arrest data between 1963 and 1986. Austin found that "there was convergence of male and female arrests rates over these 22 years for total Index offenses, aggravated assault, burglary, larceny-theft, auto theft, and arson."[47] Our own inspection of the *Uniform Crime Reports* and the National Crime Victimization Survey reveals that the trend identified by Austin has continued. Whether it will persist throughout the 21st century likely depends on whether sex roles become more or less differentiated. If they become less differentiated, the behavior of males

think
about it

How are boys and girls different? Are girls more moral than boys? Should boys and girls be punished or treated the same?

table 2-2	10-Year Arrest Trend for Juveniles, by Sex, 1996–2005	
OFFENSE CHARGED	FEMALES	MALES
Murder and nonnegligent manslaughter	−23.5%	−48.5%
Forcible rape	+22.4	−26.0
Robbery	−29.0	−34.2
Aggravated assault	−5.4	−23.4
Burglary	−34.4	−45.5
Larceny-theft	−27.7	−50.3
Motor vehicle theft	−47.1	−55.3
Arson	−3.8	−27.0
Violent crime	**−10.2**	**−27.9**
Property crime	**−29.1**	**−49.3**
Other assaults	+24.0	−4.1
Forgery and counterfeiting	−59.3	−47.8
Fraud	−28.9	−32.4
Embezzlement	−15.7	−13.8
Stolen property	−32.6	−50.1
Vandalism	−9.5	−29.8
Weapon violation	+15.4	−16.1
Prostitution	+59.0	−33.3
Other sex offenses	−26.4	−4.0
Drug abuse violations	+14.4	−13.6
Gambling	−51.4	−28.4
Offenses against family	−33.0	−38.7
Driving under the influence	+30.6	−10.9
Liquor laws	−5.2	−26.2
Drunkenness	−21.4	−42.4
Disorderly conduct	+29.3	−5.8
Vagrancy	−9.0	−34.6
All other offenses (not traffic)	−3.6	−20.9
Suspicion	−68.4	−77.3
Curfew and loitering violations	−24.5	−27.5
Runaways	−43.4	−44.6
TOTAL	**−14.3**	**−28.7**

Source: Federal Bureau of Investigation, *Crime in the United States, 2005* (Washington, DC: U.S. Department of Justice, 2006).

and females—and consequently their incidence of arrest—should become more alike. On the other hand, if sex roles become more differentiated, the present trend may reverse itself.

Data on the percentage change in arrests over the past decade corroborate this conclusion of convergence. Between 1996 and 2005, male arrests for serious *violent* crimes *decreased* by 28 percent, while female arrests declined only by 10 percent. In the same period, 1996 to 2005, male arrests for seri-

ous *property* crimes *declined* by 49 percent and female arrests *dropped* by 29 percent. Yet, even though there is consistent support for the idea that the behavior of boys and girls is becoming more similar, we must caution against misunderstanding gender differences in delinquency. Even though girls are "catching up" to boys in terms of delinquent involvement, arrest rates for males are *still several hundred percent higher* than for girls. Gender differences are even more pronounced for the most violent crimes. Joycelyn Pollock and Sareta Davis suggested that the idea that females are becoming increasingly more violent than (or as violent as males) is a myth, and that statistical increases are small when considering the total perspective of gender differences in crime.[48]

Is Race Related to Delinquency?

The study of race and delinquency has traditionally reflected larger social concerns. Throughout history, one or more oppressed groups of people have been assigned the brunt of the responsibility for crime. Today, much of the delinquency problem is blamed on young African American males. A recent study attributes this perception to the news media's routine portrayal of young African Americans as perpetrators of crime. This negative characterization has made whites fearful of being victimized by African American juveniles. Twice as many whites than African Americans believe they are more likely to be victimized by an African American than a white, even though whites are three times more likely to be victimized by a white than by an African American.[49]

Cultural values that are deeply rooted in hundreds of years of history contribute to many of our beliefs. Since the early colonial period, whites have oppressed African Americans. Along with oppression has come the presumption by whites that African Americans are lazy, aggressive, inferior, subordinate, and troublemakers.[50] The transmission of such a racist ideology that is passed from generation to generation has had a devastating impact on all African Americans, particularly children. For instance, the percentage of African American children who live in poor families is three times greater than the percentage of low-income white children. The impact of living in a low-income family goes beyond malnourishment and the ruinous consequences of poor nutrition. It also means that many of these children are more likely to endure family stress and depression, have access to fewer resources for learning, and experience severe housing problems.[51]

Nearly 16 percent (11.4 million) of U.S. children are African American. There are *five* times more white children than there are African Americans.[52] An inspection of the *UCR* indicates that a disproportionate number of African American juveniles are arrested for all serious violent and property offenses and for most of the less serious crimes. African American children are twice as likely as whites to be arrested overall, and, for murder and robbery, they are five and nine times more likely to be arrested, respectively. Most curious is that African American juveniles are 63 times more likely than whites to be arrested for gambling! (See Table 2-3.)

Self-report data offer a mixed bag of findings regarding the relationship between race and delinquency. Some studies report that African American juveniles and white juveniles are equally involved in delinquency.[53] In their nationwide survey of adolescent drug use, Lloyd Johnston and his colleagues found that African American juveniles have substantially lower rates of illicit drug use than white adolescents.[54] Yet, according to the *UCR* data shown in Table 2-3, African Americans are twice as likely as whites to be arrested for a drug abuse violation. Other self-report studies tell a different story. Jay Williams and Martin Gold found that while African Americans and whites report committing delinquency at about the same rate, African Americans report greater involvement in more serious forms of delinquency.[55] Similarly, using *NYS* data, Delbert Elliott and Suzanne Ageton discovered significant race differences for total delinquency and for predatory crimes against persons.[56] They concluded that African Americans are arrested more often because they are the more frequent and more serious offenders. Related studies further suggest that African American males are less likely to report involvement in serious crimes for which they have been arrested.[57] Research has questioned the truthfulness of the offending rates they report. Terence Thornberry and Marvin Krohn discovered that African American males substantially underreport their involvement in delinquency, a finding consistent with Barbara Mensch and Denise Kandel who detected differences among races on their level of truthfulness when answering survey questionnaires.[58] If these researchers are correct, African Americans are likely to appear *less* delinquent than they actually are.

Findings from the *NCVS* compliment *UCR* and self-report surveys. Recent analyses of *NCVS* data for 1980 through 1998 compared the rates of offending for African American and white juveniles as reported by crime victims. The study focused on the serious violent crimes of aggravated assault, robbery, and rape because these are crimes in which victims have face-to-face contact with offenders. Data from victims indicate that the serious violent offending rate for African American juveniles is higher than the rate for white juveniles.[59] From 1980 to 1998, the offending rate for African American juveniles was, on average, more than four times the offending rate for white juveniles. In comparison, the African American–to-white ratio of arrest rates reported in the *UCR* for these same offenses shows greater disparity than was found for offending. The average arrest rate for 1980 to 1998 was almost six times higher for African American juveniles than for white juveniles. For both offending rates and arrest rates, though, the ratios of African American to white rates have somewhat declined in recent years. From 1992 to 1998, the African American–to-white rates were very similar for arrests and offending. On average, African American juveniles had arrest rates that were five times greater and offending rates that were five times greater than the rates for white juveniles.

What do these data suggest about race and delinquency? Why are African American juveniles more involved in crime than whites? What explanations for the findings from *UCR*, self-report surveys, and the *NCVS* might make them more plausible? Three interrelated theoretical explanations have been advanced to explain the disproportionate involvement in delinquency among African

table 2-3   Race–Arrest Ratio for African American and White Juveniles, 2005[1]

OFFENSE CHARGED	AFRICAN AMERICAN–WHITE ARREST RATIO
Murder and nonnegligent manslaughter	6:1
Forcible rape	3:1
Robbery	11:1
Aggravated assault	4:1
Burglary	2:1
Larceny-theft	2:1
Motor vehicle theft	4:1
Arson	1:1
Violent crime	**5:1**
Property crime	**2:1**
Other assaults	3:1
Forgery and counterfeiting	1:1
Fraud	2:1
Embezzlement	2:1
Stolen property	4:1
Vandalism	1:1
Weapon violation	2:1
Prostitution	7:1
Other sex offenses	2:1
Drug abuse violations	2:1
Gambling	63:1
Offenses against family	1:1
Driving under the influence	1:5
Liquor laws	1:4
Drunkenness	1:2
Disorderly conduct	3:1
Vagrancy	3:1
All other offenses (not traffic)	2:1
Suspicion	3:1
Curfew and loitering violations	2:1
Runaways	2:1
TOTAL	**2:1**

[1]To calculate the *African American–white arrest ratio,* the total number of juvenile arrests of African Americans was multiplied by 5 (there are five times more white juveniles than African American children under age 18), and the sum was divided by the number of white juveniles who had been arrested. For an example of how to read the table, go to the column labeled "African American–White Arrest Ratio." See the ratio corresponding to the crime, murder and nonnegligent manslaughter. It is 5:1. For this crime in 2005, proportionately five African American juveniles were arrested for every white juvenile arrested.

Source: Federal Bureau of Investigation, *Crime in the United States, 2005* (Washington, DC: U.S. Department of Justice, 2006).

Americans specifically, and racial minorities generally. These are economic deprivation, family breakdown, and cultural factors.

Economic deprivation. In a series of landmark books, William Julius Wilson argued that African Americans, more than whites or any other minority group, have faced an acute shortage of economic opportunities as the result of the inequitable distribution of services and wealth. During the latter part of the 20th century, as the American economy shifted from manufacturing to more service-oriented jobs, those without the necessary credentials or skills were left behind. Over time, middle-class citizens left urban centers and migrated to the suburbs. At first, whites departed the cities, in part because of new job opportunities and in part because of prejudice against African Americans. Soon, middle-class minorities similarly relocated to suburbs.[60]

The economic problems and residential segregation created **concentrated disadvantage,** neighborhoods characterized by extreme poverty and high-crime rates in African Americans neighborhoods. This situation has caused frustration, stress, and a sense of fatalism among African Americans in their pursuit of cultural goals through legitimate means, which contributes to high delinquency rates among African Americans.[61]

Family breakdown. Economic deprivation creates a host of strains contributing to family breakdown in the African American community, led by approximately 70 percent of black children being born to unmarried parents. Other features of the culture of poverty include few male role models because of absentee fathers, overworked single mothers, and children who must largely raise themselves often by associating with their friends who often share their family background.[62] Disruptions in family structure negatively impact school performance, which contributes to the seemingly endless cycle of poverty.[63] As a result, children raised in neighborhoods of concentrated disadvantage are poorly equipped to succeed in American society.[64]

Cultural factors. The culture of poverty also contributes to serious and violent forms of delinquency. Karen Parker and Tracy Johns found that family disruption is a significant predictor of homicide particularly among racial minorities living in major American cities.[65]

Police departments have initiated street sweeps of suspected gang members in an effort to combat delinquency. Are such programs effective in controlling gang delinquency?

Similarly, John MacDonald and Angela Gover found that economic and cultural problems were particularly related to homicide committed by adolescents and young adults.[66] In fact, criminologists have provided compelling evidence for the idea that concentrated disadvantage, the most economically impoverished, racially segregated neighborhoods, is related to delinquency. Far from being a pervasive problem, serious delinquency and violence among African Americans is overwhelmingly limited to the "worst" neighborhoods in the United States, the very places that define concentrated disadvantage.[67]

Another explanation for why African Americans are more likely to commit crime is because they have developed from their life experiences a hostile view of larger society and its values. In reaction, African Americans have constructed a culture with distinctive modes of dress, speech, and conduct that are at odds with larger society. Crime is the result of African Americans not respecting the values of larger society and being more willing to flaunt social norms. Some criminologists have suggested that the culture of poverty places tremendous importance on personal appearance and self-respect perhaps because economic deprivation is so pronounced. Because of this, youths interpreted signs of disrespect or other seemingly trivial affronts as serious threats. Elijah Anderson calls this the "Code of the Street" where violence, even murder, is viewed as the normative response to signs of disrespect.[68] Given that many arguments, fights, and even homicides stem from trivial confrontations, such as bumping into another person or staring at another person in a threatening manner, it is likely that some youth subscribe to a subcultural code of the streets.[69]

think
about it

Are police practices such as racial profiling necessary for the effective control of delinquency? Why or why not?

In *Crime and Human Nature,* James Q. Wilson and Richard Herrnstein reject these explanations and suggest that differences in the arrest rates between the races can be traced to intelligence.[70] Their argument is based on evidence that shows the IQ scores of African American are, on the average, 12 to 15 points lower than whites. Wilson and Herrnstein also reject the notion that cultural bias explains the differences in IQ scores and conclude: "If lower measured intelligence is associated with crime independently of socio-economic status, and if Blacks, on the average, have much lower scores, then these facts may help explain some of the Black–White differences in crime rates."[71] (See the discussion of intelligence in Chapter 5.) Many criminologists disagree with Wilson and Herrnstein.[72] Alternatively, they propose that the race–arrest differences are a function of differential law enforcement, namely that more police patrol African American neighborhoods and receive more calls for service from residents of African American neighborhoods, resulting in more police–citizen interactions.[73] Critics of Wilson and Herrnstein also contend there is police bias that results in **racial profiling,** a practice where police use race as an explicit factor in "profiles" for guiding their decision making (see Chapter 13).

About half of all African American men say they have been victims of racial profiling. Police justify racial profiling on the basis of arrest statistics that suggest African Americans are more likely than whites to commit crime. Studies of racial profiling, however, indicate this is not necessarily the case. In Maryland, for example, 73 percent of those stopped and searched on a section of Interstate 95 were African American yet state police reported that equal percentages of the whites and African Americans who were searched, statewide, had drugs or other contraband. Other research also supports the belief that police use racial profiling. Nationally, citizens report police make traffic stops of African American male drivers more frequently than of other groups. African American drivers are more likely to report the police did not have legitimate reasons for stopping them and that police acted improperly during the traffic stop. In addition, African Americans are significantly more likely than whites to be searched after a traffic stop. Many studies of racial profiling have concluded that police actions are discriminatory and reflect racial prejudice of individual officers or organizational racism found in police departments.[74]

The relationship between race and delinquency is complex. The existing data tell a mixed story. Based on data produced for the *UCR*, from self-report studies, and from the *NCVS*, the conclusion that more African American juveniles are involved in delinquency than whites is warranted. However, studies of racial profiling, while not directly studying police–juvenile interactions, are strongly suggestive of the possibility that a juvenile's race influences the decision by an officer regarding whether to arrest (see Chapter 13).

Is Social Class Related to Delinquency?

By now you are likely not surprised to read that studies reporting on delinquency and social class have produced mixed results. Some studies report a direct relationship between social class and delinquency, while others have found no relationship or a very weak one.[75]

Research based on official data (e.g., the *UCR*) has typically found that lower-class youths are arrested and incarcerated more than middle- and upper-class adolescents. A landmark study examining the relationship between delinquency and social class was published in 1942. Clifford Shaw and Henry McKay observed a very strong relationship among delinquency rates, rates of families on relief, and median rental costs in 140 neighborhoods.[76] Follow-up research reported similar findings for a variety of measures of social class. However, relationships at the neighborhood level do not mean those factors are related at the individual level. To assume that they are is committing the **ecological fallacy.** For example:

1. Police could be biased, arresting juveniles in lower-class neighborhoods for behavior (e.g., loitering) they ignore in other neighborhoods.
2. People could leave their middle- and upper-class neighborhoods and go to lower-class neighborhoods to commit crimes (e.g., illegal drug sales).
3. Only a small number of juveniles might be committing most of the offenses in a lower-class neighborhood.

For these reasons, in the 1950s criminologists started to use self-report surveys to evaluate the relationship between delinquency and social class. These early studies revealed there was *no* relationship between them. This conclusion stirred considerable controversy. Some criminologists contended that the self-report method was not a reliable or valid tool. Other criminologists were sufficiently intrigued to conduct their own research, using other samples, to see if they would find the same thing. Often they did. Delinquency was as common among middle- and upper-class juveniles as it was among lower-class teenagers.[77]

The debate surrounding delinquency and social class has not been resolved. Contemporary criminologists have tried to clarify and summarize what is known. Charles Tittle and his colleagues report that the relationship between delinquency and social class depends on *when* and *how* the research was conducted. Not only did the relationship vary from decade to decade, but self-report

Are social class and delinquency related? Does growing up poor increase the likelihood a child will commit crime?

data yielded different results than did official data.[78] Official data in the 1940s showed a strong correlation between delinquency and social class, but the correlation weakened in later decades and fell to practically zero in the 1970s. In self-report studies, the average correlation between social class and delinquency was never high; before 1950 there were no self-report studies examining this relationship, and afterward the correlation was only very weak.[79]

These findings lend themselves to different interpretations. Perhaps the official data of the 1940s and 1950s are invalid and should not be accepted. Or the official data may be accurate, and lower-class juveniles did have a monopoly on delinquency, but middle- and upper-class teenagers have now caught up. Tittle and his colleagues reject both possibilities. They think self-report data are probably correct in showing that the relationship between delinquency and social class has not changed very much over the years and that lower-class adolescents are only slightly more likely than others to commit crime. They also think that the official data reflect bias. They believe that police and court officials discriminated against lower-class juveniles, arresting and referring them to court more often, particularly in the 1940s and 1950s, than was the case for other children. Their contention has found support in research by Robert Sampson who examined arrest decisions and found that for most offenses committed by teenagers, official police records and court referrals were structured not just by the act, but also by the juvenile's social class.[80] Similarly, John Hagan discovered that police characterize lower-class neighborhoods as having more criminal behavior than other areas.[81] Douglas Smith has perhaps captured the dynamic of the ecological fallacy "in action" best when he observed:

> Based on a set of internalized expectations derived from past experience, police divide the population and physical territory they must patrol into readily understandable categories. The result is a process of ecological contamination in

which all persons encountered in bad neighborhoods are viewed as possessing the moral liability of the area itself.[82]

The conclusions of Tittle and his colleagues and those whose research supports their claims have been soundly criticized. Michael Hindelang and his associates observed a rather consistent relationship between delinquency and social class for serious crimes.[83] John Braithwaite wonders whether Tittle and his associates really take their conclusion of no relationship between delinquency and social class seriously and queried as to whether they "adopt no extra precautions when moving about the slums of the world's great cities than they do when walking in the middle class areas of such cities."[84] Braithwaite suggests that the evidence overwhelmingly supports the notion that delinquency and social class are related.[85] Even though the connection between the delinquency and social class is sometimes inconsistent, more research identifies the presence of a significant class difference than would be expected by chance. When you consider that self-report studies exaggerate the proportion of delinquency committed by middle-class juveniles by paying too much attention to minor infractions, the "true" relationship between delinquency and social class begins to emerge. Studies of delinquency and social class based on official records have consistently found sizable class differences.

One study examining the relationship between delinquency and social class has been able to test the conflicting opinions by using such a large sample that it could include serious offenses. Delbert Elliott and Suzanne Ageton compared the self-report data of more than 1,700 juveniles representing the lower class, working class, and middle class. They concluded that the self-reporting behavior of adolescents was similar, *except for predatory crimes against persons* (robbery and aggravated assault). For these crimes, differences across the social classes were profound. For every such crime reported by middle-class juveniles, three of these crimes were committed by working-class youths, and lower-class juveniles reported four of these crimes, leading Elliott and Ageton to conclude that the behavior of lower-class teenagers is similar to the behavior of middle-class adolescents for "run-of-the-mill offenses" but lower-class juveniles commit many more serious crimes.[86]

In 1982 Gary Kleck reported that lower-class juveniles had a tendency to underreport their involvement in crime in self-report studies, to which Tittle and his colleagues responded by saying "Kleck (and others) . . . believe that poor people are not only more criminal than those of other classes but bigger liars as well."[87] The jury is out on the exact nature of the delinquency–social class relationship. From their research in 1990, Tittle and Robert Meier observed that criminologists today are no closer to understanding the relationship between delinquency and social class than they were 50 years ago.[88] A decade later, in 2000, Gregory Dunaway and his colleagues reached much the same conclusion when they reported that the impact of social class on criminality is negligible.[89] Now the delinquency–social class debate has entered the 21st century absent any agreement among criminologists.

Is Age Related to Delinquency?

Age and delinquency are related. The association between them was originally observed by the 19th-century French criminologist, Adolphe Quetelet, who noted that crimes peaks in the late teens through the mid-twenties.[90] Today, a well-established fact is the **age–crime curve,** which states that crime rates increase during preadolescence, peak in late adolescence, and steadily decline thereafter.[91] The high point of the curve is slightly different for serious violent and property offenses. Arrests for serious violent crimes peak at age 18, and then steadily decline; arrests for serious property crimes top out at age 16 and decrease consistently thereafter. Juveniles whose behavior fits this pattern are called **adolescence-limited offenders** because their delinquency is restricted to the teenage years.[92]

The age–crime curve does not apply to all juveniles. Some children begin and end their involvement in delinquency at earlier and later ages. Variation in offending patterns among juveniles has been observed across offense type, by sex, and by race. For instance, (1) violent offending by girls peaks earlier than boys and (2) African American children are more likely than whites to continue offending into early adulthood.[93] What is constant across all categories of juveniles is they commit fewer crimes as they grow older—a process that criminologists call the **aging-out phenomenon.**[94]

There are several competing explanations regarding why crime diminishes with age.[95] Some of these ideas about why people age-out of crime follow:

- Personalities change as juveniles mature. Once-rebellious adolescents often become adults who exercise self-control over their impulses.
- Adolescents become aware of the costs of crime. They start to realize they have too much to lose if they are caught and little to gain.
- Peer influences over behavior weaken with age. As juveniles grow older, the importance of their peers' opinions of them decreases.
- For males, the level of testosterone in their body decreases as they grow older and so does their aggressiveness.
- Some crimes, such as strong-arm robbery and burglary, decline with age because people lack the physical strength or agility to commit them.
- The need for money decreases. It is much more difficult for juveniles to get money than adults. As adolescents grow older, their prospects for full-time employment increase.

Although most children age-out of delinquency, others do not, and often they become chronic offenders also known as serious, violent, and chronic juvenile offenders. Typically, **chronic offenders** are juveniles who begin offending at a very young age and continue to offend as adults.

SERIOUS, VIOLENT, AND CHRONIC JUVENILE OFFENDERS

Recall from Chapter 1 that the juvenile court in the United States was established in Cook County (Chicago), Illinois. Judge Merritt Pinckney, one of the judges who presided in the nation's first juvenile court had this to say about some of the youths he met:

> A child, a boy especially, sometimes becomes so thoroughly vicious and is so repeatedly an offender that it would not be fair to the other children in a delinquent institution who have not arrived at his age of depravity and delinquency to have to associate with him. On very rare and special occasions, therefore, children are held over on a mittimus to the criminal court.[96]

Now consider this assessment from criminologist Terrie Moffitt, who developed the developmental taxonomy consisting of adolescence-limited and life-course persistent offenders (see Chapter 8):

> Longitudinal research consistently points to a very small group of males who display high rates of antisocial behavior across time and in diverse situations. The professional nomenclature may change, but the faces remain the same as they drift through successive systems aimed at curbing their deviance: schools, juvenile justice programs, psychiatric treatment centers, and prisons. The topography of their behavior may change with changing opportunities, but the underlying disposition persists throughout the life course.[97]

Although nearly a century separates these two quotations, both address the same recurrent problem in delinquency: chronic offenders. Today referred to as serious, violent, and chronic juvenile offenders, it has always been the case that a small group of serious violent youths are responsible for the overwhelming majority of serious violent crime occurring in a population. These youth have lengthy delinquent careers (duration or span), commit crimes at very high rates (frequency), are deeply committed to antisocial behavior (priority), and are most likely to commit crimes, such as murder and rape (seriousness).

Research on Delinquent Careers

Chronic offenders often commit their first serious crime before age 10 and by age 18 have achieved a lengthy police record. (See Box 2-6 for a profile of Keith, a chronic offender.) Importantly, the general profile of the chronic delinquent is remarkably similar regardless of whether the study group is from the United States or from other countries. For all intents and purposes, the most delinquent and violent youthful offenders are the same type of person across different types of societies and social contexts.[98] The remainder of the chapter explores some of the most important studies of delinquent careers and serious, violent, and chronic juvenile offenders.

Sheldon Glueck and Eleanor Glueck The first criminologists to study chronic offenders were Sheldon Glueck and Eleanor Glueck during the 1930s. Their study included 500 delinquent white males between the ages of 10 and 17 who had been committed to two Massachusetts correctional facilities, the Lyman School for Boys and the Industrial School for Boys. The Gluecks collected an array of data and created offender dossiers for each boy, including deviant and criminal history, psychosocial profile, family background, school and occupational history, and other life events such as martial and military history. The delinquent sample was matched on a case-by-case basis to 500 nondelinquent boys from the same area. Both samples were followed until the boys reached age 32. The study design permitted researchers to examine the long-term effects of early life experiences on subsequent social and antisocial behavior. In fact, the dataset is so impressive that it has been resurrected by Robert Sampson and John Laub since 1988 and used for more sophisticated data analysis.

The Gluecks' research produced some important findings. For example, an early onset of problem or antisocial behavior strongly predicted a lengthy criminal career characterized by high rates of offending and involvement in serious criminal violence. The Gluecks' used the phrase "the past is prologue" to

---

box 2-6	**A WINDOW ON DELINQUENCY**

Profile of a Chronic Offender

Keith was 16 when he was sentenced to 27 years to life for robbery and murder. He had a long history of violence. He was an only child of parents who had never lived together. By age 7, he was uncontrollable and would run away from home. His mother fought with her live-in boyfriends over Keith's behavior. Nearly every adult male with whom he came in contact physically abused him.

Problems in school led to a suicide attempt by Keith to "get back" at his mother for spanking him. Keith and a friend stole an automobile at age 12 and were arrested after they wrecked the automobile. Within days, Keith was suspended from school for assaulting a student who refused to loan him a pencil. He and a friend tortured and hanged a lamb at a nearby school. Keith was placed in a boys' home at age 13.

At the home, Keith was disruptive and hostile, and escaped several times. During one escape, he physically assaulted two girls who were 11 and 12 years old. Afterward, Keith was captured and placed in a juvenile detention center where his stay was marked by several escapes, misconduct, and fighting. Keith's final escape ended in a siege in which Keith held detention center staff and police at bay with a tire iron. The net result of all these incidents was, astonishingly, that Keith was placed on probation.

Instances of vehement tantrums, vandalism, assaults, and attempted suicide followed in an escalating pattern of violence. Keith was sentenced to 20 months in a detention facility for attacking his 21-year-old cousin with a hammer. Keith was 15 at the time. After serving one year, Keith was returned to his home, where truancy, disruptive behavior, and drug use continued. One day Keith skipped school with two of his friends. He stopped his car at a shopping center to "get some money." Keith entered a bakery, demanded money from the woman owner, and then shot her in the face when she refused to open the cash register. Keith's excuse was, "The bitch should have given me the money, it was her fault."

Source: Timothy Crowe, *Habitual Juvenile Offenders* (Washington, DC: U.S. Department of Justice, 1994), pp. 9–11.

---

capture the idea of the stability in behavior. However, the Gluecks' also found that even high-rate offenders tended to reduce their offending after they passed through adolescence into early adulthood. Similarly, even serious offenders could desist from crime, and seemingly ignore their own criminal propensity, by participating in conventional adult social institutions such as marriage, work, and military.[99]

The Gluecks were also among the first criminologists to focus on psychopathy among serious delinquents. *Psychopathy* is a personality disorder that results in severe affective, interpersonal, and behavioral problems such that psychopaths can victimize and manipulate others seemingly without conscience. The Gluecks found that psychopathy was a useful variable to differentiate delinquents from nondelinquents. They described psychopathic offenders as openly destructive, antisocial, asocial, and less amenable to therapeutic or educative efforts. Other characteristics included insensitivity to social demands of others, shallow emotionality, self-centeredness coupled with a complete lack of empathy, impulsive behavior, lack of stress or anxiety over social maladjustment, gross irresponsibility, and emotional poverty. Psychopathic youth did not appear to respond to treatment or rehabilitative efforts, instead they were unconcerned about their consistent criminal behavior. They also found that the prevalence of psychopathy was almost *20 times* more common among their delinquent sample than their matched, nondelinquent control group.[100]

Marvin Wolfgang and the Philadelphia Birth Cohorts   The landmark study that established the contemporary understanding of career offenders was *Delinquency in a Birth Cohort* by Marvin Wolfgang, Robert Figlio, and Thorsten Sellin in 1972. The study followed 9,945 males born in Philadelphia in 1945 and who lived in the city at least from ages 10 through 18. The significance of this longitudinal birth cohort design was that it was not susceptible to sampling error because every male subject was followed. They found that nearly two-thirds of the youths never experienced a police contact and that 35 percent of the population of boys had. For the minority of persons who were actually contacted by police, the police contacts were rare occurrences occurring just once, twice, or three times.

On the other hand, some youths experienced more frequent interaction with police. According to Wolfgang and his associates, persons with five or more police contacts were chronic or habitual offenders. Of the nearly 10,000 boys, only 627 members, just 6 percent of the population, qualified as chronic or habitual offenders. However, these 6 percent accounted for 52 percent of the delinquency in the entire cohort. Moreover, chronic offenders committed 63 percent of all Crime Index offenses, 71 percent of the murders, 73 percent of the rapes, 82 percent of the robberies, and 69 percent of the aggravated assaults.[101]

A second study examined a cohort of persons born in Philadelphia in 1958. Conducted by Paul Tracy, Marvin Wolfgang, and Robert Figlio, the second Philadelphia cohort contained 13,160 males and 14,000 females. Overall, the 1958 cohort committed crime at higher rates than the 1945 cohort and demonstrated greater involvement in the most serious forms of crime, such as murder, rape, robbery, and aggravated assault. Roughly the same proportion of persons, 33 percent, was arrested prior to adulthood. Approximately 7 percent of the population members were habitual offenders, and they accounted for 61 percent of all delinquency, 60 percent of the murders, 75 percent of the rapes, 73 percent of the robberies, and 65 percent of the aggravated assaults.[102] A few years later, Paul Tracy and Kimberly Kempf–Leonard collected criminal records for the 1958 sample up to age 26. Their analysis showed that juveniles who were actively involved in crime as children were more likely to be adult criminals whereas non-delinquents generally remained non-criminal in adulthood.[103]

When Marvin Wolfgang and his colleagues tracked 974 persons from their Philadelphia cohort through adulthood to age 30, they discovered that over 50 percent of chronic offenders were arrested at least four times between ages 18 and 30. In comparison, only 18 percent of persons with no juvenile arrests were ever arrested as adults.[104] The continuation of antisocial behavior across stages of the life span is known as **continuity of crime.**[105]

Cambridge Study on Delinquent Development   The most important European contribution to the study of delinquent careers is the Cambridge Study in Delinquent Development, a prospective longitudinal panel study of 411 males born in London in 1952–1953. Originally conceptualized by Donald West in

1961, the study continues presently under the guidance of David Farrington. Now more than 50 years old, the study subjects have been interviewed nine times between the ages of 8 and 46 with their parents participating in eight interviews. The Cambridge study uses convictions rather than police contacts or arrests as its unit of analysis; nevertheless, their results about serious, violent, and chronic offenders are familiar. For example, 37 percent of the sample had been convicted of some criminal offense, most commonly theft or burglary. Six percent of the sample, or 25 youths, were chronic offenders who accounted for 47 percent of all acts of criminal violence in the sample including about 60 percent of the armed robberies.[106]

Due to the richness of the Cambridge panel data, Farrington has published widely on a variety of topics pertaining to chronic offenders, the criminal behavior of their siblings and parents, and the processes by which criminal behavior is transmitted from one generation to the next. For example, youthful chronic offenders possessed a number of risk factors that forecast a life in crime. These included having a parent who had been incarcerated and having delinquent siblings. Young chronic offenders also tended to be daring, prone to trouble, impulsive, and defiant; to have low intelligence and low school attainment; and to have been raised in poverty. The most antisocial boys in childhood were similarly the most antisocial adolescents and adults. Crime also tended to "run in families" as chronic offenders often had children whose life trajectories also reflected a syndrome of antisocial behavior.[107] These findings not only lend support to the Gluecks' idea that the "past is prologue" but also show the dangers of not intervening in the lives of serious delinquents—life-course persistent criminality and lives of despair are the usual outcome.[108]

National Youth Survey   The *National Youth Survey* (*NYS*) was initiated in 1976 by Delbert Elliott and his collaborators. It is a prospective longitudinal study of the delinquency and drug use patterns of American youth. The sample contains 1,725 persons from seven birth cohorts between 1959 and 1965 and multiple waves of data have been collected since the study's inception. The *NYS* has yielded plentiful information about the prevalence, incidence, correlates, and processes related to delinquency and other forms of antisocial behavior.

Chronic offender information based on *NYS* data were generally similar to information derived from studies employing official records. For most persons, involvement in crime generally and violence specifically were short-lived and limited in scope. Individual offending rates varied greatly. Delinquents tended to dabble in a mixed pattern of offenses, not focusing on one particular type of crime. A small proportion of the sample was habitual in its delinquency. For example, approximately 7 percent of youths in the survey were serious career offenders, defined as persons who committed at least three Crime Index offenses annually. These youth accounted for the vast majority of antisocial and violent behaviors in the sample and often committed many times the number of assaults, robberies, and sexual assaults than non–career offenders. However, only 2 percent of those identified as self-reported career criminals were identified as such using official records. This suggests that serious and violent chronic offenders commit significantly more crime than their official records would indicate. Additionally, information from offender self-reports suggests that the number of career offenders might be larger than previously thought. For example, later research using additional waves of data found that 36 percent of African American males and 25 percent of white males aged 17 reported some involvement in serious violent offending.[109]

Program of Research on the Causes and Correlates of Delinquency   In 1986 the Office of Juvenile Justice and Delinquency Prevention created the Program of Research on the Causes and Correlates of Delinquency. The result was three prospective longitudinally designed studies: the Denver Youth Survey, Pittsburgh Youth Study, and Rochester Youth Development Study. The Denver Youth Survey is a probability sample of 1,527 youth living in high-risk neighborhoods in Denver. Survey respondents, which included five age groups (7, 9, 11, 13, and 15 year olds), and their parents were interviewed between 1988 and 1992. By its design, the study would obtain longitudinal data covering the 7- to 26-year-old age span to examine the effects of childhood experiences and neighborhood disadvantage on problem behaviors. The Pittsburgh Youth Study contains 1,517 boys in grades 1, 4, and 7 in public schools in Pittsburgh during the 1987–1988 school year. Data on delinquency, substance abuse, and mental health difficulties were obtained every six months for 3 years via interviews with the subjects and their parents and teachers. The Rochester Youth Development Study contains 1,000 youths (75 percent male, 25 percent female) sampled disproportionately from high-crime neighborhoods. Interviews with multiple sources are ongoing to gather data on criminal offending and related behaviors. Each study offered a "core measurement package" that provided official and self-reports of delinquent behavior and drug use; neighborhood characteristics; demographic characteristics; parental attitudes and child-rearing practices; and attitudinal measures of school performance, peer and social networks, and views about committing crime.[110]

The Denver, Pittsburgh, and Rochester studies provided a substantive glimpse into some of the nation's most crime-beleaguered communities and the youth who faced the multiple risk factors that exist there. Not surprisingly, they produced nearly identical findings about the disproportionate violent behavior of chronic offenders. Between 14 and 17 percent of the youth were habitual offenders who accounted for 75 to 82 percent of the incidence of criminal violence. Just as Delbert Elliott and his colleagues found with respondents from the *NYS*, researchers found that about 20 to 25 percent of adolescents in Denver, Pittsburgh, and Rochester tended to be "multiple problem youth" who experienced an assortment of antisocial risk factors, such as mental health problems, alcoholism and substance abuse histories, and sustained criminal involvement.

A small minority of youths were the most frequent, severe, aggressive, and temporally stable delinquent offenders. These youths, all of them males, were reared in broken homes by parents who themselves had numerous mental health and parenting problems. These boys were also noticeable by their impulsivity, emotional and moral insouciance, and total lack of guilt with which they committed crime, indeed as children they showed many of the characteristics of psychopathy.[111]

Other Studies of Serious, Violent, and Chronic Juvenile Offenders   Finally, three other important studies of delinquent careers and serious, violent, and chronic juvenile offenders are the Dangerous Offender Project, The Cambridge–Somerville Youth Study, and the Racine, Wisconsin, birth cohorts. Under the guidance of Donna Hamparian, Simon Dinitz, John Conrad, and their colleagues, the Dangerous Offender Project examined the delinquent careers of 1,238 adjudicated youth born in Columbus, Ohio, between 1956 and 1960. Overall, these youth committed a total of 4,499 offenses, 1,504 crimes of violence, and 904 violent Crime Index crimes. Even among violent juvenile offenders, a small minority whom they dubbed the "violent few" accounted for the majority of crimes. For instance, 84 percent of the youths were only arrested once for a violent crime as adolescents and 13 percent were arrested twice. The remaining 3 percent—the violent few—accumulated significantly more police contacts for violent crimes. In fact, they were arrested between 3 and 23 times.[112]

Joan McCord and William McCord used data from the Cambridge–Somerville Youth Study to study the long-term effects of early childhood experiences on later criminality. The study contained 506 impoverished males born from 1925 to 1934. The boys had been treated for a variety of behavioral problems and were tracked via official records until 1978. By age 50, approximately 30 percent had been arrested particularly those who were reared in broken homes characterized by parental conflict, parental criminality, and low levels of parental affection toward and supervision of the children. Like the Gluecks' research, the McCords' research illustrated the antecedent role of family strife and abuse in the development of habitual antisocial behavior.[113]

Lyle Shannon selected 1942, 1949, and 1955 birth cohorts from Racine, Wisconsin, that yielded 1,352, 2,099, and 2,676 respondents, respectively, to examine delinquent criminal careers over time. Shannon followed the birth cohorts well into adulthood to further explore continuity in criminal behavior. This included follow-up of the 1942 cohort to age 30, the 1949 cohort to age 25, and the 1955 cohort to age 22. Like prior studies, Shannon found that a small cohort of chronic offenders committed the preponderance of offenses.[114]

Comprehensive Strategy for Serious, Violent, and Chronic Juvenile Offenders

Are serious, violent, and chronic juvenile offenders doomed to a life of crime? Without any intervention, the answer is probably. Thankfully, the juvenile justice system has made the most severe offenders its top priority. In 1993 the federal Office of Juvenile Justice and Delinquency Prevention developed the Comprehensive Strategy for Serious, Violent, and Chronic Juvenile Offenders on the belief that a balanced approach of prevention, rehabilitation, and control could help the worst delinquents. The Comprehensive Strategy is based on five principles.

1. Strengthen the family in its primary responsibility to instill moral values and provide guidance and support to children.

2. Support core social institutions, such as schools and religious institutions, and community organizations in their roles of developing capable, mature, and responsible youth.

3. Promote delinquency prevention as the most cost-effective approach to reducing juvenile delinquency.

4. Intervene immediately and effectively when delinquent behavior occurs to successfully prevent delinquent offenders from becoming chronic offenders and perhaps progressively commit more serious and violent offenses.

5. Identify and control the small group of serious, violent, and chronic juvenile offenders who have committed felony offenses or have failed to respond to intervention and nonsecure, community-based treatment and rehabilitation services.

To accomplish these goals, the Comprehensive Strategy contains six levels of interventions and sanctions. From the least to most restrictive, these are:

1. Prevention of delinquency by reducing risk and enhancing protection.

2. Early intervention with predelinquent and child delinquents and their families.

3. Immediate intervention for first-time delinquents and nonserious repeat offenders.

4. Intermediate sanctions for first-time offenders or violent offenders, including intensive supervision for serious, violent, and chronic offenders.

5. Secure corrections for the most severe offenders.

6. Aftercare.[115]

With the Comprehensive Strategy, great strides have been made in preventing, treating, and punishing the most at-risk juvenile offenders. Serious, violent, and chronic juvenile offenders and the many outstanding prevention programs that have proven effective at reducing the continuity of delinquent careers are explored in great detail.

conclusions

No one can say exactly how much delinquency is committed or how many children commit it. This is because most crime never comes to the attention of police. It is hidden from them. Criminologists therefore are forced to estimate the nature and extent of delinquency by using a variety of measures such as the *Uniform Crime Reports, National Crime Victimization Survey,* and self-report studies, such as the *National Youth Survey.*

Some groups of children are arrested more often than others. However, nearly all children commit fewer crimes as they grow older. This does not mean all of juvenile offenders completely stop committing crime. Some children become chronic offenders. Chronic offenders typically have been found to have low intelligence, suffer from hyperactivity disorder, live in poverty, be reared by single parents, and be poorly supervised.

The next two chapters will explore in greater detail the extent and nature of youth violence and drug use particularly as they are related to the most severe types of delinquent offenders. While these two areas of delinquency do not comprise the majority of delinquencies committed by youth, they are the two that generate the greatest concern for the public and for policy makers. Juveniles are arrested nearly six times more often for serious property offenses than for

3

Violent
Youth Crime

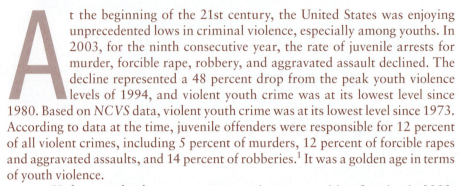

At the beginning of the 21st century, the United States was enjoying unprecedented lows in criminal violence, especially among youths. In 2003, for the ninth consecutive year, the rate of juvenile arrests for murder, forcible rape, robbery, and aggravated assault declined. The decline represented a 48 percent drop from the peak youth violence levels of 1994, and violent youth crime was at its lowest level since 1980. Based on *NCVS* data, violent youth crime was at its lowest level since 1973. According to data at the time, juvenile offenders were responsible for 12 percent of all violent crimes, including 5 percent of murders, 12 percent of forcible rapes and aggravated assaults, and 14 percent of robberies.[1] It was a golden age in terms of youth violence.

Unfortunately, the most recent news is not as positive. Starting in 2003, violent youth crime in the nation's major cities has increased. Beginning in 2004 and continuing to today, the overall violent crime rate increased for the first time in years. The number of juveniles arrested for murder increased *more than 20 percent* from 2003 to 2004 *and again* from 2004 to 2005.[2] Similarly distressing news came from across the nation. In Minneapolis, police estimate that juveniles account for 63 percent of suspects in serious felony crimes. In Boston the juvenile robbery arrest rate increased 54 percent, and the juvenile weapons arrest rate increased 102 percent in 2005. Similar increases in violent youth crime appear in Houston, Milwaukee, New Orleans, Washington, DC, and many other cities. Criminal justice practitioners attribute the increases to gangs that are arming and recruiting younger kids into their ranks.[3] For example, homicides increased 5 percent in 2005 with much of the killing attributed to gang activity in Milwaukee, Oklahoma City, Omaha, and St. Louis.[4] In 2004 and 2005 Indianapolis, Louisville, Memphis, and Phoenix violent crime rates increased from 13 to 25 percent, mostly because of juvenile offenders.[5] The recent upsurge is not limited to American delinquency. In Thessaloniki, Greece, five schoolchildren between the ages of 12 and 13 were recently charged with murdering an 11-year-old boy and desecrating the corpse.[6]

In March 2007 the Police Executive Research Forum (PERF) gathered crime data for 2006 from 56 policing agencies across the United States. Their assessment about the most recent crime trends is troubling:

> Overall, the 24-month trend, starting on January 1, 2005, is unmistakable: Among the jurisdictions filing reports with PERF, total homicides in 2006 were more than 10 percent higher than they were in 2004. Robberies increased over 12 percent; aggravated assaults increased by 3 percent; and aggravated assaults with a firearm increased nearly 10 percent. Law enforcement officials offered several explanations for the upsurge in violent crime, but among the most commonly cited reason was that young people with access to firearms and a willingness and at times to settle disputes violently. The violence was disproportionately committed by young males who dropped out of high school, were involved in the drug trade and generalized criminal activity, and who viewed even the most trivial affronts as reason enough to inflict violence.[7]

Even though general trends show declines in delinquency compared to its peak in the early 1990s, citizens, politicians, and the media continue to express concern about youth violence. Although neighborhoods and schools are much safer than in recent decades, public perceptions have changed little. People continue to believe juvenile violence is a serious threat and that it should be dealt with severely. This chapter will explore the problems of youth violence today, general trends and how they have changed over the past years, the specific problems posed by the most severe delinquents (those who have psychopathic traits), what is being done to provide treatment for serious delinquent offenders, and programs and policies that reduce adolescent violence in the future.

THE NATURE AND EXTENT OF YOUTH VIOLENCE

Based on the most recent available data collected by the Federal Bureau of Investigation, approximately 60,000 juveniles were arrested for serious violent crimes in 2005. About 36,995 youths were arrested for aggravated assault, 15,713 youths were arrested for robbery, 2,434 youths were arrested for forcible rape, and 711 youths were arrested for murder.[8] Juveniles are both perpetrators of violence and victims of violence, and their violence occurs at home, at school, and on the streets. Children are frequently victims of violence in the home, with more than 300,000 reported cases of child abuse validated each year and about 1,500 fatalities resulting from abuse (see Chapter 10). Although children are more likely to be victimized in the home, they sometimes engage in violence toward other family members often as a response to their own maltreatment.

Since 1992 more than 200 children have been killed at school, most by other students (see Chapter 11). Many students bring weapons to school, even more carry weapons while not at school. Most violence by juveniles occurs during the hours shortly after school. While the number of violent crimes by adults increases from 6 A.M. through the afternoon and evening hours, peaks at 11 P.M., and then drops hourly to a low point at 6 A.M., juvenile violence peaks in the afternoon between 3 P.M. and 4 P.M., the hour at the end of the school day. More than one in seven sexual assaults by juveniles occurs in the four hours between 3 P.M. and 7 P.M. on school days. And unlike other violent crimes, sexual assaults by juveniles on non-school days are most likely to occur between noon and 1 P.M.[9]

Patterns of Youth Violence

As shown in Figure 3-1, the arrest rate per 100,000 juveniles between the ages of 10 and 17 for the most violent offenses has declined sharply in recent years before the upsurge since 2003. From 2003 to 2004, the number of juveniles arrested for murder and nonnegligent homicide increased 21.6 percent. From 2004 to 2005 the juvenile murders increased another 20 percent, and robberies increased more than 11 percent. In the first six months of 2006, the overall violent crime rate jumped another 4 percent. The bulk of these increases were attributed to gang homicides among adolescents (see Chapter 12).[10] In spite of these recent surges in violence among adolescents, overall violent and property crime rates among juveniles are still at their lowest point in decades. For violent crimes, for instance, youth arrest rates in the early 21st century are comparable to those in 1981. According to the property Crime Index, current rates are at their lowest levels in decades, about 1,500 arrests per 100,000 juveniles.

Figures 3-2 and 3-3 illustrate the patterns of delinquency by gender and race from 1981 to 2004. Gender rates are shown for aggravated assault, simple assault, weapons offenses, and drug abuse violations. Although males have

figure 3-1   Violent and Property Juvenile Arrest Rates, 1981–2004

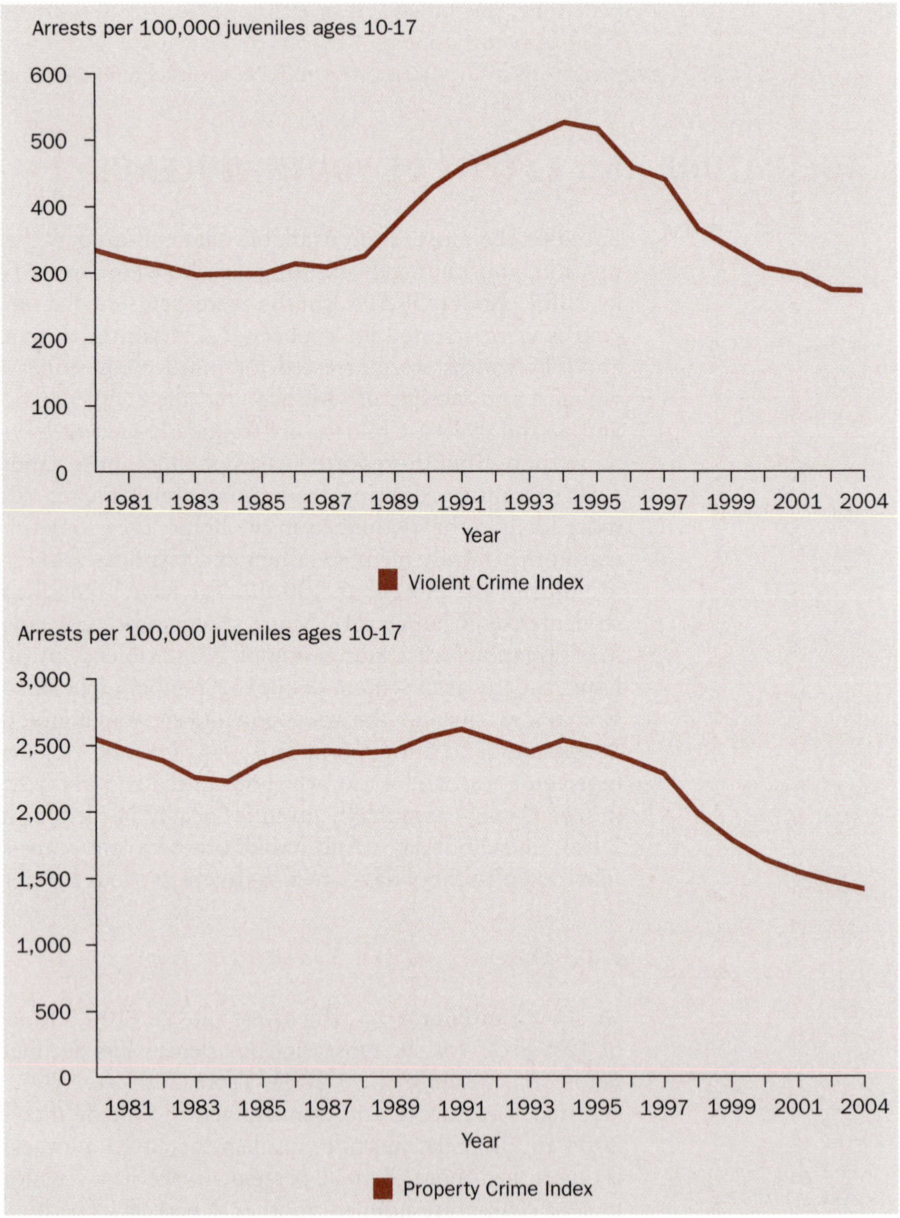

Arrests per 100,000 juveniles ages 10-17

[Chart showing Violent Crime Index arrests per 100,000 juveniles ages 10-17 from 1981 to 2004. Y-axis ranges from 0 to 600. The line starts around 330 in 1981, dips to about 300 in 1983–1985, rises sharply to a peak near 525 around 1994, then declines to about 275 by 2004.]

Year

■ Violent Crime Index

Arrests per 100,000 juveniles ages 10-17

[Chart showing Property Crime Index arrests per 100,000 juveniles ages 10-17 from 1981 to 2004. Y-axis ranges from 0 to 3,000. The line starts around 2,550 in 1981, dips to about 2,250 in 1983, rises to about 2,600 around 1991, then declines steadily to about 1,450 by 2004.]

Year

■ Property Crime Index

Source: Howard Snyder, *Juvenile Arrests, 2004* (Washington, DC: U.S. Department of Justice, Office of Juvenile Justice and Delinquency Prevention, 2006).

significantly higher arrest rates than females for all offenses, the relative "gender gap" for these offenses has decreased. There are also significant but changing offending differences in serious delinquency between African Americans and whites. For murder, robbery, aggravated assault, and serious property crimes, the "racial gap" in juvenile arrests has drastically narrowed, as African American youths have experienced sharply declining crime rates.

figure 3-2   Serious Juvenile Arrest Rates by Gender, 1981–2004

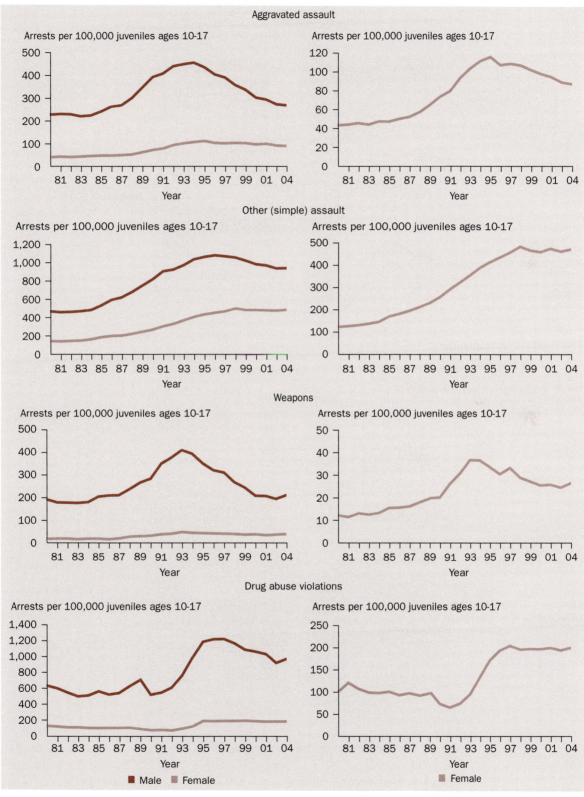

Source: Howard Snyder, *Juvenile Arrests, 2004* (Washington, DC: U.S. Department of Justice, Office of Juvenile Justice and Delinquency Prevention, 2006).

figure 3-3 Serious Juvenile Arrest Rates by Race, 1981–2004

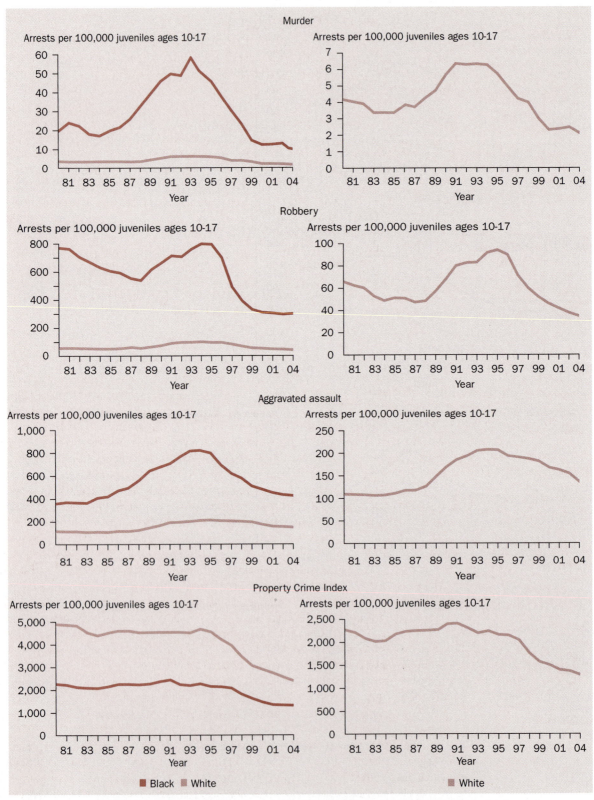

Murder

Robbery

Aggravated assault

Property Crime Index

■ Black ■ White

■ White

Source: Howard Snyder, *Juvenile Arrests, 2004* (Washington, DC: U.S. Department of Justice, Office of Juvenile Justice and Delinquency Prevention, 2006).

African Americans comprise about 16 percent of all juveniles in the United States, yet they disproportionately contribute to violent crime arrests. As described earlier, however, the race-specific arrest rates for violent offenses have declined more dramatically for African American youths since 1993 than they did for white youth. Other forms of youth violence, including forcible rape, robbery, aggravated assault, weapons violations, and other assaults (fighting), also declined after the mid-1990s, with most offense categories showing double-digit changes. Terance Miethe and Wendy Regoeczi believe that there has been *no* significant increase of homicides by girls during the 1990s and that there was *no* increase in interracial homicides involving youth during that period. Moreover, they suggest that if there was any noticeable change in youth homicides, it was that they were becoming increasingly "characterized by young, African American male offenders, instrumental motives, multiple offenders, guns, and strangers."[11] In other words, while there are fluctuations in gender by gender and race, serious juvenile violence is still disproportionately committed by young minority males.[12] (For a discussion of youth violence in European countries, see Box 3-1.)

Although it does not get the same attention as delinquency, suicide is another important form of violence affecting the lives of children and adolescents. Nearly one in five high school age youth made a plan to attempt suicide during the year, and about half actually attempted suicide. Many risk factors that contribute to violent delinquency, such as family trouble, delinquent peers, and bullying, also contribute to suicide among adolescents. For instance, Ann Burgess and her colleagues suggest that chronic bullying in schools produces students who are susceptible to committing suicide, school shootings, or both.[13] From 1999 to 2004, 11,176 juveniles committed suicide in the United States. Suicide is the third leading cause of death of adolescents after accidents and homicide. While females are more likely to attempt suicide, males are four times more likely to die from suicide.[14] Suicidal thoughts, suicide attempts, and depression can also be part of a larger set of problem behaviors that serious adolescent offenders wrestle with. Alex Piquero and his colleagues recently found that life-course persistent offenders have more mental health problems and more adverse health outcomes than adolescence-limited delinquents.[15]

Explanations for the Decline in Youth Violence

In 1997, in the third edition of this textbook, we wrote that "if there is no significant change in the tendency of youths to become involved in violence, juvenile violent-crime arrests will double in just 18 years."[16] We were looking at the most current data available at the time, but such data are always out of date by the time a book is published. Thus, in 1997 the most current arrest statistics were from 1994. The one-year decline between 1993 and 1994 did not appear to be much more than an anomaly especially after so many years of increasing youth violence. Howard Snyder and Melissa Sickmund had recently calculated estimates of juvenile violent crime for the year 2010 based on juvenile arrests for 1992 and available projections of population growth. They stated: "If current trends continue, by 2010 the number of juvenile arrests for murder is expected to increase by 145 percent over the 1992 level."[17] They also projected increases of 129 percent for aggravated assault and 66 percent for rape. Louis Freeh, Director of the FBI, stated that "the ominous increase in juvenile crime, coupled with population trends, portends future crime and violence at nearly unprecedented levels."[18] But

box 3-1   DELINQUENCY AROUND THE GLOBE
Youth Violence in European Countries

The United States is not the only country that struggles with juvenile violence. Research on recent trends in juvenile crime and violence in European Union countries suggests that the rate of juvenile violence rose sharply in the latter part of the 20th century just as it did in the United States. Since the early to mid-1980s, an increase in youth violence occurred in Austria, Denmark, England and Wales, France, Germany, Holland, Italy, Poland, Sweden, and Switzerland. Rates of youth violence increased in most of these countries even though overall youth crime rates appeared to be stable and even though crime rates were not increasing among older people. In some countries, the official figures increased between 50 and 250 percent. In England and Wales in 1986, for example, approximately 360 of every 100,000 youths ages 14 to 16 were "convicted or cautioned by the police" for violent crimes; in 1994 that figure had climbed to approximately 580 per 100,000. Increases in youth violence in Germany were even higher. In 1984 the number of 14- to 18-year-olds suspected of violent crime in the former West Germany was approximately 300 per 100,000; by 1995 that figure had more than doubled to about 760 per 100,000. Rates in the former East Germany were between 60 and 80 percent higher. Even Sweden, a country that forbids parental use of physical force against their children and prohibits professional boxing, reports dramatic increases in the number of juveniles sentenced for assault since the mid-1980s.

According to official records, victim surveys, and self-report studies, the victims of violent crimes committed by juveniles were other juveniles. In the Netherlands young people ages 15 to 17 were four times more likely than adults to be the victims of assault. Juveniles in Germany were also more likely to be the victims of violent crime than members of other age groups. In every country, young males were far more likely than young females to be violent crime victims.

Explanations for the growth in European juvenile violent crime rates parallel those used to explain youth violence in the United States: unemployment, alcohol, drugs, availability of guns, and domestic abuse. In some countries—France and Germany, for example—the problem of unemployment was exacerbated in the early 1990s by an influx of immigrants from countries that had been under communist rule. Immigrants who could not overcome language and culture barriers in order to find employment were more likely to engage in violent crimes than those who found jobs and became integrated into society.

German officials noted an increase in the use of alcohol and other drugs in the last decade, and firearms had become somewhat more available after the fall of the Berlin Wall than they had been in the past. Even though many of the German males arrested for violent crimes came from low-income households, the most common thread in their life histories is that they came from families where violence was common: they were beaten, their siblings were beaten, or one of their parents was beaten.

Ultimately, a main cause appears to be that life in many European countries is shifting toward a winner–loser culture in which many disadvantaged youth appear fated to be losers. Countries vary considerably in the mix of law enforcement and prevention efforts undertaken to deal with increased youth violence.

Sources: Mangai Natarajan, *Introduction to International Criminal Justice* (New York: McGraw-Hill, 2005); Christian Pfeiffer, "Juvenile Crime and Violence in Europe," pages 255–328 in Michael Tonry (ed.), *Crime and Justice: A Review of Research,* volume 23 (Chicago: University of Chicago Press, 1998); Hanns Von Hofer, "Criminal Violence and Youth in Sweden: A Long-term Perspective," *Journal of Scandinavian Studies in Criminology and Crime Prevention* 1:56–72 (2000); Rosemary Barberet, Benjamin Bowling, Josine Junger-Tas, Cristina Rechea-Alberola, John van Kesteren, and Andrew Zurawan, *Self-Reported Juvenile Delinquency in England and Wales, the Netherlands, and Spain* (Monsey, NY: Criminal Justice Press, 2004).

these estimates and predictions were all wrong. Why were we and so many other criminologists wrong about the direction of violent youth crime, and why did juvenile violence and crime in general decline so much and so quickly?

Frank Zimring recently said, "Criminologists are like weathermen without a satellite. We can only tell you about yesterday's crime rates."[19] However, there is also a good deal of disagreement among criminologists as they offer interpretations and explanations of the last decade's violent youth crime rates. There are a variety of explanations for why youth violence ended up declining rather than increasing. In Chapter 2, six reasons for the general decline in juvenile arrests were discussed including an improving economy, increased use of incarceration, more and better policing, changes in the age distribution of the population, the decline in the crack market, and legalized abortion. But are explanations for why youth committed fewer thefts, used certain drugs less frequently, burglarized fewer homes, and stole fewer automobiles adequate for explaining the drop in homicides, forcible rapes, aggravated assaults, and weapons violations?

Marc Ouimet examined the drop in crime in the United States and Canada to explore what caused the drastic declines in crime. Whereas American criminal justice policy included greater numbers of police, more aggressive and specialized policing tactics, and increased use of prison, Canada's criminal justice policy did not. Yet, both nations enjoyed similar reductions in crime. Ouimet believes that the causes of the crime decline in both countries lay in demographic shifts, improved work opportunities, and changes in cultural values.[20]

According to John Conklin, "Whatever caused crime rates to fall in the 1990s saved tens of thousands of lives and millions of dollars worth of property." Because nearly all categories of crime dropped after the early 1990s, Conklin argues that no single factor led to the decline. He suggests that increases in the number of police officers on the streets or police patrol practices, decreased use of crack but greater use of marijuana, more rigorous and more enforced gun laws, lower divorce rates, and even the shrinkage in the relative size of the adolescent population cannot explain the decline in violent crime *and* nonviolent crime during this period. Rather some common forces were at work, pushing all the rates down.

think about it

Violent movies abound, violence is pervasive on the Internet, poverty rates have not changed significantly over the years, and two-parent families are in decline. Yet youth violence has declined significantly. Is it possible that violent behavior is more easily deterred by swifter and more severe punishments after all?

Conklin argues that the force common to the large declines in both violent and nonviolent youth crime was essentially the harsher sentencing laws passed in the late 1980s and early 1990s, the "get-tough" attitude of the courts, the waiver of serious violent juveniles to adult criminal court, and the burgeoning correctional population. According to Conklin, "At least 10,800 murders, 2,176,000 robberies, 738,000 burglaries, and 748,000 motor vehicle thefts were prevented over the course of the decade by the incarceration of additional offenders. . . . The increase in the incarceration rate can account for the decreases in all four crime indicators."[21]

On the other hand, Alfred Blumstein and Joel Wallman believe that the decline in youth violence largely resulted from the decline in demand for crack, which reduced the need for street markets to recruit large numbers of young drug sellers, and that this was accompanied by a reduced need for street sellers to be armed (see Chapter 4).[22] In addition, Blumstein says that police were more effective in enforcing gun laws and disrupting gun markets (discussed later in this chapter) and that the economy improved so young people were able to get legitimate jobs.[23] Others contend that the focus on crack markets and lethal violence among minority youths is inaccurate. Callie Rennison and Mike Planty used *NCVS* data for the crimes of rape, sexual assault, robbery, and aggravated assault between 1994 and 2001—the era of the greatest declines. In contrast to previous findings, Rennison and Planty found that for *nonfatal* crimes, reductions among African American and urban males were modest. However, among white, nonurban males, the reductions were great. In other words, contrary to many media accounts that focus on delinquency among inner-city, minority youths, it was actually the case that rural and suburban white youths "cleaning up their act" contributed most impressively to declines in serious youth violence (excluding homicide).[24]

Finally, Frank Zimring says that upward and downward trends in youth violence tend to be cyclical in unpredictable ways because there are "no unitary trends in the recent history of youth arrests for violent crime."[25] Juvenile arrest rates for homicide, robbery, rape, and assault are rather cyclical and the cycles for the four offense categories are different. For example, he notes that while gun assaults increased after 1983, nongun aggravated assault cases increased even faster, and that although gun homicides increased, killings with knives remained rather stable.

Characteristics of Violent Juvenile Offenders

Today, as in past years, the overwhelming majority (82 percent) of youths arrested for violent crimes are males, although girls accounted for about 24 percent of those arrested for aggravated assault, 11 percent for murder, and 10 percent for robbery (see Table 3-1). Girls who murder are more likely to use knives than are boys, who tend to use guns. They are also more likely to murder family members and very young victims. For example, 24 percent of girls' murder victims were under age 3, compared to only 1 percent of boys' murder victims.[26]

Yet girls do appear to be more violent than in the past. Between 1992 and 1996 female juveniles arrested for violent crimes increased by about 25 percent, and since the mid-1990s the decline in female violence has been much smaller than the decline in male violence. Girls involved in violence are also increasingly likely to make the national news. For example, a group of high school girls were videotaped beating other girls during a hazing incident in a Chicago suburb. And 12-year-old Nicole Townes was in a coma for three weeks after being pummeled and stomped by a group of girls between the ages 13 to 15 at a birthday

think
about it

A different form of youth violence occurs when adolescent females commit infanticide. Are such acts more or less egregious than school shootings? How does gender influence lethal violence?

table 3-1   Juveniles Arrested for Violent Crimes, by Sex and Race/Ethnicity, 2005

OFFENSE	SEX		RACE/ETHNICITY		
	MALE	FEMALE	WHITE	BLACK	OTHER
Murder	89.1%	10.9%	43.0%	54.0%	3.0%
Forcible rape	98.5	1.5	64.3	34.0	1.7
Robbery	90.5	9.5	30.7	67.5	1.8
Aggravated assault	76.4	23.6	55.6	42.2	2.2
Total violent crime	81.5	18.5	48.2	49.8	2.0

Source: Federal Bureau of Investigation, *Crime in the United States 2005* (Washington, DC: U.S. Department of Justice, 2006).

party in Baltimore. According to Wiley Hall, "Around the country, school police and teachers are seeing a growing tendency for girls to settle disputes with their fists. They are finding themselves breaking up playground fights in which girls are going at each other toe-to-toe, like boys."[27]

White youths accounted for over half, or about 48 percent, of all youths arrested for violent Crime Index offenses (see Table 3-1). White youths were roughly 64 percent of juveniles arrested for forcible rape and 56 percent for aggravated assault, but only 43 percent of the arrests for murder and 41 percent for robbery. African American youths are most overrepresented in arrests for robbery and murder, and this pattern has been generally consistent over the past several decades.[28]

While some criminologists suggest arrest data may reflect police bias in arrest decisions, the use of broader measures of delinquency, such as self-report data from the National Youth Survey, provide additional support for findings of disproportionate minority involvement in violent crime (see Chapter 2 and Chapter 13). Delbert Elliott reports that at the peak age of offending (17 years), 36 percent of African American males and 25 percent of white males reported that they had committed one or more serious violent crimes and that nearly twice as many African Americans as whites continued violent offending into adulthood.[29]

Arrest disparities may not reflect differences in the *characteristics of incidents* involving white and nonwhite offenders. Using the more complete information provided in the newer National Incident-Based Reporting System (*NIBRS*) (discussed in Chapter 2), Carl Pope and Howard Snyder found that compared with nonwhite juvenile offenders, white juvenile offenders were

- Less likely to have multiple victims.
- More likely to act alone.
- More likely to commit crimes indoors.
- Less likely to possess a nonpersonal weapon, such as a firearm, knife, or club.
- Less likely to offend against adults.
- Equally likely to offend against females.
- Less likely to offend against members of another race.
- Equally likely to injure victims.
- More likely to commit crimes against family members and equally likely to commit crimes against acquaintances.[30]

Pope and Snyder suggest that these incident characteristics, rather than race, are more likely to impact arrests. They state that:

> Overall, the *NIBRS* data offer no evidence to support the hypothesis that police are more likely to arrest nonwhite juvenile offenders than white juvenile offenders, once other incident attributes are taken into consideration. This holds true when the data are analyzed in the aggregate (i.e., for all states and crimes combined), at the state level, and within each crime category. In fact, there is some evidence to support the conclusion that once a violent crime is reported to or witnessed by police, the likelihood of arrest is greater for white juvenile offenders than for nonwhite juvenile offenders.[31]

Explanations for youth violence abound, and specific explanations for why males are more violent than females, why minority youth may (or may not) be more likely to engage in violence, why older juveniles are more violent than younger juveniles, why juveniles tend to age out of violent and nonviolent crime, and why youth violence tends to be disproportionately found in urban areas, especially lower-income neighborhoods, range from consideration of biological, psychological, and developmental factors; social disorganization and social strain; patterns of socialization and peer association; and economic and power differences. These various explanations for juvenile delinquency and youth crime are examined in depth in Chapters 5 through 9.

Violent Victimization of Youth

If the middle of the 1980s marked the beginning of an upsurge in juvenile arrests for violent crime, it also marked the point at which violent juvenile *victimizations* began to increase dramatically. Between 1984 and 1993, the rate of juvenile homicide victimizations increased threefold. In 2004, for instance, a total of 1,365 juveniles were homicide victims—an average of a little under four per day. Of these victims, 504 were age 4 or younger and 176 were younger than 1 year old.[32] One 4-year-old murder victim is Emanuel Barima, who was stabbed in the neck by two brothers, one 9 years old, the other only 8. The two brothers had allegedly been teasing and bullying Emanuel's 5-year-old sister, Abigail, for months before confronting Emanuel and Abigail outside their Bronx apartment. If convicted, both young murderers could face up to 18 months in a secure juvenile correctional facility.[33] (See Box 3-2 for a discussion of the murder of very young children.)

African American males are over five times more likely than white males to be homicide victims. This young boy was the victim of a drive-by shooting. What might be done to prevent senseless violence?

box 3-2 — A WINDOW ON DELINQUENCY
The Murder of Young Children

More young children, those under age 6, die from homicide than from infectious diseases or cancer. Girls under age 6 are much more likely than girls ages 12 to 17 to be murdered, and white children under age 6 were nearly as likely as their teenage counterparts to be victims of homicide. Between 2001 and 2003, 94 infants were murdered in the United States, and 19 infants were killed and classified as negligent manslaughter. During the same time period, nearly 3,000 infants were raped, sodomized, or assaulted in the United States.

However, the actual homicide rate for very young children is likely to be much higher than official statistics suggest because they are among the most difficult to document. The deaths of very young children often resemble deaths resulting from accidents and other causes. For example, a child who dies from *sudden infant death syndrome* (SIDS) is fairly indistinguishable from a child who has been smothered. A child who has been thrown or intentionally dropped is likely to have injuries quite similar to those of a child who died from an accidental fall.

Two characteristics distinguish homicides of very young children from other juvenile victims: Such homicides are committed primarily by family members and half by the common use of "personal weapons," such as hands and feet, to batter, strangle, or suffocate victims. In addition, young boys are somewhat more likely than young girls to be victims of homicide (55 and 45 percent, respectively). Among very young children, those at highest risk of homicide are those under age one. Homicides of children in this group include a certain number appropriately classified as **infanticide** (homicides in which recently born children are killed by relatives who do not want the child or who are suffering from a childbirth-related psychiatric disturbance). The FBI does not provide data identifying infanticides as a distinct subgroup, although countries such as Britain and Canada have a special infanticide offense category in their national crime statistics. The number of infanticides rose from 4.3 to 9.2 per 100,000 between 1970 and 2000, but then declined in recent years. Infants are most likely to be murdered by their mothers during the first week of life, but after that time, males, typically a stepfather or boyfriend of the mother, are more likely. Half of all infanticides occur before the fourth month of life and the greatest risk of being murdered is on the day of birth.

FBI data do not identify victims murdered during the first six days of life (victims of what is called *neonaticide*), annually there are about 70 such victims. Two-thirds of these children were murdered by mothers, one-half of whom were under age 20. Fathers were responsible for only about 1 out of 10 of these murders. Sadly, prosecutors decline to pursue charges in 76 percent of cases involving these infant victims.

Sources: Federal Bureau of Investigation, *Crime in the United States 2005* (Washington, DC: U.S. Department of Justice, 2006), p. 23; David Finkelhor and Richard Ormrod, *Homicides of Children and Youth* (Washington, DC: Office of Juvenile Justice and Delinquency Prevention, 2001); ChildTrends DataBank, *Infant Homicide*, online at http://www.childtrends databank.org/pdf/72_PDF.pdf, accessed April 22, 2007; Federal Bureau of Investigation, *Infant Victims: An Exploratory Study* (Washington, DC: U.S. Department of Justice, 2005), pp. 359–366.

But like the juvenile homicide offending rate, the rate of homicide victimization of juveniles has declined significantly since the mid-1990s, dropping 50 percent from an all-time high of 12.1 per 100,000 in 1993. Using data from the National Crime Victimization Survey, Katrina Baum reports on recent trends in criminal victimization among children and adolescents. Since 1993, juveniles between the ages of 12 and 17 have annual rates of nonfatal, violent victimization that are about 250 percent higher than the rates for adults. Although rates are higher among juveniles than adults, overall crime rates declined for all age groups for all types of crimes since 1993, and the greatest declines were among younger teens between the ages of 12 and 14. Younger teens are more likely to be victimized by strangers, 80 percent are victimized by another adolescent, and they are slightly less likely to be victimized by a firearm. Older juveniles are slightly more likely to be victims of robbery, aggravated assault, and rape/sexual assault than are younger juveniles. Male juveniles are substantially more likely than females to be victims of violent crimes, with the exception of rape and sexual assault. [34]

Serious injuries resulting from violent crimes also differ by gender. Girls were more likely than boys to have stab wounds, while boys were more likely than girls to have gunshot wounds. And girls were also more likely than boys to be injured at home rather than in a public place or at school. [35] African American youths are victims of violence at rates higher than white youths. African American and white youth are generally likely to experience similar rates of violent victimization, although 12- to 15-year-old white youth are slightly more likely to be victims of aggravated assault, and African American youth are significantly more likely to be victims of robbery. Interestingly, African American females are nearly twice as likely as white males to be victims of aggravated assault. [36]

Juveniles comprise about 12 percent of all crime victims reported to police, but 71 percent of all sex crime victims and 38 percent of all kidnapping victims. Simple assault is the most commonly reported crime against juveniles, comprising 41 percent of all juvenile victimizations. Sexual assault accounts for almost one-third of preteen victimizations, more than twice the proportion for older juveniles. [37] Victims of juvenile violence are frequently victimized by other juveniles as 38 percent were no more than one year older or one year younger than the offender. Over 90 percent of male victims of violent crime were victimized by males; 52 percent of female victims ages 12 to 17 were victims of female offenders. Nearly all victims of juveniles knew the offender. In those incidents where the relationship was known, about two-thirds of the victims of juvenile violence were acquainted with the offender, 23 percent were family members, and only about 12 percent were strangers. [38]

In addition to the obvious negative impact of the victimization of children and adolescents, there is another problem: The cycle of violence that victimization perpetuates. Murray Straus and Sarah Savage examined the link between childhood neglect and dating delinquency in a group of nearly 7,000 students sampled from 33 universities in 17 countries. They found that about half of university students reported some form of parental neglect sustained when they were children. Nearly 15 percent of students experienced a pervasive pattern of neglect. For both genders, neglect increased the likelihood of physically assaulting a dating partner. [39] Using a large sample of Canadian youths, David Wolfe and his colleagues found that those who were maltreated as children were significantly more likely to suffer from various psychiatric problems. Maltreated boys were 200 to 400 percent more likely to suffer from depression and post–traumatic stress disorder and 200 to 340 percent more likely to threaten or abuse their dating partners. [40]

Overall, approximately 12 percent of high school students have experienced some form of dating violence and the prevalence estimates from various studies range between 9 and 57 percent. [41] Fortunately, the United States appears to be taking the victimization of children more seriously. In July 2006 Congress passed the *Adam Walsh Child Protection and Safety Act* that toughened a variety of laws that targeted offenders who victimize children. In addition, the Department of Justice created Project Safe Childhood, an initiative designed to protect children as they use the Internet.[42] In addition to these federal developments, a number of prevention and treatment programs aimed at serious youth violence are described later in this chapter.

The Role of Firearms in Youth Violence

The majority of juvenile homicide and suicide victims are killed with firearms. A frequently made claim by a segment of one side in the gun control debate is that "Guns don't kill people, people kill people." The implication is that guns do not act on their own, they are tools in the hands of people who choose to use them for carrying out violent acts. If people did not have access to guns, then they would find other deadly weapons to use. Many advocates of strict gun control take a very different view. To them, guns are, in and of themselves, evil. Guns are deadly forces that are directly responsible for the deaths or maiming of tens of thousands of people every year. If it were not for the easy availability of guns, most perpetrators would either refrain from violence altogether or, at worst, select a less deadly weapon.[43] There are more than 250 million guns in America today, and there is no question that juveniles have significantly greater access to guns in the 21st century, that guns are available through often illegal means, and that the guns they have access to are much more deadly than in the past.[44] While the number of arrests of juveniles for weapons violations *increased* by over 400 percent between 1960 and 1990, they *decreased* significantly (dropping nearly 50 percent) since 1993. In 2005 juveniles accounted for just over 20 percent of all persons arrested for weapons violations. Of those juveniles arrested and victimized, most were males, two-thirds were white, and just under a third were African American. Among all age and sex groups, males at age 18 have the highest per capita arrest rates for weapons violations, followed by males at age 17.[45]

Carrying and Getting Guns   According to the Indicators of School Crime and Safety National survey, schools are safer than they have been in decades. During the school year when the most recent data are available, 17 homicides and five suicides of school children occurred on school property.[46] A recent Centers for Disease Control and Prevention national survey of middle/junior high and high school students reported that just over 5 percent of the students said they had carried a gun to school during the month prior to the survey. Nearly 8 percent said they had been threatened or injured with a weapon on school property once or more during the preceding year.[47] In other words, few school children carry, possess, or use weapons.

Pamela Wilcox and Richard Clayton surveyed over 6,000 6th- through 12th-grade students in 21 schools and discovered that males were about 30 percent more likely than females to carry weapons to school, and that nonwhites were nearly 50 percent more likely than whites to bring weapons to school. Wilcox and Clayton also reported that students of lower socioeconomic status, students who have been threatened at school, students who report a variety of other problem behaviors, and students whose parents own guns were also significantly more likely to carry weapons to school.[48]

Surveys of only students may not provide the most accurate estimate of how many youths possess or carry guns on a regular basis. Many youths have dropped out of school, and substantial numbers are confined in correctional institutions. Joseph Sheley and James Wright surveyed students as well as 835 male juvenile inmates in six different correctional facilities. Students were asked if they currently owned a gun, and inmates were asked if they had owned a gun at the time they were arrested. About 22 percent of the students and 83 percent of the incarcerated youths reported ownership of a gun at the time in question.[49]

The media has often pointed to gang violence involving semi-automatic assault rifles and report that some police officers believe that they are "outgunned" by many of the weapons used by violent youth. Indeed, much gang violence in recent years has been characterized by the use of more sophisticated weapons (discussed later in this chapter). However, most youth violence is *not* gang-related violence, and there is evidence that the general sophistication of firearms used by juveniles did not change much throughout the decade of the 1990s. Rick Ruddell and Larry Mays examined data involving the confiscation of 1,055 firearms from juveniles in St. Louis from 1992 through 1999. They found that handguns were the most likely kind of firearm to be confiscated from juveniles and that

Children with ready access to firearms are at an increased risk for violent offending and victimization. For child safety, guns should be kept unloaded and locked in a safe place. Does the balance of child safety and protection against criminals depend on what neighborhood you live in?

most often these handguns were of the Saturday night special variety—cheap, easily concealed, and small caliber. Only 10 assault weapons were confiscated from juveniles over the 8-year period, compared to 134 nonpowder firearms (BB or pellet guns). According to Ruddell and Mays, "youths are more likely to have pellet guns, .22 caliber firearms, and Saturday night specials confiscated by the police. . . . Overall, most firearms seized from juveniles by the police have a low threat level."[50]

The **Brady Bill** mandated a five-day waiting period for the purchase of handguns, while The *Violent Crime Control and Law Enforcement Act of 1994* made it a federal crime for anyone to sell or transfer a handgun, or ammunition for a handgun, to a person under age 18.[51] The act also made it a crime for juveniles to possess a handgun or ammunition for a handgun, although there are certain exceptions: A youth may possess a handgun when it is used for farming, ranching, target shooting, or safety instruction provided the youth has his or her parent's written permission to have the handgun. However, most states already prohibit the sale of handguns to persons under age 21 and the sale of rifles and shotguns to persons under the age of 18. Therefore, if it is clearly illegal for youths to obtain guns through legitimate channels, how do they get them? It is estimated that about a third of children in the United States live in homes with firearms.[52] If there is no firearm available in the home, a youth is likely to have little difficulty in obtaining one from friends, on the street, through theft, or through an illegal purchase from a gun dealer.

In their classic study, Sheley and Wright asked students and juvenile inmates how they had obtained the guns they possessed. More than half the students said they borrowed their guns from a family member or friend, whereas most of the juvenile inmates said they had gotten their guns from friends and street sources. Both students and inmates indicated that they felt they could obtain guns with little trouble: There was little need to steal guns or to go through normal retail outlets where a friend or family member could legally purchase a gun.[53] This is fairly consistent with a recent survey of firearm use by offenders. About 40 percent of state prison inmates age 24 or younger obtained the gun used in their current offense from family members or friends. Only 7 percent obtained a gun from a retail store.[54]

Unfortunately, many young people live in social worlds characterized by crime and violence. Of the juvenile inmates, 40 percent had siblings who had been incarcerated, 62 percent reported having male family members who routinely carried guns, and 84 percent indicated that they had been threatened with a gun or shot at during their lives. Half had been stabbed with a knife, and more than 80 percent had been beaten up by someone. Students were only slightly less exposed to violent environments. Nearly half the students reported that male members of their households regularly carried guns, 45 percent reported having been threatened with a gun or shot at, and one-third of the students had been beaten up either at school or on the way to or from school.[55]

Philip Cook and Jens Ludwig believe that, at the local level, greater ownership of guns by adults is associated with the likelihood of youths carrying both guns and other types of weapons. However, they argue that while gun prevalence does not affect the decision of a youth to carry a weapon, it does affect the decision of what kind of weapon the youth will carry. This means that "the availability of guns clearly increases the likelihood that those teens that do carry weapons choose guns."[56]

Thus far, this chapter has explored topics related to a general understanding of serious youth violence, especially involvement in the most serious forms of delinquency and gun-related crimes. Within this general framework are the most serious, violent, and chronic juvenile offenders—the chronic delinquents described in Chapter 2. However, within the population of serious, violent, and chronic juvenile offenders is another important phenomenon that has yet to be examined: *psychopathy*. Only a small subgroup of serious delinquents is psychopathic, which is a serious personality disorder that impairs social development and enhances involvement in delinquency.[57]

think
about it

Is the ultimate argument for gun control that children can readily obtain them from family, friends, and their homes? What are the benefits and costs of having firearms in a family home?

JUVENILE PSYCHOPATHY

Psychopathy is a personality disorder that impairs interpersonal, affective, and behavioral functions and is closely linked to serious antisocial behavior. The disorder is significantly more likely to occur in boys as opposed to girls and does not discriminate by race, ethnicity, social class, or country of origin. In other words, psychopaths have been studied in many racial groups and in many different countries. There are several core characteristics of psychopathic individuals. They are aggressive, self-centered or narcissistic, impulsive, and prone to risky activities. They often begin getting into trouble very early in life, engage in a wide variety of antisocial behaviors, and are prolific criminals.[58] Thus far, these characteristics describe many serious, nonpsychopathic offenders as well. It is the following list of characteristics, however, that distinguishes psychopaths from other individuals. Psychopathic delinquents are callous, guiltless, and have little to no fear or anxiety. They are exploitative, manipulative, deceptive, and seemingly unable to form warm relationships with other people. They are without conscience and appear to be impervious to efforts by the juvenile and criminal justice systems to intervene.[59]

Philippe Pinel is considered the first person to clinically study the construct of psychopathy with the publication of his *A Treatise on Insanity* in 1801. Pinel described a diagnosis for people who exhibited uncontrolled rage and outlandishly immoral behavior that was without psychotic features such as delusions. In other words, people seemed to be extremely dangerous yet simultaneously in control of their emotions and mental health.[60] In 1835 James Pritchard called the disorder "moral insanity," again noting that serious criminal conduct was occurring without mental defect.[61] Many other physicians, psychiatrists, and correctional clinicians also studied psychopathy throughout the 19th and 20th centuries. The modern understanding of psychopathy was realized in 1941 with the publication of Hervey Cleckley's *The Mask of Sanity*. His work was the most systematic clinical study of psychopathy and laid the groundwork for contemporary research. Cleckley described the sheer antisocial differences between psychopaths and even the most delinquent youths:

> In repetitive delinquent behavior, the subject often seems to be going a certain distance along the course that a full psychopath follows to the end. In the less severe disorder, antisocial or self-defeating activities are frequently more circumscribed and may stand out against a larger background of successful adaptation. The borderlines between chronic delinquency and what we have called the psychopath merge in this area. Although anxiety, remorse, shame, and other consciously painful subjective responses to undesirable consequences are deficient in both as compared with the normal, this callousness or apathy is far deeper in the psychopath.[62]

The majority of research on psychopaths has centered on adult criminals in prisons or psychiatric hospitals. It was discovered that offenders presented psychopathic characteristics throughout their lives, even in early childhood and adolescence. Thus, juvenile psychopathy is an important area of research for understanding the disorder and developing ways to prevent it or reduce its negative effects.

The application of psychopathy to children and adolescents has occurred for decades. William McCord and Joan McCord expressed concerns that serious violent crime was the work of adolescent psychopaths in 1964.[63] In 1966 Lee Robins described children that appeared in local psychiatric clinics as "Boys [that] had a history of truancy, theft, staying out late, and refusing to obey parents. They lied gratuitously, and showed little guilt over their behavior. They were generally irresponsible."[64] In the 1980s as crime rates increased and criminology focused more attention on the most serious types of offenders, serious juvenile offenders also began to receive more scrutiny from researchers. In recent years, criminologists in several countries have produced an impressive knowledge-base on psychopathic traits among juvenile offenders. Some of their primary characteristics and behaviors are described next.

Characteristics and Behaviors of Psychopathic Youths

Criminologists have found that a set of traits typifies psychopathic youths. Donald Lynam and his colleagues suggest that juvenile psychopathy can be understood as a constellation of personality characteristics that contribute to delinquent behavior. The personality profile is quite negative, unfortunately. Psychopathic youths are very disagreeable and often are suspicious, deceptive, exploitative, arrogant, tough-minded, and aggressive. They are low in conscientiousness and constraint, which means that they impulsively seek to satisfy their own needs with no concern for the feelings of other people.[65] Paul Frick and his colleagues studied a sample of more than 1,100 children in third, fourth, sixth, or seventh grades to examine the stability of psychopathic traits. Again, they found that the most psychopathic children (their average age was 10 years) were highly impulsive, highly narcissistic, and highly callous and unemotional to others. Moreover, these characteristics were relatively stable over a 4-year follow-up period. This suggests that psychopathic traits develop early in life and, once established, are likely to persist throughout the life course.[66]

If the personality profile of psychopathic youths is troubling, the behavioral profile is even more unsettling particularly among institutionalized juvenile offenders. Mary Ann Campbell, Stephen Porter, and Darcy Santor found that psychopathic youths are among the most aggressive, antisocial, and delinquent children within detention centers. Although they are the most prone to externalizing problems (e.g., hurting others), and they are the least prone to internalizing problems (e.g., hurting themselves). In other words, psychopathic youths do not feel "stressed" about engaging in serious antisocial behavior. They also tend to have had the most severe criminal records, been suspended or expelled from school, often had multiple placements in foster homes and juvenile detention centers, and experienced more abuse during early childhood.[67] Several other scholars have also found that youths who present psychopathic traits have multifaceted involvement in delinquent behaviors.[68] Unfortunately, psychopathic youths appear to be impervious to the legal and moral bases of punishment. They simply do not respond to punishment by correcting their behavior, instead they appear to be unmoved.[69]

Compared to serious delinquents who are not psychopathic, juvenile psychopaths are noteworthy for their sustained criminal activity, continued criminal activity while under the supervision of the juvenile justice system, and recidivism rates upon reentering society. Michael Vaughn and Matt DeLisi studied the effects of psychopathic traits on delinquent careers among a population of institutionalized delinquents in Missouri. They found that adolescents with psychopathic personality features were 300 percent more likely to have an early onset of criminal behavior, be contacted by police, and be processed by the juvenile court.[70] In addition, youths with psychopathic traits were significantly likely to become adult career criminals.[71] Diana Falkenbach and her associates studied psychopathic features among 69 children who had been arrested and placed in a juvenile diversion program (Chapter 13). They discovered that youths with psychopathic traits were more likely to not comply with the program and be rearrested.[72] Based on data from Canadian youths between the ages of 12 and 18, Raymond Corrado and his colleagues reported that psychopathic youths are significantly likely to commit general, violent, and nonviolent delinquent acts than kids who are not psychopathic. Moreover, psychopathic youths commit crimes faster and with greater frequency.[73] Even while incarcerated, psychopathic youths present problems. Daniel Murrie and his associates studied institutionalized youths in Virginia and found that prior record for crimes of violence, record of violence that did not result in arrest, violence while incarcerated, assaulting other correctional residents with weapons, and inflicting great bodily harm were significantly correlated with psychopathy.[74] Similarly, among 85 adjudicated delinquents in Florida who were between the ages of 11 and 18, psychopathic youths accumulated more disciplinary infractions, committed more violent acts, and had worse treatment outcomes than nonpsychopathic children.[75]

Causes of Psychopathy

What causes some youngsters to be glib, deceitful, manipulative, callous, irresponsible, impulsive, mean, lacking in guilt, and so easily able to victimize others? Is their pathology innate? Did something happen to them that produced psychopathy? Does some combination of nature and nurture produce psychopathy? Based on the weight of the evidence, the best answer appears to be that it is produced by a combination of biopsychological and sociological factors—in other words, *nature and nurture* (for more on the development of antisocial behavior, see Chapter 8).

Some behavioral scientists have distinguished primary and secondary psychopaths as a way to explore **etiological**, or causal, factors of antisocial behavior. *Primary psychopaths* are persons who have brain abnormalities that impair their ability to process and express emotion, such as empathy. Their antisocial behavior is largely innate.[76] Research by James Blair and his colleagues indicates that the genetic factors produce neurotransmitter dysfunction that in turn reduces the ability of the amygdala, almond-shaped groups of neurons in the brain that control our emotional ability, to process emotional learning and socially relate to others.[77] Importantly, even the most biologically centered explanation also points to the importance of the social environment in developing antisocial behavior. In other words, even primary psychopaths respond to the influence of others in determining their behavior.

Secondary psychopaths have the same characteristics as primary psychopaths; however, the pathology in the secondary psychopath is developed often as an adaptation to some severe trauma in early life, usually parental abuse or rejection. Because of the importance of early life trauma in developing secondary psychopathy, many criminologists use the term **sociopath** to distinguish psychopathic characteristics that are largely the result of early life abuse and neglect.[78] Donald Lynam has shown how these biological and environmental factors in-

box 3-3   A WINDOW ON DELINQUENCY
Psychopaths and Violence

Psychopathic offenders are noteworthy for the extremity of their violence. In the community, psychopathic offenders are the most active, versatile, and relentless offenders; in prison, they are among the most violent and noncompliant inmates. Several criminologists have explored the nature of offending by psychopathic individuals. Stephen Porter and his colleagues compared murders committed by psychopaths and nonpsychopaths among inmates in Canadian prisons. They reported that murders committed by psychopaths were characterized by sadism and more gratuitous violence (e.g., stabbings with dozens or hundreds of entry wounds) than killings by nonpsychopathic offenders. More than 82 percent of psychopathic offenders committed these types of murders compared to 52 percent of nonpsychopathic offenders.

Katherine Ramsland researched psychopathic violence among children and adolescents and unearthed several examples:

• Sixteen-year-old Brenda Spencer received a rifle for her birthday. She used it to shoot kids at an elementary school near her San Diego home, wounding nine and killing two. A reporter asked her later why she had done it. Her answer: "I don't like Mondays. This livens up the day."
• Two bodies were found on a country road in Ellis County, Texas. One was male, one female. The boy, 14, had been shot, but the 13-year-old girl had been stripped, raped, and dismembered. Her head and hands were missing. The killer turned out to be Jason Massey, who had decided he was going to become the worst serial killer that Texas had

ever seen. He tortured animals, stalked another young woman, and revered killers like Ted Bundy. He was 9 years old when he killed his first cat and added dozens more over the years, along with dogs and even six cows. He had a long list of potential victims and his diaries were filled with fantasies of rape, torture, and cannibalism of female victims. He was a loner who believed he served a "master" who gave him knowledge and power. He was obsessed with bringing girls under his control and having their dead bodies in his possession.
• Nine-year-old Jeffrey Bailey, Jr. pushed a 3-year-old friend into the deep part of a motel pool in Florida. He wanted to see someone drown. As the boy sank to the bottom, Jeffrey pulled up a chair to watch. When it was finished, he went home. When he was questioned, he was more engaged in being the center of attention than in any kind of remorse for what he had done, and spoke nonchalantly about the murder.

Given these disturbing images, it is clear why juvenile psychopathy is such an important area of research to enable the prevention of serious youth violence.

Sources: Stephen Porter, Michael Woodworth, Jeff Earle, Jeff Drugge, and Douglas Boer, "Characteristics of Sexual Homicides Committed by Psychopathic and Non-Psychopathic Offenders," *Law and Human Behavior* 27:457–470 (2003); Matt DeLisi, "Criminal Careers Behind Bars," *Behavioral Sciences and the Law* 21:653–669 (2003); Robert Hare, "Psychopathy as a Risk Factor for Violence," *Psychiatric Quarterly* 70:181–197 (1999); Katherine Ramsland, The Childhood Psychopath: Bad Seed or Bad Parents?, online at http://www.crimelibrary.com/criminal_mind/psychology/psychopath/1.html, accessed June 3, 2007.

teract to produce psychopathy in young people. Children who present severe hyperactivity, impulsivity, and attention problems often also suffer from conduct problems. These children are very difficult to parent and manage in school and often alienate themselves from conventional peers, resulting in social isolation and labeling. Over time, the antisocial aspects of their behavior become reinforced or exacerbated while the positive aspects of their behavior become more infrequent and difficult to reinforce. Unless a major treatment intervention occurs, these "fledgling psychopaths" develop into the most serious, violent, and chronic delinquents.[79]

Treatment of Juvenile Psychopathy

Whether prevention and treatment programs specifically address the needs of juvenile psychopaths is unknown because almost all of the evaluation research has been conducted on adult offenders. By and large, criminal justice treatments attempt to increase the prosocial abilities of offenders. In the case of psychopathic offenders, the emphasis is placed on increasing empathy through intensive cognitive therapy and behavioral modification. Amazingly, prior research shows that, in some circumstances, treatment actually makes psychopaths more dangerous. Marnie Rice, Grant Harris, and Catherine Cormier evaluated an intensive therapeutic community program that included up to 80 hours of intensive group therapy per week. Whereas the treatment reduced recidivism among 146 nonpsychopathic offenders, it increased recidivism among 146 psychopathic offenders. By learning to take others' perspective and behave in socially acceptable ways, psychopaths were able to enhance their ability to manipulate, exploit, and victimize others.[80] Robert Hare and his colleagues similarly discovered that recidivism rates for psychopathic offenders that had received social skills and anger management classes were higher than those without treatment.[81] Grant Harris and Marnie Rice have concluded that "there is no evidence that any treatment yet applied to psychopaths have been shown to be effective in reducing violence or crime."[82]

Despite this grim assessment, those who have the most contact with psychopathic juvenile delinquents, probation and detention officers within the juvenile justice system, believe that the most violent and antisocial youths can still be rehabilitated. Keith Cruise and his colleagues surveyed 424 juvenile detention and probation officers and reported that many have hope that the most severe juvenile offenders can be reformed. Nearly 61 percent felt that psychopathic youths are candidates for rehabilitation, and nearly 63 percent of probation officers felt that psychopathy was changeable. This suggests that even those with the most frequent contact with juvenile offenders still detect admirable traits that suggest the youths are amenable to turning their lives around.[83] Moreover, it is too expensive *not* to treat serious delinquents who present psychopathic traits. Individual criminal careers ultimately cost society more than $1 million per offender in assorted victimization and criminal justice costs.[84] Michael Caldwell and his colleagues have reported that for every dollar spent to provide intensive treatment to violent, psychopathic delinquents, seven dollars in various costs were saved or effectively prevented.[85]

The treatment of youthful psychopathic offenders must borrow heavily from the treatment of juvenile homicide offenders. Both groups represent the extremes of delinquency and point to the need for intensive, multifaceted, and sustained treatment. Kathleen Heide and Eldra Solomon present the following treatment protocol for the most violent of juvenile offenders:

- Comprehensive cognitive behavioral restructuring.
- Prosocial skills training.
- Positive peer communities.

- Anger management and appropriate emotional release.
- Empathy training.
- Clear, firm, and consistent discipline.
- Drug and alcohol counseling and education.
- Transitional treatment including family counseling when appropriate.
- Aftercare.
- Psychopharmacological management.
- Educational and vocational programs and other activities that promote prosocial opportunities for success.[86]

VIOLENCE PREVENTION

Although youth violence has declined significantly since its mid-1990s peak, it remains well above levels observed for most of the 20th century. What can be done to ensure that youth violence continues to decline? In this final section we will consider four strategies for preventing violence by juveniles, whether psychopathic or non-psychopathic. The four strategies are (1) controlling availability of guns, (2) reducing violence in families, (3) providing community-based prevention programs, and (4) promoting treatment and get-tough approaches.

Controlling Availability of Guns

A variety of innovative policing initiatives have been designed to reduce the availability of guns to juveniles. Beginning in 1994, the New York City Police Department installed its "Compstat" approach that stressed zero tolerance of nuisance types of offending, such as loitering, turnstile jumping, vandalism, and prostitution. By refusing to tolerate even the most trivial violations, the police sent a message to offenders that any type of criminal behavior would not be permitted. Not coincidentally, youth who committed serious crimes and carried firearms also committed minor forms of delinquency; thus, they were often arrested before their nuisance offending could escalate to more serious acts. This policing approach was responsible for dramatic reductions in violence, homicides, and gun crimes in New York City.[87] In fact, even harsh critics of the program acknowledge that controlling offenders who use guns and the subsequent availability of guns resulted in crime declines.[88]

Similarly, the Richmond, Virginia, Police Department developed a coordinated antigun program with the United States Attorney's Office, known as Project Exile, to aggressively prosecute all gun arrests as federal offenses. The primary advantage is that authorities are able to use existing stricter federal gun laws and the more severe penalties available in the federal courts. Although Project Exile does not directly target youth, gun violence in the Richmond area did appear to decline after its implementation. Critics of Project Exile argue that the decline in gun violence was only a continuation of the more general decline in gun violence observed in large cities around the country and not due to the new program. A recent reevaluation by Richard Rosenfeld and his colleagues found strong violence reduction effects resulting from Project Exile.[89]

think
about it

Raising the price of guns and creating a scarcity of ammunition might reduce the ability of youths to possess firearms. Should guns be priced out of the reach of youths? Would such a policy discriminate against persons from the lower class?

Franklin Zimring suggests an alternative to banning firearms. He notes that there is a distinct political economy of adolescents. Youths have less monetary capital, lower regard for property as capital assets, and shorter monetary attention spans than adults. Adolescents with many economic wants, therefore, can be more easily distracted from investing their capital in guns. Zimring believes that raising the price of guns and creating a scarcity of ammunition for those who possess guns would have a significant negative impact on juveniles', especially younger juveniles', decisions to spend money on guns.[90]

Policies aimed only at reducing the total number of firearms in circulation in communities may not be adequate. As Marc Riedel and Wayne Welsh note, it is not the total number of guns available that leads to higher levels of violence, rather it is "the carrying of guns in high-risk places at high-risk times."[91] If this is true, the creation of new laws designed to reduce gun and ammunition availability may not be as effective as stricter enforcement of existing laws prohibiting persons from carrying concealed weapons.

Law enforcement has been attempting to reduce the availability of guns through a variety of strategies, such as targeted enforcement operations (including hot spots of gun crime and the use of gun sweeps), community-supported silent witness programs that encourage residents to report the presence of illegal guns, cooperation with the Bureau of Alcohol, Tobacco, and Firearms (ATF) to trace illegal guns, safe gun storage programs, and the creation of juvenile gun courts.[92] Box 3-4 discusses some successful approaches to getting guns off the street.

Reducing Violence in Families

A growing number of criminologists believe that the structure of the modern family and the lack of meaningful relationships between parents and children today are significant causal factors in youth violence (see Chapter 10).

Whether a victim or only an observer, children learn inappropriate techniques for resolving conflicts. Should the penalties for inflicting or exposing children to violence be more severe?

box 3-4   DELINQUENCY PREVENTION

Getting Guns off the Streets

The evidence presented in this chapter so far clearly establishes the increase in firearm crime, especially among youths. If the police could get more guns off the streets, would there be fewer firearm crimes?

The **Kansas City Gun Experiment** was designed to test this idea. For 29 weeks, from July 7, 1992, to January 27, 1993, the Kansas City Police Department focused extra patrol attention on gun-crime "hot spots" in an 80- by 10-block area of the city. The extra patrol consisted of a pair of two-officer cars, with officers assigned on a rotating basis. Four officers worked six hours of overtime each night, from 7 P.M. to 1 A.M., and two other officers worked an additional 24 nights. The overtime was funded by the Bureau of Justice Assistance Weed and Seed program.

All officers focused exclusively on gun detection, primarily through traffic stops and pedestrian checks. The experiment appears to have had a number of significant effects. Among them are the following:

- Gun seizures by police in the target area increased by more than 65 percent, while gun crimes declined in the target area by 49 percent.
- Neither the number of gun crimes nor that of guns seized changed significantly in a similar beat several miles away, where the focused patrol was not used.
- The number of drive-by shootings dropped from seven to one in the target area but doubled in the comparison beat.
- Homicides were significantly reduced in the target area but not in the comparison beat.
- Traffic stops were the most productive method of finding guns, with an average of one gun found per 28 traffic stops.
- Two-thirds of the persons arrested for gun carrying in the target area resided outside the area.
- Before-and-after surveys of citizens showed that respondents in the target area became less fearful of crime and more positive about their neighborhood than did respondents in the comparison beat.

The Kansas City Gun Experiment was replicated in Indianapolis in 1997 as part of that city's *Weed and Seed program,* but with mixed success. Directed patrols that met with greater success were more selective about which vehicles to stop and issued citations rather than warnings; they also used K-9 patrols and probation sweeps for guns. In addition, directed patrol did not seem to shift crime to surrounding areas. Where a general deterrence patrol strategy was used to maximize the number of police stops and create a sense of increased police presence, there appeared to be little impact on gun-related crime.

Boston's **Operation Ceasefire** combines a direct law enforcement attack on illicit firearms found on traffickers supplying juveniles with guns and an attempt to create a strong deterrent to gang violence. The project includes:

- Expanding the focus of local, state, and federal authorities to include intrastate firearms trafficking in Massachusetts in addition to interstate trafficking.
- Focusing enforcement attention on traffickers of the makes and calibers of guns most used by gang members.
- Focusing enforcement attention on traffickers of guns that had short time-to-crime intervals and, thus, were most likely to have been trafficked.
- Focusing enforcement attention on traffickers of guns used by the city's most violent gangs.
- Attempting to restore obliterated serial numbers of confiscated guns and subsequently investigating trafficking based on those restorations.
- Targeting gangs engaged in violent behavior.

(continued)

• Delivering an explicit message that violence would not be tolerated.
• Backing up that message by "pulling every lever" legally available when violence occurred.

A recent evaluation of gun programs found that the homicide drop in Boston was more dramatic than in 95 other large American cities, suggesting that Operation Ceasefire was particularly effective in reducing gun violence. The program has also been utilized in the most crime-ravaged parts of Los Angeles and Atlanta, and was shown to produce great reductions in gun crimes. For instance, in the six years after the intervention was begun in Atlanta, the number of homicides fell nearly 30 percent with total homicide levels at their lowest rate in 30 years.

Sources: Lawrence Sherman, James Shaw, and Dennis Rogan, *The Kansas City Gun Experiment* (Washington, DC: U.S. Department of Justice, 1995); Shay Bilchik, *Promising Strategies to Reduce Gun Violence* (Washington, DC: Office of Juvenile Justice and Delinquency Prevention, 1999); David Kennedy, Anthony Braga, Anne Piehl, and Elin Waring, *Reducing Gun Violence: The Boston Gun Project's Operation Ceasefire* (Washington, DC: U.S. Department of Justice, 2001); Edmund McGarrell, Steven Chermak, and Alexander Weiss, *Reducing Gun Violence: Evaluation of the Indianapolis Police Department's Directed Patrol Project* (Washington, DC: National Institute of Justice, 2002); Richard Rosenfeld, Robert Fornango, and Eric Baumer, "Did *Ceasefire, Compstat,* and *Exile* Reduce Homicide?" *Criminology and Public Policy* 4:419–450 (2005); George Tita, Jack Riley, Greg Ridgeway, and Peter Greenwood, *Reducing Gun Violence: Operation Ceasefire in Los Angeles* (Washington, DC: National Institute of Justice, 2005); Arthur Kellerman, Dawna Fuqua-Whitley, and Constance Parramore, *Reducing Gun Violence: Community Problem Solving in Atlanta* (Washington, DC: National Institute of Justice, 2006); Edmund McGarrell, Steven Chermak, Jeremy Wilson, and Nicholas Corsaro, "Reducing Homicide through a 'Lever-Pulling' Strategy," *Justice Quarterly* 23:214–231 (2006).

Consider this horrifying case. Laree Slack, a 12-year-old girl was being raised in a church-going, intact, two-parent family, but her parents were anything but loving. Laree's parents, Larry and Constance, became angry at Laree because she had failed to appropriately wash and put away the family's clothes one day. As punishment, Laree was ordered to "assume the position" and stand ready to be whipped. She was whipped with the same 5-foot stretch of electrical cord Larry had used earlier on Laree's 8-year-old brother. When Laree attempted to squirm away, her father ordered Laree's two older brothers to tie her face down on a metal bed frame. Larry and Constance took turns lashing Laree. When her back began to bleed, Larry untied her and turned her over and she was whipped again on her chest and stomach. Laree suffered more than 160 lashes and was pronounced dead at the hospital a few hours later.[93]

Violence within the family has far-reaching effects on children, regardless of whether they are the direct object of the violence or not. Children who observe their parents fighting or physically punishing siblings begin to internalize these acts as "normal" techniques for resolving conflicts. Exposure to violence or abuse in the home and exposure to hostile and punitive parenting are among the most important risk factors for a child's subsequent involvement in violent behavior.[94] Stephen Baron and Timothy Hartnagel's study of the violent behavior of street youth also notes that domestic violence is a significant factor in decisions to engage in violence. According to Baron and Hartnagel, "these youths also learn from their abusive home experiences that using force is a practical and effective method of gaining compliance, increasing the odds that they will use coercion to gain financial or material rewards."[95]

A variety of family factors place children at risk of violent behavior, including harsh or ineffective parenting, poor parental monitoring, poor attachment, and lack of warmth and nurturing (see Chapter 10). Parents of children with behavioral problems are more likely to engage in inconsistent and punitive discipline, and the children tend to develop aversive behaviors to affect and manipulate their family environments. The *Blueprints for Violence Prevention Initiative* has identified a number of successful strategies aimed at reducing juvenile violence by changing the individual behavior of the child by altering the social environment of the family, including home visiting, parent training, and family therapy programs.[96] Two important prevention programs in the country are explored next.

Multisystemic Therapy Multisystemic Therapy (MST) is a family and community-based treatment program that seeks to address the multiple problems of seriously antisocial and aggressive youth ages 12 to 17. The multisystemic approach is that individuals are nested within a complex network of interconnected systems that encompass family, peer, school, and neighborhood domains. The principal objective of MST is to empower parents and youth with the skills and resources needed to surmount risk factors and capitalize on protective opportunities. These empowerments include strategic family therapy, structural family therapy, behavioral parent training, and cognitive behavior therapies over a 4-month period. Despite the difficulties inherent in treating seriously antisocial people, preliminary evaluations of MST have shown 25 to 70 percent reductions in rearrest and 47 to 64 percent reductions in out-of-home placements. At a cost of a mere $4,500 per youth, MST has been ranked as the most cost-effective program in the country that targets serious and violent juvenile offenders.[97]

The Incredible Years Series One of the best programs to accomplish reduction in aggressive behavior is the Incredible Years Parent, Teacher, and Child Training Series. The Incredible Years is a comprehensive social competence program that treats conduct problems in children between the ages of 2 to 8. In six randomized trials, aggression and conduct problems have been reduced by 60 percent among the participating children and families. Other promising outcomes were increased academic competence and achievement, increased sociability and friendship-making skills, anger management and problem solving, and increased empathy among previously problem youth.[98] The Incredible Years program is one of the model prevention programs in the United States.[99]

Providing Community-Based Prevention Programs

Early American criminologists believed that the local neighborhood and community largely determined the nature and extent of various social problems, including delinquency (see Chapter 5). This theoretical perspective led to a wide variety of community-based programs, such as the Chicago Area Project, aimed at eradicating or reducing such social ills as poverty, alcohol and drug abuse, the breakdown of the traditional family, and crime and delinquency. Today, community-based programs are still operating and are targeting youth violence.

box 3-5   FROM THE BENCH

United States v. Lopez

On March 10, 1992, a 12th grade student arrived at Edison High School in San Antonio, Texas, carrying a concealed .38 caliber handgun and five bullets. Acting on a tip, school authorities confronted the student, who admitted to carrying the weapon. The student was arrested and charged by federal agents with violating the *Gun Free School Zones Act of 1990*. The student's attorney moved to dismiss the federal indictment on the ground that it was unconstitutional for Congress to legislate control over the public schools. However, the district court concluded that Congress was indeed free to regulate activities of public schools that affect interstate commerce. The student was tried and found guilty and sentenced to six months imprisonment.

On appeal to the U.S. Supreme Court, the government argued that possessing a firearm in a local school zone affects interstate commerce because the costs of violent crime are substantial and insurance costs are spread throughout the population and that violent crime reduces the willingness of people to travel to areas within the country that are perceived to be unsafe. However, the Court disagreed, holding that "the possession of a gun in a local school zone is in no sense an economic activity that might, through repetition elsewhere, substantially affect any sort of interstate commerce."

In 1996 Congress reenacted the Act [18 U.S.C. § 921(a) (25)] to include an explicit interstate commerce element. It states that: "It shall be unlawful for any individual knowingly to possess a firearm that has moved in or that otherwise affects interstate or foreign commerce at a place that the individual knows, or has reasonable cause to believe, is a school zone."

Source: *United States v. Lopez*, 514 U.S. 549 (1995).

Children rarely choose where they live. Rather, they are dependent upon their parents, or their parents' fate, with regard to the particular neighborhood in which they reside. The neighborhood may be more or less safe, inhabited by the homeless, littered with graffiti, preferred by drug dealers and users, occupied by juvenile gangs, and lacking in supportive and nurturing social institutions such as a school and church. In other words, many children, through no choice of their own, face daily lives in communities and schools that are threatening and dangerous. Increasing levels of school violence even led Congress to pass the *Gun Free School Zones Act of 1990*. However, in 1995 the U.S. Supreme Court declared the Act unconstitutional in **United States v. Lopez,** only to have Congress reenact the provisions the following year (see Box 3-5).[100]

A number of programs are emerging in a variety of communities to counter the problems of juvenile violence. Individuals as well as diverse community groups are sponsoring neighborhood and community programs to reduce violence.[101] Three of the best community-based prevention programs are reviewed next.

Promoting Alternative Thinking Strategies   The Promoting Alternative Thinking Strategies (PATHS) curriculum is a comprehensive program for promoting emotional and social competencies and reducing aggression and behavior problems in elementary school children (kindergarten through grade 5) while enhancing the educational process in the classroom. It is taught three times per week for 20–30 minutes per day and seeks to improve students' emotional literacy, self-control, social competence, positive peer instructions, and interpersonal problem-solving skills. The PATHS curriculum also focuses on the ability of the students to label, understand, and manage their feelings, impulses, and stress. In program evaluations, PATHS has been shown to improve protective factors (that insulate children from delinquency) and reduce risk factors (that propel youths toward delinquency). Other positive outcomes include increased self-control, improved understanding and recognition of emotions, more effective conflict-resolution strategies, improved thinking and planning skills, reduced depression, and fewer conduct problems. The PATHS program costs a meager $45 per student per year.[102]

Big Brothers/Big Sisters of America

For nearly 100 years, the Big Brothers/Big Sisters of America has provided mentoring, one-on-one relationships for youths between the ages of 6 and 18 from single-parent homes (which is the typical family background of violent juvenile offenders). The service is provided by volunteers who complete rigorous training and follow published, required procedures for youth mentoring. In a recent 18-month follow-up evaluation, children who participated in Big Brothers/Big Sisters of America were 46 percent less likely than control youth to begin using drugs, 27 percent less likely to being using alcohol, 30 percent less likely to hit someone, and had better academic behavior, attitudes, school performance, and relationships with parents and peers.[103] Motivated by the successes of mentoring programs like Big Brothers/Big Sisters of America, the National Faith-Based Initiative for High-Risk Youth, a Public/Private Venture of the Office of Juvenile Justice and Delinquency Prevention, uses one-on-one and group mentoring approaches to address the delinquency and mental health problems, especially depression, of high-risk juvenile offenders. Although the program has not been formally evaluated, preliminary outcomes from programs in Baton Rouge, Brooklyn, Denver, Philadelphia, and Seattle have been promising.[104]

Olweus Bullying Prevention Program

The Olweus Bullying Prevention Program is a universal intervention for the reduction and prevention of bully and victim problems. The program targets are students in elementary, middle, and junior high schools with additional interventions for students who have prior history of bullying and/or bullying victimization. Core components of the program are implemented at the school level, class level, and individual level and contain assistance from counselors, teachers, and mental health professionals. The Olweus Bullying Prevention Program has been shown to result in significant reductions in bullying and victimization among boys and girls, reductions in related delinquency problems, such as vandalism, fighting, theft, and truancy, and improvements in the school social climate. The program costs $200 per school and approximately $65 per teacher.[105] Although bullying is a historical part of the school experience, it is also a serious risk factor for serious, violent, and chronic delinquent behavior (Chapter 11).

In spite of the efforts being made to reduce the availability of guns, to reduce violence in the media, to intervene in families, and to create safer and more nurturing communities, many experts believe that the only way to reduce youth

think **about it**

Weed and Seed programs reduce youth violence. They require brief but intense law enforcement. Why are the policies not more widely used given their effectiveness? Is the American public reluctant to empower the police?

violence is by arresting violent youths and dealing with them formally within either the juvenile or adult justice system.

Promoting Blended Treatment and "Get-Tough" Approaches

There is a serious dilemma facing both criminologists and policy makers when attempting to determine the "best" treatment approach or the "most effective" punishment approach for dealing with serious, violent juveniles. Unfortunately, it is difficult to distinguish the causes of the behaviors of violent youths from those of nonviolent delinquent youths. To select primarily violent youths for participation in a particular treatment program or for transfer to criminal court for prosecution based upon assumptions about the ability to bring about rehabilitation or deterrence might be flawed. Dewey Cornell points out that, even very violent juveniles can be subdivided into smaller subgroups based upon the youths' prior adjustment problems. Cornell states, "Among violent offenders, youth convicted of the most serious violent crime, homicide, actually have less history of prior violence than do offenders convicted of less serious assaults."[106]

Regrettably, it is often the case that serious, violent, and chronic delinquents were themselves exposed to severe abuses and deprivation from very early in life. Indeed, there is some public sentiment characterized by a "what did we expect" belief about the effects of early life abuses on subsequent violence and criminal behavior. This leads many observers to wring their hands in resignation convinced that nothing can be done to stem the actions of the serious delinquents.[107] Fortunately, this is not the case. Mark Lipsey recently reviewed the literature on programs that target serious delinquents and concluded:

> the average effect on the recidivism of serious juvenile offender of those interventions that I studied are positive, statistically significant, and, though modest, not trivial . . . this evidence shows that optimal combinations of program elements have the capability to reduce recidivism by 40 to 50 percent, that is, to cut recidivism rates to nearly half of what they would be without such programming.[108]

Most treatment programs for violent youths occur within locked, secure correctional facilities, although they continue to emphasize rehabilitation and early reintegration into the community. One such treatment program is the Violent Juvenile Offender (VJO) program, designed to target chronic violent male juvenile offenders in four urban areas, Boston, Detroit, Memphis, and Newark. Youths selected for the VJO program must have been adjudicated for a Part I Index felony and must have at least one prior felony adjudication. The program involves efforts aimed at "strengthening youths' bonds to prosocial people and institutions, providing realistic opportunities for achievement, employing a system of rewards for appropriate behavior and sanctions for inappropriate behavior, and individualized treatment." To accomplish these goals, VJO youths are initially placed in small, secure treatment facilities and then gradually reintegrated into the community in phases. The second phase involves treatment in a community-based residential program, after which youths progress to the third phase, involving intensive supervision in the neighborhood.

Another treatment program for violent juvenile offenders is the Capital Offender Program (COP) in Texas. For a youth to be eligible for placement in COP, he or she must have committed a homicide and must not have been diagnosed as having a severe psychological disorder. COP is designed to promote verbal expression of feelings, to foster empathy for victims, to create a sense of personal responsibility, and to decrease feelings of hostility and aggression. Treatment includes group psychotherapy emphasizing role playing in which youths act out their life stories and reenact their crimes from their own perspectives and those of their victims.[109]

Many states have lowered the age for waiver of violent youths to criminal court or are making it less difficult to transfer such youths (see Chapter 14); have established determinate sentences for serious, violent youths adjudicated in the juvenile courts; and have permitted a juvenile's arrest and court record to be made available to schools and to adult criminal courts once a youth is prosecuted as an adult. In addition, some states have passed parental-liability laws whereby juveniles' parents are held in contempt of court for missing their children's court hearings.

Law enforcement, prosecutors, and the courts are coordinating efforts in a number of jurisdictions to develop new strategies for targeting violent juveniles. The Salinas Police Department in California created a Violence Suppression Unit consisting of 15 officers involved in aggressive patrol focusing on violent and gun-related crimes. The Seattle Police Department has established a system for tracking violent offenders and disseminating information through the department and other social service agencies to reduce the anonymity of the juveniles and refer the offenders to intervention services. A list of the 50 most violent juveniles was developed, with increased communication between police and probation, to increase surveillance of these youths and to provide for greater enforcement of their conditions of probation. In addition, enhanced prosecution for serious, violent juvenile offenders was instituted with the addition of a new full-time position in the prosecutor's office. At the same time, Seattle's Juvenile Firearms Prosecution Project provided for vertical prosecution of all juvenile firearms offenses with a Deputy Prosecutor specializing in firearm prosecutions assigned to handle all juvenile firearms offenses from initial filing of the case through juvenile sentencing. In Baltimore, the City Police Department's Youth Violence Task Force, working closely with the U.S. Attorney, ATF, FBI, and school police, identifies and targets gang members and violent offenders, and aggressively seeks their apprehension and incarceration.[110]

conclusions

Youth violence had been declining dramatically for over a decade before it began to increase again in 2004. Even though it continues to be a serious threat, it is not yet the problem it was in the 1980s and early 1990s. For some criminologists, the lower level of youth violence is primarily due to the decline in the crack market and associated lethal violence with firearms. Other criminologists, however, believe that the decrease in violence stems from more police officers on the street and a get-tough attitude by the courts, resulting in more youths being incarcerated.

The vast majority of violent youth are males, disproportionately minorities, from urban, lower-income neighborhoods where a variety of stressors and strains predominate. Juvenile victims of violence reflect similar characteristics: They are older, male, and minority youth; younger, female and white youth are significantly less likely to be victimized. Guns, especially handguns, are used in most violent incidents involving juveniles.

Is it possible to prevent youth violence? Criminologists, legislators, and policy makers differ in their opinions of the root causes of youth violence and how to respond to violence. Proposals include getting guns out of the hands of juveniles, reducing violence in the media, strengthening families, assisting schools to teach alternatives to violence, providing treatment for offenders, and getting tough on violent offenders. None of these approaches appears terribly promising on its own, but possibly a comprehensive strategy that combines the best features of each may more effectively control youth violence.

The next chapter will explore illegal drug use by adolescents, which is another area of juvenile delinquency. While both youth violence and delinquency in general have declined during the past decade, juvenile drug use has increased.

key terms

Brady Bill   Federal legislation that mandated a five-day waiting period for the purchase of handguns.

Etiology   The scientific name for the cause of antisocial behavior, such as delinquency.

Infanticide   Homicide in which recently born children are killed by relatives who do not want the children or who are suffering from childbirth-related psychiatric disturbances.

Kansas City Gun Experiment   An experiment in which the use of additional police to patrol in target areas for the exclusive purpose of gun detection significantly increased gun seizures and decreased gun crimes.

Operation Ceasefire   A gun prevention program in Boston involving direct law enforcement attack on illicit firearms traffickers supplying juveniles with guns.

Psychopathy   A personality disorder that impairs interpersonal, affective, and behavioral functions and is closely linked to serious antisocial behavior.

Sociopathy   A form of psychopathy, sometimes referred to as secondary psychopathy, which is produced from early life environmental factors such as parental abuse and neglect.

United States v. Lopez   A U.S. Supreme Court case that held that the *Gun Free School Zones Act of 1990* was unconstitutional.

4

Illegal Drug Use and Delinquency

I n terms of adolescent substance use and delinquency, the headlines are impossible to avoid. "Movies inspire children to smoke,"[1] "Survey: Parents clueless on booze, drugs at teen parties,"[2] "Meth's impact on children probed,"[3] "Many more treated for meth, pot,"[4] "Prescription drugs find place in teen culture,"[5] "More kids get multiple psychiatric drugs,"[6] and "Anti-drug advertising campaign a failure, GAO report says"[7] are just some of the thousands of news items on adolescent drug use that permeate American culture. These headlines present complex and, at times, conflicting information about the current status of substance use among children and adolescents, the effectiveness in treating substance use, and the most appropriate ways for the juvenile and criminal justice systems to respond to drugs and delinquency.

Often, children and adolescents bear the brunt of the drug problem. To illustrate, in January 2004, an 11-year-old girl was arrested for selling heroin on the streets in Miami, Florida. The police had been observing the girl for a number of weeks after being tipped off by the girl's neighbors. Over time, the girl was seen selling $10 and $20 doses of heroin from the sidewalk in front of her house, sometimes dressed in her school uniform and sometimes in her pajamas. Undercover officers finally made purchases from the girl. During one transaction, the officers indicated they wanted to purchase three bags, but the girl had only two. "The girl said she needed to check with her mom," according to Sgt. Ruben Rodriguez, a South Miami drug officer. Police believe the girl was working for her mother and a man who may be her stepfather.[8]

A recent Mayo Clinic study found that there are may be about 5 million children with ADHD and possibly a million or more with bipolar disorder, depression, obsessive-compulsive disorder, social-anxiety disorder, sleeplessness, or other phobias (see Chapter 5). Many of these children will be prescribed a drug. The American Academy of Child and Adolescent Psychiatry lists dozens of drugs that can now be used for children with emotional, physiological, or psychological problems. Specialized drugs have been developed for depression, such as Celexa, Prozac, and Zoloft; for bipolar disorder, such as Depakote and Tegretol; for ADHD, such as Adderall, Concerta, and Ritalin; and for regulating moods, such as Effexor, Lithium, and Zyprexa. Although most of these drugs were neither designed nor tested on children, an increasing number of doctors are using them to treat childhood disorders. While Adderall, a once-a-day amphetamine, has been approved to treat children as young as age 3 for ADHD, Prozac, another drug "certified" as safe for children, has been found to produce a 50 percent higher risk of suicide for children compared to children taking placebos.[9]

The United States is a drug-consuming society. From conception until death, drugs have played a varied and important role in most people's lives. Today drugs are used to block the physical pain of childbirth; to keep premature babies alive; to help gain or lose weight; to help people wake in the morning and sleep at night; to reduce anxiety, stress, and depression; and to clear up faces marked by acne. In addition, drugs prevent illnesses and overcome diseases, help to keep cancers from spreading, and reduce the pain when people are dying. Air Force fighter pilots used amphetamines in the war against terrorists in Afghanistan to stay alert during long combat missions. Drugs are used to control the hyperactive behavior of students, primarily boys, in school, and drugs are the preferred method of execution in states that use the death penalty.

Most Americans use some sort of drug on a daily basis—alcohol, aspirin, caffeine, and nicotine are but a few examples. Most drugs are used legally. As

think
about it

American culture is pro-drug. Indeed, the large baby boom cohort is notorious for its liberal attitudes toward drug use, and large percentages of Americans have experimented with a variety of illicit drugs. Because of these attitudes and behaviors, is America reaping what it has sown regarding drugs?

an adult, you can legally consume alcohol and smoke tobacco, although where you may smoke is increasingly being restricted. Even children can legally drink liquid refreshments, such as *Red Bull*, that is loaded with caffeine and buy aspirin over-the-counter. But these are not the major focus of concern when talking about the drug problem in America. The drug problem, especially for young people, involves cocaine, crack, ecstasy, heroin, LSD, and marijuana.

Each fall, over 14 million high school students return to school.[10] Many of them will enter buildings where licit and illicit drugs are stashed, sold, and used. According to the National Center on Addiction and Substance Abuse, "By the time students reach twelfth grade, 70 percent have smoked cigarettes, 81 percent have drunk alcohol and 47 percent have used marijuana. Each year, 13.2 million students (ages 12 to 17) become new users of tobacco, alcohol and drugs."[11]

The problem of adolescent drug use is complex and cannot be understood apart from the broader nature of drug use in the larger society. In this chapter, we will examine the nature and extent of the drug problem facing youth, explanations of why juveniles use drugs, the relationship between drug use and delinquency, and different ways of responding to adolescent drug use.

PATTERNS OF ADOLESCENT DRUG USE

Prior to the 1960s, adolescent drug use was relatively rare. That changed as the "drug culture" burst upon the scene in the early sixties. LSD, marijuana, "uppers," and "downers," initially used by college students and those in the hippie counterculture, eventually spread to the high school and middle school level. Whether it was an attraction to the lifestyle of the hippies, a simple interest in "getting high," or a growing alienation from the norms and values of conventional society, more youths began to turn on with an ever-increasing variety of drugs. The drugs of choice among youths vary over time, and there is a continuous flow of new drugs and rediscovery of older drugs by each generation.

Measuring Adolescent Drug Use

It is difficult to obtain an accurate estimate of the incidence and prevalence of delinquency. Consequently, a variety of different measures (arrest data, self-report surveys, and victim surveys) are used to produce the best estimates possible. Drug use is equally difficult to measure. Because illicit drug use is considered to be a "victimless crime," the *National Crime Victimization Survey* does not inquire into drug violations. One estimate of adolescent drug use comes from *Uniform Crime Reports* (*UCR*) data on people arrested for drug violations. Three additional estimates are produced from self-report surveys on drug use, such as the University of Michigan's *Monitoring the Future* survey of high school students,[12] the U.S. Department of Health and Human Service's *National Survey on Drug Use and Health*,[13] and the *National Youth Risk Behavior Survey* conducted by the Centers for Disease Control and Prevention.[14]

The past four decades have witnessed major shifts in juvenile drug use. Among both boys and girls, illicit drug use increased at an alarming rate between 1965 and 1974, with drug use by girls converging toward levels similar to that of boys. However, from the mid-1970s to the mid-1980s, arrests of juveniles for drug violations declined. Then, as crack cocaine use increased during the late 1980s, so did arrests of juveniles for drug offenses. Between 1990 and 1997, the juvenile arrest rate for drug abuse violations increased 145 percent. The arrest rate declined 22 percent between 1997 and 2003; however, the 2003 rate was still almost double the 1990 rate. The changes in adolescent drug use between 1990 and 2003 were different for males and females. For boys, arrests for drug violations increased 81 percent; for girls the increase was 184 percent.[15] Overall arrests of juveniles for drug violations have continued to drop nearly 30 percent since 2003. Today, approximately 141,000 juveniles are arrested annually for drug violations.[16]

UCR data are far from perfect. First, with respect to drug arrests, they do not distinguish between arrests for specific kinds of drugs—for example, marijuana versus crack. Second, *UCR* data reflect only those juveniles arrested for drug violations, and, as with most other victimless crimes, most people who use drugs do so out of sight of police and with others who are not likely to report their drug use to authorities. These data, in other words, do not reflect *hidden* or secret drug use; arrest data grossly underestimate the amount of drug use by adolescents today.

Each year, the Institute for Social Research at the University of Michigan examines patterns of drug use and attitudes about illicit drugs in its survey of 8th-, 10th-, and 12th-grade students and includes nearly 50,000 students in over 400 secondary schools. The annual survey conducted by the U.S. Department of Health and Human Services and funded by the National Institute on Drug Abuse measures the prevalence of illicit drug use throughout the U.S. civilian, noninstitutionalized population age 12 and older. Both of these national self-report surveys provide three different measures of drug use—**lifetime prevalence** (use of a drug at least once during the respondent's lifetime), **annual prevalence** (use of a drug at least once during the prior year), and **30-day prevalence** (use of a drug at least once during the previous month)—as well as a measure of frequency of use. The self-report survey conducted by the Centers for Disease Control and Prevention monitors six categories of health-risk behaviors, including alcohol and other drug use. Each year they survey students in grades 8 through 12 throughout the nation, combining the data with an additional 32 state surveys and 18 local surveys. All of these self-report surveys, unlike the *UCR*, provide information on the use of specific drugs.

Current Adolescent Drug Use

Based on the most recent data available, 141,035 juveniles were arrested for drug abuse violations, accounting for about 10 percent of all drug arrests. Of all juveniles arrested for drug violations, 16 percent were under age 15. Juveniles were arrested for liquor law violations (92,556 arrests) and public drunkenness (11,816 arrests) in 2005.[17] About 2 percent of 12- and 13-year-olds reported current illicit drug use with inhalants and prescription-type drugs being used without medical reason being the clear drug of choice. Slightly over 8 percent of 14- and 15-year-olds reported they currently used illicit drugs with marijuana their drug of choice. About 17 percent of youths ages 16 and 17 reported current use and, like 14- and 15-year-olds, their drug of choice was marijuana. During the month prior to the survey, about 16 percent of adolescents in grades 8, 10, or 12 reported using some illicit drug.[18]

Substantial numbers of juveniles are initiated into drug use each year. In 2006, for instance, about two million juveniles initiated marijuana use, nearly 500,000 juveniles used cocaine for the first time, and over four million youths were initiated into drinking alcohol. Interestingly, new initiates into drug use are most likely to have first tried marijuana, alcohol, or cigarettes during the summer months, as opposed to other times of the year. In the summer, teens appear to be less supervised and have more difficulty finding jobs to keep them busy.[19] Whether these youths become regular users, use only occasionally, or quit after initial use is not yet known. More than 6 percent of adolescents are diagnosed with treatment needs for alcoholism and more than 5 percent need treatment for other substance abuse.[20]

Adolescent males are significantly more likely than females to be arrested for drug offenses, with males comprising 83 percent of all juvenile drug arrests. Although boys are arrested for drug offenses more than four times as often as girls, the difference, according to Joan McCord and her colleagues, may be that boys use drugs more frequently than girls in public places, thereby increasing their likelihood of being arrested.[21] White youths comprised 73 percent of all juvenile drug offense arrests, while African American youths accounted for 26 percent of drug arrests.[22] Referrals of juvenile drug offenders to the juvenile court reflect similar racial patterns: White youths accounted for 71 percent of drug cases; African American juveniles, 27 percent; and other adolescents, 2 percent.[23] Although white youths comprise the vast majority of drug arrests and court referrals at the national level, official processing of juvenile drug offenders in many large cities suggests disparities in the opposite direction. For example, in Illinois, African Americans are 59 percent of youths arrested for drug crimes. In Cook County (Chicago), African Americans comprise 95 percent of juvenile drug offenders transferred to criminal court to be tried as adults. Furthermore, 91 percent of youths admitted to Illinois State Prisons from Cook County for drug offenses were African American. It should be noted that almost 70 percent of all juvenile drug arrests in Illinois occurred in Cook County. [24]

Alcohol-related arrests reflect a significantly different pattern and one not consistent with self-report surveys or other studies of adolescent drinking patterns. Whites accounted for more than 90 percent of all juvenile arrests for liquor law violations and public drunkenness. These arrest figures are interesting in that white and African American high school seniors report much more similar frequencies of alcohol use. Six percent of white seniors reported heavy monthly alcohol consumption, compared to five percent of African American seniors. White seniors are more likely, however, to be "binge" drinkers. About 36 percent of white seniors reported consuming five or more drinks in a row on one or more occasions during the two-week period prior to the survey, compared to only 12 percent of African American seniors.[25]

Trends in Drug Use

During the last third of the 20th century, adolescents were using illicit drugs at rates never before seen in this country. By 1975 the majority of youths (55 percent) had used an illicit drug by the time they left high school. By 1981 this figure had increased to 66 percent, but then gradually declined to 41 percent in 1992. In 2003 it had again risen to 51 percent. However, the patterns do vary somewhat depending upon the specific illicit drug (see Table 4-1). In 2006

table 4-1	Percentage of High School Seniors Reporting Ever Having Used Specific Drugs, 1975–2006						
DRUG	1975	1980	1985	1990	1995	2000	2006
Alcohol	90.4	93.2	92.2	89.5	80.7	80.3	72.7
Cigarettes	73.6	71.0	68.8	64.4	64.2	62.5	47.1
Marijuana	47.3	60.3	54.2	40.7	41.7	48.8	42.3
Tranquilizers*	17.0	15.2	11.9	7.2	7.1	8.9	10.3
Cocaine	9.0	15.7	17.3	9.4	6.0	8.6	8.5
Hallucinogens	16.3	13.3	10.3	9.4	12.7	6.9	8.3
Heroin	2.2	1.1	1.2	1.3	1.6	2.4	1.4

*Reflects only drugs used without a doctor's prescription.

Source: Lloyd Johnston, Patrick O'Malley, Jerald Bachman, and John Schulenberg, *Monitoring the Future, National Survey Results on Drug Use, 1975–2006* (Bethesda, MD: National Institute on Drug Abuse, 2007).

the proportion of adolescents ever having tried any illicit drug in their lifetime was 21 percent, 36 percent, and 48 percent for youths in grades 8, 10, and 12, respectively. In other words, half of the students today have tried an illicit drug, which during adolescence includes cigarettes and alcohol, by the time they finish high school. According to the *Monitoring the Future* survey, estimates in 2006 represented the fifth consecutive decline in teen drug use.[26]

Marijuana Use   The percentage of high school seniors reporting that they had ever tried marijuana rose during the last half of the 1970s and reached a peak in 1980, with 60 percent admitting having tried the drug at least once in their lifetime. Since 1980, marijuana use by seniors steadily and significantly declined, dropping to slightly over 40 percent in 1990. Unfortunately, as with adolescent drug use generally, marijuana use rose during the 1990s. By 2006, 42 percent of the seniors reported having used marijuana at some point in their lifetimes, and 32 percent reported marijuana use annually.

Cocaine Use   The percentage of high school seniors reporting having ever tried cocaine nearly doubled between 1975 and 1985 when 17 percent of seniors reported having tried cocaine. Cocaine use declined over the next two decades, reaching a low of only 8 percent in 2003. Today, only about 9 percent of high school seniors reported ever using cocaine. Perhaps more important, the percentage of seniors reporting use of cocaine during the prior 12-month period dropped noticeably from 13 percent in 1985 to only 3 percent in 1992, but then rose again to 5 percent in 2006. The use of crack cocaine by seniors during the prior year, a figure never very high, dropped from nearly 4 percent in 1987 to 2 percent in 2006.

Other Drug Use   The use of other drugs by high school seniors followed the broad trends in adolescent drug use, generally declining between the mid-1970s and the late 1980s. The use of drugs, such as amphetamines and LSD, both popular in the late 1960s and early 1970s, fluctuated during the period between 1980 and 1995 and then fell noticeably in recent years. Ecstasy (MDMA) use was first measured among high school students in 1996 with fewer than 5 percent reporting having used the drug during the past year. After increasing to 9 percent in 2000, ecstasy use among seniors declined to only 4 percent in 2003 (see Box 4-1). Heroin use by seniors has never been widely accepted. However, the decade of the 1990s showed a very steady increase in its use, rising from less than 1 percent in 1991 to nearly 3 percent in 2000 and declining again to 1 percent in 2006. Overall drug use trends have varied by grade level. The youngest respondents, 8th graders, have shown the largest proportional drop in their use of nearly all of the illicit drugs since the recent peak rates of the 1990s. In 2006 the declines in drug use among 8th graders have stabilized. On the other hand, the older teens in 10th and 12th grades are today showing the greatest declines in drug use.[27]

Sometimes adolescents discover that over-the-counter, nonprescription medicines can produce a desired "high." One of the latest drug fads involves cough and cold medicines containing dextromethorphan, or DXM. More than 120 such medicines, including Robitussin can be purchased at grocery, drug, and discount stores throughout the nation. When taken in heavy doses, they can produce a loss of motor control and hallucinations similar to the effects of phencyclidine (PCP). Adolescents do not have to drink entire bottles of syrup to go "Robotripping." They can simply pop a number of pills, such as Coricidin HBP Cough and Cold tablets, which contain a more potent dose of DXM.[28]

Alcohol and Cigarette Use   While use of illicit drugs has broadly declined, alcohol use by high school seniors remained fairly steady between 1975 and 1990, but then declined over the next 15 years. Cigarette smoking by seniors also has declined, with reported lifetime prevalence dropping from about 74 percent in 1975 to 47 percent in 2006. Overall monthly smoking rates fell by between 30 and 50 percent among students in grades 8, 10, and 12 as smoking was increasingly viewed as more dangerous and socially unacceptable. Like drug use among seniors, eighth-grader drug use fluctuated during the period between

None of the eventual outcomes of hard-core drug use are positive. Given this, why are drugs so prevalent in the United States? Why do many Americans express tolerance toward illegal drugs?

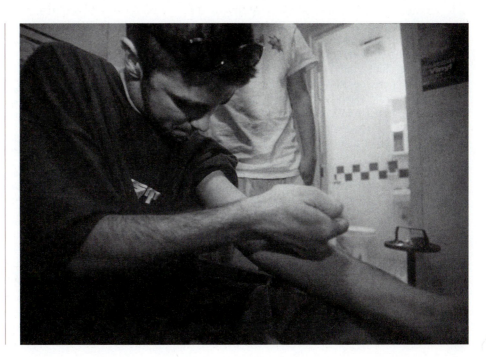

box 4-1   **A WINDOW ON DELINQUENCY**

The Science of Ecstasy/MDMA

The use of ecstasy or MDMA among young people has been a major concern in recent years. Part of the problem with ecstasy is the inaccurate belief that it is a relatively harmless drug, an innocent high that can be purchased for about $25 per dose. Ecstasy use can result in severe and irreparable damage to the human body. MDMA (3,4 methylenedioxy-methamphetamine) belongs to the amphetamine family of compounds and has properties of both stimulants and hallucinogens. Even though MDMA does not produce true hallucinations, as a result of being under the influence of the drug, users often report feelings of distorted time and perception, which lasts four to six hours.

Ecstasy works in the brain by increasing the activity levels of the three major neurotransmitters: dopamine, norepinepherine, and serotonin. It especially increases serotonin, which is involved in mood regulation, sleep, pain, emotion, appetite, and other behaviors. By increasing the production of these neurotransmitters, MDMA also depletes them. In addition, MDMA affects the cardiovascular system, such as the pumping ability of the heart, and the ability of the body to regulate its internal temperature. Since MDMA users often engage in strenuous activity (e.g., dancing at clubs), MDMA's effects on the heart could increase the risk of heart damage or other cardiovascular complications.

Exposure to MDMA rapidly and persistently destroys a key marker of serotonergic function in regions known to have a high density of serotonin neurons, including the striatum and cortex. More detailed examination of this structural damage shows that MDMA appears to prune, or reduce in number, serotonin axons and axon terminals. Eighteen months after a short course of MDMA, investigators found that some brain regions had substantial loss of serotonin axon terminals, while a few others had more serotonin axon terminals. This pattern is a hallmark of axon pruning, since nerve cells will often grow replacement terminals upstream of the damaged terminals. These results, then, are evidence not only of MDMA's neurotoxicity, but of the brain attempting to rewire the serotonin system after damage. This effect is particularly damaging for developing brains and thus can result in birth defects. If female users erroneously believe that ecstasy is a harmless drug, the long-term effects of MDMA use during pregnancy are potentially severe.

Finally, MDMA present users with an array of psychiatric changes as the result of ecstasy abuse, including increased obsessive traits, anxiety, paranoia, disturbed sleep, and substance abuse disorders. Indeed, the use of MDMA along with other drugs, such as cocaine, is troubling. Acute drug intoxication is the leading cause of death among MDMA mortalities, the second leading cause of death is homicide. Overall, the science behind MDMA illustrates emphatically that ecstasy is a very dangerous substance.

Sources: National Institute on Drug Abuse, *Ecstasy: What We Know and Don't Know about MDMA A Scientific Review,* online at http://www.drugabuse.gov/PDF/MDMAConf.pdf, accessed April 21, 2007; Tom Ter Bogt and Rutger Engels, "Partying Hard: Party Style, Motives for and Effects of MDMA Use at Rave Parties," *Substance Use and Misuse* 40:1479–1502 (2005); Joachim Uys and Raymond Niesink, "Pharmacological Aspects of the Combined Use of 3,4-methylenedioxy-methamphetamine (MDMA, Ecstasy) and Gamma-Hydroxbutyric Acid (GHB): A Review of the Literature," *Drug and Alcohol Review* 24:359–368 (2005); James Gill, Jonathan Hayes, Ian deSouza, Elizabeth Marker, and Marina Stajic, "Ecstasy (MDMA) Deaths in New York City: A Case Series and Review of the Literature," *Journal of Forensic Sciences* 47:121–126 (2002); Kenneth Tardiff, Peter Marzuk, Kira Lowell, Laura Portera, and Andrew Leon, "A Study of Drug Abuse and Other Causes of Homicide in New York," *Journal of Criminal Justice* 30:317–325 (2002).

table 4-2 Percentage of Eighth-Graders Reporting Ever Having Used Specific Drugs, 1991–2006

DRUG	1991	1993	1995	1997	2000	2003	2006
Any illicit drug	18.7	22.5	28.5	29.4	26.8	22.8	20.9
Marijuana	10.2	12.6	19.9	22.6	20.3	17.5	15.7
LSD	2.7	3.5	4.4	4.7	3.9	2.1	1.6
Cocaine	2.3	2.9	4.2	4.4	4.5	3.6	3.4
Heroin	1.2	1.4	2.3	2.1	1.9	1.6	1.4
Alcohol	70.1	67.1	54.5	53.8	51.7	45.6	40.5
Cigarettes	44.0	45.3	46.4	47.3	40.5	28.4	24.6

Source: Lloyd Johnston, Patrick O'Malley, and Jerald Bachman, *Monitoring the Future: National Results on Adolescent Drug Use: Overview of Key Findings 2006* (Bethesda, MD: National Institute on Drug Abuse, 2007).

1991 and 2006. As shown in Table 4-2, while lifetime use of *any* illicit drug increased, the increase was largely due to increased marijuana use, with very modest increases in use of cocaine and heroin. Eighth-grader use of LSD, alcohol, and cigarettes actually fell nearly by half.

One word of caution is needed in considering findings from these surveys. The school survey (including 8th-, 10th-, and 12th-graders) does not provide information on youths who are absent from school (about 18 percent of the enrolled students) or youths who have dropped out of high school (about 15 percent for this survey). These two groups of students are likely to be among the most vulnerable to serious drug use.[29] The National Household Survey of 12- to 17-year-olds also underestimates serious drug use by adolescents. It does not include institutionalized youths, transients, and people unable to be identified through normal census identification procedures. It is important to recognize that adolescent drug use is not confined to the United States. A discussion of drug use by juveniles in a variety of countries is found in Box 4-2.

Changes in Adolescent Attitudes Toward Drugs

Many youths today perceive illicit drugs to be relatively dangerous or at least risky. The *Monitoring the Future* survey of adolescent drug use provides some interesting findings (see Table 4-3). Students in 8th, 10th, and 12th grades were asked how much they thought people risked harming themselves if they engaged in certain patterns of drug use. The differences between 8th and 12th graders in their perceptions of risk are very interesting. Eighth-grade students were significantly less likely than seniors to see a great risk in taking LSD regularly, in trying cocaine powder occasionally, and in smoking one or more packs of cigarettes per day. Seniors, on the other hand, were less likely than 8th graders to see great risk in smoking marijuana regularly, taking MDMA (ecstasy) or crack occasionally, and drinking one or two alcoholic beverages nearly every day.

Perceptions of risk are not necessarily shared between parents and children. For example, a study by the Partnership for a Drug Free America reported that 33 percent of the parents surveyed thought that their children viewed marijuana as harmful, although only 18 percent of the 13- to 18-year-olds felt that smoking marijuana was risky.[30]

box 4-2   DELINQUENCY AROUND THE GLOBE
Adolescent Drug Use in Other Countries

The use of illicit drugs by adolescents is not unique to the United States; youths around the world experiment with and use a variety of drugs in ways not too dissimilar to their American counterparts. The International Self-Reported Delinquency Project (ISRD) has examined drug use and delinquency among respondents in Belgium, England and Wales, Finland, Germany, Greece, Holland, Italy, Northern Ireland, Portugal, Spain, Switzerland, and the United States. Research has found that, like American youths, adolescents from around the globe demonstrate a multifaceted involvement in drug use and delinquency. For example, a survey of 21,000 Spanish youths ages 14 to 18 found that the use of cocaine has increased dramatically in recent years. Only 5 percent of 18-year-olds had used cocaine at least once in 1994, compared to 9 percent in 1998. There was a threefold increase in cocaine use by 16-year-olds during the same period, with 2 percent having used cocaine at least once in 1994 compared to 5 percent in 1998.

Over 1,700 tenth-graders in Bogota, Colombia, were surveyed in 1997 and nearly 90 percent reported having used alcohol at least once during their lifetime, and 54 percent reported they started drinking before age 12. Some 77 percent of the youths reported having used tobacco at least once during their lifetime, with 60 percent reporting tobacco use during the 30 days prior to the survey. Eleven percent of the youths reported having used marijuana at least once during their lifetime. Slightly more than one-third of the students reported having first used marijuana when they were 15 or 16 years old; although about 5 percent indicated they first experimented with marijuana before age 9.

In a survey of nearly 1,600 Australian adolescents ages 14 to 19, it was reported that about 45 percent of the respondents had used marijuana at least once in their lifetime, and 78 percent of that group had used it during the year prior to the survey. The use

of marijuana significantly increased with age: 24 percent of 14- to 15-year-olds had tried marijuana at least once, compared to 47 percent of 16- to 17-year-olds and 63 percent of 18- to 19-year-olds. The average age of first use of marijuana was 14.6 years old. Even though the proportion of adolescent males having ever tried marijuana changed little between 1995 and 1998, the proportion of females reporting having ever used marijuana nearly doubled during the same period, increasing from 24.4 percent in 1995 to 45.2 percent in 1998. While many Australian youths who had tried marijuana stopped using the drug, about 21 percent of those who continued to smoke marijuana reported using it on a weekly basis and 7 percent smoke it daily.

Although both licit and illicit drug use by youths in Taiwan is substantially lower than among American youths, the Taiwanese government is concerned about its apparent increase in use and related social and health problems. A survey of approximately 2,200 13- to 18-year-olds was conducted in a rural county in Taiwan. Seven percent of the youths reported tobacco use, 2 percent reported chewing betel gum, nearly 2 percent currently drank alcohol, and 1 percent reported illicit drug use. Males ages 13 to 15 were much more likely than females to use tobacco (9 percent compared to 3 percent), but they were only slightly more likely to use alcohol (4 percent compared to 2 percent) or illicit drugs (0.7 percent compared to 0.4 percent).

Smoking is considered to be the greatest substance abuse problem among adolescents in China. Almost all of the 320 million smokers in China began smoking as teenagers, with the average age of onset being before age 15. Most youths initially experimented with smoking out of curiosity. Chinese youths also obtain a degree of status in smoking foreign-brand cigarettes, especially Marlboro. The Chinese government is attempting to counter the "cool" image of the teenage

box 4-2   **DELINQUENCY AROUND THE GLOBE**
Adolescent Drug Use in Other Countries —continued

smoker by advertising campaigns designed to portray adolescent smokers as social misfits.

Sources: Xavier Bosch, "Survey Shows Cocaine Use by Spanish Adolescents on the Rise," *The Lancet* 355:2230 (2000); Kow-Tong Chen, Chien-Jen Chen, Anne Fagot-Campagna, and K. M. V. Narayan, "Tobacco, Betel Quid, Alcohol, and Illicit Drug Use Among 13- to 35-Year-Olds in I-Lan, Rural Taiwan: Prevalence and Risk Factors," *American Journal of Public Health* 91:1130–1134 (2001); Tsung Cheng, "Teenage Smok-

ing in China," *Journal of Adolescence* 22:607–620 (1999); Miguel Prez and Helda Pinon-Prez, "Alcohol, Tobacco, and Other Psychoactive Drug Use Among High School Students in Bogota, Colombia," *Journal of School Health* 70:377–380 (2000); Amanda Reid, Michael Lynskey, and Jan Copeland, "Cannabis Use Among Australian Adolescents: Findings of the 1998 National Drug Strategy Household Survey," *Australian and New Zealand Journal of Public Health* 24:596–602 (2000); Martin Killias and Denis Ribeaud, "Drug Use and Crime Among Juveniles: An International Perspective," *Studies on Crime and Crime Prevention* 8:189–209 (1999).

table 4-3   Perceived Harmfulness in Drug Use by 8th, 10th, and 12th Grade Students, 2005

PERCENT SAYING "GREAT RISK" IF THEY:	8TH GRADE	10TH GRADE	12TH GRADE
Smoke marijuana regularly	73.2	64.9	57.9
Take LSD regularly	40.0	60.7	69.3
Take MDMA (ecstasy) occasionally	52.0	71.3	59.3
Take crack occasionally	68.7	76.2	64.8
Take cocaine powder occasionally	64.0	71.3	61.9
Take heroin occasionally without using a needle	75.3	83.6	76.2
Take one or two drinks nearly every day	31.3	31.7	25.3
Smoke one or more packs of cigarettes per day	59.4	67.7	77.6

Source: Lloyd Johnston, Patrick O'Malley, Jerald Bachman, and John Schulenberg, *Monitoring the Future: National Results on Adolescent Drug Use: Overview of Key Findings, 2006* (Bethesda, MD: National Institute on Drug Abuse, 2007).

Although adolescents perceive drug use as carrying risks, they are also quick to report that most drugs are "fairly or very easy" to get. Understandably, high school seniors are more likely than 10th-graders and 8th-graders to report drugs as easy to obtain. While nearly 93 percent of the seniors said alcohol was "fairly easy to get," only 83 percent of the 10th-graders and 63 percent of the 8th-graders so indicated. About three times as many seniors as 8th-graders report marijuana and MDMA are easy to obtain, and seniors are about twice as likely to say LSD and heroin are fairly easy to get.[31]

One reason youth find drugs, especially marijuana, easy to obtain is that they usually receive drugs from close friends. For example, over 60 percent of youth age 12 to 17 who used marijuana obtained it for free or shared someone else's marijuana. Only about one-third of youthful marijuana users obtained the drug through a purchase, and such purchases were most likely to be from someone they had just met or did not know well. And the majority of marijuana-using youth obtained the drug from a friend, regardless of whether they bought it or obtained it for free or shared it.[32]

Clearly, high school and middle school students use drugs and find drugs rather easy to obtain. Sometimes they can be obtained from other students who deal drugs within the school. Just how many students bring drugs to school is less well documented than the number of students who bring guns to school (see Chapter 3), but enough school administrators are concerned about the problem to bring police to school to conduct sweep searches of lockers and sometimes even random searches of students (see Chapter 11). And sometimes, these searches may legally cross the line. For a discussion of a controversial drug raid in a South Carolina high school, see Box 4-3.

CAUSES OF ADOLESCENT DRUG USE

Theories of juvenile delinquency, ranging from early classical and neoclassical theories that emphasize free will and choice to deterministic theories that blame crime on biological, psychological, and sociological factors will be discussed in later chapters. All these perspectives provide good, strong explanations for why youths use illicit drugs or legal drugs inappropriately; however, in this section our focus will be on five approaches based on the sociological perspective as they apply to the causes of adolescent drug use.

Double Failure by the Individual

In *strain theory,* Robert Merton argued that in a competitive and materialistic society in which success through legitimate avenues is attainable by relatively few individuals, those unable to achieve success may choose deviant modes of adaptation to deal with their failure (see Chapter 6).[33] An individual who chooses *retreatism* as an adaptation rejects both the cultural goal of success and the approved means to achieve success. Merton suggests that moral scruples also prevent the individual from choosing criminal means to achieve success as well. Richard Cloward and Lloyd Ohlin believe that the avoidance of illegitimate means is due not to the constraint of the person's scruples but, rather, to the lack of opportunity to utilize such means in the pursuit of success.[34] Regardless of who is right, drug use is seen as deriving from failing to "make it" in conventional society as well as failing to achieve success in the criminal world. The person has failed twice and, consequently, retreats into a world of drugs.

More than four decades after Cloward and Ohlin introduced their theory, Stephen Baron and Timothy Hartnagel interviewed 200 homeless adolescents living in a large western Canadian city and found that perceived lack of opportunities for viable employment contributed to delinquency and drug use. Moreover, the effects of many young people who were similarly disaffected by their job prospects contributed to worsening drug involvement.[35] Similarly, Robert Agnew's *general strain theory* is an extension of the "double failure" idea. He contends that various sources of strain contribute to depression and an escapist withdrawal from society into drug use (see Chapter 6). Nicole Leeper Piquero and Miriam Sealock have tested this idea and found that social strain did contribute to feelings of depression, especially among young females.[36] In turn, depression is an important factor that can plunge adolescents into serious drug abuse.[37]

think
about it

The retreatist alcoholic or drug addict is a social type described by Merton and Cloward and Ohlin. Are retreatists living evidence that certain people lack the capacity to participate in society? Are retreatists useful for other members of society since they provide a point of comparison to measure life success?

box 4-3   A WINDOW ON DELINQUENCY

A Drug Raid in School

It was 6:45 A.M. on a Wednesday morning in early November 2003. The video surveillance cameras at Stratford High School in Goose Creek, South Carolina, were running. Students were walking down the school hallway with backpacks on their backs. Two girls talked with each other as they passed by a group of boys gathered next to their lockers. Suddenly, three police officers with guns drawn rushed toward the boys. In the commotion, the two girls with the backpacks and one of the boys fell to the floor. Students farther down the hall looked to see what was happening. Eleven more police officers entered the hallway. One officer wrestled a boy to the ground while another officer held his gun in both hands, swinging it back and forth in front of the students. A few minutes later the drug dogs entered the hallway and began to sniff the backpacks. Nearly 130 students either sat or lay on the ground or were on their knees, hands over their heads. At least a dozen of the youths were restrained with flex-cuffs or disposable, plastic strip handcuffs. No drugs were found and no arrests for drugs were made. One student, a ninth grader, was charged with filing a false police report after claiming an officer shoved her to the floor during the search. A review of the video tape showed that the girl was not in the hallway during the drug raid.

What happened? Or perhaps more important, why did what seemed to be such an inappropriate police drug raid in a school happen? School administrators had been told some weeks earlier that students were bringing drugs to school and that drug sales were occurring on school property. The principal contacted the police, who began an investigation. After monitoring the school's surveillance cameras for a number of days, the police were convinced they saw what appeared to be organized drug activity with students acting as lookouts and others concealing themselves from the cameras. With consent of the school administrators, the police arrived early at the school that morning and got themselves into position. Teachers had been assigned locations to secure the hallway and to keep other students from entering. School officials said they had no idea the police would draw their guns during the raid. A Goose Creek police lieutenant said that the officers drew their guns "as a matter of officer safety" and that the students placed in cuffs had failed to "respond to repeated police instruction."

Civil lawsuits have been filed on behalf of 38 students who claim their rights were violated. Some parents had asked that criminal charges be filed against the police and school officials. In July 2004, the state attorney general decided such charges would not be forthcoming, although he said that "such raid tactics are well suited for a crack house, but not a school house."

Sources: Tony Bartelme, "School Raid Raises Questions About Drug War," *The Post and Courier,* online at http://archives.postandcourier.com/archive/arch03/1103/arc11161451970.shtml, accessed April 21, 2007; "State Investigating High School Drug Sweep," online at http://www.thestate.com/mld/thestate/news/local/7215835, accessed April 21, 2007; "Police, School District Defend Drug Raid," online at http://www.cnn.com/2003/US/South/11/07/school.raid/, accessed April 21, 2007; "Drug Raid Accountability," online at http://www.charleston.net/stories/070404/edi_04edit2.shtml, accessed April 21, 2007.

However, a number of ethnographic studies do not support the double failure theory of drug use. This research suggests that many persons, at least among those who use expensive drugs and heroin, have reasonably successful criminal lifestyles.[38] According to Charles Faupel and his colleagues, the theoretical notion that drug users are double failures is seductive because people who are not part of the drug culture cannot understand why a person would use drugs in the first place: "Why else would anyone use drugs or become addicted? Surely, they would prefer another lifestyle! The evidence suggests, however, that, indeed, many addicts *do* freely choose a drug-using lifestyle, indeed preferring it to nine-to-five routines."[39]

Learning to Use Drugs

Edwin Sutherland was among the first criminologists to suggest that delinquent behavior is learned (see Chapter 6). The idea that a youth learns delinquent behavior through an interactive process has been extended by integrating Sutherland's principles of differential association with theories of operant conditioning drawn from the field of psychology. *Social learning theory* argues that a person's behavior is the result of group-based reinforced learning situations.[40] According to Erich Goode, adolescents learn to define behaviors as good or bad through their intimate interactions with other youths in certain groups. Different groups express different norms regarding illicit drugs and differentially reward or punish the use or distribution of drugs by members of the group.[41] Often times, social groups that condone substance use similarly engage in other forms of risky behavior. Angela Gover explored the social learning approach to adolescent drug use based on data from 5,545 high school students. Gover found that teens tended to associate with other peers who use drugs and alcohol, were sexually promiscuous, and committed crimes, such as drunk driving. Moreover, youths in these social groups were also significantly likely to be victimized in romantic relationships.[42] In short, the group processes that encouraged drug use similarly influenced delinquency and victimization.

Adolescent drug use, then, is positively reinforced by exposure to drug-using role models, approval of drug use by peers, and the perceived positive or pleasurable effects of the drug itself. To the extent that the individual's drug use is also not negatively reinforced either by bad effects of the drug or by statements or actions by parents, peers, or authorities, drug use will persist. There is strong empirical support for the idea that social learning processes form a causal basis for adolescent substance use.[43] For instance, Jacquelyn Monroe examined the effects of social learning and teen smoking based on data from the National Center for Health Statistics and found that associating with delinquent peers, identifying with delinquent peers, holding delinquent definitions, and imitating delinquent peers significantly predicted tobacco use.[44]

Might this learning process involve something as simple as watching people use drugs in movies? While Sutherland argued that learning needed to occur in face-to-face, intimate interactions, he had not anticipated the impact of the media culture in the late 20th century. One study that examined the effect of viewing smoking in movies on adolescent smoking initiation was conducted by Madeline Dalton and her colleagues using a surveyed sample of 3,547 children between the ages of 10 and 14 who had never tried cigarettes. The youth were then followed up 13 to 26 months later with a survey inquiring into their current use of cigarettes and which of 50 popular movies they had watched during the study period. Findings from the study strongly suggest that youth who watched the most movies judged to have the greatest portrayal of smoking were about "three times more likely to initiate smoking than those with the least amount of exposure."[45] Moreover, children with parents who *did not* smoke were significantly *more* susceptible to the impact of watching smoking in movies.

Subcultural Socialization into Drug Use

Another explanation for adolescent drug use is that youths begin to use drugs and continue to do so because of their involvement in social groups in which drug use is reinforced. Drug subcultures vary. For many adolescents, membership in one drug subculture may bring involvement in other drug subcultures, for instance, alcohol-using, marijuana-using, cocaine-using, heroin-using, or multiple drug-using subcultures. As an adolescent's involvement in a drug-using subculture deepens, he or she becomes increasingly socialized into the values and norms of the group, and drug-using behavior is likely to ensue. Howard Becker described the process of becoming a marijuana user through interaction with a marijuana-using subculture. For an individual to become a marijuana user, three events must occur. First, one must *learn the proper technique* for smoking marijuana to produce the desired effects. Second, one must *learn to perceive the effects and connect them* with marijuana. And third, one must *define the effects of marijuana smoking as pleasurable*. The smoker "has learned, in short, to answer 'Yes' to the question: 'Is it fun?'"[46]

But learning to smoke marijuana is not enough to become a regular user. A juvenile must also establish a reliable means of supply, keep his or her drug use secret from others who may disapprove, and neutralize moral objections to marijuana use held by conventional society. Becker suggests that fulfilling these conditions requires involvement in a group that regularly uses marijuana.

Goode believes that the socialization process within a drug subculture involves much convincing of new users that they have nothing to fear from the drug. He has identified five elements critical to the person's decision to use marijuana:

1. The perception of danger or lack of danger.
2. The perception of any benefit from use of the drug.
3. The attitude toward users of marijuana.
4. The closeness to those advocating use of marijuana.
5. The closeness to those who are trying to get them to smoke marijuana.

Goode also found that heavy users of marijuana are more involved with friends who also used marijuana, as well as other drugs, and who were generally more involved in the drug subculture.[47] Brian Kelly studied the marijuana subculture among relatively affluent youths in the New York City vicinity. He found that a rather intricate culture, complete with a specific sense of style, clothing, music, and language, was devoted to marijuana use among these teens. Moreover, important normative differences existed between using marijuana from a "bong" versus from a "blunt."[48] Denise Kandel contends that the process of socialization into drug use is selective.[49] Among early adolescents, drug and alcohol use tends to be more situational or even accidental. The specific activities of the immediate peer group greatly influence the behavior of the individual: If the youth has friends who drink, he or she will be more likely to drink; if the youth has close peers who are drug users, he or she will be more inclined to try drugs; and if he or she hangs out with friends who disapprove of alcohol and drug use, he or she will not be inclined to use either. In later adolescence, youths who have begun to use drugs or alcohol will gradually break away from non-drug-using peers and move toward peers who do use them. Andy Hochstetler has chronicled the drug-fueled lives of young adult offenders. Almost all of their offending careers began during early adolescence when they socialized entirely with other drug-abusing peers. Over time, their decisions to engage in various forms of delinquency were often simply a need to obtain more drugs and continue partying.[50]

Finally, it is important to recognize that the effects of *subcultural socialization* on substance use are not always negative. There exist among young people several social cliques that serve to promote healthy, prosocial forms of behavior where there is peer pressure to avoid drug use and delinquency. One example is the Straight Edge movement, an identifiable group characterized by vigilantly anti-drug attitudes, vegetarianism, and hardcore or punk music.[51] Thus, some subcultures can effectively insulate adolescents from substance use and delinquent behavior.

Weakening of Social Controls

think
about it

Peer pressure, particularly as it applies to adolescent drug use, denotes a negative connotation. This does not have to be the case, however. Can positive, strong-willed teens also be role models for their peers and provide healthy pressure? Did such persons exist at your high school?

Social control theory argues that delinquency is the result of an absence or weakening of the social control mechanisms that ensure conformity (see Chapter 6). Without established social controls, people will pursue their self-interests, including pleasure. A strong social bond to conventional social institutions reduces the likelihood of deviation from normative expectations, whereas weakening of the bond releases the individual from the constraints of the norms.[52]

To the extent that a youth is strongly *attached* to conventional others (parents, peers, or teachers), is strongly *committed* to conventional institutions, is heavily *involved* in conventional activities, and strongly *believes* in conventional norms, he or she is unlikely to violate society's laws and use drugs. Conversely, if any of these elements of the social bond are weakened, the juvenile becomes more likely to deviate, and drug use becomes more probable. Michael Maume and his colleagues examined the effects of marital attachment and delinquent peer association on marijuana use. They found that young persons with strong attachments to their spouses were significantly likely to desist from marijuana use regardless of the number of drug-using peers that they had. This suggests that "cutting the grass" is likely among young people who strongly bond to society through marriage.[53]

Recent analysis of data from the 2006 National Survey on Drug Use and Health provides support for the idea that social controls reduce the likelihood of a youth getting involved in drug use. For example, youths age 12 to 17 who participated in one or more school-based, community-based, or church- or faith-based activities during the prior year were less likely to have used cigarettes, alcohol, or illicit drugs in the past month than youths who did not participate in such activities in the past year.[54] In addition, youths who attended religious services 25 times or more during the prior year were less likely to use alcohol, cigarettes, or illicit drugs than youths who attended fewer than 25 times, and youths who reported that religious beliefs are a very important part of their lives were less likely to use drugs than were youths who reported that religious beliefs were unimportant to their lives.[55] Finally, more than three million youths were considered to be school dropouts. More than half of school dropouts smoked cigarettes during the six months prior to the survey, although dropouts did not appear to be any more likely than nondropouts to use illicit drugs.[56]

Family Conflict and Poor Parenting

Delinquency frequently occurs as a result of dysfunctional dynamics within the home and most often in homes characterized by poverty, disruption, and conflict. It is no surprise that the same conditions produce drug use among children:

> Rare in the ghetto today are neighbors whose lives demonstrate that education is meaningful, that steady employment is a viable alternative to welfare and illegal pursuits, and that a stable family is an aspect of normalcy. . . . More and more families, stressed and depleted, are surrounded by others in similar straits. This concentration of the persistently poor, unskilled, alienated, unemployed, and unmarried is central to the development of children who grow up in such a setting.[57]

These children often turn to drugs. Parental failures, fighting, extreme or inconsistent discipline of children, lack of communication, physical and sexual abuse, emotional distance, and disrupted marriages all take their toll on children. Drug use may help ease the pain of criticism and serve as an escape from the fears of the next assault by an abusive parent. (See discussion of *differential oppression theory* in Chapter 7.)

It has been reported, for example, that adolescent drug use is associated with strict or inconsistent parental discipline. Anthony Jurich and his colleagues found that adolescents who use illegal drugs daily are more likely to have parents

Adolescents are more likely to develop substance abuse problems if they were raised in homes characterized by family conflict. Does family conflict lead to delinquency and drug use generally, or are youths who use drugs also more likely to argue with their parents?

with laissez faire or authoritarian patterns of discipline rather than democratic ones or to have parents who were inconsistent in their disciplinary patterns (see Chapter 10).[58] In addition, a number of studies report that parental conflict in child-rearing philosophy and inconsistent or restrictive discipline were associated with both marijuana and alcohol use among children.[59]

Emotional distance, perceived lack of love, or outright conflict with parents has also been associated with adolescent drug use. Rafaela Robles and her associates reported that among Puerto Rican high school students, those who felt their parents were disgusted with them and those who were not close to their fathers were more likely to be drug users.[60] Other studies discovered that adolescent drug use was greater among children who perceived lower levels of parental love or negative parental attitudes expressed toward them.[61] Rick Kosterman and his colleagues found that the likelihood of adolescent initiation into marijuana and alcohol use was reduced by proactive family management practices, such as monitoring, applying rules and discipline, and employing reward practices, while bonding to mother appeared to have little or no effect.[62]

Broken homes, divorce, separation, and abandonment by the father have also been correlated with adolescent drug use.[63] Stephan Quensel and his colleagues examined the relationship between family structure and adolescent drug use among more than 3,300 15-year-olds. They found that cigarette smoking and marijuana and alcohol use was significantly higher for youths living in single-mother families than for those living in traditional two-parent families, and this held true for both boys and girls.[64] Research also suggests that lack of supervision by parents when children come home from school is related to adolescent drug use. Peter Mulhall and his associates report that *latchkey children* (middle school youth who were home alone after school two or more days per week) were significantly more likely to have used alcohol during the prior month, to consume more alcohol, and to drink to intoxication than were nonlatchkey children. Furthermore, latchkey youth were more likely to have used marijuana and to have smoked cigarettes during the prior month.[65]

The relationship between child maltreatment and the child's ensuing drug use has also been explored. Ann Burgess and her colleagues compared a group of youngsters who had been sexually abused as children with a group of non-abused youths. They discovered a strong connection between the childhood experience of sexual abuse and later drug use.[66] Richard Dembo and his associates studied 145 youths confined in a detention center in a southeastern state and found that both male and female youths who had been sexually abused were much more likely to be current drug users.[67] More recent studies using more sophisticated methodologies have also looked at this relationship.[68] In addition, Timothy Ireland and his colleagues reported that maltreatment of children from childhood through adolescence significantly increases the likelihood of drug use. They note, however, that if the maltreatment is limited to childhood and does not continue on into adolescence, it presents only a minimal risk of subsequent drug use.[69]

More than six million children lived with at least one parent who abused or was dependent on alcohol or an illicit drug during the previous year. Moreover, parental use of drugs and alcohol also has been found to have a direct effect on the child's likelihood of using drugs.[70] One study found that 78 percent of parents who used marijuana also had children who were drug users suggesting that children imitate their parent's drinking habits.[71] Parents who drank were likely to have children who also drank, while parents who abstained were likely to have abstaining children. Denise Kandel and her colleagues examined parental influences on marijuana use, comparing the *baby boom generation* and their children. They discovered that children of parents who had *ever* used marijuana were about three times as likely to have ever used marijuana as the children of parents who had *never* used the drug. The influence was similar for mothers and fathers and sons and daughters. In addition, parents who perceived little risk associated with marijuana use had children with similar beliefs, and adolescent attitudes had the strongest association with adolescent marijuana use of any of the adolescent characteristics examined in the study.[72]

DRUG USE AND DELINQUENCY

Does illegal drug use lead to acts of delinquency? Conversely, does delinquency lead to drug use? Is the drug use–delinquency relationship spurious; that is, are they related only because they are both caused by some other factors? Or is there a reciprocal relationship between drugs and delinquency with drug use leading to delinquent behavior and delinquency leading to drug use? What exactly is the relationship between adolescent drug use and delinquent behavior? These questions have puzzled criminologists for some time. The reason that the drugs–delinquency relationship appears to be multifaceted is that it applies to two general but largely distinct groups within the population, *adolescence-limited* and *life-course persistent offenders* (see Chapter 2 and Chapter 8).

Drugs and Delinquency

Although many studies have led criminologists and policy makers to believe there is a causal link between drug use and delinquency, the exact nature of the relationship has not been established.[73] Scott Menard and his colleagues explored the relationship between drugs and crime from adolescence into adulthood and reported that "the drug–crime relationship is different for different ages and for different stages of involvement in crime and drug use" and that "initiation of substance use apparently is preceded by initiation of crime for most individuals." However, they note that in later stages of involvement the relationship becomes reciprocal. That is, adolescent involvement in serious illicit drug use appears to "contribute to continuity in serious crime, and serious crime contributes to continuity in serious illicit drug use."[74]

Many studies confirm an association between alcohol and drug use and general patterns of delinquency, but again with no causal relationship established.[75] John Welte and his colleagues studied the drugs–delinquency connection and found that a general deviant syndrome *did not* explain specific problem behaviors, such as drug use. Although drugs and delinquency were correlated, their ultimate causes seemed to be distinct. In other words, adolescent substance abuse was not simply part of a teen's larger involvement in crime.[76] Others have shown that marijuana use is highly associated with a variety of delinquent behaviors. Youths who smoked marijuana during the past year were more likely than youths who did not to have engaged in fights, stolen things worth more than $50, carried a handgun, and sold illegal drugs. Furthermore, youths age 12 to 17 who had run away from home in the past year were more likely than youth who did not run away to have used marijuana, alcohol, or an illicit drug.[77]

David Altschuler and Paul Brounstein reported that although drug use and drug trafficking were correlated with other delinquent activities, "still, for every type of crime reported in the past year, only a minority of offenders reported ever using drugs while committing the crime. . . . Most youths appear to commit crime for reasons completely independent of drugs."[78] Even though most serious delinquents were found to be regular users of alcohol and drugs, the vast majority of their instances of drug and alcohol use occurred without crimes, and most crimes occurred without prior substance abuse.

Other criminologists have reached slightly different conclusions. Colleen McLaughlin and her colleagues discovered in a study of 25 male juveniles committed to Virginia juvenile correctional facilities for murder or voluntary manslaughter that over half of the murderers were known drug dealers, compared to less than 10 percent of all juveniles incarcerated in the state. In addition, 28 percent of the murder incidents were regarded as drug related. Perhaps more important, they found that none of the drug-related murders involved offenders who did not have some history of illicit drug use. Drug use by homicide victims was also a significant contributor to murder incidents. Victims who had recently used drugs were more likely to be killed in a drug-related incident than victims who did not use drugs.[79]

David Huizinga and his colleagues reported on findings from research on the causes and correlates of delinquency conducted in Pittsburgh, Denver, and Rochester. More than 4,000 youths were surveyed in the three cities. In each city they detected a statistically significant relationship between persistent delinquency and persistent drug use, and this was true for both males and females. Huizinga and his associates note that "for males, the majority of persistent serious delinquents were not drug users, but the majority of drug users were serious delinquents. . . . [And that] among females, delinquency is a stronger indicator of drug use than drug use is an indicator of delinquency."[80] But as we noted at the beginning of this section, the finding of significant relationships between drug use and delinquency does not answer the question: Which causes which? In the final analysis, it is most prudent to conclude that there is a co-occurrence between drug use and delinquency.

Drugs, Delinquent Friends, and Delinquency

There is research to suggest that associating with peers who are delinquent, who use drugs, or who are both delinquent and drug users is strongly related to both delinquency and drug use. Criminologists who have examined self-report responses from a national sample of 1,725 youths have concluded that there was a causal relationship between prior delinquency and involvement in delinquent peer groups and subsequent drug use.[81] Other studies report similar findings. Research by Helen Garnier and Judith Stein found that the most significant predictors of both drug use and delinquency were having peers who engaged in the behaviors. They also noted that youths select friends who are more like themselves, sharing similar values, backgrounds, *and* behaviors, including drug use.[82] Moreover, Andrea Hussong reported that the strongest predictor for adolescent drug use was the extent of drug use by the youth's best friend.[83] It thus seems that having strong bonds to delinquent peers increases the risk of both delinquency and drug use for all youths.

Drug use by girls does not appear to be as likely to lead to delinquency as it does for boys. However, are girls who use drugs likely to experience different kinds of problems than boys who use drugs?

Juveniles who belong to gangs are significantly more likely to engage in drug use than are adolescents who are not members of gangs. Similarly, joining a gang is often a precursor to drug use. In addition, juvenile gang members, and even gangs themselves, are often explicitly organized for the purpose of drug trafficking. Research has consistently confirmed that gang members are extensively involved in drug sales, especially marijuana and cocaine.[84] In addition, as youths are more involved in delinquency and drug use, they are significantly more likely to fall into long-term life trajectories involving a variety of precocious transitions. Marvin Krohn and his colleagues report that alcohol and drug use during early adolescence increases the risk of becoming pregnant or impregnating someone, dropping out of school, becoming a teenage parent, and living independently from parents. These consequences, in turn, increase the likelihood of drug and alcohol use as the youths become young adults. Krohn and his colleagues conclude that these youths are then greatly disadvantaged in their ability to form stable adult lives and more likely to turn to deviant lifestyles.[85]

A Developmental Taxonomy, Drugs, and Delinquency

The reason that the drugs–delinquency relationship appears to be multifaceted is that it applies to two general but largely distinct groups within the population, *adolescence-limited* and *life-course persistent offenders*. As the label implies, adolescence-limited offenders engage in drug use and delinquency during middle to late adolescence largely in response to the ambiguous transition from child to adult status. Most youth fit into this category. For this group, delinquent involvement often includes less serious forms of conduct and is short-lived. In terms of drug use, the "normal" adolescence-limited delinquent will experiment with marijuana, alcohol, and tobacco but mostly abstain from trying more illicit narcotics, such as heroin, cocaine, and methamphetamine. The popular notion of the high school student drinking beer on weekends or occasionally smoking marijuana meshes with the idea of the adolescence-limited offenders. For most, the brief period of experimentation does not become problematic or lead to larger problems with substance abuse or antisocial behavior.[86]

For youths on the life-course persistent pathway, drug use is part of a larger behavioral pattern of delinquency. Even during adolescence, life-course persistent or chronic delinquents experience an array of overlapping behavioral problems that mutually reinforce one another but ultimately stem from some other cause, a phenomenon called **comorbidity** (see Chapter 2). Youngsters on the life-course persistent pathway suffer from several neurocognitive deficits that interact with early life disadvantage, such as abusive, erratic, or antisocial parenting, to propel them down an antisocial pathway. Experimentation with alcohol and other substances occurs very early in life, often during childhood, and at times is even introduced and promoted by parents. Early use of drugs and alcohol is disastrous for healthy human development. According to the National Epidemiologic Survey on Alcohol and Related Conditions, 47 percent of persons who begin drinking alcohol before age 14 will be dependent on alcohol at some point during their lifetimes—a prevalence estimate that is *five times* greater than among persons whose onset of alcohol use occurs at age 21.[87] Grace Barnes and her colleagues studied the drugs–delinquency link among nearly 20,000 students in 7th through 12th grades and found that children who experimented with alcohol very early in life were significantly likely to have further alcohol problems and high levels of drug use and delinquency.[88]

Not all criminologists use the developmental taxonomy discussed here; however, an array of social and medical scientists distinguish between drug use that appears to be normative, experimental, and unproblematic and drug use that appears to be part of a larger antisocial behavioral syndrome.[89] A host of "global explanations" have been offered to explain the antisocial behavioral syndrome.[90] One of the most popular is low self-control. Denis Ribeaud and Manuel Eisner discovered that low self-control, particularly its subcomponents risk-seeking and impulsivity, accounted for involvement in delinquency and substance abuse among a large sample of 9th graders in Switzerland.[91] Other criminologists suggest that aggression and impulsivity,[92] gang membership,[93] and societal-poverty factors[94] primarily explain the syndrome approach to drugs and delinquency.

RESPONDING TO ADOLESCENT DRUG USE

Conventional wisdom and much academic scholarship holds that American drug policy is almost entirely based on drug interdiction and law enforcement, excessive prosecution of drug offenders, and overall a punitive, punishment-based approach in responding to substance abuse.[95] Although the United States does take a punitive stance toward substance use compared to some other countries, American drug policy blends a variety of methods to address the drug problem. The President's National Drug Control Strategy for 2006 until January 2009 contains a three-pronged strategy including prevention, treatment, and interdiction. First, an integral part of drug prevention is the *Above the Influence* initiative that consists of multiple media educational programs to promote drug-free living among children and adolescents. Second, drug treatment is highlighted by the President's *Access to Recovery* program that expands treatment options and the use of drug courts, instead of traditional criminal prosecution, to rehabilitate offenders with substance abuse problems. Third, the Bush Administration seeks to disrupt drug markets using the resources of federal, state, and local criminal justice systems.[96] In the next section we will examine four ways to respond to adolescent drug use.

Control Response

The control response to adolescent drug use places an emphasis on the arrest and prosecution of drug dealers and drug users. When the *Anti-Drug Abuse Act of 1988* was created, it was believed that a mostly control-based response to substance abuse would create a drug-free America within 10 years—a goal obviously not achieved. Legislation and guidelines were established to provide greater support for federal, state, and local law enforcement agencies and to allocate funds for the expansion of the nation's prison system. Of course, the Anti-Drug Abuse Act had only modest success in reducing adolescent drug use in recent years.

Each year, in an attempt to emphasize and strengthen federal efforts in attacking the problem of illicit drugs in the lives of juveniles, the White House Office of National Drug Control Policy produces a *National Drug Control Strategy*. The *National Drug Control Strategy* budget for 2008 is $12.9 billion, including $18 million for student drug testing programs, $130 million to continue its National Youth Anti-Drug Media Campaign begun in 2001, and up to $59 million to fund about 100 new local community anti-drug coalitions working to prevent substance abuse among young people (see Box 4-4).[97]

Juvenile Drug Courts

The drug court movement is a combination of an outgrowth of the early crackdown on drugs in the 1970s and 1980s and the emerging interest in developing community-oriented, diversionary alternatives to the traditional criminal and juvenile courts for handling drug cases. Drug courts aim to integrate a variety of alcohol and drug treatment services with justice system case processing and to provide continued monitoring and testing of participants. Juvenile drug courts, although modeled on adult drug courts, place greater emphasis on coordinating treatment for juveniles involving the courts and the youths' families and schools in a community, rather than institutional, environment.[98]

According to the National Association of Drug Court Professionals, there are more than 1,600 drug courts in the United States with nearly 200 devoted exclusively to adolescents. Unfortunately, there are few published evaluations of the effectiveness of juvenile drug courts. Initial studies suggest some positive impact in reducing drug use and other forms of delinquency; however, more recent research raises questions about the ability of drug courts to accomplish their goals.[99] For example, Nancy Rodriguez and Vincent Webb examined data from the first three years of the Maricopa County (Phoenix) juvenile drug court program and compared the outcomes for 114 youths placed in the drug court with 204 juveniles placed on standard probation. They found "no significant difference in marijuana use between youths in drug court and those on standard probation. . . . [And that] youths in drug court were 2.7 times more likely to test positive for

---

box 4-4 **DELINQUENCY PREVENTION**

National Youth Anti-Drug Media Campaign

The White House Office of National Drug Control Policy (ONDCP) has established a five-year campaign designed to harness the media to educate America's youth to reject illegal drugs. Tapping into advertising, television programming, movies, music, the Internet, and print media, the campaign focuses on primary prevention. The initial media campaign began in 1999 with four- to six-week advertising programs providing various specific anti-drug messages often supplemented with local coalitions and other partners amplifying these messages by adding their own messages and conducting related local events and activities.

In 2000 the Office of National Drug Control Policy launched a new "brand" for youth audiences. Advertisers and marketers have long used "branding" to create a consistent identity for a product or company and, through repeated exposure, keep the image top of mind for the consumer. The ONDCP conducted research to find out if young people would embrace the idea of an "anti-drug"—something important enough in their lives to stand between them and drugs. Not only did teens and younger adolescents find ownership and empowerment in the idea of an "anti-drug" brand that reflected their own values and passions (i.e., Soccer, My Anti-Drug; Dreams, My Anti-Drug), they suggested that the brand could serve as an invitation to other youths to reflect on what their anti-drugs might be. ONDCP partnered with youth organizations nationwide in launching "my anti-drug." Through community outreach efforts, the YMCA, Future Farmers of America, Girl Scouts, and Boys and Girls Clubs were among numerous groups working with youths within their own organizations to participate.

Media initiatives also targeted multicultural audiences. For example, within the American Indian community, print advertising was developed that not only reflects the values that exist within Native culture but also lays the groundwork for extending the campaign's prevention message within local community-based programs. During much of the media campaign, advertising reached 95 percent of America's youth eight times a week and communicated messages in eight languages to youths and adults of various ethnic groups.

Since its inception, the media campaign's messages have become ubiquitous in the lives of America's youth and their parents. From network television advertisements to school-based educational materials, from murals to Internet websites, and from local soccer competitions to national youth organizations, the campaign's messages reach Americans wherever they are—work, play, school, worship, and home.

In 2007 the White House announced it was budgeting $130 million to continue funding of its anti-drug advertising campaign and expanding its strategy to include information for teens and parents to promote early intervention against drug use.

Sources: The White House, *The National Drug Control Strategy,* 2001 (Washington, DC: Office of National Drug Control Policy, 2001); The White House, *National Drug Control Strategy,* 2004 (Washington, DC: Office of National Drug Control Policy, 2004); The White House, *National Drug Control Strategy,* 2007 (Washington, DC: Office of National Drug Control Policy, 2007).

---

cocaine than youths in the comparison group."[100] Moreover, only 15 juveniles (30 percent) of the youths actually successfully completed and graduated from the drug court program.[101] (See Chapter 14 for a discussion of juvenile drug courts.)

Drug Testing in Schools Efforts to control the drug problem have also involved a call for more extensive drug testing; however, the issue of drug testing is controversial. Who should be tested? How accurate are the tests? Are tests for all illicit drugs equally accurate? Are such tests in violation of constitutional rights ensuring protection against self-incrimination and the right to privacy?

Many school districts require drug tests of high school athletes. The Supreme Court, in *Vernonia School District 47J v. Acton,* held that it was constitutional for schools to require that all students participating in interscholastic athletics sign a form consenting to a urinalysis drug test at the beginning of the season for their sport.[101] The Court's position raised questions. For example, should students participating in other extracurricular activities, such as debate, marching band, or school government also be tested? Should teachers and school administrators be required to take similar drug tests? If there is a legitimate concern about possible injury due to the student's activity, then should students enrolled in certain science or vocational courses where potential danger exists with chemicals and hazardous machinery be tested? And because studies have found that first drug use often occurs prior to entering high school, should drug testing begin in middle school or even earlier?

The Court answered some of these questions in 2002 when it decided a case brought to it by 16-year-old Lindsay Earls. When Earls began her sophomore year at Tecumseh High School in Oklahoma, she was confronted by a new school drug policy that required mandatory drug testing of all students participating in *any* extracurricular activity. This included athletics, the band, choir, academic team, color guard, and Future Farmers of America. Earls was a member of the school's choir, marching band, and academic team, and she objected to what she regarded as an intrusive testing process. Earls said that she had been pulled out of class three times and sent to the vice principal's office to fill out forms and then taken to a bathroom where a teacher would stand outside the stall while she produced her urine sample. Earls believed that if students were not using drugs, then they should not have to prove their innocence. Lindsay and her family contacted the ACLU, which accepted the case and it went into the courts, eventually ending up in the U.S. Supreme Court. The Court held, in **Board of Education of Pottawatomie County v. Earls,** that such testing was not an unconstitutional intrusion on the students' privacy rights.[102] (See Box 4-5 for a brief discussion of the Court's ruling.)

The Court's decisions in both the *Vernonia* and *Earls* cases were based on the belief that drug testing of students would likely aid in reducing the drug problems believed to exist in the schools. By 2003 drug testing of high school athletes occurred in only 5 percent of schools, and testing of students in any extracurricular activities occurred in only 2 percent of schools. But does drug testing of students reduce the likelihood of students' use of illicit drugs? Ryoko Yamaguchi and his colleagues found that it does not. They concluded that for adolescent students, school drug testing was not significantly related to the prevalence or the frequency of student use of marijuana or other illicit drugs. Furthermore, drug testing of student athletes was not related to their use of marijuana or other illicit drug use.[103]

Police Crackdowns A rather different approach to control adolescent drug use is found in the efforts of the Vallejo Community Consortium in Vallejo, California, working with the Fighting Back Partnership of Vallejo to pass the 1999 Teen Party Ordinance. This ordinance authorizes the police department to recoup any costs associated with calls for service involving teenage parties where alcohol and illegal substances are used. Parents of teens are asked to repay the costs of the service calls for each reported incident. Copies of the ordinance and

box 4-5   FROM THE BENCH
Board of Education of Pottawatomie County v. Earls

Lindsay Earls, a 16-year-old girl, objected to her school's policy requiring warrantless random drug testing as a condition for any student to participate in any school-sponsored extracurricular activity. The school board believed that a drug problem existed in the school and that it was not limited to students involved in athletics. The U.S. Supreme Court, in a 5 to 4 decision, following its earlier ruling in *Vernonia* in 1995, cited the "special needs" of public schools that permit school searches without the traditional Fourth Amendment requirement of individualized suspicion prior to a search. The Court ruled that

A student's privacy interest is limited in a public school environment where the State is respon-

sible for maintaining discipline, health, and safety. Schoolchildren are routinely required to submit to physical examinations and vaccinations against disease. . . . [S]tudents who participate in competitive extracurricular activities voluntarily subject themselves to many of the same intrusions on their privacy as do athletes. Some of these clubs and activities require occasional off-campus travel and communal undress. All of them have their own rules and requirements for participating students that do not apply to the student body as a whole . . . . We therefore conclude that the students affected by this Policy have a limited expectation of privacy.

Source: Board of Education of Pottawatomie County v. Earls et al., 536 U.S. 822 (2002).

think
about it
Emile Durkheim viewed punishment as highly moral. How would Durkheim assess acquiescence in the drug war? Does society have an obligation to combat drug use and vice generally?

a pledge are mailed to the parents of all middle and high school students in the district. Parents are asked to sign the pledge, signifying that they will make their home a safe place for teens.[104]

Other jurisdictions have employed *police crackdowns,* short-term periods of intensive law enforcement, to target substance use, drug dealing, and delinquency among adolescents and young adults in some of the nation's most impoverished, crime-plagued neighborhoods. For example, the Philadelphia Police Department conducted *Operation Safe Streets* that entailed the use of 214 officers enforcing crime in the highest drug-activity street corners spanning the summers of 2000 and 2002. An evaluation by Brian Lawton and his colleagues reported that the crackdown did significantly reduce violent and drug crimes at the target sites.[105] Police crackdowns on drugs *do not* always have the expected effects. Samuel Nunn and his colleagues reported that a crackdown in the Brightwood neighborhood in Indianapolis resulted in reductions in all types of crime except drug-related calls for service.[106]

Education, Prevention, and Treatment

In 1884 New York state passed legislation to make anti-alcohol teaching compulsory in the public schools. Forty years later, Richmond Hobson, a leading prohibitionist, warned of "demonic drug pushers" seducing young children into drug addiction by such practices as hiding heroin in snow cones. Hobson eventually founded a number of national organizations for educating the public about the evils of drugs. Lectures and brochures were prepared and provided to hundreds of school systems for use during a week set aside in February as "Narcotics Week."[107] Henry Anslinger, director of the Federal Bureau of Narcotics, published a widely read article in 1937 titled "Marijuana: Assassin of Youth," in which he described murders, debauchery, and the seduction of innocent girls as a consequence of marijuana smoking. And in 1936 the movie *Reefer Madness,* depicting many of the same marijuana-induced behaviors, was produced under the Bureau's guidance. These efforts were attempts at "educating" the public, especially the young, about the dangers of drug use. However, in retrospect, they appear to have been little more than scare tactics, misinforming rather than informing.

Education and Prevention in School   Today, alongside law enforcement strategies, rational and informed education about the nature and effects of drugs is finding wide acceptance. Media campaigns—including cartoon characters, popular songs, and costumed actors who appear as talking brain cells—are aimed at young children. One example is the *Protecting You/Protecting Me* prevention program sponsored by Mothers Against Drunk Driving that targets children in grades one through five. Protecting You/Protecting Me helps reach children before they have fully shaped their attitudes and opinions about alcohol use, and by extension drug use. Students learn what commercials do and do not communicate about alcohol use, ways to resist peer pressure, how to talk to parents and friends about alcohol, how to make informed decisions, how to manage stress without alcohol, and other important life lessons about healthy, substance-free living. Evaluation studies indicated that children who participate in Protecting You/Protecting Me benefit across a variety of outcome measures and it is considered a model program by the U.S. Department of Health and Human Services and Center for Substance Abuse Prevention.[108]

Like the anti-alcohol provision of the 1884 New York law, anti-drug education has become a standard part of school curricula. Many schools offer "refusal-skill training" or "resistance training" to students through such programs as **Drug Abuse Resistance Education (D.A.R.E.),** begun in 1983. The D.A.R.E. program is aimed at children in kindergarten through 12th grade and is designed to equip students with appropriate skills to resist substance abuse and gangs. The objectives of D.A.R.E. include:

- Acquiring the knowledge and skills to recognize and resist peer pressure to experiment with tobacco, alcohol, and other drugs.
- Enhancing self-esteem.
- Learning assertiveness techniques.
- Learning about positive alternatives to substance use.
- Learning anger management and conflict resolution skills.
- Developing risk assessment and decision-making skills.
- Reducing violence.
- Building interpersonal and communication skills.
- Resisting gang involvement.[109]

School-based prevention programs often combine teaching about the negative consequences of drug use with clearly stated policies on use, possession, and distribution of drugs. Anne Arundel County schools in Maryland claim to have reduced the number of school drug offenses by more than 80 percent since 1980 after implementing their anti-drug program. They present a simple and straight-forward policy:

> Any student caught selling or distributing drugs is immediately expelled. When a student is caught using or possessing drugs, the school notifies the police, calls his parents, and suspends him for one to five school days. In order to return to school, the student must participate in counseling and agree to participate in the district's after-school drug program. Students caught using or possessing drugs a second time are expelled.[110]

However, such programs have been criticized for reducing the school drug problem by adding to the already high dropout problem. Numerous studies have found D.A.R.E. to have *no* significant impact on reducing drug use among students exposed to the program. Dennis Rosenbaum and Gordon Hanson conducted a six-year evaluation of D.A.R.E. and found it had no long-term effects in reducing drug use.[111] Susan Ennett and her colleagues also evaluated the D.A.R.E. program and concluded that, although there were modest positive short-term effects, overall the program appeared to have no effect on reducing alcohol or tobacco use compared to a control group.[112] Richard Clayton and his colleagues examined the impact of the D.A.R.E. program over a five-year period and also reported no significant difference in drug use between students in the D.A.R.E. program and a control group of students.[113]

Finally, Donald Lynam and his associates conducted a 10-year follow-up study of over 1,000 sixth-grade students who participated in Project D.A.R.E. during the 1987–1988 school year. These students were surveyed again 10 years later. There were no differences at age 20 between D.A.R.E. participants and students who did not participate in the program for use of alcohol, cigarettes, marijuana, and other illicit drugs. In addition, the researchers found no effect of the program on individuals' attitudes toward drug use. The only significant finding of difference was that youth at age 20 who received the D.A.R.E. program had lower self-esteem scores than students who did not receive D.A.R.E.[114] D.A.R.E. officials eventually admitted the program must be revised. With nearly $14 million in support from the Robert Wood Johnson Foundation, a revised program was launched in six cities in the fall of 2001. Major changes were intended to reduce the use of local police, while increasing lectures to students and involving youths in more active ways.

Drug Treatment Programs   Not all communities have adequate drug treatment programs, and where programs exist, the access for juveniles to existing drug treatment may depend on community sociodemographics and local public perceptions toward drug treatment. Yvonne Terry-McElrath and Duane McBride report that higher than average median income communities are less likely to use juvenile drug courts than less affluent communities and that more affluent communities were more likely to provide drug treatment for juvenile offenders as a part of traditional probation.[115] Today, there are well over 5,000 drug treatment programs in the United States. These programs fall into one of five categories:

1. *Detoxification programs,* which are usually conducted on an inpatient basis and are designed to end the user's addiction to drugs.

2. *Chemical dependency units,* which are generally inpatient programs, lasting three to four weeks.

3. *Outpatient clinics,* which offer counseling and support.

4. *Methadone maintenance programs,* in which heroin addicts are treated by means of methadone, a prescribed drug that "blocks" the craving for heroin.

5. *Residential therapeutic communities,* at which drug users may spend up to 18 months in a highly structured program.

In providing effective drug or alcohol treatment for juveniles, programs face an additional problem that stems from the issues of consent and parental notification. Most states allow treatment for drug abuse of youths without parental consent, although some states restrict services to treatment for either drug or alcohol abuse, but not both. Furthermore, a few states require that a youth's parents be notified before services are provided. Such requirements can interfere with a youth's perception of the acceptability of treatment: He or she may simply find it easier to avoid seeking care.[116]

Despite these problems, some drug treatment programs produce outstanding outcomes. The Life Skills Training program targets middle and high school students and consists of general self-management skills, social skills, and information and skills specifically related to drug use. Life Skills Training costs only $7 per student and has resulted in alcohol, marijuana, and tobacco reductions ranging from 50 to 75 percent. Other long-term evaluations indicated poly-drug use reductions of 66 percent and pack-a-day reductions of 25 percent.[117] Stanley Kusnetz has identified several programs that are working well for adolescents. Bridgeback is an outpatient program in Los Angeles. Youths come to Bridgeback as self-referrals or as referrals from schools, community agencies, or the juvenile court (about 80 percent of all referrals). The philosophy of Bridgeback is that a person learns from those with whom he or she identifies. Providing positive role models, the program also tries to help the adolescent search for and examine basic beliefs, attitudes, and habits.

The Bridge is a residential therapeutic center in Philadelphia. Its primary goal is to create an atmosphere in which clients will feel comfortable, develop peer relationships for support, take responsibility for themselves, and learn problem solving related to their personal lives. Even though nearly 50 percent of clients are referred by the juvenile court, self-referrals, family and school referrals, and referrals by other community agencies are common. Clients receive a minimum of 10 hours of therapy a week, with emphasis on developing awareness and life skills. Counseling is combined with an educational program that offers nearly 30 hours of classroom experience a week, as well as vocational guidance and job placement. The staff at the Bridge believe that adolescent drug users, with proper motivation and development of skills, can develop an appreciation of their personal worth, learn how to make decisions, set goals and accept consequences.[118] Overall, drug treatment programs that address the multiple needs (e.g., psychiatric problems, family problems, poverty) of youths offer the best chance for rehabilitation.[119]

Decriminalization

Critics of current drug control strategies argue that punitive measures will fail because profits from the sale of illegal drugs are too great and the pleasurable reinforcements of using drugs are too strong. Lester Thurow has stated, "If our goal is to deprive criminals of large profits from selling drugs, economic theory and history teaches us that legalization is the only answer."[120] Others have called for a national 10-year experiment in which cocaine, heroin, and marijuana would be *decriminalized*. If the experiment fails, the country could return to present policies that are viewed as being relatively ineffective.[121]

Essentially, **decriminalization** of some drugs involves relaxing enforcement of existing laws. For example, decriminalizing marijuana might mean that police would not make arrests for simple possession of small amounts of the drug. Possession of marijuana still technically would be illegal; the law would just not be enforced. **Legalization,** on the other hand, involves eliminating many of the laws currently prohibiting the distribution and possession of drugs, but not necessarily eliminating all regulation. Alcohol is legal, but it is regulated in terms of who may sell it, where it may be sold, and how old a person must be to buy it.

Advocates of decriminalization or legalization contend that an immediate consequence of the reform would be the production of less-expensive drugs, produced and sold under government regulations and control and in accordance with standardized quality control. In other words, decriminalized drugs would contain no surprise additives or contaminants and their lower cost would reduce potential black market profits, and thus the economic attractions of importing and dealing would be eliminated. In addition, advocates argue that many drugs currently criminalized are not as harmful as certain of the legal prescription drugs that are widely available.

think
about it

A point that is often lost in the incessant pro-drug/anti-drug dialogue is the message that would be sent by legalizing drugs. Would such a policy be an admission of defeat?

Critics of decriminalization or legalization are quick to point out that either decriminalizing or legalizing particular drugs would increase their use and abuse. If drugs such as marijuana and cocaine were inexpensive and readily available, adolescents who currently refrain from drug use would be drawn to drugs in large numbers. Evidence for this may be found in the Alaskan experience when the Alaska Supreme Court decriminalized small amounts of marijuana for personal use in 1975. Even though marijuana remained illegal for children, the perception that marijuana was harmful decreased, and marijuana use rates among Alaskan youths increased significantly. Recent national surveys have found increasing support for legalization of marijuana. In 2002 fully 34 percent of respondents indicated support for legalizing marijuana compared to only 24 percent in 1983. In addition, 80 percent supported the use of marijuana for medical purposes. On the other hand, a survey of voters by the Family Research Council found that 80 percent of respondents rejected the legalization of drugs like cocaine and heroin, with 70 percent indicating strong opposition.[122]

Erich Goode believes that it may not be possible to eliminate marijuana use through legal controls such as those used in the Netherlands. Furthermore, Goode argues against any decriminalization or legalization of drugs such as cocaine and crack. He claims that both are immensely pleasurable and, therefore, are strongly reinforcing drugs that have devastating personal consequences for the user.[123] In addition, James Inciardi and Duane McBride contend that policies to decriminalize drugs are elitist and racist because they would result in increasing levels of drug dependence in low income and minority communities: Decriminalization represents a program of social management and control that would serve to legitimate the chemical destruction of an urban generation and culture.[124]

Other critics of current drug policies argue for a *harm reduction* approach to the problem. **Harm reduction** involves using a public health model to reduce the risks and negative consequences of illicit drug use. A harm reduction approach is guided by the idea that it is more appropriate to *manage* drug abuse than to attempt to stop it entirely. Minimizing harm can include changing national drug policies and laws (for example, ending drug prohibition, reducing sanctions for drug violations, and changing drug paraphernalia laws), establishing needle and syringe exchange programs, expanding methadone treatment programs and establishing treatment on demand, and providing counseling programs that promote safer and more responsible drug use.[125] But if punitive measures do not work; if education, prevention, and treatment programs are only marginally effective; and if decriminalization could possibly add to the drug problem, how should society respond to adolescent drug use?

Changing Lives and Environments

When social scientists have studied adolescent problems, generally they have explored a specific problem such as delinquency, drug use, running away, or teenage pregnancy in isolation from the others. However, these adolescent problem behaviors may have a common origin.[126] Therefore, adolescent drug use and programs designed to respond to it cannot be studied apart from the larger social milieu in which the child develops. Most juveniles using cocaine and crack live in the inner cities where poverty, unemployment, homelessness, broken families, lack of hope, and a multitude of related problems are pervasive. In an attempt to stop adolescent drug use and delinquency before they start, several programs are focusing specifically on improving children's lives and environments. Some of the following examples provide overlapping services, but each clearly makes a difference.

Preschool education programs help reduce the risks of later school failure and frustration, which often lead to drug use. The Head Start program is one of the most effective early interventions for changing children's lives. Children who have participated in Head Start are less likely to become involved with drugs, be delinquent, quit school, or have unwanted pregnancies. In Missouri, the Parents As Teachers (PAT) program sends teachers into homes of preschoolers every six weeks to educate parents about each stage of the child's development. The PAT program is now included in the Harvard Family Research Project being conducted in five states to improve family support and education. Early evaluations indicate that PAT children have better problem-solving skills and language ability than children not in the program.

Strengthening the family can have immeasurably positive consequences in the lives of children, ranging from reducing conflict and abuse to improving communication, affection, and respect. In Tacoma, Homebuilders established a team of professionals with social work, psychology, and counseling backgrounds to provide services to any family deemed by juvenile justice, child welfare, or mental health agencies to be in imminent peril of having the child removed from the home. Through intensive interventions with the family and the use of community resources, the professionals help clients regain control over their lives. The TOGETHER! project in Lacey, Washington, targets drug abuse prevention to children and families living in low-income apartment complexes. TOGETHER! rents an apartment in each complex and offers after-school and summer programs promoting a drug-free climate for children through activities ranging from homework assistance and skills building to conflict resolution and peer pressure resistance training. Drug abuse information is disseminated to parents at family potluck dinners and informal coffee hours.

Health care for adolescents is critical for establishing a foundation for success. Programs such as WIC (a supplemental food program for women, infants, and children) and Children's House (an innovative pediatric and child care program in New Haven, Connecticut) provide needed nutrition plus a combination of comprehensive health care and family support. Follow-up evaluations of the Children's House program found significant positive effects for both children and their mothers. Only 28 percent of Children's House children suffered from serious school adjustment problems compared to nearly 70 percent of children in a control group.

Job training and placement are important in changing the lives of lower-class children who may often be tempted by the easy money to be had from selling drugs. One model job placement program is Jobs for Youth (JFY) in Chicago. Each year nearly 1,000 youths are placed in jobs after a careful screening process. Volunteers from the local business community help them prepare for job interviews, and the JFY staff members remain in contact with the youths during their first two years.[127] Only with a comprehensive, sustained and multifaceted approach can the cycle of juvenile delinquency and substance abuse be broken.[128]

conclusions

Drugs are widely used, and even though most drug use is legal, many adolescents are involved in the use of illicit drugs. Adolescent drug use is one of the most important problems facing children today. In spite of declines in reported drug use during much of the 1980s, juvenile drug use increased in the early 1990s, began to decline again, and then once again increased, at least for certain drugs.

Sociological theories suggest that the causes of adolescent drug use are varied. Strain theory blames drug use on the youth's failure to make it either in the legitimate or the illegitimate world. Social learning theory argues that adolescents learn to use drugs from peers much as they learn other forms of social behavior. According to social control theory, the weakening of social controls allows an adolescent to become involved with drugs. Subcultural socialization theories hold that involvement in a delinquent subculture in which drugs are used is likely to result in drug use by the youth.

How should society respond to adolescent drug use? A punitive or control response has emphasized the War on Drugs mentality as well as extensive anti-drug advertising and drug testing in schools. Education, prevention, and treatment responses have become very popular. Unfortunately, few school-based education and prevention programs, such as D.A.R.E., are effective, and treatment programs that do reduce drug use cannot meet the demands of the growing number of clients. Decriminalization or legalization of drugs raises many questions. Should all drugs be made legal and subject to regulation, or should only certain drugs be legalized? If the latter, which drugs? Would decriminalization or legalization of some drugs lead to greater use of those drugs by adolescents? Finally, attempts to change the lives and environments of children assume that drug use is only one facet of a larger, more complex milieu of social problems facing today's youth. Poverty, unemployment, homelessness, abuse, and lack of hope create an environment in which drug use, as well as other forms of delinquency, is likely to occur. However, possible solutions to these larger problems may be within reach. Among programs found to be effective are those ones that provide preschool education, prevent teenage pregnancy, and strengthen the family. The next section of this book will explore a variety of theories of juvenile delinquency, including ones explaining drug use.

key terms

30-day prevalence   The use of a drug at least once during the previous month.

Annual prevalence   The use of a drug at least once during the prior year.

Board of Education of Pottawatomie County v. Earls   The Supreme Court held that mandatory drug testing of students involved in any extracurricular activity was constitutional.

Comorbidity   The overlapping behavioral problems that mutually reinforce one another but ultimately stem from some other cause.

Decriminalization   Relaxing of the enforcement of certain laws, for example, drug laws.

Drug Abuse Resistance Education (D.A.R.E.)   A program aimed at children in kindergarten through 12th grade, designed to equip students with appropriate skills to resist substance abuse and gangs.

Harm reduction   Using a public health model to reduce the risks and negative consequences of drug use.

Legalization   The elimination of many laws currently prohibiting drugs, but not necessarily eliminating all regulation.

Lifetime prevalence   The use of a drug at least once during the respondent's lifetime.

section 2

Explaining Delinquency

IN SECTION 2 theories of delinquency that have guided scholarship and policy development during the 20th and 21st centuries are discussed. Some of the theories are specific to juveniles while others apply to both children and adults. To help guide your reading, the major idea of each group of theories and its juvenile justice policy applications are summarized in the table at the end of this introduction.

In Chapter 5, individual theories of delinquency are reviewed. These theories reject the idea that the environment is entirely responsible for behavior and instead blame delinquency either on free will or on personal traits such as personality, temperament, genetics, brain chemistry, and so on. We have dichotomized individual theories into *choice* and *trait* explanations. Choice theories stem from the Classical School of Criminology and emphasize an individual's ability to make choices. Trait theories can be traced to the disciplines of biology and psychology that are part of the Positive School of Criminology. They attribute delinquency to individual traits that the child has little or no control over. Once, choice and trait explanation were viewed as the "opposite" of sociological theories that use environmental factors to explain crime. Today, individual and environmental theories of delinquency are viewed as complementary, not competing. Now, criminologists increasingly argue that nature *and* nurture, rather than nature *or* nurture, explain delinquency.

Chapter 6 examines sociological theories, such as cultural deviance, strain, and social control. These theories look at how the child's environment influences his or her behavior. Cultural deviance theories examine a child's interactions with social, cultural, and ecological factors that lead to delinquency; strain theories evaluate the role of a variety of stressors, including blocked

(continued)

opportunities that may push children into delinquency; and social control explanations of delinquency study how closely bonded or connected children are to family, peers, and the school.

Critical theories are discussed in Chapter 7. Two perspectives are represented, labeling and conflict theories. Labeling theories attribute delinquency to the interactions between individuals and other people or groups. The unequal distribution of the power to define behaviors as delinquent, the inability of some youths to resist the application of stigmatizing labels, and the process by which juveniles may move from unwitting or spontaneous acts to behavior associated with more organized social roles and delinquent identities are among the concerns explored by these theories. Conflict theories assess the relationship among economic, social, and political factors and how they interact to produce delinquency.

Chapter 8 focuses on developmental or life-course theories of delinquency. These theories draw on earlier schools of criminological thought by integrating the strongest elements of them, such as social control and social learning. Developmental theories also focus on protective factors and risk factors associated with changes in behavior as people mature, conceptualizing delinquency as a pattern of behavior rather than a discrete event. Because of their human development approach, developmental theories have been explicitly linked with public policies, such as prevention, that result in many positive outcomes.

Female delinquency theories are discussed in Chapter 9. A significant criminological reality is that nearly all theories of delinquency have been built around patterns of male delinquency and may not necessarily apply well when trying to explain why girls commit crime. After a brief examination of the development of female gender roles and identities, the chapter discusses biological and developmental theories, sociological theories, critical and feminist theories, and differential oppression theory in terms of their relevance and applicability to female delinquency ●

Overview of Criminology Theories and Their Policy Applications

THEORY*	MAJOR PREMISE	POLICY APPLICATION†
Choice Theory		
Classical and neoclassical (5)	Children commit crimes because they anticipate more benefits from violating the law than from conformity.	Fixed-time sentences, shock probation, boot camps
Trait Theory		
Biological theories (5)	Crime is caused by a biological deficiency *inside* the offender.	Segregation; sterilization
Psychodynamic theory (5)	Crime is caused by an overdeveloped or underdeveloped superego.	Psychotherapy or aversion therapy
Behavioral theory (5)	Criminal behavior is learned.	Token economies
Cultural deviance theory (6)	Crime is caused by disorganized neighborhoods.	Chicago Area Project
Strain theory (6)	Crime is caused by society telling children what to seek without providing the means.	Project Head Start
Social control theory (6)	Weak bonds between child and conventional others leads to delinquency.	Police Athletic League
Critical Theory		
Labeling theory (7)	Crime is caused by societal reactions to behavior.	Diversion programs; decriminalization of offenses
Conflict theory (7)	Crime is caused by imbalances in power.	Programs that equalize power, such as Project Head Start
Developmental Theory (8)	Crime is caused by many cumulative factors that vary from childhood to early adulthood.	Age-appropriate interventions, interrupting cycle of crime
Female Delinquency Theory (9)	Crime is caused by a patriarchal social structure that differently defines and responds to crime among girls.	Programs to reduce family and sexual violence and programs that equalize power between gender groups

* The chapter in which each theory is discussed is shown in parentheses.

† Social policies often derive from multiple theories. For example, the objectives of Project Head Start are to reduce strain and to make relations among children more equal. Its origin can be traced to both strain and conflict theories.

Individual Theories of Delinquency: Choice and Trait Explanations

The study of juvenile delinquency spans more than 200 years. Criminologists have constructed **theories** or integrated sets of ideas to explain and predict *when* and *why* children will commit crime. Many theories are discussed in this chapter and the following three chapters because *ideas have consequences.* You will notice that *different* theories lead to *different* policy recommendations. How a theory explains delinquency determines what social policies will be suggested to prevent it. Criminologists, for example, who think delinquency is rooted in faulty brain chemistry, may suggest drug therapy as a remedy. Alternatively, criminologists who believe delinquency is caused by economic deprivation may call for prevention policies aimed at providing equal access to legitimate opportunities.

WHAT THEORIES ARE

Theories are ideas criminologists use to explain facts. They represent the views of experts who live in a particular place at a particular time. Because theories are based on real-life experiences, as societies change so do the experiences of its citizens. New experiences generate new ideas that lead to new theories. While there are many theories to choose from, some theories are better than others. Theories are evaluated on the basis of three criteria: (1) simplicity, (2) testability, and (3) empirical validity. Each criterion forms its own continuum. A theory can be very strong on one or more of the criteria and weak on others.

Theories may be very complex or quite simple. A good theory effectively summarizes many separate observations into an easily understood statement. Simplicity is a virtue because the purpose of theory is to reduce a large body of information into a few simple laws, as the theories of Newton and Einstein did in physics.

A good theory is testable. Others must be able to refute or verify it. A good theory also makes clear and concise predictions that (1) confirm or modify the theory, (2) expand the parameters of the theory, and (3) have practical application. Some theories are not testable because their main concepts are unclear, not measurable, or both. For example, in Edwin Sutherland's *theory of differential association* (see Chapter 6) the concept of "differential association" cannot be verified because no one can monitor all of the interactions of a juvenile over an extended period of time.

If a theory is simple and testable, then a third feature to look for is whether it is supported by scientific evidence. Do research findings support the theory and its predictions? Some theories give rise to many predictions, and research tests could be carried out in many different settings and with many different samples and research methods.

Next, specific theories are discussed. Since there is *no* perfect theory, our goal is to provide you with a thoughtful, carefully crafted, and objective analysis of the most current literature, free of discipline jargon, so you may make an informed decision about what theory is best. Our discussion begins with **individual theories,** which blame delinquency on either free will or personal traits such as temperament, genetics, and brain chemistry. These theories reject the idea the environment plays an exclusive or primary role in the onset of delinquency.

Theories rooted in individual differences have a very long and steady history. They are more popular today than they have been for a long time. There are two types of individual theories: choice theories and trait theories. *Choice theories* can be traced to the Classical School of Criminology that emerged in the 18th century. They assume that children have free will and are rational and intelligent people who make informed decisions to commit crime based on whether they will benefit from doing so. *Trait theories* can be traced to the writings of Charles Darwin whose ideas in the 19th century gave rise to the Positive School of Criminology. These theories lay the blame for delinquency on biological, psychological, and biosocial factors over which children have very little control, such as defective brain chemistry, hyperactivity, or a disturbed personality.

CHOICE THEORY

Return for a moment to the opening photo for this chapter. It shows the damage caused by 15-year-old Charles Bishop who committed suicide by crashing his stolen plane into a building in Tampa, Florida. Bishop left a suicide note expressing support for Osama Bin Laden and the terrorist attacks on the United States. What does this event suggest about the rationality of people who commit crime? Do rational people smash into buildings with airplanes? Do they exercise free will? Are they intelligent? Do they seek to maximize pleasure and minimize pain? If you answered yes to these questions, you likely will agree with the causes of crime expressed in choice theories from the **Classical School** of Criminology. These theories state that juveniles are rational, intelligent people who have **free will** or the ability to make choices. Young people calculate the

Most delinquent acts are minor offenses. When young people commit these crimes, do they weigh the costs and benefits of their action before they act? Could crimes such as shoplifting be prevented by increasing punishment?

costs and benefits of their behavior *before* they act. Crime is the result of their imagining greater gains coming from breaking the law than from obeying it. In the same way, children who skip school first determine the likelihood of getting caught against the potential fun they will have. Similarly, juveniles who commit serious crime weigh the pleasure they imagine they will receive against being arrested, prosecuted, convicted, and sent to prison. Since behavior is a conscious decision children make, they may be held responsible for their choices and their consequences.

Cesare Beccaria

A leading figure of the Classical School was Cesare Beccaria who formulated his ideas about crime control during the 18th century when the criminal justice systems throughout Europe were cruel and ruthless and exercised a callous indifference for human rights. People were punished for crimes against religion, such as atheism and witchcraft, and for crimes against the state, such as criticizing political leaders. Worse yet, "offenders" were rarely told why they were punished. No one was exempt; any person could be hauled off to jail any time for any reason. Wealthy persons were generally spared the most torturous and degrading punishments, which were reserved for ordinary citizens who sometimes were burnt alive, whipped, mutilated, or branded.[1]

These conditions inspired Beccaria to write an essay titled, *On Crimes and Punishments,* in which he laid the framework for a new system of justice that emphasized humanity, consistency, and rationality. According to Beccaria:

1. Social action should be based on the utilitarian principle of the *greatest happiness for the greatest number.*
2. Crime is an injury to society, and the only rational measure of crime is the extent of the injury.
3. Crime prevention is more important than punishment. Laws must be published so that the citizenry can understand and support them.
4. In criminal procedure, secret accusations and torture must be abolished. *There should be speedy trials, and accused persons should have every right to present evidence in their defense.*
5. The purpose of punishment is to prevent crime. Punishment must be *swift, certain,* and *severe.* Penalties must be based on the social damage caused by the crime. *There should be no capital punishment.* Life imprisonment is a better deterrent. Capital punishment is irreparable and makes no provision for mistakes.
6. Imprisonment should be widely used, but prison conditions should be improved through better physical quarters and by separating and classifying inmates as to age, sex, and criminal histories.[2]

On Crimes and Punishment has become one of the most influential essays ever written. It was the basis for the 1791 criminal code of France and for salient ideas found in the United States Constitution such as (1) people are innocent until proven guilty, (2) people cannot be forced to testify against themselves, (3) people have the right to counsel and to confront their accusers, and (4) people have the right to a speedy trial by a jury of their peers.

---

theory in a nutshell

Cesare Beccaria

Beccaria believed that people were rational and intelligent beings who exercised free will. They commit crime because they imagine greater gains coming from crime than from conformity. For punishment to be effective, it must be certain, severe, and administered swiftly.

Jeremy Bentham

A second pioneer in the reform of criminal justice in the 18th century was the English economist Jeremy Bentham, who believed that *people seek pleasure and avoid pain*. Bentham's view was that the "best" punishment was one that produced more pain than the pleasure the offender received from committing the crime. Punishment, in other words, must "fit the crime," and no single punishment was always best; rather a variety of punishments should be used.

> ### theory in a nutshell
> #### Jeremy Bentham
> Bentham argued that the purpose of criminal law was to provide for the "greatest happiness for the greatest number" of people. He also proposed that the "punishment must fit the crime" and that no single punishment was always best.

Bentham's ideas radically transformed the 19th-century English penal code, called "The Bloody Code," because people were executed for harmless and minor offenses such as stealing turnips, associating with gypsies, and damaging fish ponds. Between 1820 and 1861, the number of capital crimes in the Code was reduced from 222 to 3 (murder, treason, and piracy) largely because of Bentham's work.[3]

think
about it

Bentham suggested that the punishment should fit the crime. Does the criminal justice system in the United States do this for serious felonies? Should legal condemnation and punishment match the barbarity of certain crimes?

The Neoclassical School

In spite of its good intentions, the Classical School ultimately failed because of its own rigidity. Its major weakness was not taking into account *why* people committed crime, only that they did. Their theories held *all* people equally responsible for their behavior. Those who committed similar crimes received comparable punishments, regardless of why the crime was committed. In other words, the Classical School focused on the criminal *act* and not the criminal *actor*. Yet, in reality, people are different. Young children, the insane, and the incompetent are not as responsible for their behavior as adults, the sane, and the competent. The idea that there are real differences among people led to the creation of the Neoclassical School.

Social reformers of the **Neoclassical School** were sympathetic to what the Classical School wanted to achieve. They agreed that people were rational, intelligent beings who exercised free will. However, they also thought some crimes were caused by factors beyond the offender's control. **Mitigating circumstances,** or factors such as age or mental disease, might influence the choices people make and affect a person's ability to form criminal intent or *mens rea* (guilty mind). This is why today, children under age 7 cannot *legally* commit a crime—they are believed to be incapable of having a guilty mind.[4]

The introduction of mitigating circumstances at criminal trials gave rise to the principle of **individual justice,** the idea that criminal law *must* reflect differences among people and their circumstances. Individual justice produced a series of important developments including the insanity defense and the inclusion of expert witnesses; perhaps most important, it was the cornerstone for a new explanation of crime that blamed delinquency on individual traits or characteristics that were in place *before* the act was committed. The foundation of this new way of thinking about crime was *scientific determinism*, which depended on the scientific method to explain crime and was the focus of the Positive School of Criminology. These theories are discussed later in this chapter and in Chapters 6, 7, and 8.

Where Does the Modern Classical School Theory Fit In?

In the 1960s criminologists started to question the effectiveness of rehabilitation. A flurry of evaluation studies of rehabilitation programs concluded that *some* treatment works *some* of the time for *some* offenders in *some* settings.[5] This unconvincing endorsement of the rehabilitation model led to the proposal that criminals need to be punished. One advocate of this change was James Q. Wilson, who said:

> Wicked people exist. Nothing avails except to set them apart from innocent people. And many people, neither wicked nor innocent, but watchful, dissembling, and calculating of their chances, ponder our reaction to wickedness as a clue to what they might profitably do.[6]

In this view, the reason to punish crime is that if crime is not punished, people "on the fence" will think crime pays and possibly commit it.

About the same time other criminologists were busy constructing "new" theories. Ronald Clarke and Derek Cornish introduced **rational choice theory**, in which they charged that delinquents are rational people who make calculated choices regarding what they are going to do *before* they act. Offenders collect, process, and evaluate information about the crime and make a decision whether to commit it after they have weighed the costs and benefits of doing so. Crime represents a well thought-out decision. Offenders decide where to commit it, who or what to target, and how to execute it.[7]

Research has found that many offenders *do* select a specific location to commit crime. Bruce Jacobs has reported that crack cocaine street dealers like to operate in the middle of a long block because they can see everything in both directions.[8] It also has been reported that offenders pick their crime targets only *after* they study the behavior of potential victims.[9] Criminals also learn how to avoid arrest. Successful crack cocaine dealers, for instance, know where to hide drugs on their person, on the street, and at home.[10]

A similar explanation is the theory advanced by Lawrence Cohen and Marcus Felson. Their **routine activities theory** examines the crime target or whatever it is the offender wants to take control of, whether it is a house to break into, a bottle of beer, merchandise from a department store, or illegally downloading music off the Internet. Cohen and Felson argue that before a crime will be committed three elements must converge: (1) motivated offenders, (2) suitable targets, and (3) an absence of people to deter the would-be offender.[11] Crime therefore increases when there are vulnerable targets (e.g., keys left in the ignition) and only a few people to protect them (e.g., police).[12]

There are two problems with rational choice and routine activity theories. They (1) do not identify factors that motivate offenders to commit crime and (2) overlook factors that cause the criminalization of some behavior (smoking marijuana) and not other behavior (drinking alcohol).[13] Nonetheless, both theories force us to recognize that *every crime is a unique event*. Crime may have as much to do with situational factors and free will as it does with the offender's psychology.

MONEY

SEX

DRUGS

PRESTIGE

CONCERN ABOUT CRIME

Mike Keefe '93

Source: Mike Keefe. Used with permission from dePIXion Studios, Inc.

Are Offenders Rational?   Are offenders rational? Do rational people murder their friends? Do they stab to death a 10-year-old child walking home from school? Do they drop a playmate from a 14th-floor window because he would not steal candy?[14] Juveniles committed each of these crimes. Research on whether offenders are rational has produced mixed results. Studies have found that street criminals, prostitutes, thieves, drug dealers and users, burglars, robbers, serial killers, and rapists do calculate the risks of getting caught. Gang leaders have been reported to be rational decision makers when they are determining who their enemies are, what business deals to make, the likelihood of being caught, and how to recruit new members. However, others who commit the same offenses have been found to exercise less rationality than might be expected.[15] Kenneth Tunnell studied the motivations of chronic property offenders and concluded:

1.   They do not consider the legal consequences of their behavior.
2.   They focus on rewards and not risks, believing they will not get caught.
3.   They do not consider the law, arrest, or imprisonment.[16]

Ronald Akers suggests that the concept of rationality is itself problematic. If to be rational means to have full and accurate access to *all* potential outcomes of behavior, classical theories are unrealistic because such predictable situations do not exist. If to be rational means to make a decision based on the available information, then offenders certainly have "limited rationality." With limited rationality, the emphasis upon free will and autonomy, which is the cornerstone of the classical argument, is lost.[17] The information that is available may be faulty or the individual's assessment of the situation may be incorrect. People may not be as free to rationally choose between alternative courses of action as these theories suggest.

Are Crimes Rational? Are Offenders Amoral?   Under some circumstances, predatory crimes like robbery are rational. However, what about bizarre crimes such as personal crimes of violence? Are these crimes rational? It is tempting to blame them on biological impulses and psychological delusions. Violence, however, may be rational in circumstances where offenders believe it will produce desired rewards. When rival gangs fight, the reward is reputation. Boyfriends assault girlfriends to win arguments. Children murder classmates to stop being bullied. To put it differently, *some* juveniles *some* of the time in *some* situations may see violence as an effective way to get what they want.[18]

Another reason why some juveniles make some bad choices is their lack of morality and not whether they are rational. James Q. Wilson thinks juveniles who behave badly do so because they have not had a sense of morality instilled into them:

> The moral relativism of the modern age has probably contributed to the increase in crime rates. . . . It has done so by replacing the belief in personal responsibility with the notion of social causation and by supplying to those marginal persons at risk for crime a justification for doing what they might have done anyway.[19]

Psychologist Hans Eysenck, who blames juvenile violence on parental and societal permissiveness, agrees. According to Eysenck, how young people are reared today has produced a serious problem: They have not developed a conscience because they have not been taught to connect their misbehavior with a negative outcome. Delinquency is the price we pay for society and parents who are not doing their job.[20]

Choice Theory and Delinquency Prevention

Choice theories aim to prevent delinquency in one of two ways; either through the *justice model* or the *utilitarian punishment model*. Both models hold children responsible for their behavior. They both assume children are rational, intelligent beings who exercise free will. Children calculate whether to commit crime based on the rewards and punishments they imagine they will receive *before* they act. The models differ on the reasons why they punish. The justice model punishes offenders because of the social harm they have caused; the utilitarian punishment model punishes offenders to protect society.

The Justice Model   In *We Are the Living Proof* David Fogel introduced the **justice model,** an idea that promoted imposing fixed-time sentences, abolishing parole, and using prisons to punish offenders. Fogel argued that **indeterminate sentences** or sentences of varying time lengths (5 to 10 years, for example), should be abolished and replaced with **determinate sentences** or sentences with a fixed amount of time, because the courts cannot discriminate between offenders who can be reformed from those who cannot. A more fair system would be one where people who committed similar crimes received equivalent punishments.

Fogel's thinking is grounded in **retribution**, the idea that cr[...] punished because of the social harm they have caused. *Punishment* [...] *desert.* Underlying retributive philosophy is that punishment be based [...] riousness of the crime and culpability of the offender. In addition, when s[...] ing offenders, it is wrong to consider their needs. Sentences should only re[...] the penalties criminals deserve for breaking the law.[21]

Critics complain that Fogel's remedies pander to a correctional policy of despair rather than one of hope. There also is not much empirical support that the justice model leads to a more humane and impartial criminal justice system. To the contrary, some state legislatures have established determinant or fixed-time sentences as a way to create more punitive sentences.[22]

The Utilitarian Punishment Model   At the core of the **utilitarian punishment model** is the idea that offenders must be punished to protect society. According to Ernest van den Haag:

> If a given offender's offenses are rational in the situation in which he lives—if what he can gain exceeds the likely cost to him by more than the gain from legitimate activities he does—there is little that can be "corrected" in the offender. Reform will fail. It often fails for this reason. What has to be changed is not the personality of the offender, but the cost–benefit ratio which makes his offense rational. The ratio can be changed by improving and multiplying his opportunities for legitimate activity and the benefits they yield, or by decreasing this opportunity for illegitimate activities, or by increasing their cost to him, including punishment.[23]

In van den Haag's opinion, punishment *deters* crime. If he is right, then it should be possible to prevent crime by punishing offenders more severely. Support for

Boot camps employ grueling mental and physical regiments in an effort to instill discipline and self-worth in young offenders. Do boot camps work? In what ways does the effectiveness of boot camps matter to the general public? What is the allure of get-tough responses to delinquency?

delinquency

...a has steadily increased in popularity, based on research findings pub-
...by criminologists who calculated the risk of *actual* time served for each
...index offense. For a person who commits a crime, the likelihood of serv-
...on time is very, very low; however, as time served has increased, the
...te has dropped (see Box 5-1).

...nals must be
...*is their just*
...on the se-
...ntenc-
...fect

---

box 5-1   **DELINQUENCY PREVENTION**

Does Crime Pay?

One proposal for preventing delinquency is to increase the punishment received for committing crime. This is the recommendation of Classical School criminologists who believe people weigh the costs and benefits of committing crime before they act. The juvenile crime rate is high because, for many people, the benefits of committing crime outweigh the costs or even the likelihood of incurring costs.

One way to measure the "cost of crime" is to estimate the *actual punishment* received, which can be calculated by multiplying the following probabilities:

- Being arrested for a crime after it is committed.
- Being prosecuted if arrested.
- Being convicted if prosecuted.
- Going to prison if convicted.

The product of this calculation is then multiplied by the median time served for an offense. Consider the crime of burglary.

- For every 100 burglaries committed, about 50 will be reported to the police.
- Data from the Federal Bureau of Investigation show that about 13.8 percent of all reported burglaries will be cleared by arrest, or about 6.9 burglaries of the 50 reported.
- About 9 out of every 10 arrests for burglary will be prosecuted, or 6.2 out of 6.9.
- Two-thirds of the resulting 6.2 prosecutions will result in felony convictions, or

4.2 felony convictions out of every 100 burglaries.

- Of these convictions, 1.9 felons will be sent to prison, while the remaining 2.3 will receive some combination of probation, fines, or jail time.
- The overall probability of doing any prison time for burglary is 1.9 percent.

Once in prison, a burglar will stay there for a median time of about 18.5 months. An estimated 1.7 of every 100 burglaries reported to the police resulted in prison time, so the median prison term per act of burglary in only 9.4 days (1.7 percent × 18.5 months × 30 days per month). This expectation of prison time per crime is, of course, heavily influenced by the chances of getting caught. However, on the average, a rational, risk-neutral criminal should find burglary profitable so long as what is stolen is worth more than nine days in prison. In addition, researchers have found that crime provides human, social, and personal capital to offenders with the ambition and motivation to be successful criminals. For them, the perception truly is that crime does pay.

Sources: Carlo Morselli and Pierre Tremblay, "Criminal Achievement, Offender Networks, and the Benefits of Low Self-Control," *Criminology* 42:773–804 (2004); Bill McCarthy and John Hagan, "When Crime Pays: Capital, Competence, and Criminal Success," *Social Forces* 79:1035–1059 (2001); Morgan Reynolds, "Why Does Crime Pay?" (Dallas: The National Center for Policy Analysis, 1992); Morgan Reynolds, *Does Punishment Deter?* (Dallas: National Center for Policy Analysis, 1998); Morgan Reynolds, *Crime and Punishment in America: 1999* (Dallas: National Center for Policy Analysis, 2000).

Fogel's thinking is grounded in **retribution,** the idea that criminals must be punished because of the social harm they have caused. *Punishment is their just desert.* Underlying retributive philosophy is that punishment be based on the seriousness of the crime and culpability of the offender. In addition, when sentencing offenders, it is wrong to consider their needs. Sentences should only reflect the penalties criminals deserve for breaking the law.[21]

Critics complain that Fogel's remedies pander to a correctional policy of despair rather than one of hope. There also is not much empirical support that the justice model leads to a more humane and impartial criminal justice system. To the contrary, some state legislatures have established determinant or fixed-time sentences as a way to create more punitive sentences.[22]

The Utilitarian Punishment Model   At the core of the **utilitarian punishment model** is the idea that offenders must be punished to protect society. According to Ernest van den Haag:

> If a given offender's offenses are rational in the situation in which he lives—if what he can gain exceeds the likely cost to him by more than the gain from legitimate activities he does—there is little that can be "corrected" in the offender. Reform will fail. It often fails for this reason. What has to be changed is not the personality of the offender, but the cost–benefit ratio which makes his offense rational. The ratio can be changed by improving and multiplying his opportunities for legitimate activity and the benefits they yield, or by decreasing this opportunity for illegitimate activities, or by increasing their cost to him, including punishment.[23]

In van den Haag's opinion, punishment *deters* crime. If he is right, then it should be possible to prevent crime by punishing offenders more severely. Support for

Boot camps employ grueling mental and physical regiments in an effort to instill discipline and self-worth in young offenders. Do boot camps work? In what ways does the effectiveness of boot camps matter to the general public? What is the allure of get-tough responses to delinquency?

this idea has steadily increased in popularity, based on research findings published by criminologists who calculated the risk of *actual* time served for each Crime Index offense. For a person who commits a crime, the likelihood of serving prison time is very, very low; however, as time served has increased, the crime rate has dropped (see Box 5-1).

---

box 5-1   DELINQUENCY PREVENTION

Does Crime Pay?

One proposal for preventing delinquency is to increase the punishment received for committing crime. This is the recommendation of Classical School criminologists who believe people weigh the costs and benefits of committing crime before they act. The juvenile crime rate is high because, for many people, the benefits of committing crime outweigh the costs or even the likelihood of incurring costs.

One way to measure the "cost of crime" is to estimate the *actual punishment* received, which can be calculated by multiplying the following probabilities:

- Being arrested for a crime after it is committed.
- Being prosecuted if arrested.
- Being convicted if prosecuted.
- Going to prison if convicted.

The product of this calculation is then multiplied by the median time served for an offense. Consider the crime of burglary.

- For every 100 burglaries committed, about 50 will be reported to the police.
- Data from the Federal Bureau of Investigation show that about 13.8 percent of all reported burglaries will be cleared by arrest, or about 6.9 burglaries of the 50 reported.
- About 9 out of every 10 arrests for burglary will be prosecuted, or 6.2 out of 6.9.
- Two-thirds of the resulting 6.2 prosecutions will result in felony convictions, or

4.2 felony convictions out of every 100 burglaries.

- Of these convictions, 1.9 felons will be sent to prison, while the remaining 2.3 will receive some combination of probation, fines, or jail time.
- The overall probability of doing any prison time for burglary is 1.9 percent.

Once in prison, a burglar will stay there for a median time of about 18.5 months. An estimated 1.7 of every 100 burglaries reported to the police resulted in prison time, so the median prison term per act of burglary in only 9.4 days (1.7 percent × 18.5 months × 30 days per month). This expectation of prison time per crime is, of course, heavily influenced by the chances of getting caught. However, on the average, a rational, risk-neutral criminal should find burglary profitable so long as what is stolen is worth more than nine days in prison. In addition, researchers have found that crime provides human, social, and personal capital to offenders with the ambition and motivation to be successful criminals. For them, the perception truly is that crime does pay.

Sources: Carlo Morselli and Pierre Tremblay, "Criminal Achievement, Offender Networks, and the Benefits of Low Self-Control," *Criminology* 42:773–804 (2004); Bill McCarthy and John Hagan, "When Crime Pays: Capital, Competence, and Criminal Success," *Social Forces* 79:1035–1059 (2001); Morgan Reynolds, "Why Does Crime Pay?" (Dallas: The National Center for Policy Analysis, 1992); Morgan Reynolds, *Does Punishment Deter?* (Dallas: National Center for Policy Analysis, 1998); Morgan Reynolds, *Crime and Punishment in America: 1999* (Dallas: National Center for Policy Analysis, 2000).

think
about it
Boot camp instructors
use physical coercion,
verbal abuse, and
harsh discipline
to help delinquent
youths understand the
consequences of their
misdeeds. How does this
harsh approach reconcile
with neoclassical
thought?

Several delinquency prevention programs are based on the utilitarian punishment model. In *shock probation,* offenders experience fear through a short period of incarceration preceding probation. In *boot camps,* offenders are drilled and tormented for 60 to 90 days. In *Scared Straight,* juveniles attend presentations at adult prisons where hardened convicts and inmates serving life sentences yell and scream threats of assault and rape at them, letting them know what will happen if they come to prison. Research evaluating the effectiveness of these programs has generally found they are not very successful at deterring chronic juvenile offenders (see Chapter 15).[24] In fact, instead of controlling crime, they tend to increase it. Anthony Petrosino and his colleagues conducted a systematic review of Scared Straight programs and found that youths who went through the program had higher rates of offending than youths who did not. In their words, "on average these programs result in an increase in criminality in the experimental group when compared to a no-treatment control. According to these experiments, doing nothing would have been better than exposing juveniles to the program."[25]

TRAIT THEORY

If *choice theory* is correct, juveniles weigh the cost and benefits of committing crime *before* they act. Children who sell drugs, for instance, do so because they believe they will make a profit and get away with it. If caught, they believe that they will not be prosecuted, and if they are prosecuted, not punished too severely. In contrast, *trait theories,* which are rooted in the biological and medical sciences, contend juveniles commit crimes because of particular traits, characteristics, deficits, or psychopathologies that they possess.

Early theories of delinquency were crude, deterministic, and were implicated in dubious, even diabolical social policies, such as eugenics (see Box 5-2). These dark moments in criminology created considerable distaste for perspectives that attempt to explain crime by focusing on the individual traits of criminal offenders. Instead, environmental accounts of delinquency, such as those advanced by sociologists, predominated. Most theories discussed in this text are sociological in scope because criminology is dominated by the sociological perspective. Unfortunately, a consequence of this is that many sociologists have limited understanding of biological explanations of human behavior.[26] In fact, in his presidential address to the American Sociological Association, Douglas Massey advised:

> Somehow we have allowed the fact that we are social beings to obscure the biological foundation upon which our behavior ultimately rests. Most sociologists are woefully ignorant of even the most elementary precepts of biological science. If we think about biology at all, it is usually in terms of discredited eugenic arguments and crude evolutionary theorizing long since discarded in the natural sciences.[27]

This chapter examines several trait theories of delinquency. These theories range from relatively crude attempts to typify delinquents as subhuman to explanations suggesting defective personalities. Over time, these approaches evolved from deterministic, simple notions of human behavior to multidisciplinary

box 5-2   A WINDOW ON DELINQUENCY
The Dark History of Biological Criminology

Francis Galton coined the term *eugenics* to describe the science of improving the human race through better breeding. According to eugenicists, an inherited substance in the blood called "germ plasma" that is present at conception determines *all* of an individual's mental, moral, and physical characteristics. The moment someone commits a crime that fact is encoded in their blood and is transmitted to their offspring. In 1877, Richard Dugdale used this idea to study intelligence and deviancy. In *The Jukes,* he located more than 1,000 descendants of Ada Jukes and found they included 140 criminals, 280 paupers, 40 people with venereal disease, and assorted other deviant types. Dugdale concluded that the Jukes suffered from "degeneracy and innate depravity." In *The Kallikak Family,* Henry Goddard traced the descendants of Martin Kallikak, who "had two lines of progeny, one from a 'feebleminded' barmaid and the other from a 'respectable' girl of a good family." The illegitimate union produced many paupers, criminals, alcoholics, and mentally deficient people, while there were few of these types found among descendants of the legitimate union.

Eugenics remained popular in the early 20th century. It had become so much a part of the American landscape that laws were passed making it illegal for African Americans and whites and for Asian Americans and whites to marry. In 1922 and 1924 federal laws were passed to restrict the immigration of southern and eastern Europeans into the United States. Large numbers of the "inferior" people who already lived in the United States were institutionalized and sterilized. In 1907 Indiana passed the first sterilization law, with Connecticut following soon after. In total, 33 states passed laws prescribing the compulsory sterilization of the feebleminded, mentally ill, and chronic criminal offenders. In spite of these statutes, sterilization did not gain widespread acceptance in the United States until the 1920s. In 1927 the U.S. Supreme Court ruled in *Buck v. Bell* that sterilization laws were constitutional. Borrowing from the Court's reasoning in *Buck,* the German Nazi government passed legislation that provided the legal basis for sterilizing at least 350,000 people. The second Supreme Court case involved an Oklahoma law that prescribed the involuntary sexual sterilization of chronic criminal offenders. In 1942 in *Skinner v. Oklahoma,* the Court ruled that involuntarily sexual sterilization of criminals was unconstitutional. With such a dark history, it is easy to understand why biological approaches to criminology are at times controversial.

Sources: Richard Dugdale, *The Jukes* (New York: Putnam, 1877); Henry Goddard, *The Kallikak Family* (New York: Macmillan, 1912); *Buck v. Bell,* 274 U. S. 200 (1927); *Skinner v. Oklahoma,* 316 U. S. 535 (1942).

research that centers on the importance of traits, environments, and the interaction between traits and environments.

Biological Theories

The idea that criminals are abnormal is very old. It can be traced to the Positive School of Criminology, which marked a shift in thinking about crime from the *act* to the *actor*. Charles Darwin was largely responsible for this change. In *On the Origin of Species*, he argued that God had not created *all* the species of animals and that people had evolved from lower forms of life over millions of years. Then, in *Descent of Man,* Darwin proposed that (1) God had not made people in his own image and (2) there were very few differences between people and animals. Darwin's ideas captured the attention of 19th-century criminologists who called themselves *Positivists* because they believed using the scientific method was the best way to study crime. These scholars formed the **Positive School** of Criminology. They attributed crime to factors that were in place *before* the crime was committed, and they believed that it was their job to discover what the factors were. Contrary to choice theory, in trait theory explanations, free will has nothing to do with why people commit crime; crime is caused by an antecedent condition that precedes the act. The first trait theories were rooted in the offender's biology.

Atavism   The Italian criminologist Cesare Lombroso constructed the first trait theory of crime, when he argued that you could tell how highly evolved someone was from their physical appearance. Applying Darwin's teachings, Lombroso theorized that criminals were **atavistic beings** or throwbacks to an earlier, more primitive stage of human development. They more closely resembled their ape-like ancestors in traits, abilities, and dispositions. Because criminals were not so highly evolved, they possessed **stigmata** or distinctive physical features, such as an asymmetrical face, an enormous jaw, large or protruding ears, and a receding chin that distinguished them from ordinary people. Through no fault of their own, criminals were incapable of obeying the complex rules and regulations of modern society and should be placed in restrictive institutions, like prisons.[28]

Years later the English economist Charles Goring challenged the validity of Lombroso's findings. Goring compared the physical measurements of 3,000 English convicts on 43 traits with similar measurements from a sample of university students. He found *no* evidence of a physical type of criminal.[29] Goring's conclusion remained unchallenged until 1939, when Harvard anthropologist Earnest Hooton discovered that Goring had ignored his own data that refuted his argument (and supported Lombroso). Upon reexamining Goring's data, Hooton found relative differences between criminals and nonoffenders.[30] What is interesting is that more than 125 years after Lombroso made his claims, Zeynep Benderlioglu and his colleagues found that men and women with asymmetrical extremities—ears, fingers, or feet of different sizes or shapes—were more likely to react aggressively when annoyed or provoked. The researchers argued that factors such as smoking or drinking during a pregnancy might stress a fetus in various ways, causing slight physical imperfections and also poorer impulse control.[31]

Body Type   In 1949 William Sheldon theorized there was a relationship between body type and delinquency, an idea known as **somatotype** theory. Sheldon identified three ideal body types: *Endomorphs,* who are relaxed, comfortable, extroverted "softies"; *Mesomorphs* who are active, assertive, and lust for power; and *Ectomorphs* who are introverted, overly sensitive, and love privacy. Sheldon tested his thesis by "typing" the bodies of 200 incarcerated juvenile offenders and 4,000 male college students. He found that delinquents were more likely to be mesomorphs and much less likely to be ectomorphs. He detected no significant differences between the groups on endomorphs.[32] His research has been replicated as other criminologists continue to search for a link between mesomorphy and delinquency. Sheldon Glueck and Eleanor Glueck compared the body types of 500 delinquents and 500 nondelinquents and also found that delinquents were more likely to be mesomorphs.[33] Juan Cortes and Florence Gatti typed 100 delinquents and 100 high school students and reported similar findings, that 57 percent of the delinquents and only 20 percent of the nondelinquents were mesomorphs.[34]

If there is a relationship between body type and delinquency, it could be linked to temperament. For instance, Adrian Raine, David Farrington, and their colleagues studied the effects of body size on delinquency among a sample of 1,130 children. They found that large body size at age 3 was predictive of increased aggression at age 11. Large children tended to be more fearless and stimulation-seeking, but the effects of body size on delinquency remained after controlling for temperament.[35] However, there may be other explanations. Mesomorphs may be more effective at acting out their frustrations and desires than more delicately built children. Possibly, being muscular enables mesomorphs to be admitted into delinquent gangs. It could be that since masculinity allows someone to more easily dominate others, it encourages the use of violence and threats. Muscularity may be a sign of masculinity and physical toughness, so boys with muscles feel they need to play the role of the "tough guy." Finally, maybe the relationship researchers have found between mesomorphy and delinquency results from juvenile justice officials, particularly police, regarding mesomorphy as a sign of danger and reacting differently toward mesomorphs than they do toward other body types.

Autonomic Hypoactivity and ADHD   In hindsight, early trait theories of delinquency seem almost laughable in their crudeness. However, scholarly investigations of the biological or physiological differences between serious delinquents and nondelinquents continue. Today, this line of research examines internal factors, such as heart rate, brain activity, and brain structure, not external differences, such as physical appearance. The most consistently documented biological correlate of delinquency is autonomic hypoactivity or an underaroused system marked by a low resting heart rate. Low resting heart rate is more commonly found among males than females, among chronic offenders than normative delinquents, among violent offenders compared to nonviolent offenders, and among prisoners than those in the community. The relationship between low resting heart rate and antisocial behavior has been replicated in samples from Canada, England, Germany, Mauritius, New Zealand, and the United States.[36] David Farrington examined the predictors of violence using 48 sociological, psychological, and biological independent variables. He found that low resting heart rate was the most robust and consistent predictor of crime.[37]

Several explanations for why resting heart rate is so predictive of crime have been offered. There are important differences among people in how their brains are structured and how information is processed. A growing body of literature confirms that criminality is tied to differences in brain structure, which affects people's ability to exercise self-control (frontal lobe) and respond to environmental changes (temporal lobe). For some people, their brains produce more or fewer chemicals than they need. A brain, for example, that produces too little *serotonin,* may cause a behavioral condition that has been coupled with impulsivity, aggression, and violent offending.[38] A possible consequence for children with brains that produce too little serotonin, which is one of the neurotransmitters that sends communications between the brain and nerve cells, is **attention**

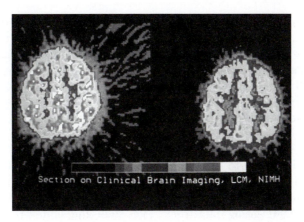

Section on Clinical Brain Imaging, LCM, NIMH

Brain scan images produced by positron emission tomography (PET) show differences in the brains of an adult with ADHD (right) and an adult without ADHD (left). Has sociological criminology been completely misguided by ignoring the role of biology in behavior? Whatever the effects of all theories of delinquency, are they all subservient to a simpler explanation: the human brain?

deficit/hyperactivity disorder (ADHD), the most common neurobehavioral disorder of childhood. A physician in Providence, Rhode Island, who was studying the causes of delinquency, discovered ADHD in the 1930s when he stumbled across a way to calm rowdy boys by giving them stimulants. Since low arousal is an unpleasant physiological state, youths seek stimulation to increase their arousal levels to normal levels. The stimulant helps arousal levels achieve normal levels. The discovery led to the creation of the first generation of drugs to treat ADHD.[39]

ADHD is generally recognizable by its symptoms, which include inattention and hyperactivity, that cause difficulty in school, poor relationships with family and peers, and low self-esteem. Children with ADHD are more than just fidgety; their "motor" is running all of the time. They run, jump, climb everywhere, constantly lose and misplace things, have difficulty following simple instructions, have trouble finishing work, and need constant reminders to remain on task. When these children want something they go for it without thinking of the consequences. Immediate gratification is the driving force. ADHD symptoms usually appear before age 4, but children often are not diagnosed with the disorder until they enter school where they talk excessively, interrupt teachers, and sometimes commit physically dangerous acts. It is not easy, however, to determine whether a child has ADHD or some other disorder. In one study more than half of the children who received medication for ADHD did not have it.[40]

It is estimated that between 4 and 12 percent of the school-age population of children age 6 to 12 are diagnosed with ADHD, and the disorder is approximately five times more common in boys than in girls.[41] A national estimate of the adult prevalence of ADHD is 4 percent based on the National Comorbidity Survey Replication.[42] Since ADHD is a relatively stable disorder, the adult prevalence should be consistent with ADHD estimates in children and adolescents. ADHD in girls, however, may be as common as it is among boys and might

think about it

Children with ADHD are difficult to parent and educate because of their consistently disruptive behavior. Should ADHD children be medicated to control their behavior? What are the benefits and costs of medicating children?

be underdiagnosed because girls with ADHD have developed more passive and acceptable coping strategies than boys.[43] Rather than being rebellious, ADHD girls often are inattentive and misdiagnosed as being lazy or spacey when they are not.[44] Teresa Nadder and her colleagues have found that the symptoms of ADHD are similar for boys and girls.[45] Compared to girls who do not have ADHD, girls with the disorder are more likely to smoke and to have conduct disorder, depression, anxiety, alcoholism, substance abuse problems, anorexia, and bulimia.[46]

The cause of ADHD is not entirely known. In the mainstream media, it has been tied to heredity, prenatal stress, neurological damage, food allergies, family turmoil, and more. In fact, ADHD is almost entirely caused by genetics. Soo Rhee and his colleagues assessed the genetic and environmental influences of ADHD using data from 2,391 twin and sibling pairs from Australia. They found that between 85 and 90 percent of ADHD symptoms were directly attributable to genes.[47] Studies by behavioral geneticists have reported that youths with a particular genetic abnormality are likely to develop ADHD.

There are many negative consequences of having ADHD.[48] For instance, children with ADHD are more likely to be depressed, have speech and language impediments, and have learning disabilities. They also engage in more problem behaviors throughout their lives. In turn, they are arrested and adjudicated delinquent and become adult criminals much more often than non-ADHD children.[49] Nondelinquents with ADHD have been found to have better cognitive functioning and verbal skills than ADHD delinquents, who have more cognitive defects than non-ADHD delinquents. When James Satterfield and his colleagues compared 110 children with ADHD and 88 normal children, he found that ADHD children were more likely to be arrested for a serious crime and were 21 times more likely to be institutionalized for antisocial behavior.[50] Recently, Travis Pratt and his colleagues conducted a meta-analysis of 20 studies that examined the effects of ADHD and delinquency. They found a consistent relationship between the disorder and crime, making ADHD an important risk factor for antisocial conduct.[51]

The most common treatment for ADHD is drug therapy, specifically physicians prescribing methylphenidate (Ritalin) or an amphetamine (Adderall and Dexedrine). Between 2000 and 2006, prescriptions for drugs to treat ADHD increased nearly 60 percent.[52] Sales of these drugs are nearly $1 billion annually. With children as young as 5 years old being prescribed methylphenidate or an amphetamine, some experts worry about the potential long-term side effects of these drugs such as psychosis, mania, loss of appetite, depression, sleep problems, moodiness, and stunting of growth.[53] Matthew Hutson reports that about 5 percent of children who are prescribed Ritalin complain of psychotic, delusional episodes where they believe that bugs are infesting their bodies.[54] Research indicates that children metabolize medications differently than adults and that their brains are developing much more rapidly. Some studies have demonstrated that the maturing neurotransmitter system in children's brains is so sensitive to drugs that the drugs may cause permanent changes in adult life.[55]

Frontal Lobes and Executive Functioning   On September 13, 1848, a freak accident affecting railroad worker Phineas Gage would lead to an important scientific discovery about the human brain and its control of behavior. While Gage was setting railroad track, an explosives accident sent a tamping iron, three feet long and weighing about 13 pounds, through his cheekbone and out the anterior frontal cortex of his head. Amazingly, not only did Gage survive the accident, but he also appeared to be generally okay, suffering minimal blood loss. His personality was another story. Before the accident, Gage was a responsible, hard-working, disciplined, congenial man who got along well with others. After the accident, Gage was highly impulsive, egocentric, irresponsible, irreverent, and did not get along well with others. He seemed entirely different in personality and temperament.[56]

The Gage accident is commonly used to illustrate the role of the human brain, and various sections of the brain, to control different aspects of our behavior. With the advancement of neuroimaging techniques, such as magnetic resonance imaging, functional magnetic resonance imaging, and positron emission tomography, neuroscientists have learned a great deal about the workings of the brain and about how different parts of the brain are responsible for different tasks. One of the more significant discoveries—and one that has direct application to delinquency—focuses on the functions and operations of the prefrontal cortex.[57]

The human brain consists of two main areas: the cerebral cortex and the subcortex. The subcortex is located beneath the cerebral cortex and contains the brainstem, the midbrain, and the forebrain. The subcortex performs many duties, but it is primarily responsible for many of the lower-order functions of humans, such as the regulation of breathing and the activation of reflexes. Although the subcortex is essential to life, most research examining the neurological basis of antisocial behaviors has focused on the cerebral cortex.[58]

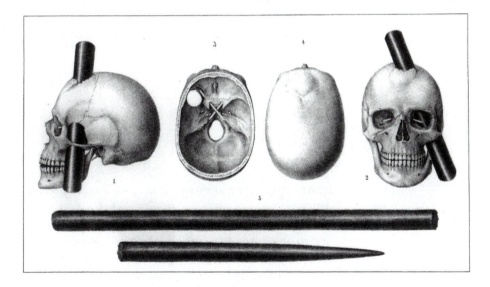

Phineas Gage's injury damaged the frontal lobes of his brain, which house the executive functions that control many human behaviors. Is the case of Phineas Gage proof that conventional and delinquent behavior is purely under the control of the brain? As more is discovered about the brain, will neurology render sociology obsolete as an explanation of crime?

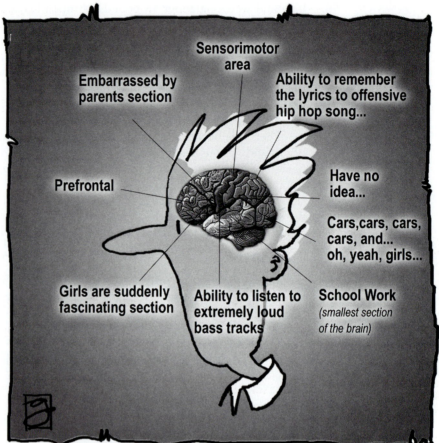

Sensorimotor area

Embarrassed by parents section

Ability to remember the lyrics to offensive hip hop song...

Prefrontal

Have no idea...

Cars, cars, cars, cars, and... oh, yeah, girls...

Girls are suddenly fascinating section

Ability to listen to extremely loud bass tracks

School Work *(smallest section of the brain)*

Anatomy of a Teenager's Brain

Source: Copyright 2007 Gary Olsen, Dubuque Schools. Used by permission.

There are two hemispheres (a left hemisphere and a right hemisphere) of the human brain and the cerebral cortex is found on the outer edges of both. Each hemisphere can be artificially divided into four different lobes: the frontal lobe, the temporal lobe, the parietal lobe, and the occipital lobe. Each lobe performs specialized functions, but the lobes most likely to be related to antisocial behaviors and traits are the two frontal lobes (one corresponding to each hemisphere).

The coordinated activities of the frontal lobes are referred to as *executive functions,* which are a cluster of higher order cognitive processes involving initiation, planning, cognitive flexibility, abstraction, and decision making that together allow the execution of contextually appropriate behavior.[59] Terrie Moffitt describes the day-to-day operations of the frontal lobes in this way:

[T]he normal functions of the frontal lobes of the brain include sustaining attention and concentration, abstract reasoning and concept formation, goal formulation, anticipation and planning, programming and initiation of purposive sequences of motor behavior, effective self-monitoring of behavior and self-awareness, and inhibition of unsuccessful, inappropriate, or impulsive behaviors, with adaptive shifting to alternative behaviors. These functions are commonly referred to as "executive functions," and they hold consequent implications for social judgment, self-control, responsiveness to punishment, and ethical behavior.[60]

Executive functioning has clear implications for involvement in delinquency because it deals with regulating impulsive tendencies, controlling emotions, sustaining attention, appreciating behavioral consequences, and inhibiting inappropriate conduct. Research has linked frontal lobe damage and impairments in executive functioning to delinquency, especially among life-course persistent offenders[61] and psychopaths.[62]

In addition to injuries like those sustained by Phineas Gage, there are multiple causes of brain damage that impact human behavior. Researchers have shown that genetic risks relating to the polymorphism monoamine oxidase A (MAOA) predispose persons to impulsive behavior and affect the frontal lobes.[63] Other explanations point to the biosocial underpinnings of delinquency. Kathleen Heide and Eldra Solomon documented how prolonged abuse and neglect of children can lead to biological changes in the ways that their brains process and respond to social stimuli. These environmentally induced changes in brain chemistry place individuals at greater risk for delinquency, especially the most serious forms of violence.[64] Heide and Solomon's work points to the essence of biologically based theories of delinquency, namely the interconnections between genes, biological functioning, and the social environment. The interplay between nature and nurture is complex and reciprocal, and the following sections highlight how *nature and nurture* combine to produce delinquency.

Nature–Nurture Interplay: How Does Biology Work?

Early biological theories of crime pointed to features on the human body as evidence of criminality. Today, it is understood that biology affects behavior through its heritability, for instance, characteristics people inherit from their biological parents, and its direct effects on human behavior, such as brain functioning. The following section highlights how biological factors translate into social behavior, including delinquency.

An individual's genetic composition, or **genotype,** is largely responsible for shaping, structuring, and selecting environments that allow optimum gene expression.[65] The ways that genes connect with environmental conditions is referred to as a *gene X environment* correlation. Gene X environment correlations (rGE) are important explanations for why there is often a relationship between an individual's personality or temperament and the environment he or she inhabits. Most personalities and temperaments are partially heritable, and many are mostly genetically created. People with certain personality traits, like a penchant for thrill-seeking, are apt to find themselves in dangerous or risky situations, such as bungee-jumping, skydiving classes, or riding motorcycles without wearing a helmet. An individual with a cautious or docile disposition would probably pass up the opportunity to jump out of an airplane in favor of a less hazardous and more mundane activity. In this case, the genes responsible for the creation of personality characteristics are also the genes responsible for the creation of the environment. There are three main types of rGEs—passive, evocative, and active—each of which accounts for a unique process by which genetic factors influence or otherwise mold the environment.[66]

Passive rGEs build upon the fact that parents pass along two different elements to their children: genes and an environment. Since children receive half of their genes from each parent and are born into environments that are largely created from, or reflect, their parents' genetic makeup, a child's genetic propensities are correlated with the environment in which that child is born. This type of rGE is referred to as a passive rGE because the child does not have an active voice in choosing his or her genotype or their familial environment—they are passively passed on from parent to offspring.

For example, intelligence is a highly heritable individual characteristic. Children who are born to intellectually savvy parents are likely to have high cognitive capabilities. At the same time, intelligent parents are also likely to provide an environment that stimulates their child's brain development. The child thus has a genetic predisposition to be "smart" and also lives in a home environment that promotes intelligence. Without considering the possibility that the parents' genes are partially responsible for their child's intelligence, it would appear on the surface that the environment is the main cause of their child's IQ. In reality, however, the familial environment is so closely intertwined with genetic influences that only genetically sensitive research designs are able to parcel out the relative effects of genes and the environment.

Evocative rGEs are the second type of rGEs and reflect the fact that people elicit certain responses from the environment based, in part, on their genes. A person with one genotype may evoke one type of response from the environment, whereas another person, with his or her own unique genotype, may evoke a completely different response. For example, family researchers have long recognized that parents treat their children very differently depending upon how their children behave. Parents will likely regularly reprimand, punish, and discipline a difficult and taxing child. The sibling, however, who has an easy-going personality and who is relatively obedient, will be much more enjoyable for the parents to rear, and punishment will be less frequent. In this case, children, depending on their unique genotypes, evoke differential responses from their parents.[67] These different familial environments are correlated with the child's genetically influenced temperaments. Evocative rGEs can be best summarized by stating that certain genetic polymorphisms elicit particular responses from the environment, and these responses are correlated with the person's genotype.

The brain of an unborn child develops rapidly. Fifty-thousand neurons per second are generated during the gestation of a fetus; 200 billion nerve cells throughout the body begin firing signals to an infant's brain with its first breath; 3 billion learning connections per second are made in a child's brain.

Active rGEs have the most relevance for criminologists because they help to explain why some adolescents associate with delinquent peers.[68] Youths actively seek out and select environments or niches that are compatible with their personalities and other genetic predispositions. For some adolescents, especially those with a genetic proclivity to engage in mischief, antisocial friendship groups may be alluring and seductive. Other youths, however, particularly those who are not genetically predisposed to become involved in delinquency, may veer away from deviant peers and select more prosocial youths to befriend. According to the logic of active rGEs, the individual person plays an integral role in identifying and selecting environments that reinforce their genetic makeup.[69]

Intelligence   The relationship between intelligence and delinquency has had a colorful history. In 1575, the Spanish physician Juan Huarte formally defined **intelligence** as the ability to learn, exercise judgment, and be imaginative. Since the 16th century, scientists have designed different ways to measure intelligence. In 1905 Alfred Binet and Theophile Simon developed the first standardized IQ test. In 1912, the German psychologist William Stern introduced the idea of an "intelligence quotient" or IQ, contending that every person had a mental age that could be represented by an **IQ score,** which is the ratio of the individual's mental age multiplied by 100 and divided by his or her chronological age. The "average" ability for any age is 100, which is the level at which mental age and chronological age are equal.

Early Research   Most of the early researchers who studied intelligence said very little about the heritability of intelligence. The idea that intelligence might be inherited was popularized in 1916 by Stanford University professor Lewis Terman, who revised the Binet–Simon test and renamed it the Stanford–Binet Intelligence Test, which is widely used today. At the beginning of the 20th century, criminologists who were trained in medicine or in psychology made some inflated and inflammatory claims about the relationship between intelligence and crime. They suggested that people of low intelligence were easily led into lawbreaking by more clever people and did not realize that committing an offense in a certain way often led to getting caught and being punished.

One psychologist, Henry Goddard, who coined the term "moron," administered intelligence tests to prison and jail inmates and he discovered that 70 percent were "feebleminded." This very high percentage of low-intelligence inmates led the public, social reformers, and state legislators to conclude that low intelligence predisposed people to commit crime. Goddard's conclusion stood unchallenged for more than a decade.[70] In 1926 in a study comparing more than 1,500 delinquent males with a group of male nondelinquents, John Slawson found no relationship between IQ and criminality.[71] Replications and extensions of Slawson's pioneering work seemed to confirm his findings. In 1928 Barbara Burks who studied the intelligence of children of mentally deficient parents reported that when the children were placed in foster homes with a nurturing environment, their IQ scores reached normal levels.[72] In 1931 Edwin Sutherland evaluated IQ studies of delinquents and refuted the idea of there being any significant relationship between IQ and delinquency.[73]

Intelligence and Delinquency   Whereas the linkage between intelligence and delinquency was generally rejected and even considered a taboo subject for study, contemporary research, which is more methodologically sophisticated, consistently reports a connection between IQ and delinquency. In a landmark study, Travis Hirschi and Michael Hindelang found that *IQ is a better predictor of involvement in delinquency than race or social class* and that the IQ of the average delinquent is about eight points lower than nondelinquents.[74] Others have confirmed their conclusion. Donald Lynam and his colleagues reported that IQ predicted delinquency even when controlling for important correlates of delinquency, such as social class, race, and academic motivation. They also found that the relationship between intelligence and delinquency varied by race. For African Americans, the effect of IQ was mediated or accounted for by school performance; however, this was not the case for whites.[75] Leslie Leve and Patricia Chamberlain reported that girls with low intelligence among other factors were significantly likely to have an early onset of antisocial behavior, which often sets the stage for a sustained delinquent career.[76] Intelligence has also been linked to the most serious forms of criminal behavior. Jean-Pierre Guay and his colleagues evaluated the intelligence–crime link among 261 sex offenders and 150 nonsexual violent offenders in Canada. They found that sex offenders have significantly impaired cognitive abilities compared to other criminals in areas, such as vocabulary, comprehension, arithmetic, mental math computations, object assembly, letter–number sequencing, and perception.[77]

How intelligence affects delinquency remains a mystery. There are at least five possibilities. *First,* intelligence might have no effect. It may be that both intelligence and delinquency are caused by some third variable (a spurious relationship), such as social class. This hypothesis is commonly held, but it has received no empirical support. Within the same social class, students with lower IQs have been reported as having higher rates of delinquency. Indeed, the idea that intelligence is unrelated to delinquency is a myth.[78]

Second, Adrian Raine and his colleagues found that criminal offenders are more likely to suffer from brain dysfunction as a result of birth complications, environmental toxins, and head injuries, which lead to problem behaviors and having a low IQ. Early brain damage causes cognitive deficiencies that produce an array of endless problems for children, such as school failure and low self-esteem, which lead to delinquency.[79]

Third, the relationship between intelligence and delinquency may be confounded by moral reasoning and cognitive empathy, which is the ability to understand and share in another person's emotional state or context. Darrick Jolliffe and David Farrington reviewed 35 studies of cognitive empathy, intelligence, and delinquency. They found that persons who have weak cognitive empathy are more likely than others to be criminal offenders, and this effect was particularly pronounced among violent offenders. Interestingly, the linkages between cognitive empathy and crime disappeared once intelligence was considered. From this perspective, both delinquency and ability to empathize with others are controlled by intelligence.[80]

Fourth, some contend that intelligence influences delinquency *indirectly,* that is, the effect is transmitted through school-experience variables. One purpose of IQ tests is to predict how well a person will do in school, and though they are not perfect, IQ tests do have a reasonably good prediction record: students who perform well on IQ tests tend to get good grades. School performance (grades) affects various aspects of the student's life, particularly the student's attitude toward school. Students who receive good grades find school more enjoyable than those whose grades are poor, and they seem to be more accepting of a school's authority. Students who can tolerate the school's authority are not as likely to break the rules and are less likely to become delinquent. Looking at the issue from this perspective, we can say that low IQ leads to lower grades in school, lower grades lead to disliking school, disliking school leads to rejecting its authority, and this rejection of authority leads some students into delinquency.[81] Jean McGloin and her colleagues found that intelligence did not directly predict delinquency, but did predict poor school performance, association from deviant peers, and low self-control. In turn, all of these variables were directly related to delinquency.[82] Similarly, Chris Gibson and his colleagues reported that the independent effect of low intelligence *interacts* with family adversity to explain delinquency.[83]

Fifth, Thomas Bouchard and his colleagues contend the abilities measured by IQ tests are partly genetic. Verbal abilities may be as inheritable as nonverbal abilities. Their theory is based on data from the Minnesota Twin Study, a 10-year longitudinal study of identical twins (twins that develop from one fertilized egg) and fraternal twins (twins that develop from two eggs fertilized at the same time) who were reared apart, that found evidence of a strong genetic component in many psychological traits, including IQ. With respect to intelligence, the researchers concluded that 70 percent of the influence on IQ scores is genetic and 30 percent comes from the environment. According to Bouchard and his colleagues, "Although parents may be able to affect their children's rate of cognitive skill acquisition, they may have relatively little influence on the ultimate level attained."[84]

Hormones and Puberty   It is easy to recognize the effects of "raging hormones" and puberty on behavior during adolescence. For many parents, the years when their children are teenagers are the most challenging as parents. Over the years, many criminologists have explored the effects of hormones and puberty on delinquency, particularly the potential effects of testosterone, which is a hormone largely responsible for the maintenance of secondary sex characteristics in males.[85] Testosterone is also a correlate of aggression. James Dabbs and Robin Morris evaluated the relationship between testosterone, social class, and antisocial behavior using a large sample of 4,462 American military veterans. The majority of the sample, about 4,000 veterans, had normal testosterone levels and 446 veterans had high testosterone levels. The latter group had significantly greater levels of childhood and adult delinquency; narcotic, marijuana, and alcohol use; sexual promiscuity; and military AWOL. Further, socioeconomic status moderated the independent effects of testosterone, as risk ratios were twice as great in the low compared to high socioeconomic status (SES) groups.[86] Alan Booth and Wayne Osgood similarly found a significant and strong relationship between testosterone and deviance and surmised that this relationship was mediated by the influence of testosterone on social integration and prior delinquency. Both of these studies demonstrate that hormonal factors interact with social and environmental conditions to produce various behavioral effects.[87]

Hormonal effects on delinquency have also been found among correctional samples and among more extreme forms of antisocial conduct. James Dabbs and his colleagues reported a relationship between testosterone level and criminal violence among a sample of 89 male prisoners. Among the 11 offenders with the lowest testosterone levels, 9 had committed nonviolent offenses. Among the 11 offenders with the highest testosterone levels, 9 had committed violent crimes.[88] It has also been reported that inmates who had been convicted of murder, rape, and child molestation had significantly higher testosterone levels than offenders convicted of other felonies. Moreover, testosterone level significantly predicted inmate infractions, and inmates with high hormonal levels tended to commit the most serious types of misconduct, such as assaulting inmates and other acts of overt confrontation.[89] Higher testosterone levels have also been reported among homicide offenders who were convicted of premeditated, more "ruthless" types of murder.[90]

The relationship between puberty and delinquency is multifaceted and important for both teenage boys and girls. Richard Felson and Dana Haynie found that adolescent boys who are more physically developed than their peers are more likely to engage in violent and property crimes, drug use, and sexual activity. The effects of puberty on delinquency were direct and not explained by other individual factors. Felson and Haynie concluded that the effects of puberty on delinquency are stronger than the effects of social class, race, and family structure."[91] Among adolescent girls, early pubertal development leads to more strained relationships with parents and "party"-related deviance.[92] Dana Haynie and Alex Piquero also reported that adolescents who go through puberty early are more likely to be the victims of crime, and this effect is stronger among physically developed girls who are dating.[93] Finally, Kevin Beaver and John Wright examined how puberty related to adolescent development and delinquency among a national sample of 6,504 youths. They found that among boys and girls, early puberty contributed to greater association with delinquent peers, and, in turn, delinquency. However, the effects of puberty on delinquency were more pronounced among males than females. During puberty, boys tended to have poorer impulse control, to have more negative interaction styles with parents and peers, and to associate more frequently with other delinquent boys.[94]

Family, Twin, and Adoption Studies　　Criminologists have commonly utilized family studies to examine the heritability of antisocial behavior. In family studies, index subjects, known as *proband*, who present the trait or behavior under investigation, such as criminality, are compared to a control group of persons who do not present the trait or behavior. From these study groups, the prevalence of the trait is examined among first-degree relatives (children, siblings, or parents) of the proband and control subjects. Genetic effects are inferred or estimated when the trait or behavior is more prevalent among relatives of the proband than control group. Sheldon and Eleanor Glueck used family study designs to examine the heritability of crime among their classic samples of delinquent youth. In their sample of male delinquents, the Gluecks found that the prevalence of family member arrest was nearly 200 percent greater among proband than controls.[95] For females, the prevalence of family member arrest was about 160 percent higher among proband than controls. In short, the Gluecks provided speculative but empirically compelling evidence that crime "runs in the family."[96]

Robert Cloninger, Samuel Guze, and their colleagues produced even stronger evidence for the heritability of crime in their studies of the transmission of sociopathy among families. In a study of 519 first-degree relatives of sociopathic males, the prevalence of sociopathy among proband subjects was more than 330 percent higher than among controls.[97] Cloninger and Guze found even stronger effects among female index subjects using arrests and sociopathy di-

MZ twins have similar levels of criminality. Why do criminologist trained sociologists ignore or dis

agnosis as outcomes. The prevalen
nearly 700 percent greater among
provided compelling evidence that
tential, including sociopathy, are l
and David Farrington examined
tions using data from 344 famili
Cambridge Study in Delinquent
whether the effect of parent cor
mediated through the quality o
sion, child rearing, and family s
from family environment and
ment influences may determin
aspects of the family environ
criminality is the strongest fa
illustrate, children of murderers are a staggering 2,
commit violent crimes than children whose parents were not mura

Another way to evaluate the impact of heredity on behavior is to study
twins. There are **monozygotic twins** (MZ) or identical twins, which have identical DNA and come from one fertilized egg; and **dizygotic twins** (DZ) or fraternal twins, who come from two separate eggs fertilized at the same time. Fraternal twins are no more alike genetically than non-twin siblings. If there is a
genetic factor in delinquency, MZ twins should be more alike than DZ twins.
This similarity is called *concordance,* which occurs when both twins share a
characteristic. For example, if one twin is delinquent and the other twin also is
delinquent, there exists *concordance* with respect to delinquency. Conversely, if
one twin is delinquent and the other is not, this is called *discordance.*

In 1929 Johannes Lange published the first study of twins and criminality.
He examined 37 twin pairs: 13 MZ twins and 17 DZ twins (seven pairs could
not be classified). In each pair at least one twin had been in prison. In 10 of the
13 MZ pairs, the other twin had also been in prison, while in only two of the
17 DZ pairs had both twins served prison sentences.[103] Karl Christiansen completed the earliest comprehensive twin study in Denmark. He identified 3,586
twin pairs born between 1870 and 1920 that were listed in the Danish Twin
Register. Christiansen reviewed police records and court documents for each
twin set. A total of 926 twins belonging to 799 of the pairs had committed at
least one criminal offense. He computed the criminal concordance rates for the
sample and found much greater concordance between crime and the criminal
careers of MZ twins than for DZ twins.[104]

David Rowe and Wayne Osgood examined the genetic and environmental
causes of antisocial behavior using a sample of 168 MZ twin pairs (61 males, 107
females) and 97 same-sex DZ twin pairs (38 males, 59 females). They explored
the frequency with which the youth committed assorted interpersonal (violent),
property, and nuisance offenses during the prior year. Rowe and Osgood found
that more than 60 percent of the variation in antisocial acts and delinquent peer
associations was accounted for by genetic factors. Among male twins, genes explained 61 percent of the variation and environmental factors explained 39 percent of the variation. For female twins, genes accounted for 64 percent of the
variation with environmental factors explaining the remaining 36 percent.[105] In
a subsequent study, David Rowe examined the common-family environmental,
within-family environmental and hereditary components of antisocial behavior.

as
often
miss this
fact?

Common-family environmental components, which included social class, child rearing styles, parental attitudes, parental religion, and other factors, *did not* influence antisocial behavior, but heredity did. The primary genetic antecedents of antisocial behavior were deceitfulness and temperamental traits, such as lack of empathy, anger, and impulsivity.[106] It has also been reported that the concordance rates for self-reported delinquency among MZ twins to be much higher than for DZ twins. MZ twins also were found to have more delinquent friends than DZ twins do. Genes predispose some children to select friends who are delinquent.[107]

Another way to evaluate the relationship between heredity and behavior is by studying adoptees. Adopted children usually have little or no contact with their biological parents. Therefore, to the extent that their behavior resembles the behavior of their biological parents, an argument can be made that genes influence behavior.

Barry Hutchings and Sarnoff Mednick compared the criminal records of 662 adopted sons with criminal records of their biological and adoptive fathers. When both the biological and adoptive fathers had a criminal record, 36 percent of the sons were criminal; when only the biological father had a criminal record, 22 percent of the sons were criminal; when only the adoptive father was criminal, 12 percent of the sons were criminal; and when neither of the fathers were criminal, only 10 percent of the sons had a record.[108]

Mednick and his associates matched the court convictions of 14,427 male and female adoptees with the court convictions of their biological mothers and fathers and their adoptive mothers and fathers. They found that the criminality of the child was more closely related to the criminality of the biological parents. Follow-up research has produced similar findings.[109] In a Swedish study of nearly 900 male adoptees, it was reported that the criminal histories of children were more similar to those of their biological parents than to their adoptive parents.[110] In follow-up research, Raymond Crowe analyzed arrest records of 52 adoptees who had been separated from their incarcerated biological mothers. He compared them to a group of adoptees whose biological mothers had no criminal record and discovered that the adoptees of the "criminal" mothers were about 500 percent more likely than the adoptees of "noncriminal mothers" to have an arrest record.[111] He also found that adoptees with "criminal mothers" were more likely than adoptees with "noncriminal mothers" to be diagnosed with antisocial personalities.[112]

Nurture–Nature Interplay: How Does Environment Work?

Behavior is under the control of the brain, which is constructed of complex neural circuits that begin to form shortly after conception and grow and change throughout life as genes and cells *interact* with the environment. For instance, researchers found that teens who played violent video games and then performed simple tasks used different parts of their brain than children who played other, nonviolent video games. Apparently, playing violent video games makes children's brains fire differently, especially affecting the ability to concentrate and modulate emotion. This could potentially make a child more aggressive since video games can affect brain physiology.[113]

The brain directs people's activities in everyday life, but the activities themselves shape how the brain processes information throughout life. The environment, in other words, contributes to both the brain's contents and to its wiring. However, the brain of an unborn child is not a miniature of an adult's. Rather, it is a dynamically changing structure that is adversely affected by outside contaminants in social environments. This section reviews some of the unfortunately many environmental conditions that are known to cause serious biological damage to developing children, create risk factors for delinquency, and preclude health human development.[114]

Maternal Cigarette Smoking   The public health costs of cigarette smoking are alarming. Each year, secondhand smoke kills 49,000 adult nonsmokers via heart disease and lung cancer. Nearly 500 newborns die from sudden infant death syndrome induced by secondhand smoke. Also each years, children experience nearly 800,000 ear infections and 200,000 episodes of asthma related to smoking.[115] Beyond the dangers of secondhand smoke is "thirdhand smoke," which is the particles and gases given off by cigarettes that cling to walls, clothes, furniture, skin, and hair. Thirdhand smoke can linger for months depending on the ventilation and level of contamination. Since crawling babies explore the world by touching—and tasting—anything they can get their hands on, the environmental effects of cigarette smoke and its byproducts are disastrous.[116]

Mothers who smoke while pregnant and parents who smoke around their children may be foreshadowing a tendency to place personal desires ahead of a concern for the potential long-term detrimental consequences for their children. Many criminologists have explored maternal smoking as a risk factor for delinquency and other problem behaviors. Nancy Day and her colleagues studied the effects of prenatal nicotine exposure on preschoolers' behavior and produced several distressing findings. Children whose mother's smoked while pregnant

Maternal cigarette smoking during pregnancy is one of the most powerful environmental causes of delinquency. Given the tremendous damage that nicotine inflicts on the body, should smoking during pregnancy be a crime? Is it already sufficiently limited by informal social controls?

were significantly likely to be emotionally unstable, physically aggressive, and socially immature and to have oppositional defiant disorder. Tobacco exposure was the strongest predictor of oppositional and defiant behavior among children at age 3. At age 10, these children had severe deficits in learning and memory.[117]

Patricia Brennan and her colleagues studied the long-term effects of maternal smoking during pregnancy among a birth cohort of males from Denmark. Controlling for a host of predictors of crime, they found that children whose mother's smoked while pregnant with them were significantly likely to engage in persistent criminal behavior into adulthood. In fact, smoking contributed to violent and property offending even when the males were age 34.[118] Maternal smoking during pregnancy also caused psychiatric problems among the males well into adulthood.[119] Chris Gibson and Stephen Tibbetts similarly found that prenatal and perinatal exposure to maternal smoking contributed to an early onset of delinquency and police contacts.[120] Recent reviews have concluded that maternal smoking during pregnancy is a formidable risk factor for delinquency and related problem behaviors.[121] Moreover, this important public health threat is wholly preventable.

Alcohol   Alcohol, the #1 drug of choice of children and adolescents, is another major environmental risk factor for delinquency. The U.S. Surgeon General reports that 1 in 12 women use alcohol at some point during their pregnancy, and the effects of alcohol on the fetus range from cognitive problems to severe growth deficiencies.[122] Each day, roughly 7,000 children under age 16 take their first drink of alcohol. By age 18, one in four children is exposed to family alcoholism or alcohol abuse. In terms of prenatal exposure and abuse within their families, alcohol poses a significant threat to healthy social development. Alcohol use among children, particularly among those who begin drinking in elementary and middle school, increases the likelihood of depression and other psychiatric problems, poorer school performance, health problems, and delinquency.[123]

Overall, the greatest environmental threat posed by alcohol use and abuse is that it places children and adolescents into social circumstances and friendship networks that increase the likelihood of delinquency. For instance, Jason Ford found that heavy drinking among adolescents reduces their social attachment to family members and others in the community. Alcohol abuse also increases involvement in other acts of delinquency, which in turn contributes to greater drinking. Problem drinking, in other words, does not occur in isolation. Instead, it weakens an individual's bond to society.[124] Other large-scale projects conducted in Canada, Norway, and the United States linked early exposure to alcohol and problem drinking to aggression, victimization, and general delinquency.[125]

think about it

Chemical toxins, such as leaded paint, are a significant health risk to children. What are the implications for the social development of children exposed to such paint? Do you think exposure to leaded paint and delinquency are related?

Chemical Poisoning   Few people blame delinquency on environmental toxins and chemicals. However, a growing body of evidence suggests that chemical pollutants such as mercury, a dangerous neurological toxin, are especially harmful when ingested by children. Much of this mercury is emitted into the air from coal-burning power plants. Mercury pollution from power plants ends up being deposited into waterways and accumulating up the food chain, where it ends up on our dinner plates. For instance, Colorado posted health warnings for nearly 20,000 acres of lakes warning people to limit fish consumption. Exposure to mercury causes damage to the brain, kidneys, and cardiovascular system. Those most vulnerable are young children whose brains are still developing. Pregnant women, new mothers, and women who may become pregnant are especially at risk. In a recent study by the Centers for Disease Control and Prevention, it was reported that one in six women of childbearing age have enough mercury in their bodies to put the health of their children at risk.[126]

While chemicals do not cause children to commit crime, they indirectly affect behavior by interfering with the ability of the brain to perceive and react to the environment. Besides mercury, another toxin that adversely affects brain functioning and may cause changes in behavior in children is *lead*. In the 1970s and 1980s the United States phased out leaded gasoline, which had poisoned more than 65 million children over the more than 50 years it was used. Public-health advocates had warned politicians for many years that using lead in gasoline was dangerous. During these decades, lead pollution caused learning disabilities, hearing loss, reduced attention spans, and lower IQs—as it has for centuries. For instance, renowned composer Ludwig van Beethoven died in 1827 as the result of lead poisoning.[127] Yet, more than seven million tons of lead was burned in the United States before it was banned. The good news is that now that lead is illegal, the percentage of children with elevated blood lead has decreased dramatically in the past three decades.[128]

Lead gets into the bodies of children in different ways. A pregnant woman may transmit lead to her children. Another possibility is that children will ingest lead through dust particles traveling in the air or by eating sweet-tasting lead-based paints peeled or chipped from walls. Lead-based paint was banned in the United States in 1978, but it is still found in many homes. A recent discovery found that candy and candy wrappers from more than 100 brands sold in California, most of them from Mexico, have tested positive for dangerous levels of lead, and nothing is being done about it. The lead from wrappers seeps into the candy and, when eaten by children, enters their bloodstream.[129]

Once lead enters a child's body, it makes its way into the bloodstream, then into soft body tissue (which includes the brain and kidneys), and finally into the hard tissue (bones and teeth).[130] Children are more susceptible to low levels of lead poisoning than adults because their nervous systems are developing faster, they are exposed to more lead, and their lead absorption rate is higher. A high

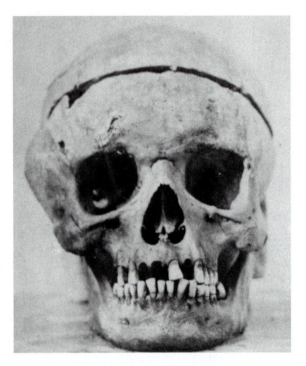

Lead poisoning caused the death of famous composer Beethoven in 1827 and is linked to numerous developmental disorders in children. How do the devastating effects of lead confirm both sociological and biological theories of delinquency? Could the rise in behavioral and developmental disorders, such as ADHD and autism, be caused by environmental pollutants such as lead?

percentage of the lead children absorb is not eliminated from their bodies for 20 or more years (see Box 5-3).

Lead damages a child's internal organs, causes brain and nerve damage, and results in intelligence and behavioral problems, particular in children. Lead poisoning has also been connected to delinquency. Herbert Needleman and his colleagues published a report that showed bone lead levels are much higher in adjudicated delinquents than in nondelinquents regardless of race. In an earlier study, Needleman and his associates reported that children with high levels of bone lead were more aggressive, self-reported more delinquency, and exhibited more attention difficulties. Lead poisoning also interfered with school performance.[131] In a related study of 900 boys, Deborah Denno concluded that lead poisoning was a principal predictor of delinquency and chronic criminality in adulthood.[132]

Children are differentially exposed to lead poisoning. The children most susceptible to lead poisoning are poor, African American children. Their environments, including their homes and schools, are much more likely to be heavily contaminated with lead and other toxins than are the environments other children live in. It has been found that lower-class African American children are eight times more likely than affluent white children to have high and dangerous levels of lead in their blood. Lead poisoning also differs by age. Children be-

box 5-3 A WINDOW ON DELINQUENCY

Poisoned Schools

Children are among the most powerless people in society. They are exposed to many dangers they can do nothing about. One place they face danger is in school. We are not talking here about school violence, but the danger children face in school when they are exposed to pesticides that are applied on school grounds and hazards from new schools that are built on or near land contaminated by chemicals.

An increasing amount of scientific evidence indicates that exposure to chemicals harms children in a variety of ways, including asthma, cancers, and learning disabilities. The Environmental Protection Agency (EPA), for example, has recently determined that the pesticide Dursban, a common pesticide used to control termites, poses significant health risks to children. Chemicals like Dursban harm the nervous, hormone, reproductive, and immune systems of growing children, which may lead them to be hyperactive, slow to learn, disruptive in school, and afflicted with certain types of cancer.

Children are more susceptible to environmental toxins than adults because they are growing more rapidly and their immune systems are less able to handle toxins. In many schools the lives of children are endangered on a daily basis from exposure to toxins. This is because those schools:

1. Are built on contaminated land or near an industrial, commercial, or municipal site (e.g., chemical plant, airport, freeway, or landfill) that daily releases toxic chemicals into the air and surrounding community.

2. Spray toxic pesticides to kill pests that subsequently contaminate carpets and floors and leave pesticide residue behind in the sprayed areas.

3. Apply weed killer and toxic fertilizers throughout school grounds, exposing children to residues as they play sports and use playground equipment.

4. Are poorly maintained, which provides a habitat for pests, molds, and allergies, and allows toxic residues to accumulate.

There also are no federal guidelines regulating where schools can be built. Only California has a policy that guides the location of new schools. In the other 49 states, cash-strapped school districts build new schools on whatever land they can afford. Many new schools have been proposed for locations on old industrial land that has been poisoned with toxic chemicals. Other schools have been proposed near industrial plants that release toxins on a daily basis. Too many existing schools are already located on poisoned sites.

Sources: Poisoned Schools (Falls Church, VA: Center for Health, Environment and Justice, 2001). The full report is available online at http://www.childproofing@chej.org, accessed April 20, 2007; Tamara Henry, "Schools on Contaminated Ground, Groups Says," *USA TODAY*, March 19, 2001:6D.

tween the ages of 2 and 4 years old are most likely to suffer from elevated blood lead levels. Children under age 1 are the least likely to have been poisoned by lead.[133]

Nutrition Are children what they eat? Does the food children ingest affect their behavior? Is a partial remedy for delinquency to change the diets of children? These questions have puzzled criminologists ever since 1942 when Hugh Sinclair suggested that poor diets, particularly ones deficient in vitamins B3, B6, and omega-3 essential fatty acids, were a cause of antisocial behavior and

These students eating lunch at Jones College Prep High School in Chicago are confronted with a bank of vending machines, which typically are filled with junk food. Must the brain be properly nourished to function efficiently? Does poor nutrition lead to aggressive behavior?

persuaded the British government to supplement the diet of all children with cod-liver oil and orange juice.[134] Today, nutrition is as important as ever as a health factor among children and adolescents. In the United States, about one-third of children are overweight or at risk of being overweight. Nearly 70 percent of adolescents purchase junk food and soda for lunch from vending machines in their schools.[135]

Research has time and again shown a link between nutrition and behavior. Stephen Schoenthaler and his colleagues have conducted a variety of studies examining the association between diet and aggressive behavior. They conducted an experiment on 80 working class children who had been formally disciplined for violating school rules during the school year. Half of these children were administered a daily vitamin–mineral supplement for four months, while the others received placebos. Children who took the vitamin–mineral supplement exhibited a 47 percent lower mean rate of antisocial behavior than the children receiving the placebos. This finding affirmed other research that has consistently revealed reductions in disciplinary actions in incarcerated children who received a vitamin–mineral supplement. Moreover, the greatest decrease in rule-violating behavior is among children who previously have been identified as chronic offenders (see Chapter 2).

Schoenthaler also has examined the relationship between diet and intelligence in more than 200 elementary school children, half of whom received vitamin–mineral supplements and half of whom received placebos. Again, significant differences between the groups emerged. After only three months, children receiving the vitamin–mineral supplement exhibited an average 16-point higher net gain in IQ scores than the matched placebo sample. Finally, in a series of three randomized controlled experiments in which half of 66 elementary school children, 62 confined teenage delinquents, and 404 confined adult felons received dietary supplements (the other half received placebos), Schoenthaler found that, for all three groups of subjects, those who received dietary supplements showed less aggressive behavior.[136]

Bernard Gesch and his colleagues have replicated and extended some of Schoenthaler's work in their study of 230 young adult prisoners. Like Schoenthaler, the Gesch team administered dietary supplements to half of their sample; the other half received placebos. The two inmate groups were matched on their number of disciplinary incidents as well as on their IQ scores, verbal ability, anger, anxiety, or depression. After 142 days the subjects were compared. It was found that inmates who received the dietary supplements had 26 percent fewer offenses and the greatest reduction in offenses was for serious violent incidents, which had a 37 percent decrease.[137] Richard Carlton and his colleagues reported similar findings. In their study of 20 learning-disabled students, the researchers found that dietary supplements dramatically improved their school performance both academically and behaviorally within weeks or months of beginning treatment.[138]

The long-term consequences of poor nutrition and malnutrition among children are severe. Jianghong Liu and his colleagues found that children who were malnourished at age 3 were more likely than other children to be aggressive and hyperactive at age 8, to exhibit aggressive, externalizing behaviors at age 11, and to exhibit conduct disorder and hyperactivity at age 17.[139] No one suggests that nutrition is the only cause of delinquency. The evidence from the United States and Great Britain suggests, however, that violent behavior might be reduced significantly with dietary supplementation in schools and correctional institutions. It is becoming clearer that a healthy diet improves brain function, intelligence, and performance in school. All of these variables have been linked to delinquency.

Psychological Theories

Some criminologists believe the cause of delinquency is psychological. After all, many delinquents live in dysfunctional homes and often find themselves in conflict with family members, neighbors, peers, classmates, and teachers. This is a "red flag" that these youth may have disturbed personalities or a mental disturbance that causes them to commit crime. Support for their belief comes from the fact that many delinquents *do* display antisocial characteristics. However, psychologists disagree on *why* many delinquent youth are mentally disturbed. Two prominent psychological theories of delinquency are psychodynamic theory and behavioral theory.

Psychodynamic Theory According to *psychodynamic theory,* unconscious mental processes that developed in early childhood control our personality. The author of this theory is the Austrian physician Sigmund Freud, who theorized that the personality consists of three parts: the id, ego, and superego.[140] The *id,* which is present at birth, consists of blind, unreasoning, instinctual desires and motives. The id represents basic biological and psychological drives; it does not differentiate between fantasy and reality. The id also is antisocial and knows no rules, boundaries, or limitations. If the id is left unchecked, it will destroy the person. The *ego* grows from the id and represents the problem-solving dimension of the personality; it deals with reality, differentiating it from fantasy. It teaches children to delay gratification because acting on impulse will get them into trouble. The *superego* develops from the ego and is the moral code, norms, and values the child has acquired. The superego is responsible for feelings of guilt and shame and is more closely aligned with the conscience. In mentally healthy children, the three parts of the personality work together. When the parts are in conflict, children may become maladjusted and ready for delinquency. Freud did not write specifically about delinquency. However, he did influence criminologists, who took his ideas and applied them to the study of crime.[141] Their theories have blamed delinquency on children having either an *underdeveloped* or *overdeveloped superego*.

In the case of the *underdeveloped superego,* the socialization process has been inadequate or incomplete. The superego is too weak to curb the impulses and drives of the id. The child's behavior becomes a direct expression of the id—for example, "If you want something, steal it." But delinquent behavior may also be indirect. Socialization inhibits the open expression of unacceptable urges, but that does not mean they disappear; they may merely become unconscious. In this way, delinquent behavior may be a symbolic expression of unconscious impulses. That is why, for example, an adolescent with an unresolved Oedipus complex may "murder" his father in a figurative way, like forging checks drawn on his bank account or killing a person who represents the authority of his father, such as a police officer.

Sometimes delinquent behavior is the result of too much socialization, which produces an *overdeveloped superego*. Impulses and urges of the id may elicit strong disapproval from the superego. This ongoing conflict causes the ego to experience guilt and anxiety. But since the ego knows that punishment must follow crime, the ego will lead the child to a commit crime to minimize guilt. To ensure punishment, the ego will unconsciously leave clues.

Psychodynamic theory is widely subscribed to by practicing psychologists who apply the theory in the treatment of adolescent offenders. Critics worry the theory rests on questionable assumptions. First there is *no* evidence of a causal link between a child's "state of mind" and his or her behavior. It also is arguable whether personality consists of an id, ego, and superego. These are traits Freud constructed, and there is no scientific evidence that any or all of the elements are present.

theory in a nutshell

Sigmund Freud

Freud believed that unconscious mental processes developed in early childhood control our personalities. The personality consists of three parts: the *id, ego,* and *superego.* In mentally healthy children, the three parts of the personality work together. When the parts are in conflict, children may become maladjusted and ready for delinquency.

Behavioral Theory   In contrast to psychodynamic theory, *behavioral theory* proposes that behavior reflects our interactions with others throughout our lifetime. A leading behaviorist was the Harvard psychologist B.F. Skinner, who

Source: By permission of Leigh Rubin and Creators Syndicate, Inc.

turned to the scientific method in his studies rather than relying on unobservable mental processes (Freud). Skinner theorized that children learn conformity and deviance from the *punishments* and *reinforcements* they receive in response to their behavior. He believed that the environment shapes behavior and that children identify those aspects of their environment they find both pleasing and painful; their behavior is the result of the consequences it produces. He concluded that children repeat rewarded behavior and terminate punished behavior.[142]

Some behaviorists have used Skinner's theory as a springboard to expand the idea. The behaviorist Albert Bandura argued that learning and experiences couple with values and expectations to determine behavior. In his *social learning theory,* Bandura suggests that children learn by modeling and imitating others.[143] For example, children learn to be aggressive from their life experiences and learn aggression in different ways; for instance, by seeing parents argue, watching their friends fight, viewing violence on television and motion pictures, and listening to violent music. What children learn

theory in a nutshell

B. F. Skinner

Skinner argued that behavior is a consequence of the reinforcements and punishments it produces. Delinquents have had delinquency reinforced (and not punished) by others, either intentionally or unintentionally.

If children learn
behaviors by
watching and
imitating others,
what consequences
should there be for
adults who behave
badly in the presence
of children? Jail?
Prison? Sterilization?
Treatment?

is that aggression is sometimes acceptable and produces the desired outcome. If Bandura is correct, is it possible children learn to be aggressive and commit violent crimes from what they see in the media? Putting it differently, is there a relationship between media violence and crime? Criminologists have studied these questions for more than 70 years. In 1933 Herbert Blumer concluded from conversations with young people that movies did influence their behavior.[144] Decades later the evidence suggests they still do. For instance, in 1979, shortly after release of *The Warriors,* three murders were committed that bore striking resemblances to acts in the film. Roughly 20 deaths have been blamed on *The Deer Hunter.* One incident involved a teenager who died after shooting himself with a .38-caliber handgun while playing Russian roulette, just as in the movie. The would-be assassin of President Reagan, John Hinckley, Jr., identified with Travis Bickle, the character played by Robert De Niro in *Taxi Driver.* After seeing the film 15 times, Hinckley became obsessed with Jodie Foster, who played the teenage prostitute. In *Taxi Driver,* Bickle entertained the thought of assassinating a political candidate and stopped only after the plan had failed. Four days after watching *Born Innocent,* three teenage girls attacked a 9-year-old girl on a California beach and raped her with a bottle, just as it was done in the movie. The victim's mother filed an $11 million negligence suit against NBC, accusing the company of being responsible for the rape. The Supreme Court ruled that networks are not liable for damages unless they willfully seek to induce violence.

Other reports of violence have been linked to *Boyz N' the Hood, Natural Born Killers, Money Train, Juice, Scream, Scream II, The Man in the Iron Mask;* and two television series, *South Park* and *Jackass.* When *Boyz N' the Hood* was released in July 1990, two people were killed and more than 30 injured near or outside movie theaters. Research has linked *Natural Born Killers* to at least 100 murders, and former Senator Robert Dole suggested that Columbia Pictures should share the blame for the torching of New York City subway

think
about it

Many people believe that the media causes crime. Should the media be censored to protect against inflaming fans? Or, would such a policy be fruitless because virtually anything can serve as the inspiration to violence for a psychologically unstable person?

clerk Harry Kaufman, the victim of a copycat crime from a scene in *Money Train*.[145] Following the premier of *Juice*, a movie about four African American juveniles, in which one of the juveniles gets involved in a robbery that ends in murder, violence broke out at theaters across the country. For instance, in Chicago a 16-year-old was shot and killed by a stray bullet from a fight between two boys waiting for tickets to the last show. In Philadelphia an 18-year-old was paralyzed from the chest down after he was shot coming out of the movie. In New York City a 16-year-old was stabbed in a theater during a quarrel with another teenager.[146] More re-cently, two teens obsessed with *Scream* and *Scream II* were convicted of murder. They stabbed their victim 45 times with four knives and a screwdriver. In the movies, victims were knifed by killers obsessed with horror movies.[147] Finally, a 9-year-old girl reenacting a scene from *The Man in the Iron Mask* hanged herself with a shoelace. Newscasters have also blamed at least one school shooting on Comedy Central's television show *South Park*, and MTV's *Jackass* was blamed when a 13-year-old Connecticut boy laid himself across a barbecue grill and suffered severe burns. Experts have blamed the video game, *Tomb Raider*, for the precipitous increase in violent crime committed by adolescent females.[148]

theory in a nutshell

Albert Bandura

Bandura thought children learn how to behave from others whom they model and imitate. Delinquent behavior is learned from direct, face-to-face interaction or by observing others in person or symbolically in literature, films, television, and music.

A persistent stream of data suggests a strong connection between children seeing violent entertainment and then behaving aggressively. Of more than 3,500 published studies on the topic, all but 18 have reported a positive association between media exposure and violent behavior.[149] An esteemed panel of social and behavioral scientists concluded that the evidence points "overwhelmingly to a causal connection between media violence and aggressive behavior" in children. Viewing violent entertainment affects children in at least one of three ways: (1) children see violence as an effective way to settle conflicts; (2) children become emotionally desensitized toward violence in real life; and (3) entertainment violence feeds a perception that the world is a violent and mean place and increases the fear of victimization.[150]

In spite of strong evidence of a relationship between media violence and behavior, a few criminologists continue to believe that other factors may be equally or more to blame for juvenile violence. They contend that juvenile violence stems more from family breakdown, peer influence, and the proliferation of guns in society than media violence. While there are studies that suggest the impact of media violence on children's behavior is short-lived,[151] new research on the topic consistently reports the opposite. Lowell Huesmann and his colleagues have linked violent TV viewing at ages 6 to 9 to adult aggression for both sexes. They surveyed 329 adults in the late 1970s and interviewed them and their spouses or friends and checked crime records 20 years later. As children, the participants were rated for exposure to televised violence after they chose 8 favorite shows from 80 popular shows for their age group and indicated how much they watched

Sega's House of the Dead 2 is a popular violent video game. The game, labeled "M" for mature audiences, is not supposed to be sold to anyone under 17, but children can easily buy violent video games. Do violent video games cause some children to commit crime? Should there be laws to make it harder to sell violent video games to children?

them. Researchers assessed the programs for amount of physical violence. As young adults, the men who scored in the top 20 percent on childhood exposure to violence were about twice as likely as other men to have pushed, grabbed, or shoved their wives during an argument in the year preceding the interview. Women in the top 20 percent were about twice as likely as other women to have thrown something at their husbands.[152]

A related study by Gina Wingood and her colleagues found that teens who spend more time watching the sex and violence depicted in the "reel" life of "gangsta" rap music videos are more likely to practice those behaviors in real life. After studying 522 African American girls between the ages of 14 and 18 from nonurban, lower socioeconomic neighborhoods, the researchers found that compared to those who never or rarely watched these videos, the girls who viewed these gangsta videos for at least 14 hours per week were far more likely to practice numerous problem behaviors. They were (1) three times more likely to hit a teacher; (2) nearly three times more likely to get arrested; (3) twice as likely to have multiple sexual partners; and (4) almost twice as likely to get a sexually transmitted disease, use drugs, or drink alcohol.[153] These and the many hundreds of other studies on the topic of media violence, aggression, and crime, have lead the American Psychological Association to conclude that viewing violence on TV and other mass media *does promote aggressive behavior,* particularly in children.

Trait Theory and Delinquency Prevention   Social policy based on biological theories recommends that offenders receive drug therapy or possibly be isolated from the general population. Because offenders cannot control their debilitating condition on their own, public safety mandates that when the cause of the behavior is known, it must be neutralized. Practically speaking, offenders will likely submit to drug therapy to control their impulses, be institutionalized, or both. As shown in Boxes 5-1 and 5-2, previous attempts to prevent delinquency in accordance with trait theory were cruel and unsuccessful. Fortunately, contemporary biological criminology is biosocial in its perspective and points to the critical importance of both biology and environment in producing delinquency. Many environmental risk factors, such as maternal smoking, alcohol, and environmental toxins, can be reduced through education, public policy, and enforcement.

Prevention is another way to reduce delinquency particularly among the youngest potential offenders who present biological risk factors for crime. In her review of the promise of prevention as it relates to neurobiological research, Diana Fishbein concluded:

> As a result of the ineffective, unidimensional approaches of the past, we are now defaulting to the mental health and criminal justice systems with troubled individuals. Rather than ignoring the warning signs in childhood and waiting until adulthood to put these systems into motion, spending billions of dollars for legal remedies that do not produce favorable outcomes, the provision of sorely needed services and interventions to high risk individuals can yield far greater benefits.[154]

Early intervention in the lives of at-risk children can help to promote factors that insulate children from delinquency, minimize or erase the risk factors that contribute to delinquency, and overall try to equalize the life chances for all children and adolescents to develop into healthy, prosocial adults.

Psychological theories recommend two strategies for preventing delinquency, and both are widely practiced today. If psychodynamic theory is correct, if children's instinctual drives are not controlled, they will experience internal conflicts that will manifest themselves in delinquent behavior. Delinquency is a symptom of deep-seated psychological problems. Offenders need counseling to acquire an understanding of the cause of mental disturbance. The use of psychodynamic theory in juvenile justice peaked in the 1950s when influential groups championed counseling, group therapy, and established correctional techniques. In turn, these and other groups seized upon the idea imbedded in psychodynamic theory that it was possible to identify "predelinquents" before they committed any crimes. Today these children are labeled "at-risk" youths. Prevention programs were developed for children in need. These antidelinquency programs marked the beginning of the child-guidance movement, the goal of which was to neutralize latent delinquency in the preadolescent.

Behavioral theories blame delinquency on the interaction between children and their environment. Social policies derived from this approach emphasize teaching children alternative ways of living. One very popular application of behavioral theory is *behavior modification therapy,* a method for changing behavior through conditioning. Behavior modification was widely practiced in the late 20th century to treat maladaptive behaviors such as overeating, drug use, alcoholism, and smoking. Two behavior modification therapies used then and still practiced today are aversion therapy and operant conditioning. In *aversion therapy,* children are taught to connect unwanted behavior with punishment. Juvenile alcohol offenders may be required to receive treatment where they must ingest a drug that causes nausea or vomiting if they drink alcohol. The underlying idea of aversion therapy is that children will connect drinking with unpleasantness and stop drinking to avoid the ill effect. *Operant conditioning* uses rewards to reinforce desired behavior and punishment to abort behavior. One example of the application of operant conditioning with juvenile delinquents is found inside of many juvenile reformatories where the **token economy,** a system of handing out points that can be exchanged for privileges such as watching TV and punishing behavior by taking those same privileges away, is in place.

Theories answer the questions of why and when something will likely happen. They are important because *ideas have consequences*. Two broad types of theories were discussed: *choice theories* and *trait theories*. Choice theories assume children are rational and intelligent people who make informed decisions to commit crime based on whether they will benefit from doing so. *Trait theories* blame delinquency on factors over which the individual has very little if any control, such as defective brain chemistry, hyperactivity, low intelligence, and personality.

The Classical School of Criminology represents choice theories. Besides theorizing that people are rational, intelligent beings who exercise free will, these theories also state that people commit crime because they imagine it to be in their best interests. Classical theorists also think punishment deters crime and that the best punishment is one that is certain, swift, and severe. The Classical School failed because of its rigidity. It gave rise to the Neoclassical School, which introduced the ideas of mitigating circumstances and individual justice and laid the groundwork for the Positive School of Criminology.

Trait theories go hand-in-hand with the Positive School. The trait theories discussed in this chapter represent more than 150 years of thinking about crime. Trait theories that emphasize the biology of the offender blame delinquency on heredity or some other trait located *inside* of children. They find the cause of crime in faulty brain chemistry, heredity, or intelligence, for example. On the other hand, trait theories that stress the importance of individual psychology examine the connection between an individual's mental health and crime.

Sociologists, believing that delinquency is the product of a child's social environment, have largely rejected Classical or choice theories. They have also been critical of both biological and psychological theories. They are concerned that biological theories do not clearly state the *specific* behavior they want to account for. It is not enough to explain something called "antisocial behavior," because it is too vague. After all, not all "antisocial" behaviors are dysfunctional, and not all legal behaviors are moral or acceptable. Sociologists have made similar criticisms about psychological theories. They criticize these theories for being difficult to test because their main concepts are so loosely defined. Consequently, the relationship between, for instance, an antisocial personality and delinquency has not received much empirical support. For some children, personality is a major determinant of whether they will commit delinquency; for others, personality does not matter very much.

Both biological and psychological theories assume that the causes of delinquency have very little to do with social factors such as the environment, poverty, or racism but instead stems from some trait children possess. Flaws, defects, or deficiencies in their constitution are the best explanations of delinquency. By the early 20th century, sociologists started to develop delinquency theories of their own that highlighted the role of social forces. In Chapter 6, three groups of sociological explanations are reviewed: cultural deviance, strain, and social control theories.

key terms

Atavistic beings   The idea that criminals are a throwback to a more primitive stage of development.

Attention deficit/hyperactivity disorder (ADHD)   The most common neurobehavioral childhood disorder.

Classical School   A school of thought that blames delinquency on the choices people make.

Determinate sentences   Prison sentences of a fixed amount of time, such as 5 years.

Dizygotic twins (DZ)   Fraternal twins who develop from two eggs fertilized at the same time.

Free will   The idea that people choose one course of action over another.

Genotype   A person's genetic composition.

Indeterminate sentences   Prison sentences of varying time lengths, such as 5 to 10 years.

Individual justice   The idea that criminal law must reflect differences among people and their circumstances.

Individual theories   Theories that blame delinquency on personal traits such as temperament, genetics, and brain chemistry.

Intelligence   The ability to learn, exercise judgment, and be imaginative.

IQ score   The ratio of one's mental age multiplied by 100 and divided by their chronological age.

Justice model   A corrections philosophy that promotes flat or fixed-time sentences, abolishment of parole, and use of prison to punish offenders.

Mitigating circumstances   Factors that may be responsible for an individual's behavior, such as age, insanity, and incompetence.

Monozygotic twins (MZ)   Identical twins who develop from one fertilized egg. MZ twins have identical DNA.

Neoclassical School   A school of thought that considers mitigating circumstances when determining culpability for delinquency.

Positive School   A school of thought that blames delinquency on factors that are in place before crime is committed.

Rational choice theory   Suggests that delinquents are rational people who make calculated choices regarding what they are going to do before they act.

Retribution   A punishment philosophy based on society's moral outrage or disapproval of a crime.

Routine activities theory   Argues that motivated offenders, suitable targets, and absence of capable guardians produce delinquency.

Somatotype   The idea that criminals can be identified by physical appearance.

Stigmata   Distinctive physical features of born criminals.

Theories   Integrated sets of ideas that explain and predict phenomena.

Token economy   A system of handing out points that can be exchanged for privileges such as watching TV and punishing behavior by taking those same privileges away.

Utilitarian punishment model   The idea that offenders must be punished to protect society.

6

Sociological Theory: Cultural Deviance, Strain, and Social Control

Trait theories blame delinquency on factors inside of the child. In the early 20th century, sociologists challenged this idea and began to blame delinquency on factors outside the individual. The first sociological theories to advance this new position were called cultural deviance theories, which assumed children are incapable of committing "deviant" acts. Even though children may commit deviant acts by the standards of the larger society, they are not committing deviant acts by the standards of their own neighborhoods. Cultural deviance theories see deviance as conformity to a set of values not accepted by the larger society. A second group of explanations, strain theories, contends that people are moral animals, committing crimes when they are under extreme pressure. The pressure comes from people having legitimate desires. Children, for example, desire success as everyone tells them they should, but they are unable to attain success by following the legitimate rules of society. Out of desperation they turn to crime to acquire the unattainable, which they may consider rightfully belongs to them. The final group of theories discussed is social control theories. These theories contend that if a child's bond or tie to society has been broken, he or she is "free" to commit delinquency. At the core of control theories is the Hobbesian question: Why do children obey the rules of society? Social control theories take deviance for granted, and conformity to rules needs to be explained.

CULTURAL DEVIANCE THEORY

Cultural deviance theory believes that delinquency is a natural result of conditions that exist within certain neighborhoods in cities. This theory was popular in the early 20th century when the Northeast and Midwest were undergoing rapid population growth resulting from the migration of Southern African Americans and European immigrants looking for industrial jobs to cities such as Boston, Chicago, New York, and Philadelphia. Many of the new residents were poorly educated, had few marketable skills, and did not speak English. To accommodate this growth, large cities expanded outward. Wealthy residents moved to the suburbs, leaving the poor and uneducated behind to fend for themselves in the old, run-down inner cities.

Clifford Shaw and Henry McKay

Two criminologists who were curious about this transformation as it emerged in Chicago were Clifford Shaw and Henry McKay. They concluded that delinquency was by caused by the neighborhood in which a child lived. Instead of focusing on individual traits, Shaw and McKay studied the impact of the "kinds of places" (neighborhoods) that created conditions favorable to delinquency.[1] They discovered that delinquency rates declined the farther one moved from the center of the city. They reached this conclusion after dividing Chicago into five concentric circles, or zones. At the center was the Loop, the downtown business district where property values were highest (Zone I). Beyond the Loop was the zone of transition (Zone II), containing an inner ring of factories and an outer ring of "first-settlement colonies, of rooming-house districts of homeless men, of resorts of gambling, bootlegging, sexual vice, and of breeding places of crime."[2]

Zones III and IV were suburban residential areas, and Zone V extended beyond the suburbs. Delinquency rates were highest in the first two zones and declined steadily as one moved farther away from the city center (see Figure 6-1).

Shaw and McKay had a ready explanation for their findings. Neighboring railroads, stockyards, and indus-

theory in a nutshell

Clifford Shaw and Henry McKay

Shaw and McKay believe that run-down areas of a city create social disorganization, fostering cultural conflicts that allow delinquency to become a tradition.

tries made Zone II the least desirable residential area, but also the cheapest. Therefore, people naturally gravitated to this area if they were poor, as many immigrants to the United States were. What did these findings say about delinquency? Shaw and McKay interpreted the findings in cultural and environmental terms. Delinquency rates remained stable in certain Chicago neighborhoods, regardless of the race or ethnicity of the people who lived there. Areas high in delinquency at the turn of the century were also high in delinquency 30 years later, even though many of the original residents had moved away or died. Shaw and McKay explained their finding in the following way:

- *Run-down areas create social disorganization.* Cities such as Chicago were expanding industrially, their populations were increasing, and segregation was forcing new immigrants into the slums. These immigrants were not familiar with the city's geography or culture; they arrived with different languages and work experiences; and they immediately faced new and overwhelming problems, including poverty, disease, and confusion.

figure 6-1   Zones of Delinquency in Chicago, 1900–1933

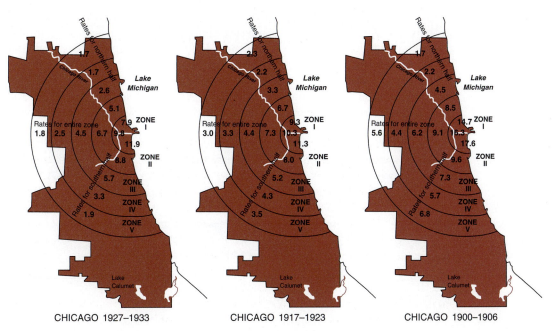

- *Social disorganization fosters cultural conflicts.* In low-delinquency areas of the city, there typically was agreement among parents on which values and attitudes were the "right" ones, with general consensus on the importance of education, constructive leisure, and other child rearing issues. Local institutions, such as the PTA, churches, and neighborhood centers, reinforced these conventional values. No such consistency prevailed in high-delinquency areas. The norms of a variety of cultures existed side by side, creating a state of normative ambiguity, or anomie (cultural conflict). This condition was aggravated by the presence of individuals who promoted an unconventional lifestyle and defined behaviors such as theft as an acceptable way to acquire wealth. This value system could count on the support of criminal gangs, rackets, and semi-legitimate businesses.

- *Cultural conflict allows delinquency to flourish.* Children raised in low-socioeconomic, high-delinquency rate areas were exposed to both conventional and criminal value systems. They saw criminal activities and organizations in operation daily. Successful criminals passed on their knowledge to younger residents, who then taught it to even younger children. Delinquency became a tradition in certain neighborhoods through the process of **cultural transmission,** where criminal values are passed from one generation to the next.

- *Allowed to flourish, delinquency becomes a full-time career.* Children in these Chicago neighborhoods dabbled in delinquency early in life, perhaps by age 5 or 6. Initial offenses were trivial, but their acts became increasingly serious, and delinquencies often became group efforts (see Figure 6-2).

think
about it

Even in the worst neighborhoods the majority of residents are law-abiding, suggesting that individual flaws explain delinquency. How would biologists, psychologists, and sociologists differently address this issue?

Relatively few sociologists went about testing Shaw and McKay's work. That changed in 1989 when Robert Sampson and W. Byron Groves published research findings supporting their general ideas.[3] Follow-up assessments of Shaw and McKay's theory have also found support for their propositions. Robert Sampson and Lydia Bean, for instance, used Shaw and McKay's thesis in their research on rural America and discovered the rate of juvenile violence was strongly correlated with rates of poverty concentration, single-parent families, and racial isolation.[4] Wayne Osgood and Jeff Chambers used Shaw and McKay's propositions in their research in rural American and discovered the rate of juvenile violence was strongly correlated with rates of residential instability, family disruption, and ethnic heterogeneity.[5] Additional support for Shaw and McKay's work also has been reported by Christopher Lowenkamp and his col-

figure 6-2   Mapping Delinquency Theory: Clifford Shaw and Henry McKay

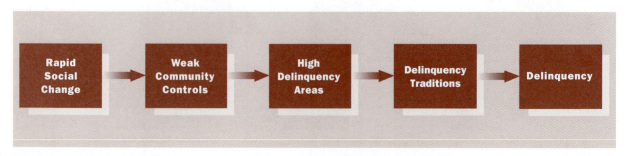

Rapid Social Change → Weak Community Controls → High Delinquency Areas → Delinquency Traditions → Delinquency

leagues.[6] Today it is widely accepted that social ties (e.g., friendship networks) lead to informal social controls (e.g., informal surveillance of the streets) that ease the effects of social disorganization (e.g., poverty, residential instability, racial and ethnic heterogeneity).[7] It is also clear that different types of social ties vary in their ability to produce mechanisms of neighborhood control. The impact of friendship ties, for instance, may be less than the social control exerted by more formally organized networks.[8] As has been reported by Mary Pattillo, whether social ties strengthen or weaken social controls depends on the particular neighborhood in which residents are involved as well as their specific interests. In her study of an African American neighborhood in Chicago, Pattillo found that some neighborhood networks (with law-abiding citizens) stimulated informal supervision of neighborhoods, whereas other networks that included law-abiding citizens, as well as gang members and drug dealers, undermined the neighborhood's efforts to fight delinquency.[9] For social ties to be effective at reducing delinquency, residents must develop a willingness to take action, and whether they do depends on mutual trust and solidarity among them. Robert Sampson and his colleagues have captured the core of this idea in their notion of **collective efficacy,** or the "mutual trust among neighbors combined with willingness to intervene on behalf of the common good, specifically to supervise children and maintain public order."[10] They found the degree of collective efficacy in a neighborhood is a better predictor of the violent crime rate than either poverty or racial composition. Their findings have been supported by Barbara Warner and Pamela Roundtree, who observed that concentrated disadvantage and the level of social ties affect cultural strength, which in turn significantly affects informal social control. The importance of Warner and Roundtree's study is that it illustrates the importance of weakened cultural strength in explaining informal social control in neighborhoods.[11]

Even though Shaw and McKay's theory stands on solid footing, there are questions still to be answered. For example, do people living in high-crime rate neighborhoods have different values than people living elsewhere? Edwin Sutherland inquired about this. He suggested there exists a **differential social organization** among neighborhoods.[12] Just because children in high-delinquency-rate neighborhoods might have regular contact with values that support criminality does not necessarily mean their neighborhoods are disorganized; their neighborhood might just be organized differently than other neighborhoods. However, Sutherland did agree that some neighborhoods do support greater opportunities for learning criminal values. Some inner city neighborhoods, for instance, are characterized by a predominance of delinquent gangs that pull adolescents into crime. Gangs influence the norms and behaviors of residents, causing neighborhoods to appear as though they support criminal activity, when they might not. Crime rates in such neighborhoods will likely be higher than crime rates elsewhere in the city. Children living in high-crime-rate neighborhoods are at high risk for committing crime. Having ready access to firearms increases the risk of violence, and youth who carry guns are more likely to offend (see Chapter 3).

Ruth Kornhauser thinks that all people share conventional values, including the desire to live in a crime-free neighborhood. Crime is high in some neighborhoods because the people living there have fewer opportunities to pursue conventional goals. These neighborhoods struggle to prevent crime because they lack the resources, willingness, or capacity to prevent it; not because they believe in oppositional values anchored in the community.[13] In neighborhoods with weak

If immersion in gang life is a central component of childhood socialization, is there any social policy that can preclude gang involvement? Who is most to blame if this child becomes a gang-affiliated juvenile delinquent?

conventional values, residents have little cultural support for exercising social control over others.[14] It is also possible that high-crime-rate neighborhoods lack a consensus of moral values, and residents are exposed to both law-abiding and deviant lifestyles. In other words, a segment of the neighborhood is attached to conventional values and another segment is not.[15]

That there are these differences speaks to the need for additional research. Of particular interest to criminologists is identifying just how widespread oppositional values are in high-crime-rate neighborhoods. To what extent do residents of different neighborhoods reject conventional values and norms? Are conventional values attenuated or suspended because residents have learned to expect deviant behavior on the street? Are there neighborhoods where the majority of residents believe it is acceptable to take the law into their own hands, that is, to retaliate against people who have offended or attacked them? In the final analysis, however, it is necessary that we offer a caveat regarding Shaw and McKay's theory. Sometimes their theory leads to a misinterpretation of the crime problem. Remember that findings about a neighborhood do not necessarily apply to its residents. If you use neighborhood-level data to draw conclusions about individual residents, you are committing the **ecology fallacy:** Knowledge about a neighborhood says nothing about the behavior of specific individuals. It is not necessarily true that when a high crime rate is discovered in a crowded neighborhood where the residents are poor and uneducated that those uneducated and poor individuals are criminals.

Edwin Sutherland

Among Edwin Sutherland's contributions to delinquency is his theory of differential association, where he described the process of becoming delinquent. No theory in modern criminology has had as much influence on our thinking about delinquency as this one.[16]

Sutherland first published the *theory of differential association* in 1939, revising it in 1947. The theory's basic premise is that behavior is learned through interaction with significant others, typically parents and peers. The likelihood of a youth becoming delinquent is determined by his or her interactions with both conventional and criminal associations. If a child has more contacts supporting criminal conduct than opposing it, he or she will be more likely to commit crime than someone who has more positive than negative associations. The theory consists of nine principles:

theory in a nutshell

Edwin Sutherland

Sutherland argued that delinquent behavior is learned from intimate others. Children who become delinquents have learned an excess of definitions favorable to the violation of law over definitions unfavorable to the violation of law.

- Delinquent behavior is learned; it is not inherited. Biological and hereditary factors are rejected as explanations for the cause of delinquency. Only sociological factors explain why youth commit crime.

- Delinquent behavior is learned through interaction with others by way of communication. The communication can be either verbal or nonverbal.

- Learning occurs in intimate groups. Children learn to commit crime in small, face-to-face gatherings.

- In intimate groups children learn techniques for committing crime, as well as the appropriate motives, attitudes, and rationalizations. The learning process involves exposure not only to the techniques of committing offenses but also to the attitudes or rationalizations that justify those acts.

- The specific direction of motives and drives is learned from definitions of the legal code as being favorable or unfavorable. The term, "definitions," refers to attitudes. Attitudes favoring lawbreaking are common, for instance, among people who smoke marijuana. People opposed to marijuana laws claim that these laws are senseless and discriminate against the younger generation. They also argue that marijuana does no more harm than alcohol; lawmakers who condemn drug use are uninformed killjoys.

- A juvenile becomes delinquent due to an excess of definitions favorable to the violation of law over definitions unfavorable to the violation of law. This sixth principle is the core of the theory. A parent who even hints through words or actions that it is acceptable to fight, treat women as potential conquests, cheat on income tax returns, or lie may promote delinquency in children unless these statements are outnumbered by definitions (attitudes) that favor obeying the law, for example, driving the speed limit. Definitions favorable to the violation of law can be learned from both criminal and noncriminal people.

- Tendency toward delinquency will be affected by the frequency, duration, priority, and intensity of learning experiences. The longer, earlier, more intensely, and more frequently youths are exposed to attitudes about delinquency (pro and con), the more likely they will be influenced. Sutherland used the term *intensity* to refer to the degree of respect a person gives to a role model or associate. Thus, correctional officers are not likely to become criminals, despite the positive things inmates say about living a life of crime. The reason is that officers do not respect the inmates and therefore do not adopt their beliefs, values, and attitudes.

- Learning delinquent behavior involves the same mechanisms involved in any other learning. While the content of what is learned is different, the process for learning any behavior is the same.

- Criminal behavior and noncriminal behavior are expressions of the same needs and values. In other words, the goals of delinquents and nondelinquents are similar. What is different are the means they use to pursue their goals.[17]

Differential association theory has shaped thinking about delinquency for more than a half century. A clear signal of its widespread acceptance is the many research studies testing and critiquing it. These tests generally show that children are more likely to commit crime when they associate with delinquent peers.[18] Many studies have found that children with prosocial peers are less likely to commit crime.[19] Mark Warr in fact contends that the nature of peer associations is the best predictor of delinquency:

> No characteristic of individuals known to criminologists is a better predictor of criminal behavior than the number of delinquent friends an individual has. The strong correlation between delinquent behavior and delinquent friends has been documented in scores of studies from the 1950s up to the present day . . . using alternative kinds of criminological data (self-reports, official records, perceptual data) on subjects and friends, alternative research designs, and data on a wide variety of criminal offenses. Few, if any, empirical irregularities in criminology have been documented as often or over as long a period as the association between delinquency and delinquent friends.[20]

Warr documented these statements through a comprehensive review of the large body of research on the group nature of delinquency and the role of peers in delinquency in the United States and throughout the world. Nicole Piquero and her colleagues, who studied the impact of delinquent peers on the delinquency of boys and girls, have extended Warr's study. They found that delinquent peer association is a good predictor of delinquency generally, but it is a better predictor of delinquency for boys than girls.[21]

Research has also found that peer associations have a greater impact on a child's behavior than do long-standing relationships.[22] Delinquent friends, in other words, do not have much of an effect on a child's attitudes, but rather, they have a temporary and short-term influence on the child's behavior. Delinquent behavior may not be the result of lifelong learning but a consequence of immediate and current relationships with delinquent peers (see Chapter 8). Barbara Costello and Paul Vowell have discovered that friends' attitudes and behaviors have direct effects on offending that are not mediated by the child's own attitudes. Associating with delinquent friends influences a child's behavior in ways that have nothing to do with the child's attitudes about crime.[23] These findings, however, beg for answers to questions that assess the intervening processes between friends' attitudes and behaviors and delinquency. Warr and Mark Stafford have asked: Do friends reward deviant behaviors? Does criminal profit vicariously reward friends of the offender? Do friends influence legitimate aspects of offenders' lives, such as their goals or academic successes, and thereby influence deviance? Is continued offending the result of continued contact with the same friends over time? Some research has addressed these questions, but more work is needed.[24]

A related shortcoming of Sutherland's theory is that he focused only on face-to-face interactions. This is because in the 1930s when Sutherland was writing, the influence of film, the Internet, music, and television on behavior was either non-existent or considered to have little impact. Notice that in the nine principles of his theory listed here there is no mention of how the mass media might influence behavior. This omission prompted criminologists to reexamine Sutherland's theory. Daniel Glaser introduced *differential identification theory,* where he suggested that face-to-face interactions were only one way children might learn conventional and deviant values. Children might learn values and social roles from characters in films, such as James Dean in *Rebel without a Cause.*[25] Then, C. Ray Jeffery offered a second modification to Sutherland's theory. In *differential reinforcement theory,* Jeffery said that (1) children learn from the consequences of their actions and (2) both social and nonsocial factors influence their behavior. A child who steals food, for example, may receive reinforcement from the fact that the stolen goods provide him or her with nourishment (nonsocial) and from the approval he or she receives from family and friends for being able to "get away with it" (social).[26] Building on Jeffery and his earlier work with Robert Burgess,[27] Ronald Akers has restated differential association theory to incorporate these new ideas. The result was a theory composed of seven propositions:

1. Deviant behavior is learned according to the principles of operant conditioning.

2. Deviant behavior is learned in nonsocial situations that are reinforcing or discriminating and through social interactions in which the behavior of other persons is reinforcing or discriminating for such behavior.

3. The principal part of learning deviant behavior occurs in those groups that comprise or control the individual's major source of reinforcements.

4. Learning deviant behavior includes specific techniques, attitudes, and avoidance procedures and is a function of the effective and available reinforcers and the existing reinforcement contingencies.

5. The specific class of behavior learned and its frequency of occurrence are a function of the effective and available reinforcers and the deviant or non-deviant direction of the norms, rules, and definitions, which in the past have accompanied the reinforcements.

6. The probability that a person will commit deviant behavior is increased in the presence of normative statements that in the process of differential reinforcement of such behavior over conforming behavior have acquired discriminative value.

7. The strength of deviant behavior is a direct function of the amount, frequency, and probability of its reinforcement.[28]

Central to Akers's reformulation are propositions 2, 3, 5, and 6. Propositions 2 and 3 state that learning takes place in nonsocial situations; however, most learning occurs in social interactions with significant others. Propositions 5 and 6 speak to the importance of social definitions. Children who receive an excess of definitions favorable to the violation of law over definitions unfavorable to the violation of law are more likely to commit crime.

Walter Miller

Walter Miller worked for a number of years with delinquent gangs in Roxbury, Massachusetts, just outside Boston. His experiences led him to see delinquency as an expression of a particular culture present in slum neighborhoods. Miller's contribution to deviance theory is explaining gang delinquency. His research methods have often included innovative approaches, using unobtrusive observation techniques. Miller would go to a pizza parlor and pretend to be completely absorbed in his meal and newspaper. In fact, however, he was listening carefully to what the youths around him were talking about. He took extensive notes, which were later mined for theoretical nuggets.[29] Miller's theory of juvenile delinquency is summarized below:

theory in a nutshell

Walter Miller

Miller blamed delinquency on two structural features of the lower-class: focal concerns and female-based households. Together they produce sex-role problems for boys. Boys, who need to learn to become men, must learn from women. This is inadequate, so they join together and form a gang. Status is achieved in the gang by living up to focal concerns, some of which lead to delinquency.

- The lower-class has a distinctive family structure. Female-based households and serial monogamy characterize lower-class families. Women run the household, and they go through a series of husbands or lovers. Because there are inevitably periods when no men are in their lives, women have to fend for themselves and their children.

- This family structure alienates boys, pushing them to join all-male peer groups. Miller believes that boys grow up with the traditional belief that a boy should not be told what to do by his mother, aunt, or older sister. With no fathers or father figures present, however, lower-class boys are subject to the control and authority of women. Resenting this, they seek the company of males who congregate on the street corner or in other gathering places, like the pool hall.

- In these all-male peer groups, lower-class culture is created and transmitted. Boys develop values and standards, which mirror those of lower-class culture in general.

- Lower-class culture revolves around six **focal concerns** or values, which guide behavior. The focal concerns of the lower-class are autonomy, excitement, fate, smartness, trouble, and toughness. *Autonomy* describes the resistance of lower-class youths to having their lives controlled by others. Often you hear them say such things as, "No one's gonna push me around" or "He can shove this job up his ass." Curiously, however, the actual behavior of lower-class people contradicts the cultural value of autonomy. Typically, they seek out jobs in restrictive settings where they are told what to do and when to do it, because they identify strong controls with being cared for. *Excitement* is the search for thrills, danger, or risk that often occurs as a result of excessive drinking, fighting, gambling, and promiscuous sexual relationships. *Fate* is the lower-class belief that forces beyond their control determine their lives. These forces are not religious ones; rather, they refer to whether someone is naturally lucky or unlucky. *Smartness* is the ability to avoid being outfoxed. It refers to "street smarts," or the skill to take advantage of the weaknesses of others. *Toughness* is a physical prowess that is often displayed through machismo (lack of sensitivity, and a tendency to treat women as sex objects and conquests). *Trouble* is the most important concern. Getting into and staying out of trouble are major preoccupations of lower-class people. Children are judged or assigned status by how well they do this. Focal concerns are not unique to the lower class; however, they are more significant to it than they are to the middle and upper classes.

- Strong identification with the focal concerns of lower-class culture leads to violations of the law. Lower-class adolescent boys in gangs get into trouble because they live up to the standards presented to them in lower-class culture, and according to the middle-class, these standards or values are delinquent. [30]

Strong identification with these values is why boys commit crime. Children participate in delinquency because they must live up to the standards of their neighborhood, regardless of what outsiders think about what they are doing. The focal concern of toughness, for instance, may mean the juvenile must fight when disrespected; possessing street smarts (smartness) may lead to drug dealing; and excitement may result in excessive drinking, gambling, or using of illegal drugs. The linkages among Miller's statements are illustrated in Figure 6-3.

Miller's theory is interesting and original. It focused on the culture of poverty and America's underclass, concerns that were becoming more popular in the larger society at the time Miller was writing. The notion of a culture of poverty can be traced to Oscar Lewis, who in his studies of Latin America described a situation where people resigned themselves to being poor as a matter of fate. Children growing up in this environment eventually believed the same thing about their future: No matter what they did, fate had determined that they too would be poor.[31] William Julius Wilson has also reported on America's underclass. Wilson explained why Chicago's inner city neighborhoods have

figure 6-3   Mapping Delinquency Theory: Walter Miller

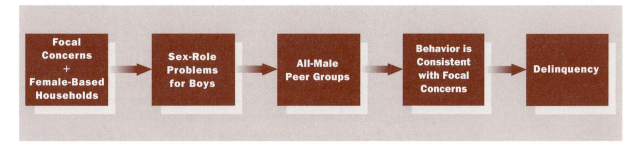

deteriorated. The deterioration has been gradual and can be blamed on structural changes that have taken place in society at large. As society became more integrated, opportunities for the professional and entrepreneurial class of African Americans increased. The members of this class moved from the inner city to the suburbs to pursue the "good life." They took with them not only their money and their businesses but also values that emphasized upward mobility. They left behind a hardcore group of chronically unemployed, unskilled, and poorly educated people who lacked the social, economic, or political base with which to prosper. Today we are seeing some of the consequences of their migration. In inner city neighborhoods, there is an underclass of "truly disadvantaged" people. These neighborhoods are riddled with social ills: homicide, violence, fetal alcohol syndrome, illegal drug use, teen pregnancy, unemployment, and so on. Worse yet, there are no indications that conditions are improving. More signs point to present conditions being the "calm before the storm."[32]

The United States is changing from a manufacturing to a service economy. In the past several decades industrial production has declined and an increasing number of jobs have been outsourced to other countries, triggering a decrease in the demand for unskilled labor. Much of the production that still exists has followed a trend of relocation, shifting manufacturing jobs to foreign countries and the suburbs. As opportunity declines, crime flourishes.[33]

The central issue, however, is not whether there is a culture of poverty or an underclass; experts agree they exist. What experts disagree on is why they exist. There are two competing lines of thought. Edward Banfield contends "birds of a feather flock together."[34] Poor people are attracted by, and relocate to, the inner city because of the presence of distinctive subcultural values that discourage personal achievement. They are looking for support for their low aspirations and lack of accomplishment. One aspect of inner city living that Banfield finds particularly disturbing is its emphasis on immediate rather than deferred gratification. Inner city residents live for the moment rather than for tomorrow. As a consequence, they achieve very little. They perpetuate their poverty and that of their children. Many of our nation's poor are irresponsible and reap what they deserve. They are responsible for their own circumstances.

Others disagree. They see the poor as victims of unfair policies that regulate the distribution of wealth. They say Banfield is "blaming the victim."[35] This alternative view claims the government purposely creates poverty because poverty is functional:

- Poverty ensures that society's dirty work will be done. Society can fill these jobs by paying higher wages than for "clean" work, or it can force people who have no other choice to do the dirty work.

- Because the poor must work at low wages, they subsidize many services that benefit the affluent. For example, domestics subsidize the upper middle and upper class, making life easier for their employers.

- Poverty creates jobs for a number of occupations and professions that serve or "service" the poor, or protect the rest of society from them, for example, welfare agencies and the criminal and juvenile justice systems.

- The poor can be identified and punished as alleged or real deviants to uphold the legitimacy of conventional norms.[36]

Poor people serve as a living example of the fate that befalls those who violate norms regarding work, family, and moral turpitude.

STRAIN THEORY

One of the building blocks of strain theory is the idea of *anomie* originally developed by Emile Durkheim, one of the founders of modern sociology.[37] Writing in the late 19th century, Durkheim wanted to understand the social change brought about by the Industrial Revolution and the impact it had on society. He believed unlimited aspirations and desires are a natural part of human nature. In order to temper the natural impulses people have and provide stability in society to ensure the greatest happiness for the greatest number, social controls are necessary. Preindustrial societies had a high degree of social cohesion and strong traditional restraints as reflected in the church and institutions, something that has been eroded in industrial societies.

In the aftermath of the Industrial Revolution with the increased complexity of society, a growth in individualization, and the continued diversification of the division of labor, social bonds weakened, leading to the disruption of the normative structure. Social controls take the form of norms as well as the sanctions that regulate the day-to-day lives of people. Durkheim observed that when a society goes through abrupt, rapid social change, such as a depression or war, the normative structure is disrupted, which can cause a period of anomie or normlessness leading to social disorganization. Without norms, some people do not have the self-control to avoid deviance; they do not understand the rules well enough and will do anything to satiate their unlimited desires.

There are many negative consequences of homelessness, including risks of delinquency and victimization among children and adolescents. What conditions contribute to homelessness and the resulting obstacles for healthy social development? Do criminologists explain this differently based on whether they are sociologists or psychologists?

A state of *anomie* can happen to the whole of society, such as during times of economic depression, famine, or war. It can also affect large groups of citizens, such as the victims of Hurricane Katrina who experienced mass migrations from one area into a culturally and normatively different one. It can also affect smaller groups of people or individuals. A family moving from one area of the country to another may encounter a different sense of normative restraints and find themselves going through as radical a change from one value system to another as they would had they been caught up in a nation-wide depression. Sometimes students going away to college for the first time experience *anomie* as they try to adjust to life outside their family structure. People bring their own norms with them only to find another set in the new locale. The meshing the old and new together can cause a radical change within individuals and society at large.

Robert Merton

In 1938 American sociologist, Robert Merton, wrote an article that expanded Durkheim's idea of anomie into what has become known as strain theory.[38] Instead of the temporary state of normlessness that Durkheim described, Merton defined *anomie* as the permanent disjuncture that exists in society between (1) cultural goals that are regarded as worth striving for and (2) institutionalized means or approved ways of reaching these goals. The main goals in U.S. society are the acquisition of wealth and status. The socially approved ways to achieve them are by getting a good education, receiving job training, and pursuing career advancement. It is easy to see that some people have a much shorter path to follow to success than those who are born to less advantageous circumstances (see Figure 6-4). The playing field is not equal in that some people have ascribed qualities (gender and race), resources (wealthy parents and the "right" connections), and environmental advantages (growing up on the "right side of the tracks" or in a family that believes in the value of education and the work ethic) that are supportive of the pursuit of the goal. However, for many children, access to legitimate means is blocked. Doors to a good education or to a good job are closed, which creates a problem, since they too desire wealth and status.

Merton believed that the strain between means and goals is always present in society and identified five ways people adapt to the frustration (see Table 6-1). Most people are "conformists," in that they buy into the system and accept both the goals defined by the culture and the socially defined means to get there. Merton uses the term *innovators* to describe those who strive for society's goals but do so through means that deviate from the norms of society. Criminals aspire to wealth yet use unacceptable means to attain it. Ritualists are persons

figure 6-4   Mapping Delinquency Theory: Robert Merton

table 6-1   Merton's Modes of Adaptation

MODES OF ADAPTATION	CULTURAL GOALS	INSTITUTIONALIZED MEANS
Conformity	Accept	Accept
Innovation	Accept	Reject
Ritualism	Reject	Accept
Retreatism	Reject	Reject
Rebellion	Reject prevailing goals and means and substitute new ones.	

Source: Adapted from Robert Merton, *Social Theory and Social Structure,* revised edition (New York: Macmillan, 1968).

think **about it**

Is it wasteful to channel resources to retreatists, such as transients, drug addicts, and alcoholics? Are they worthy of public monies? Is it inevitable that some people will not succeed in life?

who do not subscribe to the goals of society though they still participate in socially accepted means to support themselves. Assembly line workers who show up to work day after day, minding the norms of society, satisfied with their safe routines but with no hope or desire to reach the goals of success are ritualists. Individuals who have dropped out of society altogether, such as drug addicts, alcoholics, and many homeless people, neither believe in the means nor the goals of society are called retreatists. These are people who have withdrawn into what society considers a nonproductive world of their own. Finally, Merton discusses a method of adaptation he calls "rebellion." Rebels are individuals who do not subscribe to either the means society feels are legitimate or the goals that society defines. These people are visionaries or revolutionaries who define their own goals and find unique ways to achieve them.

Merton thinks children are inherently good and commit crime only when their backs are against the wall. If society was able to eliminate the conditions that produce strain, such as poverty and inequality, it may also prevent delinquency. Some criminologists believe Merton overstated the impact of strain on children. Others believe that Merton did not identify which juveniles among those who are denied access to legitimate means will commit crime. Merton also does not say much about the relationship between frustration and delinquency. Why do some children who are frustrated refrain from committing crime while others who appear to have less reason to be frustrated commit crime? Merton also does not answer an important question about the distribution of goals and means. In American society, what is the process for the assimilation of goals and how is accessibility to means to achieve those goals determined? It is also difficult to generalize, as Merton did, from the highly successful innovators to juvenile delinquents. Many juvenile offenses—for example drinking alcohol, smoking marijuana, truancy, and fighting—net very little or no money. Often delinquency is not the lucrative career Merton says it is. Margaret Farnworth and Michael Leiber believe these are unfair criticisms. They argue that critics have never really tested Merton's theory but instead tested their own misguided reinterpretation of it.[39] Nonetheless, its flaws aside, Merton's theory did inspire other criminologists to develop strain theories of their own. One who did was Albert Cohen.

Albert Cohen

In his 1955 book, *Delinquent Boys,* Albert Cohen built upon Merton's ideas and explained why urban, lower-class boys commit crime.[40] The response to Cohen's book was very favorable, and the few critics who disagreed with him felt compelled to construct rival theories.

Cohen's theory is a parable, a simple story with an obvious moral. Cohen describes the delinquencies of lower class boys as malicious, negativistic, and nonutilitarian. Malicious behaviors are committed out of spite. Delinquent boys get their kicks from bullying nondelinquents, and they show the same kind of spite toward their schools and teachers. Delinquents are also negativistic, believing their behavior is right precisely because it is wrong according to the norms and rules of the larger society. Their behavior is nonutilitarian because their activities do not produce a direct economic benefit. Cohen says delinquents "steal for the hell of it." His position is that delinquents are out to have fun, a point of view that is opposite to Merton's opinion that delinquents commit instrumental theft.

According to Cohen, the activities of delinquents show they have other traits as well, which he identifies as *versatility,* short-run *hedonism,* and *group autonomy.* Delinquents' versatility is shown in their tendency to dabble in many delinquent activities—stealing, vandalism, trespassing, truancy, and so on. Evidence of short-run hedonism is that delinquents are impatient and impulsive. They do not take kindly to rules, schedules, or organization, nor do they plan ahead, study, or practice. Future gains and goals are of no importance to them. Delinquents also exhibit group autonomy: They are close to other members of their gang but hostile to outsiders. Cohen also explains how these traits are acquired.

Americans judge children in different ways. Middle-class parents, teachers, and social workers, for example, judge the behavior of children in terms of a set of values or standards, which Cohen calls the **middle-class measuring rod.** All children, not just middle-class children, are expected to subscribe to these values:

- Ambition is a virtue. Its absence is a defect and a sign of maladjustment. Ambition emphasizes an orientation toward long-range goals and deferred gratification, an early determination to get ahead.

- Individual responsibility plays a key role in middle-class ethics. It applauds resourcefulness and self-reliance.

- Middle-class norms place a high premium on skills and tangible achievements.

- Hard work and frugality are admirable.

- Rationality is highly valued, in the sense that forethought, conscious planning, and the budgeting of time are exercised.

- The middle-class value system rewards the cultivation of manners and courtesy.

theory in a nutshell

Albert Cohen

Cohen believed that lower-class parents do not adequately socialize children effectively in terms of widely accepted values. In school, children compete for status from teachers who use a "middle-class measuring rod" to evaluate them. Lower-class children often end up at the bottom of the status ladder, causing strain that leads them to join together and form gangs, which leads to delinquency.

think about it

Many crimes are not committed for financial gain. Some armed robbers, for instance, commit crimes to obtain drugs. Rarely do they commit crime to pay their rent. Are most juveniles who commit property crimes *really* economically motivated?

- Control of physical aggression and violence, which damage personal relations, are important middle-class values.

- People should not waste time; rather, they should spend their time constructively.

- Middle-class values emphasize respect for property.

All children are expected to conform to these values. However, doing so is not so easy for some. Whereas most middle-class children may live up to them effortlessly, lower-class children may not be taught these standards, or not taught them well. Consequently, they have difficulty adopting them.

In school, regardless of their social class, children are judged by their ability to follow middle-class values. Children who do not or cannot follow them lose status or prestige and are looked down upon by teachers and fellow students. Boys frustrated by their low status come together and form a delinquent subculture that has a set of values and standards for behavior that reject middle-class norms. By making a complete change—from accepting middle-class values to rejecting them, a process called reaction formation—the youths will acquire status in the eyes of their peers. But once they adopt their new code, they lose any respect they had in the larger society; and once delinquent, they cannot turn back. Cohen thus sees delinquency as a male, lower-class phenomenon that is caused by status frustration and the inability to live up to middle-class standards. Frustrations are expressed as hostility toward middle-class norms and institutions (see Figure 6-5).

Cohen's theory is simple and logically consistent. However, research testing it has produced mixed results. It is true that academic performance and delinquency are related. The better a child's school performance, the less likely he or she will commit crime.[41] There is also substantial evidence that children commit their crimes in groups. On the other hand, empirical support is lacking for the

figure 6-5   Mapping Delinquency Theory: Albert Cohen

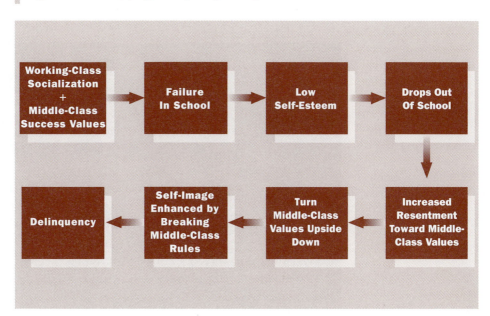

idea that delinquent boys reject middle-class values and adopt oppositional values. Lee Rainwater found that lower-class boys generally hold middle-class values but stretch them to fit their circumstances. However, they will conform to middle-class norms if they possibly can. David Downes reports that the typical response of delinquents to frustration is not rejection of middle-class values but disassociation from them. The delinquents in his study did not turn the values of their school upside down; instead, they psychologically withdrew. Steven Box observed that many lower-class boys never internalize the values of the school and teachers in the first place and are always distant from them.[42]

Richard Cloward and Lloyd Ohlin

In their book *Delinquency and Opportunity,* Richard Cloward and Lloyd Ohlin agree with Cohen that delinquency is a male, lower-class, urban phenomenon.[43] Like Merton, they think delinquency comes from the disjuncture between what children are taught to want and what is available. Adolescents who join delinquent gangs want to achieve success, but because their legitimate path is blocked, they turn to illegitimate means in the form of delinquency.

Lower-class children who want to make a lot of money but stay with their lower-class friends are the most likely to join a gang. They want, in the terminology of the 1940s and 1950s, "big cars, flashy clothes,

> ### theory in a nutshell
> #### Richard Cloward and Lloyd Ohlin
> Cloward and Ohlin identified the existence of legitimate and illegitimate opportunity structures. In both systems, opportunity is limited and differentially available depending on the where the child lives. Lower-class juveniles have greater opportunities for acquisition of delinquent roles through their access to deviant subcultures. They also have greater opportunities for carrying these roles out once they are acquired.

Strain theory contends that children are basically good. They commit crime as a last resort. The best strategy to prevent delinquency is to eliminate conditions that generate stress, such as poverty and inequality in schooling.

and swell dames." Yet they do not have a compelling urge to acquire middle-class status or a middle-class way of life.

When a lower-class boy senses he is not headed toward financial success later in life, he may blame his failure on society or himself. If he blames society, the child will likely become alienated from it and consider its rule illegitimate, especially if he thinks he is capable and deserving of success. His failing will be attributed to a closed, unfair, and discriminatory social system. Boys who feel this way may join a delinquent gang whose rules are regarded by its members as the only legitimate rules. As boys come to realize how isolated they are from the rest of society, they become closer, more cohesive, and more dependent on one another.

Cloward and Ohlin identify three delinquent subcultures. The type of subculture that develops in a neighborhood depends on how the neighborhood is organized (Sutherland) and what opportunities are available (Merton). A *criminal* subculture emerges in stable neighborhoods that provide children with illegitimate opportunities to become successful criminals. In these areas there are illegitimate opportunities to become wealthy because the neighborhood has:

- Adult role models who are successful criminals.
- Integration of age levels, which makes it possible for children to learn from their elders how to commit crime and how to handle themselves when they are caught.
- Cooperation between offenders and legitimate people, such as bail bondsmen, lawyers, and politicians.
- Control of delinquents by adult criminals, who make them cut down on unnecessary violence in favor of making money.

A second delinquent subculture is the *conflict* subculture. This subculture develops in disorganized slums, where great in- and out-migration produces social and cultural rootlessness and conflict. In these neighborhoods, children have only a few opportunities to be successful. The adult criminals who live there are failures. There is no integration of different age levels because the adult offenders have no useful knowledge to pass on. There is also little cooperation between offenders and legitimate members of the community because local lawyers and politicians have nothing to gain by associating with and assisting "losers." In addition, the adult criminals here have neither the ability nor the inclination to help neighborhood delinquents reduce their violent activity. The absence of legitimate and illegitimate opportunities frustrates children, and they vent their frustrations by turning to violence.

The third delinquent subculture is the *retreatist* subculture. Some children are eager to succeed in the criminal or conflict subculture but do not meet the standards of either one. Nor do they live up to the requirements of the conventional culture. They are double failures. They cannot succeed in any line of activity they attempt. Eventually, they give up and turn to drugs or alcohol.

Cloward and Ohlin see the cause of delinquency as a combination of the pressures to succeed and the obstacles lower-class children face. If there were opportunities for them to succeed using legitimate means, their delinquency rates would go down. However, just as there are differences in the availability of legitimate opportunities, there also are differences in the availability of illegitimate opportunities. Not everyone who wants to be a college professor, professional athlete, or rap musician can be one, nor can everyone who wants to be a drug dealer, pimp, or prostitute be successful at those endeavors (see Figure 6-6).

Cloward and Ohlin's theory was widely accepted. Scores of research studies have tested their central propositions and generally have found support for them. It is true that delinquents are more likely than nondelinquents to believe that opportunities to be successful are limited.[44] James F. Short, Jr., and Fred Strodtbeck found that not only did delinquents perceive they had fewer legitimate opportunities they also perceived they had *more* illegitimate opportunities.[45]

Robert Agnew

The theories of Merton, Cohen, and Cloward and Ohlin were developed decades ago. They were incorporated into a variety of delinquency prevention programs, but they fell out of favor during the 1970s and 1980s when violent juvenile crime soared. They were given new life, however, in 1992 when Robert Agnew introduced *general strain theory,* in which he identified many more conditions that if left unchecked would cause frustration for children. In 2005, Agnew provided a synthesis of his theory.[46]

figure 6-6   Mapping Delinquency Theory: Richard Cloward and Lloyd Ohlin

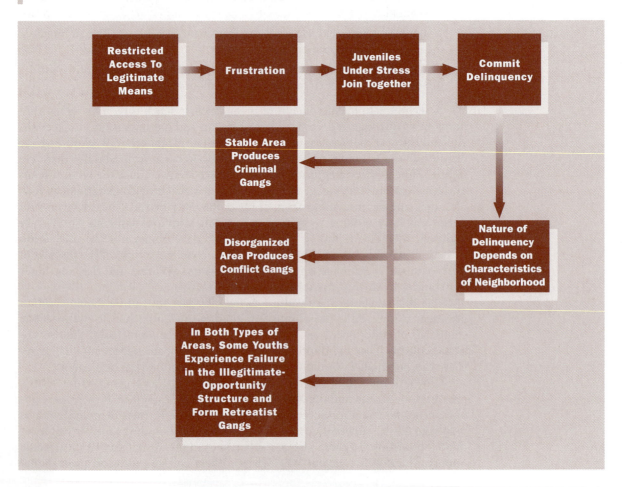

Agnew thinks traditional strain theory is limited because it only identifies one or two sources of strain: economic failure or poor school performance. Strain might come from other sources. Teenagers may experience strain in response to doing poorly in an athletic event, being fired from a job, or being "dumped" by a boyfriend or girlfriend. Regardless of its origin, strain triggers a negative emotion that sometimes leads to delinquency. The relationship between strain and delinquency, in other words, is indirect. These events may lead to delinquency if the child responds by running away from home, assaulting an abusive parent or classmate, or drinking alcohol or using illegal drugs. But only some children who experience strain commit crime.

> ## theory in a nutshell
> ### Robert Agnew
> Agnew suggested that many different sources of stress trigger a negative emotion. Whether strain leads to delinquency depends on conditioning factors the children possess, such as coping skills and intelligence. Children having fewer coping skills are more likely to commit crime.

How children react to strain depends on specific conditioning factors, such as the youth's self-esteem, intelligence, social support, coping strategies, problem-solving skills, and associations with conventional and delinquent peers. Conditioning factors provide children with the necessary tools to imagine alternative reactions and solutions to strain. Some children, for example, respond to strain by ignoring or minimizing the event responsible for it, whereas others blame themselves or others for what happened. The type of strain, who the strain is blamed on, the intensity of the strain, and the emotion the strain evokes all influence how a child might react (see Figure 6-7).

Agnew's reformulation has received some empirical support. Bill McCarthy and John Hagan found that adverse or noxious living conditions influence the likelihood of children committing crime.[47] Raymond Paternoster and Paul Mazerolle reported a positive relationship between strain and both drug use and delinquency.[48] Studying males and females, Mazerolle,[49] John Hoffman and Susan Su,[50] and Agnew and Timothy Brezina observed a link between delinquency and interpersonal strain.[51] Brezina also found that participation in delinquency reduced strain for some children and lessened the impact of negative feelings associated with it.[52] A large number of studies, including research by Lisa Broidy, Mark Colvin, and Jack Katz, as well as Nicole Piquero and Miriam Sealock, have reported that the impact of strain on delinquency partially depends on negative emotions, such as anger.[53] Ronald Simons and his colleagues recently examined the impact of strain on African American male and female children. They discovered the relationship between anger and strain is different for boys than for girls, thus suggesting that different theoretical models are needed to explain the behavior of the sexes.[54] Of particular importance in Agnew's theory is whether criminal victimization might be among the most consequential strains experienced by a child, and thereby be an important cause of delinquency. Putting it differently, is criminal victimization a potential cause of a child's future involvement in crime? Carter Hay and Michelle Evans examined this question. They found that violent victimization is a strong predictor of future participation in criminality, even when controlling for prior involvement in crime. Thus,

figure 6-7   Mapping Delinquency Theory: Robert Agnew

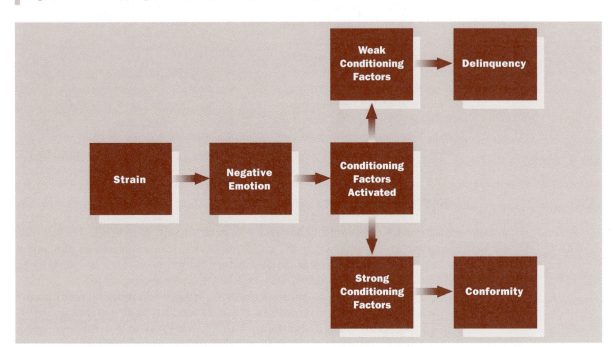

when a child is the victim of a violent crime, it increases the likelihood that he or she will commit crime down the road.[55]

At the same time, however, findings from other studies have raised questions about general strain theory. Most forms of strain have been found to have only small to moderate effects on delinquency. In other words, only some adolescents respond to strain with delinquency. The challenge facing general strain theory is to identify those factors that effect whether a youth will respond to strain with delinquency or in some other way. One promising line of inquiry is the linkage between personality and delinquency. Research suggests that strain is more likely to lead to delinquency among children who are angry and who have low self-control.[56]

Steven Messner and Richard Rosenfeld

Steven Messner and Richard Rosenfeld have also presented a modified version of Merton's work called *institutional anomie theory*.[57] Messner and Rosenfeld argue that American culture and social structure interact to produce conditions that lead to delinquency (see Figure 6-8). American culture is characterized by a culture of individualism, an orientation toward achievement, and pecuniary materialism—where the amount of money one has determines his or her worth and self-worth. These cultural factors influence important social institutions, such as the family, schools, economy, and political system. The culture permeates the entire society, thus even the most economically impoverished Americans generally subscribe to the ideals of the culture. Both poor and rich want to be independently successful. Since the poor lack opportunities and access to resources, they are effectively barred from achieving success legitimately. This creates frus-

figure 6-8 Mapping Delinquency Theory: Steven Messner and Richard Rosenfeld

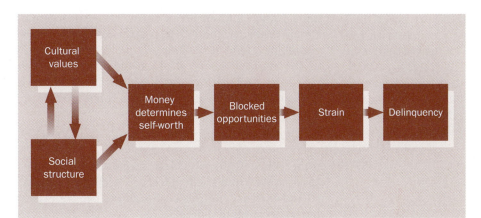

tration and anomie and is an incentive to use illegal means to achieve cultural goals.

Evaluations of institutional anomie theory have produced impressive support for it. Factors including poverty, welfare spending, social support, economic inequality, and social altruism all have been found to be related to a variety of crimes ranging from murder to property crime. Thus, although anomie is one of the oldest theoretical perspectives in criminology, it is still relevant in the 21st century.[58]

theory in a nutshell

Steven Messner and Richard Rosenfeld

Messner and Rosenfeld believe that economic and materialistic interests dominate American society. They believed that goals other than material success (e.g., being a good parent) are not important to many people today. Some children who are blocked from acquiring money legitimately will turn to crime, believing criminality is the most effective and efficient way for them to acquire wealth.

SOCIAL CONTROL THEORY

Social control can be traced to 17th-century philosopher Thomas Hobbes, who in *Leviathan* contends that humans are aggressive, argumentative, shy creatures in search of glory that would naturally use violence to master other people, their spouses, and children.[59] This profile was a quality of all people, not simply criminals. In Hobbes's view, people were basically bad, and to create order the state needed to strike fear into their hearts and punish them severely when they broke the law. Twentieth-century criminologists expanded upon Hobbes' ideas and created social control theory. These theorists assumed that without controls children would break the law. Delinquency was expected behavior. Rather than look for factors that push children into crime, the purpose of social control

t h i n k
about it

Social control theory states that people will commit crime unless obstacles are thrown in their paths and that children are hedonistic. What evidence can you use to support this dark evaluation of human nature?

theory is to identify the factors that stop or prevent children from participating in delinquency in the first place. In social control theory, what must be explained is why most children conform to society's rules most of the time. It is taken for granted that children break rules. The real question is: Why do children *not* commit crime? In the 1950s, social control theory was introduced to American criminology. One of the first criminologists to do so was Walter Reckless, with his containment theory. Reckless's theory was superseded by other social control theory explanations developed by David Matza in 1964, Travis Hirschi in 1969, and Michael Gottfredson and Travis Hirschi in 1990.

Walter Reckless

In the 1950s, Walter Reckless introduced *containment theory,* in which he focused on the child's self-concept.[60] Reckless paid attention to the role of internal and external controls on the child's behavior. He had known for some time that only certain children were chronic offenders. As a graduate of the University of Chicago with Clifford Shaw and Henry McKay as mentors, Reckless was curious about the differential response of juveniles who lived in disorganized areas. He wanted to know why some boys in high-crime neighborhoods do not get into trouble with the law. Studying this question in various ways for more than a decade, Reckless reasoned that "good boys" had a positive self-concept.

theory in a nutshell

Walter Reckless

Walter Reckless developed *containment theory.* He was curious to know why some boys living in high delinquency rate neighborhoods did not commit crime. Reckless concluded that what separated "good boys" from delinquents was that "good boys" had strong self-concepts.

Reckless identified four pressures and pulls that influence whether a child will become delinquent:

- Outer pulls or environmental factors.
- Inner pushes or psychological and biological factors.
- External containments or attachments to persons and institutions representing the existing social order.
- Internal containments or the element of a good self-concept.

Outer pulls are living conditions such as poverty and unemployment that make delinquency look like an attractive solution to a difficult problem. Inner pushes are psychological factors such as drives and motives, as well as frustration, hostility, and feelings of inferiority and biological factors like brain damage. Juveniles, however, are equipped with two lines of defense to ward off pushes and pulls. They have external containments (outer controls) and internal containments (inner controls) that insulate them from delinquency. External containments are the child's family and community ties, which buffer the immediate pressures, pulls, and pushes juveniles face, helping them to keep their behavior in check. Internal containments are strengths that stem from having a good, strong self-concept. A positive self-concept insulates children from the pressures, pulls, and pushes with which they are bombarded; it is the best defense against delinquent impulses. Research by Frank Scarpitti and his colleagues and Simon Dinitz and his associates reported that boys with strong self-concepts were less likely to be delinquent.[61]

David Matza

David Matza studied delinquency in the mid-20th century, a period of civil unrest that was highlighted by protests over civil rights and the Vietnam War. The social and political struggles Matza observed from his seat as professor at the University of California in Berkeley had a profound impact on his work. Matza came to believe that delinquency theorists had exaggerated the differences between delinquents and nondelinquents.[62] Strain theorists, such as Cohen and Cloward and Ohlin, see delinquents as part of a subculture completely committed to misdeeds, engaging in delinquency because they believe in ideas that require such behavior. These children are normal in all respects except in belonging to this subculture, which teaches them it is all right to be delinquent.

Matza finds this hard to believe and he criticizes strain theorists for not accounting for *maturational reform:* the idea that nearly all children who participate in delinquency reduce or stop such activity as they grow older. Strain theory persistently maintains that children are committed to stealing, vandalizing, and assaulting. If so, why do many delinquents modify their behavior as they reach age 18, 21, or 25? Strain theory cannot answer this question.

> ### theory in a nutshell
> #### David Matza
> Matza suggested that children are neither committed nor compelled to delinquency, and delinquents feel guilty about their misdeeds. He believes that for juveniles to feel better about themselves, they turn to *techniques of neutralization* to reduce guilt and justify their delinquencies.

Matza also suggests that if delinquents were really as committed to their misdeeds as strain theory claims, they would engage in delinquency for nearly all of their waking hours. But even the most delinquent youths spend most of their time in conventional, nondelinquent activities; they devote very little time to delinquency. Many delinquents who are caught also know they have done something wrong and feel sorry for their actions. If Matza is correct that delinquents know delinquency is wrong, why do they participate in it? He says it is because a youth may pick up cues in conversations with other youths that imply delinquency is acceptable, and that those other youths think he or she is the only one who does not want to be delinquent. Faced with this implication, he or she is reluctant to be the "chicken," the one who backs out of a delinquent escapade.

Because delinquents feel bad for what they have done, they develop **techniques of neutralization,** or rationalizations for their behavior to absolve themselves of guilt. There are five techniques of neutralization:[63]

- *Denial of responsibility* is a technique to blame the delinquent act on an outside force. The youths are drawn into situations and are helpless to act any other way. They may blame their delinquency on growing up in an abusive family, a bad neighborhood, or delinquent peers. These juveniles might say, "I couldn't help it" or "It was not my fault."

- *Denial of injury* occurs when the criminal act does not seem to hurt anyone; no one was seriously injured. A gang fight might be said to be only a private argument between consenting and willing participants. Thefts from Wal-Mart might be rationalized by suggesting that with all its wealth the company will never notice the losses from small thefts anyway. Juveniles who use this technique might say, "A criminal act hurts someone and I did not hurt anyone."

- *Denial of victim* is used when a juvenile believes what he or she did was right under the circumstances. The victim had it coming. Some adolescents will use this justification to explain their attacks on homosexuals or minorities. They might further legitimize their behavior by saying something like, "Robin Hood stole from the rich and gave to the poor because the rich deserved to be robbed."

- *Condemnations of condemners* take place when children want to shift blame from their own illegal behavior to the behavior of others. They will try to create a negative image about those who are being critical of them. They may, for example, call those who condemn them hypocrites. Juveniles may rationalize the legitimacy of their illegal drug use, for instance, by saying, "police and judges are corrupt hypocrites who are involved in the drug trade themselves."

- *Appeal to higher loyalty* is used when juveniles feel they must break the law to benefit their friends, family, or other group they are closely tied to. Illegal acts might be justified by claiming they were committed in deference to a higher authority, such as a moral or religious belief, the gang, or a racial or ethnic group. Adolescents who steal necessities of life for their family might justify their behavior on this basis.

While techniques of neutralization might be used as postevent explanations of delinquent behavior, Matza believes that the same justifications are used prior to delinquent acts to rationalize the delinquent's involvement. Techniques of neutralization ready a child for delinquency. They lessen the effectiveness of internal and external controls, thereby freeing the adolescent to commit crime.

If Matza is correct, juveniles can be delinquent without being committed to delinquency. They only need to think that the circumstances surrounding their particular involvement are exceptional. Normally, most adolescents accept conventional rules and laws, but occasionally their acceptance of the law is overridden by some other factor, such as an attack or a provocation. Then the youth may drift from acceptance of conventional values. When this happens, delinquency is possible but not inevitable. Whether delinquency occurs depends on many factors, including the juvenile's mood and his or her ability to neutralize the illegal act being contemplated.

The appeal of Matza's theory is that juveniles live in a state of flux and uncertainty. Some criminologists have criticized Matza because the central concepts of his theory are difficult to test. Matza is also vague about how children use techniques of neutralization. Nonetheless, Matza's theory has inspired others. Research examining Matza's propositions has produced mixed results. It is true that delinquents accept conventional values.[64] It is also true that most children age-out of delinquency, but possibly not without consequences. John Hagan found that past experiences of working-class males adversely affect their early adult occupational attainment.[65] Travis Hirschi found evidence for three of the five techniques (denial of responsibility, denial of injury, and condemnation of condemners), but he could not determine whether the rationalizations were in place before delinquent acts were committed or if they followed only as postevent justifications.[66] In addition, James Coleman discovered that white-collar criminals used techniques of neutralization to justify their criminal acts. The most common justification they used was "denial of injury," believing their actions did not hurt anyone.[67] Jim Mitchell and Richard Dodder have observed that delinquents use neutralization techniques to rationalize their illegal behavior.[68] Shadd Maruna and Heith Copes reported that auto thieves who were socially attached were more likely to use neutralization techniques than less-attached offenders. In addition, less-attached and more-attached thieves used different neutralization techniques. The most frequently used rationalizations for more-attached thieves were appeal to higher loyalty and denial of victim; low-attached thieves rationalized their behavior by turning to denial of the victim and denial of responsibility.[69]

Other criminologists, however, have been unable to find much support for Matza's theory. Michael Hindelang found no support for the idea that juveniles use techniques of neutralization. Adolescents who committed crime were more likely to accept delinquent behavior than juveniles who were not involved in delinquency. Hindelang was also unable to provide support for Matza's idea that delinquents disapprove of delinquency but go along with it only because their friends expect them to. Hindelang found that a juvenile's perceptions of the feelings of his or her friends have almost nothing to do with their decision to commit crime.[70] Peggy Giordano also found little support for Matza's claim that delinquents feel they are treated unjustly. In a study comparing delinquents and nondelinquents, she concluded that the two groups held similar attitudes.[71]

Travis Hirschi

In 1969, Travis Hirschi published *Causes of Delinquency,* in which he presented a detailed analysis of cultural deviance, strain, and social control theories.[72] He argued that no one should be surprised by delinquency because it is something all adolescents will do unless obstacles are thrown in their path. These obstacles are chiefly attitudes that are implanted quite effectively in most children but less so in others. These others have relatively weak bonds to society; their minds are not set firmly against delinquent activities.

Hirschi's version of social control theory is called *social bond theory.* A **bond** describes a person's connection to society. It consists of four elements: attachment, commitment, involvement, and belief. For every

Theory in a nutshell

Travis Hirschi

Hirschi wanted to know why juveniles conform. He thinks children conform because of their bond to society, which consists of four elements: attachment, belief, commitment, and involvement. The stronger the child's bond to society, the less likely he or she is to commit crime, since the child has something to lose.

Warm, healthy family relationships build strong bonds, which prevent delinquency. What are some ways that fatherhood equips children, particularly boys, to engage in successful endeavors?

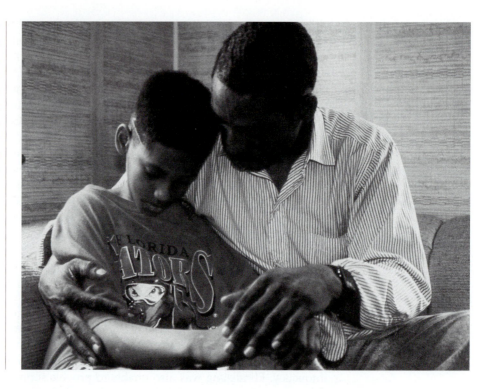

child, each component of the social bond forms its own continuum. When the continua are merged, they provide a gauge of how strongly a child is tied to society. The stronger the bond, the less likely the youth will commit crime.

The best predictor of delinquent behavior is a child's attachments to parents, schools, and peers—the primary agents of socialization. For more than 40 years, criminologists have examined the relationship between attachment and delinquency. Studies from the 1970s to the present have rather consistently reported that children who are strongly tied to parents are less likely to become delinquent; their positive feelings promote acceptance of the parents' values and beliefs. These children avoid delinquency because such behavior would jeopardize their parents' affection.[73] Interestingly, Trina Hope and her colleagues reported that adolescent girls who become pregnant and keep their babies are much less likely to commit delinquency than adolescent females who end their pregnancies through abortion.[74]

A parallel argument applies to peers. The closer juveniles are tied to their peers, the less delinquent they will be—even if their friends sometimes commit delinquency. This statement directly contradicts the more reasonable position of cultural deviance theory that closeness to delinquents will increase the likelihood of delinquency.[75]

With respect to school attachments, attitudes toward schooling and teachers are an important intervening variable in the relationship between IQ and delinquency. Juveniles with high IQs usually receive better grades than do other students. Getting better grades makes school a more enjoyable experience; thus, youths with better grades like school more than their less-successful peers. Children who like school more easily accept, or at least endure, school rules and authority and are less likely to commit crime.

Belief in the moral validity of law also has been found to reduce the likelihood that a juvenile will commit crime. Hirschi thinks that in the United States there is one belief system, and it centers on conventional values. That is, there are no subcultures that regard theft and assault as proper and permissible, contrary to the claims of cultural deviance and strain theories. Belief in the moral validity of law does seem to reduce the likelihood of committing crime.[76]

Commitment, unlike attachment, is about success, achievement, and ambition rather than respect, admiration, and identification. Recall in strain theory that thwarted ambition causes frustration, which might cause delinquent behavior—theft, in particular. Social bond theory proposes that ambition or motivation to achieve keeps juveniles on the "straight and narrow" path because they know getting into trouble will hurt their chances of success. In other words, children have a "stake in conformity." The more time and energy they have invested in building an education, a career, or a reputation, the less likely they will risk their accomplishments by committing crime. Research examining the importance of commitment has reported that children who are more heavily invested in conventional activities are less likely to be delinquent.[77]

Involvement in conventional activities has been seen as a way of preventing delinquency as early as biblical times, when sages counseled, "idle hands are the devil's workshop." Today such thinking has inspired politicians and city planners to call for more and better playgrounds and after-school sports programs to keep children off the streets. If these facilities are available, children will have less time for delinquent pursuits. Unfortunately, involvement does not have as much impact on preventing delinquency as other components of the bond to society. This is because delinquency is not a full-time job. It requires so little time that anyone, no matter how involved they are in conventional activities, can find time for delinquency if they want to.[78]

Research is generally more supportive of Hirschi than it is critical. Some studies, however, have found empirical support for social bonding variables to be weak to moderate. For instance, Marvin Krohn and James Massey found that commitment is a better predictor of delinquency than either attachment or belief.[79] Hirschi's theory also predicts female delinquency better than male delinquency and is a better predictor of minor delinquencies than serious offenses.[80] Randy LaGrange and Helen White discovered that the influence of the social bond on delinquency changes over time,[81] and Robert Agnew found that social bonding variables explain only 1 or 2 percent of future delinquency.[82] David Greenberg also reported that social control variables explain only a small amount of the variation and that much of the theory's appeal pertains to its ideological conservatism.[83]

Other concerns raised about Hirschi's theory have focused on how the different elements of the bond interact with one another. How, for example, do relationships between youths and their parents affect their attitudes about school? How do attitudes toward teachers influence a child's future work history or involvement in criminality? How are attachments to the family influenced by relationships with peers? It is important for social control theory to do a better job of explaining these relationships. Yet, in spite of its shortcomings, Hirschi's theory has inspired others to construct theories of their own. One who has is Charles Tittle who developed *control balance theory.* He explains criminality in terms of the ratio between the control imposed on a person by others and the control the individual is able to exercise over others.[84] What Tittle adds to

Hirschi is the idea that people have varying degrees of autonomy or command over their lives. Tittle predicts that individuals with either a control deficit or control surplus are most likely to commit crime. Research by Nicole Piquero and Alex Piquero testing control balance theory produced mixed support.[85] Similarly, Matt DeLisi and Andrew Hochstetler found that while control imbalances often are able to predict delinquency, they do not always do so as specified in the theory.[86]

Michael Gottfredson and Travis Hirschi

In 1990, Michael Gottfredson and Travis Hirschi published a theory of crime that departed significantly from Hirschi's earlier work. In *A General Theory of Crime,* the child's self-control, or lack of self-control, took center stage.[87] The theory is based on Hobbes' view that people are pleasure seeking and self-gratifying. They make choices based solely on the joy they imagine it will bring. Crime is committed because offenders imagine it will be gratifying. Matt DeLisi has captured the essence of self-control theory in the following anecdote:

> **theory in a nutshell**
>
> **Michael Gottfredson and Travis Hirschi**
>
> Gottfredson and Hirschi believed that delinquents have low self-control that can be traced to early childhood experiences. Parents who do not supervise their children, who do not recognize when their children are behaving badly, and who do not punish poor behavior promote low self-control in their children.

> Imagine that a female loved-one (e.g., daughter, sister, or mother) has brought home her fiancé. While the fiancé is in the other room, your loved-one briefly describes his personality and lifestyle. He is sporadically employed and generally stays at a job for only one to three months. While he has no official vocational training, he prefers work in the areas of construction and landscaping. He frequently quits or is fired because of disagreements with coworkers and supervisors. . . . He recurrently collects unemployment benefits because he chooses to avoid underemployment. For the record, the fiancé, who described school as "not his thing," did manage to graduate from high school, but found his two months in college unrewarding and quit.
>
> Socially, the fiancé enjoys going to bars and is an enthusiastic drinker. He also smokes cigarettes, dabbles recreationally with illicit drugs . . ., prefers to eat at fast-food restaurants rather than cook at home, and does not exercise. He is frequently bored and annoyed by others' expectations of him. The fiancé is friendly and only abusive, sullen, or irritable when intoxicated or when "things are not going his way." He has been "common-law married" twice and briefly engaged once before, but your loved-one is confident that their impending relationship is "the one."[88]

Many readers will recognize someone they know as having a profile similar to the fiancé. What self-control theory is curious about is why this profile is found only in some people. Or to put it differently, why do only some juveniles commit crime? Gottfredson and Hirschi think it is because they cannot resist the easy, immediate gratification that accompanies crime because they have low self-control. Children with low self-control are more impulsive, insensitive, physical (as opposed to mental), and shortsighted. They are also risk-takers with low frustration tolerance, and therefore are more likely to commit crime. In contrast, children with high self-control will be less likely throughout all periods of their lives to commit crime. Gottfredson and Hirschi also claim that differences in self-control account for most of the differences among children in criminal behavior. The relationship between self-control and crime is affected only slightly by variables that sociologists have typically blamed crime on, such as strain, peer influences, social bonds, and cultural influences. These are overshadowed by self-control or are products of self-control. In addition, Gottfredson and Hirschi propose that the effects of self-control are similar in every situation because postchildhood experiences do not influence self-control much if at all. This is because low self-control is a function of faulty child rearing. Parents help children develop self control when they (1) love a child enough to monitor and react to bad behavior, (2) supervise the child, (3) recognize naughtiness when it occurs, and (4) punish bad behavior. These children become adolescents with the self-control necessary to resist easy gratification and develop the will to succeed in school and later in the job market (see Figure 6-9).[89]

Gottfredson and Hirschi's theory has been widely tested. Research has extensively examined the relationship between delinquency and self-control, and the theory has received strong support. Measures of self-control have been found to be predictive of criminal behavior among criminals and noncriminals, college students, juveniles, males and females, and research subjects living outside the United States.[90] Callie Harbin Burt and her colleagues found that low self-control is positively associated with involvement in delinquency.[91] David Evans and his colleagues reported that self-control was related to "quality of family relationships, attachment to church, having criminal associates and values, educational attainment and occupational status, and residing in a neighborhood perceived to be disorderly."[92] Gottfredson and Hirschi have concluded that "throughout the twentieth century, evidence has accumulated that people who often lie, cheat, and steal also tend to hit other people; these same people often drink, smoke, use drugs, wreck cars, desert their spouses, quit their jobs, and come to class late."[93]

However, not all criminologists enthusiastically embrace self-control theory. Strong associations between self-control and crime have not been found for all categories of people, particularly for serious young offenders and the homeless.[94] Critics contend that a theory that blames crime on ineffective child rearing and dismisses the possibility that delinquency is a product of stress and strain (Merton), culture (Shaw and McKay), learning (Sutherland), or biology is inherently

figure 6-9   Mapping Delinquency Theory: Michael Gottfredson and Travis Hirschi

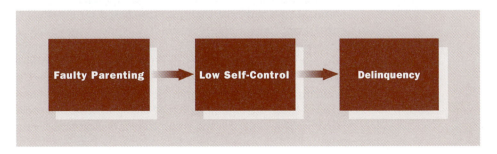

flawed. John Wright and Kevin Beaver, for example, have been able to show in a study of twins that self-control is partially genetically driven regardless of parenting styles (see Chapter 10).[95] Others, such as Constance Chapple, have been unable to find evidence to support Gottfredson and Hirschi's claim that peer groups have little or no influence on behavior.[96] Not only did Chapple find that children with low self-control were more likely to participate in delinquency, they also were more likely to be rejected by law-abiding peers, and out of necessity more likely to associate with delinquent peers. For these children it was better to have delinquent friends than no friends at all. Additionally, Gottfredson and Hirschi pay too little attention to individual differences among children and ignore differences in power in relationships between adults and children that affect the likelihood of a child's participating in crime.[97] These criticisms aside, and if we assume just for the moment that Gottfredson and Hirschi are correct, delinquency may be inevitable. If low self-control is internalized early in life, even before a child starts school, there may not be much the juvenile and criminal justice systems can do to overcome what has already been done.[98]

think about it

Some criminologists believe children with low self-control are more likely to commit crime. What does this suggest about the chances of rehabilitation or positive change for delinquents?

JUVENILE JUSTICE POLICY IMPLICATIONS

The purpose of policies based on these theories is to change the relationship between the child and his or her environment. Most public policies for preventing delinquency include components from multiple theoretical perspectives. There are few, if any, programs that are based entirely on one point of view.

Cultural Deviance Theory

Shaw and McKay and Miller believe neighborhoods are largely responsible for crime. The most comprehensive policy application of their theories is the Chicago Area Project (CAP) that began in 1931. The purpose of the CAP is to mobilize residents of high-crime neighborhoods to attack delinquency in three ways: direct service, advocacy, and community involvement. Community residents work with CAP officials to keep children out of trouble, help them when they get into trouble, and keep the neighborhood clean. Research assessing the CAP has reported it is effective for reducing the incidence and prevalence of delinquency. Other programs have spawned from the CAP, including Neighborhood Watch, Operation Weed and Seed (a federal program to combat violent crime, drug use, and gang activity in high-crime neighborhoods), and community-oriented policing (see Chapter 13).[99]

Sutherland's theory also has had a major impact on delinquency prevention. Most notable of the programs based on his theory are "detached worker programs," which place law-abiding workers into gang settings to counsel gang members about their behavior before they commit crime. Other popular applications include mentoring programs, where at-risk children are paired with law-abiding citizens who serve as positive role models for the child and the rating systems for films, music, and television. All policies based on cultural deviance theory share the common goal of changing a child's social environment in ways that make it easier for the youth to be mainstreamed into society.

Strain Theory

Programs that reduce stress and frustration prevent delinquency. Children must be provided with legitimate opportunities to achieve success. In the 1960s many delinquency prevention programs were based on these assumptions. They provided the impetus for a reform package spearheaded by Presidents John F. Kennedy and Lyndon B. Johnson. Among the Great Society reforms were a wide range of social programs, which included Project Head Start for preschool children, job training programs for adults, and financial assistance for students in postsecondary and higher education. Of these programs, Head Start is the most widely known.

Put into operation in 1965, Head Start may be the only antipoverty program embraced by both conservatives and liberals. It is a comprehensive child-development program that serves children from birth to age 5, as well as pregnant women and their families. A child-focused program, it has the overall goal of increasing the school readiness of young children in low-income families. Head Start teachers provide children with a variety of learning experiences that are appropriate to their age and development. Children are encouraged to read books, appreciate cultural diversity, express their feelings in appropriate ways, and learn how to play and interact with their classmates. Today, Head Start has an annual budget in excess of $6 billion, and nearly one million children are enrolled in its programs throughout the United States.

For years it was arguable whether Head Start was effective. Then, in 2002, results from a seven-year national evaluation of the Early Head Start program provided evidence that showed 3-year-old children completing the program performed better in cognitive and language development than those not participating. The children also developed behavior patterns that prepared them for success in school, such as engaging in tasks, paying attention, and showing less aggression. Parents in Early Head Start showed more positive parenting behavior, reported less physical punishment, and did more to help their children learn at home through activities such as reading to them.[100] In short, the Head Start program prepares children for school and has a positive impact on their social development.

Social Control Theory

Social control theory is responsible for a variety of delinquency prevention programs. The programs aim to reattach children to their parents, schools, and community by involving them in conventional and prosocial activities. These programs require parents to become active participants in children's lives. There are several popular programs based on this model. The Police Athletic League (PAL), for instance, offers children positive experiences with police and other youths.

An offshoot of the PAL is the Midnight Basketball League (MBL)—a program that provides young males in lower-class neighborhoods an opportunity to play the game of basketball to stay out of trouble. The only difference between the MBL and normal basketball is the MBL is played between 10 P.M. and 2 A.M., when young inner city males are most vulnerable to the drug culture, crime, and other negative activities. There is partial evidence that the MBL

think
about it

In West Palm Beach, Florida, police installed stereo systems that play classical music 24 hours per day in high-crime neighborhoods. Since the policy was implemented, crime has decreased. Does this example demonstrate that neighborhoods and their delinquency rates can be altered by ecological change? Why or why not?

What is the purpose of programs like Head Start? Does the very existence of such a program validate the theoretical ideas of cultural deviance, strain, and social control theorists?

is successful. In Atlanta, police records show the MBL has helped to reduce inner city crime by 40 percent. One reason is that before each game all players must attend a one-hour workshop on topics focusing on job interview skills, financial management, AIDS/HIV awareness, drug and alcohol abuse prevention, conflict resolution, and entrepreneurship. Any player who does not attend the workshop cannot play.[101]

A third important program is offered by the Boys and Girls Clubs of America, a network of more than 2,600 clubs serving more than 3.2 million school-age children. The clubs provide at-risk youths with guidance, discipline, and values from caring adults who serve as mentors, along with educational support, increased awareness of career options, and assistance for setting goals. A three-year assessment of the Boys and Girls Club programs has confirmed that the clubs have had a significant impact on reducing juvenile crime (reduced by 13 percent), drug activity (reduced by 22 percent), and the usage of crack cocaine (reduced by 25 percent).[102]

The self-control theory of Gottfredson and Hirschi does not as clearly lend itself to the development of public policy. Most delinquency prevention policies are derived from cultural deviance and strain theories. These theories rely on the deterrent and incapacitation functions of the juvenile justice system. The assumptions of popular crime-fighting strategies that focus on severity of response, such as "Three Strikes and You're Out," are not likely to be effective because "individual differences in predisposition are established prior to involvement" in delinquency.[103] In contrast, self-control theory calls for the implementation of early childhood interventions. What is needed are programs that strive to alter the course of these dispositions, such as assisting single mothers to provide capable care for their children. One program whose goals compliment self-control theory is "The Incredible Years: Parents, Teachers, and Children Training

Series." The parent-training curriculum of this series, designed for parents of children ages 3 to 12, focuses on strengthening parents' monitoring and disciplinary skills and building their confidence. The curriculum includes an 11-week basic program that uses video tapes depicting real-life situations. Parents meet in groups and cover topics such as Helping Children Learn, The Value of Praise and Encouragement, Effective Limit Setting, and Handling Misbehavior (see Chapter 10).[104] Some evidence suggests that early childhood prevention programs improve self-control and make delinquency less likely.

conclusions

This chapter has reviewed theories from three schools of sociological thought. Cultural deviance theory was the first to reject biological and psychological theories. These theories shifted attention to considering the role of the environment in delinquency, particularly the child's neighborhood. Strain theory distinguished itself by claiming that there is no unique lower-class culture. There is one culture in the United States, and it emphasizes wealth and status. However, not every person is able to achieve success because the legitimate means to it are restricted to the middle and upper classes. Thus, lower-class children are more likely to give up chasing these goals or go about achieving them in illegal ways. In contrast, according to social control theory, children are amoral, and without controls on their behavior, they will commit crime. These theories ask: Why do some children conform? They answer the question in a variety of ways. Delinquency might be explained in terms of a child's self-concept; his or her bond to parents, school, or peers; or the quality of parenting he or she has received. In the next chapter, critical theories of delinquency are discussed. These theories examine power differences among people and explain how differences in power might produce delinquency.

key terms

Bond   The glue that connects a child to society.

Collective efficacy   Mutual trust among neighbors combined with willingness to intervene on behalf of the common good, specifically to supervise children and maintain public order.

Cultural transmission   The process through which criminal values are transmitted from one generation to the next.

Differential social organization   Neighborhoods are differentially organized.

Ecology fallacy   Error in thinking that occurs when neighborhood-level data are used to draw conclusions about individual residents.

Focal concerns   The primary values that monopolize lower-class consciousness.

Middle-class measuring rod   The standards used by teachers to assign status to students.

Techniques of neutralization   Rationalizations used to explain criminality.

denial of responsibility/blame

Sociological Theory: Labeling and Conflict Explanations

B ecause children are relatively powerless, they are subject to being labeled by adults who wield greater power. It has been argued that society might produce delinquents and their delinquency through "a process of tagging, defining, identifying, segregating, describing, emphasizing, and evoking the very traits that are complained of. . . . The person becomes the thing he [or she] is described as being."[1] The theories discussed in this chapter explore the nature of the labeling process, the role of conflict, differential power, and influence in creating and enforcing the criminal law and the consequences of how adults exert power over children.

LABELING THEORY

The labeling perspective has a rich tradition in sociology, and its conceptual and theoretical foundation can be traced to the writings of symbolic interaction theorists. The labeling perspective borrows heavily from Charles Horton Cooley, George Herbert Mead, and W.I. Thomas. At the heart of labeling theory is the idea that in their everyday lives children are bombarded with different cues and clues regarding how others perceive them (Mead). Through role-playing (Cooley) and defining situations (Thomas), adolescents become keenly aware of the meanings of symbols and gestures that other children and adults use to project labels onto them.[2] **Labeling theory** thus assumes that social control (labeling) creates deviance when adolescents attach to themselves negative labels regarding their relation to others.

Labeling theory is not so concerned with individual traits (see Chapter 5) or environmental influences (see Chapter 6) that might instigate initial deviant acts. Instead it focuses on the stigmatizing effects of the juvenile justice system upon those who are labeled delinquent. The focal point of labeling theory is on the power of the social response, especially in the form of formal social control, to produce delinquent behavior. Its aim is to understand how publicly or officially "labeling someone as a delinquent might result in the person becoming the very thing he [or she] is described as being."[3] In Box 7-1 there is a brief discussion of how labeling might have contributed to Willie Bosket becoming one of New York State's most dangerous prisoners.

Frank Tannenbaum

One early expression of the labeling perspective is found in Frank Tannenbaum's 1938 book, *Crime and the Community*. Tannenbaum rejected the **dualistic fallacy**—the idea that delinquents and nondelinquents are two fundamentally different types of people. According to Tannenbaum, criminologists previously believed undesirable qualities, such as atavistic

theory in a nutshell

Frank Tannenbaum

For Tannenbaum, delinquents are actually well-adjusted people. Delinquent behavior is behavior so labeled by adults in a community. Adults, who have more power than children, are able to have children labeled "delinquent." Once children are labeled delinquent, they become delinquent.

box 7-1   A WINDOW ON DELINQUENCY

The Case of Willie Bosket

At the age of 26, Willie Bosket stabbed prison guard Earl Porter in the visiting room at Shawangunk state prison in New York. At his trial for the attempted murder of the guard, Willie explained his violent behavior as a direct product of having been labeled a delinquent at an early age and being institutionalized in the state's juvenile and adult correctional systems for most of his life. Acting as his own defense counsel, he stated to the jury: "Willie Bosket has been incarcerated since he was nine years old and was raised by his surrogate mother, the criminal justice system. . . . This being the case, Bosket is only a monster created by the system he now haunts." It is a strong claim for the effects of labeling. However, in Willie's case it is difficult to disentangle the causes and effects of the labels.

At age 6, Willie was already a troublemaker in school, throwing temper tantrums, hitting teachers, fighting with other students, and playing hooky. When he was 8 years old and in second grade, he threw a typewriter out of a school window, nearly hitting a pregnant teacher. By 9 years of age, Willie was experimenting with sex with neighbor girls. Police reports on Willie at the time included purse snatching, auto theft, threatening other children with a knife, and setting a number of fires; most of his crimes were never reported to the police. His first appearance in Family Court came as the result of his mother filing a PINS (Person in Need of Supervision) petition, which at that time was a status offense. The judge ordered Willie placed at the Wiltwyck School for Boys.

Over the next few years, Willie's disruptive and violent behavior led him to be moved from institution to institution, including both psychiatric and correctional facilities. At age 11 he was sent to the Highland School for Children where he was soon punished for throwing a chair at another boy and attacking a supervisor with a broom.

At age 14, Willie's placement expired and he was sent home. Over the next few months he was arrested five times, mostly for minor robberies and burglaries, but he received no serious sanctions for any of the crimes. According to Fox Butterfield, "by age 15, Willie claimed that he had committed two thousand crimes, including two hundred armed robberies and twenty-five stabbings." Three months after Willie turned 15, he went on a robbing and killing spree in the New York subways, resulting in the murder of two subway passengers and the serious wounding of a motorman. Although Willie was only 15 years old, the judge sentenced him to the maximum allowed under the current state law: commitment to an initial period of five years with the Division of Youth Services, and then a transfer to the adult system until he turned 21. Willie was eventually convicted of assault as an adult and sentenced to prison where additional assaults on guards resulted in his being convicted as a habitual offender, which carried a sentence of 25 years to life.

Labeling theory argues that labeling individuals causes problematic behavior. The person becomes, as Tannenbaum suggests, the thing he or she has been described as being, and according to Lemert, labeling, processing, and institutionalizing individuals only promotes recidivism. Is Willie Bosket a monster created by the juvenile justice system? Or was the labeling and official processing of Willie only a response to his violent behavior?

Source: Fox Butterfield, *All God's Children: The Bosket Family and the American Tradition of Violence* (New York: Harper Perennial, 1996).

William Bosket is a career criminal. Prior to his arrest for double homicide at age 15, Bosket had committed hundreds of armed robberies and 25 stabbings. Do such violent juvenile offenders deserve compassion from the juvenile and criminal justice systems?

physical features (Lombroso) and intellectual inferiority (Goddard), led to antisocial behavior. However, Tannenbaum rejected these notions and instead argued delinquents are rather well adjusted to their social groups.

Tannenbaum believed that delinquent activity begins as random play or adventure. Children do not think of their play as constituting delinquency, but a *play group* may later evolve into a delinquent gang as a result of conflict between the group and the community. Adults in the community might be annoyed with the group, which may be seen as playing music too loud, and then try to subdue or crush it. This usually fails, however, and the children become more defiant, turning to fellow gang members for support. When conflict between a gang and community occurs, both sides resort to name-calling. Adults call the youths' activity "delinquent" or "evil" and insist that the activity should no longer be tolerated. According to Tannenbaum:

> There is a gradual shift from the definition of the specific act as evil to a definition of the individual as evil, so that *all* his acts come to be looked upon with suspicion. In the process of identification, . . . *all* his conduct, the personality itself, becomes subject to scrutiny and question. . . . He [the child] has gone

slowly from a sense of grievance and injustice to a recognition that the defi-nition of him as a human being is different from that of other boys. . . . The young delinquent becomes bad because he is not believed if he is good.[4] (Italics added.)

Thus, calling a child "delinquent" makes it more likely that he or she will accept the description and live up to it. Labeling and stereotyping lead children to isolate themselves from the rest of the community and to associate with oth-ers similarly identified. Tannenbaum believes that the community expects the la-beled youth to act according to the label and is unlikely to believe that the child has turned over a new leaf regardless of the individual's efforts at change. This process is illustrated in Figure 7-1.

Edwin Lemert

Edwin Lemert developed the ideas of primary and secondary deviation. **Pri-mary deviation** is deviance that everyone engages in occasionally; it is "rational-ized, or otherwise dealt with as [part of] a socially acceptable role. Under such circumstances, normal and [deviant] behaviors remain strange and somewhat tensional bedfellows in the same person." This can change, however, and the person may step into a deviant or delinquent role. This role and the person's definition of himself or herself as a delinquent are affected by several factors: (1) how much delinquency the person commits, (2) how visible such acts are to the community, (3) how serious others' reactions are, and (4) how aware the delinquent is of their reaction. If the delinquency is highly visible and societal reaction is very obvious and negative, the youth will see himself or herself dif-ferently and it will be difficult for the person to hold onto past self-images and roles. The youth must choose new roles, which may be more or less deviant than the old ones. If the roles are more deviant, the adolescent has reached the stage Lemert calls **secondary deviation**:

> When a person begins to employ his deviant behavior or a role based upon it as a means of defense, attack, or adjustment to the overt and covert prob-lems created by . . . societal reaction to him, his deviation is secondary. Ob-jective evidence of the new role, in clothes, speech, posture, and manner-isms, which in some cases heighten social visibility, serve as symbolic cues to professionalization.

figure 7-1   Mapping Delinquency Theory: Labeling Theory

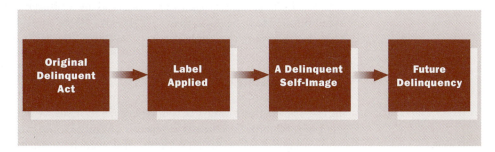

Secondary deviation involves a long process, a dynamic relationship between the person's deviation and society's reaction to it. If the adolescent is eventually stigmatized, efforts to control him or her will shift from informal to formal legal ones, and the youth will be redefined as delinquent:

> The sequence of interaction leading to secondary deviation is roughly as follows: (1) primary deviation; (2) social penalties; (3) further primary deviation; (4) stronger penalties and rejections; (5) further deviations . . . ; (6) crisis reached in the tolerance quotient, expressed in formal action by the community stigmatizing of the deviant; (7) strengthening of the deviant conduct as a reaction to the stigmatizing and penalties; and (8) ultimate acceptance of deviant social status and . . . the associated role.[5]

Lemert says that not all youths labeled "delinquent" accept this role; how receptive they are to such a label depends on their social class. If a youth comes from a family in which the parents are poor, he or she is more likely to accept the assigned delinquent role, especially if either parent is an alcoholic. This occurs because the "close identification between parents and children in our culture means that the status and self-conceptions of family members are readily transferred to children." Also, lower-class parents may be frustrated by their situation and disturbed by inner conflicts. They may be quick to label their children "bad" or "worthless," overreacting to qualities in their children that remind them of traits they despise in themselves. This leads them to reject their children and, when trouble occurs, turn them over to community agencies such as the juvenile court. Once the child arrives in juvenile court, the individual's character and deviant behavior are redefined by the court and related agencies:

> Court hearings, home investigations by social workers, clinical visit, segregation within the school system and other formal dispositions of deviants under the aegis of public welfare or public protection in many instances are cause for dramatic redefinitions of the self and role of deviants.[6]

Lemert believes that having a juvenile court record formally establishes a child's status as a deviant and segregates the child from the community. Jail experience and contacts advance this process, further ensuring that the juvenile will develop a self-concept as truly delinquent. Lemert takes it for granted that institutions fail to rehabilitate. He believes, rather, that they promote the opposite: recidivism.

theory in a nutshell

Edwin Lemert

Lemert focused on the process whereby juveniles come to define themselves as delinquents. This process involves initial minor acts of delinquency (*primary deviance*) followed by negative social responses, further primary deviance, stronger penalties, more serious deviance, formal action by authorities, and eventual acceptance of the delinquent label (*secondary deviance*).

Howard Becker

In the 1960s, there was a new intellectual ferment. A charismatic young president named John F. Kennedy entered the White House, and there was a renewed and energized focus on civil rights, followed by student protests a few years later. In sociology, labeling theory assumed new prominence and popularity; it was antiestablishment, liberal, unconventional, and "hip." Its guru was Howard Becker, who achieved fame with two books, *Outsiders* and *The Other Side*.[7]

Becker began by attacking traditional criminologists, claiming that their research was flawed because it centered on the question: Why do they do it? Criminologists assume such a question is answerable because rule breaking is inherently deviant, and some characteristic of rule breakers makes them do it. In other words, it is assumed that they are a particular kind of person. Becker disagreed, and he also suggested that criminologists often adopt the values of those in control, those who make the decisions about who is deviant and who should be institutionalized. Criminologists, in other words, play a part in the oppression of children.

Deviants are not a homogeneous group. As a result, criminologists study people who have little in common. Becker was thus curious to know how people acquire their labels, suggesting that whether an activity is "deviant" depends *on how people react to it,* not on the nature of the activity itself. That is, *behavior is neither moral nor immoral in and of itself.* Rules are not always enforced regularly or consistently; some are even allowed to lapse completely.

Next, Becker considered the process of *becoming* deviant. The first step is to commit a deviant act (even if it is unintentional). The juvenile may have no idea that others consider what he or she did as being "deviant." The next step is getting caught—which puts the spotlight on the person and his or her behavior. Now the youth acquires a new status or label such as a "slut," "mental," or "juvenile delinquent." The labeled person is presumed to be likely to engage in deviant behaviors repeatedly. Police will round up suspects (including this person) if a similar act occurs in the community at some later time. People expect the delinquent to commit other offenses, too. Thus, the *stigma,* which is a negative label, becomes generalized so that juveniles accused of one kind of deviance, such as vandalism, are also expected to lie, cheat, and steal.

This can lead to delinquency becoming a **master status,** that is, "a status that takes precedence over all other statuses or characteristics of the individual."[8] The status of "delinquent" will carry the greatest weight in the minds of others (see Chapter 1). This may be self-fulfilling. The juvenile labeled "delinquent" may not be heavily involved or interested in delinquency but may feel pressured because of labeling to sever ties with conventional people and turn to illegal activities to survive. The label may also cause conventional people to sever ties with the youth. Thus, deviance becomes a consequence of other people's reactions, not a simple continuation of the original deviant act.

The final step in the process is for the delinquent to join an organized group or gang. Gang members know how to rationalize delinquency; for example, they

theory in a nutshell

Howard Becker

Becker believed that acquiring a label depends on how other people react to the behavior and not the behavior itself. Becker saw the process of becoming a deviant in terms of a series of stages that lead to the person's deviance becoming a master status, that feature of the person that is most important to him or her as well as to others.

may regard their victims as unworthy people (con artists call their victims "suckers"). Within the gang, delinquents learn reasons to continue their participation in delinquency, and tips on how to commit acts and avoid capture are passed along to others. (Recall the discussion of Matza's *techniques of neutralization* in Chapter 6.)

Edwin Schur

Edwin Schur has made a number of significant contributions to labeling theory, most notably through his analysis of the labeling process and his recommendations for reducing juvenile delinquency through *radical nonintervention*.[9] According to Schur, the labeling process involves stereotyping, retrospective interpretation, and negotiation. *Stereotyping* of youths is rampant in juvenile courts, with officials typing youths taken into custody in ways that best fit the minimal information available. For example, a youth from a single-parent family may be viewed as unlikely to be given adequate supervision and control at home, and would be best served by being institutionalized. Retrospective interpretation is the process of reinterpreting the child's past behavior in an entirely new light on the basis of new information. Sociologist Erving Goffman thinks that retrospective interpretation frequently occurs when psychologists or psychiatrists evaluate children they believe have a mental illness. According to Goffman, "Almost anyone's life course could yield up enough denigrating facts to provide grounds for the record's justification of commitment."[10] Schur suggests that the juvenile justice system is particularly susceptible to inappropriate reinterpretation of youths because of the "vagueness with which delinquency and alleged predispositions to delinquency are defined." When examined with a cynical eye, almost every child's background has something that may suggest future trouble and delinquency. The juvenile justice system generally avoids the kind of plea bargaining or *negotiation* that occurs in the adult criminal court, perhaps because juveniles have little power or influence. The paternalistic philosophy of the juvenile court assumes that the judge and probation officer have the child's best interest in mind when making a decision. With so much discretionary power, however, court officials can be quite arbitrary, basing judgments on irrelevant and biased considerations (see Chapters 1 and 14). Schur contends that the inability of youths to negotiate effectively makes it more likely that they will be easily cast into a delinquent status, one that becomes a crucial part of their identities and increasingly difficult to disavow. Many people believe that "once a delinquent, always a delinquent."

Schur takes a rather tolerant view of delinquency by arguing that most of it is insignificant and benign instead of violent, aggressive, or harmful to other people. Therefore, punishment is unnecessary, as

theory in a nutshell

Edwin Schur

Schur thought that the best we can do for children is to leave them alone. In his idea of *radical nonintervention*, he emphasized three elements of the labeling process: *stereotyping*, *retrospective interpretation*, and *negotiation*. As these three elements work together to get the adolescent caught up in the deviant role, that role becomes increasingly difficult to disavow.

are most delinquency laws. These laws are actually counterproductive, producing more delinquency than they deter. Society should permit the widest possible diversity of behavior and not require individuals to adapt to certain standards. Only very serious violations should be brought to the attention of the courts. If juveniles are adjudicated delinquent, they should *not* be committed to correctional facilities but rather diverted to a less coercive and stigmatizing program. Schur's call for this policy of radical nonintervention is very simple: Leave children alone whenever possible.

John Braithwaite

While most labeling theorists believe that societal reaction to deviance contributes to further and often more serious involvement in delinquency, some critics argue that reacting to deviance will prevent or deter it. Ronald Akers and Christine Sellers have noted:

> Societal reaction to some deviance may actually prevent an individual from engaging in further deviant behavior. Applying a stigmatizing label and sanctions may have as much the intended consequence of deterring norm or law violation as the unintended consequence of fostering further violations.[11]

In his extension of labeling theory, John Braithwaite explores the nature and impact of *shaming*. There are two types of shaming: (1) disintegrative shaming and (2) reintegrative shaming. **Disintegrative shaming** is a form of negative labeling by the juvenile justice system consistent with traditional labeling notions that tends to stigmatize and exclude targeted youths, thereby tossing them into a "class of outcasts." For a juvenile marked as a delinquent or *pre*delinquent, legitimate avenues to membership in conventional society are severely restricted. As a result, the juvenile will likely turn to others similarly situated, and collectively they develop a delinquent subculture or gang. **Reintegrative shaming,** on the other hand, involves expressions of community disapproval, ranging from mild chastisement to formal sanctions by the court, followed by indications of forgiveness and reacceptance into the community of responsible law-abiders. The emphasis is upon a condemnation of the act rather than the actor:

> There is a stick followed by a carrot, condemnation followed by community responses aimed at binding the offender to the social order. In this case, shaming has two faces: It makes certain that the inappropriateness of the misconduct is known to the offender and to all observers, and it presents an opportunity to restore the offender to membership in the group.[12]

Braithwaite offers a thoughtful reformulation of the labeling perspective. His central proposition is that reintegrative shaming will reduce future offending, while disintegrative shaming will increase the possibility of future delinquency. A testament to Braithwaite's theory is that it is among the most empirically tested of labeling theories, although there has been mixed support. In an initial test, Toni Makkai and John Braithwaite examined changes in compliance with regulations by nursing homes in Australia and found support for the theory.[13] Carter Hay examined the effects of perceived reintegrative shaming used in parental disciplining on self-reported delinquency among American high school students. Contrary to what Makkai and Braithwaite reported, Hay found that reintegrative shaming in parental disciplining had only a negligible impact on future delinquency.[14]

think
about it

Do some delinquents deserve to be shamed and ostracized because of their illegal behavior? Isn't it helpful for society to have a "class of outcasts" as a stern reminder of what is appropriate and lawful behavior?

Jon Vagg surveyed 2,280 youths from Hong Kong and found that disintegrative shaming in which delinquents were swiftly punished and stigmatized was very effective as a method of social control. In practice, Hong Kong society preferred disintegrative rather than reintegrative shaming.[15] Similar findings on the effects of shaming on recidivism were produced from respondents in Iceland.[16] Using data from respondents in Russia, Ekaterina Botchkovar and Charles Tittle found that shaming of any sort, reintegrative or disintegrative, had negative consequences.[17] Lening Zhang and Sheldon Zhang explored the relationship between reintegrative shaming and predatory forms of delinquency using a national sample of youths. Consistent with the theory, they hypothesized that parent and peer disapproval of delinquent behavior and forgiveness of the transgressor would contribute to lower delinquency. The findings were mixed. Parental forgiveness and peer shaming reduced the likelihood of predatory delinquency. However, peer forgiveness significantly increased the likelihood of predatory delinquency.[18]

Braithwaite's theory has also found its way into criminal justice practice. For instance, many jurisdictions have developed drug courts to process offenders who have substance abuse problems but minimal other criminal history. By avoiding traditional criminal courts, drug offenders can focus on treatment and rehabilitation and avoid potentially stigmatizing labels that arise from criminal prosecution. Terance Miethe and his colleagues evaluated the effectiveness of drug courts in Las Vegas as it relates to reintegrative shaming. Their findings were contrary to the theory. Persons processed in drug courts had significantly *higher* recidivism rates than comparable defendants who were prosecuted in traditional criminal courts.[19] Lawrence Sherman and his colleagues conducted experiments among Australian offenders that applied *reintegrative shaming* principles to 1,300 violent offenders, drunk drivers, adolescent property offenders, and shoplifters. The offenders were randomly assigned to traditional court or to reintegrative conferences as a formal response to their crime. The reintegrative conferences significantly reduced recidivism among violent offenders and drunk drivers but not among the other two groups.[20] Finally, Kenneth Jensen and Stephen Gibbons reported that shame is a powerful emotion that can help serious delinquents, even career criminals, to repudiate their criminal lifestyle, desist from crime, and re-join conventional society.[21]

Evaluation of Labeling Theory

Research testing the core assumptions of the labeling perspective has produced mixed results. In support of labeling theory are a number of studies that have reported on the impact of *formal* sanctions on delinquency. Many of these studies have concluded that juveniles who are formally processed through the juvenile justice system and who have formal contact with other social control agents are more likely to report greater delinquency than those who have not.[22] For instance, Jon Bernburg and his colleagues studied the effects of juvenile justice intervention on subsequent delinquency among youths in the Rochester Youth Development Study. Controlling for relevant factors such as gender, race, poverty, substance use, delinquency, and gang membership, youths who had been processed and labeled by the juvenile justice system were more likely than other youths to continue to commit crime. Further, youths who were labeled had increased gang involvement and association with delinquent peers. In other words, the tarnishing effects of the juvenile justice system only worsened the antisocial behavior of adolescents who were labeled.[23] Identical results were produced in a study of delinquent boys in Iowa. Boys who were involved in the criminal justice system associated with more delinquent peers, had higher recidivism rates, and became more antisocial as a result of their delinquent label.[24]

It has been argued that higher recidivism rates among juveniles processed by the juvenile or criminal justice system makes sense because these are the very types of delinquents that are the most violent, dangerous, and recidivistic (see Chapter 15). In other words, the labeling effects shown by system intervention could reflect selection bias in the types of adolescent offenders that are studied. A recent study suggests, however, that the negative labeling effects of criminal justice intervention are real. David Myers compared 494 violent youths, some of whom were prosecuted as adults and some as juveniles, and controlled for several factors pertaining to the criminality or dangerousness of the juveniles. Even with these controls, youths processed as adults had higher recidivism rates than youths processed as adolescents.[25]

In research examining the impact of *informal* sanctions on a juvenile's identity, David Ward and Charles Tittle concluded that the application of informal sanctions "significantly affects the likelihood that an offender will develop a deviant identity and that such identities significantly affect the likelihood of recidivism."[26] Support for this position has been reported by both Karen Heimer and Ross Matsueda who discovered that delinquency is produced by interactions between the youth and a referenced delinquent group or conventional others, such as parents, in which such factors as motives, norms, attitudes, and gestures coalesce into self-reflected delinquent identity.[27] Heimer has also argued that structural gender inequality affects the meaning that actors give to themselves, situations, and behaviors, such as delinquency. A youth's definition of a situation as favorable or unfavorable to delinquency is affected by significant others and reference groups he or she considers in the process of role taking, and these others and groups are shaped by the youth's gender. According to Heimer, the delinquency gender gap "emerges in part because inequality teaches girls to express their motivations through behavior that differs from that of boys."[28] In short, the meaning of behavior varies across gender. These observations regarding role-taking behavior may also apply to boys. Dawn Bartusch and Ross Matsueda reported that the negative effects of informal labels are greater for boys than for girls, especially for boys with strong self-identities as males.[29] Mike Adams and his colleagues discovered that informal labeling by teachers and peers had a more significant impact on the child's self-conception than formal labeling by police or the juvenile court. Being sent to the principal's office or shunned by peers also has a greater impact on the child's self-concept than the actions of his or her parents.[30] Indeed, informal social control and the various "labels" that parents, friends, neighbors, and other relatives affix to youths can affect their conduct.[31]

However, other studies have *not* found support for the claims of labeling theory. There are two major criticisms of the labeling perspective: (1) The theory disregards the actual behavior of the deviant and instead focuses on the *image* of the deviant being coerced by the labeling process, and (2) the key concepts of the theory are vague and imprecise making it difficult to empirically validate its core propositions.[32] Charles Thomas and Donna Bishop, for instance, reported *no* evidence for the idea that sanctioning offenders pushes them toward acceptance of a deviant label.[33] Steven Burkett and Carol Hickman found that official processing of youths charged with marijuana offenses affected changes in girls' identities but not boys, although the identity changes in the girls did not lead to future delinquency.[34] Jack Foster and his colleagues concluded that youths who had been officially labeled *did not* feel it made much of a difference. Labeling, in other words, *did not* have much impact on their self-concept or what they thought was possible to achieve.[35] When John Hepburn compared official delinquents with nondelinquents, he found that arrest record had *no* direct influence on self-concept.[36] Finally, some research has produced findings opposite of what labeling theory predicts. It has been reported that youths sent to juvenile court have lower rates of future delinquency than those handled less severely.[37] To put it differently formal intervention *decreased* the likelihood of future offending.

Juvenile Justice Policy Applications

think about it

If labels have such formidable power, why don't parents label their children as "gifted," "intelligent," or "athletic?" In turn, why don't youths affix a positive label to themselves and then allow the self-fulfilling prophecy to occur?

One fairly consistent finding from research on labeling is that official labels produce a negative effect when applied to *not-so-serious* offenders. Official or formal labeling *does not* have much of an impact on more serious delinquents. In the minds of these youths, the official label may be just one facet of their life to which they have become acclimated. Labeling theory also suggests that formal intervention by the juvenile justice system only instills a deviant self-identification and thereby increases delinquency. The logical policy implications of labeling theory are to either (1) ignore delinquent acts, (2) react informally, diverting the individual away from the juvenile justice system, or (3) bring the offender, victim, and community together to "right the wrong" and to restore justice. Whatever the juvenile justice system might do, it should do less, that is, decline to formally intervene in the lives of children unless absolutely necessary and divert youths at every possible stage in the juvenile justice process.

Such an approach may require, in the terms used by Schur, policies of *radical nonintervention*. He argues that we overcriminalize youths, bring too many into the juvenile justice system, and enforce unnecessary laws. Therefore, we should consider fully removing status offenses and related violations of court orders produced by such offenses from the system. We also should remove all but the most serious juvenile offenders from the nation's juvenile corrections system.

Diversion programs at both the police and court level should be used whenever possible. The use of police diversion programs, such as Big Brother/Big Sister of America and Police Athletic League Clubs has been extensively developed around the country (see Chapter 3 and Chapter 13). Court diversion provides a variety of alternatives ranging from informal adjustment and mediation to referral of adolescents to youth service bureaus and community youth boards (see Chapter 14). A number of diversion programs also exist at the correctional stage. For example, wilderness programs, such as Vision Quest, Outward Bound, the Stephen French Youth Wilderness Program, and the Florida Associated Marine Institute, combine fitness, survival skills, and personal challenges as alternatives to secure institutional placements.[38] Diversion programs exist today, but they are not nearly as popular as they once were in the mid-1970s. The lack of empirical evidence in support of the labeling theory and concerns over diversion actually "widening the net" and bringing more youths into the system raised serious questions as to its usefulness. Labeling theory and diversion policies were clearly on the decline by the late 1970s.

Mentoring children is a rewarding experience and might prevent delinquency. However, most Americans do not mentor youths. Why? What are the reasons to not become involved in the lives of children?

The one variation in labeling theory that appears to be most appealing to policy makers today might be that of John Braithwaite and his advocacy of reintegrative shaming (see Chapter 14). Three practical policy implications may be derived from Braithwaite's work:

1. Expressing the community's disapproval of the delinquent act through the use of informal agencies or institutions of social control.

2. Integrating the repentant role with rehabilitation programs.

3. Increasing media coverage of not only the delinquent acts of juveniles, but also of individual juvenile offenders who may then be held up as examples of successful reform following their delinquencies.

Restorative justice programs also have drawn upon Braithwaite's ideas extensively. These programs bring the offender, victim, and community together to respond to less serious forms of delinquency and attempt to collectively assist in the rehabilitation process (see Chapter 14). Restorative justice programs have been attempted in juvenile courts, juvenile corrections, victim's organizations, school-based treatment programs, and community-based social service programs.[39] Overall, the outcomes of programs rooted in reintegration/restorative justice are mostly positive. For instance, Jeff Latimer and his colleagues analyzed 35 studies of restorative justice and found that the approach was more effective at reducing recidivism than traditional correctional methods.[40]

CONFLICT THEORY

Cultural deviance, strain, and social control theories share similar assumptions about the organization of society. They see society as being organized around functionally interdependent institutions. Each institution has a function, or reason, for existing as it does. In a healthy society, one in which all the institutions are functioning smoothly together, there is social order. Social values are shared throughout society and are the basis for the creation of laws. These theories assume that there is a consensus on appropriate norms in society; they do not question why institutions are organized as they are, nor do they question why law has developed as it has. Juvenile delinquency is behavior identified and prohibited by law because it violates consensual norms and values of society.

Conflict theory challenges these assumptions. It rejects the idea that society is organized around a consensus of values. **Conflict theory** contends that in its normal state, society is held together by force, coercion, and intimidation. The values of different groups are often the basis of conflicting interests between those groups. Law represents the interests of those groups that have obtained the power or influence to determine the legislation. The first theorists to articulate a conflict view of social relations were Karl Marx and Friedrich Engels.

Karl Marx and Friedrich Engels

Karl Marx and Friedrich Engels saw delinquency as stemming from competition between social classes over scarce resources as well as from the historical inequality of the distribution of resources. Writing in the latter half of the 19th century, Marx and Engels argued that the character of every society is determined by its particular mode of economic production. The primary conflict in society is between the material forces of production and the social relations of production. By "material forces of production," they meant the ability of a society to produce material goods. The concept of "social relations of production" refers simply to relationships among people, especially those relationships that are based upon property, and the manner in which material goods produced are distributed. The primary relationship in industrialized societies reflects the incompatible economic interests of the owners of the means of production (the *bourgeoisie*) and people who sell their labor (the *proletariat*). The class conflict between these two groups produces (both directly and indirectly) the conditions for delinquency.[41]

Because the *bourgeoisie* controls the means of production, it can also control all aspects of social life *even the production of ideas*, which includes the ideas that create the criminal law and the ideological or philosophical beliefs that become the basis for policies of law enforcement. According to Marx and Engels, law and its enforcement are tools of the powerful designed to protect their own economic interests. The police, courts, and correctional system of society operate to control the working class. Behaviors prohibited by criminal law or selectively enforced by the police and courts reflect acts or values that threaten the interests of the dominant class. (This process is illustrated in Figure 7-2.)

theory in a nutshell

Karl Marx and Friedrich Engels

Marx and Engels believed that the ruling class in capitalist societies is responsible for the creation and application of criminal law. Acts threatening interests of the bourgeoisie will be handled by criminal law. In addition, they believed that crime reflected the demoralization of the surplus population, which consists of unemployed and underemployed workers.

figure 7-2   Mapping Delinquency Theory: Conflict Theory

Marx and Engels also produced a modest explanation of crime and delinquency. They believed that crime is the product of a demoralized working class. It is part of human nature to work and be productive, yet capitalist societies create large surplus populations of unemployed and underemployed workers. Over time, unproductiveness leaves the individual demoralized and vulnerable to crime and vice. Marx and Engels called adult criminals and their juvenile counterparts the *lumpenproletariat*, the "dangerous class," and described them as a "parasite class living off productive labor by theft, extortion and beggary, or by providing 'services' such as prostitution and gambling. Their class interests are diametrically opposed to those of the workers. They make their living by picking up the crumbs of capitalist relations of exchange."[42]

Willem Bonger

Willem Bonger was an early 20th-century Marxist criminologist and the author of *Criminality and Economic Conditions* published in 1916. Bonger saw modern capitalist society as being divided into two classes: a ruling class and a ruled class. Furthermore, he viewed capitalism as being based on competition and profit making. Indeed, Bonger believed that economic production is carried on exclusively for profit. More important, he argued that because capitalism brings about

egoistic impulses (selfishness and personal ambition) it makes people less sensitive to the misery or happiness of others. In more "primitive" societies, people lived in a state of communism, and modes of production were designed for personal consumption, not exchange: "They had neither rich nor poor; their economic interests were either parallel or equal . . . the interest of one was the same as that of his comrade." *Altruistic impulses*, a concern for the wellbeing of others, were developed and encouraged.[43]

theory in a nutshell

Willem Bonger

Bonger argued that capitalism engenders *egoistic impulses* in all people, which inhibit tendencies toward developing a sense of responsibility to the larger group. For Bonger, the solution to delinquency was clear: A socialist society, built upon socialist modes of production, will produce *altruistic impulses* in all people. When adolescents are motivated by altruism, they will be unlikely to commit crimes against others.

However, the modern class structure found in capitalism inhibits tendencies toward mutual helpfulness and, instead, fosters social irresponsibility. The egoistic tendencies of capitalism have "weakened the moral force in man which combats the inclination toward egoistic acts, and hence toward the crimes which are one form of these acts."[44] According to Bonger, crime and delinquency reflect the egoistic behavior fostered by the desire to get ahead and to think only of personal need and desires.

Capitalism also creates conditions that encourage delinquency. In Bonger's time, child labor was still extensively practiced in industrialized countries, and he saw the exploitation of child labor as a singularly capitalist phenomenon—one that contributes to delinquency in many ways. On the one hand, labor forces the child to think only of his or her own interests, thereby instilling egoistic feelings. Paid labor also makes children more independent at an age when they most need the guidance of others. Finally, Bonger believed that involvement in paid labor brings children "into contact with persons who are rough and indifferent to their well-being."[45] All these factors increase the child's vulnerability to the enticements and pressures of delinquency.

For Bonger, the solution to crime and delinquency was to be found in the construction of a socialist society. In a society based upon socialist mode of production, altruistic influences would be dominant, both in the behaviors of individuals and in the legal system. Altruistic adolescents would be more likely to help others instead of taking advantage of vulnerable people. "Such a society will not only remove the causes which now make men egoistic, but will awaken, on the contrary, a strong feeling of altruism."[46]

However, not all conflict theorists base their ideas on the economic competition between classes or the unequal distribution of economic resources. Thorsten Sellin and George Vold explored the nature of group conflict in socially heterogeneous societies. They contend that groups in society reflect associations based on common interests such as the pursuit of goals or the protection of vested interests, such as power, wealth, and status.

Thorsten Sellin

Thorsten Sellin's *Culture and Conflict in Crime* was one of the first textbooks to argue that delinquency was the product of conflicting norms. Sellin distinguished between *crime norms,* norms found in the criminal law, and *conduct norms,* norms that are specific to localized groups and that may or may not be consistent with crime norms.

Crime norms reflect rules that prohibit specific conduct and provide punishments for violations. The particular character of the laws, the specific conduct prohibited, and the punishments provided for reflect the character and vested interests of those groups able to influence legislation. According to Sellin, "In some states these groups may comprise the majority, in others a minority, but the social values which receive the protection of the criminal law are ultimately those which are treasured by dominant interest groups."[47]

Conduct norms, on the other hand, reflect the values, expectations, and actual behaviors of groups in everyday life. Conduct norms can be very specific to particular groups, may be shared by many diverse groups, and may conflict with each other. Conduct norms are not necessarily the norms found in criminal law and at times may directly conflict with crime norms. Sellin answered the question of just what conduct norms are likely to be incorporated into the criminal law this way:

> The conduct which the state denotes as criminal is, of course, that deemed injurious to society, or in the last analysis, to those who wield the political power within that society and therefore control the legislative, judicial, and executive functions which are the external manifestations of authority.[48]

As societies become more heterogeneous and complex, the likelihood that group norms will collide with crime norms increases. In turn, delinquency rates will be higher in neighborhoods with the greatest diversity of group norms. Sellin believed that urban neighborhoods with a variety of recently arrived immigrant groups living in close proximity would have a higher level of delinquency than suburban neighborhoods where residents had little contact with "outsiders." Sellin's emphasis on the normative conflict that arises in neighborhoods compliments the work of cultural deviance theory, particularly that done by Shaw and McKay (Chapter 6).

theory in a nutshell

Thorsten Sellin

Sellin believed conflict naturally arises between the *conduct norms* of groups and the *crime norms* reflected in criminal law. The specific behaviors prohibited by law, as well as the punishments specified by the law, will reflect the character and vested interests of those groups with sufficient power to influence the legislative process.

George Vold

In 1958, George Vold published *Theoretical Criminology* in which he argued that human nature leads people into groups. Groups form because common interests draw people together. As new interests arise, new groups are created. However, "groups come into conflict with one another as the interests and purposes they serve tend to overlap, encroach on one another, and become competitive." This competitiveness generates a continuous struggle to maintain or even enlarge the position of one's own group relative to others. This conflict may eventually lead to the creation of new laws. "Whichever group interest can marshal the greatest number of votes will determine whether there will be a new law to hamper and curb the interests of the opposing group."[49]

Not surprisingly, group members who support the new law are more likely to obey it and call for its strict enforcement. People who oppose it are less sympathetic to it and, consequently, more likely to violate it. People with little power or influence have little impact on the legislative process. Therefore, behaviors reflecting their interests are more likely to be legislated as criminal by groups that have the necessary influence.

Richard Quinney

Richard Quinney is widely regarded as one of the most influential conflict theorists of the late 20th century. He contends that criminal laws are consciously created mechanisms that enable the ruling class to maintain political and economic control over the rest of society. This basic Marxian framework is found in Quinney's 1974 book, *Critique of Legal Order,* in which he states:

1. American society is organized around advanced capitalism.
2. The state exists to serve the interests of the dominant capitalist class.
3. Social and economic order are maintained and perpetuated by the ruling class through the application of criminal law.
4. Crime control is accomplished through the criminal justice system, which is administered by governing elites. This system of law and control represents ruling-class interests and is designed to establish domestic order.
5. The inherent contradictions of advanced capitalism require the oppression of the lower classes through the coercion and violence of the legal system.
6. The crime problem can be solved only by the collapse of capitalism and the creation of a new society built upon socialist economic principles.[50]

It is interesting to note, however, that Quinney's views had shifted substantially by the time he prepared the second edition of his book, *Class, State, and Crime.* In this work, rather than relying entirely on a Marxist critique of capitalist society, Quinney considers the problem of crime and delinquency within a religious context: "The contemporary capitalist world is caught in what Tillich, going beyond Marx's materialistic analysis of capitalism, calls a *sacred void,* the human predicament on both a spiritual and sociopolitical level."[51] Citing Old Testament prophets, Quinney suggests that a "prophetic understanding" of reality is necessary for a proper analysis of crime and justice and states that Marx was wrong about religion being an "opium of the people." Quinney does maintain an essentially Marxian orientation: "The socialist struggle in our age is a search for God at the same time that it is a struggle for justice in human society."[52]

John Hagan

John Hagan, who focused on the role of the mother as a worker, suggests a different approach to explaining delinquency in his *power-control theory.* According to Hagan, children's participation in delinquency is affected by the relative position of fathers and mothers in the workplace:

> Positions of power in the workplace are translated into power relations in the household and . . . the latter, in turn, influence the gender-determined control of adolescents, their preferences for risk taking, and the patterning of gender and delinquency.[53]

Delinquency is a male-dominated phenomenon because of the class structure of modern patriarchal families. The *patriarchal family* consists of a husband whose employment outside the home carries some degree of authority and a wife who is not employed outside the home. This type of family is more likely to socially reproduce daughters like their mothers—females who focus on domestic labor and consumption, activities preparing them for a cult of domesticity. The sons in patriarchal families are more likely to be prepared to participate in the external labor force in direct production.

The opposite of the patriarchal family is the *egalitarian family,* in which both parents are employed in positions of authority outside the home. Here, both males and females engage in consumption and production activities equally. In egalitarian families, parents attempt to socially reproduce both sons and daughters for entry into the production sphere of the labor force.

In the patriarchal family, females are both instruments and objects of informal social control. While both fathers and mothers exert control over their daughters much more than over their sons, daughters are even more controlled by their mothers than by their fathers. In egalitarian families, parents redistribute their informal controls in a manner that treats sons and daughters more equally.

The relationship between parents and daughters in patriarchal families is also responsible for her significantly lower interests in risk-taking (an activity viewed as more acceptable for sons). Patriarchal families teach daughters to avoid risk-taking, while egalitarian families are more likely to encourage both sons and daughters to take risks. Consequently, patriarchal families are characterized by large sex-ratio differences in common forms of delinquency. In egalitarian families, where girls are treated more like their brothers, minimal differences in common delinquency are detected.

Tests conducted by Simon Singer and Murray Levine have lent support to power-control theory. They reported that gender differences in delinquent behavior were largely tied to variations in parental authority.[54] Brenda Blackwell and her colleagues found partial support for Hagan's theory when they found that it explained gender differences in delinquency in their study of middle-school and high-school students in a small Florida city.[55] However, other tests of power-control theory have found little or no support for it. Gary Jensen and Kevin Thompson examined data from three surveys conducted between 1964 and 1979 that were based on samples 3 to 30 times larger than the Toronto sample used by Hagan and his associates. Whereas Hagan had predicted significant relationships between (1) social class and delinquency and (2) gender and class, data produced by Jensen and Thompson did not support these hypotheses. They suggest the lack of supportive findings may be the result of differences between American and Canadian youths or methodological differences between the two studies.[56]

Merry Morash and Meda Chesney-Lind have reported mixed support for power-control theory. They found that girls were less delinquent than boys in each type of family. Furthermore, the key explanatory variable was not the mother's relative workplace power but rather the absence of a father and presence of a stepfather, as well as the quality of the child's relationship with his or her parents. Their data also yielded several other important findings:

> In some types of families, boys were controlled more than girls. Specifically, if the mother was alone and unemployed, she controlled more of the decisions about boys than about girls, and was more punitive toward boys. The family with an unemployed mother alone also differs from other types in that the children identify less with their mother.[57]

Daniel Curran and Claire Renzetti argue that Hagan's theory defines patriarchal control in the home as simply "parental supervision" and is thus too narrowly conceived.[58] James Messerschmidt suggests that it may be incorrect to assume that the authority a person has at work translates in exactly the same way as authority in the home and family.[59] Finally, Ronald Akers takes the theory to task claiming that although Hagan's own Canadian study supported the theory, the findings from other studies are much less supportive:

> The class and gender differences, the low involvement of fathers in exercising parental control, and other internal family variables have no or very weak effects on delinquency. The gender differences in delinquency are about the same for patriarchal and egalitarian families. . . . Furthermore, the effects of family control variables on delinquent behavior are equally weak for both males and females.[60]

Mark Colvin and John Pauly

Mark Colvin and John Pauly's **integrated structural-Marxist theory** argues that serious delinquency results from the reproduction of coercive control patterns tied to the relationship between production and class structure in capitalist societies. Their approach assumes that the "objective structure of social relations [is] grounded in the process of material production under capitalism." The struggle between the three major classes (capitalist, working, and petite bourgeoisie) produces distinctive "fractions" within each major class. The different control structures, operating within the various fractions of the working class, "solicit and compel certain types of behavior from individuals and shape ideological orientation for the individual in relation to the agents and apparatuses of social control."[61] Within the working class there are three important fractions:

1. Fraction 1 is primarily composed of workers located in very competitive, secondary-labor-market industries. Given the minimal job security and dead-end nature of the work, control tends to be simple and coercive.

2. Fraction 2 provides greater job security than Fraction 1, largely as a result of the unionization and protective contracts that are more common within it. The control structure relies more on the worker's consciously bonding to work and authority on the basis of the possibilities of promotions and wage increases.

3. Fraction 3 comprises mainly workers located in jobs that provide greater amounts of independence and require or expect individual initiative. Controls in Fraction 3 take a more bureaucratic, normative form in which the worker is manipulated through valued symbols and statuses.

Coercive control patterns that exist for lower-class parents in the workplace are reproduced in the home, shaping the parents' behavior as they interact with each other and their children. Fraction 1 parents, holding jobs that are inferior, tightly controlled, lacking in personal authority, and regulated by superiors through coercive means, reproduce these control patterns in the home. This leads to the increased alienation of the child from authority in general. In addition, the use of coercive controls in the home, including physical punishment, tends to weaken the bond between parent and child.

Social bonds of lower-class adolescents may also weaken in the school setting. Colvin and Pauly argue that control structures of schools are designed to support the labor requirements of capitalism. Consequently, these structures use coercive controls similar to those in the workplace.

When entering school, the child, with initial bonds produced in a family control structure, confronts a new structure of control. The school, like parents' workplaces, contains gradations of control within various "tracks" that are exercised over students. A child with negative initial bonds is likely to be placed in a control structure at school that parallels the coercive family council structure that produced the child's negative bond.[62] According to Colvin and Pauly, the reproduction of coercive controls in school is accomplished in four ways:

1. IQ and aptitude testing are likely to identify more negatively bonded children for placement in lower-levels tracks.

2. Negatively bonded children may give behavioral cues to school authority figures that identify them as potential "problem students." Such cues may be self-fulfilling, with the child becoming what he or she is expected to become.

3. The differential placing of lower-class students into lower-level tracks will lead to greater strain and alienation.

4. Differential financial resources of schools in lower-, working-, and middle-class neighborhoods will produce differences in the availability of rewards and punishments in the school settings. Schools with fewer resources will rely on more coercive controls.

School control structures lead to differential patterns of rewards and punishments, resulting in differential reinforcement or weakening of social bonds. Lower-class adolescents who have become alienated at home and school are more likely to join peer groups composed of similarly alienated individuals. Criminal, violent, or delinquent patterns of behavior will emerge from these relationships. Colvin and Pauly's approach may be summarized as follows:

1. Parents' *class position* is negatively associated with their experience of coercion in *workplace control structures,* a situation that leads to more alienated bonds in lower-class parents.

2. Alienated parental bonds contribute to the development of more coercive family control structures, which result in more alienated initial bonds in juveniles.

3. Juveniles with alienated initial bonds will more likely be placed in more coercive school control structures, reinforcing the juveniles' alienated bonds.

4. Juveniles' reinforced alienated bonds lead to greater association with alienated peers who form peer-group control structures, which interact with class-related, community and neighborhood distributions of opportunities to create qualitatively different paths of delinquent development.

Recent tests of Colvin and Pauly's theory have found only modest support for their claims. Studies by Steven Messner and Marvin Krohn and by Sally Simpson and Lori Elis have reported the basic relationship between social class and delinquency is largely structured by gender.[63] These researchers suggest that traditional gender controls in the home interact with workplace controls to produce more rigid discipline and control for girls.

Mark Colvin

Nearly two decades after Colvin and Pauly published *integrated structural-Marxist theory,* Colvin developed a second integrated theory using a conflict framework he called differential coercion theory. Colvin defines coercion as a force that causes a child to behave in a certain way out of the fear and anxiety it creates. According to Colvin, children who are exposed to coercive environments are more likely to develop social–psychological deficits that increase the possibility of committing crime.[64] Differential coercion theory borrows heavily from published works showing that aversive family interchanges and coercive disciplining patterns are strong correlates of juvenile delinquency in adolescents. Indeed, research supports the idea that children who are physically abused and who receive erratic discipline are more likely to commit crime.[65] Some examples of the types of coercive interchanges Colvin identifies include physical attacks, teasing, humiliation, yelling, and threats. Through aversive family interchanges, coercion becomes the mechanism children growing up in these environments learn to use when they find themselves in undesirable situations. Children bring what they learn from coercive family interactions into other social settings. These are the children who are more likely to become "early starters" in delinquency and life-course persistent or career offenders.[66]

> ## theory in a nutshell
>
> ### Mark Colvin
>
> As an advocate of *differential coercion theory,* Colvin argued that children who are exposed to coercive environments are more likely to develop social–psychological deficits that increase the possibility of their committing crimes. He defined coercion as a force that causes a child to behave in a certain way out of the fear and anxiety it creates. Children who grow up in coercive environments are more likely to behave inappropriately in settings they find to be unpleasant.

Colvin identifies two dimensions of coercion: the *strength* of the coercive force, which ranges from no coercion to total coercion, and the *consistency* with which coercion is applied or experienced. Children usually experience coercion on either a more or less consistent basis or an *erratic* basis. Juveniles who experience coercion erratically will develop a different set of social–psychological deficits than children who experience coercion consistently. The most notable difference between them is the direction of their anger and the degree of self-control induced in the child. Erratic coercion leads to anger directed at *others* because the child's perception of unjust and arbitrary treatment is heightened as a result of an unpredictable schedule of coercion. Erratic coercion also induces low self-control. Coercion that is applied inconsistently teaches children that they cannot control the consequences of being punished because the punishment occurs randomly and not as a predictable outcome of their behavior. Thus, when children believe their punishment is random, there is no pattern or incentive for them to learn self-control.

On the other hand, coercion that is applied more or less consistently leads to a different outcome. It produces *self*-directed anger and a rigid type of self-control that is based on a steady fear of reprisal from external sources. Colvin argues that erratic coercion creates children who are prone to committing predatory crime, whereas consistent coercion produces children who are submissive. While children who experience consistent coercion are less likely to commit crime, they are more likely to experience mental illness, an idea that finds support in John D. Hewitt and Robert M. Regoli's work on female delinquency and *differential oppression theory* (discussed later in this chapter).[67]

While consistent coercion might prevent crime in theory, it is very difficult for adults to maintain such consistency in their interpersonal relations in practice with children since it requires constant monitoring to detect noncompliance. Except for extreme situations of monitoring, such as that exercised over females in highly repressive, patriarchal households, consistent coercion typically becomes erratic because of the difficulty it causes for adults who are trying to maintain close surveillance. Consequently, the crime-controlling effect of consistent coercion is short-lived. It thus seems that coercion may be best at controlling delinquency when it is coupled with an array of social supports in which coercion remains subtle and in the background and used only as a last resort when social supports fail to create compliance.

Finally, Colvin distinguishes between *interpersonal* and *impersonal* forms of coercion. The first occurs within direct interpersonal relations of control (e.g., adults and children). The second, which is grounded in Merton's strain theory (see Chapter 6), is linked to pressures from larger structural arrangements that create an indirect experience of coercion. On the one hand, interpersonal coercion uses the threat of force and intimidation to create compliance in interpersonal relations. These micro-levels of coercive processes of control might involve the actual or threatened use of physical force or the actual or threatened removal of social supports. Impersonal coercion, on the other hand, results from pressure arising from structural arrangements and circumstances beyond the individual's control that produce stress, frustration, anxiety, desperation, and anger. These macro-level sources of coercion may include economic and social pressures that stem from unemployment, poverty, or competition among groups. The experience of coercion can involve the removal of social supports at both the micro-level of interpersonal relations (e.g., love, food, and clothing) and the macro-level of social and governmental structures (e.g., unemployment benefits, health care, and housing).

Francis Cullen

In 1994 Francis Cullen advanced *social support theory* as a general framework for criminology and criminal justice. Social support is defined as the perceived and actual amount of instrumental and expressive or emotional supports that one receives from primary relationships, social networks, and communities. Having a neighbor, friend, or family member to help with babysitting, job searching, and bill paying and to provide other advice and counsel are examples of social support. Across multiple levels of social life, social support may be provided informally and formally through churches, schools, governmental assistance programs, and even the criminal justice system.

According to Cullen, social support is theoretically important to criminology because it serves as a protective factor that both insulates persons from delinquency and assists in the process of correctional rehabilitation. In this sense, social support is applicable to crime prevention and offender treatment. In particular, Cullen's "general" proposition is that, all things being equal, individuals—from would-be offenders to those who have already broken the law—who receive higher levels of social support will be at a lower risk for engaging in wayward behavior in the future.[68]

In the correctional setting, social support may serve as a resource and safety net to help steer former delinquents and prisoners along conventional pathways. Indeed, in subsequent work, Cullen and his colleagues note that the social support approach was particularly suited to rehabilitate prisoners since recidivism has been shown to be reducible via programs that develop interpersonal skills, provide support counseling from caring providers, and furnish multiple social services. Thus, social support theory predicts that much of the potentially harmful effects of prison conditions on an inmate's behavior can be mediated by the provision of social support.[69] In fact, Cullen and Colvin have linked their theories by showing that social support is an important way to reduce the noxious effects of social coercion in people's lives.[70]

> ## theory in a nutshell
>
> ### Francis Cullen
>
> Francis Cullen's *social support theory* contends that the perceived and actual amount of instrumental and expressive or emotional supports that one receives from primary relationships, social networks, and communities can insulate youths from delinquency. In addition, social support is an important way to help former offenders desist from crime and reconnect or reintegrate into conventional society.

Criminologists have produced impressive empirical support for *social support theory* using an array of data sources and analytic methods. Using the National Youth Survey, for instance, John Wright and his colleagues found that familial social support, or family capital, was positively related to moral beliefs, time spent studying, and grades, and negatively related to having delinquent friends. Youths who had a strong family support system were also more likely to exercise, maintain a healthy lifestyle, and be committed to their jobs. In addition, youths who had family support had few criminal friends and were less likely to use drugs. Overall, Wright and his associates reported that family social support produced other beneficial forms of social support or capital, reduced delinquency over a six-year period, and exerted effects for a range of outcomes associated with prosocial adult development.[71]

Benjamin Cornwell examined the effects of social support on mental health outcomes using data from the nationally representative Add Health Study and found that adolescents with reduced parental and friendship support experienced higher levels of depression than youths who had greater connectedness with their peers and families.[72] Elise Peplin and Victoria Banyard found that social support mediated the effects of child maltreatment on developmental outcomes in young adults. In other words, people who were mistreated as children could overcome the harmful effects of maltreatment with emotional and other forms of support from friends and family.[73]

Researchers have shown that although the general public holds many punitive attitudes in regards to punishing delinquents, they also advocate social support. Melissa Moon and her colleagues reported that citizens believe in the importance of rehabilitation to change delinquents and support prevention programs. In fact, some people are even willing to volunteer their time to provide social support to juvenile delinquents.[74] Social support is also linked to crime at the aggregate level. Travis Pratt and Timothy Godsey examined the relationship between a society's degree of social support and its murder rate among 46 nations. They found that nations with greater levels of social support have lower violent crime rates; nations that do not invest in social support tend to have more homicides.[75]

Robert M. Regoli and John D. Hewitt

In their **differential oppression theory**, Robert M. Regoli and John D. Hewitt contend that children have little power to influence their social world. Children have almost no choice regarding whom they associate with and have limited resources available to influence others or to support themselves independently of adults. Therefore, they have the least access to resources that could allow them to negotiate changes in their environment.[76] In comparison to parents, teachers, and other adult authority figures, children are relatively powerless and are expected—often required—to submit to the power and authority of adults. When this power is used to deny children self-determination and impede them from developing a sense of competence and self-efficacy, it becomes oppression.[77]

> ## theory in a nutshell
> ### Robert M. Regoli and John D. Hewitt
> Regoli and Hewitt think that children develop in an arena of oppression that affects who and what they become. Oppression begins with the assumptions adults hold about the need for order and, subsequently, the form that order should take. Children are differentially oppressed, some more frequently and more severely than others. Children who experience more frequent and severe forms of oppression are more likely to adapt to their oppression through delinquency.

According to Regoli and Hewitt, *all* children are oppressed. The amount of oppression children experience falls on a continuum, ranging from simple demands for obedience to rules designed for the convenience of adults to the physical, sexual, and emotional abuse of children. They contend that the problem behaviors of children, including crime and delinquency, drug and alcohol abuse, and mental disorders can be understood as adaptive reactions to oppressive social situations created by adults. Many children grow up under oppressive conditions that fail to support their developmental needs; the psychological, emotional, or physical consequences that a child suffers depend on the duration, frequency, intensity, and priority of the oppression and on the child's stage of development. The theory of differential oppression is organized around the following four principles (see Figure 7-3):

1. Because children lack power due to their age, size, and lack of resources, they are easy targets for adult oppression.

2. Adult oppression of children occurs in multiple social contexts and falls on a continuum ranging from benign neglect to malignant abuse.

3. Oppression leads to adaptive reactions by children. The oppression of children produces at least four adaptations: passive acceptance; exercise of illegitimate coercive power; manipulation of one's peers; and retaliation.

figure 7-3 Mapping Delinquency Theory: Differential Oppression Theory

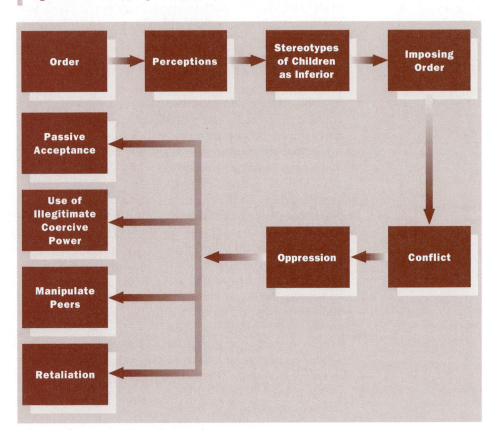

4. Children's adaptations to oppression create and reinforce adults' views of children as being inferior, subordinate, and ready to make trouble. This view enables adults to justify their role as oppressor and further reinforces children's powerlessness.

Forms of Oppression The term *oppression* is a summation of the abusive, neglectful, and disrespectful relations many children confront. Oppression of children by adults occurs in multiple social contexts and falls on a continuum ranging from benign neglect to malignant abuse; it occurs whenever adults act in ways that belittle or trivialize children as being something less than authentic and feeling human beings. Children are exposed to different levels and types of oppression that vary depending on their age, level of development, and beliefs and perceptions of their parents. While there are occasions when adults exercise power over children out of sincere concern for the child's welfare, Regoli and Hewitt focus on the times when an adult's use of power over children is about the needs and interests of the adult rather than the child. In fact, much of the oppression children suffer stems from their parent's inability to meet their needs, either because adults are uninformed about what the needs of children are at various stages of development or because they are not capable of responding to those needs. Oppressive structural forces, such as poverty, social isolation, and residing in a disadvantaged neighborhood also negatively influence parenting practices. However, the underlying source of adult oppression may be found in the mistreatment they received as children and continue to experience as adults. Therefore, the oppression adults inflict on children is likely a part of a chain of coercion and abuse that is transmitted from one generation to the next.[78]

Healthy development requires that social contexts provide opportunities for children to fulfill their physical, intellectual, psychological, and social developmental needs. Unfortunately for many children, rather than being supportive and nurturing, the social contexts in which they are surrounded are oppressive and damaging. Using a developmental–ecological perspective can provide a means for understanding how the oppression of children is likely to occur within multiple social contexts that may interact to produce harmful outcomes for children. These contexts include both micro-level relationships with family and friends and macro-level structural elements, such as race, class, neighborhood, and age, which expose individuals to more or less oppression of different types.

Micro-Level Oppression   The most severe and damaging oppression adults inflict upon children is officially defined as maltreatment. The major forms of child maltreatment include physical abuse, sexual abuse, neglect, and emotional abuse. According to the most recent data, about three million cases of child abuse or neglect involving over five million children were reported to the various state protective services. Sixty percent of these cases were referred for investigation, and slightly less than one-third of the investigated cases resulted in a disposition of either substantiated or indicated child maltreatment. About 60 percent of the victims suffered neglect, while nearly 20 percent suggested physical abuse, and another 10 percent were sexually abused.[79] Official data are reinforced by the findings from a self-report study based on a national sample of 3,346 adults in which 63 percent of parents reported they had used at least one form of psychological aggression on their children in the previous year.[80]

Certain parenting styles are more likely to oppress children. Some parents oppress children as they attempt to impose and maintain adult conceptions of social order. Such parents may view their children as extensions of themselves rather than as individuals and therefore feel free to impose their will on their children.[81] In any case, the children are required to obey rules designed to reinforce adult notions of right and wrong behavior. In an attempt to exert greater control over their children, parents and other adults often use coercion or force. According to Richard Gelles and Murray Straus, American cultural norms regarding violence in families prescribe that it is acceptable to hit a child if he or she is doing something wrong and "won't listen to reason." Such coercion may become excessive, lead to physical harm and long-term psychological damage, and is a mechanism for transmitting an ageist ideology that diminishes the value of children in relation to adults across society.[82]

Other parents oppress children through neglectful parenting that fails to meet their children's physical, emotional, and educational needs. Examples of physical neglect include the refusal of or delay in seeking health care, abandonment, expulsion from the home, refusal to allow a runaway to return home, and inadequate supervision. Emotional neglect includes inattention to the child's needs for affection, refusal of or failure to provide needed psychological care, and spouse abuse in the child's presence. The allowance of chronic truancy, failure to enroll a child of mandatory school age in school, and failure to attend to special educational needs are all examples of educational neglect. Generally, neglect occurs anytime a caretaker permits a child to experience suffering or fails to provide one of the basic ingredients essential for developing a child into a physically, intellectually, emotionally, and psychologically healthy person. Although single incidents of neglect may have no noticeable harmful effects, in some cases, they can result in death. Chronic patterns of neglect also may result in developmental delays or emotional disabilities. According to W. I. Munkel, "Neglected children suffer hurts in their bodies, their minds, their emotions, and their spirits."[83]

Macro-Level Oppression   Macro-level social forces such as poverty also oppress children. Children living in poverty are more likely to experience oppression than children living in more affluent conditions. This oppression can be viewed developmentally and is likely to be cumulative as children continue to grow and develop in destitute conditions. During the early years, socioeconomic disadvantage oppresses children by impairing their physical health status at birth and providing less access to resources that may moderate the negative consequences of those problems. For healthy development, young children need exposure to stimulating materials or experiences. Unfortunately, children living in poverty are less likely than their wealthier counterparts to have access to these materials or experiences. Often their homes are unsafe, lacking heat and adequate plumbing. In addition, they have increased exposure to chemical toxins such as lead, which are associated with cognitive deficits, lower school achievement, and long-term impairment of neurological function.[84] Rather than receiving cognitively stimulating experiences, young children living in disadvantaged neighborhoods may rarely leave their home. Environmental and work-related conditions often limit their access to the outdoors. Poor children are more likely than nonpoor children to live in housing located in commercial and industrial areas, which often lack safe outdoor places for children to play and limit opportunities for social interaction and cognitive development.[85]

Poverty and economic disadvantage also have oppressive influences on school-age and adolescent children. During middle childhood and adolescence, children increasingly come into direct contact with their neighborhoods through involvement in school, youth serving organizations, and informal neighborhood groups. For young people, the physical features of their neighborhood establish the boundaries of their social universe. Some neighborhoods offer youth a variety of supervised instruction and structured activities, while others send the majority of the children out on the street.[86] Due to the restricted tax base in poor neighborhoods, limited public resources are available to support the education, recreation, and health needs of youth and their families. In contrast, youth in wealthy neighborhoods have opportunities that poor children are not offered, like summer camp, music lessons, sports training, home computers, and special tutoring. Instead, adolescents in dilapidated inner-city neighborhoods have higher exposure to physical danger, criminal activity, and drug use.[87]

Because successful adaptation at each stage of youth development is influenced by earlier developmental histories, long-term exposure to oppressive living conditions typically results in worse developmental outcomes for children. African American and Hispanic children are more likely than white children to experience persistent poverty and to live in areas of concentrated poverty.[88] For instance, Thomas McNulty and Paul Bellair found that concentrated poverty is so segregated by race that virtually no white children live in the worst neighborhoods that some African American and Hispanic children do.[89] High-risk contexts such as poverty, chronic stress, and child maltreatment may have lasting effects when they damage or impair crucial adaptive systems such as adult–child attachment, intelligence, and self-regulation of emotions and behavior. Persistent poverty is consistently found to have more adverse effects than transitory poverty on children's cognitive development and school achievement. Children living for long periods in impoverished conditions experience more negative life events and adverse conditions that may place demands on their coping resources well beyond what they can handle.[90] Consequently, exposure to chronic adversity exacts a toll on a child's mental, physical, and emotional health. This may trigger a cycle of lifelong deficiencies encompassing many contexts of their lives:

> Children who enter school with few resources, cognitive difficulties, and self-regulatory problems often have academic problems, get into trouble with teachers, are more likely to be rejected by peers and are at risk for disengaging from normative school and peer contexts, which sets them up for considerable difficulties.[91]

Since many social problems are significantly clustered and correlated with concentrated poverty, cumulative oppression and its ensuing pathways to long-term developmental problems are much more frequent for children who endure lifelong exposure to impoverished social environments.

Adaptations to Oppression Most children adapt to oppression through *passive acceptance* and subsequent obedience—an obedience built upon fear, which derives from implied threats and intimidation. This adaptation is characterized by the child's passive acceptance of their subordinate and inferior status. It is more common among females due to higher status generally afforded males and to generally low female involvement in delinquency.[92] Since children are inundated by adult domination, they quickly learn that obedience is expected. Such adaptations among children are similar to the passive acceptance of the slave role, adaptations of prison inmates, and immersion in the cycle of violence for battered women. These children outwardly accept their inferior positions, but they develop a repressed hatred for their oppressors, adapting to the structures of domination in which they are immersed. Once a situation of violence and oppression has been established, it engenders an entire way of life and behavior for those caught up in it, oppressors and oppressed alike. Both are submerged in this situation, and both bear marks of oppression. The oppressed are likely to believe they have no purpose in life except those the oppressor prescribes for them.

Passive children do not fully explore personal autonomy; they never become the "author of their own life" so to speak. This repression results in negative self-perceptions that may manifest themselves in a wide range of problem behaviors including alcoholism, drug addiction, eating disorders, low self-esteem, and psychiatric disorders.[93]

A second adaptation to oppression is the *exercise of illegitimate coercive power.* Many adolescents are attracted to delinquency because it helps them to establish a sense of autonomy and control. This anticipatory delinquency is a yearning for adult status.[94] Delinquent acts can immediately and demonstratively make things happen and provide the child with a sense of restored potency

Source: 1989 Jules Feiffer. Reprinted with permission. All rights reserved.

denied him or her by adults and parents. Sexual misbehavior, illicit use of drugs or alcohol, and violations of the criminal law derive greater symbolic importance for the child to the extent that they demonstrate resistance to adult attempts to exert control over his or her behavior.

A third adaptation is the *manipulation of one's peers*. This is an attempt by the child to become empowered. Through the manipulation of others within the peer group, a child who has experienced oppression at the hands of adults may acquire a sense of strength and control or a degree of empowerment not otherwise felt. Gerald Marwell suggests that "at any given point of time this potential [for social power] lies primarily in the opinions of the actor held by those with whom one interacts. If one is thought strong, one, by and large, is strong, or at least, may use 'strength' to manipulate others."[95] The school bully is an example, so is the child who spreads gossip in hopes of gaining status and prestige in the eyes of others. Unfortunately, the mere involvement of a child with his or her peers leads many adults to view the involvement as problematic in itself. Adults may then react by exercising even greater control over the child's interaction with others.

The fourth adaptation is *retaliation,* which may include delinquent acts ranging from property crimes to violent offenses. It is the most severe and least common of the adaptations to oppression. Retaliation is more common among males than females. Children may engage in retaliation to get back at the people or the institutions they believe are the source of their oppression. School vandalism sometimes occurs because a student is angry with a teacher or principal. Some children may strike directly at their parents or peers by assaulting or killing them. Others try to hurt their parents by turning inward by becoming chronically depressed and contemplating or committing suicide.[96]

Confronted by oppressive forces, children, to put it simply, adapt. Adults individually or collectively affect children, and children react. Intuitively, this should make sense. The theory of differential oppression contends that people first interpret, then people proceed, or, to put it differently, people interpret something (e.g., who children are in relation to them), then people see *them* (children) as they interpreted *them*. And even though children *as a group* are oppressed, the impact is most significantly experienced at the individual level. Oppression is differentially experienced, both in its application and impact. Children adapt differentially and the individual reasons for how particular children adapt are generally unknown. Even children growing up in the same family, in the same neighborhood, and experiencing similar oppressive situations will often exhibit different adaptations.

Current research has well established the connection between oppression and the problem behaviors of children. Future research is needed to explore why one child adapts to abuse by passively accepting the situation and developing an eating disorder and low self-esteem, while another child experiencing similar abuse adapts by manipulating or bullying others, perhaps even abusing age peers, and yet still another child retaliates by murdering the offending adult. For statistical information about the status of children in the United States, see Box 7-2.

Evaluation of Conflict Theory

Conflict theories have been criticized for a number of reasons. Jackson Toby, for instance, contends that conflict theory is nothing more than a rehashing of the traditional liberal approach of helping the underdog. He claims that most crime is for profit and luxury, not for survival.[97] Conflict theory has also been accused of relying too heavily on historical and theoretical approaches that fail to produce testable hypotheses. Statements or postulates offered tend to be untestable; they are not subject to scientific verification and instead must be accepted as a matter of faith. In addition, Francis Allen[98] and David Shichor[99] state that

---

box 7-2   **A WINDOW ON DELINQUENCY**

Each Day in America

4	children are killed by abuse or neglect
5	children commit suicide
8	children are killed by firearms
77	babies die before their first birthday
192	children are arrested for violent crimes
383	children are arrested for drug abuse
390	babies are born to mothers who received late or no prenatal care
1,839	babies are born without health insurance
1,887	public school students are corporally punished
2,411	babies are born into poverty
2,261	high school students drop out
2,383	children are confirmed as abused or neglected
4,302	children are arrested
17,132	public school students are suspended

Source: Children's Defense Fund, *Each Day in America, 2007,* http://www.childrensdefense.org/site/PageServer?page name=research_national_data_each_day, accessed June 16, 2007.

conflict theory oversimplifies and overemphasizes the political and economic nature of juvenile delinquency. Their concern has received some support from J. A. Sharpe, who analyzed patterns of law violations in England between the 15th and 19th centuries and found little evidence to support the claims of conflict theorists that crime and delinquency increased with the development of capitalism.[100]

Ronald Akers has taken conflict theory to task for portraying modern society as too heterogeneous for the general population to arrive at any significant value consensus. Instead of viewing society as a precarious balancing of crisscrossing, conflicting, and competing interest groups, Akers contends "society is also held together by the larger or smaller number of widely supported values, common assumptions, and images of the world. This is a chief factor in providing some continuity and unity in a diversified society."[101] Akers also notes that most delinquency cannot be explained by group conflict inasmuch as most delinquency is *intra*group in nature—that is, committed by members *within* the group against other members *within* the group by outsiders.

Donald Shoemaker is critical of the suggested direct link between capitalism and delinquency. He questions the existence of such a link because (1) delinquency is widespread in the middle- and upper-middle classes; (2) juveniles appear to have little concern for their status in the economic system; (3) racial and ethnic factors have as much or more influence on crime and delinquency as social class factors do; and (4) there is a failure to demonstrate "a necessary connection between capitalism per se and industrial or demographic conditions within a society."[102]

Despite these critiques, criminologists in the 21st century continue to show the relevance of conflict theory to explaining delinquency and helping offenders rehabilitate and reintegrate into society. Propositions derived from conflict theory have been linked to overcoming abuse,[103] homicide rates,[104] racial profiling by the police,[105] and coercive encounters between the police and the public.[106] Social support theory, in particular, holds promise for applicability to criminal justice practice. Recent research indicated that social support was linked to inmate misconduct at both the individual and the facility level. Shanhe Jiang and his colleagues analyzed data from the National Survey of Inmates in State and Federal Correctional Facilities, which encompassed more than 9,000 inmates and 275 correctional institutions and found that inmates who received telephone calls from their children were significantly less likely to accumulate rule violations than those without contacts from their children. At the structural level, facility participation in religious programs was negatively related to facility rule violations.[107] Similarly, Jiang and Thomas Winfree reported that (1) female inmates have greater social support than male inmates based on calls, mail, and visits from their children; (2) male inmates experience greater social support from their spouses; and (3) inmates with more social support commit fewer prison infractions per month.[108] It has also been reported that ex-convicts that have greater social support are better able to successfully transition from the status of inmate to the status of citizen.[109]

Nonetheless, critics of conflict theory must reconcile the fact that research connecting the more extreme forms of oppression of children including beatings, sexual abuse, hitting, slapping, screaming, ridicule, verbal insults, and serious neglect and deficiencies in child care to subsequent delinquency is substantial.[110] Several studies illuminate this relationship, including Cathy Spatz Widom and

Michael Maxfield's research on more than 1,500 children; James Unnever and his colleagues' study of coercion and delinquency for 2,472 students from six middle schools; Stephen Baron's research on Canadian skinheads; and a series of studies conducted by Lisa Hutchinson Wallace and her colleagues.

The research by Widom and Maxfield is interesting because it updates data initially collected in 1988 on the link between child abuse and offending with newer data. Their study followed 1,575 cases from childhood through young adulthood and included a study group of 908 substantiated cases of childhood abuse or neglect and a comparison group of 667 children who had not been officially recorded as abused or neglected. Both groups were matched on sex, age, race, and family socioeconomic status. According to Widom and Maxfield:

> Those who had been abused or neglected as children were more likely to be arrested as juveniles (27 percent versus 17 percent), adults (42 percent versus 33 percent), and for a violent crime (18 percent versus 14 percent). . . . The abused and neglected cases were younger at first arrest, committed nearly twice as many offenses, and were arrested more frequently.[111]

Unnever and his associates tested core propositions from *differential coercion theory*. They evaluated whether involvement in delinquency was related to four coercive environments: parental coercion, peer coercion, school coercion, and neighborhood coercion. They found consistent support for the theory: Students exposed to coercive environments were more likely to develop social–psychological deficits and be involved in relatively more serious delinquency.[112]

Baron examined the violent behavior and political consciousness of Canadian male street skinheads. Using the framework of Regoli and Hewitt's *differential oppression theory,* he discovered, as the theory would predict, that skinheads come from homes characterized by extreme violence and oppression. Their family and school experiences destroy any trust these young people might have for authority and they model the violent behavior of their oppressors. As such, they are themselves vulnerable to violent behavior. According to Baron:

> Their serial abuse negates their ability to empathize with others and leaves them vulnerable to frustration, while their familial oppression exposes them to violent cultural influences and leads them to seek opportunities for deviance.[113]

Their violence also was exacerbated by their oppressive school experiences that inspired their proneness to violence by stifling their creativity and individuality through an environment the skinheads characterized as being dictatorial and authoritarian. They reacted to these conditions through detachment and attack. By withdrawing, the skinheads found themselves in a situation where the only doors open to them were ones that fueled their violence. Baron concluded that the political consciousness of the skinheads he interviewed was tied to their long histories of experiencing oppression.

In a series of empirical tests, Lisa Hutchinson Wallace and her associates provided a comprehensive evaluation of how differential oppression theory might be used to explain school delinquency. Wallace and her colleagues assessed three of the four adaptive reactions set forth in the theory. They reported that students who perceive themselves to be oppressed by teachers frequently adapt to oppression through *passive acceptance* and the use of marijuana, beer, wine, and other types of alcohol. In addition, Wallace and Seydlitz found oppression by teachers and having low self-esteem to be predictive of more serious forms of drug abuse, such as ecstasy, heroin, and cocaine use. Children who are the victims of verbal and emotional abuse from their parents are also likely to have low self-esteem. This low self-esteem in turn leads to increased victimization from other peers who take advantage of them.[114]

Oppression resulting in the use of *passive acceptance* is not limited to substance abuse. Wallace reported on the effects of oppression in student experiences with delinquency in the schools. She found that students oppressed by teachers were more likely to be the victims of school delinquency than those who had not experienced such oppression. In an effort to examine the relationship of oppression in the home to other forms of victimization, Wallace and Mueller studied the linkage between parental oppression and peer victimization. They noted that children who had experienced parental oppression were more likely to be *both* verbally and physically abused by their peers. Further, findings indicated that self-esteem played a significant role in future victimization, as children who were oppressed by their parents but who exhibited high levels of self-esteem were less likely to be victimized by their peers.

In looking at the relationship between differential oppression and the *use of the exercise of illegitimate coercive power,* Wallace was able to reveal that students who experienced oppression by parents and teachers were more likely to commit acts of low-level delinquency within the school. Low levels of self-esteem increased students' use of this particular adaptive reaction. Finally, Wallace tested the role of oppression in the use of *retaliation.* Though the measures Wallace used were only indicative of students' thoughts of retaliation, she found that oppression by parents and teachers significantly increased retaliatory thoughts by students. As with *exercise of illegitimate coercive power,* low levels of self-esteem increased the likelihood of this reaction.[115]

Juvenile Justice Policy Applications

Conflict theories have had little direct impact on either juvenile justice policy or broader social policy. Federal and state legislative bodies have been understandably hesitant to consider policy changes that would require a restructuring of the larger society along socialist lines. Similarly, they have generally balked at dramatically redefining crime to either include broadly accepted business and economic practices associated with capitalism or to exclude "revolutionary" crimes of the economically or socially deprived or marginalized underdog.[116]

However, conflict theory has contributed in many ways to the discourse within criminology and the larger society on the need to reduce structural inequalities based upon economic, social, racial, and gender differences and to eliminate discriminatory practices within the juvenile and adult justice systems. Differential oppression theory has led to recent calls for adults to refuse to define children as objects and instead empower them with the essential fundamental constitutional rights adults enjoy. At minimum, seriously abused and neglected children should be quickly removed from dangerous and threatening home environments and placed in foster care or group homes designed to provide loving and supportive adult care and supervision.

conclusions

The theories discussed in this chapter represent explanations that have focused on the impact of interactions, inequalities in power, conflict, and oppressive relations between adults and children. Unlike strain and social control theories, labeling theory shows little interest in the immediate causes of individual delinquency, being more concerned with reactions to behavior and imbalances in power that stem from social arrangements. These theories tend to side with the adolescent and view the juvenile justice system in a critical light.

Labeling theory assumes that social control efforts produce more serious problem behaviors, especially juvenile delinquency. The social response to acts socially defined as delinquent results in individuals engaging in such acts being labeled as delinquents. It is the interactional process and impact of the response and label that is of greatest interest to labeling theorists. If there are solutions to the problem of delinquency, they are to be found in the juvenile justice system doing less, not more.

Conflict explanations of delinquency assume that social order in contemporary, heterogeneous societies is maintained through coercion, force, and confrontation. These theories stress the effects of economic and political power, influence, and group interests on the development and enforcement of law. Solutions to delinquency from the conflict perspective largely focus on major social and economic structural changes designed to eliminate discriminatory laws and legal processes and equalize wealth and power. For example, differential oppression theory assumes that children develop in an arena of oppression. This oppressive environment has consequences for what children become and who they are in relation to adults. Adults impose their sense of order on children, whom they see as being inferior, which leads to maladaptive responses by children, including delinquency. Differential oppression theory, then, argues that the solution to delinquency lies not so much in reforming the juvenile or changing the juvenile justice system, but in changing adult perceptions of who children are: Children must be seen as equally valuable, autonomous, and independent human beings.

key terms

Conduct norms   Rules that reflect the values, expectations, and actual behaviors of groups in everyday life. They are not necessarily the norms found in the criminal law.

Conflict theory   Theory that argues that society is held together by force, coercion, and intimidation and that the law represents the interests of those in power.

Crime norms   Criminal laws that prohibit specific conduct and provide punishments for violations.

Differential coercion theory   Theory that states that children who are exposed to coercive environments are more likely to develop social-psychological deficits that increase the possibility of their committing crimes.

Differential oppression theory   Delinquency is the culmination of a process that begins at conception and evolves through adolescence; the more a child is oppressed, the greater the likelihood he or she will become delinquent.

Disintegrative shaming   A form of negative labeling by the juvenile justice system that stigmatizes and excludes targeted youths, tossing them into a class of outcasts.

Dualistic fallacy   This idea questions the notion that delinquents and nondelinquents are two fundamentally different types of people.

Integrated structural-Marxist theory   Serious delinquency is the result of the reproduction of coercive control patterns tied to the relationship between production and class structure in capitalist societies.

Labeling theory   Assumes that social control leads to deviance; how behavior is reacted to determines whether it is defined as deviant.

Master status   The status of an individual that people react to first when they see or meet him or her for the first time.

Primary deviation   Deviant behavior that everyone engages in occasionally.

Radical nonintervention   An approach to juvenile justice whereby police and the courts would, whenever possible, "leave children alone."

Reintegrative shaming   The expression of community disapproval of delinquency, followed by indications of forgiveness and reacceptance into the community.

Retrospective interpretation   The process of reinterpreting the child's past behavior in an entirely new light on the basis of new information.

Secondary deviation   Deviant behavior based on the youth's taking on and accepting the deviant role as part of his or her identity.

Social support   The perceived and actual amount of instrumental and expressive or emotional supports that one receives from primary relationships, social networks, and communities.

Developmental Theories

8

Developmental theories of delinquency constitute a diverse group of explanations that share several important features. While they borrow heavily from other schools of criminological thought, developmental theories (1) pull together or integrate the strongest elements of earlier theories, (2) suggest that the key risk factors associated with delinquency change as individuals grow older, (3) contend that the key protective factors associated with delinquency also change as people age, and (4) view delinquency as a pattern of behavior rather than an isolated event. Developmental theories are not as interested in accounting for why a child commits a particular delinquent act as they are in seeking to identify those factors that drive an individual's entire criminal career.

WHAT IS DEVELOPMENTAL THEORY?

Over the past decade, **developmental theories,** sometimes called life-course theories, have become among the most popular theories in criminology. Developmental theories operate on the assumption that antisocial behavior, such as delinquency, *has to develop* and is not simply the manifestation of an underlying condition. Rather than attributing crime to the pathologies of the individual (e.g., damaged frontal lobes, low self-control, bad temper, or psychopathy) the developmental perspective points to life-experiences that mold individuals and send them along trajectories or pathways (see Chapter 5). These life trajectories can be positive, such as going to school or playing on a sports team, or negative, such as joining a criminal gang. Thus, developmental theories assert that everyday problems with family, school, and work can snowball into larger problems, such as alcohol and drug use, gambling, and delinquency. Daniel Nagin and Raymond Paternoster capture the central idea of developmental theory:

> Correlation between past and future behavior is not based on the predictive power of the initial distribution of criminal propensity or conventional opportunities and characteristics of the population. It is instead based upon the fact that some actions have dynamically increased the subsequent probability of crime by weakening previous inhibitions or strengthening previous incentives for criminal activity.[1]

Developmental theories have become popular with criminologists for two main reasons. First, earlier theories of delinquency were usually designed to explain whether juveniles were likely to become delinquent during a certain period of time or how much trouble they were likely to get into. Accordingly, they devoted little attention to the time ordering of potential causes of misbehavior and the acts of misbehavior themselves. Many theorists simply assumed that key risk factors, such as exposure to violent behavior, weak bonding, or status frustration, caused delinquency soon after they were experienced. Alternatively, some criminologists, such as Gottfredson and Hirschi (see Chapter 6), proposed that a *static* characteristic, such as a lack of self-control, was responsible for causing both delinquency and other problem behaviors. They assumed that the effect of low self-control persisted throughout one's life and that the characteristic itself was relatively stable across life. Additionally, traditional criminologists did not usually devote much attention to *how* events that occurred during one part of a person's life (e.g., childhood) may influence behavior during later stages (e.g., adolescence). Indeed, the few criminologists that considered this issue failed to allow for the possibility that key risk factors might change as people mature.

Second, traditional theorists have often treated delinquency exclusively as an outcome measure. That is, they have only been interested in examining why risk factors such as bad parenting, poor school performance, or association with deviant peers *cause* delinquent behavior. What they have not done is to allow for the possibility that delinquency itself may have important causal effects on its own presumed risk factors.[2] For example, in Robert Agnew's general strain theory he suggests that delinquency is the product of different types of strain, all of which can lead to delinquent behavior, depending on several conditioning factors (see Chapter 6). However, Agnew's theory does not explicitly state that delinquency itself can produce strain. For instance, Agnew would contend that being expelled from school should produce strain, which under the right circumstances might drive a youth to delinquent behavior. Yet it is also possible that committing delinquency, for example, going to school under the influence of drugs or stealing from another student's locker can be an important factor in why a youth is suspended or expelled. In such a situation, the delinquent act *precedes* or comes before the student's experience of strain. Accordingly, it would be less likely for the strain of being expelled to be the cause of the delinquent behavior.

Developmental theories are different from other criminological theories in how they approach these issues. First, rather than being interested in predicting

"It seems like only yesterday you were a juvenile offender."

Source: © The New Yorker Collection 2001, Danny Shanahan from cartoonbank.com. All rights reserved.

the *prevalence* or the *incidence* of delinquency, developmental theories explain changes in the progression of delinquent behavior over time, which criminologists call the **delinquent career**. Instead of being interested only in understanding why a juvenile has committed a crime, or how many crimes he is likely to commit in the following year, a developmental theorist is more interested in explaining why the youth who seemed to be a "good kid" throughout his childhood suddenly started getting into trouble as a teenager. For example, while a social control theorist might try to determine whether a troubled teenager's attachment to her parents is currently weak or strong, a developmental theorist is likely to be interested in the teen's entire history with his or her parents. The developmental theorist would contend that the parenting a child received at various ages is as important to understanding his or her present behavior as is the parenting that the child is currently receiving.

think
about it

If the seeds of delinquent behavior are planted in early childhood, is it too late to do anything when teenagers begin misbehaving? Should society require parenting classes to make sure that everyone "gets it right" during childhood?

In formulating their explanations, developmental theorists look beyond what happened in the lives of children immediately before they got into trouble. Instead, they try to determine what has occurred in an individual's life for many years prior to the criminal or delinquent incident. These life situations are classified into two broad categories: risk factors and protective factors. **Risk factors** are situations, settings, events, or characteristics that increase the likelihood that one will become delinquent. **Protective factors** are situations, settings, events, or characteristics that decrease the likelihood that one will become delinquent. Protective factors shield youths from contexts that contribute to delinquency or provide the resiliency to avoid crime. A list of common risk factors for delinquency appears in Box 8-1.

Finally, some developmental theorists explicitly recognize that delinquency itself has an impact on the factors that are typically assumed to cause it. So, while strain theorists like Merton, Cohen, Cloward, Ohlin, and Agnew might argue that juveniles who become frustrated by their lack of access to legitimate means often band together to commit crimes, developmental theorists would assert that the very act of committing crime is likely to push children further into delinquent subcultures.[3] After all, juveniles who routinely break the law will probably become ostracized by their nondelinquent peers and have little choice but to associate with other youths more like them.

DEVELOPMENTAL THEORY AND THE AGE–CRIME CURVE

Much of the early impetus for the creation of developmental theory came from a growing understanding of the **age–crime curve**, which is a line showing that crime rates increase during preadolescence, peak in middle adolescence, and steadily decline thereafter (see Figure 8-1).[4]

Remarkably, the curve did not seem to depend on the type of crime being studied, where the investigation occurred, which ethnic, racial, or socioeconomic group subjects belonged to, or whether they were male or female. In all cases, the shape of the age–crime curve tended to be very similar. So for example, although most criminologists would agree that *proportionally,* inner-city, African American males engage in more delinquent acts than middle-class, white females, the delinquent behavior of both groups tends to peak during adolescence. Young children and mature adults from both groups commit relatively few crimes when compared to their teenage counterparts.[5]

box 8-1   **A WINDOW OF DELINQUENCY**
Developmental Risk Factors for Delinquency

CHILD FACTORS

Difficult temperament
Impulsive behavior
Hyperactivity (occurring with disruptive behavior)
Impulsivity
Substance use
Aggression
Early onset disruptive behaviors
Withdrawn behaviors
Low intelligence
Lead toxicity

FAMILY FACTORS

Parental antisocial or delinquent behaviors
Parental substance abuse
Parental child rearing practices
Poor supervision
Poor communication
Physical punishment
Poor parent–child relations
Parental physical and/or sexual abuse
Parental neglect
Maternal depression
Mother's smoking during pregnancy
Teenage motherhood
Parental disagreement on child discipline
Single parenthood
Large family size
High turnover of caretakers
Low family socioeconomic status
Unemployed parent
Poorly educated mother
Family access to weapons (especially guns)

PEER FACTORS

Delinquent siblings
Delinquent peers
Rejection by peers

SCHOOL FACTORS

Poor academic performance
Old age for grade level
Weak bonding to school
Low educational aspirations
Low school motivation
Dysfunctional school

NEIGHBORHOOD FACTORS

Neighborhood disadvantage
Disorganized neighborhood
Availability of weapons
Media portrayal of violence

Source: Adapted from Rolf Loeber and David Farrington, "The Significance of Child Delinquency," pages 1–24 in Rolf Loeber and David Farrington (eds.), *Child Delinquents: Development, Intervention, and Service Needs* (Thousand Oaks, CA: Sage, 2001).

figure 8-1   Representative Age–Crime Curve

Representative Age–Crime Curve

Level of Delinquency vs *Age (years)*

The universality of this finding led criminologists to ask a number of important questions. First, is the age–crime curve universal? Does it accurately represent the behavior of all adolescents, or is it a composite of many different patterns of delinquent development? To better understand these distinctions, see Figure 8-2. Second, what causes the near universal spike in delinquent behavior experienced in adolescence? Criminologists began wondering whether it was simply that teenagers are exposed to higher levels of risk factors than people of other ages. For instance, some began wondering whether teenagers might experience higher levels of strain than younger children or adults. Perhaps lower-class teens were simply more likely to become frustrated with the inequities of the school system, much like Cohen originally suggested (see Chapter 6).

On the other hand, some criminologists theorized that there could be something unique about young people going through this developmental period that may explain their behavior. To put it differently, perhaps it was not so much the fact that external factors affecting teenagers were unique, but rather that young people themselves perceived them differently. Perhaps teenagers place greater or lesser importance on certain risk factors than people of other ages, For example, Sung Jang and Marvin Krohn have shown that parental attachment may be more important to younger children than to teens.[6] So, while a strongly bonded child finds it almost impossible to engage in delinquency, an older adolescent, even one with a strong bond to her parents, may still feel free to engage in illegal activity. Similarly, Persephanie Silverthorn and Paul Frick contend that young children look up to their teachers and place a great deal of importance on their schoolwork. These prosocial influences help keep young children out of trouble. However, as people grow older, the importance of these factors fades, and the world of delinquency opens up.[7]

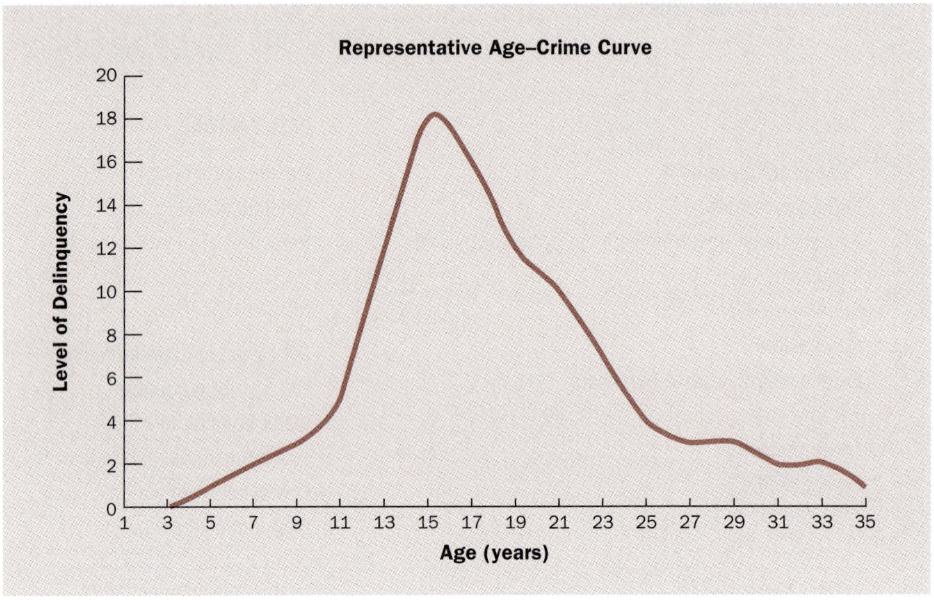

think about it

If most adolescents age-out of delinquency, why spend time and money on delinquency prevention?

figure 8-2   Various Delinquent Trajectories

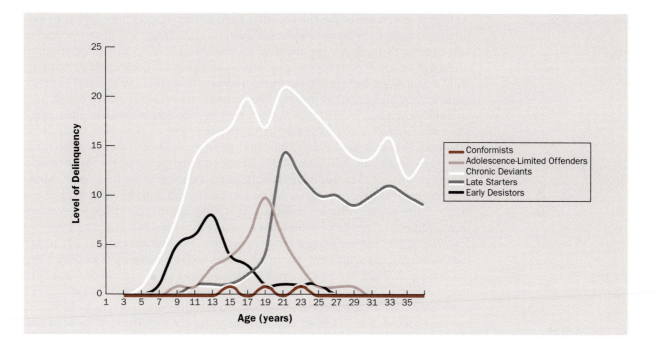

These types of observations sparked interest in developmental theory. In fact, research into these issues continues today. While most criminologists believe the curve represents a composite of different developmental pathways, those who believe that some individual-level construct accounts for crime do not. They reject the argument that delinquent behavior and the factors that influence it fluctuate over time.[8] Instead, they suggest that a child's **delinquent propensity,** an inner or constitutional indicator of criminality that influences the likelihood of becoming delinquent, is established during childhood and remains virtually unaltered thereafter. Richard Herrnstein described this rationale in the following way, "It would be an overstatement to say 'once a criminal always a criminal,' but it would be closer to the truth than to deny the evidence of a unifying and long-enduring pattern of encounters with the law for most serious offenders."[9] In other words, life events and circumstances may have subtle influences on one's behavior at any given point in time, for example, getting a good job or starting a family may temporarily keep a person with low self-control out of trouble, but not indefinitely. Along these lines, some criminologists assert that people with high delinquent propensity will relapse into antisocial lifestyles and eventually engage in behavior that jeopardizes their jobs and families and thereby fall back into antisocial, self-destructive, and ultimately delinquent behavior. The next section reviews the major developmental theories in criminology and explores ways that the theoretical ideas attempt to explain how both conventional and delinquent, or good and bad behavior, develop over the life-course.

DEVELOPMENTAL THEORIES OF DELINQUENCY

At first glance, some of the theories discussed in this chapter may appear to have little in common with one another. However, two things will become clear as you explore them. First, the theories borrow heavily from earlier perspectives offered in an array of academic disciplines including developmental psychology, child psychology, human development and family studies, behavioral genetics, criminology, and criminal justice. The concepts on which they are based, such as poor parenting, problems in school, and association with delinquent peers, are not new, rather they are factors that criminologists have long considered. However, this *new* set of developmental theories considers many of the traditional risk factors in a different light. Developmental perspectives focus on *how* the importance of these individual components varies over the life course. Moreover, many of the theories describe how experiencing a given risk factor at one stage of life might influence behavior at subsequent stages of life—something that traditional theories of delinquency usually did not do.

One of the first sociologists to propose the idea that events that occur during one stage of life can have strong influences on later behavior was Glen Elder. According to Elder, historical events, such as economic depressions and wars might affect a variety of developmental outcomes, including delinquency. Precisely *when* such events occur in an individual's life is important to how they are experienced. For example, one would not expect the effects of an economic depression to be the same on individuals who experience it as young children as compared to those who experience it as teenagers. Moreover, **precocious transitions,** key life events that occur too early in life, are likely to have adverse effects on development.[10] This in turn can start a cycle of undesirable outcomes into motion. For example, adolescents who become parents early in life may find it difficult to finish school and achieve a stable position in the job market, which can push them into lifestyles characterized by poverty, substance abuse, and crime. It is believed that the greater the number of precocious transitions an individual experiences, the more likely he is to engage in problem behaviors. Thus, a boy who becomes sexually active at age 11, fathers a child at age 14, drops out of school at age 15, and marries at age 16 is more likely to participate in crime than a boy who experiences only one of these precocious transitions.[11]

Gerald Patterson

Gerald Patterson's *coercive exchange theory* explores how early parenting influences delinquent behavior. He focuses on the exchanges that take place between parents and children immediately after the children have misbehaved. If the parents consistently react to antisocial behavior with fair, effective discipline, the children quickly learn that misbehavior carries unpleasant consequences. In turn, the children learn to behave and abide by societal rules. However, if parents fail to monitor their children and if parental discipline is lax or inconsistent, children fail to internalize this important lesson. Worse, some children actually learn to use extreme misbehavior, such as temper tantrums, to discourage parental discipline. This situation is called a **coercive exchange,** and when it occurs, the usual roles become reversed, and the child ends up controlling the behavior of the adult.[12]

think
about it

How practical is Patterson's advice? Are there situations where social norms *force* parents into coercive exchanges? Should parents spank children to stop a temper tantrum?

Imagine, for example, a situation in which a child sees a toy in a store and asks her parents to buy it. The parents decide that the toy is too expensive and refuse. The child reacts by becoming angry, stomping her feet and using a loud, assertive voice to demand that the parents reconsider. This situation is embarrassing and uncomfortable for the parents. At this point, the parents can react in at least one of two ways. First, they can give in and buy the child the toy to avoid making a scene in the store. Second, they can reassert their authority and, if necessary, discipline the child for throwing a temper tantrum.

Although the first alternative will likely be easier on the parents, Patterson argues that choosing it sets a dangerous precedent. First, it teaches children that they can force their parents to reconsider a negative answer by increasing their level of misbehavior. Therefore, misbehavior can be used as a method of getting exactly what a child wants. Second, if the parent gives in, the child's temper tantrum ceases and that is a negative reinforcement that teaches the parent to give in to future confrontations. Patterson believes that such early exchanges can have profound effects on children's development. Children who are inconsistently disciplined, especially those who master coercive exchanges, grow up to be teenagers and adults who commit crimes. Such individuals are taught to defy authority figures, reject rules, and use violence and other forms of misbehavior to solve their problems.

Patterson was one of the first scholars to differentiate the two general classes of offenders, those whose onset occurred early in life and those whose onset occurred later in life. Other criminologists, such as Terrie Moffitt, have utilized this conceptualization in their theories. Early starters are exposed to inept, coercive, or authoritarian parenting. These experiences instill an overall negativity that leads to rejection by conventional peers, dislike of school, anger, low self-esteem, and mental health problems such as depression. As early as fourth grade, these children are identifiable for their school failure and are especially prone to associate with similarly situated peers.[13] Early starters are often arrested by age 14 and are most likely to engage in chronic criminality.[14]

By comparison, such problems are not expected from late starters, individuals whose onset of delinquency occurs after age 14. Late starters are delinquents who are particularly prone to the influences of delinquent peers if their parents poorly monitored their behavior. For late-starting, or "normal" delinquents, the significant relationship between delinquent peer association and delinquency is so robust that it has been found to mediate other known correlates of crime such as socioeconomic status. Patterson's theory has enjoyed a great deal of empirical support, and his approach has proven crucial in demonstrating the contributions that families and peers have in producing delinquent behavior.[15]

theory in a nutshell

Gerald Patterson

Patterson focuses on the exchanges that take place between parents and children immediately after the child misbehaves. If parents consistently react to antisocial behavior with fair, effective discipline, children learn that misbehavior carries unpleasant consequences. However, if parental discipline is lax or inconsistent, children are likely to become teens who engage in delinquency.

Terrie Moffitt

Like Patterson's work, Terrie Moffitt's developmental taxonomy suggests that there are two types of delinquents: adolescence-limited and life-course persistent offenders (see Chapter 2). **Adolescence-limited offenders** comprise the bulk of the delinquent population; approximately 90 percent of delinquents are of this type. Adolescence-limited offenders are generally able to resist any antisocial impulses that they may have and are by and large law-abiding citizens. As their label implies, however, adolescence-limited offenders engage in delinquency for a brief period during their teen years. Driving their deviance is the ambiguity of puberty and adolescent development. During this phase, youths often have difficulty grappling with quickly changing expectations and responsibilities that are a function of age, such as obtaining a driver's license, dating, having a job, the demands of peer relationships, and the overall angst of being a teenager. By observing the delinquent behavior of serious delinquents, a process Moffitt calls "social mimicry," adolescence-limited offenders believe that a certain level of autonomy and adult reinforcement actually comes from "bad" behavior.[16]

A desire for adult status is the primary motivation for delinquent behavior in that their delinquency consists of generally low-level offenses, such as under-age drinking, marijuana use, shoplifting, and vandalism. Alex Piquero and Timothy Brezina studied offending patterns of about 2,000 males and found that adolescence-limited offenders, as theorized by Moffitt, engaged in rebellious but not violent forms of delinquency during the difficult stages of puberty.[17] Seth Schwartz and his colleagues similarly found that young people are less likely to conform to societal rules as they transition into adulthood.[18] Because adolescence-limited offenders are portrayed as nonserious delinquents, criminologists have tended to pay less attention to them. Nevertheless, studies of criminal careers have generally demonstrated that a substantial group of delinquents limit their antisocial conduct to the teen years.[19]

Life-course persistent offenders have received much more empirical attention from criminologists because such offenders are considered to be the most threatening to society. According to Moffitt, two types of neuropsychological defects, verbal and executive functions, give rise to an assortment of antisocial behaviors. Verbal functions include reading ability, receptive listening, problem-solving skill, memory, speech articulation, writing, and in short, verbal intelligence. Executive functions relate to behavioral and personality characteristics, such as inattention, hyperactivity, and impulsivity (see Chapter 5). Children with these neuropsychological deficits are restless, fidgety, destructive, noncompliant, and can be violent.[20]

As these children age, their tendencies toward antisocial behavior create friction in most of their social interactions with family, school, and peer groups. This causes life-course persistent children to be shunned and ostracized both by other adolescents and adults, such as parents and teachers. This social rejection pushes them to begin associating with other problem children and encourages further misbehavior. Eventually, life-course persistent offenders become locked in cycles of increasingly serious misbehavior and negative reactions that culminate in adult criminal careers, a process known as **cumulative disadvantage**.[21] Two other circumstances cause disadvantages for children with life-course persistent offender characteristics. First, such children often resemble their parents in terms of temperament, personality, and cognitive ability. In this way, the parents of life-course persistent offenders are themselves poorly tempered, impulsive, and prone to use violence to resolve disputes. This cycle of disadvantage further worsens the child's social development.[22]

Second, such children are disproportionately raised in impoverished home environments that are appalling by material, social, and health standards. One of the more damaging environmental factors is early exposure to lead, which is more commonly found in environments characterized by poverty. For instance, Douglas Ris and his colleagues supervise the Cincinnati Lead Study, which is a longitudinal examination of the effects of lead exposure on adolescent development. They report that children who have been exposed to lead have increased educational and cognitive risks and that the effects are more pronounced in boys than girls.[23] Bruce Lanphear and his colleagues similarly report that children who are exposed to lead and mercury suffer from an array of behavioral problems, intellectual deficits, and health problems that limit their development.[24] In September 2006, researchers surveyed 4,704 children from the *National Health and Nutrition Examination Study* to examine the long-term consequences of exposure to environmental lead. It was discovered that children with the highest blood–lead concentration were more than *400 percent* more likely to develop ADHD than children with lower lead exposure. Indeed, lead exposure accounts for more than nearly 290,000 excess cases of ADHD in American children.[25] Although children with ADHD are not the same as Moffitt's life-course persistent offender group, they are related concepts.

Once thrust into impoverished circumstances, youths described as life-course persistent offenders continually behave poorly and face consequences that narrow their options for future success. As Moffitt stated in her original conceptualization of the taxonomy, the behavioral repertoire of the life-course persistent offender is limited to negativity, rejection, and delinquency. It is well documented that such youths often suffered through adverse childhoods, demonstrated an array of problematic and antisocial behaviors, and generally led lives of crime and involvement with the criminal justice system.[26] Most sad of all, many of the environmental causes that wrought harm on this group could have been prevented.

theory in a nutshell

Terrie Moffitt

Moffitt believes delinquents are either *life-course persistent* or *adolescence-limited* offenders. Life-course persistent offenders suffer from a variety of psychosocial deficits. The process of *cumulative disadvantage* frequently turns them from troubled adolescents into career criminals. Conversely, adolescence-limited offenders become involved in delinquency during a brief period of teenage rebellion.

Robert Sampson and John Laub

According to Robert Sampson and John Laub, the development of delinquency is influenced by factors ranging from structural conditions, such as socioeconomic status and family structure, to individual traits like temperament, to traditional social control concepts, such as bonding, attachment, and supervision. Unlike many earlier theorists, however, they argue that the importance of these factors varies over the life course. Specifically, Sampson and Laub's *age-graded theory of informal social control* argues that informal social controls such as involvement in family, work, and school, *mediate* structural context and explain criminal involvement even in the face of the underlying level of criminal propensity. Like theorists who favor "kinds of people" explanations for delinquency, Sampson and Laub acknowledge that people differ both in their underlying criminal propensity and the likelihood of placing themselves in troublesome situations. Unlike other theorists, however, they suggest that people acquire different amounts of social capital from informal social control networks and this social capital explains the continuity in antisocial behaviors across various life stages. Persons with low social capital and past criminal involvement mortgage their future life chances—a process referred to as the *cumulative continuity of disadvantage*. On the other hand, the development of conventional adult social bonds or experiencing particular *turning points* can "right" previously deviant pathways such as juvenile delinquency, unemployment, and substance abuse, and place an individual onto a trajectory toward more successful outcomes. Rather than viewing the causes of delinquency as overly simplistic and deterministic, Sampson and Laub stress that *change or dynamism* characterizes criminal careers since even the most active offender desists over the life course. For instance, 60-year-old criminals are not as active and violent as they were at age 17, and Sampson and Laub's theory helps to account for such changes.[27]

Their theory has been very influential. Their own research applies modern statistical methods to data of 500 officially defined delinquents and a matched sample of 500 nondelinquents originally collected by Sheldon Glueck and Eleanor Glueck. Overall, they have found that family processes, such as the amount of maternal supervision, parental discipline style, and attachment to parents are among the most robust predictors of serious delinquency. These family variables largely mediate background social class factors and predict delinquency even when considering the antisocial dispositions of both children and their parents.[28] By the term "mediate," Sampson and Laub mean that if adults are currently involved in the "right" types of behavior, such as having a job or marriage, they can stop committing crime even if they had an extensive criminal background. On the other hand, even previously nondelinquent people may begin engaging in crime during adulthood if they are not effectively bonded to society through marriage, work, military, or some other positive social institution.

Even though Sampson and Laub's theory stresses the importance of local life circumstances, they do not entirely ignore the negative consequences of antisocial behavior that occurs during childhood. For instance, they found that childhood delinquency was predictive of an array of deviant characteristics in adulthood. However, such relationships often disappeared once adult social bonds were considered. In their words, "adult social bonds not only have important effects on adult crime in and of themselves, but help to explain the probabilistic links in the chain connecting early childhood differences and later adult crime."[29]

Sampson and Laub's theory helps us to understand the entire life-course or human development aspects of delinquency. While poverty and family circumstances set the *initial conditions* for delinquency, in that children born in disadvantaged areas are more likely to be exposed to criminogenic conditions, these factors do not directly explain why these children are more likely to grow up delinquent. Instead, they influence what is likely to happen to the children as they grow up. Young people born into impoverished, disorganized neighborhoods are more likely to experience scholastic difficulties and are less likely to have good relationships with their parents. As adolescents, they are less likely to build strong ties within their families and experience frequent and effective parental supervision. For their part, impoverished parents will be more likely to work long hours and to have less time to devote to their children. Taken together, these factors will increase the risk that disadvantaged children will begin spending time in the company of other disadvantaged children, in settings where delinquency is likely to take place. For example, while middle- and upper-class children are likely to spend much of their time at home, in organized extracurricular activities, or in places where there is at least some adult supervision, many lower-class children will spend much of their time hanging out on street corners—a setting where gang recruitment is a very real possibility.

In general, Sampson and Laub suggest that problems experienced during the early stages of life have adverse effects on later stages. If a child experiences structural disadvantage, this makes it more likely that he or she will experience poor parenting in early adolescence, which in turn will lead to increased associations with delinquent peers later in adolescence. These steps represent the "building blocks" of a typical *delinquent career.* However, Sampson and Laub do allow for the possibility that important life events, or **turning points**—which are key life events that can either drive someone toward delinquent behavior or initiate the process of desisting from it—can "derail" delinquent careers and push people back onto prosocial developmental pathways. Two of the most important turning points are marriage and steady employment. Imagine, for example, a situation in which a delinquent boy who spends much of his time on the street in the company of gang members is able to land a steady job and then meets a prosocial girlfriend. According to Sampson and Laub, this young man should thereafter spend much less time associating with his delinquent peers and will less often find himself in situations where delinquency is both possible and encouraged. He may also come to realize that he now has much to lose by being delinquent. He may, for example, begin to think that committing crimes with his friends is not worth the risk of getting arrested, fired, or rejected by his new girlfriend. Over time, Sampson and Laub suggest that this boy will become more deeply involved in a conventional, pro-

> ### theory in a nutshell
>
> #### Robert Sampson and John Laub
>
> Sampson and Laub argue that the development of delinquency is influenced by many factors, ranging from structural conditions, to individual traits, to traditional social control concepts. The importance of these factors varies over the life course. Problems experienced during the early stages of life have adverse effects at later stages. Sampson and Laub also suggest that key life events can "derail" delinquent careers and move individuals back to prosocial developmental pathways.

social lifestyle, and eventually his delinquent career will end (see Figure 8-3). Therefore, this theory not only offers an explanation for how children become delinquent but also an argument for how delinquent youth and adults are able to "go straight."[30]

figure 8-3 Mapping Delinquency Theory: Sampson and Laub's
Life Course Theory

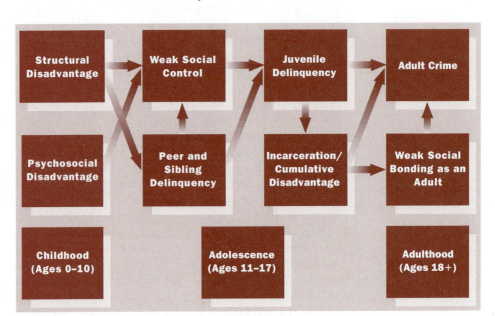

Terence Thornberry

Terence Thornberry's *interactional theory* is another important developmental
approach, which stresses that all human behavior occurs in the context of social interaction. Social interaction affects everyone and is complex, overlapping,
multidirectional, or reciprocal. For example, children who are attached to their
parents are likely to harbor conventional values and beliefs (of course, provided
that the parents harbor and teach such values and beliefs) and thus likely be
committed to school. Over time, a serious commitment to school will bolster
one's support of conventional beliefs and solidify relationships with parents,
who will be pleased the child is performing well in school. Conversely, children
who are not committed to school are likely to weaken their relationship with
their parents and more likely to initiate or strengthen relationships with peers
who are not committed to school. Social interactions that lead to both prosocial
and antisocial values and behaviors are constantly in flux, overlapping, and in
the process of development.[31] In other words, the causes and consequences of
delinquency are difficult to separate.

These ideas have been supported with data from the Rochester Youth Development Study, a panel study of middle-school children from Rochester, New
York. As conceptualized, school and family bonding variables predict delinquency, which in turn weakens school and family bonding.[32] Once involvement
in delinquency has begun, its interactional effects are often difficult for youth
to overcome. Delinquent behavior and association with delinquent peers have a
synergistic effect whereby antisocial or delinquent beliefs become increasingly
important to the youth. In other words, their delinquent beliefs and persona
become hardened, further impacting what types of people delinquent youth
associate with. For this reason, desisting from crime is a process, not a discrete

event, whereby offenders gradually transition from a social network centered on delinquency to one centered on conventional behavior. Most important for developmental theory, Thornberry's theory asserts that one's involvement in social institutions such as family, school, and work are directly, indirectly, and variably related to delinquency. Additionally, there is considerable behavioral change and responsiveness to parents, peers, and social institutions *within individuals* as they pass through adolescence.[33]

Like many theories of delinquency, *interactional theory* suggests that the roots of delinquent behavior begin with structural disadvantage, particularly low socioeconomic status. This results in low initial levels of parental attachment, belief in conventional values, and commitment to school. These factors, in turn, lead to increased associations with delinquent peers and the promotion of delinquent values, both of which are subsequently related to delinquency. Thornberry believes that the importance of key factors change as people age. For example, he argues that the importance of parental attachment declines as people move from early to late adolescence.

Based on *interactional theory,* the more delinquent a child becomes, the more likely he is to experience all other criminogenic factors. Terence Thornberry and Marvin Krohn recently extended interactional theory to explain continuity and changes in the offending careers of serious offenders. Suppose that an adolescent boy has a very poor relationship with his parents. This makes it less likely that he will spend much time at home and more likely that he will associate with delinquent peers. Together, these factors increase the probability that he will engage in delinquent behavior. The more delinquency he commits, however, the more likely he is to continue associating with his delinquent peer group as opposed to his parents or other prosocial friends. If the parents become aware of his delinquent behavior, it may also create family strife that will further damage the boy's relationship with his parents, causing him to spend even less time at home. These developments in turn will further increase the probability of deeper involvement with the delinquent peer group and more serious delinquent behavior. Eventually, the boy may become hopelessly locked into an amplifying cycle of delinquent behavior.[34]

> ## theory in a nutshell
>
> ### Terence Thornberry
>
> Thornberry believes that delinquency begins with structural disadvantage, which leads to initially low levels of parental attachment, belief in conventional values, and commitment to school. These factors lead to increased associations with delinquent peers and elevated delinquent values, which subsequently lead to delinquency. Thornberry also suggests that delinquency itself can initiate an amplifying cycle that leads to more serious delinquency.

Joseph Weis, Richard Catalano, and J. David Hawkins

Since 1981 Joseph Weis, Richard Catalano, J. David Hawkins, and other researchers at the University of Washington have conducted the **Seattle Social Development Project,** which is a longitudinal study of more than 800 children who were enrolled in fifth grade in 1985 in 18 of the Seattle public elementary

figure 8-4   Mapping Delinquency Theory: Thornberry's Interactional Theory

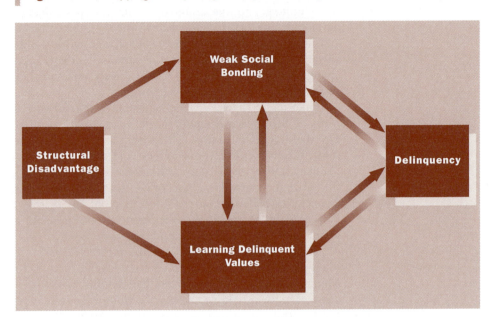

schools. The study is based on the researchers' *social development model,* which claims that the causes of delinquency are complex, multifaceted, and ultimately the outcome of an individual's journey along overlapping prosocial and antisocial paths. The social development model is rooted in the theoretical traditions of differential association, social control, and social learning and focuses on four specific periods of development: (1) preschool, (2) elementary school, (3) middle school, and (4) high school. According to the theory, socializing agents such as family, school, peers, and others teach and inculcate both "good" and "bad" behaviors to children. At each stage of development, children are faced with risk and protective factors toward delinquency. Four factors comprise the socialization processes occurring during the four periods of development, these are (1) opportunities for involvement in activities and interactions with others, (2) the degree of involvement and interaction, (3) the skills to participate in these involvements and interactions, and (4) the reinforcement forthcoming from performance in activities and interactions.[35]

An interesting component of the social development model is its explicit focus on developmental processes across various stages of childhood development for all types of individuals. In other words, the theory views antisocial behavior and the risks for antisocial behavior generally and not prescriptively for high-risk groups. Perhaps because of this, some of the empirical tests of the social development model are slightly at odds with the claims of other developmental theories. For example, researchers have found that the theory is applicable or can be generalized to males and females and children from divergent social class backgrounds.[36] Although it is well known that these groups have varying involvement in delinquency and victimization, the processes by which they are exposed or protected from delinquency reflect commonality, not differences in development. Similarly, children whose crimes onset occurred at different ages nevertheless followed similar developmental patterns toward violent behavior at adulthood.

Overall, the social development model speaks to the delinquencies and conventional behaviors of many social groups.[37] It claims that social structure sets the initial condition for how strongly an individual is likely to be bonded to conventional society. For poor children, this bond is typically weak. Disadvantaged adolescents usually see little opportunity or hope for prosocial involvement. They also lack the skills necessary to succeed in the conventional world. However, such children frequently have access to delinquent opportunity structures and possess the skills necessary to excel at delinquency. Therefore, they usually begin associating with delinquent peers and end up on antisocial developmental pathways. Just the opposite is true for more affluent children. Not only are such youth socialized with the skills necessary to succeed in conventional society, they often lack access to illegitimate opportunities. They also frequently have much to lose by engaging in delinquent behavior and often form strong bonds with parents, teachers, and prosocial friends who push them toward conventional developmental pathways. Finally, the theory is heavily geared toward delinquency prevention, and its authors have painstakingly identified the mechanisms by which social institutions and socialization agents promote healthy (e.g., protective factors) and maladaptive development (e.g., exposure to risk factors).

theory in a nutshell

Joseph Weis, Richard Catalano, and J. David Hawkins

Weis and his colleagues believe that disadvantaged youths see little opportunity for prosocial involvement and lack the skills necessary to succeed in the conventional world. These youths also have access to delinquent opportunity structures and possess the skills necessary to excel at delinquency. Thus, they frequently associate with delinquent peers and participate in crime. However, early interventions may interrupt this process.

Ronald Simons

Ronald Simons and his colleagues have empirically tested many of the developmental theories described in this chapter. Based on data from an ongoing longitudinal study of more than 450 Iowa families, Simons and his colleagues are able to examine how antisocial behavior that occurs during childhood and adolescence affects various outcomes in adulthood. Like Sampson, Laub, Patterson, and others, Simons shows that both delinquency and prosocial behavior are long-term processes heavily affected by participation in social institutions. Additionally, Simons and his colleagues are among a relatively few criminologists who have studied individuals living in rural areas. As such, they can consider the multiple routes that adolescents may take in becoming delinquent and see if traditional pathways are limited to youths living in urban settings. For instance, the researchers have reported that association with deviant peers, socioeconomic status, and parenting techniques can steer youths into positive or negative pathways. Late starters, or persons initially engaging in delinquency after age 14, who were in strong marriages were significantly less involved in crime than their peers who were single or in problematic marriages. Simons and his colleagues argue for "consideration of the manner in which peer friendships, as well as other social relationships, may operate to amplify or moderate the antisocial tendencies fostered by ineffectual parental behavior."[38] In other words, they have shown that criminal propensity as measured by childhood and adolescent misconduct often disappears once the effects of family, school, and peers are considered. The importance of this point cannot be missed. It means that informal social control networks and mundane experiences, such as getting married, having a job, or being in school, are more powerful explanations of delinquency than latent, kinds-of-people trait explanations (see Chapter 5).[39]

A unique contribution from Simons' research relates to how a romantic relationship with a prosocial partner can help "derail" a delinquent career. Simons suggests that individuals who have been delinquent throughout their adolescent years and those who have become strongly committed to a deviant peer group are not likely to form stable unions with nondelinquent partners. They are unlikely to associate with the same groups as prosocial individuals and will not appear to be attractive partners to potential prosocial mates. This stems from the fact that many serious delinquents and their prospective romantic partners will have poor social skills, substance abuse problems, lengthy criminal records, little education, and a poor work history. Instead, chronically antisocial individuals are likely to become romantically involved with other antisocial individuals because they often come into contact with them. This process, known as **assortative mating,** leads to continued involvement with deviant peer networks, dysfunctional domestic relationships, and a lack of success in the job market. All of these factors predict a continuation of delinquent careers into adulthood.[40]

Interestingly, the effect of romantic relationships on delinquency appears to work differently for males and females. Regardless of gender, delinquency and affiliation with delinquent peers led to having an antisocial romantic partner as a young adult. However, romantic relationships exerted more influence on girls than boys. More recent research by Dana Haynie and her colleagues also reported that during adolescence, delinquency by girls is more dependent on romantic partners than for boys.[41] Why is that the case? For a variety of reasons, males and females draw potential romantic partners from very different groups. Especially during adolescence, it is not uncommon for girls, even prosocial girls, to date delinquent boys. Conversely, it is highly unlikely that conventional boys will date delinquent girls. Andrea Leverentz found that formerly delinquent girls almost exclusively date former drug users or ex-offenders.[42] Because of this, girls are more susceptible to the delinquent influences of their significant others (see Figure 8-5).

think
about it

If assortative mating leads to adult crime, should steps be taken to restrict it? Would you favor a measure to deny marriage licenses to couples when both have criminal records?

theory in a nutshell

Ronald Simons

Simons thinks adolescents with a long history of delinquency, who have become committed to a deviant peer group, are unlikely to form stable unions with prosocial partners. Instead, they often become romantically involved with other antisocial individuals, which leads to their continued involvement in delinquency.

EVALUATION OF DEVELOPMENTAL THEORY

The individual building blocks of developmental theories, such as poverty, neuropsychological deficits, weak bonding, association with delinquent peers, coercive exchanges, and assortative mating, are all associated with criminality. Most

figure 8-5   Mapping Delinquency Theory: Simons and Assortive Mating

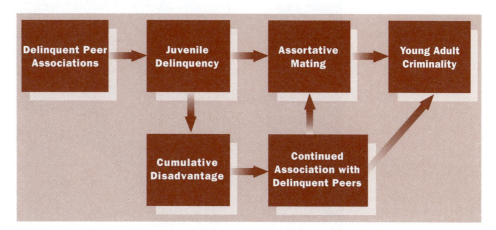

criminologists agree that adolescents can follow more than one pathway to delinquency and that the key predictors of misbehavior likely change over time. Many also recognize that the risk and protective factors associated with delinquency are involved in reciprocal causal relationships. As a whole, the developmental perspective has enjoyed widespread support within the research community.[43] For example, consider the following point about the developmental differences between individuals whose delinquency first appears during childhood as compared to those whose onset occurs during adolescence:

> The taxonomy of childhood versus adolescent-onset antisocial behavior has been codified in the *DSM-IV* [produced by the American Psychiatric Association], presented in many abnormal psychology and criminology textbooks and invoked in the NIMH [National Institute of Mental Health] Factsheet, *Child and Adolescent Violence Research,* the U. S. Surgeon General's report *Youth Violence,* the World Health Organization's *World Report on Violence and Health,* and the National Institutes of Health's *State-of-the-Science Consensus Statement in Preventing Violence.*[44]

Thus, in part due to their real-world application, developmental theories of delinquency have been extremely successful.

Of course, developmental theories are not perfect. Although the theories pay lip service to social structure, developmental theories are overwhelmingly individualistic. For instance, Per-Olof Wikstrom and Robert Sampson argue that (1) studies of developmental pathways neglect the influence of a wider social context, (2) research on individual risk factors has largely failed to specify the causal mechanisms that link the risk factors to acts of crime or delinquent pathways, (3) research on environmental influences has largely failed to specify the causal mechanisms that link social context to crime, (4) interactions between individual characteristics and community contexts are poorly understood, and (5) existing approaches to crime prevention and policy are poorly integrated.[45] Thus, if developmental theories claim to take a multilevel, comprehensive perspective on delinquency, they must do a better job of including sociological influences on behavior.

Christopher Dankovich was charged as an adult for murder for stabbing his mother 111 times. Should all youths charged with murder be prosecuted and punished as adults regardless of their age or circumstances?

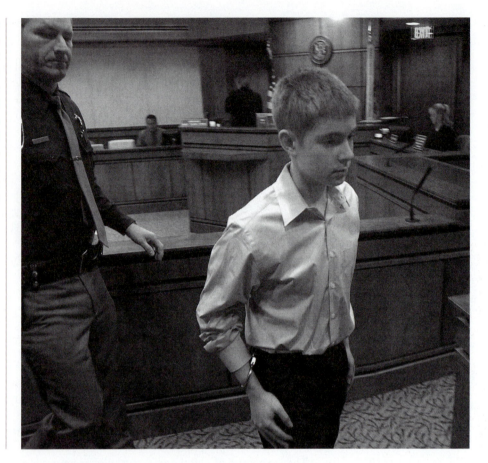

Developmental theories can also be criticized for not being theories at all, but rather descriptive models of how conventional and delinquent behavior unfolds over time. Michael Gottfredson states that most development theories lack parsimony, have difficulty explaining the versatility or generality of delinquency, and minimize the evidence of criminal propensity, whereas general theories of crime account for these issues.[46] Developmental theories are also similar with their focus on social institutions as determinants of behavior and offer only slight variations in terminology. For instance, Janet Lauritsen argues that it is unclear how developmental theories differ from one another in that they all strive to understand reciprocal relationships among families, peers, schools, and individuals. Lauritsen also believes that these theories fail to consider family composition and the various ways that different types of families can affect a youth's development.[47] Furthermore, although developmental theories stress development, the theories (with the exception of Moffitt's developmental taxonomy) ignore the earliest stages of individual development. For instance, Robert M. Regoli and John D. Hewitt's *differential oppression theory* (see Chapter 7) provides specific attention to the potential contextual effects of conception, pregnancy, infant care, and ways that adults create oppression in the lives of their children on delinquency. In other words, much development in the earliest points in life can propel youths down conventional and delinquents pathways.[48]

There is less than complete agreement regarding exactly how many delinquent pathways are open to adolescents, and precisely how the different risk factors are related to one another. For example, Moffitt's theory suggests that adolescents can follow one of three possible developmental pathways. She believes that most individuals will fall into the adolescence-limited group. Substantially smaller numbers either will become life-course persistent offenders or will never engage in delinquency. However, as shown in Figure 8-2, adolescents may actually follow many distinct developmental pathways. For example, a recent study by Amy D'Unger and her colleagues explored how many distinct "types" of offender classifications exist in famous birth cohort studies from London, Philadelphia, and Racine. D'Unger reported that four or five distinct classes emerged, which is certainly a more complex account than Moffitt's developmental taxonomy suggests.[49] Margit Wiesner and Deborah Capaldi agree and report the existence of six distinct groups of offenders. Two of the groups in their study age-out of crime by early adulthood, while two clearly do not. There are substantial differences between these groups in terms of the total amount of offending that occurs over the delinquent career. One group engages in a generally low level of offending, one engages in a moderate level, and two engage in high levels. Additionally, a substantial number of individuals were found to engage in sporadic offending over the life course. No clear developmental pattern is evident in this group.[50] This last finding is particularly difficult to reconcile with Moffitt's taxonomy since it fits neither the life-course persistent nor the adolescence-limited categories.

There is also dispute regarding exactly how the building blocks that constitute the different developmental models are related to one another. For instance, interactional theory indicates that most of the effect of peer deviance on delinquency is *direct*. That is, when a child begins associating with deviant individuals, he or she is automatically placed at higher risk for delinquent involvement. Conversely, the *social development model* indicates that much of this effect is *indirect* because associations with delinquent peers lead to delinquent behavior only after an individual has learned a deviant value system from the peer group and has had time to internalize it. Thus, it is the learning of deviant values that directly causes delinquency, not the association with delinquent peers. In general, however, none of these issues represent a serious challenge to the developmental perspective.[51] It is likely that developmental theories will continue to provide a foundation for many future studies of juvenile delinquency, but as more studies are conducted, it is also likely that modifications will be made to the existing developmental theories. Perhaps an integrated developmental perspective will emerge that will systematically consider the insights offered by the theorists discussed in this chapter.

Researchers are also currently testing how well developmental theories apply to different groups of children under various conditions (see Box 8-2). For example, it remains an open question whether particular developmental theories apply universally to both males and females and to adolescents from different cultures and social class backgrounds. Thus far, the findings of this research have generally supported the universality of developmental theories. Delinquent development appears to take place in roughly the same way throughout North America, South America, Europe, Asia, and Australia.[52] Moreover, initial investigations suggest that both boys and girls follow similar pathways to delinquency although boys are more often on chronically deviant pathways. However, more

box 8-2 A WINDOW ON DELINQUENCY

Child Rearing Revisited

There is a long-standing debate about whether it is better for children to be raised entirely by their parents, especially their mother, or with the help of other adults in daycare. In 2006, the National Institute of Child Health and Human Development published somewhat controversial findings from its Study of Early Child Care and Youth Development. The findings included the following:

- The average child spends 27 hours a week in nonmaternal care over the first 4.5 years of life.
- During the first 2 years of life, most childcare occurs in the family home.
- Knowing simply whether a child was ever in nonmaternal care provided little insight into a child's development.
- Children who were cared for exclusively by their mothers did not develop differently than those who were also cared for by others.
- Children in *higher quality* nonmaternal childcare had somewhat *better* language and cognitive development during the first 4.5 years of life.
- Such children were also somewhat more cooperative than those who experienced lower quality care during the first 3 years of life.
- Children with *higher quantity* of experience in nonmaternal childcare showed somewhat *more* behavioral problems in childcare and kindergarten than children who experienced fewer nonmaternal hours of care.
- Children who attended childcare centers had somewhat better cognitive and language development but also showed more behavioral problems in childcare and kindergarten.

The study produced the somewhat counterintuitive finding that children raised in environments without their mother may actually have healthier development. However, the difference between quality and quantity of childcare was important. Quality childcare produced educational benefits, while a higher quantity of childcare produced behavioral problems.

The study also showed the strength of social class. Children showed more cognitive, language, and social competence and more harmonious relationships with parents when parents were more educated, had higher incomes, and provided home environments that were emotionally supportive and cognitively enriched. These family effects were mutually important to children whether they had little or much childcare.

Thus, perhaps the "parents versus childcare" debate is now over and the central issue is quality of child rearing. Indeed, all the developmental theorists believe that quality child rearing, or positive care giving, is crucial to healthy human development. What features typify quality or positive care giving? They include:

- Providing a low adult-to-child ratio.
- Offering small classroom size.
- Making available more educated childcare practitioners.
- Showing a positive attitude.
- Having positive physical contact, such as an encouraging pat on the back.
- Responding to child vocalizations.
- Asking questions of children.
- Praising, encouraging, singing, and teaching.
- Encouraging social, language, and cognitive development.
- Reading.
- Eliminating negative interactions.

When care giving consists of these kinds of interactions between adults and children, healthy development flows. When it does not, antisocial development flows. A common thread in all theories of delinquency is the importance of family and the relationship between adults and children.

Source: National Institute of Child Health and Human Development, *The NICHD Study of Early Child Care and Youth Development* (Washington, DC: U.S. Department of Health and Human Services, 2006).

work remains to be done. Many of the best-known studies in this area have been based exclusively on samples of boys or have drawn their samples from relatively restricted geographical areas. Nevertheless, it is likely that developmental theory will continue to be very influential in guiding research in the area of juvenile delinquency for years to come.[53]

JUVENILE JUSTICE POLICY APPLICATIONS

Developmental theories blame delinquency on many different causes, ranging from psychosocial deficits to weak social bonding. Therefore, developmental theories suggest a wide range of juvenile justice policy implications, many of which are consistent with those suggested in earlier chapters. Developmental theories that borrow heavily from the social control perspective would likely agree that reconnecting children with their parents should be an important part of any intervention strategy. Similarly, since some also incorporate the strain perspective into their theory, there should be a focus on providing children with legitimate opportunities to succeed. Providing skills training and mentoring for disadvantaged elementary and junior high school students can act as a powerful shield against criminogenic influences. Alternatively, since Gerald Patterson's theory is more closely associated with Albert Bandura's behavioral perspective (see Chapter 5), it implies that consistent punishment of negative behavior is the key to preventing delinquency. If it is desirable to avoid the criminogenic consequences of coercive exchanges, then parents must be taught how not to become trapped in them. This clearly implies the need to provide parents with training. Young mothers and fathers must be taught to recognize coercive exchanges when they occur and have the necessary tools to prevent them from continuing. In his review of developmental theories, David Farrington argues that a variety of preventive measures can be taken to delay the onset of delinquency, especially parenting, life skills, and social skills training for parents so that they can better recognize how to enhance protective factors and minimize risk factors.[54]

Developmental theories extend the policy implications of earlier explanations of crime by making policy makers aware of the fact that events experienced during one stage of life might continue to have important consequences at subsequent stages. Because developmental theorists believe that the most important predictors of delinquency vary as people age, their theories imply that interventions that may be highly effective during one stage of life may no longer work at the next. Finally, since these theories integrate existing explanations of delinquency and because research using developmental perspectives has identified a variety of pathways that youth might follow into delinquency, this set of theories strongly cautions against a one size fits all approach to delinquency intervention.

To illustrate, a child's ties to his or her parents are the key to predicting delinquent behavior in early adolescence. Adolescents who are weakly bonded to their parents are at particularly high risk.[55] As adolescence progresses, however, the importance of parental attachment wanes and peer relationships become more important as key predictors of delinquent behavior (see Chapter 12). As adolescence gives way to early adulthood, *assortative mating* becomes a key process that predicts continued involvement in delinquency. Young adults who form

box 8-3   DELINQUENCY AROUND THE GLOBE
Targeting Predelinquents in England

A proposal by English Policing Minister Hazel Blears has reignited an important debate that first arose among criminologists in the 1960s with the advent of labeling theory. Blears suggested the implementation of a program that would "target" and "track" up to 125,000 English children with incarcerated fathers. The rationale for this policy is that research has found that children with incarcerated family members are more likely to become involved in delinquency than juveniles who do not have incarcerated relatives. The proposed program would target this population of at-risk children and provide their families with extra support throughout childhood and adolescence. The program would consist of parenting skills training, social work visits, after-school activities, and other measures designed to foster prosocial behavior.

On the surface, the program appears to be consistent with the lessons of developmental theory. It acknowledges that childhood experiences can influence adolescent behavior. It also targets known criminogenic risk factors, such as poor parenting and a lack of scholastic commitment. Moreover, there is no doubt that criminal justice resources are finite, as there is only so much money available for delinquency prevention programs. If one can concentrate these resources only on potential delinquents, rather than diluting it on the entire population, one can afford to spend more on each at-risk child. However, critics have pointed out that the program runs the risk of stigmatizing the children whom it is designed to help. In effect, if the system labels the children of incarcerated fathers as potential delinquents, it may create a self-fulfilling prophecy. If authorities repeatedly tell a child that he will grow up to be a criminal, they run the risk that the child might eventually get the message.

The proposed intervention also faces a second important hurdle. The central lesson of developmental research is that children must be targeted by *the correct intervention* if they are to stay out of trouble. After all, it is clear that children follow different pathways to delinquent behavior. For some, particularly those with neuropsychological deficits, the cycle of misbehavior begins in early childhood. However, for others, involvement in delinquency represents a normal period of adolescent rebellion. These children, even if they have fathers in prison, may not need to be tracked and targeted from childhood. Their families may not want additional help from the criminal justice system. Yet the proposed program appears to treat all 125,000 children as equals. It is not possible to say whether this program will be beneficial or if it will end up stigmatizing and labeling those whom it intends to help. If developmental theorists are correct, the program will likely help certain children while proving harmful for others.

Sources: BBC News Online, online at http//www.news.bbc .co.uk/nolpda/ukfs_news/hi/newsid_3568000/3568492 .stm, accessed April 30, 2007; *Evening Times Online,* online at http//www.eveningtimes.co.uk/, accessed April 30, 2007; *The Independent Digital,* online at: www.news.independent.co.uk/ uk/politics/story.jsp?story=551894, accessed April 30, 2007.

strong bonds with prosocial partners are more likely to mature out of crime than those who do not.[56]

If these developmental theorists are correct, it is necessary to design different types of delinquency prevention programs for adolescents of different ages. For middle and junior high school children, delinquency prevention programs might focus on family ties. Programs aimed at building good relationships and effective communication between parents and their children would probably be most effective. This would also be true for programs that give parents the opportunity to spend more time with their children. By high school, however, such programs might be discontinued. Instead it would be more important to focus on peer pressure, gang involvement, and other issues related to the peer groups of at-risk children. By late high school, intervention strategies should probably begin focusing on making effective transitions to the job market and teaching older adolescents how to avoid dysfunctional personal relationships.

Developmental theories also imply that the same intervention strategy is not likely to work for all people, even those of the same age. For example, the most serious and violent delinquents will be more difficult to help than normal delinquents. Different subpopulations require different interventions. For life-course persistent offenders, the roots of their misbehavior are often psychosocial deficits and the process of cumulative disadvantage. Consequently, Moffitt's theory suggests trying to minimize the deficits themselves or interrupting the disadvantage process. It would be important to identify problem children as early as possible and teach them effective anger management and impulse control skills. Furthermore, it would be important to try to minimize any stigmatization or secondary deviation caused by excessive reactions to initial misbehavior, in this regard, as Moffitt would likely agree with labeling theory (see Chapter 7). It appears that many school districts, which are now doing their best to keep problem students integrated with others, are following this approach. Although school administrators likely do not use the same terminology as Moffitt, such programs are an equivalent to trying to minimize the process of cumulative disadvantage by not separating difficult children from their peers and keeping them in the mainstream educational system.[57]

Victor Battistich and his colleagues have demonstrated that this approach may be successful with their evaluation of the Child Development Project, which is a comprehensive, 3-year program involving over 5,500 elementary school children from 24 schools distributed throughout the United States. Battistich and his colleagues found that the program increased prosocial behavior, academic achievement, attachment, and commitment to school. Additionally, the program reduced substance abuse among all students. In schools that had been more effective at implementing the program, the treatment effects were even stronger, resulting in significant declines in marijuana use, weapons possession, car theft, truancy, and threatening behavior.[58]

For adolescence-limited offenders, these types of measures may not be necessary. Moffitt argues that these children commit delinquency largely from a desire to appear grown up. It is unlikely they need early childhood skills training, in fact providing it would likely be wasteful and even counterproductive. It is also less important to worry about a labeling or cumulative disadvantage process developing for this group of juveniles. Even though fewer criminologists are willing to accept a "boys will be boys" view of delinquent behavior, Moffitt's theory suggests that this might be acceptable, at least for adolescence-limited offenders who mostly engage in minor delinquency. Such individuals will likely age-out of crime by themselves when they enter adulthood. Thus, interventions for adolescence-limited children could conceivably be limited to situational responses to each delinquent act. These responses should probably be kept as informal as possible, as involving the formal criminal or juvenile justice systems may do more harm than good. If these ideas sound familiar, they are precisely what Edwin Schur advocated years ago with his notion of radical nonintervention.

Still it should be acknowledged that because developmental theory is relatively new, there has been relatively little applied research exploring how

think
about it

Is there a place for "get tough on crime" initiatives within developmental theory? Can a "scared straight" or a boot camp program be considered a turning point?

box 8-4   DELINQUENCY PREVENTION
The Seattle Social Development Project

The Seattle Social Development Project is one of the longest running studies in the field of developmental criminology. The study was initiated in 1981 at the University of Washington by Joseph Weis and J. David Hawkins. It is based on a prospective longitudinal panel design, which means that it follows a group of subjects over a period of many years in order to develop an understanding of the various developments that occur throughout the life course. At its inception, the project enrolled 808 fifth graders from 18 public elementary schools in Seattle, Washington. Follow-up research continues to this day, as the subjects are now in their late twenties and many are starting families. What makes the Seattle project different from other long running developmental studies of delinquency is its focus on intervention and change. From the start, Hawkins and his colleagues sought not only to understand *why* children got into trouble but also to discover *how* the process could be interrupted.

The Seattle approach is multifaceted. The researchers believe that delinquency prevention must focus on family, schools, peer groups, and the community. Parents must be taught how to communicate and interact with their children in ways that encourage good behavior. Teachers are encouraged to use inclusive learning strategies that promote scholastic commitment in *all* students and not just those who show an affinity for learning. Perhaps most important, the adolescents themselves must be made to believe that they can achieve success through prosocial behavior. To this end, they must be taught the skills necessary to succeed in the conventional world and the value system associated with a prosocial lifestyle. In practical terms, this equates to showing children that they have much to gain by studying and working hard and much to lose by becoming involved in deviant peer groups, gangs, and delinquent activity.

Does the Seattle project prevent delinquency? The available research strongly suggests that it does. Repeated studies have found that children receiving the program interventions are less likely to be involved in delinquency, substance abuse, and other antisocial behaviors when compared with subjects who do not receive any interventions. Importantly, the treatment effects are not limited to delinquency prevention. Follow-up studies of the youths into early adulthood continue to show that children who received the interventions are healthier, lead more successful, conventional lives, and are significantly less likely to engage in crime, substance use, and other harmful acts. Indeed, the longer subjects participate in the program, the more effective it seems to be. For instance, Catalano and Hawkins have shown that children enrolled in a program called "catch them being good" from grades 1 through 6 did significantly better than those who only participated in grades 5 and 6. The research is also unique in that it has synthesized its theories and research findings into practical, step-by-step programs that can be implemented by delinquency prevention agencies or school administrators. As such programs are implemented in more and more areas, researchers will have the opportunity to see developmental theory in action and to determine whether it is an effective delinquency prevention strategy.

Sources: J. David Hawkins, Richard Catalano, Rick Kosterman, Robert Abbott, and Karl Hill, "Preventing Adolescent Health Risk Behaviors by Strengthening Protection During Childhood," *Archives of Pediatrics and Adolescent Medicine* 153:226–234 (1999); J. David Hawkins, Jie Guo, Karl Hill, Sara Battin-Pearson, and Robert Abbott, "Long-Term Effects of the Seattle Social Development Intervention on School Bonding Trajectories," *Applied Developmental Science* 5:225–236 (2001); J. David Hawkins, Rick Kosterman, Richard Catalano, Karl Hill, and Robert Abbott, "Promoting Positive Adult Functioning Through Social Development Intervention in Childhood," *Archives of Pediatrics and Adolescent Medicine* 159:25–31 (2005); Heather Lonczak, Robert Abbott, J. David Hawkins, Rick Kosterman, and Richard Catalano, "Effects of the Seattle Social Development Project on Sexual Behavior, Pregnancy, Birth, and Sexually Transmitted Disease Outcomes by Age 21 Years," *Archives of Pediatrics and Adolescent Medicine* 156:438–447 (2002).

effectively it might guide criminal justice policy compared to older theories. Many of the theories are still in an infancy stage, and some have not been tested in the real world. One notable exception is the Seattle Social Development Project.

conclusions

Interest in developmental theories of delinquency was sparked by the observation that delinquent and criminal behavior seems to trend almost predictably over time. In other words, it has been repeatedly observed that most illegal acts are committed by adolescents and young adults as opposed to young children and mature adults. Some criminologists, particularly those with backgrounds in developmental psychology, began to recognize that deviant behavior is governed not only by what is currently happening in an individual's life, but also by what has happened in the past. As criminologists subjected the age–crime curve to more sophisticated testing, they discovered that it was not nearly as universal as once thought. Although most delinquency did occur in adolescence and early adulthood, children exhibited very different patterns of behavior. This led developmental theorists to consider what causes these different patterns and to develop theories that could account for them. Developmental theories borrow heavily from earlier work but ultimately move beyond it by paying special attention to the roles of time, maturation, and social institutions on delinquent behavior.

Developmental theory has important juvenile justice policy applications. It suggests that in order to reduce delinquency, policy analysts must develop age-appropriate interventions and interventions that are tailored to particular groups of troubled children. A one-size-fits-all philosophy is not likely to be successful when the available research clearly suggests that multiple risk factors are associated with deviant development for diverse groups of children at different stages of the life course. In the next chapter, our attention will turn to one specific group of offenders, *females*. The chapter explores how the development of delinquent behavior and the experience of being delinquent are conditioned by gender. It also demonstrates how criminology has historically been a male-dominated discipline and how feminist criminologists have reacted to and addressed this problem.

key terms

Adolescence-limited offenders   Juveniles whose delinquent behavior is confined to their teenage years.

Age–crime curve   The notion that crime rates increase during preadolescence, peak in middle adolescence, and steadily decline thereafter.

Assortative mating   The concept that people choose mates that are similar to themselves.

Coercive exchange   A test of wills in which a child uses misbehavior to extort a desired outcome from his parents.

Cumulative disadvantage   The process by which successive misbehavior leads to a serious detriment for an individual's life chances.

Delinquent career The pattern of delinquent behavior that an individual exhibits over the course of his or her life.

Delinquent propensity The likelihood of committing delinquency and other antisocial acts; it is a trait that is largely set in early childhood.

Developmental theories Theories that focus on an individual's entire life course, rather than one discrete point in time.

Life-course persistent offenders Individuals who suffer from a number of neuropsychological deficits that are likely to cause them to engage in delinquency throughout their lives.

Precocious transitions An important life event (e.g., pregnancy) that is experienced too early in life.

Protective factors Situations, settings, events, or characteristics that decrease the likelihood that one will be delinquent.

Risk factors Situations, settings, events, or characteristics that *increase* the likelihood that one will be delinquent.

Seattle Social Development Project A leading study in the creation and application of developmental theory.

Turning points Key life events that can either drive someone toward delinquent behavior or initiate the process of desisting from it.

Female Delinquency Theories

"Criminology, like most academic disciplines, has been concerned with the activities and interests of men."[1] For over a century, the study of delinquency has focused almost exclusively on the behavior of males. In part, this reflects the simple reality that male law violating exceeds that of females in both frequency and seriousness. But it also reflects the fact that criminology, as a discipline, has been dominated by men who see the world through their own eyes. In addition, the vast majority of people who create laws, who prosecute and defend offenders, and who administer the juvenile corrections systems have been, and continue to be, males.

The United States has historically been a patriarchal society. **Patriarchy** refers to a social, legal, and political climate that values male dominance and hierarchy. Patriarchy affects not only social structures including the family and the economy, relationships, and definitions of appropriate social roles, but also how people, both males and females, perceive the world around them. Gender stratification as a product of patriarchy has led to unconscious assumptions about male and female behavior and misbehavior.

To the extent that patriarchy extends into the academic arena of criminological research, the delinquent behaviors of girls and the causes of those behaviors have largely been invisible. Even though sex is one of the most statistically significant factors in predicting delinquency, criminologists have rarely shown much concern in including girls in their samples. Joanne Belknap states that

> When the researchers did include girls in their samples, it was typically to see how girls fit into boys' equations. That is, rather than include in the study a means of assessing how girls' lives might be different from boys' lives, girls' delinquency has typically been viewed as peripheral and unnecessary to understanding juvenile offending and processing.[2]

think
about it

How might our understanding and conceptualization of delinquency differ if females had historically dominated criminology instead of males? If so, why?

When females have been studied as delinquents, it has nearly always been in comparison to males: why girls are *less* delinquent than boys, why girls commit *less* serious crimes, why girls are *more* likely to be arrested for status offenses, and how the causes of female delinquency *differ* from those of male delinquency.

In Chapter 2, we provided a discussion of sex differences in patterns of delinquency. Although both the amount and seriousness of female delinquency has increased over the past few decades, many of the stronger correlates predictive of male delinquency, such as associating with antisocial peers, having an antisocial personality, and holding antisocial attitudes, have also been found to be strong predictors of female delinquency.[3] This chapter, however, examines specific theories and explanations of female delinquency. We will begin by examining how patriarchy and gender stratification affect the lives of girls as they grow up. Such an examination is critical for understanding the nature of female delinquency and the appropriateness of explanations put forth to explain it.

GROWING UP FEMALE

In Charlotte Brontë's 19th-century novel *Jane Eyre,* the young protagonist paces the roof of Thornfield Hall, frustrated over the contrast between her confined existence and the possibilities that lie in the larger world:

Women need exercise for their faculties and a field for their efforts as much as their brothers do; they suffer from too rigid a restraint, too absolute a stagnation, precisely as men would suffer; and it is narrow-minded in their more privileged fellow-creatures to say that they ought to confine themselves to making puddings and knitting stockings, to playing on the piano and embroidering bags.[4]

The frustration that came from realizing the unfair situation she and other women faced in life because of their sex was not unique to Jane Eyre. In generation after generation, young girls have experienced the same frustration after realizing the same unfairness. Somehow, their place in society has been defined as being different from that of boys. But Jane Eyre's sense of a self-identity as a female was perhaps more consciously formed than that of many other young girls, and such awareness may, in part, explain why some girls feel more frustration than others over their defined place in society.

Throughout most of human history, girls have grown up in societies that have viewed them as being "inferior" to boys. Jean Stafford illustrates the pervasiveness of the belief that girls are inferior in her novel *The Mountain Lion*. Ralph, at age 11, already senses his superiority to his 9-year-old sister, Molly:

It was natural for her to want to be a boy (who *wouldn't*) but he knew for a fact that she couldn't be. Last week, he had had to speak sharply to her about wearing one of his outgrown Boy Scout shirts: he was glad enough for her to have it, but she had not taken the "Be Prepared" thing off the pocket and he had to come out and say brutally, "Having that on a girl is like dragging the American flag in the dirt."[5]

What accounts for Jane Eyre's confinement to an existence less fulfilling than that of the men of her community or for Ralph's assumption of his superiority over his sister? The differences between girls and boys suggested in these two passages reflect widely held perceptions of the superiority of boys over girls. The relegation of girls to more restricted lives also reflects patriarchal society, in which males have managed to maintain control over females. For both girls and boys, one's sense of self and of oneself in relation to others is highly influenced by society's perceptions of gender roles. In patriarchal societies, growing up female is quite different from growing up male and has significant implications for how girls confront their lives. (Box 9-1 provides a look at one consequence of preferential treatment of boys in India.)

The limits that patriarchal societies impose on girls even extend to criminal behavior. In some circumstances, the ways that gender is defined means that certain types of delinquency are viewed as typically male or typically female. In the case of crimes, such as prostitution, patriarchal society frames the crime almost entirely as a female problem. In other ways, patriarchal society and its gender roles serve to insulate girls from delinquency. For instance, Jean Bottcher has shown that traditional gender roles insulate girls in very high-risk, crime-ridden communities from delinquency because the criminal population believes that girls should engage in certain behaviors, such as taking care of children, and not others, such as hanging out and getting into trouble.[6]

box 9-1	**DELINQUENCY AROUND THE GLOBE**

Preferential Treatment of Boys in India

It is true that in patriarchal societies, such as the United States, boys receive preferential treatment over girls. This fact is reflected in a variety of ways, one being that the study of American delinquency has focused almost exclusively on the behavior of boys.

But the situation of boys receiving preferential treatment over girls is not unique to the United States. For example, in contemporary Indian society, female fetuses are targeted for abortion at a much higher rate than male fetuses. Advances in ultrasound technology have made it possible for pregnant women in India to determine the sex of their fetuses for about $11. Because boys are more valued than girls in India, increasing numbers of women are aborting female fetuses because family elders want boys, not girls. The reason: Boys are important because they have to look after all the property.

Early figures from the census indicate that female fetuses are regularly being aborted, continuing a trend that started in the 1980s. The number of girls per 1,000 boys dropped in 2001 to 927 from 945 in 1991 and 962 in 1981. The fall in the ratio of girls to boys over the past decade has been the most pronounced in the richest states where more people can afford ultrasound tests, and abortions are more easily obtained. Some researchers estimated that 10 million female fetuses have been aborted in the past 20 years. Although these estimates have been disputed, it is clear that patriarchal societies express a clear preference for boys. While this situation may be subtle or debatable in the United States, it is less disputable in other countries.

Sources: Celia Dugger, "Female Fetuses Targeted for Abortions in India," *Denver Post,* April 22, 2001:16A; Associated Press, "Indian Experts Dispute Female Abortions Study," ABC News, online at: http://www.abc.net.au/news/news items/200601/s1545961.htm, accessed May 1, 2007.

The Development of Girls' Gender Roles

Creating **gender–role identities** begins at birth (or even at the fetal stage, given ultrasound identification of the child's sex) with the announcement of "It's a girl!" or "It's a boy!" Almost immediately, in describing their infants, parents start using typical gender stereotypes. In one study, parents described boy babies as being firm, large-featured, alert, and strong, while girl babies were characterized as delicate, fine-featured, soft, and small.[7] Parents also respond to toddlers differently on the basis of the child's sex. They discourage rough-and-tumble play by girls and doll play by boys. They listen to girls and respond to them more attentively when girls are gentle or talk softly, but they attend more to boys when boys demonstrate assertiveness. Parents encourage dependence in girls and independence in boys.[8] By age 4 or 5, children have become aware of their gender and the behaviors appropriate to it.[9] Although prescriptions and proscriptions regarding gender roles have shifted in many ways over the past few decades (i.e., women now comprise the majority of college enrollments and law school admissions, participate extensively in professional sports, engage in street-level police patrol, and even die in combat in the armed forces), a great amount of everyday socializing into gender roles has not changed significantly.

think
about it

Data from international studies indicate that boys are more involved in delinquency than girls in all countries. What are the implications of this for those who argue that gender-role identities and gender socialization explain delinquency? In your opinion, what percentage of delinquency is explained by socialization and what percentage is explained by biological factors?

For example, recent research has also shown that early adolescent daughters of mothers who are employed in the workforce are more likely to hold nontraditional gender–role attitudes than daughters of unemployed mothers.[10]

Girls' gender roles are reinforced through toys and games in early adolescence. Boys frequently are given toys that encourage creativity and manipulation, such as construction and chemistry sets, while girls are given toys that encourage passivity and nurturance, such as stuffed animals and dolls. Girls are more likely to play in small, unstructured groups; their games have few rules and emphasize cooperation rather than competition. Boys, on the other hand, typically play in larger groups, often teams; their games have more complex rules and often emphasize cooperation to facilitate competing.[11]

Going to school provides both girls and boys with opportunities to learn the *four R's:* reading, riting, rithmetic, and (gender) roles. Conscious and unconscious patterns of interaction between teachers and students as well as the formal and informal activities of girls and boys in school encourage stereotyped gender roles. Girls receive reinforcement from teachers for being passive, verbal, and dependent, while boys are encouraged to explore, examine how things work, and be independent.[12]

Schools also provide avenues to develop self-esteem. For boys, the avenues are being tough, developing a good physique, participating in sports characterized by competition, aggressiveness, being cool and not showing emotions, and being good at something. The avenues for building self-esteem in girls have traditionally been more problematic, emphasizing such things as being pretty, being popular, being liked as sociable and pleasant, and being preoccupied with body weight, which may lead to anorexia or bulimia. Teachers encourage boys to be more assertive in the classroom, have higher expectations for male students, and believe that male students are better at math and science.[13]

Should boys and girls be socialized in near-identical ways to eliminate gender differences? If so, should girls be raised like boys or should boys be raised like girls?

The socialization into sex-appropriate gender roles for adolescents is also reinforced in the home. In traditional family arrangements, girls continue to be kept more dependent and cloistered through closer supervision and more restrictive rules. Parents encourage girls to stay at home or in close proximity to their mothers, to avoid risks, and to fear social disapproval.[14] Girls generally join groups later than boys, are less likely than boys to have a regular meeting place outside the home, and are less likely to belong to single-sex groups at all.[15] Parents typically encourage boys, on the other hand, to be independent, aggressive, and group-oriented, and they allow boys to date earlier than girls, to stay out later than girls with their friends, to be left alone at home, and to participate in organized activities.[16]

All agents of socialization, including the family, schools, work, and even the juvenile justice system, play a part in gender socialization and shaping girls' gender roles. Stephen Gavazzi and his colleagues studied the life histories of 305 youths who had been detained in juvenile facilities. Female delinquents were significantly more likely than boys to be detained for family violence and psychiatric problems. However, the family violence problems were noteworthy because girls were likely to be detained for exhibiting "out of control" types of behavior and not obeying their parents. Although male delinquents similarly caused their parents trouble, they were not detained for violating gender roles within the family. Instead, boys were detained for more serious violent and property delinquent acts.[17]

Girls' Identities

What are the effects of these gender–role socialization patterns on girls' identities and self-esteem? The patterns lead many girls to identify with traditional female roles, anticipate economic dependence and a more restricted adult status, and accept political, social, and sexual privileges secondary to those of boys. Such socialization creates narrower boundaries of opportunities for girls than for boys and instills in them a self-perception of powerlessness and dependence. Girls also learn that to be feminine means to nurture, and therefore they focus on relationships.[18] Carol Gilligan suggests that girls are raised to identify with the primary caretaker, the mother, and therefore experience a strong bonding relationship that becomes a model for the rest of their lives.[19] But this emphasis on relationships, or "making connections," encourages in adolescent girls the development of a "morality of response," or "ethic of care," that emphasizes the creation and maintenance of interdependence and responsiveness in relationships.[20] Males, on the other hand, develop values or ethics of justice, fairness, rationality, and individuality. Female moral reasoning, which focuses on care, connection, and relationships, thus is likely to discourage girls from framing attitudes and responses to situations in ways that would produce competition, conflict, or aggressiveness.[21]

Gender identity has been shown to influence delinquency. One study that speaks to this was conducted by Lisa Broidy and her colleagues who compared gender differences in empathy and delinquency. They used two very different samples, 425 high school students from Philadelphia and 232 youths who had served time in the California Youth Authority. Across all groups, empathy was negatively related to serious violence, meaning that adolescents who can empathize with other people and potential victims are unlikely to physically harm

think
about it

Inadequate parental socialization may produce children with low self-control. Based on the disproportionate role of women in parenting and nurturing, are they to blame for children having low self-control? Or, are "dead-beat" dads the main culprits for children with low self-control?

them. On the other hand, youths who cannot feel the common humanity of other people can fairly easily use physical force against them. Perhaps because of their gender socialization, girls were significantly more empathetic than boys in terms of emotional and behavioral expression. Broidy also found that female delinquents were more empathetic than male nondelinquents.[22] Girls, then, begin to operate very early within a network of intimate interpersonal ties that reinforce a more nurturing and caring role. And because girls are more likely to define themselves relationally, they do not develop the same precise and rigid ego boundaries common to boys.[23] According to Erik Erikson, "Much of a young woman's identity is already defined in her kind of attractiveness and in the selective nature of her search for the man (or men) by whom she wishes to be sought."[24]

In a 3-year study of 100 teenage girls in London, Sue Lees explored some of the problems of identity for adolescent girls. Lees found that a girl's sexuality is central to the way she is judged in everyday life.

> To speak of a woman's reputation is to invoke her sexual behavior, but to speak of a man's reputation is to refer to his personality, exploits, and his standing in the community. For men sexual reputation is, in the main, separated from the evaluation of moral behavior and regarded as private and incidental.[25]

While a boy's social standing is typically enhanced by his sexual exploits, a girl's standing can be destroyed by simple insinuations; therefore, she is often required to defend her sexual reputation to *both* boys and girls. The use of slang terms and insults, such as *slut* or *whore,* functions to control the activities and social reputations of girls. A girl need not actually have slept with a boy to have her reputation threatened. As one girl commented: "When there're boys talking and you've been out with more than two you're known as the crisp they're passing around. . . . The boy's alright but the girl's a bit of scum."

The possibility of being labeled "bad" or a "slut" is a form of moral censure reflecting dominant perceptions of departure, or potential departure, from male conceptions of female sexuality. More important, such terms are applied to "any form of social behavior by girls that would define them as autonomous from the attachment to and domination by boys."[26] According to Meda Chesney-Lind and Randall Shelden, teenage girls are coerced into cultivating a hegemonic, heterosexualized "teen femininity" that "recreates and reinforces the sexual double standard by labeling girls who are too overtly sexual as 'sluts,'" and that ties a girl's self-esteem and prestige far more to externals (primarily male approval) than is typical for boys. Consequently, girls are steered into acceptable or "legitimate" forms of sexual and social behavior characterized by having a steady boyfriend, being in love, and, eventually, getting married. In many ways, a girl's apparent sexual behavior is seen as a barometer, testing her capacity to learn appropriate codes of social conduct with boys.[27]

Gendered Pathways into Delinquency

Today, the understanding of the gender–delinquency relationship owes much to the developmental (or life-course) perspective that is currently popular in criminology (see Chapter 8). The developmental perspective is interested in the ways that life events occurring during childhood impact outcomes during adolescence and adulthood. Negative events or circumstances, often called *risk factors,* increase the likelihood that young people will be delinquent. Positive events or circumstances, often called *protective factors,* decrease the likelihood that young people will be delinquent (or help them desist from crime if they have already engaged in delinquency). In fact, Joanne Belknap describes developmental criminology as being directly compatible with feminist perspectives on crime.

> In many ways the life-course perspective is seemingly pro-feminist in nature: It purports to address significant childhood and adult experiences and to view how these, particularly social bonds, are related to delinquent, criminal, and deviant behavior.[28]

A handful of scholars have examined how pathways into delinquency unfold into delinquent careers among women. Marguerite Warren and Jill Rosenbaum studied 159 women who had been incarcerated in California. They found that women had similar criminal careers as men in the sense that there was a generalized involvement in many types of crimes, such as violence, property, and drug offenses. However, women were disproportionately likely to have arrests for prostitution, theft, forgery, fraud, and drug violations.[29] Other criminologists have also shown that women's offending careers contain mostly arrests relating to drug abuse.[30] Compared to male delinquents, female offenders have significantly more extensive victimization histories, including sexual, physical, and emotional abuses. Often, this abuse begins at home when girls are very young especially if there is a nonbiological male parental or authority figure in the household. A typical response to this abuse, consistent with Regoli and Hewitt's *theory of differential oppression,* is for girls to run away from home where the exposure to street life often leads to delinquency (see Chapter 7). Sooner than later, the victimization, oppressive home life, and vulnerabilities of the street lead to drug use.[31] Indeed, Ronald Mullis and his colleagues describe the typical female delinquent as one who is young and impoverished, is likely to have experienced abuse or exploitation, abuses drugs and alcohol, is likely to have unmet medical and mental health needs, lacks hope for the future, and perceives life as oppressive.[32]

The gendered part of this development centers on the ways that female offenders live on the streets and sustain their drug and delinquent careers. In many ways, the abuses that female criminals experience reflect their sexualized and subordinated status in a patriarchal society. Using a sample of women that had been arrested a minimum of 30 times, Matt DeLisi found that ironically, it is through the status of sexual object that many female offenders survive, namely through prostitution. Along with theft, forgery, and fraud, prostitution is the primary way that women on the streets get money, and the money is often quickly used to obtain drugs to numb themselves.[33] Cathy Spatz Widom chronicled the "cycle of violence" whereby physical abuse, sexual abuse, and neglect incurred during childhood dramatically increase the risks for delinquency and a host of maladaptive behaviors during adolescence and adulthood. This effect is especially strong among girls who are sexually abused.[34] In this way, the gendered pathway to delinquency illustrates a cycle where one type of abuse and victimization engenders many more, a process that Abigail Fagan calls the "gender cycle of violence."[35]

To what extent are delinquencies among girls acts of rebellion against the constraints of these restricting and oppressive sex roles imposed in adolescence (see Box 9-2)? If they are not revolts, what may account for girls' involvement in

delinquency? When they do violate the law, why are their delinquencies generally less serious, and how might we account for the increasing involvement of
girls in delinquent behavior? Finally, how adequate are male-oriented criminological theories in explaining female delinquency?

THEORIES OF FEMALE DELINQUENCY

Criminology as a discipline has, by and large, been the domain of males. It thus
should be no surprise that earlier explanations of female delinquency reflected
male perceptions of females. For the most part, those perceptions evolved from
beliefs about biological differences between males and females. Even when sociological explanations of delinquency entered the mainstream, theories were
largely developed from studies of boys. Girls were still viewed as "naturally"
less delinquent. The relative inattention given to female delinquency was also
due in part to the fact that most criminological theory has been policy driven;
that is, because males made up most of the delinquent population in the courts
and correctional institutions, policies designed to respond to delinquency sought
out theories that dealt primarily with boys.

---

box 9-2   **A WINDOW ON DELINQUENCY**
Attractiveness, Socialization, and Delinquency

Attractiveness is an important characteristic that influences how people are
differently viewed and evaluated in a
variety of ways. Researchers in Canada find
that parents often treat their own children
differently with attractive children benefiting
from more attention. For example, attractive
children, defined as those with good facial
symmetry, cleanliness, nice attire, and other
features, get more positive attention, get less
negative attention or punishment, and are
better protected than their less attractive siblings. Consistent with the arguments of feminists who believe that our patriarchal society
defines people in sexual terms often based on
attractiveness, these findings are intriguing.

Attractiveness has also been found to be
a correlate of delinquency. Naci Mocan and
Erdal Tekin have studied the effects of attractiveness on delinquency and other life
outcomes among a national sample of Americans between the ages of 18 and 26. Being
very attractive reduces involvement in crime.

Being unattractive increases criminal involvement in a variety of crimes, such as burglary
and drug violations. Attractiveness also has
a significant and independent effect on relationships with teachers, grades, high school
social history, adult vocabulary, and labor
market performance. These effects are *especially pronounced* for females. Finally, very attractive women, but not very attractive men,
receive more favorable treatment from the
criminal justice system; that is, they are more
likely to receive positive discretion, such as
being let go with a warning instead of being
issued a ticket. In some circumstances, it
certainly pays to be considered attractive. If
women garner human capital from their looks,
it is likely that looks will continue to be a
source of status in society.

Sources: H. Naci Mocan and Erdal Tekin, "Ugly Criminals"
(Cambridge, MA: National Bureau of Economics Research,
2006); Jeffrey Kluger, "Taming Wild Girls," *Time,* May 1,
2006:54–55; Laura Roberts, "Ugly Children Get Less Attention," *The Scotsman,* April 14, 2005:1.

As more women entered the field of criminology beginning in the 1980s, they brought with them a greater interest in female delinquency, its nature and causes, and how its origins may differ from those of male delinquency. In this section we will examine biological and psychological theories of female delinquency, consider how sociological theories may apply to girls, and look at the more recent feminist and critical theories.

Biological and Psychological Theories

Although the earliest explanations of delinquency located its causes in demons and, later, in free will, they did not make causal distinctions on the basis of the sex of the delinquent. It was not until the rise of the Positive School of Criminology in the 19th century, with its emphasis on biological and psychological causes of behavior, that female law violators were seen as uniquely "different" from male criminals (see Chapter 5).

In *The Female Offender,* published in 1895, Cesare Lombroso and William Ferrero applied to females the principles of Lombroso's earlier work on the male criminal. Inasmuch as criminals were viewed as "throwbacks," or atavistic by their nature, the female criminal was also seen as biologically distinct and inferior to noncriminal women. Lombroso and Ferrero believed that women were lower on the evolutionary scale than men and therefore closer to their "primitive" origins. Consequently, female criminals were not as visible as their male counterparts and showed fewer signs of degeneracy than males.

According to Lombroso and Ferrero, women are naturally more childlike, less intelligent, lacking in passion, more maternal, and weak—characteristics that make them less inclined to commit crimes. Women also share other traits with children: their moral sense is deficient and they are "revengeful, jealous, [and] inclined to vengeances of a refined cruelty." However, because "women are big children; their evil tendencies are . . . more varied than men's, but generally . . . latent. When . . . awakened and excited they produce results proportionately greater." Therefore, when a woman does turn to crime she is "a monster," as "her wickedness must have been enormous before it could triumph over so many obstacles."

> ## theory in a nutshell
>
> ### Cesare Lombroso and William Ferrero
>
> Lombroso and Ferrero contend that female criminals are biologically distinct and inferior to noncriminal women. Women were lower on the evolutionary scale than men; thus, criminal females were not as visible as male offenders and showed fewer signs of degeneracy.

For Lombroso and Ferrero, women's criminality is a product of their biology, but this biology also keeps most women from crime. To the extent that woman's nature is antithetical to crime, and with criminality seen as a characteristic more common to men, the female criminal not only is an abnormal woman but is biologically more like a man, only "often more ferocious." It should be noted that Lombroso and Ferrero believed that most female delinquents were only "occasional criminals," as were most male delinquents. The physical features of these occasional female delinquents did not appear to reflect any atavistic degeneration and that their basic moral character was essentially the same as that of their "normal sisters." [36]

In *The Unadjusted Girl,* published in 1923, W.I. Thomas postulated that males and females are biologically different. Although both males and females are motivated by natural biological instincts leading to "wish fulfillment," how they approach the fulfillment of the wishes differs. Thomas identified four distinct categories of wishes:

- The desire for new experience.
- The desire for security.
- The desire for response.
- The desire for recognition.

Thomas believed that women by nature have stronger desires for response and love than men and that they are capable of more varied types of love as demonstrated by maternal love, a characteristic atypical of males. This intense need to give and receive love often leads girls into delinquency, especially sexual delinquency, as they use sex as a means to fulfill other wishes.

However, Thomas did not believe girls are inherently delinquent. Rather, their behaviors are the result of choices circumscribed by social rules and moral codes designed to guide people's actions as they attempt to fulfill their wishes. Girls, more than boys, are limited by their gender roles in society and consequently are more likely to become demoralized and frustrated as they perceive deprivations.

The origins of female delinquency, according to Thomas, are found in the girl's impulsive desire to obtain "amusement, adventure, pretty clothes, favorable notice, distinction and freedom in the larger world. . . . Their sex is used as a condition of the realization of other wishes. It is their capital." Unfortunately, such impulsive behavior is also likely to drive girls into the arms of boys who will take advantage of them, frequently leading to pregnancy, prostitution, and eventual ruin. [37]

In *The Criminality of Women,* published in 1950, Otto Pollak argued that women are as criminal as men but their criminality is hidden or "masked." The masking of their crimes and delinquencies is a result of "natural" physiological differences in the sexes, as well as the tendency of males to overlook or excuse offenses by women. Pollak believed that the physiological nature of women makes them more deceitful than men. With less physical strength than men, women must resort to indirect or deceitful means to carry out crimes or to vent their aggression; women also are more likely to be "instigators" and men "perpetrators" of crime. Pollak further argued that social norms force women to conceal their menstruation each month and to misrepresent or conceal information regarding sex from their children, at least for some time. According to Pollak, social norms "thus make concealment . . . in the eyes of women socially required and commendable . . ., condition[ing] them to a different attitude toward veracity than men." [38]

In Pollak's view, lower rates of crime among females reflect men's deference and protective attitude toward women, whereby female offenses are generally overlooked or excused by males, a premise known as the **chivalry hypothesis.** Male victims of female delinquencies, police officers, prosecutors, judges, and juries, Pollak suggested, are hesitant to report, arrest, prosecute, or convict women. Thus, the actual rate of female delinquencies is much higher than official statistics reported.

Recent Biological and Developmental Explanations
The idea that girls' behavior is largely controlled by their biology, physiology, or sexuality continued to appear in studies for some time, although today it is rare to find expressions of the "natural" inferiority of girls in criminological literature. Instead, many of the more recent studies from this perspective suggest that girls' biological nature interacts with social forces, usually those found in the family.

In *Delinquency in Girls* published in 1968, John Cowie and his associates describe female delinquency as being dominated by sexual misbehaviors. They argue that female delinquents are unhappy and that "their unhappiness is commonly related to disturbed emotional relationships with the parents." Delinquent girls often come from families characterized by low moral standards, poor discipline, conflict, and disturbed family relations. In addition, delinquent girls are more likely than delinquent boys to have pathological psychiatric problems and overall impaired physical health. That girls are less likely than boys to be delinquent is accounted for, in part, by girls being more timid and lacking in enterprise.[39]

The idea that girls are led to sexual delinquencies because of dysfunctional families and unsatisfactory peer relations is also presented in Clyde Vedder and Dora Somerville's *The Delinquent Girl*. Feeling unloved and disapproved of by family and peers, girls are likely to engage in sexual delinquency to gain acceptance and love. Official female delinquency, according to Vedder and Somerville, is dominated by five offense categories: running away, incorrigibility, sexual offenses, probation violation, and truancy (listed in order of decreasing frequency). They suggest that running away and incorrigibility are typically the less "serious" charges filed when such behavior is actually nearly always linked to sexual misbehaviors. To "protect" the girl, officials are more likely to charge her with the more innocuous offense, thus masking the true extent of sexual delinquency among girls.[40]

Some recent attempts to link biological and physiological factors to female delinquency have stressed the effects of hormonal differences between girls and boys. Normally, males produce six times as much testosterone and twice as much androgen as females. Females, on the other hand, produce estrogen in excess of males. These hormonal differences appear to be associated with many of the basic masculine and feminine characteristics of males and females and may have some effect on gender–role behavior. A number of researchers have reported higher levels of testosterone among violent female offenders than among those considered nonviolent.[41] Even though hormonal changes in females linked to the premenstrual phase of the menstrual cycle, known as *premenstrual syndrome* or PMS, may increase irritability, no connection has been found between irritable modes and aggressive behavior, and many of the changes in mood may be due to other factors, such as stressful external events.[42]

Other studies have focused on early physical development and the impact of puberty on girls and delinquency. For example, Dana Haynie examined whether parents treat daughters who are more physically developed differently than less physically developed girls and whether early physical development in girls is related to delinquency. Using data from the *National Longitudinal Study of*

Adolescent Health, Haynie found that girls who are more physically developed than their peers and who are more developed overall are more likely to report smoking cigarettes, drinking alcohol, smoking marijuana, exhibiting disorderly conduct, selling drugs, having gang membership, participating in group fights, and having shot or stabbed someone compared to girls who report average or lower pubertal development. Haynie suggests that this may be due to the more physically developed girl's increased social distance from parents, increased association with male adolescents, greater exposure to older friends, and greater likelihood of involvement in romantic relationships.[43] Terrie Moffitt and her colleagues' continuing analysis of data from the Dunedin Study report similar findings. They found that most antisocial girls' behaviors appear to be related to an attempt to escape a *maturity gap*. That is, their biological maturity has outpaced their social maturity, and they begin to associate with older peers or peers who appear to be older. Moffitt and her colleagues also note that "females are most antisocial soon after puberty and when they are under the influence of relationships with males, who are more antisocial than females on average."[44]

In 2005, Lee Ellis presented the *evolutionary neuroandrogenic theory,* which asserts that (1) aggressive and acquisitive criminal behavior evolved as an aspect of human reproduction, especially among males, and (2) the probability of aggressive and acquisitive criminal behavior is linked to neurochemistry, notably gender-related hormones that promote "competitive/victimizing" behavior. In theorizing that males are more biologically prone to criminal behavior than females, the assumption is that this gender difference in behavior must be related to the one chromosome that males and females do not share, the Y-chromosome. Ellis argues that the Y-chromosome is important because testosterone promotes competitive/victimizing behavior related to brain functioning. Ellis developed the theory to help move criminology beyond strictly social environmental theories toward a new, more comprehensive paradigm that envisions behavior as stemming from the interaction among biological factors rooted in evolutionary history, learning, and social environmental factors.[45]

Sociological Theories

Biological and developmental theories of female delinquency continued to dominate the literature long after theories of male delinquency had shifted to the role of social forces. Their popularity reflected the lingering belief, even among many sociologists, that biological differences between females and males also determined their social behaviors. In this section we examine the ideas of several theorists whose work influenced the development of major bodies of criminological theory.

Durkheim provided the first sociological explanation for why gender differences in homicide exist and how gender murder rates may change across various stages of societal development. Durkheim's ideas were reexamined by criminologist Bruce DiCristina in 2006 who suggested that Durkheim rejected a biological reason for women's lower homicide rates and argued that because women were less active in collective life, they experienced less exposure to the causes of homicide. Durkheim also noted that opportunities to commit homicide differed between the genders and also observed that the effects of gendered socialization caused "homicidal passions" to be ignited in men and not women. Thus, Durkheim's argument is that men have higher rates of homicide than women because their social structural location provides them with greater homicidal opportunities and their socialization has provided them with the "seeds of strong homicidal passions."[46]

Sociological theories of delinquency stressed male patterns of behavior almost exclusively. Misbehavior by girls was treated as extraneous, marginal, and irrelevant. In his 1927 study of 1,313 gangs, for example, Frederic Thrasher devoted only slightly more than one page to the handful of female gangs he found. He attributed the relative absence of girl gangs to the fact that the traditions and customs underpinning socially approved patterns of girls' behaviors are contrary to the activities of gangs. The few girls who did become involved in gangs were accounted for in stereotypic and simplistic terms: "The girl *takes the role of a boy* and is accepted on equal terms with the others. Such a girl is probably a tomboy in the neighborhood."[47]

Clifford Shaw and Henry McKay's studies of the impact of social disorganization on delinquency included analyses of more than 60,000 male delinquents in Chicago. While Shaw and McKay noted the persistence of high delinquency rates in particular zones of the city and argued that these rates were linked to characteristics of the community rather than to the groups of people living in them, they made only brief reference to female delinquency. Delinquency was implicitly defined as a part of the male domain. Whether female delinquency was also a product of social disorganization was not explored.[48] Barbara Warner suggests that social disorganization theory essentially ignores cultural influences, such as gender socialization, on crime.[49] In fact, criminologists have begun to investigate the role of gender in Shaw and McKay's theory. For example, Walter DeKeseredy and his colleagues note that women who live in socially disorganized neighborhoods report higher levels of domestic violence and fear of crime than women living in more affluent neighborhoods.[50]

Robert Merton's strain theory also fails to address the issue of female crime and delinquency. No attempt was made by Merton or his followers to apply his typology of adaptations to women, even though interesting but contradictory implications for females could have been derived from his work.[51] For example, Ruth Morris suggests that the goals of women are fundamentally *relational,* for example, marriage, family, and friends, in contrast to the material goals typically pursued by men. She argues that because most women have lower material aspirations and their goals are more accessible, they do not experience the same stressful conditions as men and therefore are less likely to turn to delinquency. On the other hand, Morris argues that women do have aspirations similar to men, for example, jobs, education, and money, but are denied the same opportunities to achieve them. If this is so, it would follow that female rates of delinquency should be higher than the rates for men.[52] In 2006 Ozden Ozbay and Yusuf Ziya Ozcan tested Merton's strain theory among nearly 2,000 high school students in Ankara, Turkey. Although they found gender differences in terms of educational aspirations and expectations, none were significantly related to delinquency. In fact, upper-class boys and girls were more likely than lower-class youths to commit delinquency, a direct refutation of the theory.[53]

General strain theory has been extended by Robert Agnew and his associates in an attempt to account for differences in the nature and causes of female delinquency. It is argued that females experience different types of strain and respond differently to strain than males, thus producing different behavioral

think
about it

Will female involvement in delinquency ever match or exceed male involvement? Which social factors might facilitate or prevent this from occurring?

outcomes. For example, females experience strains from abusive situations, from excessive demands of family members, problems in maintaining relational networks, low prestige in work and family roles, and restrictions of their behavior as females. Female response to strain also varies and is likely to be tied to gender differences in coping skills, a sense of mastery, and of positive self-esteem. According to Broidy and Agnew, boys experience strains that are more likely to lead to serious property and violent crimes, while girls' strains lead to domestic violence, running away, and self-directed delinquencies, such as drug use. Many of the strains experienced by girls involve greater levels of social control and limitations on opportunities to engage in delinquency. While both boys and girls may respond to strain with anger, the anger of girls is usually tied to emotional problems, such as depression, anxiety, and shame, which also decrease the likelihood of involvement in other-directed delinquent behavior.[54]

In a recent test of Broidy and Agnew's hypotheses, Nicole Piquero and Miriam Sealock examined data from 150 youths detained in juvenile detention facilities. While they found that both males and females who reported more strain were also more likely to self-report higher levels of delinquency, they also found no significant differences in the amount of strain experienced between females and males. What appeared to differ was that females reported higher levels of anger and depression and lower levels of physical and cognitive coping resources than did males. Moreover, and as Piquero and Sealock note,

> The effect of strain on delinquency was not diminished after [they] controlled for negative emotions, and this was especially the case among males. . . . On the other hand, the results indicated that among females, anger was positively related to interpersonal aggression even when strain was not significant in the model, an effect that was not observed for males.[55]

Walter Miller also seemed unconcerned with explaining female delinquency in his classic article on lower-class culture and gang delinquency. His analysis of the "focal concerns" of the lower-class is limited to male adaptations and assumes that such aspirations are exclusive to the lower class. That is, these definitions of "masculinity" are exclusive to the lower class rather than common to all social classes.[56] Eileen Leonard suggests that Miller's focal concerns are not particularly relevant to females even in the lower class: "Given their different location in society, they [girls] are unlikely to be as concerned as males about trouble, toughness, smartness, excitement, fate, and autonomy."[57] Leonard further suggests that if lower-class males and females did have the same focal concerns and if these concerns alone explained the development of delinquent subcultures, their delinquency rates would be similar.

Albert Cohen explicitly defined the problem of delinquency and the development of the delinquent subculture as a male phenomenon. Still, he devoted 11 pages to a discussion of why his work did *not* apply to girls. According to Cohen, boys and girls have different adjustment problems requiring different solutions. The delinquent subculture develops largely as a response to the problems faced by boys and is not an appropriate response for dealing with the problems of girls arising from the female role. Boys, Cohen says, are most interested in their own achievements compared with those of other boys; girls are more interested in their relationships with boys. According to Cohen, "It is within the area of these relationships . . . that a girl finds her fulfillments *as a girl*. It is no accident that 'boys collect stamps, girls collect boys.'" Cohen does recognize the existence of female delinquency, but he defines it primarily as sexual delinquency. According to Cohen, "sex delinquency is one kind of meaningful response to the most characteristic . . . problem of the female role: the establishment of satisfactory relationships with the opposite sex."[58] In a feminist critique of Cohen's work, Ngaire Naffine states:

> The message from Cohen is manifest. Men are the rational doers and achievers. They represent all that is instrumental and productive in American culture. Women's world is on the margins. Women exist to be the companions of men and that is their entire lot. . . . While men proceed with their Olympian task of running all aspects of the nation, women perform their role of helpmate.[59]

Richard Cloward and Lloyd Ohlin's work on delinquency and opportunity focused exclusively on male delinquency produced by the frustrations associated with the unequal distribution of both legitimate and illegitimate opportunities. Females are important only as they contribute to the difficulties boys have in developing a clear masculine image. Boys, in their attempts to establish themselves as males in female-dominated homes and schools, often experience strain:

> Engulfed by a feminine world and uncertain of their own identification, they tend to "protest against femininity." This protest may take the form of robust and aggressive behavior, and even of malicious, irresponsible, and destructive acts.[60]

Because girls are seen as having no difficulty in adapting to their own prescribed female roles within this feminine world, they do not experience this strain. The fact that girls also experience similar unequal distributions in opportunities and that some girls *do* become delinquent was apparently of no interest to Cloward and Ohlin.

Edwin Sutherland offered his *theory of differential association* as a general theory of crime that explains all types of law-violating behaviors. However, he made *no* reference to females or to how differential association may account for their lower rates of delinquency. The implication in his work is that, compared with boys, girls encounter more anticriminal patterns and are exposed to fewer criminal associations and definitions favorable to violation of law. Years later, Sutherland noted that the differences in rates of male and female delinquency are explained by differential associations: "Parents and other intimate associates define one kind of propriety for girls and another for boys, and exercise one kind of supervision over girls and another over boys."[61] Sutherland presumably believed that girls who do become delinquent have less parental supervision and thus develop the same kind of delinquent associations as those developed by delinquent boys (see Chapter 10).

While Sutherland did not specifically test the impact of differential associations on gender differences in delinquency, other criminologists have. Numerous studies have looked at how girls' association with delinquent friends affects their likelihood of engaging in delinquency.[62] Kristan Erickson and her colleagues conducted a longitudinal analysis of gender differences among students from six high schools in California and three high schools in Wisconsin. They found a significantly greater positive effect of having delinquent friends on subsequent delinquency for males than for females.[63] Karen Heimer and Stacy De Coster found that girls learn fewer violent definitions than boys, on average, although the impact of violent definitions on violence is equal across gender.[64] Xiaoru Liu and Howard Kaplan studied 2,753 junior and senior high school students in Houston, Texas, and found that even though females and males engaged in similar levels of minor delinquencies, exposure to delinquent peers was more positively associated with delinquency for males than for females.[65] Finally, Lonn Lanza-Kaduce and his colleagues studied the links between gender, alcohol use, and sexual behavior among students selected from eight universities. They found that men and women who were members of fraternities and sororities were most likely to use alcohol before having sex compared to students who were not Greek-society members, whether male or female. Fraternity men were most likely to use alcohol before having sex, followed in frequency by sorority women. Social learning/differential association theory can help in explaining why sorority women frequently engaged in drinking before sex, in that they tend to associate with fraternity men who are engaging in the same behavior. Less academic success measured by grades had a greater impact on females in increasing alcohol use before sex compared to men with less academic success.[66]

Travis Hirschi's notion of the *social bond*, reflecting a social control perspective, provides a framework for explaining differences in rates of female and male delinquency, although Hirschi himself never explored this possibility. Hirschi's explanation of delinquency was developed from his analysis of a sample of about 4,000 boys; girls were intentionally excluded from the analysis. Coramae Richey Mann commented on this exclusion:

> Travis Hirschi stratified his samples of race, sex, school, and grade. He included 1,076 black girls and 846 nonblack girls; but in the analysis of his data Hirschi admits "the girls disappear," and he adds, "Since girls have been neglected for too long by students of delinquency, the exclusion of them is difficult to justify. I hope I return to them soon." He didn't.[67]

Because social control theory appears to be one of the most powerful explanations of juvenile delinquency generally, it is understandable that criminologists would soon test its application for explaining female delinquency. For example, Rachelle Canter reported that girls had stronger bonds to their parents than did boys, although this attachment had a greater inhibitory effect on delinquency for boys.[68] Other studies have observed that boys are more likely than girls to be negatively influenced by their attachments to delinquent friends and are subsequently more likely than girls to engage in delinquency and substance abuse.[69] A recent study of homeless and runaway youths by Constance Chapple and her colleagues similarly discovered that boys are more likely to get arrested than girls primarily because they have stronger attachments to delinquent peers.[70] On the other hand, some studies have found no differences in boys' and girls' attachment to their parents; gender differences in attachment to parents and peers seem to provide more protection for girls than for boys and consequently reduce the severity of delinquency among girls.[71]

In an extension of social control theory, Michael Gottfredson and Travis Hirschi argue that delinquency is more likely to occur among youth who lack self-control, and this is equally true for girls and boys. Gottfredson and Hirschi also suggest that gender differences in delinquency "appear to be invariant over time and space."[72] The explanation for this difference is found in the substantial gender differences in self-control resulting from early childhood socialization. Girls are socialized to be less impulsive and less risk-taking, more sensitive and verbal rather than physical, more resistant to temptations, and more obedient. It is this difference in socialization, rather than differences in levels of attachment or parental supervision as suggested in social bond theory, that accounts for gender differences in frequency and seriousness of delinquency.[73] Heimer and De Coster argue that female delinquency is controlled through subtle, informal social controls, whereas males are "permitted" to use interpersonal violence.[74] Interestingly, several scholars, including George Higgins and Richard Tewksbury, report that the processes of instilling self-control in children work differently for boys and girls.[75] Teresa LaGrange and Robert Silverman found that the effects of self-control on delinquency operate differently among 2,095 Canadian high school students.[76] Brenda Sims Blackwell and Alex Piquero report similar gender differences using a sample of American adults.[77] While self-control is useful as a general theoretical concept, it seems to explain delinquency better among men than women.

> ## theory in a nutshell
>
> **Michael Gottfredson and Travis Hirschi**
>
> Gottfredson and Hirschi blamed delinquency on low self-control. Girls are less delinquent than boys because girls are socialized to be less impulsive, less risk-taking, more sensitive and verbal rather than physical, more resistant to temptations, and more obedient.

Recent tests of the general theory provide support for the idea that differences in *self-control* largely account for the gender differences in delinquency. Boys exhibit lower self-control than do girls, and this has direct effects on delinquent behavior.[78] Low self-control may also be predictive of female delinquency *and* victimization. Eric Stewart and his colleagues studied a group of 466 drug-using offenders in Atlanta between 1998 and 2000. They found that young women with low self-control are both more likely to engage in risky behaviors and to have higher levels of violent victimization than those with higher self-control.[79]

Writing from the labeling perspective, Edwin Schur argues that women are negatively labeled with great regularity as "aggressive," "bitchy," "hysterical," "fat," "homely," and "promiscuous." According to Schur,

> Judgments such as these, and the social reactions that accompany them, represent a very potent kind of deviance-defining. They may not put the presumed "offender" in jail, but they do typically damage her reputation, induce shame, and lower her "life chances."

Through the process of labeling, an informal form of social control over females is maintained. Earlier in this chapter we discussed how the development of girls' identities worked to keep women in their "place" and how girls were devalued through use of such terms as *slut* or *whore*. See Box 9-3 for a discussion of sexual labeling and control of girls. According to Schur, "When women are effectively stigmatized, that reinforces their overall subordination and makes it more difficult for them to achieve desired goals." Furthermore, the differential enforcement of status offenses for girls can be seen as punishment for "violating or threatening to violate gender-related norms."[80] Current research similarly shows that labels differently affect men and women. Brenda Geiger and

Although adolescent girls and boys frequently engage in harmless bantering, kidding, and joking with each other, all too often the informal verbal interactions take on an insidious, demeaning, and manipulative flavor designed to facilitate boys' control of girls. Mark Fleisher suggests that the use of insulting terms in the verbal dueling of girls and boys in the Freemont area in Kansas City helps to establish social hierarchies, allows for the release of tensions without violence, and defines group membership and friendships. "Boys call girls by the standard list of insulting terms, including bitch, rotten bitch, stank bitch, pussy, cunt, and slut, among others. Girls retaliate with a vengeance, shouting, bastard, prick, pussy, bitch, little dick, . . . among others. Girls call one another by the standard list of insults." The seeming equality of insults, however, masks the actual inequalities in the relationships. According to Fleisher:

Girls think about relationships as moral contracts; boys don't. Beyond the street rhetoric of the gang, girls' implicit construction of relationships, especially with boys, includes fairness, reciprocity, and equality. . . . In what they perceive to be long-term relationships, girls feel an inherent responsibility toward the boys with whom they are involved, but the boys feel neither reciprocity nor fairness nor equality.

Elijah Anderson's study of the informal street code that guides interactions between boys and girls in the inner city of Philadelphia reflects a similar pattern of control in relationships. While many girls "offer sex as a gift" in their attempt to gain a boy's attention, boys define the exchange as only a means to enhance their self-esteem. According to Anderson, "The girls have a dream, the boys a desire. The girls dream of being carried off by a Prince Charming who will love them. . . . The boys often desire either sex without commitment or babies without responsibility for them." The boys want to "score" with as many girls as possible—the more girls he has sex with, the higher his esteem in the eyes of his male peers. "But the young man not only must 'get some'; he also must prove he is getting it. This leads him to talk about girls and sex with any other young man who will listen." Labels may also be used to control boys. If his peers suspect him of becoming too committed to a girl, they are likely to sanction him with "demeaning labels such as pussy, pussy-whipped, or house-husband."

Many of the interviews Mark Totten conducted with 90 Canadian boys ages 13 to 17 in Ottawa, Ontario, reflected the boys' willingness to use demeaning labels to control girls. Steve, a 15-year-old, responded to Totten's question "Do you like girls?"

No, not really . . . I think most of them are stupid bitches. I'll call them bitch, slut, whore all the time. They're always trying to show me up—make me look stupid, like a goof. . . . It's all about knowing your place in society. Some girls do, but most girls don't know what they're supposed to do. . . . We all think that girls should do what we want them to. And it pisses us off when they don't. So I've seen some of them when they've hit girls. And all the time we are just joking around, calling them names—slut, cunt, whore, bitch, fat cow—we all do it.

When boys label girls in this manner as part of their oppression and control of girls, it should not be surprising that boys also express an attitude of negative fatalism with regard to future generations of girls. Philippe Bourgois spent 5 years studying the neighborhood culture of the crack trade in East Harlem. Getting girls pregnant seemingly produced some ambivalence. Many boys took pride in noting how many girls they had impregnated. Luis, for example, bragged about getting a number of girls pregnant in just a 9-month period, but then referred to them as "holes out there." The ambivalence came from thinking about the possibility of the pregnancy producing a daughter. According to one youth, "That's why I would never want to have a daughter, if I was to get my girl pregnant. I couldn't handle the fact of having a baby, and then I have to see her being a ho." And an 11-year-old commented about his mother's pregnancy: "He told us he hoped his mother would give birth to a boy 'because girls are too easy to rape.'"

Sources: Elijah Anderson, *Code of the Street: Decency, Violence, and the Moral Life of the Inner City* (New York: W.W. Norton, 1999); Philippe Bourgois, *In Search of Respect: Selling Crack in El Barrio* (New York: Cambridge University Press, 1995); Mark Fleisher, *Dead End Kids: Gang Girls and the Boys They Know* (Madison: University of Wisconsin Press, 1998); Mark Totten, *Guys, Gangs, & Girlfriend Abuse* (Peterborough, Ontario: Broadview Press, 2000); Deborah Prothrow-Stith and Howard Spivak, *Sugar & Spice and No Longer Nice: How We Can Stop Girls' Violence* (San Francisco: Jossey-Bass, 2005).

think
about it

Edwin Schur argues that females are regularly labeled as "aggressive," "bitchy," "hysterical," or "promiscuous." With such an assortment of negative labels, shouldn't girls be more involved in delinquency?

Michael Fischer conducted a study where offenders were given various labels, such as criminal, prostitute, drug dealer, and incompetent parent. Male offenders were able to ignore or justify each label and still form a positive self-image. Conversely, female offenders were negatively affected by the labels, especially the charge of being an incompetent parent—regardless of whether it was true.[81] As Schur theorized, females appear to feel devalued by pejorative or negative labels.

Marxist–Feminist Theories

Marxist–feminist theories combine the notions of patriarchal male dominance in the home and interpersonal relationships with male control of the means of production. In such an environment, the criminal justice system "defines as crimes those actions that threaten this capitalist–patriarchal system."[82] For example, James Messerschmidt argues that in societies characterized by patriarchal capitalism, male owners control workers, and men control women. Thus, under patriarchal capitalism, women experience *double marginality:* Women are subordinate to both capitalists and men.

Messerschmidt suggests that girls are less likely to be involved in serious delinquencies for three reasons: (1) Most crimes are "masculine" in nature; physical strength, aggressiveness, and external proofs of achievement are facets of the male personality. (2) Because women are subordinate and less powerful, they have fewer opportunities to engage in serious crimes; and (3) males control even illegitimate opportunities, and females are relegated to subordinate roles even in criminal activities. When women do engage in crime, their criminal activity is usually a response to their subordinate and powerless position in patriarchal capitalist society. Such activity may take the form of *privatized resistance,* such as alcoholism, drug abuse, or suicide, or of *accommodation,* which are generally less serious economic crimes including shoplifting and embezzlement.[83]

> **theory in a nutshell**
>
> **James Messerschmidt**
>
> Messerschmidt thinks that girls commit less serious delinquency than boys for three reasons: they lack physical strength, they have fewer opportunities to commit crime, and they occupy subordinate roles even in criminal activities.

Ronald Akers and Christine Sellers have raised important questions about Messerschmidt's general reliance on the patriarchal social structure as an explanation of all types of crimes committed by both females and males. They believe that, for the theory to truly be testable, it would be necessary to be able to measure the specific nature and impact of patriarchy in different parts of society, as well as to examine the relationship of gender inequalities and male and female crime patterns within a cross-cultural perspective.[84] One such test, conducted by Darrell Steffensmeier, Emilie Allan, and Cathy Streifel, involved the examination of arrest data for homicide and major and minor property crimes in a wide range of societies. Steffensmeier and his colleagues found that neither "gender inequality" nor "female economic marginality" was related to female–male arrest ratios in different societies. They noted, instead, that arrest ratios were more significantly related to the degree to which women had access to consumer goods and to the general formalization of social control within the societies. These findings provide very little support for Messerschmidt's claim that patriarchal inequalities produce the gender differences in crime patterns.[85]

Power-control theory, developed by John Hagan and his associates, argues that girls engage in less delinquency because their behavior is more closely monitored and controlled by parents, especially the mother, in patriarchal families. In *patriarchal families* the father works outside the home and has control over others, while the mother stays at home and raises the children. Because the father has a higher control position than the mother, he maintains control over both the wife and the children in the home. *Egalitarian families,* on the other hand, are characterized by a lack of gender differences in the consumption and production spheres. Both parents work and have control positions outside the home, and both share child rearing responsibilities within the home. Parental control is redistributed so that the control over daughters is more like that over sons, and daughters, like sons, are prepared to enter the production sphere and are given greater opportunities for risk taking. This differential treatment leads boys in such families, more so than girls, to engage in greater risk taking, and, consequently, delinquency.[86]

However, Meda Chesney-Lind and Randall Shelden suggest that this is "essentially a not-too-subtle variation of the **liberation hypothesis** that women's liberation directly led to increases in female criminality. Now, mother's liberation or employment causes daughter's crime."[87] They argue there is no evidence to support Hagan's claim that as women's participation in the labor force increases,

Female behavior has historically been defined by stereotypical conceptions of femininity. Does this photo invoke any delinquent imagery? If so, why?

so too will female delinquency. It should be noted, however, that Roy Austin's analysis of labor force participation, divorce rates, and female arrests for minor, major, and occupational offenses *does* lend support to the claim that female liberation is associated with an increase in female criminality.[88]

Hagan and his associate have extended their work to more specifically consider gender differences. Their *gendered power-control theory* links delinquency to subsequent gendered patterns of feelings of anger, despair, and aggressiveness as youth move through adolescent life-course stages. They argue that lower levels of instrumental control of males compared to females in more patriarchal families increases the likelihood of males moving from more direct aggressive delinquency to the use of alcohol and drugs. Alternatively, they believe that "in more patriarchal families higher levels of relational control of females compared with males may yield sequences in which females more often move from indirect, relational involvements in delinquency to feelings of depression."[89]

Numerous tests of power-control theory have been conducted over the past two decades and they have met with mixed findings. For example, Simon Singer and Murray Levine analyzed data from 705 high school youth, and 560 parents and found that, consistent with power-control theory, parents exerted less control over boys than girls, and mothers exerted greater control over girls. However, they also found that boys were more delinquent than girls in egalitarian households, which is contrary to the theory's predictions.[90] Merry Morash and Meda Chesney-Lind, found, in their analysis of the National Survey of Children, that sex differences in delinquency were present regardless of patriarchal or egalitarian family structures.[91] While Hagan and his associates assumed that single-parent families were sufficiently similar to his classification of egalitarian families, other researchers questioned the assumption. Michael Leiber and Mary Ellen Wacker examined data from two samples of juveniles living in single-mother households in Washington and Iowa. Associations with delinquent peers were related to delinquency; however, they found no support for power-control theory.[92] Christopher Uggen examined the relationship between parents' perceptions of their workplace power and control and the delinquencies of their children. He found that "Parental power and control in the workplace increases the rate of arrest among males and decreases it among females. Maternal authority position, in contrast, dramatically raises the risk of arrest among females and reduces this risk among males."[93] Finally, Kristin Mack and Michael Leiber explored how race differences in delinquency between African Americans and whites could reflect differences in household structure; however, they found that for both racial groups, boys simply committed more delinquency than girls regardless of household structure.[94]

Daniel Mears and his colleagues suggest that sex differences in delinquency are more appropriately explained by how girls and boys are differentially affected by the same criminogenic factors due to differences in their moral development. They argue that "the primary socialization of women instills moral values that strongly discourage behavior that hurts or harms others." Thus, moral evaluations by females counteract criminogenic conditions, such as dysfunctional family organization, poverty, and exposure to delinquent friends. Not only are boys more likely than girls to have delinquent friends, it appears that boys also are more likely than girls to be strongly affected by their delinquent peers. According to Mears and his associates, this "reflects the greater effect of moral evaluations in counteracting peer influence among females."[95]

Many feminist criminologists have called for the development of a "feminist" theory of female delinquency, but *no* clearly articulated theory has emerged. The work of Chesney-Lind may come closest. Girls' lower involvement in delinquency is explained by the emphasis placed on their developing nurturing relationships. Chesney-Lind contends that children, female or male, who identify with a nurturing parent who cares for others are likely to develop identities built on an ethic of care and concern for others rather than identities conducive to harming others. It is also noted that men can take on nurturing roles and, since sons can identify just as easily with a nurturing father as with a nurturing mother, such identification can promote prosocial behavior in boys.[96]

> ## theory in a nutshell
> ### Meda Chesney-Lind
> Chesney-Lind argued that girls are less delinquent because they are more often socialized to be nurturing and thus develop identities emphasizing caring for others rather than causing harm to others.

Feminists acknowledge that girls do become delinquent and that any feminist theory of female delinquency must take into consideration the various influences of gender. From this perspective, female delinquency is accounted for by the gender and sexual scripts in patriarchal families that lead girls, more than boys, to be victims of family-related sexual abuse. In patriarchal societies, male–female relationships are unequal, and young women are defined as sexual objects and seen as sexually attractive by older men. Girls become more vulnerable to both physical and sexual abuse because of norms that give males control over females and keep them at home where victimizers have greater access to them. Furthermore, victimizers, usually males, can call upon official agencies of control to keep girls at home. The juvenile court has historically been willing to uncritically support parental control and authority over daughters. Girls who react to abuse by running away from home are often returned to their parents by juvenile authorities. If girls persist in running away, the court may then incarcerate them. Girls who successfully run away often find themselves unable to enroll in school or to obtain reasonable jobs so that they may then be forced into the streets, where their survival may depend on petty crimes such as theft, panhandling, or prostitution.[97]

Differential Oppression Theory

Differential oppression theory also provides a framework for understanding why girls become delinquent as well as why they are less inclined to delinquency than males. This theory argues that adults oppress children as they attempt to impose and maintain adult conceptions of social order. Children are perceived as objects, devalued, and defined as inferior to adults; consequently, they experience a sense of powerlessness and marginality. Adults impose their social order on children frequently through oppressive means. But oppression falls on a continuum, ranging from simple demands for obedience to rules designed for the convenience of adults to the physical or sexual abuse of children. Adults' perceptions of children as inferior, subordinate, and troublemakers allow adults

think about it

Low female involvement in delinquency seriously challenges most criminological theories. Do female offenders require separate theorization? Why might scholars be unwilling to develop "separate but equal" explanations for delinquency based on sex?

to rationalize their oppressive acts. Generally, the more oppressed the child is, the more likely she or he will become delinquent.[98]

Girls in patriarchal societies, however, are **doubly oppressed.** They are oppressed as children *and* as females. The four modes of adaptation include

- Passive acceptance of one's status.
- Manipulation of peers to gain power.
- Exercise of illegitimate coercive power.
- Retaliation.[99]

Most girls adapt to oppression through *passive acceptance* of their subordinate and inferior status. Their obedience is built upon fear, which derives from implied threats and intimidation. However, this passive acceptance may be only a façade, presenting to the oppressor the appearance of conformity. Girls outwardly appear to accept their inferior positions but develop a repressed hatred for their oppressors, adapting to the structures of domination in which they are immersed. Once a situation of violence and oppression has been established, it engenders an entire way of life and behaviors for those caught up in it.[100]

Some girls adapt to their oppression through the exercise of *illegitimate coercive power.* They are attracted to delinquency because it helps them to

Differential oppression theory contends that girls turn to prostitution because it helps establish a sense of power and autonomy. What are other reasons girls turn to prostitution? Is sex a form of social capital for them?

establish a sense of autonomy and control. This anticipatory delinquency is a yearning for adult status. Delinquent acts can immediately and demonstratively make things happen. Sexual misbehavior, illicit use of drugs or alcohol, and violations of the criminal law derive greater symbolic importance for the girl to the extent that they reflect her own control over her behavior. The "sneaky thrill" that accompanies shoplifting, drug use, or illicit sexual encounters, for example, is not simply a product of the rush of the act but a consequence of the girl knowing that *she* is controlling the event.

Through *manipulation of one's peers,* girls who have experienced oppression at the hands of adults may acquire a sense of strength and control or a degree of empowerment not otherwise felt. Bullying younger or smaller children at school may be a form of displacement of a girl's anger at a parent or teacher (see Chapter 11). Girls also verbally bully or manipulate peers, especially female peers, in an attempt to establish social hierarchies, eliminate competition for attention, release tensions without violence, or define group membership and friendships.[101]

Girls may engage in *retaliation* or "getting back" at the people or the institutions they believe are the source of their oppression. Some adolescent girls who are severely physically or sexually abused by parents may retaliate by striking directly at their parents, assaulting or killing them. Not only larger, stronger girls strike back at an abusive parent. Some smaller, physically weaker children may fight back by compensating with speed and choice of weapon. For example, a young girl may wait until her parents are asleep and then torch the home. Or, she may retaliate by striking at a substitute, such as a younger sibling who is viewed as representative of her parents. Finally, many girls retaliate against their parents by turning inward—by becoming chronically depressed or contemplating or committing suicide. According to the Centers for Disease Control and Prevention, one in four female students surveyed had seriously considered attempting suicide during some time during the 12 months prior to the survey, 16 percent had made a specific plan to attempt suicide, 11 percent had actually attempted suicide, and 3 percent made a suicide attempt resulting in an injury, poisoning, or overdose requiring medical attention.[102]

Adult conceptions in patriarchal societies of the *girl as female* (relational, nurturing, and passive) contribute to their oppression. This reinforces traditional gender roles and, subsequently, to the girl's identity as "object." Treated as an object, a girl may adapt by developing an identity through relationships with boys; she does not have to "prove" her own worth as long as she is "related" to a proven person. Consequently, her delinquencies may be indirect and relational. Being defined as a female object may also reinforce the identity of the girl as a "sexual object." In this case, adaptations may take the form of sexual delinquencies and prostitution.

But oppression of girls as females also carries with it a reinforcement of more domestic, passive, relational, and nurturing roles that often exclude them from the outside world of male street–peer groups. Not only are girls more closely monitored and kept closer to home; they are encouraged to identify with their mothers and to concentrate on building and maintaining relations. In addition, girls learn to anticipate economic dependence and the need to develop intimate interpersonal ties through which a sense of value and self-esteem may be gained. At the same time, they are discouraged from pursuing independent acts and risk-taking activities. As girls develop identities that reinforce positive, prosocial, and nurturing relations with others stressing caring and fairness, they are less likely to engage in behaviors harmful to others.

Differential oppression theory, as applied to female delinquency, builds on earlier work stressing differences in social-

ization patterns of girls and boys and views the role of socialization of adolescent girls within the context of oppression. While male adolescents experience the oppression of being a child, female adolescents experience the *double* oppression of being a female child. The socialization of girls leads not only to their being less likely to engage in delinquency in general but also to their likelihood of engaging in particular forms of delinquency.

Juvenile Justice Policy Applications

Criminological theorizing about delinquency has typically focused on male, rather than female, delinquency. The same criminological gaze through male eyes has led to a marginalizing or minimizing of policies and programs aimed at preventing or treating female delinquency. Recognizing this, Meda Chesney-Lind argues that "girls involved in the juvenile justice system are particularly invisible in terms of programming." According to Chesney-Lind, most programs offered for females are based on stereotypes of "girls' issues," such as teen pregnancy, sexual abuse, or gang violence, and focus on intervention in the lives of girls already in trouble rather than on prevention for girls who are at risk of involvement in delinquency. Moreover, most traditional delinquency programs for girls have been built around commonsense understandings about what adolescent boys need. These may sometimes work for girls, or for some girls, and sometimes they may not.[103]

There are approaches that Chesney-Lind believes may be effective, including policies and programs designed to protect girls from physical and sexual violence, to reduce the risk of HIV-AIDS and pregnancy, to deal with unemployment and job training, to locate safe and affordable housing, to assist in managing family problems and stress, and to develop a sense of empowerment (see Box 9-4 for additional discussion on female delinquency programming). Finally, Chesney-Lind suggests that programs for at-risk girls need to create separate time and space for girls, separate from boys, so that issues related to sexism will not be overshadowed by boys' more disruptive behavior.

box 9-4   **DELINQUENCY PREVENTION**
Improving Programming for Girls

A model for developing appropriate female delinquency prevention programs through the identification of special needs of female adolescents may be found in a series of studies undertaken by Barbara Bloom and her colleagues. This needs assessment gathered information on the needs of girls and young women in California through extensive interviews and focus groups with juvenile justice personnel, including judges, probation officer, and program staff, as well as with girls and young women around the state. Data were collected for the following issue areas:

• Factors contributing to delinquency and other risk behavior.
• Types of problems experienced by girls and young women.
• Types of help and services needed.
• Obstacles in seeking help.
• Program gaps and barriers.
• Effective program elements.

The researchers noted a number of findings. First, family issues, including parent–child conflicts, parental absence, parental drug use and criminality, and lack of parent–child communication were believed to significantly contribute to female offending. Second, emotional, physical, and sexual abuses were significantly related to delinquency, yet few programs address the girls' specific needs. Third, while running away from home is likely to lead to delinquency, there are very few safe options for girls who believe they can no longer live at home. Fourth, although drug abuse typically leads to other delinquent behaviors, there are few substance abuse programs, including prevention and residential care that specifically focus on the needs of girls. Fifth, adolescent females' attitudes of independence and ambivalence toward parental discipline and guidance appeared problematic, often leading to resistance to seeking help from adults. Sixth, because school difficulties and negative attitudes toward school often lead to excessive truancy and dropping out, schools were identified as key locations and opportunities for early intervention for at-risk girls. Finally, early sexual activity by girls is related to other risky behaviors and is predictive of delinquency and suggestive of the need for special female-focused sex education programming.

Bloom and her associates also found significant barriers to effective programming for female delinquents. These barriers included such problems as deficiencies in funding and resources, especially for female-focused programs; family resistance, especially lack of parental involvement or support; long waiting lists for services; and girls' distrust and fear of people in positions of authority.

Many suggestions for program change were offered. Most respondents said that greater and improved information about what works for girls was needed and that existing programs should be designed to address the wide range of specific problems, issues, and needs of girls. Programs should use gender-specific models to address issues of care and services for girls, and a gendered focus should apply to aftercare and follow-up services. In addition, training and education of those working with girls in the juvenile justice system must provide understanding into the unique dynamics of female crime; the needs of girls are very different from those of males. Finally, programs should be designed to address the particular situations of girls in society and tailored to the real-world problems of girls. All of these efforts should be gender specific and gender appropriate.

Sources: Barbara Bloom, Barbara Owen, Elizabeth Deschenes, and Jill Rosenbaum, "Moving Toward Justice for Female Juvenile Offenders in the New Millennium: Modeling Gender-Specific Policies and Programs," *Journal of Contemporary Criminal Justice* 18:37–57 (2002); Barbara Bloom, Barbara Owen, Elizabeth Deschenes, and Jill Rosenbaum, "Improving Juvenile Justice for Females: A Statewide Assessment in California," *Crime & Delinquency* 48:526–552 (2002); Barbara Bloom, Barbara Owen, Jill Rosenbaum, and Elizabeth Deschenes, "Focusing on Girls and Young Women: A Gendered Perspective on Female Delinquency," *Women & Criminal Justice* 14:117–136 (2003); Joanne Belknap and Kristi Holsinger, "The Gendered Nature of Risk Factors for Delinquency," *Feminist Criminology* 1:48–71 (2006); Kristy Holtfreter and Merry Morash, "The Needs of Women Offenders: Implications for Correctional Programming," *Women & Criminal Justice* 14:137–160 (2003); Amy Farrell, "Women, Crime, and Drugs: Testing the Effect of Therapeutic Communities," *Women & Criminal Justice* 11:21–48 (2000).

conclusions

The study of delinquency over the past century has focused almost exclusively on male behavior. The marginal treatment of females reflects the realities of a patriarchal society in which males control the sexuality and labor of women. Girls grow up in a society in which they are presumed to be "inferior" to boys and are socialized into sexually stereotypic gender roles beginning at birth.

Early explanations of female delinquency stressed the biological and developmental differences between the constitutional makeup of females and that of males: Female delinquents were seen as atavistic, inferior, unadjusted, and inherently deceitful. More recent biological and developmental theories have explored girls' emotional problems and differences in hormonal levels and early physical development as factors leading to delinquency.

Early sociological theories shifted attention from individual characteristics or flaws to the role of social forces in delinquency. Although they often ignored female delinquency or saw it as irrelevant in explaining the real problems of crime, more recent tests of many of the theories appear to provide partial explanations for gender differences in patterns of delinquency. Marxist and feminist theories, stressing the effects of patriarchy and capitalism in society on females, have focused attention on the role of control and supervision of girls in limiting their activities, including delinquency. Finally, differential oppression theory emphasizes the impact of the *double* oppression that girls face as children and as females. These modes of oppression account for both the lower rates of female delinquency as well as the particular adaptive reactions of girls to oppression, which often include delinquency.

key terms

Chivalry hypothesis   The notion that lower rates of crime among females reflect men's deference and protective attitude toward women whereby female offenses are generally overlooked or excused by males.

Differential oppression theory   The theory that provides a framework for understanding why girls become delinquent as well as why they are less inclined to delinquency than males.

Doubly oppressed   The idea that adolescent girls are oppressed both as children and as females.

Gender–role identities   Individual identities based on sexual stereotypes.

Liberation hypothesis   The belief that changes brought about by the women's movement triggered a wave of female crime.

Patriarchy   A social system that enforces masculine control of the sexuality and labor power of women.

Power-control theory   The theory that emphasizes the consequences of the power relations of husbands and wives in the workplace on the lives of children.

section 3

The Social Context of Delinquency

outline

PREVIOUS SECTIONS OF the text examined the nature of juvenile delinquency as it has come to be defined, measured, and explained. How delinquency is defined and measured largely determines how criminologists explain it. The theories and explanations that have evolved, however, must also be connected to the social reality of delinquency. This section examines juvenile delinquency within its societal context.

Juvenile delinquency is closely tied to those social groupings or institutions where children spend most of their time: with the family, in school, and with friends. Chapter 10 examines the family and the issues that directly or indirectly contribute to a child's delinquency. The traditional functions of the family, socializing of children, inculcating moral values, regulating sexual activity, and providing material, physical, and emotional security, as well as the traditional structure of the family, have undergone substantial change during the past 40 years. Many of the changes have caused increased tension, anxiety, and conflict within the family. Single-parent families, working mothers, and inadequate parenting skills have been identified as contributing to delinquency. So, too, have the problems of divorce, including custody battles, forced visitation, and failure to pay court-ordered support for noncustodial children. To whatever extent basic parenting skills and structural change within families impact the likelihood of delinquency, current research is rather consistently suggesting there are even greater effects produced by familial maltreatment of children.

Children spend close to half their waking hours in school. Chapter 11 explores how schools are not only locations of adolescent crime, but may directly or indirectly contribute to the problem of youth crime. Although violent

(continued)

crime has declined in schools in recent years, students and teachers are still victimized. Bullying has recently gained national attention as a possible correlate, if not cause, of school violence. Schools continue to grapple with the problems associated with both high rates of dropouts and troublesome students who stay in school. To what extent do the built-in stresses and conflicts of the schooling process, the temptations and pressures of peers, and the enforcement of school rules with sanctions ranging from suspensions to corporal punishment contribute to disruptive behaviors and more serious delinquencies?

Chapter 12 looks at juvenile delinquency within the context of peer groups and gangs. Are children more likely to violate norms and laws when with their friends? Are juvenile gangs simply more formal and violent expressions of more normal school and neighborhood peer groups? Why do juveniles form gangs? How do the cultural experiences of various racial and ethnic groups affect the development of juvenile gangs? Although criminologists ponder the difficulties in defining gangs, local law enforcement and politicians often draw upon statutory definitions to support get-tough approaches to gang suppression. Might intervention and prevention policies provide a more effective long-term solution to the gang problem? ●

10

The Family and Delinquency

The family is the most important social institution. The earliest and most critical stages of a child's socialization occur within the family. The family is largely responsible for instilling in children important moral and religious values and understanding about right and wrong. However, as a Chinese proverb states, "No family is perfect; nobody's family can claim they do not have problems." Family problems, however, vary greatly in both type and magnitude (See box 10-1). The problems of some families may be minor and produce only small consequences for family members. Other families may experience greater problems, and the impact on its members may be significant. One problem families often face is juvenile delinquency.

The family has long been considered an important player in producing or reducing delinquency. For example, in 1915 Douglas Morrison wrote that "among social circumstances which have a hand in determining the future of the individual it is enough for our present purpose to recognize that the family is chief."[1] How do families contribute to the delinquent behavior of their children? In this chapter, after discussing traditional functions of the family, we will explore the effects of varying family structures, family dynamics, and parenting styles on delinquency.

TRADITIONAL FUNCTIONS OF THE FAMILY

Traditionally, the family has performed four principal functions: the socialization of children, the inculcation of moral values, the reproduction and the regulation of sexual activity, and the provision of material, physical, and emotional security.

The Socialization of Children

The family is the first and most important social unit to affect children; it is the first social world the child encounters. Socialization is the process through which children learn the ways of a particular society or social group so that they can function within it. Individuals learn the attitudes, behaviors, and social roles considered appropriate for them from already-socialized individuals, typically parents and other family members. Through the socialization process in families, the personalities, values, and beliefs of children are initially shaped. Families aid in the development of stable and emotionally secure individuals and enhance the cognitive and language development of children by providing a variety of intellectually rich and stimulating experiences. Parents and older family members also serve as role models, transmitting educational values, and provide environments in which children can safely develop a sense of autonomy.[2] But families are not isolated groups. Rather, they exist within a larger social and cultural context and will reflect the family's particular class, ethnic, racial, religious, political, and regional characteristics. This means that a child's socialization is somewhat selective, depending on the background and contextual experiences of his or her particular family.[3]

box 10-1   A WINDOW ON DELINQUENCY

Family Violence in the United States

Family violence is a troubling public-health problem that produces many negative consequences for children. These include increased school problems, alcohol and substance abuse, delinquency, and mental health problems, such as depression. Witnessing, perpetrating, or being the victim of family violence during childhood or adolescence also significantly increases the likelihood that a child will use violence against partners and family members. How prevalent is family violence? The following snapshot contains national data from surveys conducted by the Bureau of Justice Statistics and databases maintained by the Federal Bureau of Investigation.

• The rate of family violence is 2 victims per 1,000 U.S. residents age 12 or older.

• Between 1998 and 2002, about 4 million violent family crimes were committed, which is 11 percent of all violent victimizations.

• 49 percent of all family violence is perpetrated against a spouse.

• Simple assault is the most common form of family violence.

• Between 1998 and 2002, about 0.5 percent incidents of family violence were murders.

• About 75 percent of family violence occurs in or near the victim's residence.

• Women comprise 73 percent of family violence victims, including 84 percent of spousal assault victimizations.

• About 75 percent of the perpetrators of family violence are men.

• Most family violence victims are white (74 percent) and between the ages of 25 and 54 (66 percent). Most family violence offenders are also white (79 percent) and age 30 or older (62 percent).

• About 60 percent of family violence victimizations are reported to police.

• Of the two million incidents of family violence reported to police from 1998 to 2002, 36 percent resulted in an arrest.

• About 75,000 offenders are currently serving time in state prisons for family violence convictions.

Sources: Matthew Durose, Caroline Wolf Harlow, Patrick Langan, Mark Motivans, Ramona Rantala, and Erica Smith, *Family Violence Statistics* (Washington, DC: U. S. Department of Justice, 2005); Kathleen Sternberg, Michael Lamb, Eva Guterman, and Craig Abbott, "The Effects of Early and Later Family Violence on Behavior Problems and Depression," *Child Abuse & Neglect* 30:283–306 (2006); Rochelle Hanson, Shannon Self-Brown, Adrienne Fricker-Elhai, Dean Kilpatrick, Benjamin Saunders, and Heidi Resnick, "Relations between Family Environment and Violence Exposure among Youth: Findings from the National Survey of Adolescents," *Child Maltreatment* 11:3–15 (2006).

At a theoretical level, families are also the primary locus for teaching children self-control, which is a major inhibitor of delinquency. You may recall from Chapter 7 that Michael Gottfredson and Travis Hirschi argue that adolescents who have low self-control are more likely to participate in delinquency than are youth with greater self-control, and the primary "'cause' of low self-control is ineffective child-rearing."[4] While we will discuss parenting or child rearing practices at greater length later in this chapter, a key ingredient in the socialization of children is the development of an appropriate level of self-control. Unfortunately, our own families and even our *family structure* can contribute to delinquency. In 2006 economists that study birth order discovered that merely having an older sibling increases the likelihood that younger brothers and sisters will misbehave. Younger siblings were 3 to 7 percent more likely to smoke cigarettes, drink alcohol, smoke marijuana, and be sexually active if they had an older brother or sister. While the purpose of the family is to socialize children for positive behaviors, inappropriate socialization can have negative consequences (See box 10-2).[5]

Inculcation of Moral Values

One of the most critical aspects of socialization is the development of moral values in children. Moral education, or the training of the individual to be inclined toward the good, involves a number of things, including the rules of society and the development of good habits.[6] Youth who have developed higher levels of prosocial moral reasoning, such as operating according to empathetic motives and internalizing values that would lead youth to act in ways to benefit others and society, are less likely to engage in aggressive behavior and delinquency.[7] Although the church and school complement the family in both teaching and setting examples of moral behavior, it is in the family where the development of

---

box 10-2 **A WINDOW ON DELINQUENCY**

Prisoner Parents and Its Effects

Children who grow up to be well-functioning adults experience security and stability as they develop and are effectively socialized to take on roles in society. Children who grow up in families where a parent is incarcerated may have experiences that do not promote development into a well-functioning adult. In other words, having mom or dad in prison is not normal and probably will result in many negative outcomes for children. What are these outcomes?

Anne Dannerbeck examined 1,112 juvenile offenders in Missouri, 31 percent of whom had a parental history of incarceration. She found that parents who had previously been imprisoned:

• Exhibited lower levels of effective parenting.
• Exhibited higher levels of ineffective parenting.
• Exhibited more substance abuse problems.
• Exhibited more psychiatric problems.
• Were more likely to physically abuse their children.
• Were more likely to lose their children to out-of-home placement.

• Were significantly more likely to have children with serious delinquent histories.

The multifaceted negative effects of prisoner parents on children are not limited to the United States. For instance, Joseph Murray and David Farrington evaluated the effects of parental imprisonment on a cohort of London boys during the first 10 years of life. The results were dramatic. Boys whose mother or father had been imprisoned were significantly more delinquent than their peers who had more normal upbringings. In fact, the independent effect of parental imprisonment continued to predict antisocial behavior and crime when the boys were 32. In short, prisoner parents inflict a variety of serious risks on their children, many of which continue to cause problems into adulthood.

Sources: Anne Dannerbeck, "Differences in Parenting Attributes, Experiences, and Behaviors of Delinquent Youth With and Without a Parental History of Incarceration," *Youth Violence and Juvenile Justice* 3:199–213 (2005); Joseph Murray and David Farrington, "Parental Imprisonment: Effects on Boys' Antisocial Behavior and Delinquency through the Life-Course," *Journal of Child Psychology and Psychiatry* 46:1269–1278 (2005); David Farrington and Brandon Welsh, *Saving Children from a Life of Crime: Early Risk Factors and Effective Interventions* (New York: Oxford University Press, 2007).

moral virtue or good character is effectively formed or left unformed.[8] Robert Coles puts it this way:

> Good children are boys and girls who in the first place have learned to take seriously the very notion, the desirability, of goodness—a living up to the Golden Rule, a respect for others, a commitment of mind, heart, soul to one's family, neighborhood, nation—and have also learned that the issue of goodness is not an abstract one, but rather a concrete, expressive one: how to turn the rhetoric of goodness into action, moments that affirm the presence of goodness in a particular lived life.[9]

Similarly, the Children's Defense Fund advocates that every child deserves a moral start in life, meaning that he or she should be taught the enduring values of honesty, hard work, discipline, respect for self and others, responsibility, and doing unto others as they would have done to themselves.[10]

Emile Durkheim believed the integrative function of religion was crucial for maintaining social order. Social cohesion was enhanced through shared values and norms generally originating from religious practice. When parents view religion as important, communicate religious values and practices to their children, and involve their children in religious activities, inclinations toward delinquency are reduced. Religious beliefs, according to Bruce Chadwick and Brent Top, have long been understood to be the foundation for moral behavior, and thus, "the more religious a person is, the less likely he or she will be to participate in delinquent or criminal behaviors."[11]

There is much evidence that an adolescent's religiosity, typically measured by religious participation, including church attendance, private prayer, Bible study, discussing one's belief in God with others, belief in this-world or other-worldly sanctions, and attitudes and behaviors reflecting an individual's commitment to the religious teachings of his or her faith, is negatively related to delinquency.

In families, children learn the ways of society. They learn attitudes, behaviors, and social roles. The children in this family are learning about the importance of education.

A recent meta-analysis of 60 published studies conducted over the last 30 years examining the relationship between religion and delinquency concluded that "religious behavior and beliefs exert a significant, moderate deterrent effect on individuals' criminal behavior."[12] A recent study by Byron Johnson and his colleagues examined the impact of religiosity on over 2,300 at-risk African American juveniles living in poverty tracts in Boston, Chicago, and Philadelphia. They found that church attendance, even after controlling for background and other nonreligious variables, such as secular bonding and informal social controls through the family and school, has an independent effect on nondrug crime, drug use, and drug dealing among the disadvantaged youth.[13] Other studies also find a religion to have a deterrent impact on delinquency. For example, Brent Benda and Robert Corwyn looked at random samples of youth from two public schools in the inner-city of a large, East Coast city and from three rural public schools in the South. They concluded that "religion is inversely related to crime among adolescents in both urban and rural public schools," although it did not appear to affect illicit drug use. Benda and Corwyn speculate that drug use may have reached a widely "normalized" level of acceptable behavior within teen culture.[14]

Interestingly, the most frequently cited work on this topic is "Hellfire and Delinquency" published by Travis Hirschi and Rodney Stark. They reported that there was no link between religiosity (based on church and Sunday school attendance and belief in Hell) and delinquent behavior.[15] The popularity of the study's findings "that religion fails to guide teenagers along the straight and narrow was soon enshrined in undergraduate textbooks."[16] Subsequent research, however, consistently found strong negative effects of religion on delinquency. Stark accounts for the relative uniqueness of their findings as a product of their study being done in the Far West where there is very low religious involvement compared to other regions of the country. Studies conducted in the East, South, Midwest, and Mountain states have consistently found an adolescent's religiosity, especially when reinforced by family and peer religiousness, to have a preventative effect on delinquency.[17] Today, Stark is not hesitant to state: "Other things being equal, religious individuals will be less likely than those who are not religious to commit deviant acts."[18]

Reproduction and Regulation of Sexual Activity

The family is the traditional social unit for sexual reproduction. The family teaches children society's norms about sexual conduct, what is acceptable, and what is unacceptable. In the family, children learn at what age, with whom, and under what circumstances they may engage in sexual relationships. Children also learn in the family about the consequences of sexual activity; that is, if pregnancy occurs, who is responsible for the care and maintenance of the infant and how such care should be provided.[19]

Provision of Material, Physical, and Emotional Security

Families are the primary providers of the material well-being of their members. The family clothes, feeds, and provides shelter. Parents or older siblings provide supervision and monitoring of younger children to ensure their safety and obedience. In addition, the family provides for the physical security of its members, and the mere presence of family members in the home functions to protect the family from potential thieves, vandals, and burglars.[20] Finally, the family provides emotional security to its members by giving encouragement, support, and unconditional love.

The provisions that families, especially parents, provide to children are cumulative. In many ways, some of the best predictors of a child's life outcomes are his or her parents' backgrounds. Steven Levitt and Stephen Dubner suggest that "who" your parents are is more meaningful in explaining children's success or failure than their parenting ability. Levitt and Dubner found that a child with at least 50 children's books in his or her room scores about five percentile points higher than a child with no books, and a child with 100 books scores another five percentile points higher than a child with 50 books. Highly educated, well-paid parents who waited until age 30 to start families have children with the highest test scores. Other important parenting factors, such as TV watching, whether mom worked, whether children went to museums, and whether the child attended Head Start, did not affect test scores nearly as much. Levitt and Dubner suggest that parenting techniques are highly overrated when it comes to assessing the material and human resources of children. By the time most parents pick up a book on parenting technique, it's too late. Many of the things that matter most were decided long ago, such as the parents' education, how hard they worked to build careers, who they married, and how long they waited to have children.[21]

The world, however, is not perfect, and many families fail miserably at achieving one or more of these goals. Families, unfortunately, often transmit values that promote violence or criminality and undermine the development of positive self-concepts among children. Too often, families fail to inculcate moral values or virtues in their young. Too many families fail to teach proper sexual conduct. And too many families fail to provide adequate material, physical, and emotional security to its members when parents divorce or fail to marry in the first place or when they engage in disreputable or criminal behavior, thereby ignoring the primary needs of the children. Such failures of the family are not new, but there is evidence that recent changes in the family have significantly contributed to problem behaviors, including delinquency.

think about it

Is sexual behavior during adolescence intrinsically delinquent?

THE CHANGING FAMILY

A number of changes in the American family during the past few decades have prompted both controversy and debate over the meaning and implications of the trends. In 1970, 85 percent of children under age 18 lived with both mother and father; by 2005, only 67 percent of children lived with both parents. Approximately 20 million children live with one parent, 17.2 million lived with their mothers and 3.5 million, with their fathers. It is expected that during the first decade of the 21st century a majority of children will spend a portion of their childhood in families with only one parent.[22] In 2006, for the first time in American history, the majority of households (50.2 percent) were comprised of unmarried couples.[23] Also in 2006 nearly 40 percent of babies born in the United States were out of wedlock, births that were once referred to as "illegitimate births." Whereas once out-of-wedlock births were considered taboo, today they are so commonplace that they are statistically almost the norm.[24]

This trend is troubling. According to James Q. Wilson:

> Compared to children who are raised by their biological father and mother, those raised by mothers, black or white, who have never married are more likely to be poor, to acquire less schooling, to be expelled or suspended from school, to experience emotional or behavioral problems, to display antisocial behavior, to have trouble getting along with their peers, and to start their own single-parent families. These unhappy outcomes afflict both girls and boys, but they have a more adverse effect on boys.[25]

Changes in the American family produce many unintended consequences, including the most serious forms of delinquency. For example, Jennifer Schwartz has examined whether family structure influences the murder rate. It does. Counties with greater levels of family disruption, defined as single-parent, female-headed households, have higher murder rates than counties with traditional family structures. Schwartz found that a 1 percent increase in a community's level of family disruption increased homicides by women 11 percent and by men 25 percent. In places where at least 20 percent of the households are female-headed, the male homicide rate is 125 percent higher while the female homicide rate is 55 percent higher.[26]

There are many other changes in the 21st century American family. Some of these changes are good, some are bad, and some are just different. For example, the United States is becoming a more adult-focused society after being child-focused for decades. Longer life expectancy, delayed marriage and child rearing, and more childlessness equate to a longer life without children. In a way, raising children, once central to most adults' lives, has become a niche in the life course.[27] On the other hand, other research indicates that both married and single parents are spending more time with their children, almost as much as they did 40 years ago. Also, men perform more housework than ever before.[28] How does this relate to satisfaction with family life? The Pew Research Center conducted a poll of 3,000 Americans and found that family ties are as strong as ever. About 42 percent of adults see or talk to a parent daily, an increase of 10 percent from 1989. Nearly 80 percent of adults have daily contact with distant relatives each day usually through e-mail or telephone. Overall, 72 percent of adults indicated that they were very satisfied with their family life.[29]

Perhaps because of these changing trends, persons in other countries hold conflicting opinions of the American family. According to family researchers, persons living in certain Asian, African, and South American countries consider the American nuclear family of husband, wife, and children (and not extended relatives and in-laws) to be the ideal family composition. American families are also lauded for marriages based on love and companionship (rather than arranged marriages), material comfort, and independence. However, American families are criticized for placing too much emphasis on work and not enough emphasis on children as well as being selfish and overly individualistic.[30]

Single-Parent Families

What might account for the increase in **single-parent families**? Linda Gordon and Sara McLanahan point out that in 1900 only about 5 percent of all children in single-parent homes were living with a parent who was divorced or had never married. Most of the parents in these homes were widowed.[31] However, by the early 21st century only about 5 percent of all female-headed households with children had experienced the death of the father; about 37 percent had experienced parental divorce; and in 36 percent of these homes, the parents had never married. The remaining 22 percent of the households were classified as "married, spouse absent."[32]

Nearly one million American teenagers become pregnant each year. About 40 percent abort their pregnancies. The birthrate for teenagers ages 15–18 was 42 per 1,000. Teenage birthrates vary by race. For example, the birthrate for white, non-Latino teenagers was 27; for African American teenagers, 64; and for Hispanic teenagers, 82. Teen birthrates also vary by location. For example, the teen birthrate in Miami (174 per 1,000) is six times that in San Francisco and Seattle (28 per 1,000), and teen birthrates in most large cities are well above the national average; 41 of the 50 largest cities had birthrates above the national average. Most teenage births are to unmarried teenagers. Although the birthrate for unmarried teenagers has fallen since 1991, births to unmarried girls ages 15–17 accounted for 88 percent of teen births, while about 97 percent of births to girls younger than 15 years were unmarried.[33]

Single-parent families are not evenly distributed across racial and ethnic groups. Today, approximately 23 percent of white children, 35 percent of Hispanic children, and 64 percent of African American children are being raised by a single parent. Single-parent families also are disproportionately at or near the poverty level: The poverty rate for single-parent families is approximately five times higher than for two-parent families. Eight percent of children in two-parent families live in poverty, while 33 percent of children in female-headed families are at or below the poverty level. And although race and ethnicity are related to poverty, such dramatic differences in family poverty rates are not a function of race or ethnicity. Only 10 percent of African American children living with their married parents live in poverty, while nearly 50 percent of African American children living in female-headed households live below the poverty level.[34]

Teenage mothers are three times more likely than other teenagers to drop out of school, and they will earn less money than unmarried mothers who did not have their first child until they were in their twenties. They are also likely to spend longer periods of time living in poverty. For instance, Sara Jaffee and her colleagues studied the effects of teenage motherhood on their children 20 years later. About 40 percent of the negative life outcomes that these youths experienced, such as delinquency, unemployment, school failure, and adult crime, were directly and independently explained by their mother giving birth as a teenager.[35] Overall, teenage childbearing is costly to taxpayers, with the federal government spending about $40 billion each year to assist families that began with a teenage birth.[36] Travis Hirschi points out; however, the teenage mother herself should not be targeted as the primary problem. According to Hirschi, "the teenage mother is not the problem. . . . The problem is the mother without a husband. Her children are likely to be delinquent, and she is likely to have more of them." He argues there should be two parents for every child and that delinquency can be reduced by improving the quality of child-rearing practices. This means strengthening the bonds not only between parents and children but also between husbands and wives.[37]

What about teenage fathers? What are the consequences of fatherhood for adolescent boys? Somewhere between 2 and 7 percent of male teenagers are

think
about it

How do the various data on the disintegration of the African American family suggest a causal relationship to delinquency?

fathers. Teen fatherhood is associated with growing up in poverty and hanging out with friends who engage in delinquency and other problem behaviors. Like teenage mothers, teenage fathers experience many negative educational, financial, social, health, and other developmental consequences. They are more likely to drop out of school and to enter the workplace earlier than their peers and to earn less money than their peers when they reach their mid-twenties. Interestingly, boys who become teenage fathers are also likely to engage in a variety of other problem behaviors, such as status offenses, disruptive school behavior, and illicit drug use. According to Terence Thornberry and his colleagues:

> Young fathers tended to be troubled young men who were significantly more likely than their matched controls to have engaged in varied serious acts of delinquency in the year of fatherhood and in the year after. . . . They were more likely than non-fathers to have had a court petition alleging delinquency, to be drinking alcohol frequently, to be involved in drug dealing, or to have dropped out of school.[38]

Unfortunately, teen fathers are unlikely to be in a position to provide financial, emotional, or other parental support for their children, and thus are likely to be poor role models. As Thornberry and his associates note, "Their legacy to their children is likely to be one of socioeconomic disadvantage, poorer health, and poorer education, among other hardships."[39]

There is also an interesting relationship between teenage fatherhood and serious delinquent behavior. That is, chronic delinquents are significantly more likely to father children than are less seriously delinquents and nondelinquents. Evelyn Wei and her colleagues' analysis of a sample of youth in the Pittsburgh Youth Study found that by age 19, nearly half of the serious repeat offenders had caused at least one pregnancy and about one-third had fathered at least one child. They also report that "repeat serious delinquents were not only more likely to father children during adolescence; many had fathered multiple children, accounting for 65 percent of the offspring produced by teenage fathers. And although these youth produced many children, they were less likely to be living with or to spend time with their children."[40]

Children in poor, single-parent families, especially those headed by teenage mothers, clearly face special difficulties. They are more likely to experience chronic psychological distress, to engage in health-compromising behaviors, including drug and alcohol use, cigarette smoking, and unprotected sex, to perform less well academically, to be expelled or suspended from school, to drop out of school, to suffer from mental illness, to commit suicide, to have trouble getting along with their peers, and to start their own single-parent families.[41] Jeffrey Grogger reports that the sons of adolescent mothers are nearly three times more likely to be incarcerated at some point in their twenties than the sons of mothers who delay childbearing until they are in their early twenties.[42]

Economic and emotional supports are critical for single-parent families, and relatively few noncustodial fathers provide it. For example, about one-third of families with children receive none of the financial support awarded by courts, and families who do receive support receive only about 60 percent of the award. Furthermore, noncustodial fathers are unlikely to have much, if any, contact with their children. Based on a National Survey of Children report, about 26 percent of noncustodial divorced fathers manage a visitation with their children on just a bimonthly basis, and 23 percent had no contact with their children ages 11 to 16 in the previous 5-year period. Fathers never married to the mothers of their children had much less contact with their children.[43]

Of course, not all children being raised in single-parent homes live in poverty, nor are all born to unmarried or teenage mothers. Many children are being raised by a divorced parent. The process and consequences of divorce on children may have negative effects independent of the mother's age or economic status. It is not unusual for intact families to be fraught with conflict between husbands and wives or for a pervasive silence to be cast over the members as each attempts to avoid provoking outbursts in others. Frequently, relations improve after divorce or separation. However, much current research suggests that both the structural reality of single parenting as a consequence of divorce and the very process of going through divorce produce adverse consequences for the children in the family.[44] The adverse consequences are often long-lasting. Frances Rice and her colleagues report that family conflict increased the likelihood of children experiencing clinical depression during childhood and adolescence.[45]

Each year about 2 percent (nearly 2 million families) of all married couples get divorced, and more than half involve children under age 18. According to the National Center for Health Statistics, about 12 percent of couples divorce within 3 years of getting married, 20 percent within 5 years, and 33 percent within 10 years.[46] Those who divorce and then remarry are even more likely to find the subsequent marriage falling apart, and multiple divorces are harder on the children. Children who have experienced multiple divorces are more likely to report higher levels of anxiety and depression, to fail in school, and eventually to have more troubled marriages of their own than are children who have experienced a single divorce or children whose families remain intact. Frank Furstenberg and Andrew Cherlin estimate that 15 percent of all children in divorced families will see the parent they live with remarry and redivorce before they reach age 18.[47] The Family Research Council has long believed that marriage and keeping a family intact provides numerous benefits to family members, both adults and children, and to society (See box 10-3).

Single Parents, Divorce, and Delinquency

think
about it

Given the implications of divorce on delinquency and the maladjustment of children, should divorce become a criminal offense? If there were criminal consequences of getting divorced, how would the American family change?

The relationship between single-parent families and delinquency has been widely studied, and much research reports that children from single-parent families are more likely to become delinquent than children from two-parent families.[48] For example, Ann Goetting found that only 30 percent of the children arrested for homicide in Detroit over an 8-year period lived with both parents.[49] Edward Wells and Joseph Rankin's analysis of 50 studies led them to conclude that the effect of the single-parent family on delinquency is real and consistent, of relatively low magnitude; the effect is greater for minor offenses, weaker for serious offenses.[50] Furthermore, Michelle Miller and her colleagues surveyed about 500 students in 11 public schools and reported that adolescents in single-parent families are more likely to engage in both serious and minor delinquencies than are youths in two-parent families.[51] Finally, William Comandor and Llad Phillips analyzed the impact of family structure on a youth's involvement with the criminal justice system using data from the National Longitudinal Survey of Youth. They concluded "the most critical factor affecting the prospect that a male youth will encounter the criminal justice system is the presence of his

---

box 10-3 **A WINDOW ON DELINQUENCY**

Marriage Benefits

HOW MARRIAGE BENEFITS CHILDREN

• Children living with married parents are safer than children living with single parents because they are less likely to be abused or neglected.

• Compared to children in single-parent families, children raised in married-parent homes have better emotional and physical health and engage in fewer risky behaviors, such as premarital sex, substance abuse, delinquency, and suicide.

• Children with married parents do better academically and fare better economically.

• Children raised in intact homes are less likely to cohabit and more likely to view marriage positively and maintain life-long marriages.

HOW MARRIAGE BENEFITS ADULTS

• Married people have better emotional and physical health and live longer than do unmarried people.

• Married couples have greater incomes than do single adults, and the longer they stay married, the more wealth they accumulate.

• Married couples enjoy greater sexual satisfaction than do unmarried people.

• Married women are safer than unmarried women. Never-married, cohabiting, separated, and divorced women experience higher rates of domestic violence than do married women.

HOW MARRIAGE BENEFITS SOCIETY

• Marriage helps ensure that human life is protected and cherished, since married women are less likely to abort their children than are unmarried women.

• Marriage makes homes safer places to live, because it curbs social problems such as domestic violence and child abuse.

• Communities with more married-parent families are safer and more attractive places to live because they are less likely to have substance abuse and crime among young people.

• Married people are more likely to be healthy, productive, and engaged citizens, benefiting businesses and, ultimately, the economy.

Sources: Bridget Maher, *The Benefits of Marriage* (Washington, DC: Family Research Council, 2004); James Q. Wilson, *The Marriage Problem: How Our Culture Has Weakened Families* (New York: HarperCollins, 2003).

---

father in the home. All other factors, including family income, are much less important."[52]

Explanations offered to explain the greater likelihood of delinquency for children from single-parent families include suggestions that (1) single parents can less effectively supervise their children; (2) children in single-parent families grow up too fast; (3) single mothers give adolescents greater say in what they can do or give too early autonomy, thus reducing control over youths; (4) children from single-parent families are more susceptible to peer pressure; and (5) children in single-parent families experience lower levels of parental attachment.[53]

The Impact of Divorce on Children

What impact does the breakup of a family have on children? According to Ronald Simons and his colleagues, divorced parents make fewer demands on their children, provide less monitoring, are more likely to display hostility, and tend to use less effective disciplinary techniques than are married parents. Each of these factors contributes to greater likelihood of delinquency.[54] Mavis Hetherington reports that in the year following the breakup, children in single-parent families are more likely to suffer psychological distress, but in the long run they cope more successfully than children in intact families where parents do not get along. She sees three major effects of divorce on women that heavily affect children: They are overloaded from both work and child rearing, they face financial strain, and they are likely to be socially isolated.[55]

Divorce also may produce "family wars," in which relatives and friends pick sides and attempt to "win" by attacking the former spouse. Children are caught in the middle, often being defined as victims or expected to accept new definitions of the former spouse. In either case, the stress produced for the child may manifest itself in many ways. Some studies have found a relationship between father absence and a host of social and emotional ills, including decreased school performance and self-control, and increased rates of psychological disturbance, drug use, gang affiliation, and involvement in violent crime.[56]

Judith Wallerstein and Joan Kelly studied families in the early stages of breaking up, after 18 months apart, and after 5 years. In the first period, both parents typically felt the pinch of a lower standard of living and were depressed and lonely. Mothers were also overburdened by having to juggle bread-winning and homemaking roles and had to stay up late to do so. Children were often upset and thoroughly opposed to the divorce. Children became more angry, aggressive, and unruly during this initial stage of the breakup, partly because of their deteriorating relationship with their mother. Eighteen months later, some mothers were still depressed, but parent–child relations were healing and children themselves improved, with fewer feeling deprived or lonely. At the 5-year point, conditions were slightly worse than at 18 months. Among children, there was increased evidence of anger and depression.[57]

Judith Wallerstein and Sandra Blakeslee published results from a study in which 60 families and 131 youths were interviewed at 1-, 5-, 10-, and 15-year intervals after divorce in an attempt to discover both short- and long-term effects of divorce. After 5 years, one-third of the children were doing well, but another third were significantly worse off, suffering both academic and psychological difficulties. Some specific consequences of divorce on children are the result of the diminished capacity of parents to supervise in almost all dimensions of child rearing. In the process of divorce, parents spend less time with their children and are less responsive to their needs. Wallerstein and her colleagues recently published their findings from follow-up interviews with these same 131 subjects, now 25 years after divorce.[58] Reflections by some of these subjects on the effects of having to make court-ordered visits with noncustodial parents are presented in Box 10-4.

Constance Ahrons argues that many divorces are actually "good," producing what she calls the binuclear family, one that spans two households continuing to meet the needs of the children. If the divorce is managed correctly, the divorcing parents and children will be able to emerge as emotionally healthy as they were prior to the divorce.[59] For some, divorce is so "good" that the process of getting divorced is becoming easier and less expensive. Today, there are "do-it-yourself" online divorce services that allow couples to legally divorce, without needing to hire attorneys, for as little as $250. Online divorces are also fast and convenient, often taking as little as 3 months.[60] However, Elizabeth Marquardt believes that there are no good divorces when it comes to children. She contends the concept

box 10-4   FACE OF DELINQUENCY

Court-Ordered Visitations

Numerous studies confirm that most children are adversely affected by the divorce of their parents and the struggle of the custodial parent to provide for the well-being of the children in the absence of the other parent. But do court-ordered visitations with the noncustodial parent aggravate the adjustment difficulties of the child? Paula was only 4-years-old when her parents separated. Her father reentered her life when she was 8, and got a court to grant him rights to regular visitation. By the time Paula was 13, she had accumulated a police record of drug use, public drinking, and theft. She had also become sexually active with two 17-year-old boys. How much of her delinquency might be attributed to the consequences of court-ordered visits with her father? Are court-ordered visits always in the child's best interests?

Judith Wallerstein and her colleagues have studied the effects of divorce on children (and parents) for over 25 years. Paula was just one of the many children who reported that being subjected to court-ordered visitations made them feel like "nonpersons" with no right to express opinions or preferences or to question the visitation arrangements imposed on them. Thousands of children, many as young as 8 or 9, make lengthy and complicated plane trips by themselves to comply with the court's orders. While Paula did not have to fly to visit her father, the court did require that she visit her dad for two weekends each month, that holidays be rotated every other year, and that Paula reside with her father during the month of July. According to Wallerstein, "The visiting schedule was set up on the basis of a compromise meeting the demands of both parents. The wishes and needs of [Paula] were never consulted or considered."

The courts and parents rarely discuss with children how they will spend time on their visits. Little, if any, thought is given to how visits might cut into the child's social life or friendships, or how they may disrupt school activities, including participating in sports or doing homework. Paula's visits with her father generally involved her spending the weekend watching television or videos or accompanying her father on his errands. Sometimes she was left in his apartment when he went out on dates. Paula dreaded the month-long visit during July. "When summer comes, all the other kids in my class look forward to it. . . . I hate July. It's terrible for me. Last July I cried the whole month and thought, why am I being sentenced? What crime did I commit?"

Years later, Paula reflected on the court-ordered visits. She said: "I hated it there. I don't think it's good for children to spend two weekends with one parent and then go back to the other home. It's really hard. When you're a child, you're trying to discover who you are and to have friends. Their plan was totally disruptive to me. My friends got so they wouldn't even invite me on the weekends I was home."

When Wallerstein asked Paula "How did you manage?" Paula replied, "I would pretend all weekend to myself that I wasn't really there."

Instead of building relationships, court-ordered visitation frequently brings further deterioration. Wallerstein notes that most of the children in her study who were required to make court-ordered visits "were very angry at the parent they had been ordered to visit. All rejected the parent whom they were forced to visit when they got older."

No easy solution is likely to be found, but it seems only reasonable that the courts, at a minimum, should allow children the right to participate in developing the plans that will affect their lives and to recognize that children change and that court-ordered visitation for very young children should be reviewed each year and modified as the child's life changes.

Source: Judith Wallerstein, Julia Lewis, and Sandra Blakeslee, *The Unexpected Legacy of Divorce: A 25 Year Landmark Study* (New York: Hyperion, 2000), pp. 174–187.

of a good divorce is an adult-centered vision. Children of divorce must go from a world that seemed safe to going back and forth between two worlds, often perceived by the children as polar opposites, left without clear guidance on right and wrong, and required to keep secrets about the different households.[61]

Remarrying after divorce does not necessarily eliminate the negative effects of the divorce. Children raised in stepfamilies do less well in school, experience higher levels of family conflict, have more adjustment problems, and are more likely to engage in delinquency than are children in two-parent, never-divorced families. Children in stepfamilies are two to three times more likely to engage in delinquency. There is evidence that while a stepfather seems to increase the likelihood of delinquency, the presence of a stepmother may reduce it, although only a very small percentage of children from divorce live with stepmothers.[62] Cesar Rebellon's analysis of data from the National Youth Survey suggests that youth who have been raised in the long-term presence of a stepparent are more likely to engage in violent delinquency than youth with minimal or no exposure to a stepparent.[63]

Working Mothers and Latchkey Children

Most women participate full time or part time in the labor force today. Three-fourths of married women with children between the ages of 6 and 17 are employed; 78 percent of single mothers with children in this same age group are employed. But mothers with much younger children are also working outside the home. Today, more than 10 million women with children under age 6 were employed: This includes 58 percent of married women and 66 percent of single women with children under age 6.[64] Some criminologists ask whether there is a connection between women in the labor force and delinquency.

Research has found one definite effect of mothers being in the labor force: They have less time to spend with their children. But Russell Hill and Frank Stafford report that college-educated working mothers try hard to compensate: They cut down on time spent sleeping and relaxing more than they cut down on time spent with their children. The same authors also note that by the time children reach adolescence, parents in general spend only an hour or two per week in nurturing them and thus, under these circumstances, there is little difference between working and nonworking mothers in the time they give.[65] Therefore, having less time to spend with her children does not necessarily mean that the mother is failing to perform her role adequately. Keith Melville states that "when working mothers derive satisfaction from their employment and do not feel guilty about its effects, they are likely to perform the mother's role at least as well as non-working women."[66]

Studies examining the effects of mothers' employment on children and their development have produced mixed results. For example, Matthijs Kalmijn reports that mothers who work in high-status jobs lead to positive school effects for their children. They report that sons and daughters do better academically, are more likely to complete high school, attend college, and eventually graduate.[67] Jay Belsky and David Eggebeen found that a variety of measures of adjustment, such as behavior problems, insecurity, and sociability, reflected no negative effects of employment of mothers.[68]

Travis Hirschi's comparison of sons of homemakers, women who worked part time, and women who worked full time found that 20 percent of sons of full-time working mothers, 17 percent of sons of part-time workers, and 16 percent of sons of homemakers were delinquent. With differences this small, we can safely say that there is at most only a weak relationship between delinquency and mothers' employment status.[69]

But what about working fathers? Between 80 and 90 percent of married and single fathers with children are employed. In the past, traditional gender roles guided fathers into bread-winning rather than into child rearing and care-giving roles, which were considered the primary domains of mothers. However, David Popenoe notes that with the majority of mothers now in the labor force, "men are being asked to return to domestic roles. Fathers are badly needed as comprehensive child-rearers on an equal basis with mothers."[70] But conflicts between fathers' and mothers' employment schedules not only reduce the time fathers have available for care giving, but competing schedules also contribute to increased stress and role conflict between husbands and wives. Only when fathers work different schedules than their wives are they more likely to provide care for their children.[71]

When both mothers and fathers are employed outside the home with overlapping schedules, most children are faced with the prospect of coming home to empty houses. The number of **latchkey children,** that is, children who regularly care for themselves without adult supervision after school or on weekends, has increased dramatically. More than three million children ages 6 to 12 spend 5 or more hours a week unsupervised or in the care of a young sibling. More than 10 percent of these unsupervised children spend 10 or more hours alone while their parent or parents are at work.[72] Many experts feel that latchkey children, especially those in their teenage years, are more susceptible to opportunities for getting involved in delinquent situations.

Laurence Steinberg thinks latchkey children face a variety of subtle fears and worries, such as exposure to dangers while alone and increases in their susceptibility to peer pressure. They have less adult supervision and are therefore more vulnerable to peer pressure to engage in delinquent acts.[73] Latchkey children are likely to "find other [children] who are coming home to empty houses. They create a peer-group culture, and it's likely to be an ugly culture—a culture of destroy, of break, of acting-out."[74]

In a study of behavioral consequences of leaving children in self-care, students who spent 11 or more hours a week in self-care were twice as likely to use alcohol, tobacco, and marijuana as children of the same age whose after-school time was supervised.[75] A recent national longitudinal study on adolescent health of more than 12,000 middle and high school students conducted by Michael Resnick and his associates found the presence of parents at home at key times during the day, such as early morning, after school, evening meal, and at bedtime, provided moderate protection against emotional distress for children, reduced the frequency of use of alcohol and marijuana, and delayed adolescents' initiation of sexual intercourse.[76]

With the numerous problems posed by self-care, it is understandable that many parents turn to childcare providers. More than 60 percent of children under age 6 are cared for on a regular basis by caregivers other than parents. Nearly 80 percent of children under age 5 are in some sort of childcare arrangement during a typical week, with 49 percent cared for by nonrelatives. Preschoolers spend an average of 28 hours per week in childcare.[77] But children who spend a large amount of time in daycare may be more likely to develop behavioral

think
about it

Latchkey children are disproportionately from the working class. Are criminologists projecting their views of appropriate parenting in lamenting the latchkey child? In other words, is the latchkey child only a problem for middle-class parents who can afford to stay at home?

problems than children who spend less time or children cared for only by parents. About 17 percent of children who spend over 30 hours a week in nonparental childcare are more demanding, more noncompliant, and more aggressive, compared to only 6 percent of children who spend less than 10 hours a week. They are also more likely to engage in hitting, bullying, and explosive behavior and to demand a lot of attention.[78] The solution may be problematic. Some critics argue that instead of reducing the time spent in childcare, high-quality childcare should be expanded.

According to a recent University of Colorado study, only 8 percent of daycare facilities were determined to be *high-quality* operations. What distinguished "high-quality" childcare? They provided intense, personal attention over an extended period of time—the same thing that real mothers do. Thus, instead of expanding childcare, other critics argue that mothers should be urged to work less and spend more time with their children. The difficulties in finding high-quality childcare may be one of the factors contributing to the recent trend of more working married mothers with very young children choosing to leave the workforce and stay home. While about 72 percent of mothers with children under age 18 continue to be in the workforce, the proportion of working married mothers with children under age 3 dropped from 61 percent in 1997 to 58 percent in 2002.[79]

PARENTING IN FAMILIES

The relationships among broken homes, absent fathers, and working mothers have been extensively studied, but research findings are inconsistent. There exists a body of research that suggests the most important determinant of whether a child will be involved in delinquency is the quality of the parent–child relationship rather than family structure alone.[80] For example, a study of nearly 2,500 middle and junior high school students in Dade County (Miami), Florida, reported that a strong attachment between parent and child significantly reduced the likelihood of delinquency, while family structure had only a weak indirect effect.[81] In addition, Marc Zimmerman and his colleagues studied the effects of family structure and parental attachment among 254 African American male adolescents from a large East Coast city. Regardless of family structure, their time spent with father and their perceptions of his emotional support were associated with lower levels of delinquency and marijuana use.[82] Perhaps delinquency has more to do with family process than with family structure, an idea proposed by sociologists more than 50 years ago.[83] The link between family process variables and delinquency is examined next.

Parenting Skills

A standard assumption is that married adults automatically know how to be good parents. Presumably there is some universal commonsense transmitted from one generation to the next. Effective parenting depends on many things. Interactions within the family and the quality of parenting change as a child's misbehavior or delinquency increases over time. Often parents become angry and short-tempered with a child who consistently gets into trouble or disillusioned when they find they cannot believe what the child tells them. Over time, parent–child conflicts may escalate, or the relationship between parent and child may become more distant and alienated. In circumstances where the child's antisocial behavior is directed against the parents, many parents are less able to exercise reasonable parental authority and may even abdicate parental responsibilities altogether.

Gerald Patterson found the type of deviance children engage in most is the type parents tolerate most. In the case of children who steal, for example:

> Many of the parents maintained that since they had never actually seen their child steal, they could not prove that their child had stolen, and therefore could not punish the child. In numerous instances, someone else had actually seen the child steal, but the child's "story" would be accepted by the parents, who would then rise to the child's defense and accuse others of picking on the child. As the parents used the word "steal," it could be used as a label only if it could be proven, which was usually impossible; ergo the child did not really steal, ergo no punishment could be applied.[84]

James Snyder and Gerald Patterson have identified two divergent disciplinary styles that characterize families with delinquent children: enmeshed and lax. Parents who practice the *enmeshed* style are overly inclusive in what they define as problematic behavior. Even trivial misbehaviors by the child result in sharp parental reactions ranging from cajoling to verbal threats. But enmeshed parents "fail to consistently and effectively back up these verbal reprimands with nonviolent, nonphysical punishment . . . [and] inadvertently provide more positive consequences for deviant child behavior." At the other extreme, parents who engage in the *lax* style tend to be very liberal in what they define as excessive or antisocial behavior.

Solving problems and negotiating disagreements or conflict are ways to forestall violence. Snyder and Patterson believe that parental violence often erupts at the end of a chain of events that began with a trivial incident like the child "sneaking" candy or food. To avoid such violence, parents must learn to break the chain and learn techniques of negotiating a settlement before minor matters get out of hand.[85] (See Box 10-5 for more on family intervention strategies to reduce delinquency.)

It is arguable, however, whether Patterson's prescription can be effective for all parents. Travis Hirschi has identified a few problems with Patterson's approach:

> The parents may not care for the child (in which case none of the other conditions would be met); the parents, even if they care, may not have the time or energy to monitor the child's behavior; the parents, even if they care and monitor, may not see anything wrong with the child's behavior; finally, even if everything else is in place, the parents may not have the inclination or the means to punish the child.[86]

Hirschi also reminds us that families with more children face greater strain on parental resources such as time and energy. And single-parent families are strained even more:

> The single parent . . . must devote a good deal to support and maintenance activities that are at least to some extent shared in the two-parent family. Further, she must do so in the absence of psychological or social support. As a result, she is less able to devote time to monitoring and punishment, and is more likely to be involved in negative, abusive contacts with her children.[87]

box 10-5 | DELINQUENCY PREVENTION
Reducing Delinquency by Strengthening Families

Juvenile delinquency is greatly affected by the family environment, including structures and dynamics of parenting. Much research has established the importance of improving families and parenting practices as a means of combating delinquency. In an attempt to identify the most effective methods or practices for providing parents with the critical skills needed to strengthen families and promote resilience to delinquency in high-risk youth, the Office of Juvenile Justice and Delinquency Prevention launched its Strengthening America's Families Initiative in the mid-1980s. Evaluations of more than 500 family-focused prevention strategies were reviewed in 1999 to identify those deemed most effective. Among those strategies regarded as exemplary models are the following:

- **The Incredible Years: Parents, Teachers, and Children Training Series.** The parent-training curriculum of this series, designed for parents of children ages 3 to 12, focuses on strengthening parents' monitoring and disciplinary skills and building their confidence. The curriculum includes an 11-week basic program that uses video tapes depicting real-life situations. Parents meet in groups and cover topics such as Helping Children Learn, The Value of Praise and Encouragement, Effective Limit Setting, and Handling Misbehavior.

- **Strengthening Families Program.** This 14-week family skills training program is designed to reduce risk factors for substance abuse and other problem behaviors. The program includes three separate courses: Parent Training, Children's Training, and Family Life Skills Training. Families with children ages 6 to 10 attend the program as a family. The parents and children attend separate sessions for the first hour of the program and then come together as a family for the second hour to practice the skills they have learned. Parents learn strategies for effective family communication, problem solving, and limit setting while children learn about communication, social skills, and ways to resist peer pressure.

- **Prenatal and Early Childhood Nurse Home Visitation Program.** This program is designed to improve the health and social functioning of low-income first-time mothers and their babies. Nurse home visitors develop a supportive relationship with the pregnant mother and family and provide them with information on personal and environmental health, maternal roles, life-course development, and the value of support from family and friends. The home visits continue until the child reaches age 2, with the frequency of visits varying depending on the child's age.

- **Multisystemic Therapy (MST).** The primary goals of this intensive home-based family treatment are to reduce rates of antisocial behavior in youths ages 10 to 18, reduce out-of-home placements, and empower families to resolve difficulties. Goals are developed in collaboration with the family, and family strengths are used as levers for change. MST treats factors in the youth's environment that are contributing to behavior problems in addition to addressing individual characteristics of the youth such as poor problem-solving skills, academic difficulties, or association with deviant peers.

Sources: Rose Alvarado and Karol Kumpfer, "Strengthening America's Families," *Juvenile Justice* 7:8–18 (2000); Carolyn Webster-Stratton, *The Incredible Years Training Series* (Washington, DC: Office of Juvenile Justice and Delinquency Prevention, 2000); Virginia Molgaard, Richard Spoth, and Cleve Redmond, *Competency Training: The Strengthening Families Program: For Parents and Youth 10–14* (Washington, DC: Office of Juvenile Justice and Delinquency Prevention, 2000); Stephen Bavolek, *The Nurturing Parenting Programs* (Washington, DC: Office of Juvenile Justice and Delinquency Prevention, 2000).

Parental Supervision

Patterson's rules of parenting also note the need for effective parental supervision, such as establishing a set of "house rules" and clearly communicating them. House rules should cover whom the child associates with, places considered off limits, curfews, and when the child should be home from school. Parents must be aware of the child's performance in school as well as school attendance, the possibility of drug or alcohol use, and the activities the child is involved in with friends. "Good supervision . . . indirectly minimizes the adolescents' contact with delinquency—promoting circumstances, activities, and peers." [88]

Commonsense suggests that unsupervised children are more likely to participate in delinquency, and substantial research confirms the relationship. Grace Barnes and Michael Farrell studied a sample of 699 adolescents and their families and found that high parental monitoring, when combined with high parental support, was the key factor in preventing delinquency. [89] Jaana Haapasalo and Richard Tremblay examined aggressiveness in samples of more than 1,000 boys in Montreal in an attempt to predict which boys would become "fighters" and which would be "non-fighters." They concluded that non-fighters appeared to be the most supervised and that low levels of supervision were associated with higher levels of fighting. [90]

Although the findings from a variety of studies report poor parental supervision to be a significant contributor to delinquency, [91] Sung Jang and Carolyn Smith suggest that parental supervision and delinquency is reciprocally related. Their analysis of data from 838 urban adolescents led them to conclude that although parental supervision has a significant negative impact on delinquency, the impact of supervision varies over time with its influence declining as adolescents mature. They also found that weak parental supervision not only promotes delinquency, but to the extent the child is delinquent, his or her participation in delinquency leads to a further erosion in the perception of effective parental supervision. [92]

John Wright and Francis Cullen argue that parents who are supportive of their children, for example, encouraging hobbies, facilitating special lessons or activities, and are involved in a child's activities, are more likely to provide greater supervision and to exhibit a stronger attachment than less supportive parents. According to Wright and Cullen, "parents who are nurturing, reliable, and closely attached to their youths and who provide guidance in the form of rules and supervision reduce the delinquency of their adolescents." [93] Positive parenting involves interactions between parent and child that have positive effects on interpersonal, academic, and work skills for the child and that reinforce conventional values and norms. Positive parenting requires a consistent approach to the child, as well as positive feedback when the child behaves as desired.

Parenting Styles

The style of parenting influences the behavior of children. According to Diana Baumrind, there are two critical aspects of parents' behavior toward children: parental responsiveness and parental demandingness. *Responsiveness* is the degree to which parents are supportive of the needs of their children. *Demandingness* is the extent to which parents demand age-appropriate behavior from children. [94]

Parents will vary on each dimension. They can be supportive and demand much (*authoritative*) or rejective and demand much (*authoritarian*). Similarly, parents can be supportive and demand very little (*indulgent*) or rejective and demand little (*indifferent*). A description of these four parenting styles follows.

Authoritative parents are warm but firm. They set standards for the child's conduct but form expectations consistent with the child's developing needs and capabilities. They place a high value on development of autonomy and self-direction but assume the ultimate responsibility for their child's behavior. Authoritative parents deal with their child in a rational, issue-oriented manner, frequently engaging in discussion and explanation with their children over rules and discipline.

Authoritarian parents place a high value on obedience and conformity, tending to favor more punitive, absolute, and forceful disciplinary measures. These parents are not responsive to their child and project little warmth and support. Verbal give-and-take is uncommon in authoritarian households because authoritarian parents believe that the child should accept without question the rules and standards established by the parents. They tend not to encourage independent behavior and, instead, place importance on restricting a child's autonomy.

Indulgent parents behave in responsive, accepting, benign, and more passive ways in matters of discipline. They place relatively few demands on the child's behavior, giving the child a high degree of freedom to act as he or she wishes. Indulgent parents are more likely to believe that control is an infringement on the child's freedom that may interfere with healthy development. Instead of actively shaping their child's behavior, indulgent parents view themselves as resources the child may or may not use.

Indifferent parents are fairly unresponsive to their child and try to minimize the time and energy they must devote to interacting with the child or responding to the child's demands. In extreme cases, indifferent parents may be neglectful. They know little about their child's activities and whereabouts, show little interest in their child's experiences at school or in his or her friends, and rarely consider the child's opinion when making decisions. The child is typically ignored except when making demands on parents, which often results in hostile or explosive responses toward the child.

Parental Attachment

Another way parents influence the behavior of children is through emotional closeness. Presumably, children who like their parents will respect their wishes and stay out of trouble. Research supports the conclusion that the children least likely to turn to delinquency are those who feel loved, identify with their parents, and respect their parents' wishes. On the other hand, delinquents often lack a supportive relationship with their fathers, have minimal supervision of their activities, are closer to their mothers, and come from broken homes. Strongly attached children also are more likely to have more open communication with parents, and youths who have problems communicating with either parent or who communicate less frequently are more likely to engage in serious forms of delinquency.[95]

Likewise, parental love may reduce delinquency because it is something children do not want to lose. Randy LaGrange and Helen White found this to be true especially for juveniles in middle adolescence. They suggest that attachment to

"Your mother and I are feeling overwhelmed, so you'll have to bring yourselves up."

Source: © The New Yorker Collection 1999 David Sipress from cartoonbank.com. All rights reserved.

a positive role model is important because it functions as a "psychological anchor" to conformity.[96] For some adolescents, the attachment to parents is reflected in their family pride. Establishment of a positive family identity appears to significantly reduce levels of delinquency for white and African American youths.[97] Weak attachments may also have a greater negative impact on female adolescents. For example, Angela Huebner and Sherry Betts report that attachment bond variables explain three times more delinquency among girls than boys.[98]

Finally, the positive effects of attachment vary somewhat in single and intact families. Michelle Miller and her colleagues found that attachment to mothers and fathers in intact families was negatively related to delinquency. However, in single-mother households, parental attachment was negatively related to serious delinquency, but was inconsistently predictive of minor delinquency.[99]

Parental Deviance

Studies show that children with criminal parents are more likely to participate in delinquency. Donald West and David Farrington's longitudinal study of British boys led them to conclude that delinquency is transmitted from one generation to the next: Criminal fathers are likely to produce delinquent sons.[100] John Laub and Robert Sampson similarly conclude: "Parental deviance of both the mother and father strongly disrupts family processes of social control, which in turn increases delinquency."[101] Helen Garnier and Judith Stein's analysis of data from the 18-year longitudinal Family Lifestyles Project led them to conclude that early maternal drug use was linked with adolescent drug use "signaling a more deviant lifestyle to which children were exposed and which could increase their exposure and attraction to deviant peers."[102]

One of the best studies of family deviance was conducted by David Farrington and his colleagues who were interested in the interrelationships among offending by three generations of relatives and the concentration of offending in

The sins of the parent(s) are often visited on the child. Delinquents are more likely to have parents who abuse drugs or alcohol, commit crimes, or beat them.

families. They also studied how far criminal relatives predict a boy's delinquency based on data from 1,395 Pittsburgh boys aged 8, 11, or 14. They found that offenders were highly concentrated in families; if one relative had been arrested, there was a high likelihood that another relative had also been arrested. Arrests of brothers, sisters, fathers, mothers, uncles, aunts, grandfathers, and grandmothers all predicted the boy's delinquency. The most important relative was the father; arrests of the father predicted the boy's delinquency independently of all other arrested relatives. In fact, boys whose father had been arrested were *500 percent more likely* to be arrested themselves.[103] When parents are involved in deviant lifestyles, for example, crime or illicit drug use, they are less likely to be conscientious and responsible parents. It is ineffective parenting, not necessarily the deviant activities modeled by the parents, that increases the child's risk of delinquency.

THE MALTREATMENT OF CHILDREN

Parenting methods affect a child's behavior. Some parents are too harsh, too irritable, and too inconsistent in discipline. Other parents are too neglectful and preoccupied with building their careers. Many of the problem behaviors of children are tied to the behavior of parents and other adults who have regular contact with children. Regoli and Hewitt's *theory of differential oppression* suggests that adults generally, and parents particularly, attempt to establish and maintain order and social control in the home in ways that are broadly oppressive of children (see Chapter 7). In more rigid and authoritarian families, when children violate the rules they are punished, often severely. Its more severe form, maltreatment, includes physical and sexual abuse, physical neglect, inadequate supervision, emotional neglect, educational maltreatment, moral–legal harm, and excessive corporal punishment. In response to such maltreatment, a child is likely to develop a sense of powerlessness, leading to negative and often harmful adaptations, such as delinquency and adult criminality. A list of risk and protective factors for child maltreatment appears in Box 10-6.

---

box 10-6	A WINDOW ON DELINQUENCY
	Child Maltreatment: Risk and Protective Factors

Child maltreatment produces $24 billion in direct costs related to the criminal justice and social service responses to child maltreatment cases each year. The indirect, long-term economic consequences are estimated at $69 billion annually. In other words, each year the United States pays nearly $100 billion in costs to respond to child maltreatment. The pain and suffering to child victims is in many ways incalculable.

A combination of individual, family, community, and societal factors contribute to the risk of child maltreatment. For example, children younger than 4 years are at greatest risk of severe injury or death. Children under 4 years account for nearly 77 percent of all injuries, and infants under 12 months account for 44 percent of deaths. There are a variety of risk and protective factors that are linked to child maltreatment.

RISK FACTORS

- Disabilities or mental retardation in children.
- Social isolation of family.
- Parents' history of domestic violence.
- Family disorganization, dissolution, and lack of cohesion.
- Family violence.
- Substance abuse in family.
- Young, single, nonbiological parents as caregivers.
- Parental stress and mental health problems.

PROTECTIVE FACTORS

- Supportive family environment.
- Nurturing parenting skills.
- Stable family relationships.
- Household rules and monitoring of the child.
- Parental employment.
- Adequate housing.
- Access to health care and social services.
- Caring adult role models or mentors.
- Communities that support parents and take responsibility for preventing abuse.

Sources: Centers for Disease Control and Prevention, *Child Maltreatment: Fact Sheet* (Atlanta: National Center for Injury Prevention and Control, 2006); U.S. Department of Health and Human Services, *Child Maltreatment 2005* (Washington, DC: U.S. Government Printing Office, 2007).

Nature and Extent of Maltreatment

How extensive is the maltreatment of children, and what are its consequences? Parents kick, bite, punch, and beat their children with belts, boards, extension cords, fists, wooden spoons, broom handles, hairbrushes, coat hangers, and bull whips. Parents also threaten their children with guns, knives, and baseball bats.[104] Children are often beaten unconscious and sometimes killed by parents or other guardians. Such maltreatment produces consequences for the child, the family, and the larger community. Children who experience maltreatment are more likely to become unhealthy adults with increased risks for smoking, alcoholism, substance abuse, eating disorders, obesity, depression, suicide, and other problems.[105]

About 3.3 million cases of child abuse or neglect involving the maltreatment of more than 6 million children are reported to state child protective services agencies each year. About 62 percent of reported cases are referred for investigation and 29 percent of the investigated cases result in a disposition of either substantiated or indicated child maltreatment. About 63 percent of the estimated 899,000 victims of maltreatment suffered neglect, while 17 percent suffered physical abuse, and just over 9 percent were sexually abused. About 7 percent of the victims suffered from emotional maltreatment. The highest victimization rates by age were for children under age 6 (17 per 1,000), and rates declined as age increased. Victimization rates by race–ethnicity varied from a low of 4 per 1,000 for Asian–Pacific Islander children to 25 for African American children. About 49 percent of child victims of maltreatment were male, while 51 percent were female. The youngest children, those from birth to 3 years, accounted for 77 percent of all child maltreatment offenses resulting in death. They are also most likely to experience recurrence of maltreatment during their childhood. Generally, the rates of victimization decline as children become older. About 80 percent of child victims were maltreated by one or both parents. Maltreatment by both mother *and* father accounted for 19 percent of the cases, 18 percent involved victimizations by father, and mother-only victimizations accounted for 41 percent.[106]

Although the corporal punishment of children is presently prohibited in nine countries (Austria, Cyprus, Denmark, Finland, Germany, Italy, Latvia, Norway, and Sweden), over 90 percent of American parents report having spanked their children by age 3 or 4. Corporal punishment is more likely to be used in *authoritarian* style parenting, where discipline is inconsistent or developmentally inappropriate, or where there is minimal parent–child communication. Even small amounts of physical punishment can have an adverse effect on the psychosocial development of children and have been found to predict intelligence failure, emotional dysfunction, impaired ability to empathize, hostility, depression, conduct disorders in children, and criminality and violence in adulthood.[107]

Approximately 1,460 children die of maltreatment, 42 percent from neglect, 28 percent from physical abuse, and 29 percent from multiple maltreatment types. Infant boys younger than 1 year had the highest rate of fatalities at 17.3 deaths per 100,000 boys. Infant girls younger than 1 year had a rate of 14.5 deaths per 100,000 girls. In those cases in which children died as a result of abuse or neglect, 58 percent involved mothers as perpetrators and 42 percent involved fathers.[108]

Maltreatment, Corporal Punishment, and Delinquency

The nonlethal consequences of maltreatment frequently include delinquent, aggressive, and violent behavior by its victims. According to Gail Wasserman and Angela Seracini, when compared to nonmaltreated children, maltreated toddlers have been found to be significantly more likely to respond with fear, threats, or aggressive behavior to another child's distress; abused and neglected children are significantly more aggressive in their interactions with peers; and abused preschool and elementary school–age children are perceived by parents and teachers to have higher rates of externalizing behavior at home and at school.[109]

John Lemmon's study of a cohort of 632 male juveniles from low-income families reported a significant impact of maltreatment on initiation and continuation of delinquency. The maltreated boys had significantly higher scores on all measures of delinquency, were more likely than their nonmaltreated counterparts

think
about it

Corporal punishment is often criticized. However, is it possible that spanking is an effective means of anticipatory socialization for children? Does spanking send the message that behavior has consequences? Does spanking prepare youths to face the legal consequences of their delinquency?

to be referred to the juvenile court, and were more likely to be adjudicated delinquent. The maltreated group comprised the overwhelming majority of youths in the juvenile justice system, accounting for 84 percent of those youths receiving placement dispositions and 78 percent of those transferred to criminal court for prosecution. The maltreatment group also accounted for most of the serious delinquencies by juveniles: 78 percent of aggravated assaults, 83 percent of robberies, and 86 percent of weapons offenses. Male delinquents who had been maltreated were significantly more likely to be persistent and violent offenders, while nonmaltreated delinquents tended to be routine, infrequent offenders.[110]

Timothy Ireland and his colleagues report that persistent maltreatment dramatically increased the risk of chronic delinquency in both early and late adolescence. Persistent maltreatment through childhood and adolescence and maltreatment limited to adolescence was predictive of both delinquency and drug use. On the other hand, children who were maltreated only during childhood, rather than in adolescence, were no more likely than controls to engage in violent delinquency in early adolescence.[111] Jane Siegel and Linda Williams conducted a prospective study of 206 women treated in a hospital emergency room. Women reporting childhood sexual abuse were twice as likely as the nonabused group to have been arrested as juveniles for violent offenses; they were also nearly twice as likely to have been arrested as adults and to have engaged in violent offenses and five times more likely to have been arrested for drug offenses.[112]

Cathy Spatz Widom reports results from four studies conducted in different parts of the country over the past 25 years. In the Midwest, abused and neglected children were more likely to be first arrested about one year earlier

Children who observe their parents fighting or physically punishing siblings are more likely than children who do not observe these events to regard them as normal ways of resolving conflicts.

than matched nonmaltreated children and significantly more likely to become chronic offenders. Findings from a subset of data from the Rochester Youth Development Study confirmed that both self-reported and official delinquency was significantly related to child maltreatment. A study out of North Carolina found maltreated children to have higher rates of reported delinquency and violence than controls, while research conducted in Washington State concluded that abused and neglected children were about *five times* more likely to be arrested for nonviolent delinquencies and *11 times* more likely to be arrested for violent offenses than their matched controls. These studies, when taken together, suggest support for the "cycle of violence" hypothesis whereby children who experience maltreatment grow up to become perpetrators of violence.[113]

Even though few people would ever condone child abuse and neglect, many parents both condone and advocate the use of corporal punishment as a form of discipline. But corporal punishment also produces negative consequences. Although low-impact spanking, when used with young children by warm and caring parents, *does not* appear to be predictive of later adolescent conduct problems, more severe forms of corporal punishment are associated with delinquency. Longitudinal studies have found a strong relationship between severe punishment such as slapping, kicking, shoving, and hitting and both self-reported and official delinquency.

A number of studies report physical punishment to be more widely accepted among African Americans than among whites. White parents may be more tolerant of moderate misbehavior, but African American parents may perceive the consequences of disobedience as more serious in their neighborhood context in which respect for authority might reduce harassment by the police. Firm discipline is believed to help protect the child from the variety of dangers in the child's social environment. For example, Delores Smith and Gail Mosby examined Jamaican child rearing practices and found it to be highly repressive and severe, with flogging the most common form of corporal punishment. Children are disciplined for a variety of misbehaviors, ranging from lying and stealing to being impolite and failing to complete their chores. Such punishment was found to be highly related to depression, post–traumatic stress disorders, prostitution, teen pregnancy, criminality, and violence.[114] See Box 10-7 for a discussion of how Sweden's antispanking law affected rates of child abuse in that country.

Beyond corporal punishment, the juvenile justice system has developed special courts to deal with family violence and other family issues that relate to delinquency. One such set of courts is the **Family Dependency Treatment Courts** established in Reno, Nevada, in 1994. These are family courts that specifically adjudicate child welfare cases involving child abuse and neglect and parental substance abuse. Family Dependency Treatment Courts strive to ensure that children are safe and provided for while providing support, treatment, and access to social services to help parents get sober. Brief stints in jail for the substance-abusing parent are used as incentives to participate in the program. Family Dependency Treatment Courts use a multidisciplinary team of child protective workers and drug counselors to address the needs of the family. The ultimate goal is to unify the family in a healthy environment. Although there are not formal evaluation studies, anecdotal information from child protective workers and drug counselors suggest that both children and parents feel that the hands-on, specialized attention that Family Dependency Treatment Courts provide is helping reduce family-related problems.[115]

box 10-7	DELINQUENCY AROUND THE GLOBE

Has Sweden's Antispanking Law Reduced Child Abuse?

Nearly two-thirds of Americans approve of spanking, down from 74 percent in 1946. College-educated parents are twice as likely to disapprove of spanking than are those who didn't complete high school, and whites are about twice as likely to disapprove of spanking as are African Americans. Many antispanking advocates express concern that spanking children produces a variety of psychological and behavioral problems, including delinquency. Other antispankers are concerned that spanking a child is just the beginning of a slide down the slippery slope toward more serious forms of child abuse. For example, recent surveys report that nearly 20 percent of parents admit hitting their children on their bottoms with brushes, belts, or sticks, while another 10 percent report spanking their children with "hard objects." In addition, about two-thirds of mothers with children under 6 years of age report spanking them at least three times a week.

In 1979 Sweden passed the first law in the world prohibiting parents from spanking their children in a major effort to reduce child abuse. Eight other countries have passed similar laws (Austria, Cyprus, Denmark, Finland, Germany, Italy, Latvia, and Norway). Did Sweden's antispanking law reduce child abuse? Most of the evidence suggests that it *did not.* Robert Larzelere, director of residential research at Boys Town in Nebraska, has examined all published studies evaluating the Swedish spanking ban and concludes that "it has made little change in problematic forms of physical punishment." While significantly fewer Swedish parents than American parents spanked their children or hit them with an object, more serious forms of physical punishment occurred more frequently in Sweden during the year after the ban than in the United States. Furthermore, Swedish police records indicate that reported child abuse of children under the age of 7 actually increased 489 percent from 1981 to 1994.

Larzelere also reports that "the rate of beating a child up was three times as high in Sweden as in the United States, the rate of using a weapon was twice as high, and the overall rate of very severe violence was 49 percent higher in Sweden than the United States average." Moreover, "the rate of pushing, grabbing, or shoving was 39 percent higher in Sweden than the average rate in the United States." Larzelere concludes that although parents in Sweden were significantly less likely than American parents to spank their children, they were also significantly more likely to use physical aggression and to engage in child abuse than their American counterparts.

Larzelere believes that parents need to be empowered with "milder, effective disciplinary tactics" incorporating limited spanking. He and other experts argue that it is not so much whether parents spank their children, but how they spank them. Most "limited spanking" advocates argue that children under 2 years of age should never be spanked because the risk of serious physical injury is too great and that spanking adolescents may actually increase their misbehaviors. Spanking, they believe, is most effective with children between the ages 2 and 6; spankings should be done in private to reduce humiliation, never done in anger, and applied only with an open hand on the child's bottom.

Sources: John Lyons and Robert Larzelere, "Where Is Evidence that Non-Abusive Corporal Punishment Increases Aggression?" Paper presented at the XXVI International Congress of Psychology, Montreal, August 18, 1996; Lynn Rosellini, "When to Spank," online at: http://Usnews.com/usnews/issue/980413/13span.htm, accessed May 1, 2007; J.E. Durrant, "Evaluating the Success of Sweden's Corporal Punishment Ban," *Child Abuse & Neglect* 5:435–448 (1999); Robert Larzelere, "Child Abuse in Sweden," online at: http://www.people.biola.edu/faculty/paulp/sweden2.html, accessed May 1, 2007.

conclusions

Few people would contend the family has no effect whatsoever on whether a child becomes delinquent. But what is the nature of that effect? What aspects of the family are most significant in this arena? Is it the inculcation of moral values? Is it the structure of the family? Is it working mothers? Or does it have more to do with parenting styles and degree of supervision? This chapter has explored these issues and presented what often appear to be conflicting findings from research.

Studies suggest the relationship between divorce and single-parent families and delinquency exists but that it is strongest for girls and for less serious offenses. However, this finding may be misleading. Possibly, the relationship between broken or single-parent homes and delinquency may seem weak because these variables are separated by a number of important intervening variables. In other words, the absence of one parent may affect delinquency by producing weak attachments between the parent and child. Parenting skills have a considerable effect on delinquency. Patterson's techniques for making children more conforming to conventional norms include reinforcing conformity and providing sane punishment for transgressions. But reinforcement alone is not enough, Patterson discovered, particularly with very problematic children. Research shows that parents can be taught how to be more effective and, in turn, their children's misbehavior will decline.

Child maltreatment, including corporal punishment, abuse, and neglect, is extensive. Nearly three million cases of abuse and neglect are reported each year, and about 1,500 children die each year as a result of maltreatment. The maltreatment of children also creates an oppressive environment that produces a variety of negative outcomes, including drug use, teen pregnancy, low academic achievement, emotional problems, and juvenile delinquency.

While the family is the most critical social institution, children may actually spend more time in direct interaction with other children and adults in another major social institution, the school. For at least 9 months every year, from about age 5 until age 18, children spend nearly half their waking hours in school. Does this time in school deter or contribute to problem behaviors in children? The next chapter will explore the relationship between school and delinquency.

key terms

Authoritarian parents   Parents who place a high value on obedience and conformity, tending to favor more punitive, absolute, and forceful disciplinary measures.

Authoritative parents   Parents who are warm but firm; they set standards of behavior for their child and highly value the development of autonomy and self-direction.

Family Dependency Treatment Courts   Family courts that specifically adjudicate child welfare cases involving child abuse and neglect and parental substance abuse.

Indifferent parents   Parents who are unresponsive to their child and may, in extreme cases, be neglectful.

Indulgent parents   Parents who are more responsive, accepting, benign, and passive in matters of discipline and place few demands on their child.

Latchkey children   Children who regularly care for themselves without adult supervision after school or on weekends.

Maltreatment   Severe mistreatment of children, including physical and sexual abuse, physical neglect, lack of supervision, emotional maltreatment, educational maltreatment, and moral–legal maltreatment.

Single-parent families   Families composed of children and one parent who is divorced or widowed or who was never married.

Socialization   The process through which children learn the norms and values of a particular society or social group so that they can function within it.

Schools and Delinquency

The United States has a long and noble history of providing free public education. The origin of this achievement can be traced to the Massachusetts Act of 1642 that instructed parents to provide children with education and literacy. Unfortunately, many parents did not, and the Puritan authorities reacted by ordering every town to provide free public schooling. More than two centuries later, in 1852, Massachusetts passed the nation's first **compulsory school attendance law** that required *all* children between age 8 and 14 to attend school for a minimum of three months each year. *Truant officers*, whose job was to check for school absences, were hired to enforce the law. As shown in Table 11-1, by 1929, compulsory education laws had been passed in all states.[1]

Although the face of education has changed greatly over the past 350 years, it is arguable whether the purpose of schooling has changed very much. Is the role of the school today different than it was in Colonial America when it was to prepare children to accept and adapt to the lives they are born into? Or has the function of public schooling changed significantly? Is the purpose of school today to open new doors to the world for children, to stimulate their imagination, and to give them the skills necessary to enhance their lives? The correct answer to these questions is probably, "It depends."

Today, nearly 50 million children are enrolled in public schools.[2] In addition, more than 1.1 million students are home-schooled, which represents more than 2 percent of all students.[3] Some children attend schools blessed with an abundance of resources, dedicated teachers, a culture of learning, and endless educational enrichment opportunities. Other children toil in dysfunctional, racially divided, overcrowded schools with high rates of teacher absenteeism and few resources and opportunities. Regrettably, there are many examples of social inequality in American schools. For instance, a national survey sponsored by the U.S. Department of Education found that 37 percent of Hispanic students aged 12 to 17 attend schools where organized street gangs operate within their school. For African American children, 29 percent report street gangs in schools, and for other minority children, 22 percent report gangs in schools. For whites, just 14 percent report attending schools where street gangs are a presence.[4] Wayne Welsh and his colleagues report that nonwhite children are significantly more likely to attend schools that are unsafe with high levels of student misconduct and delinquency.[5] African American and Hispanic children are also more likely to attend schools that have high levels of disorder that in turn fosters a negative school climate and negatively affects learning.[6] Graham Ousey and Pamela Wilcox report that nonwhite children are significantly likely to attend schools characterized by a subcultural school culture that places a priority on misbehavior and delinquency as opposed to learning.[7] Overall, the disparities in American schools, which are divided by social class, race, and ethnicity, are described by the literary scholar and author Jonathan Kozol as "savage inequalities," "the shame of the nation," and evidence of Apartheid.[8]

Widespread inequality in schooling produces countless consequences for children, particularly for low-income juveniles.[9] Yet, regardless of whether schools are well funded or poorly funded, all schools are a microcosm of larger society, where children are subordinate to adults. In schools, teachers wield power and students exercise little control over their education. The educational interests of the nation, state, school district, administrators, and teachers

table 11-1	State Compulsory School Attendance Laws[1]				
STATE	**ENACTMENT**	**AGE LIMITS**	**STATE**	**ENACTMENT**	**AGE LIMITS**
Alabama	1915	7-16	Missouri	1905	7-16
Alaska	1929	7-16	Montana	1883	7-16[10]
Arizona	1899	6-16[2]	Nebraska	1887	7-16
Arkansas	1909	5-17[3]	Nevada	1873	7-17
California	1874	6-18[4]	New Hampshire	1871	6-16
Colorado	1889	7-16	New Jersey	1875	6-16
Connecticut	1872	7-16	New Mexico	1891	5-18
Delaware	1907	5-16[5]	New York	1874	6-16[11]
D.C.	1864	7-17	North Carolina	1907	7-16
Florida	1915	6-18	North Dakota	1883	7-16
Georgia	1916	6-16	Ohio	1877	6-18
Hawaii	1896	6-18	Oklahoma	1907	5-18
Idaho	1887	7-16	Pennsylvania	1895	8-17
Illinois	1883	7-16	Rhode Island	1883	6-16
Indiana	1897	7-16	South Carolina	1915	5-16
Iowa	1902	6-16[6]	South Dakota	1883	6-16
Kansas	1874	7-18[7]	Tennessee	1905	6-17
Kentucky	1896	6-16[8]	Texas	1915	6-18
Louisiana	1910	7-17	Utah	1890	6-18
Maine	1875	7-17	Vermont	1867	7-16
Maryland	1902	5-16	Virginia	1908	5-18
Massachusetts	1852	6-16	Washington	1871	8-18[9]
Michigan	1871	6-16	West Virginia	1897	6-16
Minnesota	1885	7-18[9]	Wisconsin	1879	6-18
Mississippi	1918	6-17	Wyoming	1876	6-16[2]

1. Date of enactment of first compulsory attendance law.
2. Ages 6 to 16 or 10th grade completion.
3. Must have turned 17 by October 1.
4. At least 16 and have graduated high school or passed California High School Proficiency Exam and obtained parental permission.
5. Must have turned 5 by August 31.
6. Must have turned 16 by September 15.
7. Eligible for waiver at 16.
8. Must have turned 6 by October 1.
9. Eligible for waiver.
10. Age 16 and completion of 8th grade.
11. Age 16 and completion of school year.

Source: U.S. Department of Education, *State Compulsory School Attendance Laws* (Washington, DC: National Center for Educational Statistics, 2007).

prevail. The teacher is the taskmaster whose job it is to impose the curriculum upon students, whether children learn anything or not. Under these circumstances it is not surprising that some students find school to be hostile and uninviting, where the teacher–student relationship is characterized by structured

Educators in several states have banned purses from classrooms because the bags could hold firearms and compromise school safety. Are zero-tolerance school policies where seemingly innocent items, such as purses, are illegal worthwhile?

conflict, and where teachers coerce students into obedience and teach them to follow routines and submit to authority. Some students feel they are in a powder keg waiting to explode, and many act out in inappropriate ways that are dangerous to them, their classmates, and their teachers.

VIOLENCE AT SCHOOL

There is not a shortage of shocking incidents of violence in schools in the United States, including highly publicized killings, homicides, and other acts of violent delinquency. For example, in May 2006, 12 boys between ages 6 and 8 at an elementary school in St. Louis were suspended for the entire school year after sexually assaulting a second-grade girl during recess.[10] On March 8, 2000, Kayla Roland, age 6, was shot in the neck in her first-grade classroom with a .32-caliber pistol and died a half hour later. Her killer, Dedrick Owens, also only 6 years old, had quarreled with Kayla on the playground the day before. Dedrick, already known as a bully, had found the loaded pistol lying under blankets on the floor of his home and brought it to school tucked in his pants. After shooting Kayla, Dedrick ran into a nearby bathroom and tossed the gun into a trashcan. Once in police custody, Dedrick sat quietly drawing pictures after indicating to the police that he thought he had done something "naughty."[11]

Source: Jeff Stahler © Columbus Dispatch/Dist. by Newspaper Enterprise Association, Inc.

In the past decade the United States has witnessed a series of shockingly violent episodes taking place in the nation's high schools. These events included a principal and student killed in Bethel, Alaska; three students killed and five more wounded in West Paducah, Kentucky; one teacher and five students killed in Jonesboro, Arkansas; a teacher killed and a student wounded in Edinboro, Pennsylvania; and a teacher and 13 students killed at Columbine High School in Littleton, Colorado. In the wake of the Columbine mass murder, some students attempted to imitate the rampage. For instance, one week after Columbine, a disgruntled teenager who had dropped out of school killed a student and wounded another at the W.R. Meyers High School in Taber, Canada. In Pennsylvania, 52 bomb scares were reported the week after Columbine. Other bomb scares or plots to "copy cat" the Columbine Massacre were attempted in 17 states.[12]

Shootings in high schools, though generally rare, have been part of the school landscape during much of the second half of the 20th century. Even in the 1950s, a number of movies, such as *High School Confidential* and *Blackboard Jungle,* focused on violence in high schools. But before the late 1980s and early 1990s, when juvenile gun violence had risen so dramatically, shootings in schools typically involved only single victims, and students in the lower grades rarely witnessed the violence and were even more rarely the victims of violence. With the shooting of Kayla Roland, America's elementary schools were no longer seen as inviolate islands of safety for children. Guns were now being brought into first-grade classrooms and 6-year-olds were being shot to death (see Box 11-1).

Perhaps due to the great amount of media attention given to the series of incidents involving multiple-shooting victims in schools, school violence and bullying have replaced drive-by shootings and gang-related violence as the country's greatest concern involving the safety of its children (see Figure 11-1). However, school-associated violent deaths are rare. According to the most recent Indicators of School Crime and Safety survey, children are approximately *75 times* more likely to be murdered away from school than at school.[13]

box 11-1   DELINQUENCY AROUND THE GLOBE
School Violence Around the World

School violence is a worldwide problem. As the following examples illustrate, the typical offender is a male who shoots a male victim because of an interpersonal dispute in a school classroom or hallway, and then kills himself, leaving many questions unanswered. Below are listed a few examples of school violence that have recently taken place in the United States and elsewhere around the world.

- October 2, 2006: Charles Roberts, 32, man enters the West Nickel Mines School, a one-room Amish schoolhouse in Lancaster County, Pennsylvania, and kills five girls (aged 7–13) and himself.
- September 27, 2006: Duane Morrison, a 53-year old drifter, entered Platte Canyon High School in Bailey, Colorado, saying that he had a bomb. Morrison took six female students hostage, sexually assaulted them, killed one of the students, and then committed suicide.
- July 27, 2006: Five children aged 12 and 13 beat an 11-year-old boy to death after school in Thessaloniki, Greece.
- March 21, 2005: Jeffrey Weise, 16, killed five students, four adults, and himself at Red Lake High School in Minnesota.
- September 3, 2004: More than two dozen terrorists belonging to a cell formed by radical Chechen rebel leader Shamil Basayev killed more than 150 children who they had taken hostage at a school in Beslan in southern Russia.
- June 1, 2004: The throat of 12-year-old Satomi Mitarai was slit and her arms slashed with a box-cutter by an 11-year-old classmate who left her to bleed to death in Tokyo.
- April 29, 2002: Dragoslav Petkovic, 17, opened fire with a handgun shortly after noon at his high school in Vlasenica, Bosnia-Herzegovina, killing one teacher and wounding another before taking his own life.
- April 26, 2002: Robert Steinhaeuser, 19, who had been expelled from his high school in Erfurt, Germany, returned to the school and shot and killed 13 teachers, two students, and a police officer before killing himself.

- February 19, 2002: A 22-year-old gunman in Munich, Germany, killed his former boss and a foreman at the company that fired him, then went to a high school where he shot the school's headmaster when he was unable to find the teacher he was after. He then shot another teacher in the face and set off home-made bombs before killing himself.
- June 8, 2001: Mamoru Takuma forced his way into Ikeda Elementary School in Osaka, Japan, stabbed to death 8 students and injured 13 others.
- March 26, 2001: An arson fire at the Kyanguli Secondary School in Kenya killed 67 students. Two students were charged with murder.
- April 28, 1999: A 14-year-old, who had been bullied, opened fired at his high school in Taber, Alberta, Canada, killing a 17-year-old student and wounding another student.
- May 21, 1998: Kip Kinkel, 15, murdered his mother and father, and then went to Thurston High School in Springfield, Oregon, where he killed 2 students and wounded 25 others.
- October 1, 1997: A 16-year-old boy killed two students and wounded seven others at his high school in Pearl, Mississippi.
- March 13, 1996: Thomas Hamilton, 43, dressed in black and wearing earmuffs to protect him from the noise, entered an elementary school in Dunblane, Scotland, and sprayed 105 bullets into the gym striking 29 people before killing himself. Sixteen 5- and 6-year-olds and a teacher died.

Sources: Valeria Korchagina, "Russians' Grief Mixes With Anger at Officials," *USA TODAY,* September 7, 2004:8A; National School Safety Center, *School-Associated Violent Deaths Report* (Westlake Village, CA: National School Safety Center, 2006); Audrey Mcavoy, "Japanese Girl, 12, Slain by Schoolmate," *Boulder Daily Camera,* June 2, 2004:3B; Judy Keen, "A Year After Minn. Shootings, Questions, Pain Remain Fresh," *USA TODAY,* March 21, 2006:4A; Matt DeLisi, "The Columbine High School Massacre and Criminal Justice System Response: An Exploratory Case Study," *Social Science Journal* 39:19–29 (2002); Amy Bounds, "Schools Try to Increase Security After Shootings," *Boulder Daily Camera,* October 4, 2006:1A; Costas Kantouris, "Schoolchildren Accused of Killing Boy," *Des Moines Register,* July 27, 2006:5A.

With 32 victims, the mass murder at Virginia Tech in 2007 was the deadliest mass killing in modern American history. In the wake of the Virginia Tech tragedy, what factors were cited as "causes" of the event? How do these factors relate to theories of delinquency? Can aberrant events such as this be predicted or understood with existing theories, or do they defy explanation?

figure 11-1   Student Deaths in American Schools

SCHOOL YEAR	TOTAL DEATHS
2006–2007	13
2005–2006	27
2004–2005	39
2003–2004	49
2002–2003	16
2001–2002	17
2000–2001	31
1999–2000	33

Source: Greg Toppo, "High-Tech School Security Is on the Rise," *USA Today,* October 10, 2006: 7D.

Yet shootings at schools have galvanized public concern about school safety, even though research studies have found schools nationwide are safe. Two nationwide studies of school homicides have been conducted by the Centers for Disease Control and Prevention in collaboration with the U.S. Departments of Education and Justice. The first study covered a two-year period and identified 68 students who were killed on or near school grounds or at school-related events.[14] Most of the victims were male and were killed with firearms. These homicides represent less than 1 percent of all youth homicides in the period studied, and the estimated incidence of school-associated violent death was 0.09 per 100,000 student-years. Those at greatest risk of being killed were racial or ethnic minority males attending senior high schools in urban school districts. The homicide rate in urban schools, for example, was nine times greater than the rate in rural schools. The most common motives were an interpersonal dispute or gang-related activities.[15] The second study updated the figures. It identified 177 students age 5 to 19 who were killed over a 5-year period; the vast majority of the homicides (84 percent) involved firearms. School-associated homicides remained at less than 1 percent of all homicides among students, but the frequency of homicides involving more than one victim increased.[16]

Most school crime is nonfatal. The National Crime Victimization Survey found that the rate of serious violent crimes against youths age 12 to 18 was about one-half as great when they were at school as when they were not. At school, the highest victimization rates were among male students and younger students (ages 12 to 14). The rate was highest in urban schools and lower at suburban and rural schools. Overall, the rate of serious violent crimes at school remained relatively stable for the past 15 years at about 6 to 13 per 1,000 students. The Monitoring the Future survey, which asks high school seniors whether they have been victims of violence, corroborates the stability of this trend. The percentage of seniors reporting that they had been injured with a weapon at school remained stable at about 5 percent since 1990. The same victimization rate is reported by the National Study of Delinquency Prevention in Schools.[17] A snapshot of school crime statistics appears in Box 11-2.

think
about it

One reason schools are characterized by delinquency is they warehouse people ages 14 to 18. These are among the most criminogenic ages. Is a school-delinquency connection inevitable given the age effect?

Bullying at School

Bullying is the use of one's strength or status to intimidate, injure, or humiliate another person of lesser strength or status. It occurs whenever students are picked on or made to do things they do not want to do. There are four kinds of bullying:

1. *Physical bullying,* which involves hitting, kicking, spitting, pushing, and taking personal belongings.
2. *Verbal bullying,* which includes taunting, teasing, name calling, and making threats.
3. *Emotional bullying,* which encompasses spreading rumors, manipulating social relationships, or engaging in social exclusion, extortion, or intimidation.
4. *Sexual bullying,* which involves sexual harassment and actual abuse.

Bullying must be distinguished from other forms of peer aggression or conflict; bullying always involves a power imbalance between the bully and the victim.[18] Although both boys and girls bully, there are clear gender differences. Girls mostly commit emotional and verbal bullying whereas boys are more likely to physically bully. There are several important risk factors or warning signs that a child may bully his or her peers. Bullies are impulsive, hot-tempered, and lack empathy. They have difficulty following rules, are often bored and frustrated, and have low interest in school. Bullies are likely to be raised in homes where there is little parental warmth and involvement in addition to harsh and inconsistent parental discipline.[19]

Prevalence of Bullying   Bullying is widespread in the United States and in other countries. A national study found that 30 percent of students are involved in bullying either as a bully (13 percent), a victim (11 percent), or both a bully and a victim (6 percent). A study by the National Institute of Child Health and

box 11-2   A WINDOW ON DELINQUENCY
School Crime Statistics

Delinquency is extensive in American schools. For example, in 2006:

• About 1.4 million nonfatal crimes occurred; nearly 900,000 were thefts.

• More than 583,000 violent crimes, such as rapes, sexual assaults, robberies, simple and aggravated assaults were reported.

• There were 21 students killed at school representing less than one homicide per million students enrolled.

• About 4 percent of students reported being victimized at school; most of the reported cases were theft.

• Boys were more likely than girls to be threatened or injured with a weapon at school.

• More than 150,000 teacher victimizations occurred, including more than 50,000 violent victimizations.

• Ten percent of teachers in central city schools were threatened with injury by their students.

• More than 81 percent of public schools experienced at least one violent incident, and 36 percent reported the incident to the police.

• Nearly 20 percent of public schools reported weekly student acts of disrespect toward teachers, 13 percent reported verbal abuse of teachers, and 3 percent reported widespread disorder in the classroom.

• Twenty-four percent of students reported that street gangs are present in their schools.

• Twenty-five percent of high school students reported that someone had offered, sold, or given them illegal drugs on school property.

• Thirty-six percent of high school students reported having been in a physical fight in the past year.

• About six percent of students skipped school out of fear of victimization.

Source: Rachel Dinkes, Emily Forrest Cataldi, Grace Kena, Katrina Baum, and Thomas Snyder, *Indicators of School Crime and Safety: 2006* (Washington, DC: U. S. Department of Justice, 2006).

Human Development estimated that 1.7 million American children in grades 6 through 10 can be identified as bullies. This study found that 11 percent of students reported bullying others "sometimes" (moderate bullying) and 9 percent admitted to bullying others "once a week" or more (frequent bullying). Bullying occurs most frequently from 6th to 8th grade, with little variation seen among urban, suburban, and rural areas.[20]

The National Center for Education Statistics reported increases in the percentage of students victimized by bullying in recent years. While crime at school as a whole has declined in recent years, bullying is one of the few problems to increase in prevalence. Almost 10 percent of students reported that they had been bullied at school in the last 6 months. Nine percent of all males and 7 percent of all females surveyed (ages 12 to 18) reported experiencing bullying during the past 6 months. The percentage of students who reported that they had been bullied increased for each racial–ethnic group except African American students. About 6 percent of African American students in both years reported they had been bullied. The percentage of students bullied increased from 5 percent to 9 percent for white students, from 4 percent to 8 percent for Hispanic students, and from 3 percent to 7 percent for other, non-Hispanic students.[21]

Consequences of Bullying   Bullying has long- and short-term consequences for both those who are bullied and those who are bullies. Bullies and their targets are more likely to engage in violent behavior, such as frequent fighting or carrying a weapon than other youths. Victims of bullying grow up to have more depression and lower self-esteem than other adults. Children who are bullied also are more likely to feel lonely, to have trouble making friends, and to get along poorly with classmates. Sometimes they are insecure, embarrass easily, and are fearful of attending school. The impact of chronic childhood bullying often follows them into adulthood where they face substantial risks of suffering from depression, schizophrenia, and committing suicide.

Children who bully are also affected by their behavior, and bullying is usually only one of their problems. They might also abuse animals, vandalize buildings, shoplift, drop out of school, fight, and use illegal drugs and alcohol. Dan Olweus and Susan Limber found that bullies are more likely to be *chronic offenders* and adult criminals. They also reported that 60 percent of boys who bullied in grades 6 through 9 were convicted of at least one crime as adults, compared with 23 percent of boys who did not bully. More strikingly, 40 percent of boys who bullied had three or more convictions by age 24, compared with only 10 percent of boys who did not bully.[22] Matt DeLisi suggests that many of the most serious career criminals began their careers in violence as bullies at school.[23]

think
about it

Is bullying a social problem or a minor nuisance that many people experience in their lives? Why might bullying contribute to school shootings?

Prevention of Bullying   Peter Gill and Max Stenlund recently conducted a case study where three friends of a bully acted as police officers to intervene when a classroom bully started to victimize other students. The three peers forcefully pinned the bully to the ground and commanded him to stop harassing and using violence toward others. Seeing the class bully being physically overpowered reduced the perception among students that he was to be feared. In addition, the case study provided a deterrent to the bully because he did not like the experience of being physically handled.[24] Unfortunately, examples like this are likely the exception.

Research shows that bullying can have lasting adverse effects on children, but that carefully implemented school programs may substantially reduce bullying.[25] Bullying at school can be reduced by approximately 30 to 70 percent, according to Dan Olweus, whose program was implemented throughout Norway. His approach has been adapted for use in many schools in other countries, including the United States. The basic program involves school-wide, classroom, and individual interventions. School-wide rules and sanctions that emphasize a climate intolerant of bullying behaviors are reinforced by regular classroom discussions. Individual students receive consistent supervision and discipline, accompanied by parent involvement and in some cases, mental health interventions.[26] The Olweus Bullying Prevention Program is so effective that is has been recognized as a model program by the Office of Juvenile Justice and Delinquency Prevention and the Substance Abuse and Mental Health Services Administration.

Teacher Victimization

Some crime victims in schools are teachers. In addition to the personal toll that violence may take on teachers, those who worry about their safety may have difficulty teaching and may leave the profession altogether. From 2001 to 2005, teachers were the victims of 1.3 million nonfatal crimes at school, including 817,000 thefts and 473,000 violent crimes (rape or sexual assault, robbery, aggravated assault, and simple assault). Among the violent crimes committed against teachers during this 5-year period, there were about 48,000 *serious* violent crimes accounting for 10 percent of the violent crimes, including rape or sexual assault, robbery, and aggravated assault. On average, 21 violent crimes were committed for every 1,000 teachers, and teachers were victims of two serious violent crimes per 1,000 teachers, annually.

During the same 5-year period, the annual rate of violent victimization for teachers varied according to their sex and their instructional level. For example, urban teachers were more likely than rural and suburban teachers to be victims of violent crime (28 vs. 13 vs. 16 crimes, respectively, per 1,000 students). Teachers in urban areas were more likely than those in rural areas to experience theft at school (42 and 26 crimes per 1,000 teachers, respectively).

Teachers also are threatened and attacked by students. Data on the extent to which students make threats or physically attack elementary and secondary teachers provide a snapshot of this problem. In a recent survey teachers were asked whether they had been threatened with injury or physically attacked by a student in the previous 12 months. The survey results indicate that about 10 percent of elementary and secondary school teachers are threatened with injury by a student at their school. Each year about 4 percent of teachers are physically attacked by a student. Teachers in central city schools were more likely to be threatened with injury or to be physically attacked than teachers in urban fringe or rural schools. For example, 11 percent of teachers in central city schools had been threatened with injury by students, compared with 8 percent each in suburban and rural schools.

Teachers' reports of being victimized or attacked by a student vary according to the level and sector of their school. Secondary school teachers were more likely than elementary school teachers to have been threatened with injury by a student (10 percent vs. 8 percent); however, secondary school teachers were less likely to have been physically attacked (2 percent vs. 6 percent). Public school teachers were more likely than private school teachers to be victimized by students in school: 10 percent of public school teachers had been threatened with injury, compared with 4 percent of private school teachers. Likewise, students had physically attacked 4 percent of public school teachers and 2 percent of private school teachers. Among teachers in central city schools, those at public schools were four times more likely to be targets of threats of injury than their colleagues in private schools (14 percent vs. 3 percent) and about three times more likely to be targets of attacks (6 percent vs. 2 percent).[27]

Perceptions of School Violence

Although the overall risk of violence and injury at school has declined, students and their parents report being increasingly apprehensive about their schools. Students are more fearful about being attacked or harmed at school, and they often avoid certain places within their schools. Some teenagers skip school for fear of getting hurt, and many parents are afraid for their children at school.[28] A Gallup poll found that nearly half of the parents surveyed feared for their children's safety when they sent them off to school, whereas only 24 percent of parents reported this concern in 1977. Shortly after the shootings at

Columbine High School in Littleton, Colorado, 74 percent of parents said that a school shooting was very likely or somewhat likely to happen in their community.[29]

Public perceptions about school safety seem at odds with the evidence that the risk for serious violence at school has not changed substantially over the past 20 years. For instance, Pamela Wilcox and her colleagues compared the objective and subjective experiences with school crime among nearly 4,000 middle school students in Kentucky. Students reported that although the most serious forms of school crime occasionally occur, they are "overrated" in the sense that most students did not experience violence. Instead, losing their property due to theft was overwhelmingly the most common type of school delinquency. Wilcox also found that students reported a substantial amount of fear of crime at school especially for offenses, such as simple assault, theft, and sexual harassment. Students who had previously been victimized at school were significantly more likely to report feeling less safe and perceive that various types of school crime were common.[30]

But several indicators of violence did increase during the epidemic, such as school fights, gangs, drug use, and students carrying weapons to school. While gangs and weapon carrying have declined recently, the rates of drug use and physical fighting are high and have not changed since the 1990s. Today's students are still more likely to be carrying guns than those of the earlier eras, and the proportion of students reporting that they felt too unsafe to go to school has not changed since the peak of the violence epidemic in the mid-1990s. These findings add to the concern that the violence epidemic is not yet over.[31]

SCHOOLS, CHILDREN, AND THE LAW

Schools are in a constant struggle to promote a climate that fosters learning and teaching. To control the behavior of students, schools put into place many rules and regulations. The student handbooks children receive when they enter secondary school are roughly the same across the nation. They list behaviors that are violations of school policy and the consequences for violating them. For instance, in some schools students cannot bring toys to school, wear their hair in any style, or wear spaghetti straps. Students who violate school rules often are disciplined. The most common form of discipline is to remove the student from the activity or specific area for a "time-out." For more serious violations, students are required to have their parents sign and return a discipline form. If a student continues to misbehave, the principal, teacher, student, and parents will confer to discuss the situation. Sometimes students are expelled or suspended from school, and in some school districts, in some states, students are physically punished.

Suspension and Expulsion

Students are suspended or expelled from school for violating school rules or for having a dangerous health condition, such as lice. Students who face suspension have specific legal rights. In 1976, in *Goss v. Lopez,* the Supreme Court decided that students who face suspension for 10 days or less must receive a hearing.

School shooters, such as Kenneth Bartley, often generate policy discussions about toughening laws against juvenile offenders. While school shootings are often deadly and receive massive media coverage, they are rare compared to other serious forms of delinquency. Why does the public focus so much attention on school shootings?

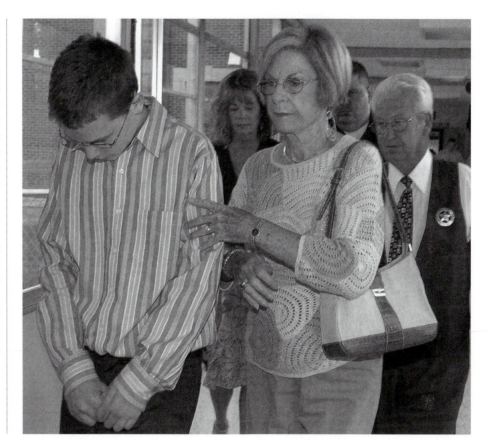

However, at the hearing they *do not* have the right to an attorney or the right to cross-examine and confront witnesses. Within 24 hours following a suspension, the principal must provide the student's parents with a written statement describing the reason why the child was suspended. The principal must also make a reasonable effort to hold a conference with the parents before the student is readmitted to school (see Box 11-3).[32]

Students who face expulsion are guaranteed a more exhaustive list of rights than students who may be only suspended. Students who face expulsion have a right to a hearing, the right to know the qualifications of the hearing examiner, and the right to appeal the decision to the school superintendent or school board. Some children are more likely to be suspended than others. Of the more than three million children suspended from school every year, over 30 percent are African American, even though only 17 percent of the total student population nationwide is African American. In fact, nearly 1 in 8 African American children are suspended every year, while only 1 of 30 white students is suspended annually. These data have led civil rights groups to contend that, like police who stop juveniles on the basis of their race, teachers and school officials discipline African American students more often and more harshly than whites. The result is that African American students are more likely to fall behind in their studies and abandon school altogether.

The issue before the Court in *Goss v. Lopez* was whether the suspension of a student for a period of up to 10 days without a hearing constituted a violation of their due process rights. Several public high school students (including D. Lopez) were suspended from school for misconduct but were not given a hearing immediately before or after their suspension. School authorities in Columbus, Ohio, claimed that a state law allowed them to suspend students for up to 10 days with a hearing. The students brought legal action claiming that the statute was unconstitutional because it allowed school authorities to deprive students of their right to a hearing, violating the due process clause of the Fourteenth Amendment.

The Court said that education is a property interest protected by the Fourteenth Amendment and any suspension requires prior notice and a hearing. Permitting suspension without a hearing is, therefore, unconstitutional. The Court said that oral or written notice of the charges brought against a student must be given to the student who is being suspended for more than a trivial period. If he denies the charges, the student must be given a hearing. The hearing may be an informal one where the student is simply given an explanation of the evidence against him and an opportunity to tell his side of the story.

Source: Goss v. Lopez, 419 U.S. 565 (1975).

Corporal Punishment

Corporal punishment is the infliction of pain as a penalty for a student who violates a school rule.[33] Teachers and other school officials hitting students for breaking school rules have a well-documented history. In the 17th century in Jesuit schools, it was expected that teachers would hit students. Serious student offenders were "stripped in front of the whole community and beaten until they bled." Whipping was a teaching aid. One student complained, "My master . . . beat me horribly; he used to seize me by the ears and lift me off the ground."[34]

In America during the Colonial era, corporal punishment was also widely practiced. Disobedient students were tied to the whipping post and beaten. Violence against students was justified on the basis of an assertion in the Old Testament attributed to Solomon in the Book of Proverbs: "He that spareth his rod hateth his son; but he that loveth him chastiseth him betimes."[35] Thus, the "right thing to do" was for teachers to physically punish unruly students.[36]

By the end of the 20th century and into the early 21st century, discipline problems in schools were a daily occurrence. Teachers tried to control students through threats, intimidation, and beatings. Today, as is shown in Table 11-2, corporal punishment in schools is prohibited in every industrialized nation except the United States and one state in Australia. The U.S. Supreme Court has issued two rulings on the corporal punishment of students. In 1975, in *Baker v. Owen,* the Court decided that teachers could administer reasonable corporal punishment for disciplinary purposes.[37] In 1977 in *Ingraham v. Wright,* the Court added that corporal punishment does not violate the cruel and unusual punishment clause of the Eighth Amendment (see Box 11-4).

table 11-2	Worldwide Ban on Corporal Punishment

Except for the United States and one state in Australia, all industrialized nations have banned corporal punishment in schools. The following list shows a sample of the trend toward prohibiting corporal punishment that dates as far back as the 1700s.

YEAR	COUNTRY	YEAR	COUNTRY
1783	Poland	1970	Germany
1820	Netherlands	1970	Switzerland
1845	Luxembourg	1982	Ireland
1860	Italy	1982	Greece
1867	Belgium	1986	United Kingdom*
1870	Austria	1990	New Zealand
1881	France	1990	Namibia
1890	Finland	1996	South Africa
1900	Japan	1998	American Samoa
1917	Russia	1998	Kenya
1923	Turkey	1999	Fiji
1936	Norway	1999	Zimbabwe
1949	China	2000	Zambia
1950	Portugal	2000	Thailand
1958	Sweden	2000	Trinidad and Tobago
1967	Denmark	2004	Canada
1967	Cyprus		

* Includes England, Scotland, Wales, and Northern Ireland.

Source: National Coalition to Abolish Corporal Punishment in Schools, 2007, available at http://www.stophitting .com/disatschool/, accessed June 25, 2007.

However, while school authorities may hit children, the Court, in *Garcia v. Miera* (1987), held that the extent of the punishment must not be excessive. In *Garcia,* a 9-year-old New Mexico girl was held upside down and struck five times with a broken wooden paddle leading to bleeding and permanent scarring. She was paddled a second time 3 months later causing severe bruising. The 10th Circuit Court of Appeals found that school officials had used excessive force in administering corporal punishment and by doing so violated the student's federal constitutional right of substantive due process. Both the school district and the administrators were liable for damages suffered by the student. The *Garcia* case makes it clear that school officials can be sued, and the results can be time-consuming and expensive. But what happens if parents object to the use of corporal punishment on their children? The 4th Circuit Court of Appeals considered this question in **Hall v. Tawney** and ruled parents have *no* constitutional right to exempt their children from corporal punishment in public schools.[38]

Teachers, principals, coaches, and bus drivers physically punish nearly 400,000 students each year. While this number may be alarming, it represents a steep drop from the 1.4 million students who received corporal punishment in 1980. In spite of this trend toward the elimination of corporal punishment in public schools, about 5,000 children annually are beaten so badly that they require medical attention. Furthermore, more than 90 percent of the reported

box 11-4   FROM THE BENCH

Ingraham v. Wright

In *Ingraham v. Wright,* the Court was asked to decide whether school authorities have the right to use corporal punishment. The case involved James Ingraham who was a junior high school student in Dade County (Miami), Florida. Ingraham was paddled 20 times by the school principal, Willie Wright, for not leaving the stage of the school auditorium promptly. Principal Wright hit Ingraham repeatedly on the buttocks with a 2-foot long wooden paddle. When Ingraham went home, his mother examined him and then took him to a local hospital. At the hospital, doctors prescribed pain pills, ice packs, and a laxative and recommended Ingraham stay home from school for one week.

The Court ruled that the "cruel and unusual punishment clause" of the Eighth Amendment

does not apply to corporal punishment in schools and the "due process clause" of the Fourteenth Amendment does not require the school to give students notice before punishing them. The Court declared that corporal punishment is not "cruel and unusual" punishment because it is the traditional method for maintaining discipline in public schools. The Court also argued that the punishment must be reasonable and that if the punishment is extreme, criminal charges may be brought against the offender. In other words, school authorities may hit children, but the extent of the punishment cannot be excessive.

Source: Ingraham v. Wright, 439 U. S. 651 (1977).

think about it

For most students, the threat of paddling is an effective means of social control. But for some bullies, paddling may be viewed as a status symbol of achievement. Should paddling be used more widely?

incidents of corporal punishment in schools nationwide took place in only 10 states.[39] African Americans and males are hit most often. Boys, who comprise 51 percent of the student population, receive 80 percent of the beatings administered at schools. Similarly, African Americans constitute about 17 percent of the students nationwide, but are hit 40 percent of the time.[40] For a look at which states permit corporal punishment, see Figure 11-2.

The reasons why corporal punishment is banned vary, but they include the following:

1. It perpetuates a cycle of child abuse by teaching children to hit someone smaller and weaker when angry.

2. Injuries occur. Bruises are common. Broken bones are not unusual. Children's deaths have occurred as a result of corporal punishment in U.S. schools.

3. Corporal punishment is used much more often on poor children, racial and ethnic minorities, children with disabilities, and boys.

4. Schools are the only institutions in America in which striking another person is legally sanctioned. Corporal punishment is prohibited in prisons, in the military, and in mental hospitals.

5. Educators and school boards may be sued when corporal punishment is used in their schools.

6. Schools that use corporal punishment often have poorer academic achievement; more vandalism, truancy, pupil violence; and higher drop out rates.

figure 11-2   U.S. States Banning Corporal Punishment

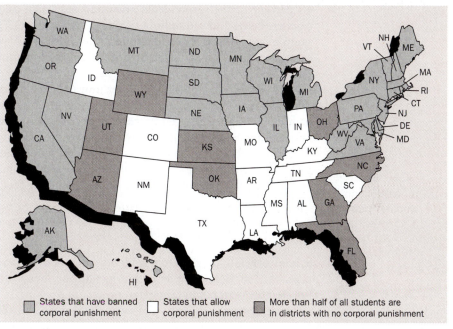

| States that have banned corporal punishment | States that allow corporal punishment | More than half of all students are in districts with no corporal punishment |

Source: Adapted from the National Coalition to Abolish Capital Punishment, 2006, available at www.stophitting .com/disatschool/, accessed June 27, 2007.

7. Corporal punishment is often *not* used as a last resort. It is often the first resort for minor misbehaviors.

8. Alternatives to corporal punishment, such as time-out, losing recess, and calling parents, have proven their worth. Alternatives teach children to be self-disciplined rather than cooperative only because of fear.

Research examining the effect of corporal punishment on children has found that it may lead to more serious problems for the juvenile, the school, and other students through increased aggression and depression.[41] Andrew Grogan-Kaylor found that children who are paddled have an earlier onset of antisocial behavior, which often portends a variety of behavioral problems. In addition, the effects of corporal punishment on delinquency appear to be longer lasting among boys than girls.[42] Emily Douglas and Murray Straus explored the experience of corporal punishment as a child as it related to adult dating behavior. Using a sample of 9,549 students in 26 universities in 19 countries, they found that being spanked as a child exerted an independent effect on assault in adult dating behavior. Adults who were paddled as children, in other words, are more likely to use violence in romantic relationships when they are at university.[43]

In the United States, there is currently a nationwide movement to prohibit corporal punishment in public schools. (Private schools are not affected by state and federal laws on corporal punishment.) More than 40 professional organizations including the American Academy of Pediatrics, American Bar Association, American Medical Association, American Psychiatric Association, and the

National Education Association oppose corporal punishment, but these groups face stiff opposition and an unsympathetic public. In a national opinion poll, 48 percent of the respondents answered *yes* when asked: "Do you agree with teachers being allowed to inflict corporal punishment?"; about 44 percent of the sample said *no;* and 8 percent voiced "no opinion." Nevertheless, the movement to end corporal punishment in public schools continues to move forward (see Table 11-3).[44]

Does corporal punishment deter unwanted behavior? No widespread deterrent effects of corporal punishment have been found whether the spanking or paddling was administered by parents or teachers. Instead, the effects of corporal punishment are a range of physical, psychological, emotional, and behavioral problems.[45] Ralph Welsh found that corporal punishment produces fear and anger in students. When the fear subsides, the anger remains. Angry students are more likely to strike out at whomever and whatever they blame for their pain and suffering.[46]

Searches and Seizures

think
about it

Should schools use dogs to search for contraband such as explosives and drugs? Are such measures unnecessary forms of social control or viable steps toward preventing delinquency?

School officials may search students and their lockers without consent. This may seem to violate the Fourth Amendment, but it does not. The standard is lowered for searches in schools to protect and maintain a proper educational environment for all students. This was the decision reached in ***Thompson v. Carthage School District.*** Ramone Lea was expelled from Carthage High School after school officials found crack cocaine in his coat pocket while looking for guns and knives reported to be on school grounds. The district court awarded $10,000 to Lea in damages for "wrongful expulsion" because the search had violated his Fourth Amendment rights. The Carthage School District appealed the ruling to the U.S. Court of Appeals, which concluded that under the circumstances the search was constitutionally reasonable.[47]

| **table 11-3** | Corporal Punishment in U.S. Public Schools, 2005 |

In 2005 in the United States, 301,016 students were recipients of corporal punishment. Today, 29 states and the District of Columbia have banned corporal punishment (Ohio and Utah have limited bans). Data on the remaining 21 states are listed below.

STATE	NUMBER OF STUDENTS HIT	STATE	NUMBER OF STUDENTS HIT
Alabama	37,390	Mississippi	45,197
Arizona	64	Missouri	6,875
Arkansas	34,113	New Mexico	1,119
Colorado	71	North Carolina	4,866
Florida	9,223	Ohio	621
Georgia	25,189	Oklahoma	17,046
Idaho	7	South Carolina	2,781
Indiana	1,605	Tennessee	37,419
Kansas	46	Texas	57,817
Kentucky	2,846	Wyoming	2
Louisiana	7,200		

Source: National Coalition to Abolish Corporal Punishment in Schools, 2006, available at www.stophitting.com/disatschool/, accessed June 26, 2007.

School officials may also search student lockers because the school is the rightful owner of both the locks and lockers. Students in effect "borrow" them to store clothes, schoolbooks, supplies, and personal items necessary for school. Lockers cannot be used to store items that interfere with any school purpose. Therefore, lockers and their contents are subject to search to ensure they are being properly used.

A search of all lockers is called a **sweep search,** which can be ordered whenever a principal believes an inspection of lockers is necessary for many reasons that include:

1. Interference with a school purpose or an educational function.
2. Physical injuries or illness.
3. Damage to property.
4. Violation of state law or school rules.
5. Disposal of confiscated contraband.
6. Involvement of law enforcement officials.
7. Locker cleaning.

Contrary to the probable cause requirement of the Fourth Amendment, the decision to search lockers is based on the less-restrictive notion of reasonableness and school officials' interpretation of what reasonableness is. The "reasonable suspicion doctrine" was applied in 1985 in *New Jersey v. T.L.O.,* when the Court ruled that school officials can conduct warrantless searches of individuals at school on the basis of reasonable suspicion (see Box 11-5).[48]

---

box 11-5   **FROM THE BENCH**

New Jersey v. T.L.O.

In *New Jersey v. T.L.O.* the Court was asked to decide whether the state of New Jersey and its agent, the assistant vice-principal, violated T.L.O.'s Fourth Amendment right of protection from "unreasonable search," her Fifth Amendment right of protection from self-incrimination, and her right to due process as provided in the Fourteenth Amendment. In 1980 a teacher at Piscataway High School, New Jersey, discovered two girls smoking in the lavatory. Since smoking was a violation of a school rule, the two students, T.L.O. and a companion, were taken to the principal's office. There they met with the assistant vice-principal who demanded to see T.L.O.'s purse. Upon opening the purse, he found cigarettes and a cigarette rolling paper. He proceeded to look through the purse and found marijuana and drug paraphernalia, money, lists of names, and two letters that implicated her in drug dealing. T.L.O. argued that the search of her purse was unconstitutional.

The Court decided in favor of the school and its assistant vice-principal. The Court reasoned that to maintain discipline in school, school officials who have "reasonable suspicion" that a student has done something wrong can conduct a reasonable search of the suspicious student. A school's main objective is to educate students in a legal, safe learning environment. Police need "probable cause," a higher standard, to search people, places, and things. School officials, unlike the police, need only reasonable suspicion to search students when they suspect unlawful conduct.

Source: New Jersey v. T.L.O., 469 U. S. 325 (1985).

The decision in *T.L.O.* was affirmed in 1995 in ***Vernonia School District 47J v. Acton.*** In *Acton* the Court held that students participating in school athletic activities must submit upon request to an involuntary drug test. The *Acton* ruling thus allows schools to "seize" the urine of particular students to "search for" chemical traces of unlawful drugs, without any evidence of grounds for suspicion that drug testing is warranted (see Box 11-6). The Court's ruling in *Acton* was expanded in 2002 in ***Board of Education of Independent School District No. 92 of Pottawatomie County et al. v. Earls et al.,*** a case involving the legitimacy of a school district's drug testing policy. In *Earls* the Court decided that a school could require students to submit to a urinalysis for illegal drugs prior to participating in *any* competitive extracurricular activities such as the Academic team, Future Farmers of America, Future Homemakers of America, band, choir, pom pom, cheerleading, as well as athletics. In spite of efforts by the Court and school districts across the nation to thwart illegal drug use, research examining whether the relationship between a school having a drug testing policy and self-reported student drug use has found *no* relationship between them. As far as student drug use is concerned, it makes *no* difference whether a school has a drug testing policy in place or not.[49]

Free Speech

No one has absolute free speech. The guarantee of free speech in the First Amendment is a relative one, and no one can say what they want, when they want, wherever they want, without consequence. But even though the free speech students have in schools is more restricted than the free speech of adults, it is not entirely restricted (see Box 11-7).

One early Supreme Court ruling on the free speech of students was issued in 1943, in ***West Virginia State Board of Education v. Barnette.*** The Court held that the free speech rights of students were violated when they were required to salute the flag while reciting the Pledge of Allegiance (see Box 11-7).[50]

---

box 11-6 **FROM THE BENCH**

Vernonia v. Acton

The issue before the Court in *Vernonia v. Acton* is whether drug testing of student athletes violates their protection against unreasonable search and seizure provided in the Fourteenth Amendment? The Vernonia school district in Oregon, concerned about the drug problem among athletes and students in their community, sought to reduce the problem by creating a student-athlete drug policy. School officials worried that drug use by athletes might produce more risk of sports-related injuries. The Vernonia school district student-athlete drug policy authorized urinalysis drug testing of student athletes. James Acton refused the urinalysis test and was disallowed participation in the school's junior high football program. In a 6 to 3 decision, the Court reasoned that drug testing of student athletes was constitutional. The Court accepted the argument that student rights were lessened at school if it was necessary to maintain safety and to fulfill the educational mission of the school.

Source: Vernonia v. Acton, 515 U. S. 646 (1995).

box 11-7 — A WINDOW ON DELINQUENCY

Religion, Schools, and Students

The relationship among religion, schools, and students has evolved over the past 60 years. The Supreme Court has heard many cases where the First Amendment of the Constitution is at issue. With respect to religion, the First Amendment states:

Congress shall make no law requiring an establishment of religion, or prohibiting the free exercise of religion.

The Court has been asked to establish the boundaries that govern the relationship among religion, schools, and students. Some of the more notable Court decisions on this topic are the following:

1948: In *McCollum v. Board of Education,* the Court disallowed the practice of having religious education take place in public school classrooms during the school day.

1962: In *Engel v. Vitale,* the Court ruled it was unconstitutional for a school to require students to recite school prayers.

1963: In *Abington School District v. Schempp,* the Court overturned a Pennsylvania law that permitted the reading of 10 verses from the Bible at the opening of each school day.

1968: In *Epperson v. Arkansas,* the Court found the state law prohibiting the teaching of evolution to be unconstitutional.

1972: In *State of Wisconsin v. Jonas Yoder,* the Court ruled that compulsory schooling of Amish children beyond the eighth grade was a violation of the free exercise of religious rights.

1980: In *Stone v. Graham,* the Court ruled a Kentucky law requiring the posting of the Ten Commandments in each public school classroom in the state to be unconstitutional.

1985: In *Wallace v. Jaffree,* the Court found that an Alabama law requiring that each day begin with a one-minute period of "silent meditation or voluntary prayer" was unconstitutional.

1992: The Court ruled in *Lee v. Weisman* that the graduation prayer during a high school graduation was unconstitutional.

2000: In *Santa Fe School District v. Doe,* the Court held that official student-led prayers before a high school football game was unconstitutional.

2002: In *Zelman v. Simmons-Harris,* the Supreme Court ruled 5–4 that a Cleveland program that spends large amounts of public money on subsidizing education at religious schools was constitutional.

These rulings are based on the Court's interpretation that the First Amendment guarantees the government will not coerce any person to support or participate in religion or its exercise.

Sources: McCollum v. Board of Education, 333 U.S. 203 (1948); *Engel v. Vitale,* 370 U.S. 421 (1962); *Abington School District v. Schempp,* 374 U.S. 203 (1968); *Epperson v. Arkansas,* 393 U.S. 97 (1968); *Wisconsin v. Yoder,* 406 U.S. 208 (1972); *Stone v. Graham,* 449 U.S. 39 (1980); *Wallace v. Jaffree,* 472 U.S. 38 (1985); *Lee v. Weisman,* 505 U.S. 577 (1992); *Santa Fe School District v. Doe,* 168 F.3d 806 (2000); *Zelman v. Simmons-Harris,* 536 U.S. 639 (2002).

Twenty-six years later, in 1969 in ***Tinker v. Des Moines Independent Community School District,*** the Supreme Court revisited the issue of students' free expression. In *Tinker* several students who wore black arm bands to school in protest of the Vietnam War were suspended. The school argued that the armbands violated the dress code policy. The Court ruled in favor of the students, stating that their dress "neither interrupted school activities nor sought to intrude in the school affairs or the lives of others."[51]

think
about it

Some people are uncomfortable with the Pledge of Allegiance because God is mentioned. Should schools ever provide students with moral and religious messages?

There are some limits on a student's right to free expression, such as ***Bethel School District No. 403 v. Fraser,*** a decision in which the Court held that schools may prohibit vulgar and offensive language. On April 26, 1983, Matthew Fraser, a student at Bethel High School in Pierce County, Washington, delivered the following speech nominating a fellow student for student elective office:

> I know a man who is firm in his pants, he's firm in his shirt, his character is firm—but most of all, his belief in you, the students of Bethel, is firm. Jeff Kuhlman is a man who takes his point and pounds it in. He doesn't attack things in spurts—he drives hard, pushing and pushing until finally he succeeds. Jeff is a man who will go to the very end—even the climax, for each and every one of you. So vote for Jeff for ASB vice-president; he'll never come between you and the best our high school can be.

Approximately 600 high school students, many of whom were 14-year-olds, attended the assembly. Students were required to attend the assembly or to report to the study hall. The assembly was part of a school-sponsored educational program in self-government. During the entire speech, Fraser referred to his candidate in terms of an elaborate, graphic, and explicit sexual metaphor.

Two of Fraser's teachers, with whom he discussed the contents of his speech in advance, informed him that the speech was "inappropriate and that he probably should not deliver it," and that his delivery of the speech might have "severe consequences." During Fraser's delivery of the speech, a school counselor observed the reaction of students to the speech. Some students hooted and yelled; some by gestures graphically simulated the sexual activities pointedly alluded to in respondent's speech. Other students appeared to be bewildered and embarrassed by the speech. One teacher reported that on the day following the speech, she found it necessary to forgo a portion of the scheduled class lesson in order to discuss the speech with the class. A Bethel High School disciplinary rule prohibiting the use of obscene language in the school provides:

> Conduct which materially and substantially interferes with the educational process is prohibited, including the use of obscene, profane language or gestures.

The morning after the assembly, the Assistant Principal called Fraser into her office and notified him that the school considered his speech to have been a violation of this rule. Fraser was presented with copies of five letters submitted by teachers, describing his conduct at the assembly. He was given a chance to explain his conduct, and he admitted to having given the speech described and that he deliberately used sexual innuendo in the speech. Fraser was then informed that he would be suspended for 3 days, and that his name would be removed from the list of candidates for graduation speaker at the school's commencement exercises.

Fraser sought review of this disciplinary action through the School District's grievance procedures. The hearing officer determined that the speech given by respondent was "indecent, lewd, and offensive to the modesty and decency of many of the students and faculty in attendance at the assembly." The examiner determined that the speech fell within the ordinary meaning of "obscene," as used in the disruptive-conduct rule and affirmed the discipline in its entirety. Fraser served 2 days of his suspension and was allowed to return to school on the third day.[52]

Shortly after *Fraser*, in 1988, in ***Hazelwood School District v. Kuhlmeier,*** the Court decided that school administrators may regulate the content of student publications in public schools, but only if it served an educational purpose (see Box 11-8). The *Hazelwood* case involved a disagreement between students and school officials over administrative censorship of two pages in the school's student-run newspaper. (Students in private schools do not have First Amendment protection against censorship by their teachers and principals, who are not government employees.) The topics the students had written about were important to them: teenage pregnancy and divorce. The Court held that "censorship will only be prohibited in school-sponsored activities when school officials have no valid educational purpose for their action."[53]

The Court's decision in *Hazelwood* was widely protested on the basis that it constituted an unreasonable form of censorship. Critics complained that censorship does not enhance the education of young journalism students unless the purpose is to teach them not to report on unpopular issues. Students across the United States, however, have taken it on themselves to circumvent the censorship imposed upon them by *Hazelwood* by establishing independent student Web publications that are not under school control.[54]

On June 25, 2007, in *Morse v. Frederick,* the Supreme Court held that the First Amendment was not violated when school officials suspended students

---

box 11-8 FROM THE BENCH
Hazelwood School District v. Kuhlmeier

In *Hazelwood v. Kuhlmeier* the Court was asked to decide whether the school district violated the freedom of expression right of the First Amendment by regulating the content of its school newspaper. Kathy Kuhlmeier and two other journalism students wrote articles on pregnancy and divorce for their school newspaper. Their teacher submitted page proofs to the principal for approval. The principal objected to the articles because he felt that the students described in the article on pregnancy, although not named, could be identified, and the father discussed in the article on divorce was not allowed to respond to the derogatory article. The principal also said that the language used was not appropriate for younger students. When the newspaper was printed, two pages containing the articles in question as well as four other articles approved by the principal were deleted.

The Court held that the Hazelwood School District did not violate the First Amendment right of the students. The Court ruled that although schools may not limit the personal expression of students that happens to occur on school grounds (*Tinker v. Des Moines,* 393 U.S. 503 [1969]), they do not have to promote student speech that they do not agree with. This decision gave schools the power to censor activities such as school plays and school newspapers as long as the school finances the activities and there are grounds for the censorship. The Court said in *Tinker* that in order to censor a student's expression, the expression must substantially disrupt the school's educational process, or impinge upon the rights of others. This case broadened that guideline to include censorship of unprofessional, ungrammatical or obscene speech, or speech that goes against the fundamental purpose of a school.

Source: Hazelwood School District v. Kuhlmeier, 484 U.S. 260 (1988).

for displaying a banner that stated "Bong Hits 4 Jesus" because schools are entrusted to protect students from harmful language, including language that appears to promote substance use. Chief Justice John Roberts delivered the opinion of the Court in a narrow 5-4 ruling.[55]

EXPLANATIONS OF SCHOOL DELINQUENCY

Schools in the United States face a wide range of problems. There is violence and bullying, and some students bring weapons to school. Rules and laws generally have been ineffectual at controlling the utter chaos found in some schools. What explains school delinquency and disruption? Why do some children behave badly in school? Why might children act violently toward their classmates and teachers? We will examine three theories that attempt to answer these questions.

Loss of Teacher Authority

Paul Copperman developed a theory of delinquency that blames school crime on the loss of teacher authority, which is primarily the result of "open" classrooms established in the late 1960s. In open classrooms (1) children are permitted to study the things that interest them, virtually whenever they want to do so; (2) a wide variety of learning activities are to be made available to students within the classrooms; (3) during their learning activities children may move freely around the classroom, interacting with other students as they desire; and (4) the teacher is to behave in a democratic, nonmanipulative, warm, and respectful way toward the students, providing them with pleasant and enjoyable educational experiences. The open-education movement has spawned flexible scheduling, more electives, and lighter course loads, but in many instances such freedoms are detrimental to learning. Flexible scheduling gives students more periods during which they have no classes to attend. Teachers who see students in the hallways cannot know whether the children are legitimately unscheduled or are just skipping class. Teachers tend to give such students the benefit of the doubt, and students take advantage of this confusion to cut more classes.

Furthermore, Copperman argues that many students today can choose not only their electives but also the teachers who will conduct their required classes. Teachers, accordingly, are put in a difficult position. Without wishing to sacrifice quality, they realize they must get a reasonably large number of students to take and like their courses if they are to remain employed. Students tend to like courses that are entertaining and easy. This situation generates a popularity contest among teachers in which one of the ways to win is to inflate grades. If one teacher inflates grades, others are almost forced to follow. As a result of such pressure, standards for students are relaxed. With life so easy, students are more likely to become lazy and unmotivated. Poor study habits present no worry because the students will receive good grades anyway. As teacher expectations decrease, students work less and learn less, and their skills erode.[56]

This lack of control makes it easier for students to get away with deviant behavior, such as drug use, violence, and vandalism. If there is a great deal of free time and teachers are reluctant to intervene, delinquent and disruptive behaviors are likely to increase. For instance, Michael Turner and his colleagues found that well-run, traditional schools instilled self-control in children, which not only inhibited their delinquency but also enhanced their school performance. However, schools in the most disadvantaged neighborhoods where there has been the greatest loss of teacher authority failed to foster self-control in students and, as such, the students suffered.[57]

Gary Gottfredson, Denise Gottfredson, and their colleagues developed the idea of communal school organization, which in many ways reflects more traditional school discipline unlike the open classrooms described by Copperman. **Communal school organization** exists when teachers have shared values and expectations of learning and appropriate student behavior. Communally organized schools have activities designed to foster meaningful social and learning interactions among students to link them to school traditions. In short, communally run schools empower students, while teachers and administrators remain clearly in control. The results are positive. Based on a national survey of 254 high schools, they found that communal school organization reduces school disorder, student delinquency, and victimization of both teachers and students.[58]

James Coleman conducted a nationwide survey of nearly 60,000 students from more than 1,000 high schools. Much of Coleman's work compared public and private school students. Coleman points out that students' scholastic achievement is much higher in private schools primarily because of firm teacher control:

> First, given the same type of student . . . private schools create higher rates of engagement in academic activities. School attendance is better, students do more homework, and students generally take more rigorous subjects. . . . The indication is that more extensive academic demands are made in the private schools, leading to more advanced courses and thus to greater achievement. This is a somewhat obvious conclusion, and the statistical evidence supports it. Second, student behavior in a school has strong and consistent effects on student achievement. . . . [The] greatest differences in achievement between private and public schools are accounted for by school-level behavior variables (that is, the incidence of fights, students threatening teachers, and so forth).[59]

Private schools have fewer behavior problems most likely because they are selective in whom they admit, whereas public schools are required by law to accept any student regardless of any behavioral problems he or she may bring. Indeed, "the *average* public high school is outside the whole range of Catholic schools in the direction of more behavior problems."[60] Coleman believes that private schools have fewer behavior problems because of their disciplinary climate. Three-fourths of the private school students he interviewed said discipline in their school was strict and effective; only 40 percent of the public school students said the same about their schools. Because of higher standards of discipline in private schools, behavior problems such as absenteeism, cutting classes, threats to teachers, and fights among students are fewer. Although private schools were clearly superior to public schools during Coleman's era, this may no longer be true, at least in terms of academic achievement. The U.S. Department of Education reported in 2006 that independently run, publicly financed charter schools perform no better than comparable public schools. In fact, students in public schools perform slightly better in math and reading at the fourth- and eighth-grade levels.[61] Overall, poorly controlled and supervised schools where teachers have lost control obviously jeopardize school safety and create opportunities for delinquency to thrive.[62]

Tracking

Some criminologists have singled out tracking or ability grouping as a cause of delinquency. **Tracking** is the grouping of students into curricular categories, such as the college-preparatory, general, vocational, business, agricultural, and remedial tracks. Students in the college-preparatory track usually take a foreign language, algebra or some other form of advanced mathematics, and a science course during their freshman year in high school. Students in other tracks take different courses. Segregation and differentiation, therefore, begin very early in students' high school careers. The philosophy of tracking is to make classes as academically homogeneous as possible. Students who achieve at the same level could work at the same pace, proceeding rapidly and uniformly through the material under the supervision of the teacher. Students who were slower would not hold up high-ability students, and low-ability students could receive specialized instruction that might make it possible for them to catch up with their peers later on.

Teachers and guidance counselors decide what track a student will be placed in. Research has found that decisions regarding what track to place students in do not rest entirely on their academic abilities. The higher the family income of students, the more likely they will be placed in higher ability groups or the college-preparatory track. Conversely, students from low-income families are more likely to be placed in the vocational track or in the low-ability group. In 1949 August Hollingshead published *Elmstown Youth,* which is the first major study on the topic. He divided the population of Elmstown into five social classes at Elmstown High School where there were three tracks of study: college preparatory, general, and commercial. Hollingshead examined the social class of students in each track. Nearly two-thirds of students from upper- and upper-middle-class families were in the college-preparatory track. More than half of the middle-class and lower-middle-class students were in the general track with a large proportion in the commercial track and many fewer in the college-preparatory track. Lower-class students were overwhelmingly in the commercial and general tracks; only 4 percent were in the college-preparatory track.[63]

Sometimes teachers *expect less* from lower-class students. Perhaps the best-known study examining teacher expectations and student performance is Robert Rosenthal and Lenore Jacobson's *Pygmalion in the Classroom.*[64] The researchers gave students a standard intelligence test. Next, teachers were provided with the names of students the researchers called "late bloomers" and were told to expect a sudden burst of learning from them. What the teachers did not know was the names of the "late bloomers" were selected randomly from the class. One year later the intelligence tests were readministered. The scores of the later bloomers were compared with those of the other students who received scores on the original test similar to the group of supposed late bloomers. The researcher found that students who were identified to teachers as late bloomers made significant gains on their intelligence test scores when compared to the group of "ordinary" students. The principal inference of Rosenthal and Jacobson's study is that teacher expectations make a strong difference in the educational achievement of children. To the extent teachers expect children from poor families to fail or to struggle in school, there exists a major barrier to what these students might be capable of achieving. Interestingly, these effects are nearly identical to the effects of labeling children as delinquent in that the label may become a self-fulfilling prophecy.

Students certainly do have different academic abilities; however, there is a negative side of tracking—it might be discriminatory. The labels students are assigned are important because they may turn out to be irreversible: once assigned to a particular track, a student has little chance of ever being reassigned. Going from a non-college-preparatory track to a college-preparatory track, for instance, is difficult because schools establish prerequisites. For example, freshman algebra must be taken before a student can take sophomore geometry.[65] Walter Schafer and Carol Olexa have discovered that only 7 percent of students switch from a college-preparatory track to a non-college track, or vice versa. Furthermore, the tracks students occupy influence their future careers, determining their associates in and out of school, their grades, their participation in extracurricular activities, and their self-esteem. Tracking also affects their attitudes toward school, their chances of failing, their attendance, and their involvement in delinquency inside and outside a school setting.[66] Karen Randolph and her colleagues report that the experience of being held back to repeat first grade produces an array of educational deficits throughout children's school career. A school track that includes "flunking" first grade is very difficult to overcome.[67]

Also important is the connection between track position and delinquency. Delos Kelly correlated track position, sex, and social class with self-reports of delinquency and surprisingly found delinquency was more closely associated with track position than with sex and social class. Students on the lower tracks were more likely to be involved in gang fighting, smoking, and school expulsion.[68] Adam Gamoran and Robert Mare found some support for Kelly in their study of high school sophomores. They discovered that a student's track position was related to the probability of high school graduation and, conversely, to the likelihood of dropping out. They suggest that tracking assignments in school reinforced preexisting inequalities in achievement among students from different socioeconomic backgrounds.[69] Tracking might also serve as a proxy for other variables that are related to delinquency. Eric Stewart used data from the National Educational Longitudinal Study, which contains nearly 11,000 students from 528 high schools, and found that students who have strong school bonds are less involved in delinquency. In this sense, different school tracks reflect real scholastic and behavioral differences between children.[70] Some juveniles take school seriously and do not have time for delinquency; for others delinquency is the priority. Richard Felson and Jeremy Staff suggest that tracking does not reflect social class, IQ, or academic skills, but self-control. Tracking is organized according to students' abilities to defer gratification and display diligence, tenacity, and persistence in performing school work. Felson and Staff found that a child's self-control was the best predictor of his or her delinquency both inside and outside of school.[71]

But not all research finds that tracking is harmful or discriminatory. First, if students with equal academic ability are compared, the track they enter is not significantly affected by their social class background.[72] Second, students do not always know what track they are in. Both students and staff are often unsure what the tracks are.[73] Students in the non-college-preparatory track are most likely to misperceive their track and think they are in the college-preparatory track. Far from feeling stigmatized and frustrated, these students are unrealistically optimistic. Third, the college-preparatory track is becoming less popular as more students opt for general and vocational tracks, and many of them will still be able to enter college.[74] These findings appear to contradict tracking theory, which claims that tracking is prejudiced against particular groups of students.

Michael Wiatrowski and his associates reached a similar conclusion after looking at a national sample of 500 white males in high school and then following them for several years. They found *no* relationship between a student's track and (1) delinquency among tenth-graders, (2) delinquency among seniors, (3) extent of delinquency one year after high school, or (4) seriousness of delinquency one year after high school.[75] In a review of the study by Wiatrowski and his colleagues, Kenneth Polk agreed that it showed tracking to be less important that tracking theorists claim. However, Polk found that other school factors were important in producing delinquency. He examined the relationship between school performance (measured by high school grades) and adult criminality. The four groups compared were (1) youths with a high grade point average (GPA) and a record of delinquency, (2) youths with a high GPA and no record of delinquency, (3) youths with a low GPA and a delinquency record, and (4) youths with a low GPA and no delinquency record. When Polk looked at the adult lives of these people, he discovered, as expected, that those who had been delinquent as youths were more likely to be criminals as adults. But grades also made a difference in adult life. Students with low GPA, but no record of delinquency, were almost as likely to become adult criminals (40 percent), as were students with a delinquency record and a high GPA (50 percent). Polk's findings suggest that high school grades have a long-term effect on social behavior.[76]

Social Reproduction and Resistance

Social reproduction theory contends that schools reproduce the social class structure of society for the benefit of the economic elite. As schools perpetuate inequality, some students react by turning to delinquency. In *Schooling in Capitalist America,* Samuel Bowles and Herbert Gintis contend that the public school is the vehicle society uses to transmit existing social class differences among children into differential occupation and income opportunities. Schools are able to do this by instructing children differently depending on their social class backgrounds. For instance, schools with a high proportion of children from low-income families are more authoritarian and require more conformity to school rules than schools with a high percentage of youths from high-income families. Often lower-class children are educated to fill low-paying jobs that do not require much independent thinking and decision making. The reverse is true for upper-class children. The schools they attend socialize them to be bosses and creative and critical thinkers.[77]

One problem with this line of theorizing has been pointed out by Henry Giroux in *Theory of Resistance.* He claims that it assumes children are passive recipients of outside forces who are easily manipulated by school authorities.[78] Nearly every teacher knows this is not true; students are not easily controlled and manipulated. An ever-increasing complaint among teachers is the growing willingness of some students to challenge teachers' authority. Many students balk at blindly following teacher instructions and go out of their way to make life difficult for teachers. Some students have an agenda regarding their own lives that may have very little to do with the goals of the school, and students might resist the plans teachers and school administrators have made for them. Some students, in other words, have constructed an *oppositional culture* to the goals of the teacher and the school. In *Ain't No Makin' It,* Jay MacLeod describes how entrenched the oppositional culture is in the inner-cities of America and that schools are viewed not as opportunities for advancement but instead as a waste of time.[79]

Paul Willis tested a similar idea with a group of students with working-class backgrounds who attended an all-male comprehensive high school in an industrial area of England. The students learned to manipulate the school environment to make sure they always "had a good time." They established a peer culture that was antisocial and one that differed sharply from students they called the "ear-'oles," who in their opinion did nothing but sit and listen in school, conforming to school authority and expectations. The working-class students resented both the ear-'oles and the authority of the school. For them, the school was out-of-touch with the "real world" and had little to offer them in preparation for the life they would enter as adults. These students reacted by taking every opportunity to play pranks on the school officials, teachers, and ear-'oles, as their culture rejected the notion of upward mobility coming through schooling and the value of learning. Willis portrays their "opposition culture" as preparation for the generalized labor force these students would enter. The pranks they played in school were similar to the pranks they will play on the shop floor. The peer culture they developed was comparable to the culture of their fathers at work and the cultures they will experience when they enter the workforce. The students Willis studied created an antischool culture that played a determining role in ensuring the perpetuation of their working-class status. In his account, the culture of the school was in conflict with the culture of the students. Sometimes this conflict manifests itself in the form of school violence and delinquency.[80]

A generation later, Willis' theory is still relevant. Elizabeth Stearns and Elizabeth Glennie examined data from all public high schools in North Carolina to explore why dropouts leave school. For younger adolescents, dropping out is usually for disciplinary reasons. However, among students age 16 and older, the decision to leave school was driven by work and family responsibilities that conflicted with school demands. Lower-class youths felt "locked into" their social class position and believed that completing school would not appreciably improve their position.[81] Similarly, Roslyn Caldwell and her colleagues found that some African American students who live in disadvantaged communities *perceive* that their future is uncertain because of violence in their neighborhoods. Students with a sense of fatalism and uncertainty about the future were more likely to be delinquent and have behavioral problems in school. However, students living in the same neighborhoods who had a longer time horizon and could picture themselves going to college, getting married, and successfully transitioning into adult roles had no behavioral problems.[82] In other words, expectations of a lower-class position directly influenced school performance and delinquency.

Many criminologists have found that students who reject school in opposition to mainstream culture face a host of problems. Timothy Brezina and his colleagues found that students who harbor excessive anger against teachers, students, and school generally are at risk for delinquency and victimization in school.[83] Students who resist the social reproduction that occurs in schools face risk of social exclusion and isolation. Derek Kreager studied a national sample of youths and found that students who were socially isolated often had negative peer relationships and were prone to delinquency.[84] Priscilla Coleman and Caroline Byrd explored the correlates of school victimization and discovered that the most popular students, often those who are wealthiest and socially advantaged, had the lowest likelihood of being victimized at school. Consistent with the theory, affluent students could afford a comfortable and safe school experience whereas disadvantaged students faced a more difficult and often dangerous school experience.[85]

PREVENTING SCHOOL VIOLENCE

In the wake of highly-publicized school shootings in the late twentieth and early twenty-first centuries, schools around the country started to implement *zero-tolerance* measures to prevent future school violence (see Box 11-9). Many schools now apply zero-tolerance to *any* threatening behavior, sexual harassment, cigarette smoking, and possession of over-the-counter medications. Pottsgrove High School, just outside Philadelphia, prohibited students from driving cars to school because students might hide bombs or weapons in the trunks of their cars and banned water bottles, soda cans, and book bags unless they are made of mesh or clear plastic.

One Houston school required students to enter school through a metal detector, while another Houston school suspended two third-grade boys for possessing a small pocket-knife even though no one was threatened or hurt. In Indianapolis, a 14-year-old boy was arrested after school officials heard a rumor that the boy planned to bring a gun to school the next day. Other schools have suspended students for drawing pictures of guns or for turning in creative writing assignments that were too violent. A growing number of schools have dropped dodge ball from their gym classes and playgrounds after it came under attack by some women's groups who argued that it fostered aggression and future violence among players.

Unfortunately, zero-tolerance policies take away from school administrators the need to use commonsense and discretion to distinguish between genuine threats to school safety and innocent mistakes. If students are needlessly being suspended, then the policies appear to be backfiring.[86] In addition, few of these measures are likely to prevent school violence and might even exacerbate school violence if zero-tolerance policies are unevenly applied. African American and male students are more likely to be suspended or expelled from school than girls and white children. Even among students of similar economic and social backgrounds, African Americans are disciplined at a higher rate than whites in the same school. In addition research examining the effectiveness of zero-tolerance policies has reported that schools with zero-tolerance policies are no more orderly and secure than are schools that evaluate behavior problems on a case-by-case basis.[87]

Some school antiviolence programs attempt to reduce school-related risk factors, such as academic failure, low self-esteem, low commitment to school, and problematic peer relationships, by targeting classroom organization, management practices, and instructional strategies. Many of the more promising programs include reductions in class size, nongraded elementary schools, tutoring, computer-assisted instruction, interactive teaching, and cooperative learning.[88] For school-based interventions to be most effective, they need to start early in the school career, such as elementary school. Many schools have installed early truancy initiatives that aim to reduce chronic absenteeism among children in first through sixth grades. Cynthia McCluskey and her colleagues evaluated an

box 11-9 **DELINQUENCY PREVENTION**

Zero-Tolerance in Public Schools

Several horrific juvenile crimes have heightened the public's concerns regarding how juveniles should be treated. In response to such crimes, many public schools throughout the nation created "zero-tolerance" with respect to questionable student behavior, as well as guns and drugs. Under zero-tolerance policies, when school authorities perceive a child to be violating a school rule or law, they remove him or her from school by suspension or expulsion. In essence, these policies allow for no margin of error, even the most minor student infraction is subject to immediate school discipline. Many of these policies apply harsh penalties to innocuous conduct. Some critics of zero-tolerance policies believe they are the result of an attitude of "hyper-vigilance." Many of the decisions local school boards have made are criticized for being "by-the-book," without taking into account the particular circumstances of individual students or incidents. These "one-size-fits-all" approaches may severely punish students for violating the letter—but not the spirit—of such policies.

Nationally, several prominent incidents highlighted extreme decisions by school officials, including students who were subject to disciplinary action for bringing Advil to school, bringing a water pistol to school, or taking a slurp of Listerine (which is 22 percent alcohol) during school hours. A junior high school student from Belle, West Virginia, who gave a zinc cough lozenge to a classmate was suspended for three days. A kindergarten boy in Newport News, Virginia, was suspended for bringing a beeper on a class trip. A 9-year-old boy from Manassas, Virginia, was suspended for one day for giving breath mints to a classmate. A 13-year-old boy, who was an honor student, from Fairborn, Ohio, received an 80-day suspension for bringing ibuprofen to class, a disciplinary action that later was reduced to 3 days. A 6-year-old boy from Madison, North Carolina, who kissed a girl on the cheek, was given a 1-day suspension. An 11-year-old girl from Columbia, South Carolina, was arrested and suspended for having a steak knife in her lunchbox to cut chicken she had brought to school to eat. A 10-year-old boy was expelled for bringing a one-inch plastic knife to school. An 8-year-old girl from Alexandria, Louisiana, was expelled for bringing to school a one-inch pocketknife that was attached to her grandfather's pocket watch chain.

These stories prompted some reviews of zero-tolerance policies to look at whether there are racial disparities in the application of school discipline. A Michigan study found that while 40 percent of the students in the districts surveyed were African American, they accounted for 64 percent of school expulsions. A Seattle study found similar racial disparities. A national report, referring to zero-tolerance policies as a form of "racial profiling in schools," pointed out that African American students comprised 17 percent of the student population nationally, but 33 percent of those suspended. Over the last 25 years, studies have shown that minority students are suspended at a rate two to three times that of white students.

The many stories of excessive and inappropriate use of suspension and expulsion, as well as concerns about disparate impact of school discipline on minority youths, have led to a national backlash against zero-tolerance policies. For example, the American Bar Association recently voted to oppose zero-tolerance policies that have a discriminatory effect or that mandate either expulsion or referral of students to juvenile or criminal court, without regard to the circumstances or nature of the offense or the student's history. Similar resolutions have been approved by bar associations in a number of states. Although created with honest intentions, zero-tolerance policies have in many ways created more problems than they have solved.

Sources: David Richart, Kim Brooks, Mark Soler, *Unintended Consequences: The Impact of "Zero Tolerance" and Other Exclusionary Policies on Kentucky Students, 2003,* available at http://www.buildingblocksforyouth.org, accessed May 3, 2007; Margaret Tebo, "Zero Tolerance, Zero Sense," *ABA Journal* 86:40–48 (2000); Erin Hickey, "Zero Tolerance for Policies Depriving Children of Education: A Comment on Zero Tolerance Policies," *Children's Legal Rights Journal* 24:18–25 (2004); Jeanne Stinchcomb, Gordon Bazemore, and Nancy Riestenberg, "Beyond Zero Tolerance: Restoring Justice in Secondary Schools," *Youth Violence and Juvenile Justice* 4:123–147 (2006).

early truancy initiative in three elementary schools that were located in a lower-income area and where a significant proportion of students missed more than 30 days of school per year. The program entailed a letter to parents and a home visit from a school attendance officer. These simple procedures reduced absenteeism at the schools even among students who had been chronically absent.[89] If children are spending more time in school, it stands to reason that other educational outcomes will also improve. Other programs target chronic truants using police–school partnerships. A recent evaluation by Michael White and his colleagues found that police–school partnerships produce modest academic benefits for chronic truants; however, they do reduce school behavioral problems. Also, the partnerships help connect at-risk youths with appropriate social service and juvenile justice agencies.[90]

Other school programs focus primarily on in-school counseling and behavior modification. This approach involves group counseling, the use of time-out rooms, interpersonal and problem-solving skills training, moral education, value clarification, peer counseling, and intervention in the opening moves of escalating conflicts.[91] The National Resource Center for Safe Schools recommends a number of components be considered in planning for safe schools. These include developing emergency response planning, creating a positive school climate and culture, ensuring quality facilities and technology, and instituting links with mental health social services.[92]

Still other programs emphasize control. Control-oriented programs likely entail measures such as closing off isolated areas, increasing staff supervision, installing electronic monitoring for weapons detection, removing tempting vandalism targets, requiring students to wear only see-through backpacks, and using police or private security personnel for patrol, crowd control, investigation of criminal activities, and intelligence gathering.[93] A promising control-based program is a **School Resource Officer Program,** where a police officer works within the school to perform a variety of specialized duties. According to Peter Finn, school resource officer programs provide four important benefits for police: (1) they reduce the workload of traditional patrol officers, (2) they improve adolescent and student perceptions of police officers, (3) they create and maintain positive relationships between law enforcement agencies and schools, and (4) they enhance the agency's reputation in the community. They also benefit schools because of improved school safety, improved police response time to problems, and improved perceptions of school safety.[94]

Targeted violence in schools, or incidents in which the attacker has targeted particular persons or groups, may not be amenable to general prevention programs. An intensive study of 37 school shootings, involving 41 attackers, was conducted by the U.S. Secret Service National Threat Assessment Center. The study found:

- Incidents of targeted violence at school are rarely impulsive. The attacks are typically the end result of an understandable and often discernible process of thinking and behavior.
- Prior to most incidents, the attacker told someone about his or her idea and/or plan.
- There is no accurate or useful profile of "the school shooter."
- Most attackers had previously used guns and had access to them.
- Most shooting incidents were not resolved by law enforcement intervention.

- In many cases, other students were involved in some capacity.
- Most attackers engaged in some behavior, prior to the incident, that caused others concern or indicated a need for help.

Implications for prevention of targeted school violence reflect a number of issues. For example, because the typical student engaged in school violence did not "just snap," it may be possible to gather information about intent and planning before the incident. It is also helpful to distinguish between making a threat and posing a threat; adults should attend to concerns that someone poses a threat. Because profiling is not effective for identifying students who may pose a risk of targeting violence, school officials should focus instead on a student's behaviors and communications to determine whether the student appears to be planning or preparing for an attack. It is important to discover if a student is on a path toward a violent attack. Because other students often know about incidents in advance, it is wrong to assume shooters are "loners." Thus, it is important to gather information from a potential attacker's friends and schoolmates.[95]

How might schools gather such information? In 2005, the Houston County (Georgia) school board became one of the first school districts to enroll in the national Student Crime Stoppers program, which pays students up to $100 for information about theft, drug violations, or weapons possession on school property. Many schools use revenues from vending machines to pay student "tattlers" or "snitches" that report on the delinquency of their peers. Critics argue that the policy sends the wrong message to children that civic duty should be performed for payment. Proponents feel that student information is a proactive way to prevent delinquency and violence in schools.[96]

A more controversial approach for addressing school violence is recommended by Jackson Toby who believes schools are unsafe because of a *stay-in* problem and not a drop-out problem. In other words, there are too many students in school who disrupt teaching and learning. Stay-in students earn bad grades (Fs and Ds), disrupt classes, and interfere with the education of those students who go to school to be educated. For example, in an interview with Joe, Jackson Toby tells us about the type of student responsible for the stay-in problem in schools today:

> "I like school," Joe said. I was surprised. Most delinquents I had known hated school and did poorly in their schoolwork. "What did you like about it?" I asked. He told me about sitting in the lunchroom with his gang and having food fights, about "making out" in the halls with his girlfriends, . . . about harassing a young, inexperienced teacher. . . . "What about your classes?" I asked. "Did you like them?" "Yeah," he replied. "I liked gym." Did he like English, math, or anything else in the curriculum? "No," he replied, smiling. "They weren't in my curriculum."[97]

While Toby is unique in his argument about the stay-in problem other criminologists have documented the extensive misbehavior of students like Joe. Many times, the students with the most school problems are also the most serious delinquents. Xia Wang and his colleagues compared the school careers of 5,187 nondelinquent students to 5,187 delinquents in Florida. Other than their delinquency status, the study groups were matched by demographic and school-based characteristics. On every measure, delinquents had worse school problems than nondelinquents. Compared to nondelinquent students, delinquents had lower grade point averages, had higher absenteeism and truancy, were more likely to repeat a grade, had greater and more serious behavioral problems, and received more and harsher disciplinary actions. Moreover, the delinquency and other behavioral problems of the delinquents worsened after they were expelled or received an out-of-school suspension.[98]

Does dropping out of school lead to delinquency? Does dropping out turn a law-abiding juvenile into a delinquent? While dropouts do have higher crime rates than juveniles who continue their schooling, their rates were also higher *before* they left school. Research examining whether dropping out of school increases or decreases the likelihood of future criminality has produced mixed results. Early studies by Delbert Elliott showed that delinquency among dropouts was highest just prior to their leaving school and dropped sharply after they quit, leading Elliott to reason that school was the cause of the students' stress and frustration.[99] In contrast, Terence Thornberry and his colleagues found that dropping out of high school *increased* the likelihood of subsequent crime.[100] David Farrington and his associates also found evidence that dropping out of school *does not* decrease crime. They reported that adolescents in school committed fewer delinquencies than (1) those who had dropped out and were fully employed or (2) those dropouts who were unemployed.[101] These conflicting findings led Roger Jarjoura to hypothesize that the reason juveniles drop out of school would be related to his or her future delinquency. Jarjoura found that students who *quit* school because of family problems, financial reasons, or poor grades were not any more involved in delinquency after leaving school than before. But students who were *expelled* from school increased their involvement in drug abuse and theft after dropping out. To put it differently, sometimes dropping out leads to more delinquency and other times it does not.[102]

Finally, when a youth drops out of school is crucial to understanding how dropping out relates to delinquency. For instance, truancy has been referred to as the "kindergarten of crime" since it is often a forerunner of delinquency and other problems, such as unemployment, alcoholism, substance use, and adult criminality.[103] Eileen Garry found that when police made intensive truancy sweeps, shoplifting, purse snatching, and arrests for nuisance crimes dropped 50 to 70 percent. Thus, children who frequently miss school early in life are in trouble.[104] Jane Sprott and her colleagues argue that attending school is one of the most important protective factors against delinquency. Coincidentally, Sprott also argues against zero-tolerance policies because they remove children from school.[105]

conclusions

There is an extensive body of literature on the decline of American public schools. Anxiety over schools is relatively recent, following a long period during which education was thought to be one of our nation's greatest strengths. There is a growing concern with school violence and shootings, bullying, and teacher victimization, leading to different prevention strategies such as zero-tolerance being implemented and U.S. Supreme Court decisions regulating what clothes students may wear, searches and seizures of their personal belongings, and how they might express themselves.

Different theories have been advanced to explain the link between schools and delinquency. Paul Copperman examines loss of teacher authority, which he says is caused primarily by open classrooms that lead to less control and lower academic standards. Lack of control, in turn, makes it easier for students to get away with behaviors, such as drug use, violence, and vandalism. Tracking theory contends that students placed in non-college-preparatory tracks are stigmatized by such placement and react in many negative ways, including delinquency. Finally, according to social reproduction theory, the purpose of public schools is to serve the economic elite. Their primary function is to reproduce the existing class structure in society and when they do they cause lower-class students to become disruptive.

key terms

Baker v. Owen   Teachers can administer reasonable corporal punishment for disciplinary purposes.

Bethel School District No. 403 v. Fraser   Schools may prohibit vulgar and offensive language.

Board of Education of Independent School District No. 92 of Pottawatomie County et al. v. Earls et al.   Expands *Acton;* schools may require students to submit to a urinalysis for illegal drugs prior to participating in all competitive extracurricular activities.

Bullying   Negative acts by students carried out against other students repeatedly over time.

Communal school organization   Partnership of teachers who have shared values and expectations of student learning and appropriate student behavior.

Compulsory school attendance law   A legislative act that requires students to attend school between specific ages (e.g., 6 to 16 years old).

Corporal punishment   The infliction of physical pain as a penalty for violating a school rule.

Garcia v. Miera   School authorities that use excessive or extreme punishment against a child may be sued for damages suffered by the student and attorney fees.

Goss v. Lopez   Students who may be suspended for 10 or less days must receive a hearing.

Hall v. Tawney   Parents do not have a constitutional right to exempt their children from corporal punishment in public schools.

Hazelwood School District v. Kuhlmeier   School administrators can regulate the content of student publications in public schools for educational purposes.

Ingraham v. Wright   Corporal punishment does not violate the cruel and unusual punishment clause of the Eighth Amendment.

New Jersey v. T.L.O.   School officials can conduct warrantless searches of individuals at school on the basis of reasonable suspicion.

School Resource Officer Program   A control-based policy where a police officer works within the school to perform a variety of specialized duties.

Sweep search   A search of all school lockers.

Thompson v. Carthage School District   School officials may legally search students and their lockers without consent.

Tinker v. Des Moines Independent Community School District   Students have the right of free expression as long as their behavior does not interrupt school activities or intrude in the school affairs or the lives of others.

Tracking   The grouping of students into curricular categories, such as the college-preparatory, general, vocational, business, agricultural, and remedial tracks.

Vernonia School District 47J v. Acton   Students participating in school athletic activities must submit upon request to an involuntary drug test (urinalysis).

West Virginia State Board of Education v. Barnette   Students do not have to salute the flag while reciting the Pledge of Allegiance.

Peer Group and Gang Delinquency

P eople are social and group-oriented. Adolescents are possibly more social than adults, and they certainly are attracted to social groups, including play groups, cliques, adolescent peer groups, and gangs. In thinking about the effects of peers on adolescent behavior, it is important to consider which type of *peer effect* and which type of *delinquent* is at hand. For example, virtually everyone is affected by peers, and these peer effects influence our beliefs, attitudes, and behaviors in powerful ways. This is the very process that Terrie Moffitt has used to explain delinquency among *adolescence-limited offenders*. However, most people are never involved in gangs. Instead, youths who have multiple risk factors for delinquency and those who are already delinquent are most susceptible to gang membership. In other words, normal peer groups influence normative delinquency just as delinquent gangs influence more serious delinquency. This chapter will look closely at the nature of group delinquency with a focus on the role of peers and involvement in gangs.

GROUP DELINQUENCY

For many juveniles the most important social institution, the one they spend the most time with and are closest to emotionally, is the family. But for many others it is their **peer group,** youths of similar ages and interests who empower each other in their sense of feeling worthwhile and important. The social world of some adolescents revolves around their closest friends. They search for acceptance, status, identity, and meaning through interactions with others. The style of music, dress, and language of their peers often becomes their own. Peer group activities reflect behaviors that are symbolic of adulthood and are viewed as signs that the person is no longer a child. These behaviors often have to do with drugs, sexuality, and autonomy. Wanting to be accepted and to feel worthwhile and more grown-up, many youngsters turn to delinquent activities because of peer influence.[1]

The period of adolescence and intense peer-group activity is viewed by many as the time in a youth's life that is most likely to lead to conflict with adults, conventional institutions, and the law. As young people increasingly see a social, and perhaps moral, distance between themselves and adults, they look to the peer group for camaraderie, acceptance, and a sense of purpose. Without close parental supervision and guidance, youths are susceptible to the pulls and pushes of their peers, which may lead to minor or even major forms of deviance and delinquency.[2]

If nothing else is absolutely known about juvenile delinquency, it is that delinquency is generally a group activity. In fact, "no characteristic of individuals known to criminologists is a better predictor of criminal behavior than the number of delinquent friends an individual has."[3] As early as 1931 Clifford Shaw and Henry McKay reported that 80 percent of Chicago juvenile delinquents were arrested with co-offenders.[4] Although early research into the causal direction of the relationship between delinquency and delinquent friends suggested that delinquents are most likely to develop delinquent friendships *after* they become involved in delinquency, more recent studies consistently find that associating with delinquent friends leads to increased delinquent activity.[5] As

For many adolescents, drug use is a rite of passage—and a gateway to a delinquent career. It is normal to experiment with drugs, such as tobacco, alcohol, and marijuana, yet most people do not develop substance abuse problems from this experimentation. Why?

noted by Albert Reiss, "most young offenders have co-offenders in their offending and associate in other group activities with still other young offenders."[6]

Studies in the early part of the 20th century probably overestimated the amount of delinquency that could be attributed to groups. These studies relied on official data in which the police were more likely to arrest and refer youths to court if they congregated in packs. To counter this bias, Michael Hindelang turned to self-report data to estimate group delinquency rates. He found that some offenses are more likely than others to be committed with associates. Smoking marijuana and getting drunk, for instance, are primarily social activities. But a few crimes are more often engaged in alone, such as carrying a weapon.[7] Based on self-reported data from the National Youth Survey, Andy Hochstetler and his colleagues reported similar outcomes for crimes, such as assault, theft, and vandalism. Although the influence of delinquent peers was an important predictor of delinquency, the *presence* of other people was not always required for youths to engage in these forms of delinquency.[8] For example, as discussed in Box 12-1, delinquency in the Netherlands also involves a great deal of group activity.

Delinquency and adolescent drug use are typically social activities, and youths often participate in the same behavior as their friends. Helen Garnier and Judith Stein conducted an 18-year longitudinal study of juveniles. They observed that youths usually select friends who are more like themselves and are typically selected by other youths who seem to share similar backgrounds and values, a concept known as *homophily* (which means "love of the same," [see Box 12-2]). As a result of social selection and peer pressure, an adolescent's likelihood of using drugs or engaging in other types of delinquency increases.[9] Studies have found that close, or best friends, have a strong influence on teen behavior. A youth is about twice as likely to engage in delinquency if his or her close friend is already engaged in crime, and the strongest predictor of adolescent drug use is the extent of drug use by the youth's best friend.[10]

box 12-1   DELINQUENCY AROUND THE GLOBE
Group Delinquency in the Netherlands

For many Dutch youths, hanging around or street loitering is a preferred leisure activity. Many youths hang out in small groups and engage in troublemaking, nuisance, or intimidating behavior. More often than not, these youths are not terribly involved in crime, but when they are, they commit their crimes in groups rather than alone. Recent surveys in the Netherlands indicate the majority of delinquencies involve co-offenders. Delinquencies most often committed with others include vandalism, followed by drug violations, intimidation, aggression, shoplifting, bicycle theft, and other thefts. Younger adolescents are more likely to commit crimes with co-offenders than are older youths. And girls are more likely than boys to commit crimes with others, especially for such crimes as shoplifting and bicycle theft. Youths who commit crimes together are most likely to be friends, followed by classmates and neighborhood youths. If not engaging in delinquencies with friends, girls are most likely to co-offend with classmates, while boys co-offend with neighborhood youths.

More criminally involved youth groups also hang out and loiter, and it is understandable that the public and authorities often lump all street youth groups together. There are impor-tant differences according to Alfred Hakkert, who has divided local youth groups into nuisance groups, troublemaking groups, criminal groups, and gangs. All of these groups engage in a variety of similar behaviors, including hanging out in groups in doorways or sidewalks, getting in the way of passers-by, playing loud music, and making impudent remarks.

Nuisance groups are the least problematic, tending to simply annoy or intimidate people, especially older people, by their mere presence or incivility in encounters on the street. *Troublemaking groups* often engage in minor delinquencies, such as bicycle theft, vandalism, shoplifting, and drug use. *Criminal youth groups,* on the other hand, are likely to participate in more serious offenses, such as robberies, burglaries, auto theft, and drug dealing. Finally, *youth gangs,* organized expressly to engage in criminal activities, are involved in extortion, serious property crimes, violent thefts, and drug dealing.

Sources: Alfred Hakkert, "Group Delinquency in the Netherlands: Some Findings from an Exploratory Study," *International Review of Law Computers & Technology* 12:453–474 (1998); Finn Esbensen and Frank Weerman, "Youth Gangs and Troublesome Youth Gangs in the United States and the Netherlands: A Cross-National Comparison," *European Journal of Criminology* 2:5–37 (2005).

To the extent that one's peers and their behaviors can have serious negative influence on adolescents, what may be done to reduce the impact? What policies or practical recommendations to parents might prevent peer-related delinquency? For more than six decades, the policy implications of Edwin Sutherland's *theory of differential association* (see Chapter 6) have led parents and schools to create opportunities for children to spend greater amounts of time in supervised, productive activities. After-school, weekend, and summer recreational programs involving youths in such things as music, sports, art, scouts, computers, and church have been looked to as mechanisms for preventing children from spending time hanging out with "bad kids" or the "wrong crowd." Parents have also been encouraged to provide more quality family time with their children.

Some argue there is little convincing evidence that teen involvement in after-school programs or jobs reduce their likelihood of becoming delinquent,[11]

box 12-2   A WINDOW ON DELINQUENCY
Why Are People Group-Oriented?

For centuries, criminologists have observed the tendency for people to seek out others. This tendency is especially strong during childhood and adolescence. The link between antisocial peers and misconduct is so well-established and consistently replicated that Mark Warr contended that "few, if any, empirical regularities in criminology have been documented as often or over as long a period of time as the association between delinquency and delinquent friends." Associating with delinquent peers is another example of homophily, which means "love of the same." People often associate with others who are similar to them in terms of age, social class, race, appearance, belief system, and other factors.

Youths are so influenced by their peers that friendship networks are substantially more important than parents in determining human behavior. In her controversial and best-selling book *The Nurture Assumption: Why Children Turn Out the Way They Do,* Judith Rich Harris argues that the socialization effects of parents on children are overrated and that friendship and peer networks during the school years are who *really* socialize them. Behavioral scientists present compelling evidence that Harris is correct, namely that peers are the most powerful socializing agents. For instance, behavioral genetics research indicates that genetic and nonshared environmental factors, such as peer groups, account for nearly 100 percent of variation in delinquency. Shared environmental factors, such as home environment, explain little to no variation in delinquency.

The reason that sociologically oriented criminologists have noted the universal tendency for adolescents to be group-oriented and seek others like them is that homophily appears to be intrinsic to human nature. Neuroscientists are discovering the genetic bases of homophily and social factors, such as associating with delinquent peers. According to Anthony Walsh, "the biological events that are taking place during the teenage years should be incorporated into theories of adolescent offending. These kinds of data may go a long way to explaining the range of adolescent behaviors that [criminologists have historically] described solely in social terms." In other words, it is probable that in the 21st century, scientists will discover at the genetic level why people are group-oriented.

Sources: Mark Warr, *Companions in Crime: The Social Aspects of Criminal Conduct* (New York: Cambridge University Press, 2002), p. 40; Anthony Walsh, "Companions in Crime: A Biosocial Perspective," *Human Nature Review* 2:169–178 (2002), p. 174; Judith Rich Harris, *The Nurture Assumption: Why Children Turn Out the Way They Do* (New York: Free Press, 1999); Alessandra Iervolino, Alison Pike, Beth Manke, David Reiss, Mavis Hetherington, and Robert Plomin, "Genetic and Environmental Influences in Adolescent Peer Socialization: Evidence from Two Genetically Sensitive Designs," *Child Development* 73:162–174 (2002); H. Harrington Cleveland, Richard Wiebe, and David Rowe, "Sources of Exposure to Smoking and Drinking Friends among Adolescents: A Behavioral-Genetic Evaluation," *Journal of Genetic Psychology* 166:153–169 (2005); Judith Rich Harris, *No Two Alike: Human Nature and Human Individuality* (New York: W. W. Norton, 2006).

but studies provide positive support for youths spending more time with their families. Mark Warr, for example, reports that children who spent a great deal of time with their families every week "had low rates of delinquency *even when they had delinquent friends.*" In addition, youths who report having a close relationship with their parents are less likely to have any delinquent friends. But youths cannot be isolated from friendships, and it is difficult, if not impossible, for parents to identify or separate out the "good" child from the "bad" one.

Consequently, parents should closely monitor their children's associations, establish and maintain contact with the parents of their children's friends, and work to develop trust and open, frequent communication with their children.[12]

GANGS AND GANG DELINQUENCY

For people working in the juvenile justice system and for criminologists, concern about juvenile delinquency has historically centered more on gangs than on peer groups. But the notion of "gang" itself has been poorly understood, defined, and measured. More important, how gangs are defined has significant implications for police, policy makers, and criminologists who study gangs. Depending on how gangs are defined may lead to inaccurate estimates of the extent of the problem, misunderstanding the primary activities of gang members, and incorrect identification of the demographic composition of gangs.[13] Next we review different ways of defining gangs and the diversity of characteristics associated with gangs and gang members.

Problems in Defining Gangs

In the early 20th century the term "gang" was associated with groups in socially disorganized and deteriorated inner-city neighborhoods. It was applied to juveniles who engaged in a variety of delinquencies ranging from truancy, street brawls, and beer running to race riots, robberies, and other serious crimes. In 1927, Frederic Thrasher, in his study of 1,313 delinquent gangs in Chicago, noted that while no two gangs were exactly alike, delinquent gangs possessed a number of qualities that set them apart from other social groups. These qualities include meeting face to face, milling about, going places as a group, engaging in conflicts with other gangs and adults, and planning activities. Such collective behavior produces gang traditions, unreflective internal organizational structure, *esprit de corps,* a sense of solidarity and awareness of being a distinct group, and claims to a local territory.

This image of gangs stressed youth groups as being localized and territory-based, with social organization and traditions and with group awareness and morale fostered through conflict with authorities and other gangs. While Thrasher's work set the tone for much of the subsequent writing on gangs for many decades, it is important to note that he did not include in his definition of a gang delinquent or law-violating behavior. For Thrasher, delinquent gangs were only one type of youth group.[14]

By the 1950s the image of the gang increasingly focused on large groups of urban boys engaged primarily in violent conflict, fighting each other in battles or "rumbles" over territory or status, much like the Sharks and the Jets in *West Side Story.* The gang, from this perspective, suggests a slightly broader definition:

> [The gang is] a friendship group of adolescents who share common interests, with a more or less clearly defined territory, in which most of the members live. They are committed to defending one another, the territory, and the gang name in the status-setting fights that occur in school and on the streets.[15]

By the 1980s police, politicians, and many criminologists began to emphasize the organization and illegal activities of gangs. According to Walter Miller, a **youth gang** is

> a self-forming association of peers, bound together by mutual interests, with identifiable leadership, well-developed lines of authority, and other organizational features, who act in concert to achieve a specific purpose or purposes which generally include the conduct of illegal activity and control over a particular territory, facility, or type of enterprise.[16]

think about it

Scholars frequently disagree over the appropriate definition of gangs. Is this simply a semantic issue? Are gangs, by implicit definition, a negative, criminal phenomenon?

But the characteristics in Miller's definition do not fit all youth groups identified as gangs by either the police or criminologists. Some groups are involved in illegal activities; some are not. Some claim territory; some do not. Some use and/or sell drugs; many do not. Some engage in drive-by shootings; most do not. And some are highly organized with identifiable leadership, while others are not.[17]

Such variations have not prevented some state legislatures and police agencies from developing very narrow and specific definitions of gangs. For example, the Street Terrorism Enforcement and Prevention (STEP) Act of the California penal code defines the criminal street gang as

> any ongoing organization, association, or group of three or more persons, whether formal or informal, having as one of its primary activities the commission of one or more of the criminal acts enumerated in paragraphs (1) to (8), inclusive, of subdivision (e), which has a common name or common identifying sign or symbol, whose members individually or collectively engage in or have engaged in a pattern of criminal gang activity.[18]

The criminal acts specifically included in the Act include aggravated assault, robbery, homicide or manslaughter, drug trafficking, arson, victim or witness intimidation, and shooting into an inhabited dwelling. This definition gives police and prosecutors a basis for arresting any youth who actively participates in a criminal street gang regardless of whether the youth holds formal membership in the gang as long as the youth knows that the gang is involved in illegal activities and willfully promotes, furthers, or assists in any felonious criminal conduct by members of that gang.

Most states do not have legislatively determined definitions of juvenile gangs, however. Consequently, law enforcement agencies and criminologists generally select their own criteria for defining a gang, which means there is a lack of consensus on what is a gang. The National Youth Gang Survey included the following instruction in their survey to guide law enforcement agencies. For the purposes of the survey, a youth gang is

> A group of youths or young adults in your jurisdiction that you or other responsible persons in your agency or community are willing to identify or classify as a "gang." DO NOT include motorcycle gangs, hate or ideology groups, prison gangs, or other exclusively adult gangs.[19]

In addition, many police agencies have developed definitions of gang members reflecting the need to document youths identified as gang-involved. Their definitions typically distinguish between *associate, or "wanna be," member* and *hardcore member.* Associate or wanna be members are peripheral or fringe members, and even though they associate with full-fledged members, they may not be recognized by others as a regular member. Members comprise the core of the gang and are likely to have frequent contact with each other and to regularly engage in gang activities. Hardcore members are viewed by police as the most dangerous and most likely to be involved in serious, violent gang activity. As Charles Katz notes, some law enforcement agencies require that at least one of the nine specific characteristics found in Table 12-1 must be documented to identify an individual as a gang member.[20]

Similar to the problems of defining a gang and gang member is the problem of defining "gang-related" activity. The spread of gang violence has complicated the problem of determining those activities that are gang-related. Malcolm Klein and Cheryl Maxson report that different urban police and sheriffs' departments use different definitions of what constitutes a gang-related crime. More than half of the law enforcement agencies responding to a recent National Youth Gang Survey indicated that they use a **member-based definition,** a crime in which a gang member or members are the perpetrators of the crime, regardless of the motive. Nearly a third use a **motive-based definition,** a crime committed by a gang member or members in which the underlying reason is to further the interests and activities of the gang. About 11 percent said they used some other definition.[21]

Are Gang Members More Delinquent than Nongang Youths?

When gang membership is a known factor in group offending, clear differences in delinquency rates between gang and nongang members have been reported (see Box 12-3). Prevalence rates of delinquency and individual offending are greater for both male and female gang members than for their nongang coun-

---

▌ **table 12-1**   Documenting Gang Members

Associate/Wanna Be

1. Individual who wears colored clothing and/or uses gang hand signals consistent with suspected gangs.
2. Individual associates/corresponds with known gang members and/or is observed writing gang-related graffiti on any type of property.
3. Individual is included in group pictures of known gang members or arrested in the company of identified gang members.

Member

4. Commits criminal act as a gang member.
5. Self-admission, tattoos, or identified by a public source.
6. Identified by reliable informant and corroborated by reliable source.
7. Involved in gang retaliations, assaults, and/or drive-by shootings.
8. Past criminal/prison records for gang-related activity, gang status corroborated by law enforcement agency.

Hardcore Member

9. Individual fits criteria listed for the gang associate and gang member with the additional involvement in high-level narcotics distribution and/or commits gang-related felony crimes.

Source: Charles Katz, "Issues in the Production and Dissemination of Gang Statistics: An Ethnographic Study of a Large Midwestern Police Gang Unit," *Crime & Delinquency* 49: 496 (2003).

To be involved in a gang is perhaps the greatest risk factor for delinquency and a variety of other problem behaviors. But how large of a risk factor is gang membership? George Knox and other gang researchers from the National Gang Crime Research Center completed one of the largest, most comprehensive studies of gangs in the United States. Knox and his colleagues collected data in 17 states from 85 different correctional facilities (prisons, boot camps, juvenile institutions) on a national sample of 10,166 confined offenders, of which 4,140 were self-reported gang members.

Compared to youths who were not in gangs, gang members were significantly *more likely* to

- Have a parent who had served time in prison.
- Have psychopathic personality traits.
- Have been a bully in school.
- Have sold narcotics, especially crack cocaine.

- Have fired a gun at a police officer.
- Have been shot, stabbed, or seriously assaulted.
- Have engaged in violent, weapons-related, and drug misconduct while incarcerated.

Gang members were significantly *less likely* to

- Finish high school or have a GED.
- Attend church.
- Avoid situations involving the risk of arrest or personal injury.
- Report that the juvenile or criminal justice system deterred them.
- Report that he or she had adequate parental supervision as a child.
- Believe in conventional morality.

Source: George Knox et al., *The Facts about Gang Life in America Today: A National Study of over 4,000 Gang Members* (Peotone, IL: National Gang Crime Research Center, 2004).

terparts.[22] Others report that although gang members *do not* appear to have higher rates of delinquency or drug use *prior* to entering the gang, once they are members their rates became significantly greater than nongang youths.[23] Sara Battin and her colleagues report that gang members have higher rates of offending compared to nongang adolescents and that belonging to a gang predicted court-reported and self-reported delinquency above and beyond the contribution of having delinquent peers and above and beyond prior delinquency.[24]

The flip-side of delinquency is, of course, victimization, and prior research indicates that gang members are much more likely to be victimized than nongang youths. For instance, Dana Peterson and her colleagues explored the gang–victimization relationship among a longitudinal study of 3,500 students and a cross-sectional study of 5,935 students. While controlling for a variety of other correlates of victimization, Peterson found that youths who had ever been in a gang were more likely to be the victim of a serious violent crime. In addition, the increased risk of victimization among gang youths existed before, during, and after their gang involvement.[25]

The Rochester Youth Development Study examined the portion of delinquency in the community that could be attributed to gang members compared to nongang youths. About 30 percent of the youths reported being members of a street gang at some time prior to the end of high school. Those youths who belonged to gangs, however, accounted for the bulk of delinquent acts, especially the more serious crimes. Gang members accounted for 86 percent of the serious delinquent acts, 69 percent of the violent delinquent acts, and 70 percent of the drug sales. The study concluded that involvement in gangs substantially increases the likelihood of involvement in delinquency, particularly serious delinquency.[26] Very similar trends exist among gang youths in other major cities. In Seattle, for instance, gang members comprised 15 percent of a large sample of adolescents, but accounted for 85 percent of the total robberies in the sample. Similarly, in Denver, gang members comprised 14 percent of a sample but accounted for 79 percent of all serious, violent adolescent offenses. And in Montreal, gang members appeared in juvenile and criminal courts between *400 and 700 percent* more frequently than nongang youths.[27]

A slightly cautionary note about the findings just reported is suggested by Tom Winfree and his associates. They conclude that among youths having a progang attitude, a predisposition toward violence, especially group-context violence, may be a more important delinquency factor than actual gang membership. No difference was found between gang and nongang youths in theft crimes, other property crimes, and even drug crimes, although gang members were more likely to be involved in violent offenses.[28]

Joining and Getting Out of Gangs

Although delinquent peer groups and gangs exist in virtually all types of communities in the United States, the most violent and serious gang threats are concentrated in the most impoverished neighborhood of major cities. In this way, it is believed that socioeconomic disadvantage and family problems are the root conditions that lead adolescents to join gangs. Some youths grow up in families in which older brothers, sisters, fathers, and sometimes grandfathers are or were gang members, and thus their entry into gang life is essentially just a part of adolescent socialization. From a very young age, it is expected that they will eventually become a gang member.[29] Rachel Gordon and her colleagues report that the same risk factors that propel youths into serious delinquent careers, such as poverty, school failures, and family dysfunction also precede gang membership.[30] David Eitle and his colleagues found that racial minority status, family financial problems, and the cumulative exposure to stressful life events during childhood also contribute to gang membership.[31]

As shown in Table 12-2, many of the risk factors that have been identified as correlates of delinquency are also forerunners of gang membership.[32] There are seven general types of risk factors for gang membership:

1. *Area characteristics* include community and neighborhood measures of poverty, arrest rates, and disorganization.
2. *Family characteristics* include race, ethnicity, family structure, and family educational attainment.
3. *Parent–child relations* include the degree of attachment, involvement, and commitment between parents and children, parenting measures, abuse, neglect, and maltreatment.
4. *School factors* include the child's attachment and commitment to school, college aspirations, and test scores.

table 12-2 Risk Factors for Gang Membership	
RISK FACTOR	PERCENTAGE INCREASED RISK
Percentage in poverty	88%
Community arrest rate	79
Report of child maltreatment	78
Delinquent peers	97
Early dating	182
Precocious sexual activity	58
Negative life events	225
Depression	71
Externalizing behaviors	98
Delinquent beliefs	115
Prior general delinquency	226
Prior violent delinquency	319
Prior drug use	149

Sources: Terence Thornberry, Marvin Krohn, Alan Lizotte, Carolyn Smith, and Kimberly Tobin, *Gangs and Delinquency in Developmental Perspective* (New York: Cambridge University Press, 2003); Marvin Krohn and Terence Thornberry, *Longitudinal Perspectives on Adolescent Street Gangs* (Washington, DC: National Institute of Justice, 2006).

5. *Peer relationships* include delinquent peers, early dating, and sexual activity.

6. *Individual characteristics* include negative life events, psychiatric diagnoses, self-esteem, and delinquent beliefs.

7. *Prior delinquency* includes onset of delinquency, prior drug use, prior violence, and prior delinquency.

Several criminologists have found that gang members in Canada, Norway, Seattle, Rochester, and numerous other cities often have most of these risk factors *prior* to their initiation into gang life and that the more risk factors an adolescent has, the greater the likelihood he or she will be involved in gangs.[33] Terence Thornberry, Marvin Krohn, and their colleagues described three general ways that youths join street gangs. The first is a "kind-of-person" model known as the **selection model,** which argues that adolescents with a strong propensity for delinquency seek out gangs. These youths are already involved in antisocial behavior and commit crime whether in a gang or alone. The **facilitation model** is a "kind-of-group" model, which suggests that the normative structure of the gang along with group processes and dynamics increase delinquency among youths. According to the facilitation model, a youth's delinquency will increase during periods of gang membership and be lower both before and after that period. The third type known as the **enhancement model** combines elements of the *selection* and *facilitation* models. According to the enhancement model, adolescents who are already involved in delinquency are most apt to join a gang (selection) but, after joining, their delinquency is likely to increase significantly (facilitation).[34]

Pastor Kenneth Hammond of Durham, North Carolina, helps relocate adolescents who want out of gangs. As a social institution, has the church been overlooked as an insulator against delinquency?

Martín Sánchez-Jankowski has identified six reasons for joining a gang. They include *material incentives* (gang membership increases the likelihood of making money); *recreation* (gangs provide entertainment and a chance to meet girls); *refuge* or *camouflage* (the gang offers anonymity); *physical protection* (gangs provide personal protection from predatory elements, including other gangs, in high-crime neighborhoods); *a time to resist* (the gang provides opportunities to resist living lives similar to their parents); and *commitment to community* (gang membership provides the opportunity to demonstrate a form of local patriotism and dedication to protecting the neighborhood).[35] Making money also appears to be related to gaining the social "respect" that having money produces. Whether a youth first joins a gang to gain respect or to make money, the two often quickly become intertwined with each other.[36]

Motivations for joining gangs sometimes vary by sex. Boys are more likely to join gangs for excitement, to have a territory of one's own, for protection, for money, and for a sense of belonging. Girls, on the other hand, are more likely to join for social or associational reasons, for example because family members or friends were involved in gangs, to enhance their reputation, and for protection.[37] There are also important commonalities between boys and girls who join gangs. For instance, Jody Miller, Jenna St. Cyr, and Scott Decker found that family and neighborhood problems push both girls and boys into gangs.[38]

Many youths stay in the gang into early or even middle adulthood, although most drift in and out of gangs over the years. Some will join other organizations, such as social clubs or organized crime groups; some go to prison; some die from gang violence or drug use; and others get a job, get married, have children, and find the demands of gang membership incompatible with the new demands of family and job.[39] Gang mythology maintains the belief that once a youth joins a gang he or she is in for life; however, reality is substantially different. Leaving a gang may be risky, especially for youths who have special knowledge of serious crimes committed by gang members. It is not uncommon after a member announces his or her decision to leave the gang that a "beating out" ceremony occurs. Leaving the gang has two other risks. The police and courts may continue to treat the youth as a gang member and rival gangs may not be aware the youth quit the gang. In these instances, continued gang association might provide protection from rival gangs. However, most youths ultimately age out of gangs, and many peripheral and fringe members quit gangs without being required to give a reason for their decisions.[40]

think about it

Are the rationales youths provide for joining gangs merely excuses? Why do the majority of youths in gang-infested neighborhoods choose not to join? How does the phrase "birds of a feather flock together" apply to delinquent gangs?

Characteristics of Gangs

When Walter Miller asked police, juvenile officers, social workers, and other experts to define gangs, they agreed that gangs had the following traits: organization, leadership, turf, cohesiveness, and purpose.[41] But do all gangs exhibit these characteristics, and if so, do they possess them to the same degree? Decades of research have produced inconsistent answers.

Organization   The organizational structures of gangs have varied widely over time, from city to city, and even within cities. An example of a highly organized gang was the Vice Lords in Chicago in the 1960s.

> The most important element in the new organizational scheme was the creation of an administrative body called the "board" to deal with matters affecting the entire Vice Lord Nation. Further, regular weekly meetings were instituted with representatives from all the subgroups present. Finally, membership cards were printed with the Vice Lords' insignia—a top hat, cane, and white gloves.[42]

The Vice Lords, however, may be atypical. James F. Short, Jr., suggests that most gangs fall somewhere in the middle between crowds and mobs on the one hand and ordinary organizations on the other.[43]

Gene Muehlbauer and Laura Dodder's analysis of a suburban gang, *The Losers,* noted that its structure centered on a core group of about 10 to 12 members. These members were the nucleus of the gang and all other members were defined in relationship to this core. Alternatively, some gangs become so large they are unable to function effectively as a total unit; consequently, they divide into groupings called cliques.[44]

In their study of Hispanic gangs in California, Robert Jackson and Wesley McBride report that cliques are based primarily on age but sometimes on a specialty. In some gangs, for instance, there is a clique that specializes in violence and most of the "shooters" (gunmen) in the gang belong to that clique. Often, such cliques have a number of members who are not only capable of violence but also seek it out.[45] Joan Moore also noted age-grading in Chicano youth gangs in barrios in Los Angeles, El Paso, and San Antonio. The age cohorts, or **klikas,** appear to form every two years or so and become "salient lifelong membership and reference groups for some, but not all, members of the gang." [46]

Julie Amato and Dewey Cornell reported that different names youths use to describe gangs, such as crew, clique, posse, or mob, influence the reasoning they provide for joining the group and the type of delinquency in which they engage. Students involved in groups referred to as "gangs" had the highest delinquency rates. However, students also engaged in delinquency albeit at lower levels when involved in other groups, such as "crews." Additionally, youth involvement in groups like crews or cliques is often for social reasons to create new friendships. Conversely, gang involvement is often expressly to engage in delinquency.[47]

Leadership   Most gangs have clearly established leaders, although, like any organizational structure, this has varied over time and location. In the militaristic, or Mafia-style, model of gang leadership, the top authority position "is analogous to that of the highest ranking officer in a military unit; below him are lieutenants, sub-lieutenants, and so on. Decisions originating in higher echelons are transmitted through the ranks by a chain-of-command system."[48]

A second type of ideal leader is charismatic ruling by force of his or her personality. This leader is usually older, stronger, and revered by the gang's members. In the violent gangs studied by Lewis Yablonsky, leaders seemed to be self-appointed and often emotionally unstable. These leaders would occasionally manipulate other gang members into aggressive or violent actions just to satisfy their own emotional needs. By a combination of charisma and intimidation, the leaders of violent gangs tended to be relatively permanent in their positions, but turnover among the general membership was high.[49] Barry Krisberg suggests the only distinctive feature of gang leaders is their superior verbal ability. In the African American gangs he studied, this verbal "gift of the gab" enabled leaders to capture the attention of other members.[50]

Leadership varied greatly among the gangs John Hagedorn studied in Milwaukee. In most cases, the youth's "reputation or ability to fight was the main criterion for a leader . . . [while in other cases] someone was the leader because they knew most about gangs. . . . Some even disputed there ever was a leader."[51] In gangs whose leaders were identified, "titles" were rarely used.

Turf   According to Irving Spergel, **turf** or territoriality involves two components, *identification* and *control*. Many urban gangs identify with particular neighborhoods, parks, housing projects, or schools. At one time, crossing turf boundaries and entering another gang's territory, often clearly marked by graffiti, involved taking serious risks. However, automobiles have increased the mobility of teenagers, and slum districts have been sliced up by highways and urban renewal, blurring the old dividing lines. Identification with specific turf has been drastically altered for many gang members, largely because of frequent relocation of gang members' family residences.[52] Furthermore, according to Sánchez-Jankowski, "Gangs operate in a given area because that location is the only place they are strong enough to feel secure and in control, not because that particular territory is fundamental to their self-definition."[53]

Cohesiveness   Are gangs very close, tight-knit organizations with loyal members bound to one another by mutual friendship and common interests? Early writers thought so. Thrasher, for instance, depicted gangs as filled with happy-go-lucky youngsters, with the gang performing positive functions such as providing status for members.[54] Modern writers are sometimes equally romantic, but some criminologists disagree. Malcolm Klein says that the gang members he observed were "dissatisfied, deprived, and making the best of an essentially unhappy situation."[55] Klein adds that there are good reasons why gangs are not cohesive: The gang has few if any group goals; the membership is constantly in a state of flux, turning over rapidly; and group norms are practically nonexistent. James F. Short, Jr., and Fred Strodtbeck say that gang members fail at school, on the job, and elsewhere. These failures, along with other social disabilities, make gang members anxious and insecure about their status, and such insecurities are heightened by constant challenges and insults by other gang members.[56] Contemporary criminologists similarly note that most gangs are at best loosely organized and are most cohesive when committing delinquency.[57]

Purpose Delinquent gangs have been often thought to exist for the purpose of committing criminal offenses. Purpose is a state of mind that is difficult for gang researchers to measure. It is easier to study behavior, such as the extent to which gangs commit crime. Jacqueline Schneider's study of gangs in Columbus, Ohio, found gangs often specialize in certain offenses. By looking at the arrest offense patterns of gang leaders, she discovered that gangs tend to operate within particular crime niches. For instance, the Crips were primarily involved in violent offenses while the Freeze Crew accounted for a disproportionate number of property crimes.[58]

t h i n k
about it

In the late twentieth century gangs were responsible for hundreds of homicides each year. How might the media or academic portrayal of gang-affiliated youths contribute to the problems they pose?

Researchers have found that gang members spend most of their time on pursuits other than crime mostly just whiling away their time. For many, this involves little more than "partying and hanging out." Geoffrey Hunt and his colleague's study of ethnic youth gangs in Northern California also reports that "hanging around," "kicking back," and especially drinking were "commonplace and integral part[s] of everyday life among gang members." Fighting was seen as an activity more typical of one stage in the development of the gang. Constant fighting with other gangs happened early and helped structure the gang. As gang members grew older, their inclination was to decrease the fighting and increase the partying.[59]

THE CONTEMPORARY GANG PROBLEM

In the 1970s, only 19 states reported gang problems. The states with the largest number of gang-problem cities were California, Florida, Illinois, and Texas. Overwhelmingly, gangs were concentrated in the largest cities, such as Chicago, Houston, Los Angeles, and Miami.[60] Today, all 50 states, Washington, DC, and nearly 3,000 cities, towns, villages, and counties indicated they were experiencing some type of gang problem. Estimating the number of gang members is problematic and dependent on how criminologists define a gang. Given that limitation, the National Youth Gang Survey of law enforcement agencies across the country reported that in 2004 there were approximately 760,000 gang members in the United States. These 760,000 gang members comprise 24,000 gangs that are active in more than 2,900 jurisdictions. Although gangs are found in all types of communities, about 85 percent of all gang members lived in larger cities and suburban counties.

According to police reports, 67 percent of gang members were adults, and 33 percent were children or adolescents. The overall age of the gang population has increased in recent years due to a decline in reports of gang problems in smaller communities that typically report very young gang members and increased police attention toward older, more criminally active gang members.

Nationally, about 50 percent of the gang population was Hispanic. African Americans comprised about 35 percent of the gang population, and whites accounted for 10 percent. About 29 percent of gangs were multiethnic. Males make up more than 90 percent of all gang members. Approximately 63 percent of law enforcement agencies reported that the return of gang members from jail or prison confinement to their jurisdiction created several problems, such as increased violence and drug trafficking.[61]

It is difficult to estimate the gang population because gang members often migrate to other jurisdictions. For instance, 10 percent of the police agencies participating in the National Youth Gang Survey reported that more than half of the gang members in their jurisdiction had recently migrated from other areas. Gang members move for a variety of reasons. About 45 percent moved for legitimate reasons pertaining to family obligations or employment opportunities. However, 23 percent moved for drug market opportunities, 21 percent moved to avoid law enforcement, and 18 percent moved to pursue other illegal ventures.[62]

Randall Shelden and his colleagues point out that this expansion of the gang problem throughout the country has prompted a debate. Some in law enforcement believe there has been a *migration* of gang members from community to community, reflecting the franchising of a gang's criminal activities. An alternative perspective focuses on the *proliferation* of the gang problem. This perspective suggests the increase in the number of communities reporting gang problems only reflects the changing definitions of gang and gang member, the desire of local police to obtain increased funding to respond to the gang problem, or the movement of youths who are gang members to new communities although the reasons for the move are unrelated to gang membership.[63]

Although criminologists debate the migration versus proliferation of gangs, one point not subject to debate is that gangs negatively affect communities. James Howell has identified several ways that delinquent gangs harm young people and communities: (1) gang members commit a disproportionate amount of crime; (2) gang members are most criminally active while they are in gangs (their delinquency is lower before and after leaving the gang); (3) gang members commit more serious crimes, such as robberies and assaults; (4) there is overlap between gang membership and chronic offending, thus their delinquency is long-lasting; and (5) gang delinquency creates enormous costs. For instance, each assault-related gunshot injury has been estimated at $1 million in public costs and a single criminal career of a serious gang member can inflict costs between $1.7 million and $2.3 million. Finally, all of these issues take an enormous social toll on communities that must deal with the delinquency, victimization, social costs, and fear generated by gangs.[64]

The Spread of Gangs

Walter Miller has identified seven reasons offered by law enforcement, criminologists, and policy makers for the dramatic proliferation of gangs over the past three decades. Some of the reasons suggest a pattern of gang migration.

1. *Drugs:* Police believe the expansion of illegal drug markets increased the solidarity of existing gangs, offered incentives for the creation of new gangs, and promoted the development of widespread networks of drug-trafficking gangs.

2. *Immigration:* Major waves of immigration during the past 25 years have brought in many groups of Asians, Southeast Asians, and Latin Americans whose children have formed gangs in the tradition of Irish, Jewish, and Slavic immigrant groups during the 1800s.

3. *Gang Names and Alliances:* In the 1980s the pattern of adopting a common name and claiming a federated relationship with other gangs became increasingly common. Hundreds of small local gangs adopted the names or

claimed alliance with well-known gangs such as the Crips, Bloods, Latin Kings, and Gangster Disciples.

4. *Migration:* Some experts believe gangs that exhausted drug markets or faced violent competition from other drug-dealing gangs in a particular community simply left that area and transferred their operations to new markets in towns and cities with little existing gang presence.

5. *Government Policies:* During the 1960s some policy makers viewed urban youth gangs as representing an untapped reservoir of potential leadership for improving the quality of life for residents in low-income communities. These officials advocated recognizing gangs as legitimate community groups and enlisting them in social reform efforts. Over $1 million in federal funds were allocated to urban gangs in Chicago and New York by the Office of Economic Opportunity as part of the federal war on poverty.

6. *Female-Headed Households:* This explanation suggests that the increase in female-headed households and absence of stable adult male role models created identity problems for male adolescents who then turned to gangs for their sense of place and values.

7. *Gang Subculture and the Media:* Gangs have become "hot" market items in movies, novels, television, and music. Because the media portrayed gang members as macho, hip, cool, and victims of racism, police brutality, and government oppression, the gang subculture became viewed in a glamorous and rewarding lifestyle.[65]

However, Cheryl Maxson believes the most common reason for the proliferation of gangs into smaller communities is that gang members often move with their families to suburbs or other traditionally safer areas to improve the quality of life and to be near relatives and friends.[66] Other research suggests the recent appearance of gangs in communities that had not previously had gang problems is not the result of "migrated" gang members but, rather, the development of loosely organized cliques of age-graded neighborhood adolescents who are growing up in areas characterized by declining local economic conditions and growing poverty.[67]

Racial and Ethnic Variations in Gangs

Gangs differ significantly in their organization and structure, leadership, cohesiveness, purpose, and sense of turf. Older perceptions of gangs as similar kinds of youth groups must be reconsidered in light of the ethnic and racial diversity of gangs today.

African American Gangs   The most notable and widespread of the contemporary African American gangs are the Bloods and the Crips. These gangs have become essentially confederations of smaller sets or subsets. These sets are generally organized around neighborhoods and typically have between 20 and 30 members although a few of the larger sets may have more than 100 members.

African American gangs have little, if any, formal structure. But what these gangs lack in organizational structure, they make up in violence. Much of the violence stems from traditional rivalry and competition over turf, although fights may start from something as minor as wearing a red hat in a Crips neighborhood or showing the wrong hand sign in the wrong place. Violence between the Bloods and Crips also often results from both gangs' involvement in the drug trade. The large amounts of money from narcotics sales allow them to purchase high-powered, military-style automatic weapons. Unfortunately, many of those affected by the violence of the Bloods and Crips are innocent victims caught in the crossfire of a gang fight or in random drive-by shootings.[68] Indeed, young African American males between the ages of 14 and 24 (the prime age range for gang membership) are both the perpetrators and victims of homicide at rates that are *10 to 30 times* their proportion of the population.[69]

Hispanic Gangs   Hispanic gangs are composed of youths whose ethnic backgrounds include Mexican, Mexican American, Cuban, and Puerto Rican, among others (for a look at what has been called the most violent gang in the country, see Box 12-4). Hispanic gangs have shown a remarkable longevity over the decades, with multiple generations of family members being affiliated with the same gangs. Today, Hispanic gangs made up nearly half of the known gangs in Southern California, although only a small percentage of Hispanic youths have any gang affiliation. Nationally, 50 percent of all gang members are Hispanic.[70]

Most Hispanic gangs are organized around age cohorts, or klikas, separated in age by 2 or 3 years, and are territorially based: "For gang members the word for gang and for neighborhood is identical. *'Mi barrio'* refers equally to 'my gang' and 'my neighborhood.'" The fierce loyalty to one's barrio is the basis for much intergang violence. "Gang members feel obliged to respond with violence in defense of their barrio. This often involves repelling intruders—especially those from rival barrios—from the territory claimed by the gang." Like all racial and ethnic groups, most Hispanic gang violence is *intraracial,* that is directed against other Hispanics. For instance, Alison Rhyne and Douglas Yearwood found 80 percent of Hispanic gang violence is directed against other Hispanics.[71]

Membership in Hispanic gangs is achieved through initiation rituals designed to establish a member's loyalty to the gang. The ritual typically consists of a beating at the hands of three or four members of the gang. Serious beatings in the initiation are rare since the intent is to see if and how the would-be member stands up and defends him- or herself. The ritual is also intended to solidify the new member's integration into the gang.[72]

Much time is spent partying and drinking in casual settings or in more structured settings, ranging from residences, public parks, or isolated streets. There are typically two categories of partying. The first involves more conventional family-oriented gatherings, such as weddings, birthday parties, baptisms, and barbecues. Both male and female gang members attend such parties where beer and marijuana are casually consumed. The second type of party is more spontaneous, likely to include only male gang members, and often involves heavy alcohol and poly-drug use.[73] As Alice Cepeda and Avelardo Valdez note, "The primary objective, according to several respondents, is to get 'loaded and high.'"[74]

Asian American Gangs   Asian juvenile gangs are a relatively new development in the United States. According to Ko-lin Chin, the first Asian youth gangs developed in the Chinese section of San Francisco in the 1950s and were composed almost exclusively of American-born Chinese.[75] But with the arrival of large numbers of Hong Kong–born Chinese in the 1960s, gangs such as the Wah Ching (Youths of China) were formed as rivals to American-born Chinese gangs. These gangs soon became involved in prostitution, drugs, gambling, and

box 12-4   DELINQUENCY AROUND THE GLOBE

MS-13

A growing security threat to the United States, Mexico, and Central America is the Mara Salvatrucha (rough translation is "mob of El Salvadoran youths on guard"), or MS-13 gang. In the course of El Salvador's Civil War, children as young as 11 and 12 years old were trained and used as soldiers. The war devastated the small nation and displaced approximately one million Salvadorians, most came to the United States. Many of the youths had received military training in El Salvador, including training in explosives, booby traps, small arms, and hand-to-hand combat. El Salvadorian youths were not accepted by many of the Hispanic groups in Los Angeles and other American cities. As the youths became marginalized, they banded together for protection and formed what is now known as MS-13.

Because El Salvador's weak state created a breeding ground for criminal violence, MS-13 engages in some of the most extreme forms of terror and violence of any gang. These acts include machine-gun killings, home invasion robberies, and machete attacks. Much of the gang violence that MS-13 commits is directed toward the Latin Kings, their chief rival among street gangs. Although originally organized in single cliques, MS-13 is creating alliances to better organize their criminal activity, which includes human smuggling, drug trafficking, and an array of other crimes. MS-13 is located in 33 states and has over 250,000 members in the United States. Members are distinguished by heavy tattooing covering the body and face.

In addition to delinquency and violence, MS-13 poses a threat to national security. Al Qaeda and other Islamic terrorist groups are creating relationships with MS-13 because of their involvement in human trafficking across the United States and Mexican border. This has the potential to create a major security concern for Americans. Ultimately, Los Mara Salvatrucha and other similar type gangs pose a serious threat to border security for Mexico, Central America, and the United States. Mara Salvatrucha recruits and manipulates vulnerable youths. These youths provide fresh blood and expendable assets for the gang. The question is how the United States, Mexico, and Central American governments will react to this increasing threat.

Sources: Jeffrey Wenner, "MS-13 in Montgomery County Maryland," *Journal of Gang Research* 11:23–28 (2004); Andrew Grascia, "Gang Violence: Mara Salvatrucha—Forever Salvador," *Journal of Gang Research* 11:29–36 (2004); Shelly Domash, "America's Most Dangerous Gang," *Police: The Law Enforcement Magazine* 29:30–34 (2005); Kevin Johnson, "MS-13 Gang Growing Extremely Dangerous, FBI Says," *USA TODAY,* January 5, 2006:1A.

---

extortion. The accumulation of money, rather than fighting with other gangs over turf, dominated gang activity.[76]

Indo-Chinese gangs, predominantly Vietnamese, are the most numerous among Asian gangs today. It has been estimated that there are more than 100 Indo-Chinese gangs with thousands of members. The city of Westminster in Orange County, California, for example, has a population of 86,000 with about 25 percent Asian, and most are Vietnamese refugees.[77] Unlike Hispanic gangs, Vietnamese gangs are weakly connected to the local community and its institutions. Rather, gangs are organized around personal friendships. Consequently, members "are more likely to attack local citizens and exploit the organizations that remain in the community."[78] Although dominated by Vietnamese youths, Cambodians, Hmong, Thais, and Laotians are also found in independent ethnic gangs or in mixed gangs. In addition to Indo-Chinese gangs, there are Pacific

Islander gangs composed of Filipino, Samoan, Tongan, Fijian, and Hawaiian youths as well as Japanese and Korean gangs.[79]

A recent study of Southeast Asian gangs by Geoffrey Hunt and his colleagues reports that these gangs have little internal hierarchy or clearly defined leadership and a minimal concept of territory although they do have tattoos, colors, and patterned cigarette burns as symbols. Gang initiations are more informal than those found in Hispanic gangs. Instead of "jumping in" ceremonies, Southeast Asian gangs were more likely to evaluate potential members through a process of "kicking back" or "hanging around" that could last from a few months to a year. Hunt and his colleagues conclude that the everyday life of Southeast Asian gang members is rather similar to that of other California gangs and that these gang members like other groups make a variety of attempts to deal with and transcend the mundane.[80] Some Southeast Asian gangs operating in the United States have developed relatively unique patterns of violent crime, such as bank robbery and murders in which victims are bludgeoned to death.[81] Box 12-5 describes the violent crime of rape engaged in by some Hmong gangs.

Native American Gangs   Until recently, little attention had been paid to Native American youth gangs. Only in the 1990s did criminologists and police notice the emergence of these gangs. Attempting to estimate the number of Native American gangs and gang members is no less problematic than that posed in general gang research. However, Janice Joseph and Dorothy Taylor report the number of Native American gangs more than doubled between 1994 and 2002. Today, there are at least 113 Native gangs around the country with 55 gangs including 900 members on the Navajo Reservation in the four corners area of Arizona, Colorado, New Mexico, and Utah. Gang activity has been reported on all nine South Dakota reservations, as well as in cities ranging from Rapid City to Seattle to Albuquerque to Tulsa.[82] Joseph Donnermeyer and his colleagues surveyed a sample of junior and senior high Native American youths in reservation and urban schools in several Western states and found that about 6 percent of males and 1 percent of females reported gang membership.[83] In their survey of 212 middle school students on reservations in the upper Midwest, Les Whitbeck and his colleagues found that 6 percent of males and 4 percent of females indicated that they were in gangs.[84]

Native American gangs generally do not reflect traditional native culture, rather they identify with nationally recognized African American and Hispanic gangs. Native American gangs account for an increasing number of serious and violent crimes on reservations, including homicide, assault, rape, drug dealing, drive-by and walk-by shootings, and extortion. Marijuana is easily cultivated, and remote sections of reservations provide locations for setting up of methamphetamine labs. According to Joseph and Taylor, "Current trends indicate that Indian gangs are mirroring the gang activity occurring in the communities surrounding Indian Country."[85] Liz Martinez notes that Indian authorities are concentrating their resources on arresting and prosecuting gang members primarily because of their disproportionate involvement in crime on reservations.[86]

Gang Violence

Gang members pose a significant danger to American society in terms of their involvement in the most violent forms of delinquency. Using the National Crime Victimization Survey, Erika Harrell discovered that between 6 and 10 percent box 12-5

box 12-5   A WINDOW ON DELINQUENCY

Hmong Gangs and Rape

The number of Hmong gangs and the level of their criminal activity has been increasing in severity over recent years. While they have become involved in a wide range of crimes, such as homicides, prostitution, home invasions, burglaries, auto thefts, and the sale and distribution of drugs, the crime of rape, and especially gang rape, represents a particular concern. Following the Vietnam War, many Hmong families immigrated to the United States, first settling in California, Minnesota, and Wisconsin. Today, at least 36 states have Hmong populations. According to Richard Straka, a street officer and investigator who has worked with the Hmong community for over 10 years, Hmong gangs began to appear in the St. Paul and Ramsey County, Minnesota, area in the mid-1980s. The first Hmong gang in Minnesota, the Cobras, began as a group of teenage friends who played on a soccer team. By 1988, a number of 10- and 11-year-old Hmong youths wanted to join the Cobras but were told they were too young. As a result, they started their own gang, the White Tigers. Their early crimes included breaking into gun shops to obtain weapons. By the late 1990s, Hmong gangs were identified as major players in local gang violence. In the summer of 1999, at least 22 reported shootings and the deaths of two were attributed to Hmong gangs. Most of the shootings occurred among four rival gangs: the White Tigers, the Oroville Mono Boys, the Purple Brothers, and the Oriental Ruthless Boys.

But Hmong gangs represent a violent threat to nongang members as well. The most frequent and violent crimes against non-Hmong gang members is rape. The majority of the victims in the sexual assaults are juvenile Hmong females. In 1997 a number of girls 12 to 15 years old had arranged to meet gang members through a message service. The victims went willingly with the boys thinking they were going for a ride or to a party. Instead, gang members took them to an attic of a garage or a house, turned off the lights or put a blanket over their heads, and raped them. The gang members called this "doing the Ninja" as the victim could not identify who had sexually assaulted her.

Violent rape by Hmong gang members is not limited to Minnesota. In Warren, Michigan, several members of a Hmong gang were arrested for repeatedly raping teenage girls who they had held prisoner for nearly 3 weeks. Authorities in Fresno, California, reported a similar case in which at least 33 victims had been raped and held by gang members for periods ranging from 2 days to 3 months.

Hmong girls who have been sexually assaulted are hesitant to report the crimes. After being raped, they fear being shunned by family members who would consider them "damaged" or having "shamed" them. Gang members use this to their advantage, telling the victims that "they were no good to their families and that the gang was now their family." Some of the victims stayed with the gang members even after they were raped. They felt that they had nowhere else to go because they feared their own families more than the gang members.

Sources: Richard Straka, "The Violence of Hmong Gangs and the Crime of Rape," *FBI Law Enforcement Bulletin,* February: 12–16 (2003); John Wang, "A Preliminary Profile of Laotian/Hmong Gangs: A California Perspective," *Journal of Gang Research* 9:1–14 (2002).

of all violent victimizations were reported by victims to be committed by gang members. According to the most recent data, this equated to nearly 400,000 rapes, sexual assaults, robberies, aggravated assaults, and simple assaults committed by gang members. At the height of gang violence in 1994, gang members accounted for more than 1.1 million violent victimizations. Aggravated assaults and robberies are the violent crimes most commonly committed by gang members; however, they also commit a disproportionate number of murders. Based on the FBI's Supplemental Homicide Reports, gang youths commit between 5 and 7 percent of total murders and between 8 and 10 percent of firearm-perpetrated murders each year.[87]

Although gang violence is a national problem, it is often more destructive within certain communities (see Box 12-6). For instance, police departments in major cities, such as Denver, often underreport the magnitude of crimes committed by gang members. A recent investigative report by Denver media analysts found that the number of gang crimes per year was *10 times* the number re-

---

box 12-6   **A WINDOW ON DELINQUENCY**

The Criminology of Gang Homicide

In many American cities, gangs are responsible for a disproportionate number of homicides. During the late 20th century, gang homicides in Chicago increased almost 500 percent and accounted for 25 percent of all murders in the city. In Los Angeles, nearly 50 percent of homicides in Los Angeles County were gang-related. In Boston, about 1,300 gang members, who comprised less than 1 percent of their age group, were collectively responsible for 60 percent of all youth homicides in the city.

According to Scott Decker, the quick rise and fall of gang homicide is consistent with the organization of gangs and its generally weak leadership. Most gangs are loosely organized and seemingly waiting for something to unite them. The uniting element is a real or perceived threat from some "out" group, usually a similarly disorganized set of youths from another neighborhood or ethnic group. Very quickly, the threat is framed as an enemy to the gang. This serves to increase cohesion of the gang and justify the use of violence to "respond" to the real or perceived threat posed by the gang's enemy. Some short-lived act of violence, such as a drive-by shooting, occurs and rapidly deescalates until the process begins again. Decker described this process in seven steps:

1. Loose bonds to the gang.
2. Collective identification of threat from a rival gang, which reinforces the use of violence, expands the number of gang members, and increases cohesion.
3. A mobilizing event possibly, but not necessarily, violence.
4. Escalation of activity.
5. Violent event (e.g., homicide).
6. Rapid deescalation.
7. Retaliation.

Subsequent research has supported this model of gang homicides, in fact, Jesenia Pizarro and Jean McGloin found it was a better explanation of gang homicide than social disorganization theory. Given the haphazard nature of gang organization and violence, they believe that controlling gang access to lethal weapons and encouraging youth involvement in structured activities can reduce lethal violence among adolescents.

Sources: Scott Decker, "Collective and Normative Features of Gang Violence," *Justice Quarterly* 13:342–264 (1996); Richard Rosenfeld, Timothy Bray, and Arlen Egley, "Facilitating Violence: A Comparison of Gang-Motivated, Gang-Affiliated, and Non-Gang Youth Homicides," *Journal of Quantitative Criminology* 15:495–516 (1999); George Tita and Allan Abrahamse, *Gang Homicide in Los Angeles, 1981–2001* (Sacramento: California Attorney General's Office, 2004); Jesenia Pizarro and Jean McGloin, "Explaining Gang Homicides in Newark, New Jersey: Collective Behavior or Social Disorganization?" *Journal of Criminal Justice* 34:195–207 (2006).

ported by police.[88] In Compton and other areas of south-central Los Angeles, it is not uncommon to have one or two gang homicides per day.[89]

Comparing matched samples of gang members and at-risk youths from four high-crime neighborhoods, Ronald Huff found that gang members were 20 times more likely than at-risk adolescents to participate in a drive-by shooting, 10 times more likely to commit murder, 8 times more likely to commit robbery, and 3 times more likely to assault someone in public. The criminality of gang members is so pronounced that Matt DeLisi and his colleagues concluded:

> In addition to various forms of violence, gang members commit antisocial acts such as randomly intimidating or assaulting patrons in shopping centers and grocery stores, using and selling drugs in school, and assaulting their teachers during class. Even among samples of youths characterized by multiple risk factors for delinquency and violence, gang members are noteworthy for their strident criminality.[90]

think
about it

To avoid gang violence, should prison populations be segregated based on gang affiliation? Would such a policy be construed as acquiescence to the criminal element?

Two significant differences between contemporary youth gangs and those of earlier decades are that many of today's gangs are exceptionally violent and much of that violence occurs within school settings (see Chapter 11). In some instances, gangs have taken effective control of urban high schools. Gang violence and other gang activities in public schools had reached startling levels by the 1970s. Gang operations have been identified at all three levels of schools, including elementary, middle school, and high school. Serious assaults have been directed by gang members against other gang members, teachers, and fellow students.

However, most gang violence occurs *outside* school settings. Violence perpetrated by members of youth gangs in major cities began to rise dramatically in the late 20th century. Walter Miller attributes the growth of gang violence during this period largely to a single factor, guns. By the mid 1970s, many youth gangs were giving up their traditional zip guns, chains, and knives and turning to revolvers, shotguns, and semi-automatic rifles. Miller predicted that the problem would become worse, more violent, and more confrontational with law

Does "gangsta-rap" glorify the senseless violence of gang life or provide a glimpse into a world largely hidden from mainstream America? In what ways is gangsta-rap indicative of an antisocial subculture?

think
about it

Fraternities and sororities
on university campuses
meet many of the criteria
for gangs. What sorts
of deviance and crime
do Greek organizations
engage in at your
college? Do class and
ethnic characteristics
impact the manner in
which we conceptualize
gangs?

enforcement agencies. His prediction was correct. Youth gang homicides clearly increased. While gang-related killings in major gang cities totaled 633 in 1980, Chicago and Los Angeles alone accounted for more than 1,000 gang homicides in 1994. With more weapons available, with more gang members carrying guns, and with the reality that gangs often attract young males who enjoy violence, increased levels of serious violence came as no surprise.[91]

Gang homicides appear to have declined significantly after 1995 in most large cities that had been reporting large numbers of gang homicides. However, gang-related homicides doubled in Southern California's Orange County in recent years, and increases in gang violence have recently been reported in other cities around the nation in the early twenty-first century.[92] For instance, more than half of the over 1,000 homicides in Los Angeles and Chicago were gang-related. In 171 other major American cities, about 25 percent of homicides were gang-related, and in 2004, U.S. cities experienced an 11 percent increase in gang homicides over the previous eight-year average.[93]

Drugs and Drug Dealing by Gangs

In the summer of 2006, police in three states arrested more than 30 people with ties to the Mickey Cobras, a street gang based in the Dearborn Homes Apartments in Chicago. The gang had been selling a deadly type of heroin that was mixed with the powerful (often fatal) painkiller fentanyl. The drug concoction killed nearly 150 people and resulted in several hundred nonfatal drug overdoses.[94] The incident underscored the public belief that gang members are extensively involved in drugs and drug dealing. Are gang members more likely than nongang members to use drugs? The answer is yes, and they are more likely to do so in conjunction with other delinquent activity. Arielle Baskin-Sommers and Ira Sommers' study of methamphetamine users found that 35 percent of regular drug users committed a violent crime while under the influence. Of these violent offenders, nearly 30 percent were either active gang members or actively involved in the drug trade.[95] Jeffrey Fagan found gang members to be about twice as likely to use drugs and to use them more often than youths who are not involved in gangs.[96] Dana Peterson and her colleagues found gang youths to be disproportionately involved in drug use and that for many gang members their initiation into the gang was a precursor to their use of drugs.[97] Scott Decker and David Curry report that gang members are not only more likely to use and sell serious drugs, such as cocaine, but also are more likely than nongang adolescents to commit homicides primarily during the course of drug activity.[98] Indeed, the drug activity of gang members with all of the negative consequences that it produces has been likened to a public health epidemic.[99]

Are juvenile gangs extensively involved in drug trafficking? Ronald Huff reports that his study of four communities in Colorado, Ohio, and Florida found that gang members were extensively involved in drug sales, especially cocaine and marijuana, and that gang members sell significantly more cocaine than nongang youths.[100] George Knox and his colleagues' study of over 4,000 gang members from 17 states found that 82 percent of gang members reported that their gang has sold crack cocaine. In addition, drug trafficking for profit was one of the primary reasons for their gangs' existence.[101]

However, gang involvement in the drug trade appears to vary by ethnicity and locale. African American gangs are more involved in drug trafficking than

Hispanic, Asian, or white gangs.[102] Jeffrey Fagan notes that in Los Angeles, Chicano gangs sell small quantities of marijuana, but the crack and cocaine trade is dominated by African American gangs. In New York, the crack trade is not controlled or dominated by any particular group of street gangs.[103]

The National Youth Gang Center surveyed over 1,000 police and sheriffs' departments and reported that 43 percent of the drug sales in their jurisdictions involved gang members, although the degree of involvement varied extensively. For instance, only about 25 percent of gang members selling drugs were seen as doing so at a "high" level, and nearly half were involved at a "low" level. Although gangs are involved in drug dealing, respondents indicated that gangs did not control or manage most of the drug distribution in their jurisdictions.[104]

Some take issue with police, criminologists, and the media who overemphasize the gang–drug connection. Malcolm Klein argues that drug gangs and *street gangs* are not the same. More important, most street gangs simply do not have the necessary leadership, cohesiveness, sense of loyalty and secretiveness, or narrow focus on the mechanics of drug sales. Rather, Klein says that typical street gangs have shifting leadership, intermediate levels of cohesiveness, frequently broken codes of honor, and very versatile and independent criminal involvements. Because of these reasons, Klein believes that gangs are lousy mechanisms for drug distribution.[105] Similarly, James Inciardi and his colleagues' study of drug use and serious delinquency found that only about 5 percent of the street youths in their sample had ever been involved in gangs. Most youths involved in drug distribution saw little reason to belong to gangs.[106]

Unfortunately, criminological studies often rely on small samples and are not necessarily reflective of national trends in gang activity. The assessment of the threats posed by gangs from criminal justice practitioners is often more stark than the assessments made by academics (see Box 12-7). For example, each year the National Alliance of Gang Investigators Associations (NAGIA), a consortium of over 10,000 gang investigators in law enforcement and intelligence communities produces a national gang threat assessment. On the topic of drugs, the NAGIA reports that gangs are the primary distributors of drugs throughout the United States and that many of the fasting-growing gang-related problems pertain to drug trafficking.[107]

FEMALE GANG DELINQUENCY

It is difficult to obtain reliable estimates of the number of female gang members. Research suggests that girls may comprise up to 38 percent of all gang members.[108] However, the National Youth Gang Survey reports that less than 10 percent of gang members identified by law enforcement were female. Such a wide range likely reflects the type of data being used with the lower estimates generally based on official data and higher estimates utilizing self-report measures.[109] While the majority of gang boys are in all-male gangs, most girls join gangs with mixed gender composition. For instance, the National Youth Gang Survey reports about 39 percent of all youth gangs had female members and that only 2 percent of gangs were identified as predominantly female.[110]

Gang girls are much more likely to be involved in delinquency, especially serious delinquency than are nongang females. In general, gang girls commit

box 12-7 A WINDOW ON DELINQUENCY

The National Gang Threat Assessment

The National Alliance of Gang Investigators Alliances (NAGIA) is comprised of 15 state and regional gang investigators associations, representing over 10,000 gang investigators across the country and gang practitioners from the Federal Bureau of Investigation, Bureau of Alcohol, Tobacco, Firearms, and Explosives, National Drug Intelligence Center, and others. The NAGIA conducts a national survey to produce a national gang threat assessment. Highlights include

- Gangs are the primary distributors of drugs throughout the United States.
- Gangs are increasingly associating with organized crime organizations from Mexico, Russia, and several nations in Asia.
- Few gangs have been found to associate with domestic terrorist organizations, but gang members are most susceptible to these influences while in prison.

- There is increased fluidity between delinquent street gangs and prison gangs.
- Hispanic gang membership is increasing and spreading throughout the country.
- Indian Country is reporting escalating levels of gang activity and crime.
- About 31 percent of communities refuse to acknowledge a gang problem despite evidence to the contrary.
- Gang activity around schools and college campuses has increased.
- Depending on the region of the country, gangs are disproportionately responsible for the trafficking of marijuana, cocaine, crack cocaine, and methamphetamine.

Source: National Alliance of Gang Investigators Associations, *2005 National Gang Threat Assessment* (Washington, DC: Bureau of Justice Assistance, 2006).

fewer violent crimes than gang boys and are more inclined to commit property crime and status offenses.[111] Based on in-depth interviews with 27 female gang members in St. Louis, Jody Miller and Scott Decker noted that although girls are less often involved in violent crime than are boys, fully 85 percent of the girls reported having hit someone with the idea of hurting them.[112] Finn Esbensen and his colleagues surveyed nearly 6,000 eighth-graders in 42 different schools. While gang boys reported more delinquencies than the girls, 39 percent of the gang girls reported attacking someone with a weapon, 21 percent indicated that they had shot at someone, 78 percent said they had been involved in gang fights, and 65 percent claimed to have carried hidden weapons.[113] Gang girls are also more likely to be heavier and more frequent users of drugs than nongang girls. Geoffrey Hunt and his colleagues conducted interviews with 168 female who were currently gang members. Nearly two-thirds of the females reported using marijuana more than 50 times, with about one-fifth using marijuana on a daily basis. In addition, over 80 percent of the female gang members reported regular or somewhat regular use of such drugs as cocaine, crack, LSD, heroin, and methamphetamine.[114]

Gang girl criminality, however, may be a function of the sex structure of the gang. Girls in sex-balanced gangs were significantly less likely than the gang boys to engage in violent offenses, carry weapons, undertake drug sales, and become involved in serious property offenses. Offending by girls in majority-male gangs was more likely to reflect similar levels of involvement in delinquent activities as male members. Finally, girls in majority-female or all-female gangs reported significantly less delinquency than males in all-male gangs.

Gang girls are much less likely to be victims of violence than are gang boys, although much more likely than nongang females. Their lower rates of violent victimization are attributed to a number of factors: Gang boys tend to exclude them from potentially violent activities, girls' peripheral status as gang members reduces the likelihood of their being targets of violence by rival gang members, and girls are protected by male gang members against predatory males in the community.

Females, like their male counterparts, are generally initiated into gangs through a process of being "beaten in" or being required to assault a rival gang member or to participate in a serious crime. Some girls are tattooed with gang symbols, while others may be "blessed in" by gang members praying over the girl. More problematic are initiations where a girl is "sexed in," meaning the girl is required to have intercourse with multiple male gang members. Girls who are sexed into a gang are at much greater risk for continued sexual mistreatment and exploitation and are generally viewed by male and female gang members as weak, promiscuous, and subject to contempt and disrespect.[115]

Girls join gangs for many reasons, although many young females see the gang as an escape from family problems. Joan Moore and John Hagedorn report that in the Hispanic gangs they studied, girls were more likely than boys to come from families that were abusive. The parents of gang girls were also more likely to be alcoholic or heroin users.[116] Jody Miller also reports that gang girls are more likely to come from very dysfunctional families. For example, 71 percent of the gang girls in her study reported serious family problems, such as violence, drug addiction, and drug or alcohol abuse, compared to only 26 percent of nongang girls.[117] Anne Campbell's study of mixed-sex gangs in New York City suggests that girls generally join gangs to escape the isolation they experienced in their families while growing up. The girls she studied looked to the gang for a sense of belonging, for loyalty in relationships, and for unconditional acceptance.[118]

Other research suggests a rather different relationship between gang girls and their families. Geoffrey Hunt and his colleagues report that gang girls maintain strong ties to family members, especially mothers, sisters, and other female relatives, and that these family connections are significant elements of social support. In many ways, gangs are seen as extensions of their families. These girls had grown up around gangs and gang activities, and gangs were simply part of their daily lives. Fully 96 percent of the girls said they had family members who had been, or were currently, members of gangs.[119]

Some girls may "choose" to join gangs because they believe there is no other choice. According to Alan Turley, who studied female gang members in the six largest cities in Texas:

> Girls feel they have no choice; that eventually the male gang members will have them (sexually), so it makes sense to the girls to submit to the gang, rather than becoming female prey for the gang.[120]

On the other hand, in her study of Hispanic gangs in California, Mary Harris found that girls became members of gangs in a manner similar to joining other teenage groups. They were not pressured or coerced into membership but entered gangs through friendships and family ties. Once in the gang, the girl soon took on the attitudes of other gang members, including the willingness to fight, to be "bad," to be "tough," and to use drugs. And although she may have entered the gang through family ties, the gang soon became the girl's primary reference group, demanding stronger loyalty than either family or school. But fighting or engaging in potentially violent confrontations are not the dominant activities of gang girls any more than of gang boys. Rather, most gang girls (and boys) spend the greater part of their time together simply hanging out—watching television, listening to the radio, playing music or video games or cards, drinking beer, or smoking marijuana.[121]

GANGS AND JUVENILE JUSTICE

Several strategies for responding to the problem of youth gangs have been developed. These strategies include *neighborhood mobilization* approaches popular in the 1920s and 1930s; *social intervention* programs popular in the 1940s and 1950s; programs aimed at *creating social and economic opportunities* for inner city and at-risk youths used in the 1960s; the *suppression efforts* that emerged in the 1970s and 1980s; and the *intervention and prevention* strategies that have been given more emphasis in recent years. Even though suppression strategies continue to dominate the field today, many intervention and prevention programs are being pursued in schools and communities around the country. For many gang experts, suppression strategies combined with intervention programs appear to be the most promising approaches.[122]

Many law enforcement agencies have created special gang-units as a response to the growing gang problem. Today, there are an estimated 400 police gang-units in the United States, and over 85 percent of them have been established in the past decade.[123] About 36 percent of national law enforcement agencies (51 percent in large cities) have specialized units primarily assigned to combat delinquent gangs. Almost 50 percent of national law enforcement agencies use firearm suppression initiatives to address gang violence.[124] Police gang suppression strategies involve a variety of activities. The key elements in police gang suppression involve understanding the nature and scope of the community gang problem, gathering information and intelligence into a comprehensive database, and developing strategies that will ultimately incapacitate gang leaders and the most violent and criminally involved members and associates.[125]

Suppression

Suppression is a police response to gangs and includes selective surveillance, arrest, and prosecution of gang members. A number of states have attempted to suppress the growing gang problem by revising existing laws or by establishing entirely new legislation aimed at both gang members and gang behaviors. These laws make it possible for authorities to charge gang youths with basic criminal offenses as well as to use conspiracy laws to target gang members who may not have been physically present during the commission of a crime. In some states, conviction for a gang-related crime may limit the range of possible sentences

Police departments have initiated street sweeps of suspected gang members in an effort to combat delinquency. Are such programs effective in controlling gang delinquency? Do such policies aggravate or enhance police–community relations?

or may carry an automatic maximum sentence (see Box 12-8). At the federal level, the Violent Crime Control and Law Enforcement Act of 1994 included provisions allowing federal prosecutors to try juvenile gang members as adults if the juvenile played a leadership role in an organization, or otherwise influenced other persons to take part in criminal activities, involving the use or distribution of controlled substances or firearms.[126]

One of the most common suppression strategies is the neighborhood "sweep" in which a large number of officers sweep through a neighborhood, arresting and detaining known or suspected gang members. Another strategy involves "hot spot targeting" of known gang members and their hideouts. Police select certain gangs for intensive or saturated surveillance and harassment in an effort to apply pressure and send a message of deterrence. For instance, the Dallas Police Department conducted its Anti-Gang Initiative targeting five areas of the city that were home to seven of the city's most violent gangs. The suppression strategy included saturation or high visibility patrols in target areas in which suspected gang members were stopped and frisked, aggressive curfew enforcement whenever suspected gang members were encountered, and aggressive enforcement of truancy laws and regulations. An evaluation of the program conducted by Eric Fritsch and his colleagues found that gang-related violence decreased in both target and control areas, although the decrease was more substantial in targeted areas (57 percent versus 37 percent).[127] Programs produced similarly positive outcomes in Boston, Minneapolis, and Indianapolis.[128]

Sometimes suppression efforts produce unexpected outcomes. Susan Popkin and her associates evaluated an anti-drug initiative in the Chicago Housing

box 12-8 DELINQUENCY PREVENTION

Using the Law to Get Tough on Gangs

As the gang problem continues to grow, an increasing number of states and local communities are turning to new antigang legislation or to new interpretations of existing statutes to crack down on gangs and gang members. Included in these efforts are the use of the federal Racketeer Influenced and Corrupt Organization (RICO) Act and the Street Terrorism Enforcement and Prevention (STEP) Acts, based on the RICO model; the creation of Safe School Zones; and the use of civil gang injunctions and public congregation ordinances.

The *RICO Act* was signed into law in 1970 and was used for nearly two decades to fight the Mafia and other adult organized-crime groups. Today, however, prosecutors are turning to the RICO laws as a weapon against entrenched youth gangs partly because these laws allow prosecutors to charge gang members for simply being part of a criminal enterprise. This means that the more insulated and protected higher level leaders of gangs can be prosecuted for the criminal activities of street-level members.

STEP Acts use a pattern of specified crimes as the basis for increasing sentences of youths convicted of gang-related crimes and mandating the forfeiture of a street gang's assets. Typically, the Acts link definitions of "criminal street gang," "pattern of criminal gang activity," and "participation in a criminal street gang." According to the *California STEP Act,* criminal gang activity is the commission of one or more of seven predicate offenses on two or more separate occasions, while a criminal street gang is defined as an ongoing group that has as one of its primary activities the commission of one or more of the predicate crimes and also has a common name or common identifying sign or symbol. Participation in a criminal street gang is considered a separate offense to avoid violating constitutional rights of free association. By keeping precise records pertaining to gang incidents, the police assist prosecutors in targeting gang participants.

Some states, such as Illinois, have enacted Safe School Zone laws that enhance penalties for certain weapons violations that occur within 1,000 feet of a school, public housing property, or a public park. Violations include possessing a silencer or machine gun or carrying a pistol, revolver, stun gun, firearm, or ballistic knife when hooded, robed, or masked. However, a federal Safe School Zone law prohibiting the mere possession of a gun within 1,000 feet of a school was deemed unconstitutional.

Local governments also have begun to wage a turf war against gangs using a variety of ordinances including curfew laws, antiloitering laws, and civil gang injunctions. In addition, some courts are using nuisance-abatement injunctions against street activities of gang members, effectively prohibiting their congregating in public space. For example, the San Fernando, California, city council passed an ordinance prohibiting active gang members with recent histories of violent crime from entering its Las Palmas Park. Violation of the ordinance could result in a citation and a fine of up to $250. However, the Supreme Court, in *Chicago v. Morales,* held that a Chicago antiloitering law targeting gang members by prohibiting the gathering of two or more people in any public place was unconstitutional and vague. The Court stated that "in this instance the city has enacted an ordinance that affords too much discretion to the police and too little notice to citizens who wish to use the public streets."

Today, at least 30 jurisdictions use civil gang injunctions. Fully half of those jurisdictions are located in southern California with another four in northern California. The city of Los Angeles has obtained 17 injunctions. Injunctions prohibit a variety of behaviors, including associating with known gang members; using public pay phones, cell phones, or pages; and engaging in vandalism, drug dealing, or trespassing on private property.

Sources: Jamilah Owens and Robert Boehmer, "New Anti-Gang Laws in Effect" (Chicago: Illinois Criminal Justice Information Authority, 1993); Matthew Purdy, "Using the Racketeering Law to Bring Down Street Gangs," *The New York Times,* October 19, 1994:A1, B5; Claire Johnson, Barbara Webster, and Edward Connors, *Prosecuting Gangs: A National Assessment* (Washington, DC: National Institute of Justice, 1995); Malcolm Klein, *The American Street Gang: Its Nature, Prevention and Control* (New York: Oxford University Press, 1995), p. 184; *U.S. v. Lopez* 514 U.S. 549 (1995); *Chicago v. Morales* 527 U.S. 41 (1999); Cheryl Maxson, "Civil Gang Injunctions: The Ambiguous Case of the National Migration of a Gang Enforcement Strategy," pages 375–389 in Finn Esbensen, Stephen Tibbetts, and Larry Gaines (eds.), *American Youth Gangs at the Millennium* (Long Grove, IL: Waveland Press, 2004).

Authority. Although the program reduced drug sales and disorder, residents felt more vulnerable to gangs that lived in the projects because they retaliated against residents who cooperated with police. Another unintended consequence was that power vacuums were created after gang leaders were arrested and detained. This contributed to *more* violence and disorder.[129] Suppression efforts alone often cannot reduce gang problems; however, when paired with prevention, it is more effective. Arresting gang youths is only part of the equation; prosocial alternatives and other programs need to be provided as alternatives to gang-life.[130] Indeed, Anthony Braga and his colleagues report that antigang initiatives that balance crime-control and social services produce the strongest and most enduring effects.[131]

Another suppression strategy involves establishing specialized prosecutor programs to target gangs. Responsibilities of these specialized units include coordinating their efforts with law enforcement, creating and managing databases designed to track gangs and gang members, and the vertical prosecution of gang members. Vertical prosecutions involve a process by which an attorney or a small group of attorneys is assigned to gang cases and is responsible for handling them from inception to sentencing.[132] For example, in Orange County, California, a gang reduction program brought together the police, probation department, and prosecutor's office to create the Tri-Agency Resource/Gang Enforcement Team (TARGET). This approach permitted them to merge gang member identification, field interviews, enforcement, case preparation, witness support, vertical prosecution, sentencing, and probation into a single collaborative effort. Other gang prosecution programs around the country include

- Transfers to adult court for juvenile gang members.
- Forfeiture of cars used in drive-by shootings.
- Enhanced penalties for crimes committed near schools.
- Enhanced penalties for graffiti writing.
- Prosecution for gang recruitment.
- Prosecution for criminal conspiracy under federal RICO and similar state laws in cases of drug sales and other applicable crimes.[133]

Injunction/Abatement

An **injunction or abatement** is a civil process in which gang members are prohibited from engaging in mundane activities, such as loitering at schools or hanging out on street corners, and face arrest if they participate in these activities. Basically, gangs are defined as a public nuisance, which is anything that is injurious to health, indecent or offensive, or an obstruction of free use of property that interferes with the enjoyment of life. When gang members violate the civil injunction, they are issued a temporary restraining order, much like defendants in domestic violence cases. When gang members violate the temporary restraining order, they are legally held in contempt of court and can be charged in civil or criminal court.[134] Nationally, about 12 percent of agencies use abatement ordinances and 6 percent use civil gang injunctions.[135] Sometimes, injunctions creatively attempt to reduce gang delinquency. For example, in Cicero, Illinois, police had the vehicles of gang members towed to remove them from town. According to officials, the city could seek injunctive relief to abate the public nuisance (gangs).

The American Civil Liberties Union challenged the towing policy, and it was voluntarily suspended by the city.[136]

Do gang injunctions work? Cheryl Maxson and her colleagues evaluated a gang injunction in five neighborhoods in San Bernardino, California. Residents were surveyed about their perceptions and experiences with gangs 18 months before and 6 months after the gang injunction. In the most gang-ridden areas, the injunction resulted in less gang presence, fewer reports of gang intimidation, and less fear of confrontation with gang members. However, areas that previously had fewer gang problems reported more gang presence presumably due to the gang members fleeing the injunction area. Even with these mixed findings, total fear of crime was reduced in all neighborhoods.[137]

Intervention and Prevention

Not all gang experts believe the gang problem should be viewed in an "us versus them" context or that policy responses should be focused exclusively on suppression. Some criminologists think gangs and the problems they present are best considered within their social, economic, and cultural context.[138] For example, John Hagedorn argues that the growth of gangs in "rustbelt cities," such as Milwaukee, is largely the product of the emerging African American urban underclass. Growing unemployment, poverty, and the flight from the cities by both whites and upwardly mobile blacks have left the underclass behind in the inner city. As the poverty of the minority underclass increases, old gangs reposition themselves, new gangs emerge, and gangs generally get stronger, drawing from the increasing number of school dropouts and under- or unemployed youths looking for the only jobs in town. Moreover, the social organization of the community, the social cohesion, friendship ties, and willingness to establish

Meditation at a Buddhist temple is one policy aimed at reducing gang delinquency. Could such a policy be widely implemented? What objections might be raised regarding government funding of such programs?

and participate in informal social controls are negatively affected by joblessness. This means creating jobs and improving educational opportunities for the urban underclass.[139]

The federal Office of Juvenile Justice and Delinquency Prevention recently created a gang reduction program that supports local gang prevention and intervention program in gang-plagued communities. One of the most successful programs is Homeboy Industries in Los Angeles. Homeboys Industries is a job-training program that educates, trains, and finds jobs for at-risk youths and gang members. Among the programs and jobs that Homeboy Industries provides is silk-screening, maintenance, food service, car detailing, restaurants, and bakeries. Several free services, such as tattoo removal, counseling, job referrals, and life-skills training, are provided. The program is so successful that First Lady Laura Bush visited Homeboy Industries in April 2005 as part of her Helping America's Youth Initiative.[140]

Many communities have turned to intervention and prevention programs that target youths before they join gangs. Contemporary approaches evolved out of programs developed during the late 1960s and early 1970s, in which street workers also known as "detached workers" were assigned by social service agencies to work directly with gang members. Current programs target at-risk youths in the community who have not yet joined gangs; they are intended to help youths develop positive social relationships and find alternatives to gang participation. These programs use combinations of community-, school-, and family-based strategies, including

- Youth outreach programs.
- Establishment of community centers.
- Employment and training assistance.
- School dropout services.
- Multicultural training for teachers.
- Family intervention and training.
- Substance abuse counseling.
- Conflict mediation programs.
- Recreational activities.

According to Ronald Huff, intervention and prevention programs should be multilevel and multifaceted in light of the fact that serious adolescent gang behavior typically is the result of multiple factors. Programs should address family and peer issues, the child's psychological needs, school adjustment problems, and any ecological or neighborhood disorganization factors that affect the child. Finally, Huff believes that if these programs are to bring about "significant and sustainable change in youth behavior," they must be systematic and long-term lasting a minimum of 2 years.[141]

One program receiving considerable attention is Gang Resistance Education and Training (G.R.E.A.T.), a curriculum taught by police officers to elementary and middle school students. G.R.E.A.T. students are given the opportunity to discover for themselves the ramifications of gang violence through structured exercises and interactive approaches to learning. The officers and teachers work together to teach students to set goals for themselves, resist peer pressure,

In high-crime neighborhoods, contact with police officers is a normal occurrence. How has the normalization of crime and violence in high-crime areas desensitized residents to getting arrested or going to prison? Does the criminal justice system lose its effectiveness as a deterrent when it has become so commonplace?

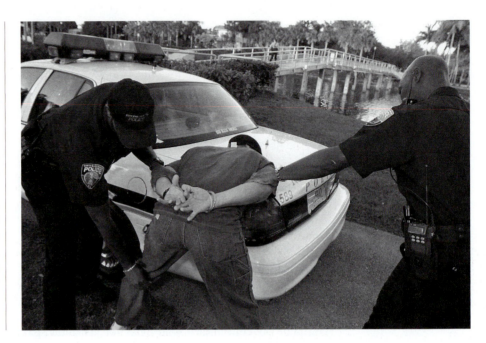

reduce impulsive behavior, enhance self-esteem, and learn to make better choices, thereby leading to reduced gang affiliation and delinquent activity. Recent evaluations of G.R.E.A.T. suggest that the program is working. Students who go through the G.R.E.A.T. program are less likely than peers who did not go through the program to become involved in gangs or to engage in most indicators of delinquency, including drug use, property crimes, and crimes against the person. These studies also indicate that G.R.E.A.T. is more effective for youth who are at higher risk for gang affiliation and delinquency, specifically, young minority males.[142]

conclusions

For many youths, next to the family the peer group contains the people they spend most of their time with. Their social world often revolves around their peers. Through peers, youths search for identity, acceptance, and meaning. Peer groups are important in the socialization of adolescents, but they also provide opportunities for youths to develop values, attitudes, and behaviors contrary to those of many adults. Many behaviors engaged in by peer groups involve delinquency. Adolescents who have delinquent friends will also be more likely to become delinquent.

However, most of the criminological research on the relationship between peers and delinquency centers on gangs. There is a mythology about gangs that depicts them as organized and cohesive, with strong leadership and an orientation to protecting their turf. Criminologists have found that, by and large, these characteristics *do not* accurately describe what most gangs are or do. It has been found that gangs do appeal to minorities and lower-class youths in large cities, that gang members have important problems as adolescents, and that they learn to cope by being aggressive, even against other members in the gang. Additionally, recent studies suggest that gang violence is increasing at a serious rate and that much of the current gang violence is related to competition in drug markets.

While legislative, law enforcement, and community strategies to combat gangs have varied greatly over the past century, there is little evidence they have been successful at stemming the tide of gangs. Like delinquency in general, gang delinquency ultimately brings youths into contact with the police, the juvenile and criminal courts, and the correctional system. Therefore, the final section of the text explores each component of the justice system and how each one responds to juvenile delinquency.

key terms

Enhancement model   Adolescents who are already involved in delinquency are most apt to join a gang (selection) but, after joining, their delinquency is likely to increase significantly (facilitation).

Facilitation model   A "kind of group" explanation that suggests the normative structure of the gang along with group processes and dynamics increase delinquency among youths.

Injunction or abatement   A civil process in which gang members are prohibited from engaging in mundane activities, such as loitering at schools or hanging out on street corners, and face arrest if they participate in these activities.

Klikas   Age cohorts within Hispanic gangs.

Member-based definition   Defining a crime as gang-related when a gang member or members are either the perpetrators or the victims, regardless of the motive.

Motive-based definition   Defining a crime as gang-related when committed by a gang member or members in which the underlying reason is to further the interests and activities of the gang.

Peer groups   Groups of youths of similar ages and interests.

Selection model   A "kind of person" explanation of gang initiation that argues adolescents with a strong propensity for delinquency seek out gangs.

Suppression   A police response to gangs that includes selective surveillance, arrest, and prosecution of gang members.

Turf   A gang's sense of territoriality.

Youth gang   A group of youths willing to use deadly violence to claim and protect territory, to attack rival gangs, or to engage in criminal activity.

section **4**

The Juvenile Justice System

outline

THE FINAL SECTION examines the American juvenile justice system and how it responds to children accused of criminal behavior. It was during the last two decades of the 19th century and the early years of the 20th century that the child-saving movement defined juvenile delinquency as a serious social problem (see Chapter 1). This new social problem was to be dealt with by a new, completely separate complex juvenile justice system. This produced major reforms in police department organization and policies, including new units dedicated to dealing with youthful offenders and new procedures for arresting, booking, and holding juveniles in custody. In addition, a separate juvenile court system was established for the adjudication of delinquents, including status offenders and dependent and neglected children. The new court viewed juvenile offenders as being in need of treatment, rather than punishment, and probation soon became the default disposition. However, not all juvenile offenders were placed on probation; an increasing number were placed in new correctional institutions intended to provide rehabilitation through schooling, vocational training, and counseling.

In Chapter 13, the historical role of police, legal limitations placed on police in arresting and interrogating juveniles, the effectiveness of community-oriented policing, and how police discretion affects which juveniles become officially identified as delinquents are examined.

Chapter 14 examines the modern juvenile court and explores the processing of juveniles through the court, detention, adjudication, disposition, aftercare, and due process issues in the juvenile court. In addition, the chapter

(continued)

explores both restorative justice programs and the transfer process whereby a juvenile may be waived to adult criminal court to be prosecuted.

Today, nearly 100,000 juveniles are confined in state or private correctional facilities on any particular day. Chapter 15 explores issues related to contemporary correctional practices, including the nature of the U.S. correctional system for juveniles and which youths are most likely to be incarcerated, how long they stay, and what happens to them while there. Differences in the treatment of youths in correctional facilities based on race, class, and particularly gender raise serious questions about juvenile corrections today. In addition, the chapter explores the incarceration of juvenile offenders in adult prisons. Finally, the juvenile death penalty was abolished on March 1, 2005, when the U.S. Supreme Court ruled in *Roper v. Simmons,* that such executions violated the Eighth Amendment of the Constitution that prohibits cruel and unusual punishment. No longer could juveniles age 16 or 17 be executed regardless of the heinous nature of their crimes. ●

Police and Delinquency

There has been a long and contentious history of tension between the police and adolescents. Criminologists often attribute this friction to the beliefs police hold that separate them from the public, especially younger citizens.[1] Many officers are secretive, defensive, and distrustful of outsiders and "see themselves as the pragmatic guardians of the morals of the community . . . the 'thin blue line' against the forces of evil."[2] To many police officers, juveniles who are involved in delinquency are part of that force of evil. Many youths, on the other hand, view the police as intrusive, anxious to find fault, and needlessly intimidating.

POLICE IN THE UNITED STATES

think about it

American policing has largely been the responsibility of males. Why? Does a person's sex influence his or her ability to police society? Because males commit most crime, is it appropriate that police officers are also disproportionately male?

Policing in the United States is done differently today than it was in the past. In the American colonies, when settlers lived in widely scattered villages, the *parish-constable system* of policing was used.[3] It was the type of police system the colonists were familiar with in England. Two of its distinctive features were the *watch and ward,* which allowed the constable to draft any male into service to guard the town at night, and the *hue and cry,* a loud call for help that was shouted by the constable or by one of the watchmen when they confronted more resistance than they could handle. The parish-constable system worked very well in the beginning, when there was little crime, and when the crime that did exist was minor.

Once the colonists settled in towns, such as Boston in 1630 and Philadelphia in 1682, they felt a greater need for police protection. Police operations became more formalized. However, the changes that were made did very little to prevent crime, which flourished well into the next century.[4]

In the 19th century a "new" police system evolved as municipal governments were forced to find fresh ways to manage highly diverse populations. Old-stock (white, northern European, Protestant) Americans were fearful of the strangers on the streets, many of whom spoke foreign languages and practiced different customs and religions. They also were concerned about the number of poor and dependent people and the worsening crime problem. The fear of crime, coupled with the feeling of a decaying society, set the stage for police reform.

Turning to England for models of effective policing, the public endorsed the idea that the government must assume responsibility for the social well-being of its citizens. The practical consequence of implementing this idea was the creation of police forces with paid full-time uniformed officers who assumed a wide range of duties, ranging from lighting the gas lamps in the evening to monitoring elections and apprehending criminals. By 1870 all big cities in the United States had full-time police departments, and by 1924 most urban police departments had established specialized juvenile bureaus, ranging from juvenile aid divisions, to speakers' bureaus, to youth crime units. This trend continued into the 1940s and 1950s, largely in response to an outbreak of delinquent gang activity (see Chapter 12). Today, nearly all police departments allocate a portion of their resources to delinquency prevention, frequently targeting curfew violators (Box 13-1).

In 1998 the U.S. Fourth Circuit Court of Appeals, in *Schleifer v. Charlottesville,* held that the curfew law in Charlottesville, Virginia, *was not* a violation of a child's rights. One hundred and ten cities established curfew laws between 1995 and 2000, and a survey of these cities reported that more than 90 percent believed that nighttime curfews are "useful tools for police officers." Police arrested more than 104,000 juveniles in 2005 for curfew and loitering law violations; approximately 28 percent of these children were under age 15. While curfew laws have become both popular and controversial in recent years, police have been arresting children for being out of their homes at night since the late 1880s.

Juvenile curfew laws appear to have come about for three basic reasons. First, industrialization and the emphasis on efficiency meant that work, and eventually child rearing, became increasingly defined by the clock. Second, the use of child labor in such activities as selling newspapers and errand running for telegraph companies meant that many youths were on the streets in the middle of the night both working and vulnerable to the temptations of alcohol, cigarettes, and prostitution. Third, the middle class, by the late 19th century, had become concerned about the proper rearing of working-class children and the need to inculcate appropriate moral values. Children, especially working-class children, who stayed out on the streets late in the evening violated both of these concerns. Children of the urban working class regularly participated in "night work" and "nightlife." That is, they played and worked on the streets at night, went to and from work in factories and sweatshops, and frequented the shopping and entertainment available in crowded working-class neighborhoods. Reformers argued that teenage boys were susceptible to immoral temptations as they walked about the streets unsupervised. Middle-class parents had the luxury of secluding their children from nighttime temptations; working-class parents appeared less concerned and granted their children much greater freedom. This freedom and lack of supervision also allowed children to learn about their sexuality.

Juvenile curfew laws responded to all three concerns. In the late 1800s and early 1900s, many towns and cities established curfews or "Children's Laws" requiring all children under age 15 without parental supervision to be off the streets by a specific time or face arrest. The curfew law in Lincoln, Nebraska, a model for many cities around the nation, set a curfew of 9 P.M. in the spring and summer and 8 P.M. in the fall and winter for children under 15. Exceptions to the law included children who were accompanied by a parent, who were running errands, or held jobs, such as newspaper delivery. Although laws were passed, they were rarely enforced. No children were arrested during the first few months of the Lincoln curfew, and only four children a year were arrested for curfew violations in Indianapolis during the first six years of the law's existence. It was not until the 1950s when baby boomers began to reach their teenage years that police began to enforce curfews in an attempt to prevent delinquency, though there was little evidence that enforcement made much difference.

Is police enforcement of curfew laws any more effective in preventing delinquency today than it was in the late 19th and early 20th centuries? Kenneth Adams conducted an analysis of 10 recent empirical studies on the impact of curfew laws on preventing crime and victimization. These 10 studies were consistent in their findings that curfews fail to reduce crime and criminal victimization. Moreover, Adams reports that the studies indicate that when crime levels do appear to change after a curfew law has been implemented, the change is just as likely to be an increase in crime as a decrease in crime.

While police enforcement of curfew laws does not appear to support goals of preventing crime or protecting youths from victimization by others, they may reinforce parental authority and reduce fear of working-class youths by middle-class adults. In addition, there is some support to suggest that the enforcement of driving curfews for juveniles may marginally reduce automobile accidents and injuries.

Sources: Peter Baldwin, "Nocturnal Habits and Dark Wisdom: The American Response to Children in the Streets at Night, 1880–1930," *Journal of Social History* 35:593–611 (2000); Kenneth Adams, "The Effectiveness of Juvenile Curfews at Crime Prevention," *Annals of the American Academy and Social Science* May:136–159 (2003); Federal Bureau of Investigation, *Crime in the United States, 2006* (Washington, DC: U.S. Department of Justice, 2007); *Schleifer v. Charlottesville,* 159 F.3d 853 (4th Cir. 1998).

Responding to the problems of juvenile delinquency in the early 20th century also created opportunities in policing for women who had previously been excluded from the profession. In 1905, Portland, Oregon, hired the first female officer, Lola Baldwin. A few years later, New York City and Washington, D.C., hired women to look after runaways, truants, and delinquent children and to otherwise discourage adolescents from pursuing criminal careers.[5]

The role of the police in regulating juvenile misconduct in the late 19th and early 20th centuries was often seen as punitive and unsympathetic to the welfare of children. According to David Wolcott, child welfare advocates, educators, and parents at the turn of the century "viewed policemen as brutish, blue-coated enforcers who would arrest a young shoplifter or a truant unable to account for himself" just to keep the child out of mischief, and "as bogeymen, warning children that if they did not, 'the cop will get you.'"[6] Wolcott notes that between 1890 and 1907, prior to the establishment of Michigan's first juvenile court, the Detroit police generally imposed a kind of "rough justice" for juvenile offenders in which youths would typically be arrested and their cases decided the same day in the police court. The police courts handled all misdemeanor cases, and thus the majority of juvenile arrests. The police decided the relatively small number of public order and status offenses informally, sending youths home after being lectured, while the majority of cases (about two-thirds of all juvenile arrests) were sent on to the police court. If convicted in police court, juveniles could face a fine of up to $100 or up to 3 months in jail. Youths arrested for felonies were sent on to the criminal courts for prosecution.[7]

By 1899, at least in Chicago and a growing number of cities, police also performed the role of juvenile probation officer. Because the *Illinois Juvenile Court Act of 1899,* which established the first juvenile court in the United States, did not provide a means of funding probation officers, the juvenile court had to rely on volunteers and contributions from philanthropic organizations[8] and a special detail of Chicago police officers assigned as police probation officers (PPOs).[9] In 1904, 21 PPOs were assigned to the juvenile court, and there were only four probation officers funded by philanthropies. During the 1920s and 1930s, approximately 30 police officers worked in the court as PPOs each year. Recruited from the ranks of regular patrol officers, wearing civilian clothing, and given no special training, PPOs carried out their primary duties of investigating complaints about juveniles and then making decisions about which cases to formally petition to the juvenile court. The majority of cases were handled by the police; juvenile cases were investigated, dismissed, or informally adjusted with youths placed on informal "police probation."[10]

In 1955 the Central States Juvenile Officers Association was formed, followed by the International Juvenile Officers Association in 1957. Both organizations worked to develop professional standards and procedures for police officers assigned to deal with juveniles. In the 1970s and early 1980s, police diversion programs emerged and quickly became very popular. However, the 1980s also saw a great number of police departments establishing specialized units to respond to juvenile gangs, violence, and drugs.

Today, nearly all police departments have either specialized juvenile units or officers who have gone through special training to deal with juveniles. For example, the Pekin (Illinois) Police Department has a Special Services Division that includes investigations, narcotics investigations, crime prevention, and a high school liaison. A sergeant in charge of the investigations unit is also responsible for overseeing cases involving juveniles. More important, a total of 26 officers on general patrol are also state-certified as Juvenile Police Officers providing an extra level of professionalism when dealing with juvenile matters.[11]

POLICE, CHILDREN, AND THE LAW

Central to understanding the relationship between the police and juveniles in a democratic society is the impact of decisions by the U.S. Supreme Court in constraining police behavior in their encounters with citizens. The most important Supreme Court decision affecting the rights of juveniles is actually a case about an adult. In 1966, in *Miranda v. Arizona,* the Supreme Court issued a ruling that forever changed all police–citizen interactions.[12] The *Miranda* case still raises many interesting questions. Who was Ernesto Miranda? What crime did he commit? Did the police treat Miranda fairly? Were his rights violated?

On the night of March 2, 1963, in Phoenix, Arizona, 18-year-old Patricia Ann Weir was walking to a bus when a man shoved her into his car, assaulted her, tied her hands and ankles, then drove to the outskirts of the city where he raped her. He then drove Weir to a street near her home, let her out of the car, and asked her to say a prayer for him.

Weir telephoned the police. Soon thereafter police picked up Ernesto Miranda and asked him whether he would voluntarily talk with them about the incident. Miranda agreed and was taken to the police station, where he willingly participated in a lineup and was identified by Weir as the rapist.

Ernesto Miranda, a seriously disturbed man with pronounced sexual fantasies, was a 23-year-old eighth-grade dropout with a police record dating from when he was age 14. During police interrogation, two Phoenix police officers told Miranda that Weir had identified him as the rapist. At that point, Miranda agreed to prepare a written confession, in which he described the incident and stated that his confession was voluntary and that he had given it with full knowledge of his legal rights. He was charged with kidnapping and rape.

When the case went to trial, Miranda's court-appointed attorney, Alvin Moore, questioned the officers about their interrogation of his client. Both officers stated that at no time during the two-hour interrogation had either of them advised Miranda of his legal right to have counsel present during police questioning.[13] Nevertheless, and over Moore's objection, the trial judge allowed Miranda's written confession to be admitted into evidence. Miranda was found guilty, convicted, and sentenced to 20 to 30 years in prison for each offense. The case was appealed to the Arizona Supreme Court, which upheld the decision of the lower court.

The case was appealed to the U.S. Supreme Court, where Miranda's new attorney, John Flynn, asked the Court to decide whether "the confession of a poorly educated, mentally abnormal, indigent defendant, not told of his right to counsel, which was not requested, can be admitted into evidence over specific objection based on the absence of counsel." On June 13, 1966, the Court announced its decision. In a 5-to-4 vote, Chief Justice Earl Warren expressed the majority opinion that Miranda's rights to protection from self-incrimination under the Fifth Amendment and to counsel under the Sixth Amendment had been violated. The Court held that "When an individual is taken into custody . . . the privilege against self-incrimination is jeopardized. Procedural safeguards must be employed to protect the privilege."[14] *Miranda* and a series of other cases decided by the Supreme Court over the next few years dramatically altered how the police dealt with juveniles.

Search and Seizure

Every crime is like a jigsaw puzzle with a few missing pieces. Police *search* for the missing pieces by investigating the premises or suspects they believe are linked to them. Related to the search is the *seizure,* where people or objects relating to the crime are taken into custody.[15] Speaking practically, what this means is the police have taken legal control over them. People are legally seized when they are not free to leave a scene, not when police only detain them for a very short time to ask them a few questions.

The **exclusionary rule,** derived from the Fourth Amendment, protects people from unreasonable searches and seizures and applies to juveniles in the same way as it does to adults. Based on the Supreme Court decision in *Mapp v. Ohio,* illegally obtained evidence may not be admissible in a criminal prosecution or in a juvenile court adjudication hearing.[16] You may recall, however, from Chapter 11 that juveniles do not have exactly the same Fourth Amendment protections regarding searches *if* searches are conducted in schools. Furthermore, school officials need only reasonable suspicion, not probable cause to conduct a search of a student. However, when juveniles are faced with searches outside school, in the public arena, police are held to the same standards used when searching adults.

Interestingly, juveniles also do not have the same Fourth Amendment protections regarding privacy and searches at home. Courts have held that parents can give third-party consent for officers to search their child's room based on their "common authority" over the premises. In other words, parents may allow police to search the home and their child's bedroom based on either parent's right to control their child or their exercise of control over the premises.[17] However, parents may not give consent to police to search a juvenile's personal effects, such as a tool box or locked suitcase unless the parent claims an established right to control over the items.[18] Parents may also conduct searches of their child's room and possessions because the Fourth Amendment protection only applies to government agents, such as law enforcement or probation officers.

On the other hand, juveniles have generally not been viewed by the courts to have authority to give similar third-party consent to police to search the home or their parent's bedroom, although state appellate courts are not in complete agreement on this issue. For example, the California Supreme Court, in *People v. Jacobs,* held that an 11-year-old was not capable of giving valid consent to search the home to locate and arrest her father.[19] The court stated that children do not have coequal dominion over the family home even though parents may choose to grant their minor children joint access and mutual use of the home. The Montana Supreme Court recently held that a youth under age 16 does not have the capacity or the authority to relinquish his or her parent's privacy rights.[20] Some courts have concluded, however, that not all minors lack the authority to consent to a search. Appellate courts in Wisconsin, Kansas, Oregon,

think
about it

Should there be any legal constraints on parental searches of their child's personal property? Should parents be required to obtain a warrant to search through emails and visited websites on their child's computer or to listen in on phone conversations?

and Georgia have held that a juvenile's ability to give valid third-party consent to search depends on a number of factors. In addition to a youth's age, courts should consider the totality of the circumstances, the child's mental maturity, and whether the child is considered able to willingly, knowingly, and voluntarily give consent.[21]

Arrest

Juveniles suspected of committing criminal acts are taken into custody rather than arrested, although the distinction is essentially euphemistic. Prior to *Gault* the courts generally held that juveniles could be taken into custody "for their own good" when, under the same circumstances for an adult, it would be considered an invalid arrest (see Chapter 14).[22] Today, the same law of arrest applies fairly equally to adults and juveniles, at least in cases where the youth is suspected of an act that would be a crime if committed by an adult.

To make a legal arrest, the police must have **probable cause,** which is a set of facts that would lead a reasonable person to believe a crime has been committed and the person to be arrested committed it. In *misdemeanor cases,* police can arrest a person *only* if the crime is committed in their presence (called the *in-presence requirement*). In *felony cases,* police may make an arrest (1) if they observe the crime in progress or (2) if they have knowledge a felony crime has occurred and have probable cause for believing a particular person committed it. But these are the rules for arresting adults. Many jurisdictions allow police to take into custody a juvenile if the officer has probable cause to believe the youth is delinquent. For instance, Illinois law states that police "may, without a warrant, take into temporary custody a minor . . . whom the officer with reasonable cause believes to be a delinquent minor."[23] In addition, most states require that juveniles taken into custody be taken to a juvenile detention facility rather than to a jail and that parents be notified of the arrest.

Juveniles may also be taken into custody for *status offenses,* such as running away, truancy, and incorrigibility; however, police are somewhat more restricted with regard to their actions in these cases. For example, in New York, when a police officer, without a court order, takes a juvenile into custody for being a runaway, he or she must take the child to a facility certified by the state for handling runaways rather than to jail or detention.[24] In Michigan, on the other hand, an officer who apprehends a juvenile for a status offense may take the youth into custody if "(1) the officer has reason to believe that due to the nature of the offense, the interest of the juvenile or the interest of the public would not be protected by release of the juvenile, or (2) a parent cannot be located or the parent refuses to take custody of the juvenile."[25]

Booking

The most significant differences in the rights of adult and juvenile suspects occur at **booking,** which is the official recording of a person into detention after arrest. Once suspects are booked, they are photographed and fingerprinted.[26] This information becomes part of the alleged offender's permanent record.

However, booking is typically handled differently when it comes to juveniles. In most states police cannot fingerprint and photograph children. Juveniles, however, may be fingerprinted and photographed on court order and then only for identification or investigative purposes to determine whether a youth's fingerprints match ones found at the crime scene, for example. In Ohio, juveniles may not be photographed or fingerprinted without consent of a judge, and even then, only for instances in which the youth is suspected of having committed a felony. In addition, all fingerprints and photographs of the child must be removed from the file and destroyed if the complaint is not filed or is dismissed after being filed.[27]

A juvenile's record may also be sealed or destroyed when a case is closed. *Sealing* a record means that it is removed from the main police files and secured in a separate file to be made available only to selected persons with designated authority. *Expunging* a juvenile's arrest record actually physically destroys the record. Some states, such as Massachusetts, allow a juvenile record only to be sealed after the child has reached the age of majority and served his or her sentence for a crime. Judges in later criminal cases against the same person may still use sealed records, even after the person becomes an adult. Massachusetts, however, does not permit a juvenile's record to be expunged.[28] However, the laws regarding both sealing and expunging of juvenile records varies among the states. For example, in the state of Washington, a person must first apply to have his or her records sealed or expunged and then meet particular statutory requirements. Eligibility depends on a variety of factors, including the person's age, seriousness of the juvenile's offense, pending criminal matters, and the amount of time since most recent conviction. A judge has the final discretionary power to agree or not to seal or expunge the record.[29] If a juvenile's record has been sealed or expunged, he or she can usually, but not in all cases, answer in the negative to questions of whether he or she has ever been arrested, convicted, and so forth.

Interrogation

In 1966 the New Jersey Supreme Court, in *In re Carlo,* held that the ultimate objective of the juvenile justice process was to arrive at the truth of a case in order to further the rehabilitation of the juvenile. In their decision, the Court stated,

> The object of the juvenile process is to make men out of errant boys. In that process we must build upon the truth. A juvenile should be led to believe that the decent thing is to come clean, to face the music. A father, inquiring as to the misconduct of his son, would feel a bit absurd if he told the son the truth may be used against him, that he has a right not to answer, and that he may consult counsel before deciding whether to talk. That scene would be absurd for a couple of reasons, and one is that is no way to teach integrity. . . . A child can be rehabilitated only in the face of the truth. . . . If a confession is obtained in circumstances which cast doubt upon it truthfulness, it has no place in the juvenile process. . . . Thus, there should be every assurance that the juvenile was not led into a false account, and to that end, at least if the offense is a serious wrong, the police should see that a parent or some relative or friend is present, if it is at all feasible.[30]

That same year, the U.S. Supreme Court decided the *Miranda* case. One year later, in 1967, in the case of *In re Gault,* the Court directed police to change their practices with respect to how juvenile suspects were treated.[31] In *Gault,* the Court extended to juveniles many of the same protections that had been established for adults in *Miranda,* including the right against self-incrimination and the right to counsel. The standard *Miranda* warning states:

> You have the right to remain silent. Anything you say can and will be used against you in a court of law. You have the right to speak to an attorney, and to have an attorney present during any questioning. If you cannot afford a lawyer, one will be provided for you at government expense.

However, a number of states believe that juveniles, especially younger children, need to be provided with a *Miranda*-style warning that is more age-appropriate. For example, Missouri has established a warning known as the *McMillian warning* as an alternative to *Miranda* for use when interrogating juveniles:

> I am a police officer, your adversary, and not your friend.
> You have the right to remain silent.
> Anything you say can and will be used against you in a court of law.
> You have the right to talk to a lawyer and have him present with you while you are being questioned.
> If you cannot afford to hire a lawyer, one will be appointed to represent you before any questioning, if you wish.
> You have the right to have a parent, guardian, or custodian present during questioning.
> Any statement you make can be used against you if you are certified for trial in adult court.[32]

Another issue that may develop when police interrogate juveniles is whether children can waive their rights to an attorney, as can adults. The validity of such a waiver may depend on numerous factors, such as the child's age, education, intelligence, knowledge as to the substance of the charge, whether the child has been interrogated before, methods of the interrogation, and length of police questioning.[33] For instance, the Wisconsin Supreme Court held that a confession made by a 14-year-old boy with only an 84 IQ, who had limited prior experience with police, who had been interrogated by the police for a total of nearly 6 hours, and who had repeatedly asked if he could call his mother or father and was told that he could not, was unconstitutional.[34]

In 1979 in *Fare v. Michael C.,* the U.S. Supreme Court ruled that there was no need for courts to impose special protections for minors during interrogation.[35] The Court held that the same standards for adults could be used to assess the constitutionality of a waiver of a juvenile's rights during questioning. As long as the waiver is done "knowingly and intelligently" under the "totality of the circumstances," it is a valid waiver. However, a child asking police to speak to a probation officer was not viewed as being equivalent to his requesting to speak to an attorney. Only a request to speak to an attorney invokes the juvenile's *Miranda* rights.

States, such as New Mexico, require that the *Miranda* warning be triggered even when a child is not under custodial interrogation but "suspected" or "imagined" to be engaged in some wrongdoing. The New Mexico Supreme Court, in 2001, held that prior to questioning, a child who is detained or seized and suspected of wrongdoing must be advised that he or she has the right to remain silent and that anything said can be used in court.[36] If a child is not advised of the right to remain silent and warned of the consequence of waiving that right, any statement or confession obtained as a result of the detention or seizure is inadmissible in any delinquency proceeding. Officers are not required to give the warning prior to asking questions about a child's age or identity, general on-the-scene questions, or when a child volunteers statements. Moreover, New Mexico law prohibits the admission of any statements made by a child under the age of 13 *in any circumstance,* and imposes a legal presumption that any statements made by children age 13 or 14 are inadmissible. According to Maria Touchet, these very restrictive standards for questioning juveniles may reflect a return to the old *parens patriae* perspective, which assumed that children do not possess the required level of understanding or cognitive abilities to control their actions. Thus, the court must determine what is in the best interests of the child.[37]

The U.S. Supreme Court in 2004 reinforced the notion that juveniles do not require special consideration when being questioned by police. The Court, in a 5-to-4 decision in *Yarborough v. Alvarado,* held that police did not need to factor in the youth and inexperience of a suspect in their decision of whether to read a juvenile his or her *Miranda* rights if the youth is *not* believed to be "in custody" (see Box 13-2). The *Miranda* warning applies only to persons who are under arrest or who, under the circumstances, reasonably believe they are not free to leave.

There are some additional constraints on police interrogation of juveniles. For example, the Texas Family Code stipulates that a juvenile's statement made to the police is not valid unless "signed in the presence of a magistrate by the child with no law enforcement officer or prosecuting attorney present."[38] And some states, such as Colorado, require a parent or guardian be present during a custodial interrogation and that both the child and parent be informed of the juvenile's right to remain silent and to have counsel appointed if requested.[39] All these issues regarding interrogation of juveniles reflect a concern about the possibility that the juveniles might feel coerced or be too easily misled about factual elements of their situations and subsequently make false confessions (see Box 13-3).

Lineups

In a police lineup adults and juveniles have similar protections. A juvenile suspected of engaging in an act that would be a crime if committed by an adult has the right to counsel at a pretrial lineup; the juvenile and his or her parents should be informed of the right to counsel and that, if necessary, one will be appointed.[40] However, some courts have held that because delinquency proceedings are not exactly the same as criminal proceedings, the right to counsel at a lineup prior to filing of formal charges is not constitutionally required.[41]

Children and adults generally have similar due process rights.[42] Police, however, have more latitude when deciding what to do with children, especially when the child is accused of committing a minor crime. This raises the issue of police discretion, the topic of the next section.

POLICE DISCRETION

Although the idea of policing is grounded in the legal order and its rules, police officers have vast discretionary powers regarding when and how to apply the law. **Police discretion** is the authority of police to choose one course of action over another.

box 13-2 FROM THE BENCH

Yarborough v. Alvarado

Michael Alvarado, a 17-year-old boy, participated in an attempted truck-jacking with a friend, Paul Soto. Soto pulled out a gun and approached Francisco Castaneda, who was standing near his truck in the parking lot of a shopping mall in Santa Fe Springs, California. Soto demanded money and the ignition keys from Castaneda, and when Castaneda refused to comply, Soto shot him, killing him. Alvarado then helped hide Soto's gun.

About a month after the shooting, Los Angeles County Sheriff's detective Cheryl Comstock left word at Alvarado's house and also contacted Alvarado's mother at work with the message that she wished to speak with Alvarado. His parents brought him to the Sheriff's station to be interviewed. They asked if they could be present during the interview and were told no; they then waited in the lobby while Alvarado went with Comstock to be interviewed. The interview lasted about two hours and was recorded by Comstock with Alvarado's knowledge. Alvarado was not given a *Miranda* warning. Part way into the interview, Alvarado began to change his story about the evening's events and then, with Comstock's appeal to his sense of honesty and the need to bring the man who shot Castaneda to justice, admitted he had helped Soto try to steal the truck. When the interview was over, Comstock returned with Alvarado to the lobby where his parents were waiting. His parents then drove him home. A few months later, Soto and Alvarado were charged with first-degree murder and attempted robbery. Alvarado's statements to Comstock were admitted into evidence at trial, and he was convicted of second-degree murder and sentenced to 15 years to life.

Alvarado's case was eventually appealed to the federal Court of Appeals for the Ninth Circuit, which reversed the conviction holding that the trial court erred in admitting Alvarado's statements to Comstock. The court ruled that Alvarado's youth and inexperience should have been taken into account by the trial court in deciding whether or not Alvarado was in custody. According to the Court of Appeals, the effect of Alvarado's age and inexperience was so substantial that it turned the interview into a custodial interrogation, thus requiring the *Miranda* warning.

The State of California appealed the Ninth Circuit Court's decision to the U.S. Supreme Court, which, in a 5-to-4 decision, reversed the Ninth Circuit and held that the youth and inexperience of the suspect did not have to be considered. The issue was whether a reasonable person would believe that he or she was in "custody" under Alvarado's circumstances. The State argued that the police did not transport Alvarado to the station or require that he appear at a particular time, did not threaten him or suggest he would be placed under arrest, and during the interview, focused on Soto's crimes rather than Alvarado's. In addition, Comstock twice asked Alvarado if he wanted to take a break, and after the interview ended, Alvarado went home. Thus, a reasonable person would have felt free to terminate the interview and leave. On the other hand, the length of the interview and the fact that Comstock did not tell Alvarado he was free to leave might suggest he was in custody.

In the final analysis, the Supreme Court held that it has never "stated that a suspect's age or experience is relevant to the *Miranda* custody analysis," and that its "opinions applying the *Miranda* custody test have not mentioned the suspect's age, much less mandated its consideration." Justice O'Connor, while concurring with the majority, wrote,

> There may be cases in which a suspect's age will be relevant to the *Miranda* custody inquiry. In this case, however, Alvarado was almost 18 years old at the time of his interview. It is difficult to expect police to recognize that a suspect is a juvenile when he is so close to the age of majority. Even when police do know a suspect's age, it may be difficult for them to ascertain what bearing it has on the likelihood that the suspect would feel free to leave.

Source: Yarborough v. Alvarado, 541 U.S. 652 (2004).

In July of 1998, the nearly naked body of 11-year-old Ryan Harris was discovered. Her face was bloodied and her underpants had been stuffed in her mouth. Two boys, age 7 and 8, were arrested 2 weeks after Harris's discovery and subsequently charged with the murder of Harris. According to the police, during the interrogation both boys made incriminating statements and confessed to the crime. When semen stains were found in the girl's underpants a month later, experts indicated that it was extremely unlikely that boys this young could have produced the semen. The prosecutor dropped the charges and the investigating detectives were quickly criticized for using "Gestapo tactics" that produced the false confessions. A few weeks after the charges were dropped, DNA evidence was linked to a 29-year-old man who was already suspected of raping three young girls earlier that year.

Although both boys recanted their confessions after only a few days, what might have led them to falsely confess to a murder they did not commit? One reason is that the police are trained to use intimidating and manipulative interrogation methods to elicit information from suspects. For example, the most widely used interrogation manual instructs police to use the same techniques with juveniles as with adults. Officers are taught to isolate suspects from outside influences, to sit close to the suspect and subject him or her to lengthy interviews, and even mislead the suspect about the presence of incriminating evidence, such as fingerprints, an eyewitness, or DNA, even when such evidence does not exist. Such techniques, especially when used on younger adolescents, may increase the likelihood of producing a false confession.

Two recent studies, one conducted by Ingrid Candel and her associates in the Netherlands and one conducted in the United States by Allison Redlich and Gail Goodman, demonstrate the relative ease by which authorities can elicit false confessions. Both studies used variations on an experimental design in which the subjects were asked to type certain keys on a computer keyboard, but specifically to not hit the Shift (Dutch study) or Alt (American study) keys. Experimenters then falsely accused the child of having hit the prohibited key, produced what appeared to be a printout of all the keys that had been hit during the session (American study), and indicated that the experiment was now over because of the resulting computer problem. When false evidence was presented, more than two-thirds of the subjects in the American study admitted that they had probably hit the prohibited key. In the Dutch study, which did not provide false evidence to subjects, 36 percent "confessed" to hitting the prohibited key.

In a related study conducted by Naomi Goldstein and her colleagues, 57 boys in a residential correction facility in Massachusetts were asked to respond to a survey. The survey presented the boys with hypothetical scenarios and asked the boys to pretend they were the suspects in the cases. Following each situation, the boys were asked, among other things, the probability that he would have offered a false confession. The scenarios were based on interrogation techniques discussed above. Over 40 percent of the boys self-reported that they would likely have made a false confession in at least one of the hypothetical scenarios and 25 percent said they definitely would give a false confession in at least one of the situations.

In all three studies, age was the best predictor of a youth offering a false confession, with younger children more likely than older children and young adults to falsely confess. Researchers generally believe that juveniles, especially younger youths, are more suggestible than their older counterparts and when suggestibility is combined with coercive and manipulative interrogation techniques, false confessions should not be unexpected.

Sources: Steve Bogira, "Who Killed Ryan Harris?" *Chicago Reader,* October 20, 2006, online at: http://www.chicagoreader.com/features/stories/floyddurr/, accessed May 3, 2007; Fred Inbau, John Reid, Joseph Buckley, and Brian Jayne, *Criminal Interrogation and Confessions,* 4th edition (Gaithersburg, MD: Aspen, 2001); Ingrid Candel, Harald Merckelback, Silvie Loyen, and Hanne Reyskens, "'I Hit the Shift-Key and then the Computer Crashed': Children and False Admissions," *Personality and Individual Differences* 38:1381–1387 (2003); Naomi Goldstein, Lois Condie, Rachel Kalbeitzer, Douglas Osman, and Jessica Geier, "Juvenile Offenders' *Miranda* Rights Comprehension and Self-Reported Likelihood of Offering False Confessions," *Assessment* 10:359–369 (2003); Allison Redlich and Gail Goodman, "Taking Responsibility for an Act Not Committed: The Influence of Age and Suggestibility," *Law and Human Behavior* 27:141–156 (2003).

When police suspect a juvenile of a crime, they can handle the matter informally or take the child into custody and refer the child to juvenile court, criminal court, or a welfare agency. Specifically, police have discretionary authority to

- Release the child with or without a lecture.

- Release the child, with or without a lecture, but write a report describing the contact.

- Release the child, but file a more formal report referring the matter to a juvenile bureau or an intake unit for possible action.

- Interrogate or search the child.

- Issue a citation for future appearance in juvenile court.

- Take the child into custody (arrest).

Most police encounters with juveniles do not end up with arrests. Stephanie Myers's analysis of data from Indianapolis, Indiana, and St. Petersburg, Florida, suggests that very few juvenile suspects are taken into custody.[43] Of the 654 juvenile suspects encountered by police, only 13 percent were arrested. Police lectured and then released 22 percent of suspects, wrote a report on the situation with 15 percent of the juveniles, interrogated 48 percent, searched 20 percent, and issued a citation to 3 percent.

Clearly, police use their discretionary authority in making decisions of whether to arrest juveniles. Some youths get arrested, but most do not. Some *groups* of youths are also more likely to be arrested while other groups are not. While the decision to arrest should be made on the basis of *legal criteria,* often it is not. Police also appear to be influenced by *extralegal factors*. In 1967 Carl Werthman and Irving Piliavin described police encounters with poor African American juveniles as very problematic. They noted that

> Street life in a typical [African American] ghetto is perceived [by police] as an uninterrupted sequence of suspicious scenes. Every well-dressed man or woman standing aimlessly on the street during hours when most people are at work is carefully scrutinized for signs of an illegal source of income; every boy wearing boots, black pants, long hair, and a club jacket is viewed as potentially responsible for some item on the list of muggings, broken windows, and petty thefts that still remain to be cleared; and every hostile glance at the passing patrolman is read as a sign of possible guilt.[44]

What has changed in the 40 years since this research was published? Are relations between police and African American children still defined by structured conflict? Is police use of discretion different today from what it once was? Sandra Browning and her colleagues studied these questions and found that African Americans today still believe "they are personally and vicariously hassled by the police . . . police surveillance is discriminatory . . . [and] clear racial differences exist in whom police officers watch and stop."[45] Their conclusion reinforces one drawn by Doug Smith, who found that suspects police encountered in lower-class neighborhoods were more likely to be arrested than those police stopped in middle- or upper-class areas.[46]

There is evidence that police today handle cases involving juveniles in a more formal, legalistic, follow-the-book manner than they did in the past. For instance, 45 percent of the juveniles taken into police custody in 1972 were handled informally within the department and released. By 2003 the percentage of

think about it

Police officers are disproportionately cynical and often harbor punitive, distrustful views of society. Why? Do the negative and sometimes depressing social circumstances that police face daily influence their perspective?

children handled informally and released dropped to 20 percent.[47] With about a fifth of these youths handled informally, is it possible that both legal and extra-legal factor might affect the arrest decision of police?

Legal Factors

There are a number of legally relevant factors that may influence police decisions to arrest, but four appear to be most common. These are offense seriousness, prior arrest record or police contacts, presence of evidence, and suspicious behavior.

Offense Seriousness   Juveniles who commit serious crimes are more likely to be arrested than ones who commit minor offenses. This is the conclusion reached by Robert Terry from a study of police dispositions of more than 9,000 juvenile offenses.[48] In a related study, Donald Black and Albert Reiss divided offenses into four types and found that the likelihood of being arrested increased with offense seriousness.[49] Moreover, as Stephanie Myers found in her analysis of data from Indianapolis and St. Petersburg, juveniles are more likely to be arrested not only for serious offenses but when a weapon is present.[50]

Police, however, do not always respond to serious crimes in the same way. They determine how they will handle a case based on three criteria. If they believe the offense was *sophisticated* (rather than amateurish), *premeditated* (rather than spontaneous), and *malicious* (rather than mischievous), they are more likely to arrest and refer the child to juvenile court rather than handle it informally.[51]

Prior Arrest Record   Police are more likely to arrest children who have a prior arrest record. Terry found that a juvenile's prior arrest record was a strong predictor of police action. In his study, first-time offenders constituted 38 percent of juveniles arrested but only 7 percent of the juveniles referred to juvenile court. At the other extreme were juveniles with five or more previous arrests. They constituted 20 percent of arrests but more than 66 percent of juvenile court referrals.[52]

Based on observations of police–juvenile encounters in two cities, Aaron Cicourel concluded that having a prior arrest record often turned an otherwise trivial event into a serious one.[53] He also discovered that a youth's prior arrest record became a more important factor when decisions were made at the police station rather than on the street. Patrol officers often lack the necessary information to take a prior arrest record into account. Patrol officers may also view past-offense history as irrelevant, since their primary concern is handling the situation they face in the least troublesome manner.[54]

Presence of Evidence   Black and Reiss also examined the role of evidence and discovered that in patrol work there are two ways suspects are connected with a crime: (1) police see the suspect commit the crime or (2) a citizen informs the police about a crime and who did it. In about half of the situations that Black and Reiss researched, police witnessed the offense. Citizens provided testimonial evidence in an additional 23 percent of the cases. The remaining cases lacked any evidence of criminal conduct. Therefore, in roughly 75 percent of the routine police–juvenile contacts, police were provided with evidence sufficient to link a suspect to a crime. In these situations, 13 percent of the suspects were arrested. In the citizen-testimony situations, 19 percent of the suspects were arrested. In only 0.5 percent of cases was a suspect arrested when there was no situational evidence available.[55] These arrest percentages illustrate the discretion police have when deciding what to do with juvenile suspects even when they have persuasive evidence that the youth committed a crime.

More recently, Kenneth Novak and his colleagues analyzed data collected in the late 1990s in Hamilton County, Ohio, and found the presence of evidence to be positively related to arrest. In cases where a greater number of evidence criteria were present, ranging from the officer hearing a confession from the suspect and hearing claims from others regarding the suspect to observing physical evidence and seeing the suspect commit the act suspects were significantly more likely to be arrested.[56]

Suspicious Behavior   A police officer's discretionary decision to stop and then possibly arrest a juvenile generally begins when the officer observes a youth engaging in what he or she believes to be suspicious behavior. Suspicious behavior is more than presenting a nonrespectful demeanor or "attitude." Such behavior includes acts that appear out of place given the particular circumstances. For instance, police may become suspicious of youths wearing long coats on a warm summer day while they walk back and forth outside a store or of youths running away from a parked car just as the car alarm goes off. In 1968 the Supreme Court held in *Terry v. Ohio* that if the police observe behavior that leads them to conclude criminal activity may be in progress and that the suspect is likely armed, they may stop and frisk him or her.[57] However, merely acting suspiciously does not provide a legal justification for an arrest.

Unfortunately, some research suggests that police perceptions of youths acting suspiciously may be related to both the sex and race of the youths. Terrence Allen found that police officers are overwhelmingly (84 percent) more likely to agree with the statement that "if two or more males are together they are probably committing a delinquent act."[58] Moreover, Geoffrey Alpert and his colleagues believe that minority status does influence whether a police officer initially perceives a youth as suspicious or not. African Americans are more likely to be viewed by police as suspicious based on nonbehavioral indicators, for example, the individual's appearance, race, and time and place he or she is observed. Race is predictive of suspicion regarding particular youths, however, it does not appear to influence the final decision by the officer to stop and question. Instead, the stop-and-question decision is more likely the consequence of a behavioral prompt, such as committing a traffic offense or matching a description of a person to "be on the look out for," such as a young, African American male wearing a blue sweatshirt and jogging pants.[59]

Extralegal Factors

There are far too many extralegal factors that may influence the arrest decision to discuss them all in a single chapter. Extralegal factors are those elements of an encounter or characteristics of a juvenile suspect or the officer that have nothing to do with the actual crime but may still influence the decision police make. Throughout this section, the most significant of the many extralegal factors are discussed.

This 10-year-old boy was arrested by Florida law enforcement officers for trespassing on hospice property for attempting to bring Terri Schiavo a glass of water. Was discretion exercised appropriately in this case?

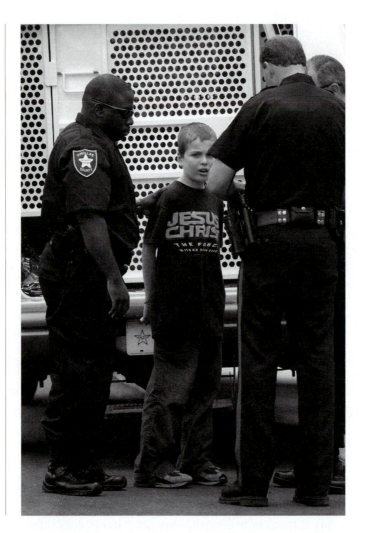

think about it

Policing is a largely reactive endeavor. Allegations that the police discriminate against African Americans by actively patrolling minority neighborhoods are largely anecdotal. How do the offender–victim relationship and official and victimization data address the issue of police bias against African Americans?

Race and Ethnicity   Race has received more attention than any other extra-legal factor. Research on the influence of race on police use of discretion has produced mixed results. Some studies concluded that race mattered, and other studies found it did not matter very much. And in at least one recent study, it was reported that police are actually more lenient with minority suspects.[60] Criminologists, however, generally believe police do treat African American and white children differently for comparable offenses or when holding prior record and presence of evidence constant.[61]

Proportionally more African American than white juveniles are arrested (see Chapter 2).[62] Therefore, police departments assign more patrol officers to African American neighborhoods than to white ones.[63] Police also stop and question African American youths at a higher rate than they do white juveniles.[64] In addition, police think African American juveniles are more likely to be involved in serious criminal activity than whites.[65] Robert Sampson reports that police tend to be suspicious of minority youths and that this suspicion leads them to stop African American and Hispanic juveniles more frequently and to make a record of these encounters. Later, when police stop and question these youths again, they are already "known" to the police and their "prior contact" with the police becomes a basis for more severe treatment.[66]

According to Joan McCord and her colleagues, the substantial research on police–juvenile encounters provides evidence of racial bias by police, although there is some inconsistency in the findings. They suggest that "such inconsistencies may arise from variations in police practice by location (e.g., particular city or rural area), variation in police practice over time as policies and administrations change, or even as a consequence of alterations in police behavior when they are under research observation."[67]

Police officers' nearly automatic suspiciousness of minority youths, coupled with discriminatory practices and beliefs on the part of police, generate feelings of hostility among African American children. In turn, African American juveniles are more likely than white youths to interact with police in a more antagonistic or disrespectful manner, which may lead to their being arrested more often.[68]

While race appears to play a role in the arrest decision, Robert Brown believes that it is not that African Americans are simply arrested because of their race, although race does appear to play a role.[69] Brown examined data based on systematic observations of street-level officers in Cincinnati during the period from 1997 to 1998. Brown reports that extralegal factors appear to have little effect on arrest decisions for white suspects, but that all of the extralegal factors measured significantly affected arrest decisions for African American suspects. Moreover, both legal and extralegal factors increased the likelihood of arrest for African Americans. For example, Terrance Taylor and his colleagues reported that African Americans, Hispanics, and Native Americans had significantly less favorable opinions of the police than whites and Asian Americans. In other words, racial or ethnic differences in police contacts might reflect attitudinal and behavioral differences between racial groups as they relate to the police.[70]

Attitude and Disrespect   Police suspiciousness of juveniles may be prompted by how youths portray themselves to police, including their demeanor, dress, and attitudes suggestive of disrespect. Piliavin and Briar's study of police–juvenile encounters was among the first that reported that police decisions were based on character cues that emerged from interactions with juveniles. Among the cues police observed were the juvenile's age, race, grooming, dress, and demeanor. A juvenile's demeanor was a principal predictor of outcome in 50 to 60 percent of the cases.[71]

Cicourel also examined the role of demeanor. He determined that police initially try to establish a "trust" relationship with the child. They interpret the child's demeanor as evidence of the youth either accepting or rejecting their trust. Failure to show the proper demeanor, such as deference to authority, contriteness, and politeness, was viewed by police as a violation of trust and resulted in a more punitive disposition.[72]

In a related study, Black and Reiss classified juveniles' demeanor as "very deferential," "civil," or "antagonistic." Excluding felonies, the arrest percentages for encounters where suspects were very deferential was 17 percent; where suspects were civil, 12 percent; and when suspects behaved antagonistically, 18 percent. When these findings are compared with those reported by Piliavin and Briar, some striking differences in the percentages of juveniles arrested within similar demeanor categories are noted. Whereas Black and Reiss reported 18 percent of their "antagonistic juveniles" were arrested, Piliavin and Briar found nearly four times that many arrests for "uncooperative juveniles." Only 4 percent of the "cooperative juveniles" in Piliavin and Briar's study were arrested, compared with 13 percent of the combined "civil and deferential suspects" in the Black and Reiss sample.[73]

Citizens who are disrespectful of police are more likely to be arrested.[74] Actually, hostile citizens are about three times more likely to be arrested than nonhostile citizens.[75] However, David Klinger argues that the suspect's demeanor does not necessarily exert an independent impact on the arrest decision. He thinks the problem with earlier studies is they did not control for hostile behavior that occurred after the arrest and therefore could not have influenced the arrest.[76] Other research suggests that "it is not the suspect's hostility that leads to arrest, but rather noncompliance or verbal resistance in front of other officers. In fact, the odds of being arrested *increase by 3.53* when a suspect is hostile and other officers are present" (italics added).[77]

Stephen Mastrofski and his colleagues examined the impact of police disrespect toward the public and by the public toward the police on arrest decisions.[78] They found that unprovoked disrespect of citizens by police is rare (only 4 percent of observed encounters) but that police were three times more likely to disrespect elementary school age youths than people over 60 years old. More important, they report that minority youths are actually less likely to be disrespected by the police than are white youths:

> There was no significant difference between the races when suspects initiated disrespect toward the police. However, contrary to expectation, minority suspects had only .6 the odds of being disrespected as white suspects who did not provoke the police. When the interaction of race and suspect resistance was tested, among resistant suspects, whites had more than twice the odds of receiving police disrespect as minorities; there was no significant difference by race among nonresistant suspects.[79]

Social Class   Data describing police practices in Oakland, California, during the late 19th and early 20th centuries indicate that police were most likely to arrest lower-class males. Is this still true today, and does it apply to juveniles? Several criminologists have examined the impact of social class on police disposition of juveniles. Some research reports that police treat poor and wealthy youths similarly for comparable offenses; other studies reach the opposite conclusion.

George Bodine divided more than 3,000 records of police dispositions of juveniles into five income-level categories. After comparing dispositions and income levels, he concluded that juveniles from lower-class areas had higher court referral rates than juveniles from upper-class neighborhoods. Bodine offered two explanations as to why. First, lower-income youths were more likely to be repeat offenders. Second, juveniles from lower-class areas tended to account for a larger proportion of offenses that generally had high court referral rates, such as petty theft.[80] Terence Thornberry analyzed data from a large Philadelphia birth cohort. He found that social class had a strong effect on police dispositions that could not be explained when controlling for offense seriousness or prior record. Thornberry also found that lower-class youths were less likely than higher-class juveniles to receive a remedial disposition and that this difference was most pronounced for serious offenses.[81]

Cicourel also found social class to be related to police referrals of juveniles to court. But as he explained, social class operates indirectly on the likelihood of court referral. Juveniles from middle- and upper-class homes fared much better after coming into contact with police because their families could mobilize resources to minimize their involvement with the juvenile justice system. Alternatively, parents of lower-class juveniles often felt that police and probation officers should intervene and help them control their children.[82]

Sex   Males are arrested in much larger numbers than females, and males generally commit more serious crimes and commit crimes more frequently. Do these differences simply reflect differences in delinquent behavior of boys and girls, or does their sex influence police decision making? Conventional wisdom tells us that a suspect's sex is likely to make a difference in police dispositions, and a good deal of recent research appears to support this notion.[83]

However, some studies find that girls are treated more leniently than boys, but other research does not. Thomas Monahan reported that (1) police treated female suspects more leniently and (2) police were more likely to arrest girls than boys for sex offenses.[84] Subsequent research has investigated one or the other of these findings. For example, Delbert Elliott and Harwin Voss concluded that girls were treated more leniently even in serious cases. They believe that the differences were not due to differential involvement in delinquency, but that official

Traditionally, female delinquents were afforded "chivalry" by the justice system. The exception to this occurred when female delinquents violated traditional gender roles. Such behavior warranted harsher treatment. Has this viewpoint of female delinquency changed? Why?

think
about it

Extralegal factors
influence the treatment
individuals receive
from criminal justice
personnel. Is the
justice system held to
an unrealistic ideal of
equality that other social
institutions are not?
If not, why?

records reflect a bias in favor of girls in serious cases.[85] Their findings have been confirmed by separate studies by Gail Armstrong and Meda Chesney-Lind.[86] On the other hand, Katherine Teilman and Pierre Landry found that police responded more harshly to girls who committed relatively minor status offenses, such as running away and incorrigibility.[87] Similarly, Ruth Horowitz and Ann Pottieger found that girls who committed serious felonies were less likely to be arrested than boys but were more likely than males to be arrested for less serious crimes.[88] Finally, Christy Visher observed that "police officers adopt a more paternalistic and harsher attitude toward young females to deter any further violation of appropriate sex-role behavior."[89] Visher also noted that "female suspects who violated typical middle-class standards of traditional female characteristics and behaviors (i.e., white, older, and submissive) are not afforded any chivalrous treatment during arrest decisions."[90]

What happens to boys and girls after they have been arrested? Do girls receive preferential treatment at the police station? Early work examining these questions showed that girls were treated more harshly.[91] Girls were more likely to be referred to juvenile court or to have their case turned over to a social service agency. Marvin Krohn and his colleagues analyzed 29 years of data on police contacts in a Midwestern city. Over those three decades, girls were more likely than boys to be referred for status offenses.[92] On the other hand, girls suspected of criminal offenses were less likely than boys to be referred to court, at least in the early years. During the later years, the pattern became mixed. However, Teilman and Landry have observed a trend toward equality in police responses to girls and boys charged with status offenses. Girls were no more likely to be referred to juvenile court than were boys.[93]

Age   Criminologists have studied the association between an offender's age and police disposition. Nathan Goldman found that older youths were more likely to be referred to juvenile court. Juveniles under age 10 were referred to court 21 percent of the time; those between ages 10 and 15, 30 percent; and adolescents 15 to 18 years old, 46 percent. In accounting for this referral pattern, Goldman proposed two possibilities. First, the offenses of very young children were typically less serious. Second, some police officers considered the offenses of young children as normal childhood escapades requiring informal rather than formal actions; others thought that formal system processing would do more harm than good; still other officers were too embarrassed to assume a police role in cases where the offender did not fit the stereotypical mold of a criminal menace to society.[94] Alexander McEachern and Rita Bauzer reported that when offense seriousness was held constant, the proportion of court petitions requested varied with age, ranging from a low of 4 percent for juveniles under age 10 to a high of 41 percent for ages 17 to 18. Police records from Santa Monica, California, also indicated that petition rates were higher for older children.[95]

Bodine's analysis of more than 3,000 juvenile dispositions showed that for both first-time and repeat offenders, the percentages of children referred to court were smaller for younger juveniles than for older ones.[96] Being young was more likely to reduce the possibility of referral for first-time offenders but not for recidivists. Police apparently will give young children a break if they do not have a prior record of delinquency.

Structure and Organization of Police Departments   James Q. Wilson studied how the social organization of a police department affects decisions officers make.[97] He hypothesized that how police handle juveniles was predominately affected by the department's organization, community attachments, and social norms. He tested this idea in a study of the juvenile bureaus in Western City and Eastern City. Western City was a more professional force, while the Eastern City department was more of a fraternal one.

The Western City department was highly bureaucratized; organizational rules were numerous and specific; and supervision was tight. Officers were likely to treat all juveniles according to a strict interpretation of departmental rules. In contrast, the Eastern City police department lacked systematic rules to guide officer decision making concerning juveniles, and supervision of their processing was minimal. Officers handled juvenile suspects primarily on the basis of personal judgment, taking into consideration individual and situational differences.

Although earlier research had indicated that department policy does not ensure consistent decision making among officers, Wilson's study suggests that when there is both centralized management and close supervision, officers in the field will more likely adhere to department policy. Richard Sundeen tested Wilson's claim regarding centralized management. He found that in departments with high bureaucratic control, the greater the policy emphasis on counsel and release dispositions, the higher the rate of counsel and release. In departments characterized by low bureaucratic control, policy emphasis had little impact on disposition rates.[98] The effect of close supervision has recently been examined in research conducted by Robin Engel. Based on analysis of data from Indianapolis and St. Petersburg, Engel reports that while the styles of individual supervisors did not have an effect on arrest decisions, "the mere presence of supervisors at police–citizen encounters—regardless of their supervisory styles—does not increase the likelihood of arrest."[99]

JUVENILES AND THE POLICE

Disparities and discrimination in police decision-making regarding which juvenile to arrest and which to release with just a warning, as well as day-to-day interactions youths may have with police, often produce negative perceptions of the police. This is especially true for minority and poorer white adolescents. In 1961 James Baldwin, in his book *Nobody Knows My Name,* described his sense of police: "He moves through Harlem, therefore, like an occupying soldier in a bitterly hostile country, which is precisely what, and where he is, and is the reason he walks in twos and threes."[100]

While relations between the police and youths in general have improved over the past half century, many tensions remain, making the work of police difficult. Recent studies of adolescent interactions with and attitudes toward police report African American and Hispanic youths are more likely than white youths to be stopped and searched by police, nearly a third of urban youths say police often use abusive language when talking with young people, and about 40 percent of young females indicated male police officers flirted, whistled, or came on to them.[101] More specifically, Delores Jones-Brown's study of 125 high school age African American males found that "A majority of the males report experiencing the police as a repressive rather than facilitative agent in their own lives and in the lives of others."[102] Obviously, many youths do not feel comfortable around police, do not trust police, and instead of seeing police as a force of community protection, perceive them to be a force of oppression as suggested by Baldwin nearly 50 years earlier.

Relations between children and police largely reflect the relations between adults and police. And as the research on police use of discretion discussed earlier in this chapter suggests, situational and individual characteristics appear to affect decisions in the moment. But the use of discretion and the context for making decisions can be changed, and the majority of police agencies around the country have been taking steps to change things, to improve relations between adolescents and law enforcement. The most comprehensive changes have come under the umbrella of community-oriented policing.

Community-Oriented Policing

Community-oriented policing (COP) got its start in the late 1970s as a way to build a partnership between the police and the public, to improve relationships, and to reduce delinquency. Community-oriented policing is different from its immediate predecessors, team policing and problem-oriented policing, inasmuch as it focuses on the neighborhood and its problems and attempts to involve residents of the neighborhood in finding solutions.[103] More specifically, **community-oriented policing** is "a new philosophy of policing, based on the concept that police officers and private citizens working together in creative ways can help solve contemporary community problems related to crime, fear of crime, social and physical disorder, and neighborhood decay."[104] It involves a major change in the role of the police, reallocating patrol officers' time, and developing partnerships with community groups. Strategies include the use of foot or bicycle patrols, assigning officers to smaller, specific areas to work in, organizing community meetings, decentralizing police stations and locating them in neighborhoods, malls, and near schools, conducting community surveys, and dealing with everyday problems and disorder in the neighborhoods.[105]

According to Robert Trojanowicz and Bonnie Bucqueroux, "juveniles represent a special problem for community policing."[106] Juveniles are not only major players in local crime, especially violent crime (see Chapter 3), but are also among the most likely to be victimized, with much of that victimization occurring within the home (see Chapter 10). Community-oriented policing provides a significant opportunity for police "to see themselves as the first line of defense in protecting our nation's children."[107] Thus, police need to be active in identifying abused and neglected children by taking opportunities to check on children when they respond to calls at residences or come into contact with families outside their homes in neighborhood settings. Police also need to develop cooperative relationships with those social agencies involved in investigating and dealing with child abuse and neglect. Lastly, COP officers are in a position to link families experiencing problems with public and private counseling programs. COP officers, thus, are able to engage in delinquency prevention at the primary level by identifying problems early, working with families, and solving problems that would otherwise eventually lead to delinquent behavior.

Youths also need to be involved in developing and implementing community policing. Unfortunately, juveniles are much less likely to be involved in community meetings with police where local programs are likely to be developed.[108] And, as noted earlier, many youths hold very negative perceptions of police as a result of having been stopped, often disrespected, and sometimes

Police officers provide service, trust, and safety to all citizens, especially children. Decades of research indicate that the general public overwhelmingly approves of the police and appreciates their public service. Yet the media often portrays the police and the citizenry as enemies, why?

illegally searched. When COP programs solicit community ideas from surveys, they should find ways of tapping into the concerns and attitudes of neighborhood youths and whenever possible, invite a representative group of youths to attend meetings. Some COP officers have developed youth-oriented programs within their departments aimed at helping officers and youths to get to know and understand one another. For instance, the "Brown Baggin' with the Blues" program, developed by the Denver Police Department, creates opportunities for children and COP officers to have lunch together. The International Association of Chiefs of Police has recognized another program, called "Kops 'n' Kids," that brings officers and children together in fun activities as an alternative to interactions based on anti-drug or antigang speeches. Officers share lunch with the children, bring their K-9s along for demonstrations, and form jogging clubs to provide positive role models and build trust. Finally, the Greeley (Colorado) Police Department developed an "Adopt-an-Officer" program in which COP officers volunteer to be adopted by elementary classes. Students visit police stations and officers and students exchange cards and share meals.[109]

Police Diversion Programs

The best of community-oriented prevention efforts sometimes fail, and youths become delinquent and come into contact with the police as suspected offenders. After police decide to take a child into custody, they must decide what to do with the juvenile. Of the children police took into custody in 2003, 71 percent were referred to juvenile court, 7 percent were referred directly to criminal court, while the remaining youths were referred to a welfare agency or handled within the department and released.[110]

Internal Diversion   The most basic form of internal diversion is *diversion without referral*. In these cases, police warn, counsel, and release the child without taking any formal action. In contrast, there is *diversion with referral,* where a youth is referred to a program administered by an agency other than the juvenile justice system. Diversion with referral usually takes one of four forms.

An *internal referral,* or an in-house diversion, is the referral of a case from one branch of the police department to another branch better equipped to handle it. In-house programs can be organized in different ways. In some departments, an officer administers the program and supervises a team of full-time professional counselors, usually civilians. In a variation of this approach, an officer serves as an administrator and directs the efforts of a team of volunteer counselors. Typical internal referral programs include community volunteer programs, recreation programs, and probation programs (see Box 13-4 for a discussion of a police diversion program in Alberta, Canada).

The goal of community volunteer programs is to identify and recruit citizens to provide assistance to problem youths. The citizens serve as Big Brothers or Big Sisters or by providing educational tutoring or employment opportunities. Police officers are responsible for identifying and developing liaisons with the citizens. Volunteers are trained in the objectives of the diversion program (for instance, counseling about drugs and alcohol) and receive additional training in child development and crisis intervention techniques.

Recreation programs are found in many large and medium-sized police departments. Athletic activities, such as Police Athletic League programs, attempt to channel the energy of delinquent youths into socially constructive activities.

box 13-4 DELINQUENCY AROUND THE GLOBE
Police Diversion Committees in Alberta, Canada

Police are not always required to formally charge youths even when there is sufficient evidence to do so. In cases where the offense is less serious in nature, the police may decide to exercise their discretion by diverting a young offender from the youth justice system and to a youth justice committee. *Youth justice committees* are groups of volunteers working in partnership with the Alberta justice system. The police may refer youths directly to youth justice committees for guidance, counseling, or direction. Importantly, if a youth fails to comply with the directions of the youth justice committee, no further action can be taken. Whether a youth complies or fails to comply, the diversionary referral does not constitute a young offender record.

First- and second-time youthful offenders who are at least 12-years-old and under age 18 at the time of their offense are eligible to be diverted to the youth justice committee. However, there are a few offenses that exclude youths from participation. These include acts or threats of violence, breaking and entering an inhabited dwelling, perjury, and all driving-related offenses. While simple possession of marijuana or its products are not excluded, all other drug offenses are. In all cases, youths considered for the program must accept responsibility for the offense and be willing to meet with the committee.

The youth justice committee diversion program is designed to allow citizens to work out differences among young offenders, victims, and community members, to provide community-based resolutions to youth crime, and to provide young offenders with an alternative to the formal court process. It is guided by the following principles:

- Young persons should be held accountable for their criminal behavior.
- There must be regard for the rights and freedoms of young persons and victims.
- The least intrusive alternatives and restrictions of a young person's freedom must be sought while maintaining the protection of the community.
- The community has a right and responsibility to participate in the youth justice system.

Once a youth referred by the police is diverted to the youth justice committee, every effort is taken to expedite the matter as quickly as possible (maximum length of involvement is 45 days). In most cases, a onetime meeting with the youth, his or her parent(s), and the victim (if willing) is sufficient to make the juvenile understand the consequences of the offending behavior. The committee will negotiate conditions to be imposed, bearing in mind the youth's age, full-time attendance at school, and time available to comply with conditions. Appropriate conditions that may be imposed include

- Personal or written apology to the victim.
- Personal service to the victim.
- Community services to a nonprofit community or government agency.
- Return property or pay restitution to the victim.

To further explore police diversion of juvenile offenders to the youth justice committee program, visit the Alberta Solicitor General website at http://solgen.gov.ab.ca/yjc.

Source: Guidelines for Police Diversion: Referrals to Youth Justice Committees, online at http://solgen.gov.ab.ca/yjc, accessed May 3, 2007.

These programs are based on the assumption that if youths are exposed to the benefits of sportsmanship, playing by the rules, and healthy competition, they will internalize these values and apply them to other spheres of life. It is believed that by having the police directly involved in these programs, relations between police and juveniles will be improved.

think
about it

The majority of a police officer's time is spent maintaining order, not performing law enforcement functions. Have attitudes toward and appreciation of police officers changed since the terrorist attacks of September 11, 2001?

Diversionary *probation programs* are designed to teach children that they must stay out of trouble. Children who are assigned to a probation program must report to police officers on a regular basis. The purpose of the meetings is to allow the juvenile to inform the police of his or her activities since the last visit and to receive encouragement, advice, or warning (as warranted) from the officers. Children who violate conditions of the program are referred to juvenile court.

External Diversion External diversion programs are an alternative to processing the child through the juvenile justice system. *External referrals* involve the police diversion of youths to programs outside the police agency. An example of an external diversion program can be found in the Honolulu Police Department's restorative justice model in which juveniles are referred to a Real Justice conferencing program. Real Justice conferences have participants (offenders, victims, and community representatives) sitting in circles and facilitated by a neutral third party. The offender is required to speak first and take responsibility for his or her actions and then to answer questions from the other participants aimed at having the youths reflect on the consequences of his or her behavior. Not all juvenile offenders are eligible to participate in this diversion program; shoplifting and runaway cases and youths who refuse to admit to wrongdoing are excluded.[111]

Police departments use four criteria to decide whether to refer youths to a community service agency: acceptability, suitability, availability, and accountability.[112]

- *Acceptability.* Police officers have a tendency to stereotype certain service agencies as soft, lenient, coddling, and permissive. Police generally view free clinics, runaway shelters, and crisis centers with suspicion. Police see these programs as catering to the vices of youths rather than controlling or preventing them.

- *Suitability.* Many community service agencies are unsuitable for use by the police. An agency may accept only certain cases, or its policies and practices may conflict with those of police. Other practical considerations that affect suitability are restrictive costs, long waiting lists, and insufficient personnel. Furthermore, many service agencies are open only between 9 A.M. and 5 P.M., making it difficult for police to utilize their services fully.

- *Availability.* Over the years, various recommendations have been made in an attempt to provide community resources where none exist. Two problems may arise regarding such resources. First, availability of resources is no guarantee of quality. Second, there is often a low level of resource awareness among police. For instance, when Malcolm Klein interviewed officers in six California cities on the availability of community resources, he found that they had little knowledge about what was available.[113]

- *Accountability.* The appropriateness of a referral can never be fully known without formal procedures for follow-up. By actively soliciting comments from referral agencies, police are better equipped to make future referrals and improve communication with service agencies. Better communication, in turn, improves coordination and the ability of agencies to respond to police needs.

conclusions

The first American police departments were modeled after the English police. They included constables and a night watch. By the middle of the 19th century, nearly all big cities had established police departments that closely resembled those we see today. With the creation of the first juvenile court in 1899, police work with juveniles changed substantially as they found themselves increasingly required to work with noncriminal, status offending youths. By the mid-1950s, police officers given juvenile assignments began to specialize and improve their professional status.

Most encounters between police and juveniles are constrained by the same rules and court decisions governing police–adult interactions, but this has not always been the case, and the courts and state legislatures provide for some differences in treatment. For example, juveniles are typically taken into custody, not arrested; booking procedures in most states prohibit fingerprinting and photographing juveniles; and youths are not given the same latitude in waiving their right to remain silent or to have an attorney present as are adults.

The police officer's discretionary decision to arrest a juvenile suspected of a crime is based on many factors. Some of the factors are legal; others are extralegal. The offense seriousness, a youth's prior record, presence of evidence, suspiciousness, and characteristics of the juvenile, such as race, sex, age, and attitude, all affect how an officer will respond to a situation. The decision to arrest a child is important because it gets the juvenile justice process started. At a minimum, an arrest may lead to a tainted reputation. In the worst case, adjudication and confinement may follow. When police take a child into custody, they must decide what to do next and they choose among alternative actions. Children may be referred to juvenile court for processing; they can be handled informally within the department; or they can be referred to an agency outside the juvenile justice system. The decision police make is based on many criteria, including offense seriousness and the availability of appropriate community resources.

Discretionary decisions by the police, especially decisions appearing to be arbitrary or discriminatory, have led to relational problems between youths and police. Recent developments in community policing have been aimed at reducing the distance between youths and cops as well as providing opportunities for police to divert many youths out of the juvenile justice system. Unfortunately, the majority of youths taken into custody by the police find their way into more formal processing. In the next chapter, we will explore the juvenile court and what happens to juveniles who enter that stage of the juvenile justice system.

key terms

Booking The official recording of a person into detention after arrest.

Community-oriented policing Police officers and private citizens working together can help solve community problems related to crime, fear of crime, social and physical disorder, and neighborhood decay.

Exclusionary rule A legal rule that states evidence police produce illegally is not admissible in court.

Miranda v. Arizona Established the right to protection from self-incrimination under the Fifth Amendment and the right to legal counsel under the Sixth Amendment.

Police discretion The authority of police to choose one course of action over another.

Probable cause   A set of facts that would lead a reasonable person to believe that a crime has been committed and that the person to be arrested committed it.

Yarborough v. Alvarado   Police do not need to factor in the age and inexperience of a suspect in their decision of whether to read a juvenile his or her *Miranda* rights if the youth is not believed to be "in custody."

JUDGE
...NY H. JOHNSON

14

The Juvenile Court

449

The origins of the American juvenile court were discussed in Chapter 1; this chapter examines the transformation of the court through the 20th century and into the early 21st century. One of the most significant changes in this transformation was the movement away from the court's traditional paternalistic and protectionist view of children to one that took an increasingly adversarial and punitive approach to dealing with them.

Less than a decade after Illinois established its juvenile court in 1899, 10 more states and the District of Columbia followed suit. By 1925 all but two states had passed juvenile codes and created special juvenile courts. When Wyoming established its juvenile court in 1945, the list was complete.[1] However, creating the juvenile court system was much easier than making it work. In many cities, juvenile courts did not function to achieve their prescribed tasks. In practically all states, reformatories and penal institutions continued to be filled with hundreds of children. In many jurisdictions where detention homes had not been provided for court use, children were still confined in jails, often with adult criminals, to await hearings.

Although the juvenile courts began to employ more full-time professional probation officers, their effectiveness was hindered by large caseloads that hampered complete investigation and treatment.[2] One consequence was that juvenile offenders made only infrequent appearances at their probation officer's station. These visits replaced the idealized home visits and were usually far too hurried and superficial to promote a meaningful exchange between the adult supervisor and the young offender.

From the juvenile court's inception, many youths accused of serious offenses were left in the adult criminal system. According to Sanford Fox, developments in the treatment of juvenile offenders, from the house of refuge movement, to the juvenile court's establishment, to the concerns in the 1970s with removing status offenders from the court system, have focused on "petty offenses and salvageable offenders."[3]

By the 1980s much of the attention and concern of the court had shifted to the growing number of serious juvenile offenders, and the watchwords became secure detention, punishment, deterrence, and waiver to criminal court. Although the juvenile court has experienced upheavals and controversies as well as varied reform movements over the years, it is still the mainstay of society's attempt to control delinquent and wayward youths (see Box 14-1 for a discussion of the juvenile courts in France).

JURISDICTION OF THE JUVENILE COURT

The juvenile justice system, and especially the juvenile court, was originally conceived to prevent future criminal conduct by paternalistically treating or rehabilitating young offenders. To achieve this goal, broad statutory authority was deemed necessary to allow the court to intervene in a wide range of situations and to bring many juveniles under its jurisdiction. In other words, the system allowed the state to intervene in the juvenile's life virtually as it pleased. Such broad jurisdiction was built on the assumption that the child's parents would be expected to be concerned with the full range of adolescent behavior—from

box 14-1 — DELINQUENCY AROUND THE GLOBE

Juvenile Justice in France

Following developments in the United States by nearly a half century, the Order of 2 February 1945 "On Delinquent Youth" established the contemporary juvenile court in France. It provided for specialized "juvenile judges," and the court's responsibility was to educate and reform delinquents. The French juvenile court gave the judge great power to inquire into the "material and moral status" of the youth's family, the child's character, school behavior and academic achievement, and past record of delinquency. In addition, judges could order psychological and medical examinations.

Hearings are not public, and except for the child and his or her parents, there are few people in attendance. Those typically involved in the hearing include the judge, two magistrate assistants, a prosecutor or deputy prosecutor, a defense attorney (either appointed or hired by the family), the court clerk, and possibly a social case worker. In minor cases, judges hold hearings in their chambers. If the child is determined to be delinquent, the judge can select from a variety of dispositions, including returning the child to his or her home, formally cautioning the child, placing the child on probation, or placing the child in a special school for delinquents or in another type of specialized children's home.

Catherine Blatier surveyed juvenile courts in four representative jurisdictions, including Paris, St. Etienne, Gap, and Rennes. Her research indicates that most cases brought before the French juvenile courts involve simple thefts. Nearly 75 percent of the cases involved theft, car or moped theft, or aggravated theft. Fewer than 8 percent involved violent crimes, and only 1 percent were drug-related. Boys committed more than 90 percent of the cases brought to the juvenile courts; nearly half of the youths were 17 or 18 years old; only about a third of both boys and girls committed their crimes alone.

Reflecting the nonpunitive approach of the French courts, dispositions during the 5 years studied suggest that very few juveniles were placed in custodial situations. For first-time offenders, 5 percent of the youths were acquitted or discharged, 35 percent of the recommendations involved a warning, 13 percent were left in the care of the family or guardian, 25 percent received formal or informal probation, 8 percent were required to pay compensation, 6 percent were only fined, 5 percent were placed in care, and only 3 percent of the youths received a sentence of institutional confinement. Second-time offenders were treated much more harshly, with 55 percent placed in institutions.

France is beginning to face more frequent and more serious delinquent behavior by its youths, including rioting involving extensive destruction of property and assaults against citizens and authorities. These offenders are also getting younger. However, French law prohibits the incarceration of children under the age of 16, and with children as young as 10 committing serious crimes, lawmakers might begin to consider some of the "get-tough" measures that many experts argue helped reduce serious juvenile delinquency in the United States in the late 1990s.

Sources: Catherine Blatier, "Juvenile Justice in France: The Evolution of Sentencing for Children and Minor Delinquents," *British Journal of Criminology* 39:240–252 (1999); Molly Moore, "As Youth Riots Spread Across France, Muslim Groups Attempt to Intervene," *Washington Post,* November 5, 2005:A1.

criminal acts to smoking and skipping school—and the court, in its *parens patriae* role, should act as a "super parent" when the natural parents were unsuccessful. Thus, the early juvenile court established jurisdiction over both criminal and noncriminal (status offenses) behavior of youths. However, during the latter part of the 20th century, nearly all states removed status offenders from the juvenile court to be handled by family or other civil courts.

The juvenile courts in most states have original jurisdiction over all youths who are under age 18 at the time of arrest. In 37 states, the District of Columbia, and the federal districts, 17 is the upper age limit for jurisdiction; 10 states set the limit at age 16; and three states (Connecticut, New York, and North Carolina) set the upper age limit at 15. Most states also set minimum ages at which a juvenile may be transferred to adult court (discussed later in this chapter).[4]

The states also establish lower age limits for juvenile court jurisdiction in delinquency matters. The lowest age of jurisdiction reflects the interests of the states in early intervention into the lives of juveniles. Ten states set the lowest age for jurisdiction at age 10, one state (Arizona) sets it at age 8, three (Maryland, Massachusetts, and New York) set it at 7, and one (North Carolina) sets it at 6. The remaining states and the District of Columbia have no specified lowest age for juvenile court jurisdiction.

The original juvenile justice system intended that youthful offenders would be handled outside of the formal, adversarial criminal justice system. But some juveniles who commit certain crimes have always been eligible for prosecution in the criminal courts through a waiver of jurisdiction process (discussed later in this chapter). While some states maintain *exclusive jurisdiction* over some crimes regardless of the juvenile's age, most states have established procedures for waiver to criminal court depending on the age–crime combination. Finally, a few states statutorily specify *concurrent jurisdiction* whereby prosecutors have the authority to file cases involving juveniles accused of certain crimes in either juvenile or criminal court.

think
about it

Most people would agree that serious violent repeat juvenile offenders are the real concern, not youths involved in petty delinquency. Should the juvenile justice system be used exclusively for youths engaging in minor offenses? Should serious violent juvenile delinquents always be prosecuted and punished as adults?

PROCESSING JUVENILE OFFENDERS

What happens when a child is brought into the juvenile court system? Typically a case flows through the system by first being reported to police, who refer it to the court. Then if the case is processed by the juvenile court intake department, the youth is formally charged by the prosecutor, the case is adjudicated in a court hearing, and the youth is possibly assigned to some form of correctional activity. At any point in this flow, a case may be diverted, dismissed, or terminated in some other way, returning the child to the outside world.

Arrest

Adult law violators are arrested by police, but juvenile offenders have traditionally been "taken into custody," reflecting the *civil* rather than *criminal* nature of the juvenile court. In fact, much of the terminology used in the juvenile court reflects this difference (see Table 14-1). States vary in their procedural rules regarding the arrest of juveniles. Many states do not require arrest warrants as they would with adults in similar circumstances.[5] Whether juveniles are only taken into custody or formally arrested, authorities must provide them with essentially the same fundamental constitutional protections that apply when arresting adults, such as probable cause and protections against unreasonable search and seizure (see Chapter 13).

table 14-1 Comparison of Terminology in the Criminal and Juvenile Justice Systems

CRIMINAL JUSTICE SYSTEM	JUVENILE JUSTICE SYSTEM
Crime	Delinquent act
Criminal	Delinquent
Arrest	Take into custody
Arraignment	Intake hearing
Indictment	Petition
Not guilty plea	Deny the petition
Guilty plea	Agree to an adjudication finding
Plea bargain	Adjustment
Jail	Detention facility
Trial	Adjudication hearing
Conviction	Adjudication
Presentence investigation	Social history
Sentencing	Disposition hearing
Sentence	Disposition
Incarceration	Commitment
Prison	Training school, reform school, youth center
Parole	Aftercare

Police are generally the first to make a formal determination on whether to process the juvenile. They also exercise discretion, and not all eligible youths are formally arrested. If police decide to arrest a child, subsequent actions are then largely determined by legal statutes. In some states, police are required to notify a probation officer or other official designated by the juvenile court; in other states, police are required to notify only the child's parents. But whenever a juvenile is taken into police custody, he or she goes to the police station for initial screening and possible interrogation, after which the police decide whether to terminate the case, divert it to an alternative program, or refer it to juvenile court for formal intake.

Court Intake

Courts with juvenile jurisdiction handle an estimated 1,600,000 delinquency cases each year. Arrest rates of juveniles fell dramatically since the mid-1990s, but there was no comparable decline in court cases. Between 1985 and 2002, the volume of the court cases handled by the juvenile courts around the country increased by 41 percent. However, delinquency cases dropped 11 percent from the 1997 peak to 2002. Juvenile cases involving crimes against the person and public order offenses each increased about 110 percent between 1985 and 2002, while drug cases increased by 159 percent. During this period, property offense cases actually dropped by 10 percent.[6] These delinquency cases were referred to the courts by a variety of sources, including law enforcement agencies, social service agencies, schools, parents, probation officers, and victims.

Once referred to the court, juveniles go through a case-screening process called intake. **Intake** procedures are designed to screen out cases that *do not* warrant a formal court hearing, such as the following:

- Cases involving matters over which the court has no jurisdiction.
- Cases in which the evidence against the child is insufficient.
- Cases that are not serious enough to require juvenile court adjudication.
- Cases in which the youth or his or her family have already compensated the victim.
- Cases that should be waived to criminal court.

The intake department may also order social history investigations, medical or psychological diagnoses, or other studies that might be used to determine the suitability of juvenile court involvement. Informal hearings, adjudications, and probation supervision are frequently administered at the intake level without referral to a judge.

While most state statutes on intake are deliberately broad, some jurisdictions have formulated specific guidelines for intake officials to consider when deciding

The use of detention has increased more rapidly for females than males. What explains the recent surge in serious delinquency among females? What unique problems do female delinquents pose?

whether to file a petition or to adjust a case informally. The seriousness of the offense is the most important element considered. A number of courts specify that certain offenses may not be adjusted or, more generally, that no felony offense may be adjusted. The range of available adjustments at the intake stage is limited only by the availability of resources in the community and the imagination of the intake staff. If a child has been referred on a minor charge and the intake officer determines that court intervention is not necessary, but feels the child needs to be impressed with the seriousness of his or her actions, the officer may lecture the child. To make the warning more impressive, the youth may be taken before a judge in his or her chambers for a stern reprimand.

The intake process often selects **informal adjustment** for cases deemed to be best handled through discretionary nonjudicial dispositions. One approach to informal adjustment is the use of a summary disposition in which the child is either simply warned; required to participate in a community service program, make restitution, or apologize to the complainant; or referred to a *diversion program* (see Box 14-2). Another approach to informal adjustment is the use of **informal probation,** in which the child is expected to comply with probationary conditions similar to that of court-ordered probation, possibly including community service, victim restitution, or voluntary probation supervision. Informal adjustment is widely used. In 2002 slightly over 38 percent of all juveniles being supervised on probation were supervised in some form of informal, or voluntary, probation.[7]

Problems with informal probation have arisen, however, since informal supervision of juveniles by probation personnel is conducted in much the same way as supervision of adjudicated children. If children and their parents are unfamiliar with juvenile court procedures, they sometimes agree to informal probation, not realizing that they have the right to a court hearing before the probation staff has any sanctioned authority over the child's behavior and that an admission of guilt, which is a requirement for diversion, will become part of the child's formal juvenile record.

Perhaps more problematic at intake is that in many jurisdictions, statements made by juveniles during interviews with a probation or intake officer may be admissible later in the adjudication hearing. Although courts have held that juveniles have no constitutional right to counsel during the informal intake process, a few states, such as Washington, have established a statutory right to counsel for juveniles at intake.[8]

Filing the Petition   If intake procedures result in a decision to submit the child to a formal court hearing, a petition is filed. A **petition** sets forth the specific charge that a delinquent act has been committed. It serves to notify the child of the claims made about his or her misconduct. The petition is the counterpart of an indictment in criminal prosecutions and a complaint in civil litigation, with the petition requesting either an adjudicatory or waiver hearing.

The prosecutor at this stage evaluates the case in terms of its legal adequacy. In any case in which a juvenile is alleged to qualify for prosecution in the juvenile court, the prosecutor submits a petition to the court. If the prosecutor decides not to file the petition, that decision is regarded as final, and the case is dismissed. If the prosecutor does file the petition, it is usually followed by a report by the intake officer on the behavior patterns and social history of the juvenile.

Disparities in Intake Decisions   About 58 percent of all delinquency cases referred to the juvenile court are officially processed. Cases involving juveniles

Roberto Potter and Suman Kakar contend the primary purpose of juvenile diversion is to divert adolescents from early encounters with the juvenile justice system. Diversion may occur at any of a number of points. For example, police utilize diversion in handling juvenile offenders, such as an officer's decision to handle a complaint informally, and juvenile courts have developed a wide variety of diversion programs, including placement of a youth on informal probation or placement in specialized counseling or treatment programs. In any of these situations, diversion is intended to suspend or terminate the official handling of juveniles in favor of some informal or unofficial alternative.

The formal juvenile court process can be suspended prior to the filing of a petition to permit the juvenile to be handled informally by community agencies, a process called *informal adjustment.* In other words, diversion allows youths to avoid formal court processing and adjudication and the stigma that typically accompanies formal action. First-time offenders charged with minor misdemeanors, repeat status offenders, or youths already participating in a community-based treatment program are generally considered good candidates for diversion programs.

Most diversion programs offer innovative approaches to treatment and rehabilitation. Early programs, such as Project Crossroads in Washington, DC, combined counseling, vocational training, and academic development opportunities for first-time offenders with no prior convictions and facing charges for a nonviolent offense. Sacramento's Project 601 aimed to reduce court costs and recidivism rates by combining crisis intervention and counseling for juveniles identified as truants, habitual runaways, or incorrigibles.

Current diversion programs may involve mediation, in which meetings are scheduled among the complainant, the juvenile, and a neutral hearing officer who facilitates communication between the disputants and helps them reach a mutually acceptable resolution to the conflict. Community youth boards are informal hearing boards that determine which, if any, services should be provided to children referred by schools, police, the juvenile court, parents, or the children themselves. While some boards only accept status offender referrals, others allow referrals of all juvenile offenders.

Diversion programs may also be designed to provide alternatives to formal placement in a correctional institution. For example, wilderness programs attempt to take streetwise youths, with their well-developed skills at conning and manipulating people, and place them in a setting where they cannot avoid taking responsibility. The goal of these programs is to increase youths' self-respect through self-discipline and through overcoming both physical and psychological challenges encountered in individual and group efforts. Two recent innovative diversion approaches, *youth courts* and *drug courts,* are discussed later in this chapter.

Are diversion programs effective? Advocates argue that such programs reduce court caseloads and costs, reduce the time staff spend in case processing, reduce the time the juvenile is involved in the juvenile justice system, and reduce recidivism. Critics, on the other hand, argue that diversion may actually increase the number of cases sent to the juvenile court as diverted youths are typically drawn from a group traditionally released by police or probation staff without further action, a process known as net-widening. Critics also note that diversion from juvenile justice processing raises fundamental issues of fairness: Selection for diversion may be arbitrary or biased; procedural rights may be overlooked or ignored; eligibility requirements may violate due process; and long-term effects may hinder the juvenile's return to society.

Sources: Roberto Potter and Suman Kakar, "The Diversion Decision-Making Process from the Juvenile Court Practitioners' Perspective," *Journal of Contemporary Criminal Justice* 18:20–36 (2002); Patrick Griffin and Patricia Torbet, *Desktop Guide to Good Juvenile Probation Practice* (Pittsburgh: National Center for Juvenile Justice, 2002); Albert Roberts, *Juvenile Justice: Policies, Programs, and Services* (Chicago: Dorsey Press, 1989); Steven Patrick, Robert Marsh, Wade Bundy, Susan Mimura, and Tina Perkins, "Control Group Study of Juvenile Diversion Programs: An Experiment in Juvenile Diversion—The Comparison of Three Methods and a Control Group," *The Social Science Journal* 41:129–135 (2004).

age 16 or older are more likely to be petitioned than cases involving younger juveniles. Regardless of offense, juvenile courts are more likely to petition cases involving males than females. For example, 63 percent of males were petitioned in 2002; only 54 percent of females were. On the other hand, African American youths are significantly more likely than white youths to be petitioned (66 versus 57 percent). Differences in likelihood of being petitioned are greatest in cases involving drugs, where 78 percent of African American juveniles are petitioned, compared with 56 percent of whites.[9]

Lisa Bond-Maupin and her colleagues examined intake decisions in a jurisdiction in which Hispanic girls are in a numerical majority. Referrals for drug offenses were rare, and there were no referrals for serious violent crimes. However, Bond-Maupin and her colleagues report that it was clear the juvenile justice system was designed for boys: "Not only were referrals of boys more common, but the overwhelming majority of probation and parole resources were allocated to referred and adjudicated males."[10] At intake, girls' cases were more likely to be handled informally as a result of intake workers viewing girls' cases as less serious or tied to family problems or the sexual behavior of the girls.

Michael Leiber and Kristin Mack report that African American juveniles "are more likely than their white counterparts at intake to be referred on for further court processing. At intake, African Americans are also more likely to be released than participate in diversion when compared to white youth."[11] However, they also note that being from a single-parent household disadvantages African American youths at intake, increasing the likelihood of receiving more severe outcomes.

Bail and Detention

Most adults are afforded the right to bail if they are arrested. **Bail** is a money or cash bond deposited with the court or bail bondsman allowing the person to be released on the assurance he or she will appear in court at the proper time. However, if a child is not released immediately to his or her parents after being taken into custody, the child must be taken to a local or regional juvenile detention facility. When no bail or bond is available for juveniles, the detention hearing is typically used when the court considers whether to release the juvenile.

Juvenile **detention** is the temporary confinement of children within a physically restricting facility pending filing of a petition, while awaiting adjudication or disposition hearings, or the implementation of disposition. The primary purpose behind detention is twofold: (1) to ensure the youth appears for all court hearings and (2) to protect the community from future offending by the youth.[12] If a youth is brought to the detention facility by the police after having been taken into custody, intake probation officers must then determine whether the youth should be released or detained. If the juvenile is to be detained, then a petition must be filed and a detention hearing scheduled within 48 to 72 hours.[13] For example, Alabama requires that a child taken into custody be released except in situations where

- The child has no parent, guardian, custodian, or other suitable person able and willing to provide supervision and care for such child.

- The release of the child would present a clear and substantial threat of a serious nature to the person or property of others where the child is alleged to be delinquent.

- The release of such child would present a serious threat of substantial harm to such child.
- The child has a history of failing to appear for hearings before the court.[14]

Juveniles also may be detained for evaluation purposes and while awaiting placement in a long-term correctional or treatment facility. And like adults detained in jail, the mere fact of being detained increases the likelihood of being adjudicated delinquent and receiving a more severe disposition.[15]

In recent years, both federal and state courts have held that a juvenile may not be detained pending trial on charges of delinquency without a prompt determination of probable cause. However, in 1984 the Supreme Court reversed this ruling in *Schall v. Martin* (discussed in more detail later in this chapter).[16] The justices upheld a New York statute authorizing the pretrial detention of an accused juvenile who, if released, may pose a "serious risk" by committing the equivalent of an adult crime. The statute provides for a detention hearing; however, a formal finding that there is probable cause to believe that the youth committed the offense for which he or she was arrested is not required prior to his or her detention.

Approximately 20 percent of all delinquency cases brought before the juvenile court result in detentions prior to disposition.[17] According to the most recent reports, a total of 329,800 juveniles were held for some period of time in detention facilities. Of the detained delinquency cases, 11 percent were related to drugs, 27 percent involved public order offenses, 29 percent involved crimes against the person, and 32 percent involved property crimes.[18]

Disparities in Detention

Race and sex disparities exist in detention as they do in arrest decisions, adjudications, dispositions, waivers, decisions about community corrections versus institutional placement (discussed later in this chapter). As Eleanor Hoytt and her colleagues argue, "Because detention is a key entry point from which youth further penetrate the juvenile justice system, decisions made at detention can have profound impact on disproportionality throughout the system."[19] These disparities or overrepresentations raise serious questions and, for many people, suggest the possibility of race and sex discrimination.

But overrepresentation may stem from factors other than discrimination. Factors relating to the seriousness and volume of crime, prior record, community characteristics, and life circumstances—such as dropping out of school or living with a single parent—may influence the decisions of police, intake officers, and juvenile court judges.[20]

Race

Secure detention was nearly twice as likely in cases involving African American youths than those involving white youths, even after controlling for general offense category. For example, 18 percent of delinquency cases involving white youths included detention at some point between referral and disposition; among cases involving African Americans, the figure was 25 percent. The most striking differences were among cases involving drug offenses and crimes against the person (see Figure 14-1). Detention was used in 16 percent of drug cases involving white youths, in 33 percent of cases involving African American youths. White youths were also noticeably less likely to be placed in detention

figure 14-1   Delinquency Cases Detained by Offenses and Race, 2006

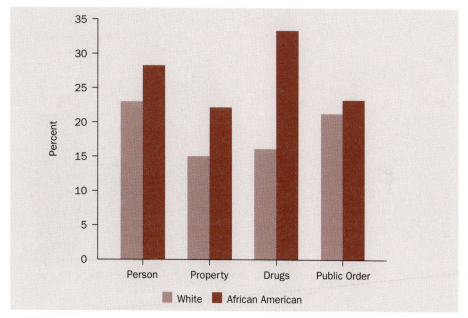

Source: Howard Snyder and Melissa Sickmund, *Juvenile Offenders and Victims: 2006 National Report* (Washington, DC: National Center for Juvenile Justice, 2006), p. 169.

in cases involving property crimes and crimes against the person. Finally, the use of detention for delinquency cases remained relatively steady for all racial groups between 1986 and 2002.[21]

A recent study by Michael Lieber and Kristan Fox illustrates how the impact of race on detention decisions is not only somewhat complex, but has a significant influence on subsequent decisions in the juvenile justice system. Lieber and Fox examined more than 5,500 juvenile court referrals in Iowa between 1980 and 2000. While legal and extralegal variables were predictive of detention decisions, race had an independent additive and interactive effect on detention. African American youths, compared to white youths were 5 percent more likely to receive detention, and African American youths charged with a drug offense were 10 percent more likely to be detained. More important, they note that "African Americans also moved further through the system because of the effect of detention on decision making at intake, initial appearance, and judicial disposition."[22]

Sex   Of juveniles charged with a delinquency offense, males are more likely than females to be held in detention. Overall, 22 percent of male delinquency cases involved detention; it was involved in 17 percent of female cases. But the use of detention has increased more rapidly for girls than for boys. Regardless of the general offense category, detention was used more often for cases involving male juveniles (see Figure 14-2). However, girls were more likely than boys to be detained for minor offenses such as status offenses and traffic offenses.

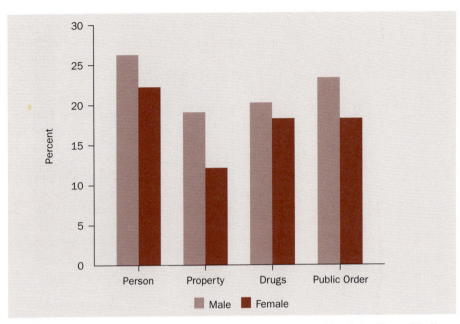

figure 14-2 Delinquency Cases Detained by Sex, 2006

Source: Howard Snyder and Melissa Sickmund, *Juvenile Offenders and Victims: 2006 National Report* (Washington, DC: National Center for Juvenile Justice, 2006), p. 169.

In addition, girls are more likely than boys to be placed in detention for probation and parole violations.[23]

Females with less extensive delinquency histories also are more likely than males with similar histories to be placed in detention, to be detained for technical violations of probation, to "protect" them, and to spend more time in detention than their male counterparts.[24]

Race and sex also appear to interact in terms of detention decisions. Christy Sharp and Jessica Simon report that in the mid-1990s approximately 63 percent of all girls in secure detention were African American or Hispanic and that African American girls were about three times more likely to be detained than white girls.[25] Bond-Maupin and her colleagues argue that the less serious nature of girls' offenses do not justify the use of detention and that it is used inappropriately to resolve school and family-based problems.[26]

Court Hearings

Even though juvenile court proceedings have historically been less adversarial than those in adult criminal court, in recent decades they have taken on many characteristics of the adversarial system. As a result of Supreme Court decisions and get-tough legislation by states, there has been a noticeable convergence between juvenile and adult court proceedings, with hearings in the juvenile court now rather adversarial in nature. However, according to Barry Feld, juvenile courts tend to operate with two competing conceptions of adolescents. On the one hand, juveniles continue to be regarded as "children" and not given all the same protections adults receive. On the other hand, juveniles are increasingly being held criminally responsible for their "adult-like" crimes. Thus, Feld believes that young offenders "receive the worst of both worlds."[27]

There are three critical court hearings facing juvenile offenders. These are the *adjudication hearing,* the *disposition hearing,* and the *waiver hearing.* The first two of these hearings are discussed next, while the waiver hearing is discussed later in this chapter.

The Adjudication Hearing   An **adjudication hearing** determines whether the child committed the offense of which he or she is accused. In delinquency cases, the required standard of evidence is *proof beyond a reasonable doubt,* the same as that needed to sustain a criminal charge in an adult court. Hearsay is inadmissible at the adjudication hearing. Juveniles have the right to confront and cross-examine witnesses and are entitled to the due process safeguards of adequate, timely, and written notice of the allegations and sufficient time to formulate a response. The right to refuse to testify is also ensured under the Fifth Amendment. Juveniles are also entitled to the assistance of counsel.

To be valid, confessions must be voluntary, corroborated by someone other than an accomplice, and preceded by the *Miranda* warning, which includes the right to (1) remain silent, (2) have an attorney present during questioning, and (3) have an attorney provided free of charge if the youth cannot afford to hire one. If the juvenile waives these rights, any statement he or she makes may be used in court against him or her. Generally, this warning is also given to the juvenile's parents so that they may assist in protecting their child's constitutional rights. After hearing all the evidence, the court may dismiss or continue the case or sustain the petition. If the petition is sustained, the court sets a date for the disposition hearing, or the judge may ask for the social investigation report and make an immediate disposition of the case.

The Disposition Hearing   The **disposition hearing** is the equivalent of the sentencing stage of the criminal court process. At this hearing the court decides what disposition is best for the child and for the community. In the early years of the juvenile court, dispositions were to be in the "best interests of the child." Thus, disposition hearings were informal, approached on a case-by-case basis, and intended to provide for the most appropriate treatment or rehabilitative strategy as a means to improve the lives of the children. Early dispositions were noncriminal, or civil, in nature and almost entirely indeterminate, whereby a judge could send a child to a state institution for an undetermined amount of time, often until the age of maturity.

The disposition hearing has retained many of the informal aspects that characterized the juvenile court system prior to the *Kent* and *Gault* decisions (discussed later in this chapter), although an increasing number of states are now using offense-based sentencing guidelines to determine appropriate sanctions. For example, in Washington State, the guidelines consider the seriousness of the offense and the juvenile's age, with younger, less serious offenders receiving more lenient sanctions.[28] In traditional disposition hearings, the judge, the probation officer, the prosecutor, the defense attorney, and the child's parents typically discuss available options. Hearsay evidence and opinions are admissible at this stage.

The judge may, to obtain more information, withhold disposition and continue the case; or the court may release the child into the custody of his or her parents or place the child on probation. Judges have a great deal of discretion at disposition. The most common disposition is probation; however, judges may sentence a youth to a correctional facility or other "out-of-home" placement. In addition, judges have a wide variety of alternative dispositions available, such as restitution, home detention, fines, and community service. If probation is the disposition, the juvenile may be referred to the probation department for formal or informal supervision. A child may also be removed from the custody of his or her parents and placed under the court's authority and be placed in a public or private facility or foster home.

Disposition decisions are made in regard to a relatively small number of juveniles, and youths who are evaluated for various disposition outcomes have already been processed through several decision points. As noted earlier, there were nearly 1.6 million juveniles eligible for referral to the juvenile court. Of these cases, 58 percent were petitioned to the juvenile court for an adjudicatory hearing (see Figure 14-3). Roughly 7,100, or 1 percent, of the petitioned cases were waived to criminal court, 32 percent were not adjudicated, and 67 percent were adjudicated as delinquent. The majority of adjudicated delinquents were placed on probation (62 percent); only 23 percent resulted in out-of-home placements, such as boot camp, ranch, privately operated facility, group home, or correctional institution.

figure 14-3   Juvenile Court Processing of Delinquency Cases, 2006

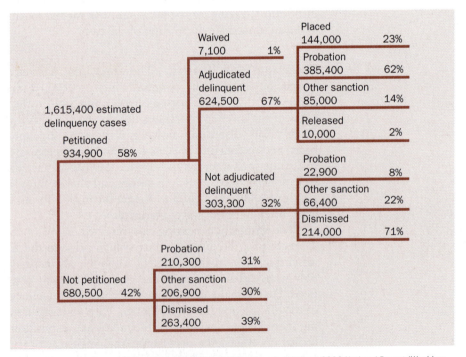

Source: Howard Snyder and Melissa Sickmund, *Juvenile Offenders and Victims: 2006 National Report* (Washington, DC: National Center for Juvenile Justice, 2006), p. 177.

Disparities in Adjudications and Dispositions Some scholars and critics have expressed concern regarding possible sex and racial disparities in court adjudications and dispositions.[29] John MacDonald and Meda Chesney-Lind report that, even though sex may not have an effect on early stages of the juvenile justice process when all relevant legal factors are controlled, once girls have been adjudicated delinquent they are more likely than boys to receive more severe dispositions than boys, especially for offenses reflecting female defiance, such as running away.[30] Unjustified disparities in particular communities have been reported in the literature, but the national statistics are less alarming. Males accounted for 74 percent of all delinquency cases handled by the juvenile courts, and cases involving males were slightly more likely than cases involving females to be adjudicated (63 versus 60 percent). Of petitioned youths, 67 percent of whites and 56 percent of African Americans were adjudicated.[31]

Minor discrepancies also appear in dispositions (see Table 14-2). Adjudicated cases involving males are more likely to result in out-of-home placement than cases involving females (25 versus 18 percent) and less likely to involve probation (61 versus 65 percent). Adjudicated cases involving African American youths are only slightly more likely to result in probation than those involving white youths (63 versus 62 percent) but much more likely to involve out-of-home placements (27 versus 21 percent).[32]

And, as noted earlier, national court statistics are typically compiled without controlling for the seriousness or context of the crime, the criminal histories of youths, the amount of harm or loss to victims in the current offense, or the youth's family or school situation. To the extent that disparities that cannot be explained by legally relevant factors exist, race and sex considerations may play

think about it

Few crimes result in arrest, a small number of cases progress through the courts, and many cases are dismissed. Why is the justice system so ineffective?

table 14-2 Percentage of Dispositions of Adjudicated Delinquency Cases

	OUT-OF-HOME PLACEMENT	FORMAL PROBATION
All cases	23%	62%
Offense		
Person	25	63
Property	23	63
Drugs	18	64
Public order	24	57
Age		
15 or younger	22	61
16 or older	25	65
Sex		
Male	25	61
Female	18	65
Race		
White	21	62
African American	27	63
Other	25	54

Source: Howard Snyder and Melissa Sickmund, *Juvenile Offenders and Victims: 2006 National Report* (Washington, DC: National Center for Juvenile Justice, 2006), pp. 174–175.

a part in the court decisions. Such concerns, in addition to the general concerns over the processing of juveniles, are best addressed by ensuring that the basic due process rights of all citizens accused of crimes apply to youths in juvenile court. But not all rights do apply, and those that do have been extended only since the mid-1960s. These concerns will be discussed a little later in this chapter.

ALTERNATIVES TO THE JUVENILE COURT

Not all youths referred to juvenile court are formally adjudicated; many have their cases dismissed, and still others end up in an alternative to the traditional juvenile court. A number of alternative courts, such as youth courts and drug courts, have emerged in the past two decades to allow for diversion from full and formal case processing. Another alternative is referral to a community-based restorative justice program. In this section we will explore these three alternatives to the juvenile court.

Youth Courts

Youth court, sometimes called teen court, peer jury, or student court, is an alternative to the traditional juvenile court, which allows young offenders to take responsibility for their acts, to be held accountable, and to receive appropriate dispositions imposed by their peers. Today, there are over 1,100 youth court programs operating in 49 states and the District of Columbia, serving between 110,000 to 125,000 youths each year, and allowing approximately 9 percent of juvenile arrests to be diverted from formal processing in the juvenile court.[33]

Youth courts not only function to divert minor delinquents from juvenile court, they also offer opportunities to large numbers of peers in the community to be involved in the decision-making process for dealing with the problem of delinquency and to learn about the juvenile justice system. Youths charged typically with minor offenses appear before their peers who perform many of the roles in a traditional juvenile court, for example, prosecutor, defense counsel, bailiff, and jury. Participation in youth court is voluntary, with referrals generally made by the police, schools, juvenile probation, or juvenile court.

About 92 percent of youth courts are *dispositional* and require an admission of guilt by the juvenile before his or her appearance in the court. The primary purpose of dispositional youth courts is to arrive at a fair and appropriate disposition after hearing the facts of the case. The remaining 8 percent of youth courts are adjudicatory and allow a youth to plead "not guilty" and have the peer jury determine the youth's responsibility.

While youth courts operate throughout the country, an increasing number of states have introduced legislation to make the courts more consistent and establish minimum standards for their operation. These statutes specify the kinds of cases to be heard, including the nature of the offense and prior record of the juvenile, as well as the types of dispositions that may be imposed. For example, many states limit the type of misdemeanors (that is, they will hear cases that carry only fines) and some states, such as Utah, exclude specific gang-related offenses. However, Mississippi gives its juvenile courts the discretion to refer *any appropriate case* to youth courts, while Rhode Island allows felony offenses to be referred to youth court but only with written consent by the chief justice of family court.

Juveniles referred to youth court are typically first-time offenders charged with minor misdemeanors, status offenses, or traffic violations. Thefts, minor assaults, disorderly conduct, alcohol violations, and vandalism are among the most typical offenses referred to youth courts.[34] Dispositions available to youth courts include written essays, apologies to victims, restitution, community service, and mandatory attendance at workshops dealing with crime, drugs, and safe driving. Youth courts in Mississippi may order youths to perform up to 112 hours of community service, apologize in person to the victim, write a research paper on an offense-related topic, or perform any other disposition authorized by the juvenile court. In West Virginia, dispositions include a requirement that the youth serve at least twice as a youth court juror.[35]

Drug Courts

Juvenile drug courts are a more recent innovation in the juvenile court alternatives basket, dating back to 1993 when the first court began operations in Key West, Florida. Today there are about 150 such courts. Most juvenile drug courts have been modeled on adult drug courts, although there are some differences in focus. For example, juvenile courts typically involve the youth's family in the treatment program.[36]

Juvenile **drug courts** are intensive treatment programs established within and supervised by juvenile courts to provide specialized services for eligible drug-involved youths and their families. The courts provide intensive and continuous judicial supervision over delinquency and status-offense cases that involve substance-abusing juveniles as well as coordinated and supervised delivery of a wide variety of support services. These services typically include substance abuse and mental health treatment, primary care, family therapy and support, literacy skills building, mentoring, education, and vocational training. Court members (including prosecutor, defense attorney, treatment provider, and school representative) act as a team in setting out a treatment plan. The key leader, however, is the judge who is generally frequently and directly involved with each youth on a face-to-face basis.

Most juvenile drug courts target juveniles who are moderate to heavy substance users and present no danger to the community. Sanctions typically used include the imposition or increase in curfew conditions, community service, and increased frequency of court and/or treatment contacts and/or random drug testing. Positive incentives are also used. These may include award of a gift voucher or a ticket to a local sporting event, presentation of a certificate or other token acknowledging the participant's accomplishments, and promotion to a subsequent program phase.[37]

Are drug courts an effective alternative to traditional juvenile courts in reducing recidivism, measured either by rearrests, reincarcerations, or renewed drug use? Studies of the effectiveness of adult drug courts, which have been in operation longer, suggest mixed results. While some studies find those who actually graduate from drug court have real success, many studies report no evidence of reductions in criminal and drug-related behavior.[38] In fact, Terance Miethe and his colleagues report that drug court is more stigmatizing than traditional court and that this leads to higher recidivism risks.[39]

Juvenile drugs courts also appear to have mixed effects, although most of the recent research suggests positive results for those youths who complete the drug court program.[40] However, a major concern noted in many evaluations is the low completion rate of youths participating in the programs. For example, Nancy Rodriguez and Vincent Webb report that the majority of juveniles in drug court were not successful at meeting program requirements and that most of these youths were subsequently placed on standard probation or sent to state-operated correctional facilities.[41] In their evaluation of the juvenile drug court in Maricopa County (Phoenix), Arizona, they found only 30 percent of youths successfully completed the program while 44 percent were institutionalized and 18 percent were placed on standard probation.

Restorative Justice

Restorative justice is a recent, and increasingly popular, alternative to both the traditional rehabilitative and more punitive juvenile justice paradigms.[42] According to Lynn Urban and her colleagues, both paradigms are "closed systems" focusing only on the offender and ignoring other important actors in the criminal event, such as victims and the community. In addition, they argue that current treatment and retributive approaches assume offenders are unable to proactively change and make amends.[43]

The focus of **restorative justice** is on restoring or repairing relationships disrupted by crime, holding offenders accountable by requiring restitution to victims or the community harmed by the crime, promoting offender competency and responsibility, and balancing the needs of community, victim, and offender through involvement in the restorative process. This entire process should be informal, nonadversarial, less punitive, less stigmatizing, and less costly than the current juvenile justice system.[44]

What Is Restorative Justice?

What Is Restorative Justice?   Recent implementations of restorative justice include a variety of approaches. For example, *victim–offender mediation programs* involve the participation of offenders and victims who have agreed to meet with a third-party mediator. The victim and offender relate their versions of what happened, and the mediator facilitates a reparative agreement. In *family group conferencing,* the offender admits the offense and then identifies a representative to attend a conference with a representative of the victim. After a discussion of the offense and the consequences for the involved parties, a plan of action is signed by the offender, victim, and police officer in charge of the case, specifying what will be done to repair the different harms. New Zealand now requires that disposition of all delinquency cases, except rape and murder, be resolved by family group conferencing. *Circle sentencing,* an updated approach originally practiced among aboriginal communities in British Columbia, Canada, and native groups in the southwestern United States, involves addressing both the criminal behavior of offending youths and the needs of their victims, the families, and the larger community. The victim, offender, representatives of the juvenile justice system, social service agencies, and community residents come together into a circle to discuss what happened, how each participant feels about the crime and offender, and their suggestions for responding to the crime and the needs of the victim and community. *Reparative probation,* used primarily in Vermont, allows nonviolent juvenile offenders to be sentenced by a hearing board composed of local citizens (and sometimes by the court) after generally private deliberation based on the board's earlier questioning of the offender and victim.[45]

Evaluation of Restorative Justice

Restorative justice programs have been operating for more than 25 years, although there have been relatively few rigorous evaluations of their effectiveness. In their review of studies looking at the impact of victim-offender mediation (VOM), Mark Umbreit and his colleagues report that

- Victims and offenders choosing to participate appear to have high levels of satisfaction with the program.
- Participants regard the proceedings as fair.
- Restitution is an element in most VOM agreements.
- About 80 percent of agreements are completed.
- VOM is at least as effective in reducing recidivism as traditional probation alternatives.
- VOM is less expensive than comparable programs.[46]

A quasi-experimental analysis of face-to-face restorative justice conferences in Australia and England also examined the impact of such programs on victims and concluded that such conferences appear to clearly assist victims in getting more of what they want out of the juvenile justice system. Victim participants report highly valuing the opportunity for meaningful involvement in their cases, including being able to ask questions they consider most important, learning just how their cases are being dealt with, and being treated with respect and fairness.[47]

Much of the attraction of restorative justice is its claim that punitive correctional approaches do significantly more harm than good. However, Sharon Levrant and her colleagues question whether restorative justice can ever really be achieved and whether it is really such a desirable alternative to current get-tough approaches to the problem of serious youth crime. They note that restorative justice advocates have failed to offer a realistic blueprint for crime control and the reduction of recidivism by serious, persistent offenders (see Chapters 2 and 3). Their criticisms include the following:

- Restorative justice systems fail to provide due process protections and procedural safeguards.
- Offenders may be coerced into participation, believing that refusal to participate in mediation will produce harsher punishments.
- Restorative justice programs may simply widen the net of the juvenile justice system to include minor offenders who would have been diverted otherwise.
- Restorative justice policies may add punishments for offenders by subjecting youths to both reparative conditions and traditional probation supervision.
- The focus on community reintegration of offenders and expanding the role of probation officers is not realistic given the current organization and limited resources of probation departments.
- There may be unintended race and class bias whereby more affluent offenders may be better able to mediate or negotiate more favorable sanctions.

think
about it

Is restorative justice an attempt to take the juvenile court back to the pre-*Kent* and *Gault* days when juveniles were handled informally, in nonadversarial hearings, and with few or no due process rights?

- Most restorative justice programs have targeted low-risk, nonviolent offenders who are unlikely to recidivate, and there is little evidence that these programs will work with more serious offenders.

- It is unlikely that restorative justice programs will have any long-term impact on altering an offender's criminogenic needs.

Levrant and her colleagues conclude, "Restorative justice remains an unproved movement that risks failure and perhaps does more harm than good. Its attractiveness lies more in its humanistic sentiments than in any empirical evidence of its effectiveness."[48]

Carol Gilligan has argued that males and females have different basic valuing systems that may affect how they are affected by rehabilitative programs (see Chapter 9). Gilligan believes males value independence, autonomy, justice, and fairness, while females value relationships and making connections.[49] If this is true, might there be a gendered effect in the impact of restorative justice programs? Lori Elis thinks so and suggests that to the extent restorative justice programs emphasize restoring relationships and strengthening social bonds, they are likely to have a greater positive impact on females. However, Elis warns that the informality of these programs and the potential for incorporating local community values based on patriarchal relationships and beliefs regarding conventional morality could also lead to a double standard regarding behavior. To the extent that this occurs, traditional gender roles are likely to be reinforced.[50]

Adam Crawford and Todd Clear raise a different set of concerns about restorative justice.[51] They suggest that restorative justice advocates assume a community consensus in response to delinquency, but those advocates fail to question just what the community *is*. What do advocates really mean by their wish to "restore" a community? A return to a preexisting state, a turning back of the clock, or a set of imagined historic traditions? In addition, to the extent that communities are hierarchical in nature, structured around power, dominance, and authority relations, will attempts to restore be able to truly bring about changes required to reduce youth crime? Moreover, not all communities are sufficiently homogeneous or integrated, nor do they all have similar resources needed to restore victims and reintegrate offenders. Perhaps more important, should young offenders who often have been the victims of abuse and marginalization by adult members of the community be expected to accept the dominant moral voice of the community as legitimate?

Inasmuch as restorative justice programs often operate outside the formal mechanisms of the juvenile justice system, it would seem reasonable to question their ability to protect the rights of juveniles accused of crimes. The informality and privacy of some restorative justice programs reflect, in many ways, the early years of the juvenile court. Unfortunately, that was also a period of denial of basic due process rights for juveniles. It is at this point that we will look at how the contemporary juvenile court provides for those rights.

DUE PROCESS ISSUES

Next we examine Supreme Court cases that have produced stronger safeguards of individual rights in juvenile court processing. The decisions in these cases are not grounded solely in legal considerations. Rather, the Court has closely examined an accumulated body of research about how the juvenile justice system really works.

The Right to Due Process

The issue of whether juveniles are protected in delinquency hearings by basic due process guarantees was first considered by the Supreme Court in 1966 in ***Kent v. United States*** (see Box 14-3), which involved a juvenile court judge's decision to waive jurisdiction and transfer a case from juvenile to criminal court without a hearing.[52]

Kent set the stage for ***In re Gault,***[53] a case handed down in 1967 which many regard as one of the most important decisions in juvenile justice. Even today, the elements of *Gault* can still shock. Gerald Gault, a 15-year-old boy, was arrested with another boy and charged with making lewd phone calls to a woman in the neighborhood. At the initial hearing, the complainant did not appear, and no transcript or record of the hearing was made. At a second hearing, with the complainant still not present, the judge found Gault to be delinquent, and he was committed to the state industrial school.

The U.S. Supreme Court overturned the verdict in a 9-to-0 decision, stating that due process rights should be applied to juveniles (see Box 14-4). Throughout the incident, both police and the court acted with almost no regard for due process. Whatever was done was justified by the doctrine of *parens patriae:* It was all for the "best welfare" of the child. Gerald Gault's "welfare" required that he be committed to the Arizona Industrial School for an indeterminate sentence. Under usual court procedure, this commitment would end at age 21. Therefore, Gerald Gault, who was 15, could have been deprived of liberty for 6 years.

---

box 14-3   FROM THE BENCH

Kent v. United States

Sixteen-year-old Morris Kent was accused of robbery, housebreaking, and rape. After an initial hearing, the juvenile court judge decided to waive Kent to adult court without giving reasons for the waiver. Kent was tried, found guilty, and sentenced to 90 years in prison. The defense appealed on the grounds that the juvenile judge should not have waived Kent to adult court without giving him a hearing, providing his attorney access to reports, and presenting a statement of reasons for the waiver.

In a 5-to-4 vote, the Supreme Court overturned Kent's conviction. The Court stated that since Kent could face the death penalty in adult court compared with only a maximum of 5 years in juvenile court, the waiver was of "critical importance" to him. Therefore, he should have been entitled to access to all reports on him, a hearing, and a statement of reasons if he was to be waived. The Court further stated that not letting Kent's attorney look at the reports was the same as a denial of counsel. The Court ruled that a hearing is necessary before a case in juvenile court can be waived to criminal court and that such a hearing should be guided by the "essentials of due process."

Source: Kent v. United States, 383 U.S. 541 (1966).

box 14-4   FROM THE BENCH

In re Gault

Gerald Gault, a 15-year-old boy, was arrested and charged with making lewd phone calls to a woman in the neighborhood. At the initial hearing, the complainant did not appear and no transcript or record of the hearing was made. At a second hearing, the complainant still was not present. After this hearing, Gault was found to be delinquent and committed to the state industrial school for a period of 5 years. On appeal to the Supreme Court, the defense stated that the juvenile court erred because the defendant had been denied the basic rights of due process guaranteed by the Fourteenth Amendment.

The U.S. Supreme Court overturned the verdict in a 9-to-0 decision, stating that due process rights should have been applied to juveniles. If Gault had been an adult, the maximum penalty would have been 2 months in jail. However, as a delinquent, he faced possible incarceration until the age of majority, or 6 years. While the juvenile court is intended to help the child by its informality, it did not do so in this case. The Court decided that the juvenile court system would be enhanced, not hindered, by granting certain due process rights to juveniles.

Source: In re Gault, 387 U.S. 1 (1967).

Justice Fortas, writing the majority opinion for the Court, was unimpressed by any appeal to *parens patriae*. He argued that "the basic requirements of due process and fairness" must be satisfied in juvenile proceedings. Fortas summed up his position by saying, "Neither the Fourteenth Amendment nor the Bill of Rights is for adults only."[54] From this premise he proceeded to challenge the very essence of the juvenile court's operation. The court's position that its activities worked for the good of the child was shown to be suspect, and its procedure, in fact, violated fundamental rights. In Fortas's own words, "Under our Constitution, the condition of being a boy does not justify a kangaroo court."[55]

Fortas argued that the proper goal of the juvenile court would not be impaired by constitutional requirements. In fact, he felt that the essentials of due process would express a fair and responsive attitude toward the juvenile. Fortas then set out the essentials of due process and described how they should apply to the adjudicatory hearing in a juvenile proceeding:

1. The juvenile has a right to counsel and to court-appointed counsel, if necessary.

2. With the aid of counsel, the child can present his or her defense and confront witnesses, who must present testimony under oath through cross-examination.

3. The child also has the right to confront his or her accuser as well as a right against self-incrimination. Since his or her freedom is at stake, this right has a special urgency.

4. To make use of the available elements of defense, the child has a right to timely notice of the charges against him or her.

The spectrum of rights elaborated in the *Gault* decision is impressive. However, the ruling has noticeable limitations. The *Gault* decision was specifically applied to the adjudicatory hearing, at which guilt or innocence is determined. The decision *did not* apply to the court intake hearing, at which the initial decision to invoke juvenile court jurisdiction is made; nor did it apply to the final stage of the process, the disposition hearing, at which the decision about what to do with the child is made.

Right to Counsel

Gault established that in adjudication proceedings the Court *must* notify both the juvenile and his or her parents of their right to retain counsel and, if indigent, to have court-appointed counsel. However, as already noted, the Court did not specify whether the right to counsel extends to other hearings, such as disposition hearings or proceedings involving nondelinquency cases. While most state juvenile codes now provide children with a statutory right to counsel, it appears that few states ensure effective legal counsel in delinquency proceedings. Barry Feld notes that many jurisdictions fail to appoint counsel or even to notify youths and their parents of the right to counsel. He also reports that lawyers represented 37 to 52 percent of the juveniles in delinquency and status offense cases in three states surveyed during the mid-1980s.[56]

Even when juveniles are represented by counsel, there are serious concerns regarding the quality and effectiveness of counsel. George Burruss and Kimberly Kempf-Leonard studied three juvenile courts in Missouri and found legal representation for juvenile felony defendants was "relatively uncommon" in all three jurisdictions; in addition, there appeared to be a significant negative effect in cases where juveniles were represented by counsel. Youths in all three courts were more likely to receive out-of-home placements when they were represented by counsel, and this finding held true even as cases escalated in seriousness as the youths' prior records got longer. The researchers speculate that these disparities may be the result of more incompetent attorneys being assigned to represent juveniles, that attorneys may be retained too late in the process in juvenile cases, and that because attorneys in juvenile cases are relatively rare, their appearance in court disrupts the traditional operation of the courtroom workgroup.[57] Alternatively, Janet Ainsworth reports that many attorneys in juvenile proceedings fail to contest prosecutors' claims, provide "lackadaisical defense efforts," rarely call defense witnesses, and provide only perfunctory cross-examination of prosecution witnesses.[58]

Judith Jones suggests that access to effective counsel for juveniles is frustrated by a number of factors. Among them are the following:

- *Caseloads.* The number of cases in the juvenile courts increased 23 percent between 1990 and 1999, resulting in too few defense attorneys available to handle delinquency cases. For example, the caseloads in Louisiana are as high as 800 per year for attorneys in the juvenile courts, and in Washington they range between 360 and 750.

- *Compensation.* Compensation levels for attorneys who represent juveniles are inadequate in many jurisdictions. For example, in Louisiana, compensation for public defenders and court-appointed defense attorneys representing juveniles ranges from $22,000 to $30,000 per year, and in Maine juvenile defense attorneys are paid $50 per hour, but there is a cap of $315 per case.

- *Use of motions.* Defense attorneys rarely file motions on behalf of their juvenile clients. For example, only 30 percent of public defenders and court-appointed attorneys surveyed by the American Bar Association Juvenile Justice Center said they filed pretrial motions.

- *Use of investigations.* Juvenile defense attorneys infrequently conduct investigations prior to court hearings. For example, in North Carolina, 44 percent of attorneys surveyed reported they rarely or never see the police report or other investigative material prior to their first meeting with their client.

- *Training.* Training designed to increase the knowledge and skills of juvenile defense attorneys rarely takes place. For example, Georgia has no training standards for juvenile defense attorneys and no funding for training and continuing education, and in Maryland, public defenders handling juvenile cases are offered a one-week training program twice a year (in 2002, only 19 attorneys attended classes in juvenile defense).[59]

Not being represented by counsel in court is even more problematic. A number of studies indicate that juveniles who are represented by counsel are placed at a distinct disadvantage compared to youths without counsel. For instance, when compared to youths not represented by counsel, youths represented by counsel are about three times more likely to receive severe dispositions, they are more likely to have their cases dismissed, and they are less likely to face confinement.[60] In addition, a recent study by Lori Guevara and her colleagues found that the presence or absence of counsel has slightly different effects depending on the race of the juvenile. Specifically, they report that white youths represented by counsel are less likely than white youths without counsel to receive probation and more likely to be incarcerated. In addition, minority youths with counsel are more likely to receive probation and less likely to be incarcerated. They note that "presence of legal counsel may be seen as an aggravating legal factor for white youths and a mitigating legal factor for nonwhite youths.[61]

Burden of Proof

Three years after *Gault,* the Court dealt with the question of "whether proof beyond a reasonable doubt is among the 'essentials of due process and fair treatment' required during the adjudicatory stage when a juvenile is charged with an act which would constitute a crime if committed by an adult," in ***In re Winship.***[62] Samuel Winship, a 12-year-old boy, was accused of stealing $112 from a woman's pocketbook. The juvenile court judge stated that the evidence did not provide for a verdict of guilty beyond a reasonable doubt but that there was a preponderance of evidence indicating that the juvenile had committed the act. The defense appealed on the ground that juveniles should have to be proven guilty beyond a reasonable doubt according to due process guarantees in the Constitution (see Box 14-5). In a 6-to-3 vote, the Supreme Court decided that juveniles have the constitutional right to be convicted only when there is *proof beyond a reasonable doubt.* The Court's reasoning was that even though juvenile court proceedings are civil and not criminal in nature, the juvenile still holds the risk of losing his or her individual freedom and there should not be a reasonable doubt of his guilt.[63]

---

box 14-5   **FROM THE BENCH**

In re Winship

amuel Winship, a 12-year-old boy, was accused of stealing $112 from a woman's pocketbook. The juvenile court judge stated that the evidence did not support a verdict of guilty beyond a reasonable doubt but that there was a preponderance of evidence indicating that the juvenile had committed the act. Winship was found delinquent and placed in a training school for an initial period of 18 months, which could be expanded until Winship reached the age of 18. The defense appealed on the ground that juveniles should have to be proved guilty beyond a reasonable doubt according to the due process guarantees of the Constitution.

In a 6-to-3 decision, the Supreme Court held that juveniles have the constitutional right to be found delinquent only when there is proof beyond a reasonable doubt. The Court reasoned that even though juvenile proceedings are civil and not criminal in nature, the juvenile still holds the risk of losing his or her individual freedom and thus there should not be a reasonable doubt of guilt.

Source: In re Winship, 397 U.S. 358 (1970).

The issue of burden of proof is also relevant in arguing whether younger adolescents should be charged or petitioned for criminal acts. For example, California law presumes that a child under age 14 is incapable of committing a crime, but this presumption is rebuttable. This is called the *infancy defense*. But should a child under age 14 be held to the same standard of criminal responsibility as older and more experienced adolescents and adults? In a 1994 decision, the California Supreme Court ruled that the state needed only to show "clear proof," not proof beyond a reasonable doubt, that at the time a minor committed a crime he or she knew it was wrong in order to proceed with a delinquency petition.[64]

Jury Trial

The issue of whether juveniles have a right to a jury trial in delinquency cases was reviewed by the Supreme Court in 1971 in **McKeiver v. Pennsylvania.**[65] Proponents argued that children convicted by the juvenile court are subject to incarceration. Therefore, since a jury trial is a constitutional right afforded people accused in criminal proceedings in which their liberty is at issue, juveniles should have the same right since their liberty also is at stake. Joseph McKeiver, a 16-year-old, was arrested after he and three other juveniles chased 20 to 30 youths and stole 25 cents from them. McKeiver was charged with robbery, larceny, and receiving stolen property. At the adjudication hearing, McKeiver's request for a jury trial was denied. Even though the testimony of two of the victims was inconsistent, McKeiver was found delinquent and was placed on probation. The defense appealed on the grounds that his Sixth Amendment right to a jury trial had been denied.

The Supreme Court, in a 9-to-0 decision, stated that juveniles *do not* have a right to a jury trial (see Box 14-6). The judges reasoned that *juveniles are not guaranteed every constitutional right,* that a jury trial would make a juvenile

Joseph McKeiver, a 16-year-old boy, was arrested after he and three other juveniles chased 20 to 30 children and stole 25 cents from them. McKeiver's request for a jury trial was denied. The case was then appealed on the ground that his Sixth Amendment right to a jury trial had been denied.

The U.S. Supreme Court, in a 9-to-0 decision, held that juveniles do not have a right to a jury trial. The judges reasoned that juveniles are not guaranteed every constitutional right, that a jury trial would make a juvenile proceeding fully adversarial, and that a jury trial is not necessary in order to have a fair hearing.

Source: *McKeiver v. Pennsylvania,* 403 U.S. 528 (1971).

proceeding fully adversarial, and that a jury trial is not necessary in order to have a fair hearing. Writing the majority opinion, Justice Harry Blackmun expressed fear that the introduction of juries would "remake the juvenile proceedings into a fully adversary process and [would] put an effective end to what [had] been the idealistic prospect of an intimate, informal protective proceeding." [66] The Court decided that a jury trial is an adult right that is not essential in juvenile proceedings. In fact, the majority played down the value of the jury in any trial, whether juvenile or criminal. The jury trial does not ensure competence in the fact-finding function of the proceedings. In the context of the juvenile proceeding, the right to a jury trial could be a distinctly negative factor because it carries with it the traditional delay, formality, and clamor of the adversary system. The majority felt that the states should be allowed to have jury trials in their own juvenile proceedings if they wished, but that such a decision would in no way be based on constitutional mandate.

Because *McKeiver did not* prohibit states from allowing trials for juveniles, a number of states permit jury trials if juveniles request them; two states permit the judge to order a jury trial; and in one state, habitual offenders may be granted jury trials. [67] In 1999, the Appellate Court of Illinois held that a juvenile charged with first-degree murder and tried in the juvenile court may not be denied a jury trial. In this case, G.O., a 13-year-old, was arrested and charged in the shooting death of Rafael Kubera. His attorney requested a jury trial and was denied because the statute under which he was charged provided for jury trials only when a juvenile is facing a determinant sentence. G.O. was found delinquent and committed to the Department of Corrections until age 21. The Court reasoned that because G.O. was neither eligible for parole nor good-time credit, the sentence was punitive and determinant and the youth should have been afforded a jury trial. [68]

Double Jeopardy

In 1975, in **Breed v. Jones,** the Supreme Court unanimously ruled that the Fifth Amendment's prohibition against **double jeopardy** forbids criminal prosecution of a juvenile after he or she has been tried in juvenile court for the same offense. [69]

Gary Jones, a 17-year-old, was accused of robbery. In this case, Gary Jones was made a ward of a California court on the basis of evidence showing that he had committed the robbery he had been charged with, and he was ordered detained pending a disposition hearing. On the date of the hearing, the court announced that because Jones was "not . . . amenable to the care, treatment and training program available through the facilities of the juvenile court" it intended to waive jurisdiction and transfer the case to the criminal court. In adult court, Jones was tried and found guilty of robbery. Jones's attorney appealed on the ground that Jones's Fifth Amendment rights had been violated because the juvenile hearing plus the adult trial constituted double jeopardy (see Box 14-7).

The U.S. Supreme Court, in a 9-to-0 opinion, held that the two procedures did constitute double jeopardy, and the ruling overturned the adult court's verdict. The Court's reasoning was that a juvenile runs the risk of losing his freedom in a juvenile court for many years and therefore is put in jeopardy, thus making a second trial double jeopardy.

The Right to Bail and Preventive Detention

The Eighth Amendment guarantee that "excessive bail shall not be required" is well established for adults charged with crimes. But what about juveniles, should juvenile courts use a different system for release and supervision prior to adjudication hearings? To be released by the court is understood to be a privilege, not a right. Juveniles *do not* have a federal or state constitutional right to bail, although some states, by statute, extend the Eighth Amendment right to juveniles to be released the same as adults charged with similar crimes. In some states, such as Nebraska, juvenile court judges are given the discretion to grant bail to juveniles; but other states, such as Oregon, specifically deny juveniles the right to bail.[70] Nebraska law allows for juveniles to be granted "bail by bond in

---

box 14-7   **FROM THE BENCH**

Breed v. Jones

Gary Jones, a 17-year-old boy, was accused of robbery. There was a hearing in juvenile court in which the judge found that Jones had committed the robbery. At the juvenile's disposition hearing, the judge decided that the juvenile should be transferred to adult court because he was "unfit" for the juvenile court. In adult court, Jones was tried and found guilty of robbery. Jones's attorney appealed on the ground that his Fifth Amendment rights had been violated because the juvenile hearing plus the adult trial constituted double jeopardy.

The U.S. Supreme Court, in a 9-to-0 decision, held that the two procedures did constitute double jeopardy and overturned Jones's criminal court conviction. The Court's reasoning was that a juvenile runs the risk of losing his freedom in a juvenile court for many years and therefore is put in jeopardy, thus making a second trial double jeopardy.

Source: Breed v. Jones, 421 U.S. 519 (1975).

such amount and on such conditions and security as the court, in its sole discretion, shall determine." Hawaii law states, "Provisions regarding bail shall not be applicable to children detained . . . except that bail may be allowed after a child has been transferred for criminal prosecution pursuant to waiver of family court jurisdiction." And the Georgia statute maintains, "All juveniles subject to the jurisdiction of the juvenile court and alleged to be delinquent or unruly, on application of the parent or guardian, shall have the same right to bail as adults."[71]

The landmark case that involves preventive detention centers on Gregory Martin, a 14-year-old, was accused of robbery and assault. He was detained prior to his adjudication hearing because the judge considered him to be at risk of committing an additional crime. At the hearing, he was found guilty and placed on probation. Martin then brought a class action suit, claiming that the court's policy of preventive detention violated the due process clause of the Fourteenth Amendment. In 1984, in *Schall v. Martin,* the U.S. Supreme Court held that preventive detention of juveniles was constitutional and articulated three primary justifications for its use (see Box 14-8).[72] These include the legitimate and compelling state interest in

1. Protecting the community from crime.
2. Protecting the juvenile from his or her own "folly" and the consequences of criminal activity.
3. Preventing the child from absconding.

Preventive detention of juveniles was determined to be constitutional when the Court upheld a New York statute authorizing the pretrial detention of an accused juvenile who, if released, may pose a "serious risk" by committing the equivalent of an adult crime. In the majority opinion, the Court held that

- While the statute provided for a detention hearing, a formal finding that there was probable cause to believe that the youth committed the offense for which he or she was arrested was not required prior to his or her detention.

---

box 14-8 **FROM THE BENCH**

Schall v. Martin

Gregory Martin, a 14-year-old boy, was charged with robbery and assault. He was detained for 15 days prior to his adjudication hearing because the judge considered him to be at risk of committing an additional crime. At the hearing, Martin was found guilty and placed on probation. Martin then brought a class action suit, claiming that the court's policy of preventive detention violated the due process clause of the Fourteenth Amendment.

The U.S. Supreme Court, in a 6-to-3 decision, held that the preventive detention policy served a legitimate state objective and did, in fact, satisfy the due process clause. One justification for the decision was that even though juveniles have gained many of the constitutional rights provided to adults, they have not been granted all of them.

Source: Schall v. Martin, 467 U.S. 253 (1984).

- The protection of society is an important goal in itself, and thus, preventive detention of juveniles is permissible.
- The juvenile justice system has no obligation to *treat* juvenile offenders.
- Preventive detention was justified for juveniles because, "children, by definition, are not assumed to have the capacity to take care of themselves." They are assumed to always be subject to the control of someone, such as their parents, guardians, or the state.[73]

PUBLIC ACCESS TO JUVENILE COURT PROCEEDINGS AND RECORDS

The cases discussed in the previous section focused on fundamental due process issues in the juvenile court. Although these decisions brought significant changes in terms of court procedure, they *did not* open the courts to the public. Most states continue to have limited public access to juvenile court proceedings and juvenile records, and many states maintain confidentiality of juveniles' names. However, public and political expressions of concern over the increasingly serious nature of juvenile crime have led to significant changes in recent years. The Supreme Court noted in *Breed v. Jones* that individuals face deprivations in both the adult and juvenile systems and that "in terms of potential consequences, there is little to distinguish an adjudicatory hearing . . . from a traditional criminal prosecution."[74] To what extent should juvenile courts lose their special protections of confidentiality and consequently thrust youths into the public spotlight?

Right to Public Hearings

Since the mid-1980s, many state legislatures made significant changes in how information about juvenile offenders is treated by the justice system. Today, 14 states have delinquency hearings open to the public. However, the courts may close hearings to the public when it is in the best interests of the child and the public. Twenty-one states open delinquency hearings for some types of cases according to age–offense criteria, typically, when the youth is charged with a serious or violent offense or if the youth is a chronic offender.[75] These changes range from allowing people or agencies with a "legitimate interest" to attend hearings to permitting the media to attend and publish stories about the proceedings.

Media Involvement

Most states permit the release of certain juveniles' names or photographs to the media, but a few still forbid publication of the juvenile's name or other identifying information, although they do not prohibit the presence of the media at hearings. At least 8 states allow the media to be present at hearings and to publish information about them, although not information identifying the juvenile. This approach is particularly popular with people who contend that private hearings make abuses of authority by the juvenile court judge more likely.

They believe that allowing the media to monitor hearings effectively restrains the abuse of power.

Supreme Court decisions have largely eroded the state's power to limit publication of lawfully obtained information. In 1974, in *Davis v. Alaska,* the Court ruled that a lower court had erred in issuing a protective order prohibiting cross-examination of a juvenile about his prior juvenile court involvement and present probation status.[76] In *Oklahoma Publishing Company v. District Court,* the Court struck down a state court injunction prohibiting the media from publishing the name or photograph of an 11-year-old boy being tried before a juvenile court.[77] The Supreme Court held that once information is "publicly revealed" or "in the public domain," its publication or broadcast cannot be restrained. In *Smith v. Daily Mail Publishing Company,* the Supreme Court further eroded the principle that the media must not disclose the identity of a juvenile, ruling that when information is lawfully obtained, the state cannot prohibit its publication.[78]

Confidentiality of Juvenile Records

Nearly all states have statutes specifying circumstances in which juvenile records may be made available to the public. Under these statutes, juvenile records pertaining to certain crimes or cases may be made part of the public record or made public in some other way. The crimes specified are typically violent or otherwise serious offenses, but sometimes more minor crimes are included. Although a few states prohibit release of the names of all juvenile offenders, at least 9 states allow the records of any public court proceedings to be made available to the public without qualifying restrictions. In several states, the court is required to release the names of juveniles adjudicated delinquent for committing certain serious offenses or repeat offenses, as well as the nature of the crimes involved. A few states also allow victims or other people potentially in danger from the youth to access the court record or at least to be informed of the youth's name and address and the outcome of the case.[79]

Destruction of Records

More than one-half of the states have provisions that permit destruction of certain juvenile court records. These statutes generally allow for the sealing or destruction of social-history files or arrest records. Docket sheets and official court files are maintained, although they may be sealed or placed in a restricted area. Many people argue for complete destruction of all juvenile records, contending that unless the records are destroyed, certain information will inevitably "leak" and harm the youth. However, others argue that total destruction of these records may place a juvenile in a more vulnerable position. After all, the conduct that brought a juvenile to court may be less serious than the label attached to his or her behavior.

Although it is sometimes argued that when an adult is facing a criminal charge, his or her juvenile record should not be considered, an increasing number of states have moved to restrict the expungement or sealing of juvenile records or to forbid entirely those restrictions on information about youths adjudicated delinquent. In a number of states, not only is the destruction or sealing of juvenile records prohibited, the law now requires that the juvenile record be taken into account in determining sentencing of an adult.

TRANSFER OF SERIOUS OFFENDERS TO CRIMINAL COURT

There is no doubt that very young people are committing more serious and violent crime than 40 or 50 years ago. Although delinquency rates during the past few years are significantly lower than in the mid-1990s, serious delinquency, especially youth violence, continues to be viewed as senseless, vicious, spontaneous, and broadly threatening (see Chapter 3). Many people and policy makers increasingly believe that handling such serious, violent youths in the juvenile justice system is not the answer to the problem. The old system, emphasizing treatment and concern for offender privacy, is believed not only to be outmoded but to be dangerous in terms of community safety. Consequently, an increasing number of juveniles are transferred to criminal court for prosecution as adult offenders.

In response to demands for getting tough and holding serious juvenile offenders responsible, many states made changes making it easier for juveniles to be transferred to criminal court to be tried as adults. Changes include the following:

- Lowering the age for waiver, for example, dropping the minimum age from 15 to 14.
- Expanding the list of crimes eligible for waiver.
- Establishing "presumptive waiver" provisions requiring that certain offenders be transferred unless they can prove they are suitable for juvenile rehabilitation.
- Excluding certain offenses from juvenile court jurisdiction, such as violent crimes against the person.
- Adding prior record provisions making certain repeat offenders eligible for waiver.
- Requiring that once an offender is waived from juvenile court or is convicted in criminal court, all subsequent cases are under criminal court jurisdiction.
- Lowering the maximum age of juvenile court jurisdiction, for example, from 18 to 16 or 15, thus allowing criminal courts to prosecute younger offenders without the need for the waiver process.[80]

Even Congress, when it passed its crime control legislation in 1994, lowered the minimum age for transferring juveniles for adult prosecution from age 15 to age 13 for certain serious violent federal offenses.[81] Over the past decade, nearly half of the states expanded their transfer laws in some way. Many states lowered the minimum age for transfer, while a few states narrowed the scope of their waiver provisions. Table 14-3 lists the youngest ages for transfer in each state.

Reasons for Transferring Juveniles

There are three primary reasons for transferring juveniles to criminal court. The first involves the seriousness of the offense. Most serious juvenile offenders, particularly those who have committed violent crimes, can be prosecuted by the criminal courts where harsher punishments, including the death penalty, may be imposed.

table 14-3 Minimum Age for Judicial Waiver to Criminal Court	
No minimum age specified	Alaska, Arizona, Delaware, District of Columbia, Hawaii, Idaho, Indiana, Maine, Maryland, Oklahoma, Oregon, Rhode Island, South Carolina, South Dakota, Tennessee, Washington, West Virginia
10	Kansas, Vermont
12	Colorado, Missouri
13	Georgia, Illinois, Mississippi, New Hampshire, North Carolina, Wyoming
14	Alabama, Arkansas, California, Connecticut, Florida, Iowa, Kentucky, Louisiana, Michigan, Minnesota, Nevada, New Jersey, North Dakota, Ohio, Pennsylvania, Texas, Utah, Virginia, Wisconsin

Note: Minimum ages may not apply to all criminal offense restrictions, but represent the youngest possible age at which a juvenile may be judicially waived to criminal court.

Source: Howard Snyder and Melissa Sickmund, *Juvenile Offenders and Victims: 2006 National Report* (Washington, DC: National Center for Juvenile Justice, 2006), p. 112.

Second, youths who are older and have extensive criminal records are believed by juvenile justice officials to be not as amenable to treatment programs provided in the juvenile justice system. Their patterns of delinquent behavior and responses to the juvenile justice system suggest that either the programs are not effective or the youths are not responsive to the treatment efforts of rehabilitative staff.[82] It is believed that the more punitive environment of adult prisons may have a positive impact on these youths by giving them a taste of adult punishment.

A third reason stems from society's frustration with serious juvenile offenders. Many citizens and criminologists are uncertain about the need for harsher punishments or the ability of adult corrections to rehabilitate these youths effectively, but they argue that long-term incarceration will at least remove these offenders from the streets for a longer period of time.

Legal Criteria for Transfer

In the *Kent* case, the Supreme Court stated there is no constitutional requirement for a separate juvenile court system; it would therefore be constitutional if states wished to prosecute juveniles and adults within a single system. However, the Court held that when such a juvenile court system is authorized by statute, a juvenile may not be deprived of his or her constitutional rights (for example, being transferred to criminal court) without ceremony. Specifically, in *Kent,* the Court stated that "there is no place in our legal system for reaching a verdict of such tremendous consequences without a waiver hearing, without effective assistance of counsel, and without a statement of the reasons"[83] for transfer of a youth. The Court was also rather critical of juvenile court procedures in general, suggesting that juvenile courts had failed to achieve its goal of rehabilitating youth in a separate judicial system. The Court stated, "There is evidence, in fact, that there may be grounds for concern that the child receives the worst of both worlds: that he gets neither the protections accorded to adults nor the solicitous care and regenerative treatment postulated for children."[84]

Along with his older brother Derek, Alex King, 13, pleaded guilty to third-degree murder and received seven years in prison for the slaying of his father. It was later discovered that the boys were induced to murder their father by an adult male who was sexually abusing Alex. Even in cases of murder, is the prosecution of children as adults ever a cut and dry case? What circumstances about the King case mitigate their lethal behavior? Who was the greater villain in this case, the boys or their abuser? Does this change your thinking about waiving children and adolescents to criminal court?

The Transfer Process

Three procedures are used for transferring youths to criminal court: judicial waiver, statutory exclusion, and prosecutorial waiver or direct file. These transfer methods are also known as *certification* or *remands* to criminal court.

Judicial Waiver   Historically, **judicial waiver,** in which the juvenile court judge is the primary decision maker, has been the most common method for transferring youths to criminal courts. It is seen as the method most consistent with traditional juvenile justice philosophy. In all states except Massachusetts, Montana, Nebraska, New Mexico, and New York, juvenile court judges may waive jurisdiction over certain cases and transfer them to criminal court.[85]

The judge, acting according to the philosophy of the *parens patriae* that guides the philosophy of the juvenile court, is believed to be in the best position to consider all relevant issues of the case. The judicial waiver method requires that the state file a motion for waiver of jurisdiction to have the juvenile tried as an adult. The court then holds a waiver or transfer hearing to determine whether a transfer is in the best interests of the child and the community.

t h i n k
about it

Should there be a
defense attorney
waiver in which the
defender of the accused
acknowledges that
certain individuals are
beyond rehabilitation? If
such a waiver did exist,
would it be used?

Statutory Exclusion   Many states have established the use of the **statutory exclusion,** whereby the most serious or persistent offenders or those over a certain age are excluded from juvenile court jurisdiction and prosecuted as adults. This procedure is based on the idea that "the 'right' of a juvenile to be in juvenile court is entirely a statutory right. It is something that is granted by legislative largess and can be summarily eliminated." [86] Or, to state it differently, some states have chosen to take away some youths' "right" to have their cases heard in juvenile court.

In 1978 New York State representatives passed get-tough legislation against violent juvenile crime. These policy makers were reacting, in part, to the increased use of 13-, 14-, and 15-year-olds by adults for the commission of serious crimes, including contract murder. If the youths were caught, the old law required that they be subject to the rehabilitative orientation of the family court, and there was no judicial procedure for transferring youths to criminal court. The new legislation lowered the age of criminal responsibility to 13 for murder and to 14 for a number of other violent and potentially violent acts, such as arson, rape, and robbery, and the criminal courts were given original jurisdiction over these offenders. [87] All 16-year-olds in New York State automatically come under the jurisdiction of the criminal courts.

Prosecutorial Waiver   The **prosecutorial waiver,** or *direct file,* gives the prosecutor the authority to decide whether to file a charge against a juvenile in criminal court. Prosecutorial waivers are used in at least 15 states. In these states, the prosecutor possesses concurrent jurisdiction over most cases involving violations of criminal law and has the discretion to file charges in either juvenile or criminal court. For example, the prosecutor may choose to file a serious charge in criminal court against a juvenile meeting the minimum-age criterion or to file the charge in the juvenile court.

Twenty-five states provide some mechanism, typically known as a **reverse waiver,** whereby a juvenile who is being prosecuted as an adult in criminal court may petition to have the case transferred to juvenile court for adjudication or disposition. Generally, if the juvenile was transferred to criminal court by direct file or statutory exclusion, the court would evaluate the petition for reverse waiver on the same grounds and using the same standards that the juvenile court would use in deciding whether to waive the youth to criminal court. In states such as Kentucky, Mississippi, and Tennessee, reverse waivers are authorized only if the juvenile court's decision to initially waive the juvenile was groundless or if other "exceptional circumstances" could be shown.

Interestingly, some states provide for a **demand waiver,** whereby a juvenile may request to have his or her case transferred *from* juvenile court *to* criminal court. Such requests are uncommon and are typically used when a youth desires to have a jury trial, believing that he or she will more likely be acquitted by a jury, or when the sentence in criminal court would be substantially shorter than one likely to be imposed by the juvenile court.

Who Is Transferred?

Just under 1 percent (about 7,000) of all petitioned delinquency cases are judicially waived to criminal court. [88] In most states, except in those that use statutory exclusion based on a youth's age or offense, the majority of juveniles who

At 15, Charles "Andy" Williams went on a shooting rampage at Santana High School near San Diego, killing 2 and wounding 13. He was sentenced to 50 years in prison. Can school shooters be prevented?

meet the statutory requirements for transfer are not transferred or even formally considered for waiver hearings.[89] Given the discretion of prosecutors, what characteristics are most important in determining who gets transferred?

Property cases outnumbered person offenses among juveniles waived to criminal court up until 1993. Between 1993 and 2002, the trend reversed and person offenses accounted for a greater proportion of waived cases. Drug and public order offenses continued to account for an increasingly smaller proportion of waived cases. For example, only 14 percent of juveniles waived to criminal court were charged with drug offenses and 9 percent were charged with public order offenses.[90]

There may be no greater disparity in juvenile justice processing than that found in sex differences in waiver. Males are significantly more likely than females to be waived to criminal court, comprising 93 percent of all waived cases. More than 87 percent of waived cases involve juveniles who were age 16 or older at the time of court referral. Significant disparities are also found in the race of the waived juveniles. According to the most recent data, white youths accounted for 62 percent of waived cases; African American youths, 35 percent of the cases; and youths of other races, 3 percent. White youths are more likely to be waived for property offenses, while African American youths are more likely to be waived for drug offenses.[91]

Transferred juveniles are more likely than nontransferred youths to have been charged with serious offenses, used firearms, caused the death of victims, or had prior arrests, adjudications, and commitments.[92] For example, in South Carolina, 32 percent of transferred youths had five or more prior court referrals, 26 percent had three or more prior adjudications, and 15 percent had two or more prior court-ordered residential placements. In Utah, 80 percent of youths approved for waiver had five or more prior referrals, 81 percent had five or more prior adjudications, and 78 percent had three or more prior court-ordered residential placements.[93]

Some critics of the transfer of juveniles to criminal court argue that transferred youths are likely to have impaired competence-related abilities compared to adult offenders. To the extent that adolescents, when compared to adults, are significantly more immature in their judgment, less competent, and less able to fully understand the legal proceedings in criminal court and their likely consequences, they are put at a great disadvantage.[94] Norman Poythress and his colleagues studied differences in a sample of direct file youths (ages 16 to 17) and young adult offenders (ages 18 to 24) prosecuted in criminal court in Florida.[95] They found few differences between the transferred youths and the young adults in those competence-related abilities and developmental characteristics likely to be significant in the adult legal process. Interestingly, they report that "where differences existed, they suggested somewhat better performance for the Direct File sample than for the Adult Defendant sample." [96]

The Impact of Race and Ethnicity in Transferred Cases

The previous discussion of characteristics of juveniles transferred to criminal court was largely based on national statistics. However, significant racial and ethnic disparities in transfers may be masked by national data.[97] It therefore may be more useful to examine the transfer process in local jurisdictions. Jeffrey Fagan and his associates analyzed transfer cases in Boston, Detroit, Newark, and Phoenix and found that African American youths were 75 percent more likely to be waived to criminal court than were white youths, although race had no independent influence on the waiver decision when seriousness of offense and prior record were controlled.[98] Similarly, Marcy Podkopacz and Barry Feld report no racial disparities in waived cases in Minneapolis when controlling for offender, offense, and court process variables.[99]

However, a study of juvenile transfers in 18 jurisdictions around the country suggests that race and ethnicity play a significant, but complex, role. Jolanta Juszkiewicz analyzed all juvenile cases filed in 18 criminal courts during the first six months of 1998.[100] The jurisdictions included cities such as Birmingham, Phoenix, Los Angeles, Miami, Orlando, Indianapolis, St. Louis, Brooklyn, Queens, Philadelphia, Houston, and Milwaukee. Disparities affecting African American and Hispanic youths were found throughout the process. For example,

- African American youths were disproportionately transferred to criminal court based on their proportion of felony arrests.
- African American youths accounted for two-thirds of all juveniles arrested for felony drug offenses but three-fourths of juvenile drug cases in criminal court.
- Disparities in some jurisdictions were extreme. For example, African American youths accounted for 30 percent of felony arrests in Jefferson County (Birmingham), Alabama, but were 80 percent of transferred cases to criminal court.
- White juveniles were more likely than minority youths to have violent offenses filed in criminal court in half of the jurisdictions.
- Conviction rates were significantly higher for white and Hispanic youths (76 and 72 percent, respectively) than for African American youths (57 percent).

- African American youths were nearly three times more likely than white youths to have their cases transferred back to juvenile court (13 versus 5 percent).

- African American (43 percent) and Hispanic (37 percent) youths were more likely than white (26 percent) youths to receive prison sentences.

- African American youths sentenced to prison had longer sentences than white or Hispanic youths for nearly all offense categories.

Significant racial disparities in transfer also were found in the Los Angeles County juvenile court for all youths transferred in 1996. According to Mike Males and Dan Macallair, compared to white youths, Hispanic youths were *6 times* more likely to be transferred to criminal court, while African America youths were *12 times* more likely, and Asian/other youths *3 times* more likely.[101] However, minority youths are significantly more likely to be arrested for serious crimes and the percentages of minority transfers are relatively close to their percentages of arrests for violent and property crimes (see Figure 14-4). White youths, on the other hand, are proportionately much less likely to be transferred when compared with their arrests for serious crimes.

But, as noted earlier, most youths who meet the offense and statutory-age criteria for waiver are not transferred to criminal court. Most are handled in the juvenile courts, and if their cases result in adjudications of delinquency, the youths then face disposition. The next chapter will examine the range of

figure 14-4 Arrests and Transfers of Juveniles in Los Angeles County, by Race

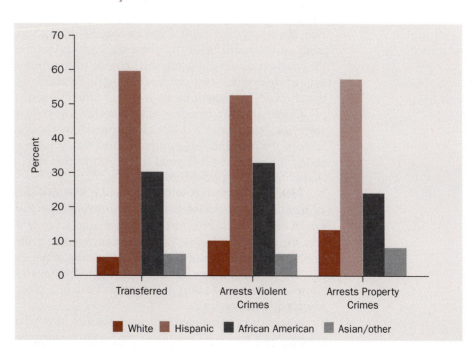

Source: Mike Males and Dan Macallair, *The Color of Justice: An Analysis of Juvenile Adult Court Transfers in California* (Washington, DC: Youth Law Center, 2000).

disposition alternatives available to the juvenile court including probation, restitution, and confinement in correctional institutions.

Sentencing Juveniles in Criminal Court

Are juveniles transferred to and then convicted in criminal court likely to be sentenced differently than other young adult offenders charged with similar offenses? While a number of studies report finding that nearly half of juveniles convicted in criminal court are incarcerated,[102] other studies report few convicted juveniles face being sent to jail or prison.[103] More recently, Megan Kurlychek and Brian Johnson addressed this question in their study of sentencing outcomes of juveniles and young adults convicted in Pennsylvania's criminal courts over a 3-year period. They found strong evidence indicating that transferred juveniles were sentenced more severely than young adult offenders. They state that "even after controlling for a host of legal and extralegal sentencing factors, transferred juveniles appear to receive sentences that are 83 percent more severe."[104] They suggest that judges may perceive greater culpability and dangerousness in transferred juveniles or that the transfer decision might indicate to judges that such juveniles are already considered incorrigible.

Blended Sentencing

In an effort to return to, or at least maintain a degree of focus on, rehabilitation of juvenile offenders and to combine the potential of rehabilitation with accountability, a number of states have implemented **blended sentences** in both juvenile and criminal courts. Blended sentences expand both disposition and sentencing options available to judges. In the juvenile courts, blended sentences allow judges to impose a juvenile disposition while also staying an adult criminal sentence. If the juvenile fails to meet the requirements of the juvenile disposition, the stay of the adult sentence may be revoked and the juvenile sent to an adult correctional facility to serve the criminal sentence. Blended sentences in the criminal courts allow juveniles convicted of crimes to receive juvenile dispositions while staying the criminal sentence. Again, failure to conform to dispositional orders may result in the stayed criminal sentence being invoked.

Criminal court blended sentencing laws have been described as a "safety valve" or "emergency exit" because they allow the court to review the circumstances of a case and make an individualized decision regarding the youth's suitability for juvenile or criminal treatment. In this way, youths are given one last chance to receive a juvenile disposition.[105]

Seventeen states allow criminal court blended sentencing. Of these states, 10 have *exclusive blended sentencing* arrangements where the criminal court has an either/or choice between criminal and juvenile sanctions. *Inclusive blend models,* in which juvenile offenders convicted in criminal court may receive a combination sentence, exist in the remaining seven states with criminal court blended sentencing (see Table 14-4). The criminal court inclusive blend model allows the criminal court to suspend the adult sanction on condition of the youth's good behavior.

Some critics of blended sentences, such as Marcy Podkopacz and Barry Feld, believe that blended sentencing produces a net-widening effect.[106] In other words, youths charged with slightly less serious crimes may be transferred to criminal

Table 14-4 Criminal Court Blended Sentencing Provisions, 2004	
PROVISION	**STATE**
Exclusive	California, Colorado, Illinois, Kentucky, Massachusetts, Nebraska, New Mexico, Oklahoma, West Virginia, Wisconsin
Inclusive	Arkansas, Florida, Idaho, Iowa, Michigan, Missouri, Virginia

Source: Howard Snyder and Melissa Sickmund, *Juvenile Offenders and Victims: 2006 National Report* (Washington, DC: Office of Juvenile Justice and Delinquency Prevention, 2006), p. 115.

court for prosecution because the judge will still have the option of sentencing the youth as a juvenile. However, Podkopacz and Feld report that judges are also more likely to revoke juvenile probation, even for technical violations, and impose incarceration sentences on youths who had received blended sentences.

STATUS OFFENDERS IN THE JUVENILE COURT

Status offenses are law violations *only* if committed by a juvenile. It is the *age status* of the individual, not the conduct that differentiates this category of offense. Status offenses are not criminal offenses, they are violations of community values and expectations of childhood.[107] Status offenders made up the majority of youths referred to the juvenile court in the first quarter of the 20th century, being brought to the court by police officers, probation officers, parents, teachers and school administrators, and even neighbors. No distinctions were made by the juvenile courts in how they handled status offenders and criminal offending youths, either in terms of adjudication or disposition. Both categories of behavior were considered delinquent offenses. The decriminalization of status offenses and the removal of this group of juvenile offenders did not come about until the early 1970s as a result of decisions by the Supreme Court and the *Juvenile Justice and Delinquency Prevention Act of 1974,* which, among other things, required the removal of status offenders from secure detention or correctional facilities.

Today, juvenile court jurisdiction continues to extend to adolescent misconduct, such as truancy, running away from home, ungovernability, curfew statute violations, and underage drinking, but how youths who engage in these proscribed behaviors are handled by the courts has changed. Most jurisdictions classify noncriminal status offending youths as MINS (minor in need of supervision), PINS (person in need of supervision), or CHINS (child in need of supervision). In some states, status offenders enter into the official system through the juvenile court intake process discussed earlier in this chapter; in other states, the case may enter through the child welfare agency. About one in five status offense cases that come to the attention of the juvenile court intake or child welfare agencies are formally processed by the courts.

Between 1985 and 2002, approximately 46 percent of runaway cases, 63 percent of truancy cases, 63 percent of liquor law violation cases, and 62 percent of ungovernability cases petitioned to the juvenile court were adjudicated as status offenders.[108] The most common status offenses referred to the court were truancy (34 percent), followed by liquor law violations (30 percent), running

think about it

Nearly 10,000 youths are detained annually for status offenses. The juvenile justice system might protect chronic runaways from dangerous home environments. On occasion, juvenile detention centers are healthier places than homes. Should the *parens patriae* doctrine still apply to juvenile justice?

away (19 percent), and ungovernability (17 percent). Females were proportionately more likely to be referred to court for status offenses than they were for delinquency offenses, accounting for 61 percent of all runaway cases and over 45 percent of truancy and ungovernability cases. However, once referred to the juvenile court, males and females were equally likely to be adjudicated as status offenders. About two-thirds of adjudicated status offense cases resulted in probation (see Figure 14-5).

Generally, the constitutional rights guaranteed by *Gault* and *Winship* do not apply to status offenders. However, some courts and some states, by statute, have extended these rights. The *Gault* decision specifically referred to the adjudication hearing in delinquency cases and left open the question of whether the protections specified in *Gault* might extend to status offenders. Some states extend some of the *Gault* protections to all status offense proceedings, for instance, the right to counsel and proof beyond a reasonable doubt in Georgia and right to counsel in Nebraska. On the other hand, many states, such as New Mexico and Tennessee, require only "clear and convincing evidence" in status offense cases instead of the higher burden of proof required by *Winship* in delinquency cases.[109] While most states prohibit hearsay evidence in status offense proceedings, a few states, such as New York and Pennsylvania, see a virtue in permitting such evidence. Finally, while some states require constitutionally or by statute that status offenders are to be protected by the right against self-incrimination, other states, such as Iowa, hold that this privilege does not apply.

figure 14-5   Percent of Adjudicated Status Offenders Placed on Probation, by Offense

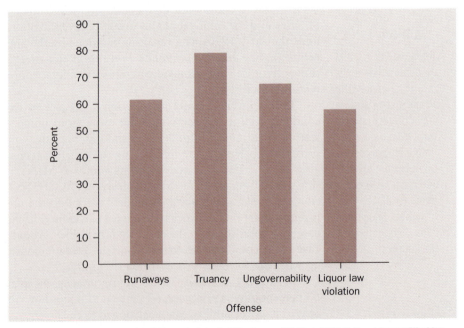

Source: Howard Snyder and Melissa Sickmund, *Juvenile Offenders and Victims: 2006 National Report* (Washington, DC: National Center for Juvenile Justice, 2006), p. 192.

conclusions

This chapter examined the nature of the juvenile courts and the specific stages and procedures of the court process, from arrest and court intake to detention and adjudication and disposition hearings. In addition, information was presented on youth courts, drug courts, and restorative justice programs as alternatives to the traditional juvenile courts.

The old juvenile court was changed dramatically in the mid-1960s as the U.S. Supreme Court, in a series of landmark cases, recognized the due process rights of juveniles and established guidelines as well as legal constraints under which the juvenile courts must operate. Other court decisions and statutes established by state legislatures have placed constraints on the public nature of juvenile court hearings, although public access to court proceedings and information has increased in recent years.

A very important issue today involves the transfer of serious juvenile offenders to criminal court for prosecution as adults. In most states, juveniles who are charged with serious violent crimes and who meet the minimum-age standard for waiver, may be transferred. Once transferred, they face the same prosecution process that adult defendants face. Some states rely exclusively on judicial waivers, but an increasing number of states permit the prosecutorial transfer of youths. Most youths tried in criminal court, however, are there as a result of legislatively mandated transfers. Given the growing get-tough sentiment of the public and politicians, it is reasonable to expect that an increasing number of youths will be tried in criminal courts for their crimes in the next few years.

This chapter also looked at a third group of juvenile offenders who sometimes enter the juvenile courts: youths who have not committed delinquent acts or crimes sufficiently serious to have them transferred to criminal court. These youths are status offenders. Their offenses are not considered crimes if committed by adults, yet their misbehaviors are seen as problematic. While status offenders have many of the due process rights of children charged with delinquencies, they do not have all the same rights.

key terms

Adjudication hearing   A hearing held to determine whether the child committed the offense of which he or she is accused.

Bail   A money or cash bond deposited with the court or bail bondsman allowing the person to be released on the assurance he or she will appear in court at the proper time.

Blended sentencing   Juvenile courts may impose adult criminal sanctions on particular types of juvenile offenders.

Breed v. Jones   Criminal prosecution of a child following a juvenile court hearing is unconstitutional because it constitutes double jeopardy.

Demand waiver   Legal mechanism whereby a juvenile may request to have his or her case transferred from juvenile court to criminal court.

Detention   The temporary confinement of children pending adjudication, disposition, or implementation of disposition.

Disposition hearing   A juvenile court hearing in which the court determines what action will be in the youth's and community's best interests; the equivalent of the sentencing stage in the criminal court process.

Double jeopardy The prosecution of an individual a second time for the same offense. It is prohibited by the Fifth Amendment.

Drug courts Intensive treatment programs established within and supervised by juvenile courts to provide specialized services for eligible drug-involved youths and their families.

In re Gault Juveniles may not be denied basic due process rights in juvenile adjudicatory hearings.

In re Winship In delinquency cases, juveniles have the right to be convicted only if there is proof beyond a reasonable doubt.

Informal adjustment Cases that are handled through discretionary nonjudicial dispositions.

Informal probation A case adjustment practice in which the child and family comply with requirements of probation personnel without a formal court order.

Intake The initial case-screening process in the juvenile court system. It is designed to screen out cases that do not warrant a formal court hearing.

Judicial waiver A method used for transferring youths to criminal court in which the juvenile court judge is the primary decision maker in determining whether the youths should be transferred.

Kent v. United States A formal waiver hearing must take place before transfer of a juvenile to criminal court.

McKeiver v. Pennsylvania Juveniles do not have a constitutional right to a jury trial in juvenile court.

Petition A document setting forth the specific charge against a juvenile.

Prosecutorial waiver Legal mechanism that allows the prosecutor to be the primary decision maker in determining whether a youth should be transferred to adult court.

Restorative justice Legal mechanism designed to restore or repair relationships disrupted by crime, holding offenders accountable by requiring restitution to victims or the community harmed by the crime, promoting offender competency and responsibility, and balancing the needs of community, victim, and offender through involvement in the restorative process.

Reverse waiver Legal mechanism whereby a juvenile who is being prosecuted as an adult in criminal court may petition to have the case transferred to juvenile court for adjudication or disposition.

Schall v. Martin Juveniles may be held in preventive detention while awaiting adjudication if they are determined to be "serious risks" to the community.

Statutory exclusion A method used for transferring youths to criminal court, whereby the most serious or persistent offenders or those over a certain age are excluded from juvenile court jurisdiction and automatically prosecuted as adults.

Youth court An alternative to the traditional juvenile court that allows young offenders to take responsibility for their acts, to be held accountable, and to receive appropriate dispositions imposed by their peers.

Juvenile Corrections

To some observers, the field of juvenile corrections appears to be only an afterthought within the history of the juvenile justice system. It has consistently been low on the list of budgeting priorities and largely ignored by national debate. To other observers, juvenile corrections has been viewed as accomplishing little more than either warehousing or coddling youthful offenders while they are in state custody. Money is expended but little reform is achieved.

It is interesting that special attention to the correctional reform of juvenile offenders predates the creation of the juvenile court by more than half a century. The first house of refuge opened in 1825 in New York for the care of wayward, neglected, homeless, and misbehaving youths (see Chapter 1). Two decades later, in 1846, Massachusetts opened the first state-run juvenile reform school, the Lyman School for Boys. In 1876 more than 50 reform schools or houses of refuge were operating around the country. By 1890 state reform schools had been established in nearly every state outside the South, and a number of states had created special reform schools for girls.[1]

Not all delinquent children were sent to reform schools. Charles Loring Brace and the other Child Savers, during the latter half of the 19th century, established a program for placing urban problem youths in apprenticeships with farm families in the Midwest and West. Brace considered such placements to be "God's reformatories" for problem children.[2]

Correctional philosophy took another turn at the end of the 19th century with the creation of the first juvenile court in Cook County (Chicago), Illinois, in 1899. Probation, or community supervision, was still in its infancy as a tool for reforming adult offenders, having been implemented at the state level in Massachusetts less than 20 years earlier. The Illinois court quickly adopted probation, and it was subsequently implemented by juvenile courts across the nation. By the middle of the 20th century, probation and a variety of more recent alternatives to institutional placement for delinquent youths became the standard court disposition.

DECIDING THE DISPOSITION

Prior to *Gault,* the juvenile court permitted judges a great deal of discretion in deciding dispositions. A judge could dismiss the case, place the youth on probation, remove the youth from his or her home to be placed in foster care, or send the youth to a correctional institution. Dispositions, from the early establishment of the juvenile court, were based on notions of rehabilitation and the desire to do what was in the "best interests of the child." This focus on treatment seemed to work fairly well through the first half of the 20th century, as most children brought to the juvenile court were minor offenders.[3]

From the mid-1960s to the early 1990s, juvenile delinquency not only increased dramatically, it increasingly involved serious, violent criminality (see Chapters 1–3). The effectiveness of rehabilitation as the sole consideration for disposition was called into question, and states began to adopt more punitive and restrictive disposition alternatives based on notions of deterrence.[4] Similar policies have emerged in a number of European countries too (see Box 15-1).

box 15-1   DELINQUENCY AROUND THE GLOBE
Punishing Juvenile Offenders in Russia and the Netherlands

Although juvenile crime rates have declined significantly in the United States during the past decade, Russia and the Netherlands have experienced increases in juvenile delinquency. Offenders, as in the United States, tend to be male (92 percent in Russia and 80 percent in the Netherlands) and to have more likely committed property crimes and social order offenses rather than violent offenses.

In Russia, local prosecutors determine what will happen with youths ages 14 to 18 arrested by police. A youth may have the case dismissed, be referred to a citizen's juvenile court for informal disposition, or be sent to a People's Court for formal adjudication. About 60 percent of juvenile offenders in Russia are convicted in the People's Courts. Prior to 1996 about 40 percent of convicted youths received suspended sentences, and between 50 and 60 percent received incarceration sentences. Since 1996, in response to rising serious delinquency, closer to three-fourths of convicted youths are sentenced to confinement in a *reformatory colony* or youth correctional facility for no more than 10 years. Juveniles are confined separately from adult offenders. First-time male offenders are typically incarcerated in a labor colony, whereas first-time female offenders more often are placed in re-educational colonies.

The Netherlands seems to take a more liberal approach in dealing with delinquent youths. Youths who are under the age of 12 cannot be held criminally responsible and may not be criminally prosecuted. Instead, they are sent home with a caution. However, if the youth committed a serious crime, then he or she may be referred to a civil court with the option of psychological counseling. Juveniles age 12 to 17 are diverted out of the justice system whenever possible at each stage of the process. In recent years, nearly half of all juveniles dealt with by the police are referred for HALT sanctions, which are similar to many police and court diversion programs in the United States. The youth must first admit committing the offense, and the case is then handled informally with an emphasis on cautioning. If the case is sent to the court and the youth is found guilty, nonpunitive sentences are most often imposed. These include fines, community sentence (either service or education), detention, and possibly placement in a juvenile institution for a maximum of 12 months if the youth is younger than 16 years old and 24 months if the youth is age 16 to 18. About half of adjudicated juveniles receive community sentences. However, as in Russia, rising rates of serious youth crime have led to a more punitive attitude toward juvenile delinquents. The Ministry of Justice is increasing the number of juvenile institutions and bed-space in current institutions. Between 1995 and 2001, the Netherlands increased the total custodial bed-space from 900 to 2,100.

Sources: James Williams and Daniel Rodeheaver, "Punishing Juvenile Offenders in Russia," *International Criminal Justice Review* 12:93–110 (2002); Dmitry Shestakov and Natalia Shestakova, "An Overview of Juvenile Justice and Juvenile Crime in Russia," pages 411–440 in John Winterdyk (ed.), *Juvenile Justice Systems: International Perspectives* (Toronto: Canadian Scholars' Press, 2002); Henk Ferwerda, "Youth Crime and Juvenile Justice in the Netherlands," pages 435–453 in John Winterdyk (ed.), *Juvenile Justice Systems;* Karin Wittebrood, "Juvenile Crime and Sanctions in the Netherlands," *Journal of Contemporary Criminal Justice* 19:435–453 (2003).

Today, about half the states use structured guidelines, mandatory offense-based minimum sentences, or determinate sentencing laws to regulate dispositions. For example, Washington State revised its juvenile code in 1977 to emphasize just deserts and implemented a determinate sentencing law aimed at protecting "the citizenry from criminal behavior"; its goal was to "make the juvenile offender accountable for . . . criminal behavior" and to "provide for punishment commensurate with the age, crime, and criminal history of the juvenile offender." [5] Recent studies of judges' disposition decisions appear to support the notion that emphasis has shifted from a *child welfare approach* toward a *crime control orientation*. For example, Brandon Applegate and his colleagues found that judges focus primarily on offense characteristics and only marginally on the offender's social characteristics. However, they note that "judges may believe that secure confinement presents the best opportunities for rehabilitating youthful felons while protecting the public" and the use of incarceration was reduced somewhat when judges believed appropriate programs were available in the community. [6] In addition, in their study of juvenile commitment decisions by juvenile court judges in Philadelphia, Jamie Fader and his associates report that dispositions are made differently for first-time and repeat offenders. [7] In cases involving first-time offenders, offense-specific variables, such as seriousness of offense and injury to victim, are viewed as key factors by judges, although significant weight is also given to child and family functioning factors. Furthermore, youths whose mothers had substance abuse problems or were known to be abusive or neglectful were more likely to be placed in institutions. [8] However, dispositions involving youths with prior offense histories were more likely to be made based on offense severity and situational factors, such as behavior since arrest, including running away from a detention facility or being arrested again.

ALTERNATIVES TO INSTITUTIONALIZATION

Most youths adjudicated delinquent for the first time are placed on probation. But probation is not the only alternative available to the court. Today, courts have a variety of dispositions to select from, including such options as home confinement and electronic monitoring, the payment of fines or restitution, and short-term placement in a boot camp.

Probation

Probation is the conditional freedom granted by the court to an alleged or adjudicated offender as long as he or she avoids further misbehavior and meets certain conditions. The majority of youths on probation have been ordered by the court to supervision at disposition after having been formally adjudicated. Approximately 62 percent of all adjudicated delinquents receive probation. [9] However, many youths who are not adjudicated delinquent voluntarily agree to abide by certain probation conditions with the understanding that if they successfully complete their probationary period, their case will be terminated without any formal processing.

Probation is based on the belief that misbehavior may be better corrected by trying to rehabilitate the juvenile in the community than in an institution.

The major goals of probation are rehabilitation and reintegration, and the principal figure in accomplishing these objectives is the probation officer. Many juvenile courts have no probation services at all, and those that do usually have large caseloads in which counseling and supervision take the form of occasional phone calls and perfunctory visits rather than carefully designed, individualized services. A recent survey conducted by the National Center for Juvenile Justice indicated that the range of probation caseload size is great, ranging between 2 and 200. The average caseload is about 41, with 30 considered optimal.[10]

Probation may be used at the front end of the juvenile justice system for first-time, low-risk offenders or at the back end as an alternative to institutional confinement for more serious offenders. The official duties of probation officers can differ between states and even between jurisdictions within a single state. In any case, the basic set of juvenile probation functions includes intake screening of cases referred to juvenile and family courts, predispositions or social history investigation of juveniles, and court-ordered supervision of juvenile offenders. Probation orders imposed by the court for supervision of juveniles usually require that the youths obey all laws, attend school regularly, periodically visit the probation officer, remain within the community, and be at home at night by a set hour. The judge has the statutory authority to frame these conditions. Some probation departments also provide aftercare for youths released from institutions; others may administer detention or manage local residential facilities or special programs.

Since probation has historically been viewed as a "favor" to a person convicted of a crime, conditions of probation were, until recently, rarely subject to judicial review. Now, however, it is generally agreed that probationary conditions for juveniles are subject to some limitations. For example, in juvenile courts, a major goal of probation is to rehabilitate the child by treatment and guidance while he or she participates in the community. If probation conditions *do not* promote this end or if they violate a youth's constitutionally protected rights, they should not be used or permitted. Examples include:

- Prohibiting association with gang members because the prohibition was not restricted to *known* gang members.
- Ordering a youth to stay away from a block on a specific street where his crime had been committed.
- Requiring the probation officer to preapprove all the persons with whom the youth associates.
- Requiring a minor to obtain satisfactory grades and practice good citizenship.[11]

A recent innovation in juvenile probation is the development of police–probation partnerships, which are designed to increase the supervision of youths. Police officers and probation officers work together to enhance supervision and to provide greater opportunities for contact between authorities and delinquent youths. Boston's *Operation Night Light* was begun in 1992 and was quickly followed by similar partnerships in Minnesota, Washington, Connecticut, and Arizona.[12] Some police–probation partnerships are limited to intensive supervision of high-risk juveniles or gang members; others, such as the programs in San Diego and Anchorage, allow for supervision of a wider range of probationers, including youths considered to be at lower risk.[13]

However, intensive probation supervision programs in general, and police–probation partnerships specifically, have been criticized for "net widening, high re-vocation rates, and related case-processing costs."[14] Although most studies report that increased supervision increases the likelihood of reporting technical viola-tions, there is little evidence that youths on intensive or partnership probation are any more likely to commit new offenses than those on traditional probation.[15]

California has developed a number of juvenile probation programs to pro-vide a more comprehensive approach to supervising juvenile offenders in the community and to provide more consistent funding for probation activities. Three innovative programs include the *Repeat Offender Prevention Program* (ROPP), which uses a multidisciplinary, multiagency, team-oriented approach; the *Juvenile Crime Enforcement and Accountability Challenge Grant Program,* which provided $50 million to help counties identify, implement, and evalu-ate community-based projects targeting at-risk youths; and the *Juvenile Jus-tice Crime Prevention Act,* which was designed to provide more stable funding for programs for juveniles that had been evaluated and found to reduce crime among at-risk youths and young offenders.[16]

Home Confinement and Electronic Monitoring

The search for dispositions offering alternatives to placement in jails, detention centers, and institutions has led to the development of various community-based programs. Drawing in part from the labeling perspective that holds that unneces-sarily punitive confinement may have adverse consequences, juvenile courts have increasingly sought the least restrictive alternatives available (see Chapter 7).

Home confinement, sometimes called *house arrest* or *home detention,* is the intensive supervision and monitoring of a person in his or her home environ-ment. Juvenile court probation departments usually administer home confine-ment programs. Surveillance consists of personal daily contacts with the youth and daily contacts with parents, teachers, and employers.[17] Juveniles are typi-cally confined to their homes unless attending school, work, or other previously agreed-upon activities. Any other time the youths are not at home, both parents and probation department supervisors closely monitor them. Advocates of home confinement programs contend the programs' costs are less than one-fourth the cost of confining youths in jail or detention centers.

A variation on home confinement is **electronic monitoring.**[18] Electronic monitoring, or tracking systems, are generally of two types: passive and active. In *passive* systems, the youth sends electronic signals via phone in response to computer-activated calls. The juvenile may respond either by inserting a special plug worn on the wrist into the transmitter or by speaking on the phone to a matched voiceprint programmed into the computer. *Active* systems are used when constant surveillance of the juvenile is desired. Traditional active systems require the youth to wear a transmitter on the ankle, neck, or wrist. The trans-mitter sends a constant signal allowing for movement to a distance of 100 to 150 feet to a receiver connected to the home telephone. The signal is then sent to a central computer that matches the signal to patterns preprogrammed for arranged absences such as school and work. The newest type of active moni-toring is the satellite-based *GPS* (global positioning system) unit. These units allow real-time tracking of the wearer, plot a subject's path, retrace a person's

think about it

Electronic monitoring allows many youths opportunities to remain in the community. Monitoring also permits closer surveillance than traditional probation. Are juveniles advantaged or disadvantaged during electronic monitoring?

Electronic monitoring of delinquents allows them to remain in the community and work toward their rehabilitation rather than being incarcerated. Unless they commit violent crimes should all adjudicated delinquents be placed on community sentences? What negative consequences arise from the confinement of adolescents? Conversely, which types of delinquent offenders probably require confinement?

movement over several days, and even determine if the youth is walking or in a vehicle.[19]

Critics of home confinement and electronic monitoring raise four concerns about the programs:

1. To what extent will juveniles, who would not otherwise be placed on supervision, be brought into the net of the juvenile justice system simply because of the convenience of these new less-restrictive programs?

2. Our society has a long-held belief that "a person's home is his castle" and should not be violated by the state. To turn a juvenile's home into a prison runs contrary to Anglo-Saxon tradition.[20]

3. If the juvenile's home is turned into a prison, what is the effect on the traditional parental role? The criminal codes of most states recognize the special relationship between parent and child. Parents are often exempt from testifying against their child or even from being prosecuted for assisting their child if he or she has escaped from a correctional facility. Will home confinement turn parents into wardens or "keepers" of their own children? Will

parents be subject to charges of contempt of court or contributing to the delinquency of a minor if they do not report violations of home detention?

4. Will electronic monitoring intrude on our nation's deeply held value of privacy and create a Big Brother atmosphere? Could a "least restrictive" program, in the long run, lead us toward acceptance of pervasive restrictions over all aspects of our lives?

Fines and Restitution

States are increasingly authorizing that restitution and payment of fines be used as disposition alternatives and be included as a condition of probation. **Restitution** is a court-ordered action in which an offender pays money or provides services to victims of the offense or to the community.[21] According to Anne Schneider, restitution programs are based on the principle that youths should be held accountable for their delinquent actions.[22] When juveniles cause damage or loss, they should repay their victims. Courts generally rely on any one of three methods to determine restitution.

1. A judge decides the amount of restitution on the basis of arguments presented by both the offender and the victim during the sentencing hearing.

2. An insurance claim is used to determine the amount to be paid by the offender.

3. The victim and offender are brought together and work out a restitution agreement that is satisfactory to both parties.[23]

A fine is a cash payment determined by the court and paid by the youth or his or her parents. Fines are seldom used as the sole disposition. Rather, they are more likely to be imposed in addition to a disposition involving probation. Part of the fine may include court costs, fees for drug or alcohol treatment, or victim compensation.

Boot Camps

Boot camps for juveniles have been a popular disposition alternative for adjudicated delinquents. Boot camps proliferated in the late 1980s and early 1990s. By 1996, there were more than 75 boot camps for adult offenders around the country and 48 juvenile boot camps were operating in 27 states.[24] After the mid-1990s, the number of boot camps declined, especially those for adult offenders. By 2000 about one-third of adult boot camps had closed, and the average daily population of boot camps dropped more than 30 percent.[25] Although boot camps for juveniles have not declined as dramatically, they have begun substituting an emphasis on educational and vocations skills for the military components traditionally emphasized.

Boot camps were designed to reduce recidivism, correctional institution populations, and costs. They were modeled after military basic training, with youths required to wear military-style uniforms, march to and from activities, and respond immediately to the commands of their "drill instructors." Daily schedules typically include drill and ceremony practice, strenuous physical fitness activities, and challenge programs. Juvenile inmates who violate rules are generally required to perform pushups as punishment.

think about it

Research asserts that boot camps do not rehabilitate delinquents. If this is true, what other benefits might boot camps provide?

Graffiti and neighborhood disorder contribute to delinquency; a sense of order reduces it. Graffiti can range from petty vandalism to signs of a serious gang problem. Why would policies that remove graffiti have crime-reducing effects?

These programs, like most boot camps for adult offenders, are designed for "midrange" delinquents, which are those who have failed with less severe sanctions, such as probation, but are not yet defined as "hard-core" or chronic delinquents (see Chapter 2). Certain offenders are typically excluded, such as sex offenders, armed robbers, and youths with records of serious violence. Most programs are available for youths in their mid to late teens, although the Mississippi boot camp program admits youths as young as 10, and two boot camps in Alabama take 12- and 13-year-olds.[26]

Juvenile boot camps are much less costly than traditional state-run correctional institutions. Based on a study of juvenile boot camps by Michael Peters and his colleagues, they estimated that the cost per offender in boot camp ($6,241) was about half the cost per offender confined in state institutions ($11,616). However, boot camps are still significantly more expensive than the costs per offender associated with traditional probation supervision ($516).[27]

Juveniles sent to boot camps usually face programs of 90- to 120-day duration. During these few months, youths are generally exposed to a militaristic environment, with in-your-face drill instructors, an emphasis on physical conditioning, and three to six hours of work detail each day. All the programs include an educational component, and most programs also include some

think
about it

"Widening the net" refers to the expansion of nonincarceration sanctions. A positive of this trend is cost savings; a negative is the expansion of the total correctional population. Is increased surveillance beneficial or problematic?

vocational education, work skills training or job preparation, and drug and alcohol counseling.

Even with their popularity among lawmakers and the public, juvenile boot camps still are controversial. Advocates of the camps argue that the structure of the programs promotes positive growth and change and creates a safer environment for youths than traditional correctional facilities. In addition, proponents believe the military model builds camaraderie among youths and fosters respect for staff. Critics argue that boot camps are generally more costly than most other traditional alternatives, such as intensive probation, and have just as high or higher recidivism rates.[28] Other critics say the camps' confrontational environment conflicts with the creation of positive interpersonal relationships and are antithetical to quality therapeutic programming. Confrontational interactions, they argue, may cause juveniles to fear correctional staff and undermine any potential for effective therapy and educational achievement. Furthermore, critics say the emphasis on group activities ignores individual youths' problems. Critics also believe the group orientation of boot camp programs, in which an entire platoon may be punished when only one member of the group misbehaved, may cause youths to view the system as unjust.[29] Ultimately, the greatest criticism of boot camps is that they foster an environment that allows aggressive and violent treatment of juveniles, treatment that sometimes leads to the death of a youth (see Box 15-2).

Are juvenile boot camps more effective than traditional correctional treatment? Early studies found no significant difference in recidivism rates for youths placed in boot camps versus those receiving more traditional correctional treatment options, although in some cases boot camp graduates had higher rates of recidivism.[30] On the other hand, boot camps provide some advantages not directly related to recidivism. Doris MacKenzie and her colleagues surveyed more than 4,000 youths in 27 boot camps and 22 traditional institutions. They reported that youths in boot camps, compared with youths assigned to traditional facilities, perceived their facilities to be more caring and just, that programs are more therapeutic and helpful in preparing them for jobs, and that they received more individual attention. In addition, while youths in boot camps more frequently reported feelings of being in danger from staff, youths in traditional facilities more frequently reported feelings of danger from other residents.[31]

CONFINEMENT OF JUVENILE OFFENDERS

The reality of confinement as a form of punishment or rehabilitation is harsh. Imprisonment is one of the most frequently criticized mechanisms for dealing with criminality. However, the range of complaints reflects inconsistent public expectations of correctional institutions.

- They should reform offenders, but they fail to do so.
- They should punish lawbreakers, but they coddle them.
- They should be secure and orderly, but there are many escapes and disturbances.
- They should operate with minimal cost to the taxpayer, but they are expensive.

box 15-2 A WINDOW ON DELINQUENCY
Juvenile Killed in Florida Boot Camp

Martin Anderson was 14 years old when he entered a Florida boot camp for juvenile offenders on January 5, 2006. Anderson had been arrested in 2005 for stealing his grandmother's Jeep Cherokee and was ordered to the camp for violating his probation after he trespassed at a school. Within hours of his arrival at the camp he had been restrained, kneed, and hit by guards. He died the next day. Although the guards claimed that Anderson was uncooperative and refused to participate in physical activities required of all new inmates, the event was caught on video tape and showed the boy being forced to the ground, being kneed in the thigh and punched in the arms, and having force applied to pressure points on his ear, all while a camp nurse stood by.

The first autopsy found Anderson died from sickle cell anemia or natural causes. However, the next day the video tape was released and an investigation began. One week later the boot camp was closed. A second autopsy found that Anderson's death was not from natural causes, but was rather a result of guards blocking the boy's mouth after forcing him to inhale ammonia capsules five times. The state's attorney general concluded that the camp guards had suffocated Anderson, causing his death.

Nearly 11 months later, a special prosecutor filed manslaughter charges against seven ex-guards and a nurse for allegedly causing the death of Anderson by culpable negligence by failing to make a reasonable effort to protect him from abuse, neglect, or exploitation and failing to give him proper care. The felony charges could result in up to 30 years in prison for each defendant.

In April of 2006, Florida Governor Jeb Bush signed into law the *Martin Lee Anderson Act,* which replaced all of the state's boot camps with juvenile facilities focusing on education and counseling.

Sources: Susan Filan, "Death Sparks Change to Juvenile Justice System," online at http://www.msnbc.msn.com/id/15936990/, accessed May 4, 2007; "Boot Camp Teen's Parents: 'It's a Good Day,'" *CNNToday,* November 28, 2006, online at: http://www.cnn.com/2006/LAW/11/28/boot.camp.death/index.html, accessed May 4, 2007.

The U.S. corrections system contains a fundamental flaw: It was developed many years ago in an era relevant to the goals of that particular time. But even though circumstances and goals have changed drastically, the system has not. Today, it may be regarded as an obstacle to significant rehabilitative efforts.

The Institutionalization of Juveniles

In 1880 nearly 20 years before the creation of the nation's first juvenile code and court, 11,468 juveniles were held in some sort of correctional facility. Of these youths, 81 percent were male, and only 11 percent were nonwhite; their average age was 13. Today, the number of juveniles incarcerated in the United States on any given day is more than 109,000. In addition to youths incarcerated in facilities specifically designated for juveniles, about 2,300 youths are held in state and federal adult correctional facilities.[32]

Not surprising, states with the largest populations also have the largest number of juveniles in custody. California has nearly 17,000 juveniles in custody on any given day, while juvenile correctional facilities in Texas have over 7,600 youths, and Florida has just over 8,200.[33] Custody rates also vary a great

Maricopa County Sheriff Joe Arpaio has taken the chain gang to another level with the first for juveniles convicted as adults. Is the chain gang a deterrent against crime? Is it better to have juveniles working in a chain gang or to sit in a cell playing cards?

deal by jurisdiction. Some, such as the District of Columbia and Wyoming, have custody rates for delinquent offenders at well over 600 per 100,000; others have dramatically lower custody rates. For example, New Hampshire has a rate of 150, while Hawaii has a rate of 97, and Vermont has a rate of only 72 (see Table 15-1).

Approximately 70 percent of youths incarcerated in juvenile facilities were held in public institutions; 30 percent were held in private facilities.[34] The average time juveniles spend in public correctional facilities varies a great deal. For example, juveniles placed in institutions in Arizona have an average length of stay of 7 to 8 months; in New Hampshire it is 8 to 12 months; and youths committed for serious crimes to Minnesota's juvenile facilities spend a minimum of 6 months and a maximum of 12 months. On the other hand, juvenile offenders in Texas spend an average of 2 months at an orientation center being evaluated and assessed prior to being sent to an institution where they can expect to spend an average of about 23 months.[35]

Race Disparities in Confinement African Americans make up a disproportionate number of youths arrested, especially for violent crimes; a disproportionate number of delinquency cases brought before the juvenile court; and a disproportionate number of youths placed in secure correctional facilities. African Americans make up about 16 percent of the youth population, yet in 2005 they were 28 percent of all youth arrested, including 39 percent of violent Index arrests and 29 percent of property Index arrests.[36] In addition, African Americans made up 29 percent of all youths referred to the juvenile court, 29 percent of ad-

table 15-1   State Custody Rates of Delinquent Offenders Held in Public Institutions (Per 100,000)

HIGHEST CUSTODY RATES		LOWEST CUSTODY RATES	
District of Columbia	625	Connecticut	210
Wyoming	606	New Jersey	199
South Dakota	564	Kentucky	185
Florida	452	Maryland	181
Indiana	415	North Carolina	169
California	392	Maine	153
Louisiana	387	Mississippi	152
Alaska	370	New Hampshire	150
Delaware	364	Hawaii	97
Nevada	362	Vermont	72
U.S. average rate	307		

Source: Howard Snyder and Melissa Sickmund, *Juvenile Offenders and Juvenile Victims: 2006 National Report* (Washington, DC: National Center for Juvenile Justice, 2006), p. 201.

judicated youths, and 33 percent of youths committed to correctional facilities. Of the estimated 144,000 delinquency cases resulting in out-of-home placement in 2002, 63 percent involved white youths, 33 percent involved African American youths, and 4 percent involved youths of other races. Nearly 28 percent of adjudicated delinquency cases involving African American youths resulted in custodial placement, compared with 21 percent of cases involving white youths and 25 percent of other minority youths.[37]

What does evidence of disparities in confinement mean? When data indicate there is an *overrepresentation* of a particular group in custody, it simply means there is a larger proportion of that group than would be expected based on their proportion in the general population. Evidence of *disparity* in custody rates means that the probability of receiving a particular outcome differs for different groups. Disparity may in turn lead to overrepresentation. *Discrimination* means that one group of juveniles is treated differently from another group of juveniles based wholly, or in part, on their race, ethnicity, or gender. However, neither overrepresentation nor disparity necessarily implies discrimination.[38]

Disparity and overrepresentation can result from factors other than discrimination. For example, research has found that minorities' higher rates of confinement are due to their disproportionate involvement in serious and violent crimes.[39] If minority youths commit proportionately more crime than white youths, are involved in more serious incidents, and have more extensive criminal histories, they will be overrepresented in secure facilities, even if *no* discrimination by decision makers occurred. For example, analysis of the FBI National Incident-Based Reporting System found that for violent crimes, no difference in the overall likelihood of arrest of white juveniles and nonwhite juveniles existed after controlling for all other incident characteristics. The likelihood of juvenile arrest was affected, however, by several other incident characteristics independent of offender race. Arrest was more likely when there was a single offender, multiple victims, victim injury, or the victim and offender were family members, rather than strangers.[40]

However, a number of other studies suggest that disparities are the result of racial and ethnic discrimination. This line of reasoning suggests that because of discrimination on the part of justice system decision makers, minority youths face higher probabilities of being arrested by the police, referred to court intake, held in short-term detention, petitioned for formal processing, adjudicated delinquent, and confined in a secure juvenile facility.[41] In addition, a few studies claim that repressive drug laws result in disproportionate numbers of African American youths being incarcerated.[42] The findings of still other studies indicate that the disparities may be the consequence of community structural factors, such as violent crime rates, minority concentration, and economic inequality, and not directly related to the characteristics of the individual offender.[43] Finally, some experts believe that differential placement of juvenile offenders in mental hospitals may contribute to minority overrepresentation in correctional facilities. For example, African American youths who exhibit very aggressive behaviors are more likely to be directed to correctional facilities while equally aggressive white youths are placed in psychiatric hospitals for "treatment." [44]

Regardless of the causes of disparities, the Office of Juvenile Justice and Delinquency Prevention established the Disproportionate Minority Confinement (DMC) Initiative in 1991 to assist states in aggressively assessing the extent of DMC in their jurisdictions. For example, Pennsylvania's DMC efforts soon discovered that, although minority juveniles represented just 12 percent of the state's juvenile population, they accounted for more than 70 percent of juveniles placed in secure confinement. These findings led to the development of special programs in five targeted communities (Harrisburg, Philadelphia, Pittsburgh, and Lehigh and Northampton Counties) designed to reduce the number of minorities confined in the state's correctional facilities. Prevention and intervention programs aimed at minority youths included educational, social, vocation, and recreational outreach; tutoring; development of life skills and job training; truancy and dropout prevention; and conflict resolution and impulse control training. By 1995 minority juveniles confined in secure correctional facilities declined from 73 to 66 percent.[45]

Based on a review of state assessment of compliance with the DMC Initiative, Michael Leiber reports that the overrepresentation of minority youths was evident in every state where adequate data were available, that overrepresentation existed at all decision points, that the decision point where minority overrepresentation was most pronounced varied by state, and that overrepresentation appeared to be greatest in those states with smaller minority populations.[46]

Decarceration of Status Offenders   In the early 1970s, the federal government pushed for elimination of all status offenders from "secure" institutions designed to house delinquent offenders. As a result of this decarceration policy, large numbers of juveniles were shifted from institutions to community-based programs such as shelter-care facilities run by local Youth Service Bureaus. By 1995 only 2.6 percent of juveniles in public facilities were held for *status offenses,* while 95.6 percent were held for delinquent offenses.[47] However, many juveniles who committed a second status offense ended up being incarcerated as a result of a process known as boot strapping, in which a youth who violates a formal court order, for example, to not run away from home, is considered to have committed a criminal offense. These youths are not technically status offenders and the original federal legislation could be sidestepped. Such practices led to revisions in the law in 2002. *The Juvenile Justice and Delinquency Act of 2002* states:

> Juveniles . . . charged with or who have committed offenses that would not be criminal if committed by an adult or offenses *which do not constitute violations of valid court orders,* or alien juveniles in custody, or such non-offenders as dependent or neglected children, shall not be placed in secure detention facilities or secure correctional facilities. (italics added)[48]

Not all states believed boot strapping to be a good practice. Taking the position that boot strapping was not "the least restrictive alternative," some states, including California, Florida, Indiana, Louisiana, Maryland, North Carolina, Pennsylvania, and Wisconsin, specifically disallowed the practice by statute.[49] More recently, the Kentucky legislature included statutory language stating: "Status offenders shall not be converted into public offenders by virtue of status conduct,"[50] thus effectively prohibiting the practice.

Institutions for Girls

The State Industrial School for Girls, the first institution in the United States built exclusively for the correction of girls, opened in Lancaster, Massachusetts, in 1856. One hundred seventeen years later, in 1973, the school closed its doors as did many other juvenile institutions in Massachusetts when a temporary reform movement of *deinstitutionalization* (intentionally removing juveniles from institutions) hit the state. The Lancaster school had served for well over a century to save young girls, especially those from the poorer classes, from the corrupting influences of urban vice and crime and to preserve family stability. During its first 50 years of operation, nearly half the girls were placed there at their parents' request. Families of the poor immigrants unable to support their children and parents simply unable to govern their teenage daughters often petitioned the state to take over responsibility. The Lancaster school provided a "homelike" milieu, emphasizing Christian family life, in which reform efforts prepared the girls for domestic work, either as wives and mothers or as paid domestic workers.[51]

This emphasis on domesticity in the correctional treatment of female juvenile offenders has continued to play a prominent role in institutions even today. In girls' reform schools, academic and vocational programs still emphasize the traditional female roles of wife, mother, and homemaker (see the discussion of vocational programs later in this chapter).[52] According to an American Bar Association (ABA) survey of juvenile facilities, the most frequent programs in girls' schools were cosmetology, business education, nursing, and food service. In contrast, the ABA found that institutions for boys were typically providing courses in auto shop, welding, and small-engine repair. Such differences in programs clearly determine differential career opportunities in the future, in terms of both job skills and wages.[53]

Even though females are half of the juvenile population and account for about 30 percent of all juvenile arrests and a little over a fourth of delinquency cases referred to the juvenile court, they comprise only 15 percent of juveniles in residential placement. Nearly a fourth of females in custody are younger than age 15, compared with 16 percent of males. Whites make up 45 percent of juvenile females in custody, while African Americans are 35 percent and Hispanics 15 percent of the correctional population.[54] Finally, while females account for 15 percent of juvenile offenders in custody, their proportion varies by offense. Moreover, females represent a much larger proportion of status offenders than delinquent offenders in custody (see Table 15-2).

Numerous studies have suggested that girls are more likely than boys to receive more-serious dispositions for less-serious offenses. And as reflected in Table 15-2, girls often end up in secure confinement for offenses for which boys would be placed on probation. John MacDonald and Meda Chesney-Lind examined the processing of nearly 26,000 juvenile cases in Hawaii over a 12-year period. They found that girls were nearly four times more likely than boys to be referred to the court for running away, and boys were 10 times more likely than girls to be referred to the court for violent offenses. However, "once girls were found delinquent, they were more likely than boys to be given a restrictive sanction for less serious offenses."[55] They note that less than 1 percent of boys given formal dispositions had been referred for running away, compared with 6 percent of the girls. However, boys were 3 times more likely than girls to receive formal dispositions for violent offenses.[56]

Living in Custody

What about the juveniles who are placed in correctional facilities? How do they adjust to their incarceration? What determines the nature of their adaptations? Institutions can be differentiated on the basis of their goals and orientations as

table 15-2   Female Proportion of Offenders in Custody, by Most Serious Offense

MOST SERIOUS OFFENSE	PROPORTION OF FEMALE OFFENDERS
Total	15%
Delinquent offenses	14
Homicide	12
Aggravated assault	16
Simple assault	25
Burglary	7
Theft	18
Drug trafficking	7
Other drug offense	15
Probation–parole violations	21
Status offenses	40
Ungovernability	59
Running away	38
Truancy	38
Curfew violation	35
Underage drinking	30

Source: Howard Snyder and Melissa Sickmund, *Juvenile Offenders and Victims: 2006 National Report* (Washington, DC: National Center for Juvenile Justice, 2006), p. 210.

well as how such differences are related to differences in the behavior of incarcerated juveniles. But few institutions operate according to a singular model; many mix treatment and custody orientations.[57]

Treatment-oriented institutions may officially promote rehabilitation of its clients, but this goal can be complicated by control or security considerations. Similarly, *custodial institutions* generally offer some minimal training or rehabilitation programs, even though their primary concern is custody. And since the mixed-goal institution attempts to combine elements of both polar types more or less equally, the result is, in terms of organizational effectiveness, often as mixed as the goals. However, comparative studies have demonstrated that the formal structure of an institution affects not only inmate responses to the institution as a whole and to the staff and programs but also assimilation into an inmate subculture. Related research has shown that as organizational orientation shifts from custody to treatment, the negative influences of confinement are either reduced or become positive.

Bernard Berk examined both juvenile detention centers and minimum-security prisons.[58] He found that inmate attitudes toward the institution were more positive in treatment-oriented than in custody-oriented institutions. He also discovered that inmate attitudes were shaped by the prison experience. Inmates who had spent long periods of time in custody-oriented institutions were more likely to hold negative attitudes than those who had been incarcerated only a few months, whereas the reverse was true at treatment-oriented prisons.

While criminologists have examined the problems of confinement in juvenile institutions, two studies stand out in terms of their extensive and intensive analyses of the nature of inmate adaptations. In a comparative study of 10 facilities in Massachusetts, Barry Feld identified four types of institutional treatment settings in terms of correctional goals, programs, and social control techniques.[59] Differences in organizational structure also had a major impact on inmates' informal social systems. In the more oppressive *custody-oriented* settings, staff roles were authoritarian and hierarchical. Staff members were strictly custodial, minimizing their contacts with inmates and attempting to maintain a high level of surveillance and control. Such practices, coupled with a high degree of institutional deprivation, gave inmates many incentives to engage in covert deviance. In this setting, there emerged a group of tough inmates who exploited weaker inmates and used violence to reinforce their own status. The use of violence by inmates, paralleling staff practices of social control, resulted in a rigidly structured authoritarian subculture in which the social distance between high- and low-status inmates was comparable to the distance between inmates and staff.

On the other hand, in *treatment-oriented* facilities that used a cottage system, substantially less hostility and aggression among inmates were observed. The greater harmony was largely due to the introduction of formal collaboration between staff and inmates, which increased the social solidarity of the entire institution and diminished incentives for violent solutions. In addition to the impact of structural and program changes on institutional climate, criminologists have reported that the greater proportion of the "hard core" juvenile being waived to adult court has resulted in fewer of these youths being sent to juvenile facilities. Moreover, most directors of juvenile facilities, whether custodial or treatment-oriented, appear unwilling to abandon the goal of rehabilitation and are thus focused on maintaining environments more conducive to positive change.[60]

But not all is completely rosy. A detailed account of the brutalizing conditions in the more custody-oriented institutions is provided by Clemens Bartollas.[61] Upon arrival at the institution, boys are subjected to a testing process by inmate leaders to determine whether the new boys will defend themselves when attacked and whether they have a history of sexual exploitation. The staff and other inmates offer little help to the new boys. The less able the youths are to defend themselves, the further down the exploitation scale they are pushed. Exploitative acts on this scale, in terms of increasing severity, are

1. Taking a victim's dessert and favorite foods at meals.
2. Taking his canteen purchases and pop and candy given to him by his parents.
3. Taking his institutional clothing, toilet articles, cigarettes, personal clothing, or radio.
4. Physically beating him or forcing him to masturbate others, play the passive role in anal sodomy, or be the receptor in fellatio.

Unfortunately, such patterns of exploitation and victimization in juvenile institutions are scarcely unique to the facilities studied by Feld and Bartollas; they have been well documented in many settings across the country over the past 25 years.[62] Extensive abuses were found in Louisiana juvenile training schools in the mid-1990s, including the placement of youths in isolation for long periods of time and restraining them with handcuffs and a lack of programming, counseling, and training opportunities.[63] Youths who committed serious rule violations in the West Virginia Industrial School for Boys were punished by being placed in small, windowless, steel-walled cells, 4 feet wide and 8 feet long, and allowed to wear only their undershorts. Other punishments included "floor time," whereby an inmate was required to stand stiffly in one position for several hours, and "bench time," in which an inmate was required to sit in a specified location with arms crossed for several hours each day for several days without talking or moving.[64]

In 2003 the Department of Justice filed a suit against the state of Mississippi over "disturbing" and "unconscionable" conditions at two of the state's juvenile correctional facilities: Oakley Training School, which holds about 325 boys, and Columbia Training School, which houses about 100 boys and 100 girls, ages 10 to 18. Among the appalling practices were the hog-tying and pole-shackling of children; requiring children to eat their own vomit; and the routine hitting, slapping, and shoving of youths by staff. On some occasions, suicidal girls were stripped and placed in isolation cells, which were windowless, empty, "dark rooms" with only a single drain in the floor to be used as a toilet.[65]

All correctional institutions contain some form of inmate culture and informal set of rules as a response to the unique circumstances experienced by inmates. While boys engage in aggressive, coercive behaviors to establish hierarchies and define social roles, girls are more likely to respond by developing family structures parallel to those outside the institution. According to Barbara Carter,

> Inmate culture in a girls' school is best understood as a complex of meanings through which the girls maintain continuity between their lives inside and outside of the institution; and as social forms established to mitigate and manage the pains of confinement and problems of intimate group living.[66]

Pseudo families are intimate relationships that substitute for those found outside the institutions. These families sometimes emerge out of continuing courtships and other times occur spontaneously. Courtship reflects traditional boy–girl relationships: recognition seeking, emotional involvement, and companionship. Consequently, such relationships can be characterized as symbolically heterosexual rather than homosexual. According to both Carter and Rose Giallombardo, this family structure involves only minor physical contact, such as hand-holding, touching, and kissing.[67] Coercive homosexual relationships often found in male institutions are rare in female facilities. Sexual roles, ranging from "mother" and "father" and "husband" and "wife" to "sister" and "cousin," also reflect traditional male–female sex roles.

According to Coramae Richey Mann, pseudo families fulfill three functions.[68] They "provide a measure of affection and belonging to girls who are lonely, isolated from their natural families, and deprived of their freedom." They offer a "form of protection from verbal and physical attacks by other inmates." And they aid the institution in maintaining social control. Institutional control is enhanced inasmuch as families, both in and out of institutions, are the primary socializing agents for the individual, teaching the rules and regulations of the institution.

Neal Shover and Werner Einstadter suggest that juvenile female inmates are less violent, less committed to an inmate code, and more likely to create pseudo families than juvenile male inmates.[69] They believe these differences may be accounted for by "differences in the preconfinement experiences of boys and girls, and traditional sex-role differences." In addition, they point out that institutionalized girls may be much more affected than boys by the loss of supportive relationships.

Treatment, Education, Vocational Training, and Recreation

Nearly all juvenile correctional facilities are organized around the following major programming areas: treatment and counseling, education, vocational training, and recreation. As noted earlier, some institutions emphasize treatment; others focus greater attention on security issues. Although the emphasis may differ, both attend to a greater or lesser degree to each of the programming areas.

Treatment and Counseling   The juvenile court was founded on the belief that juvenile delinquency was only a reflection or symptom of a deeper or more serious individual disorder, and that by taking an individualized, nonpunitive, treatment approach built on the *medical model*, which views delinquency as a disease, juvenile delinquents could be "cured" of their problems. Recent surveys of mental health disorders among institutionalized delinquents report a significant portion of institutionalized youths meet current psychiatric definitions of disorders. For example, Steven Pliszka and his colleagues found between 15 and 40 percent of detained youths had affective disorders, such as bipolar disorder and depression,[70] and a recent multistate study reported over 70 percent of youths in the juvenile justice system met criteria for at least one mental health disorder, such as disruptive disorders, substance use disorders, and anxiety and mood disorders.[71] This latter finding should not be surprising inasmuch as all the youths in the study were already defined by the court as having been involved in delinquent behavior.

The fields of psychology and psychiatry dominated the treatment of institutionalized juveniles during most of the 20th century and a variety of treatment approaches have been utilized. These include *behavior modification*, based on the work of B.F. Skinner and the use of positive and negative reinforcements to change behavior; *milieu therapy*, developed by Bruno Bettelheim, which uses all aspects of the institutional context, including peer and staff relationships; *reality therapy*, developed from the work of William Glasser, designed to help youths understand the consequences of their actions and to take responsibility for those consequences; as well as a wide variety of individual and group counseling techniques.[72]

Two very popular group treatment approaches, *guided group interaction* and *positive peer culture*, attempt to create prosocial group environments in which groups control members' antisocial actions and support conventional behaviors. Group, or peer, leaders facilitate, encourage, and reinforce conventional values and interactions in a supportive environment. However, much research on these two approaches suggests that treatment programs involving groups of antisocial youths may not be effective and may even have negative outcomes.[73] According to James Howell, "research has shown that prevention programs that create intense group interactions among homogeneous groups of antisocial youths can actually increase the forms of behavior they are intended to prevent, particularly if they do not employ leaders who control the expression and rewarding of antisocial sentiments."[74] For example, Thomas Dishion and his colleagues report that treatment approaches that gather antisocial youths into intensely interacting groups may actually promote friendships and bonds that go on to undermine the goals of the treatment and thus promote additional antisocial behavior rather.[75]

Education   Joan McCord and her associates believe that many children sent to juvenile reform schools have "significant educational needs . . . and many have not attended school recently and many perform below grade level."[76] School has generally not been a very positive experience for them (see Chapter 11). Most incarcerated youths are at least 2 years behind their peers in basic academic skills and have had higher rates of absenteeism, suspension, or expulsion from school.[77] About 33 percent of institutionalized youths read at or below the 4th-grade level, and only 20 percent read at or above the 9th-grade level.[78] Only about 10 percent of youths in public schools nationally are identified as academically disabled and in need of special education; however, between 30 and 50 percent of incarcerated youths are identified with learning disabilities.[79] Because the majority of youths placed in correctional facilities have educational deficiencies, nearly all juvenile facilities maintain some type of remedial and basic educational programming.

Institutions have to attend to the academic needs of a broad range of grades, provide basic literacy classes, and prepare youths for a traditional high school diploma or a General Educational Development (GED) certificate. While school in a juvenile correctional facility differs from traditional school in many ways, one of the most significant differences is tied to the constant arrival and departure of youths throughout the year. There is no "semester plan," and in many

Education plays a major role in the juvenile justice system as a means to empower delinquents to desist from crime and contribute to society. What deficits do serious delinquents face when they attend school while in state custody? How do cognitive factors and thinking styles contribute to both good and bad behavior?

institutions, youths are grouped according to their academic level rather than their age. Teachers then individualize learning plans for each youth based on the child's educational evaluation. Most institutions provide the normal range of subjects, including math, science, history, and English.

Vocational Training   Vocational training in juvenile correctional facilities reflects the early reference to such institutions as "industrial schools" or "training schools." Most youths sent to institutions by juvenile courts have not yet developed job skills, even though many have already dropped out of school and are looking for work. It is not uncommon for vocational programs to reflect sex stereotyping, and thus programs at boys' facilities typically include auto repair, woodworking, drafting, small-engine repair, computer programming and repair, printing, and metalworking, while programs in girls' facilities are more likely to include secretarial training, cosmetology, library services, and data entry. The relative lack of vocational programs designed to give girls the most current in-demand skills has long been a complaint and may reflect a lower level of commitment to female corrections more generally.

Recreation   Most juvenile institutions provide a wide range of recreational activities, such as basketball, softball, volleyball, billiards, art, music, table games, and sometimes swimming. While physical activity itself it seen as useful for avoiding problems of boredom and using up excessive adolescent energy, many social scientists and penologists view recreation as an important element in the institution's rehabilitative efforts. Recreation can assist with alleviating stress;

identify activities that can serve as alternatives to drug and alcohol use; foster interpersonal skills such as trust, cooperation, and teamwork; enhance self-esteem; encourage new interests; and develop decision-making and problem-solving skills.[80]

Conditions of Confinement

Dale Parent and his colleagues conducted an extensive survey and interview study of conditions or problems of confinement in juvenile institutions.[81] The most serious deficiencies observed were in the areas of living space, security, control of suicidal behaviors, and health care.

Living Space   A substantial proportion of confined juveniles have inadequate living space because of the pervasive problem of crowding in juvenile facilities. In the early 1990s, 47 percent of confined juveniles were in facilities whose populations exceeded their reported design capacities. For example, Michigan's W.J. Maxey Training School housed 450 youths in the mid-1990s and was experiencing a variety of problems, ranging from runaways, assaults, and suicides, to physical abuse by staff and even the murder of one youth. By 2002 the youth population had been reduced to fewer than 250 and most of the prior problems were significantly reduced.[82]

Security   Security practices are intended to prevent escapes and to provide a safe environment for both juveniles and staff. In the 30 days prior to the Parent survey, juveniles in the facilities studied injured nearly 2,000 juveniles and 650 staff. Juvenile and staff injury rates were higher in crowded facilities. In addition, slightly more than 800 juveniles escaped from confinement and slightly more than 800 attempted to escape but failed.

Controlling Suicidal Behavior   Incarcerated or detained youths are a high-risk population for suicide. At least 30 juveniles died while in custody in 2000, and seven of those deaths (23 percent) were the result of suicide (see Table 15-3). Even though the custody death rate is only a little more than half the death rate of juveniles ages 13 to 17 in the general population, it remains a significant concern. Each year, more than 11,000 youths engage in some form of suicidal behavior while confined in correctional facilities. Among confined male adolescents, suicidal behavior appears to be associated with depression and lack of social connections, while impulsivity and instability are associated with female suicidal behavior. Both males and females who are housed in isolation are more likely to engage in suicidal acts than youths housed in the general population, and past suicide attempts are significantly predictive of future suicide attempts.[83] To date, the only significantly effective measures for reducing suicidal behavior among confined juveniles are to conduct suicide screenings during admission and to improve the training of staff in suicide prevention.[84] Training of staff is critical because many juvenile correctional workers have inadequate knowledge of suicide risk factors.[85]

Health Care   Although confined juveniles were provided with satisfactory basic health care, Parent and his associates reported that health screenings at admission and subsequent health appraisals were often not completed in a timely

table 15-3   Causes of Death in Juvenile Correctional Facilities, 2000

CAUSE OF DEATH	TOTAL	INSIDE THE FACILITY			OUTSIDE THE FACILITY		
		ALL	PUBLIC	PRIVATE	ALL	PUBLIC	PRIVATE
Total	30	13	9	4	17	5	12
Accident*	9	2	0	2	7	2	5
Illness/natural	8	5	4	1	3	2	1
Suicide	7	6	5	1	1	0	1
Homicide by non-resident	4	0	0	0	4	1	3
Other	2	0	0	0	2	0	2

*Accidents were also the leading cause of death for youths age 13 to 17 in the general population, followed by homicide and suicide.

Source: Melissa Sickmund, *Juvenile Residential Facility Census, 2000: Selected Findings* (Washington, DC: Office of Juvenile Justice and Delinquency Prevention, 2002), p. 4.

fashion.[86] Speedy completion of health screenings are critical for ensuring that juveniles who are injured, who have acute health problems, or who are under the influence of alcohol or illicit drugs when admitted receive immediate medical treatment.

Sexually Transmitted Diseases   One factor that Parent and his colleagues *did not* consider was the issue of HIV/AIDS and other sexually transmitted diseases in juvenile facilities. However, in 1994 the National Institute of Justice and the Centers for Disease Control and Prevention conducted a survey of juvenile justice systems.[87] Forty-one (41) state systems, 32 city or county detention centers, and 27 state training schools responded to the survey. A total of 60 confined juveniles were reported to have AIDS (50 boys and 10 girls). Only two state systems reported mandatory screening of incoming juveniles. No city or county juvenile detention centers reported screening all incoming juveniles, although with the short stay and high turnover rate, it is not surprising. Of the two systems that reported screening all incoming juveniles, only one housed juveniles testing positive for HIV apart from other juveniles. Two other systems segregated juveniles with AIDS but did not report mass screening policies. None of the responding jurisdictions reported screening releasees.

Juveniles in custody are at a high risk for sexually transmitted diseases, particularly HIV and AIDS. A recent study by Linda Teplin and her associates reports that more than 90 percent of incarcerated males and over 86 percent of incarcerated females were sexually active, with 35 percent of males and 41 percent of females reporting having had unprotected vaginal sex during the month prior to the survey. In addition, among males, 12 percent reported having had anal sex, 68 percent had sex when drunk or high, and 43 percent had been tattooed. Among females in confinement, 7 percent reported having had anal sex, 52 percent had sex when drunk or high, and 45 percent had been tattooed.[88] In addition, youths with serious mental disorders and who were substance abusers were at substantially increased likelihood of engaging in HIV/AIDS risk behaviors.[89]

Other sexually transmitted diseases are more common among incarcerated youths, especially among institutionalized girls. Recent studies have found that about 2 percent of incarcerated juveniles tested positive for Hepatitis C virus (HCV), just less than 5 percent have tested positive for pelvic inflammatory disease (PID), between 16 and 27 percent of incarcerated females tested positive for chlamydia trachomatis, and between 6 and 17 percent for gonococcal infections.[90]

JUVENILES IN ADULT PRISONS

Some juvenile offenders are considered either to *not* be amenable to treatment in the juvenile justice system or to be repeat, serious, and dangerous offenders in need of long-term incapacitation. These offenders are often waived or transferred to criminal court to be prosecuted as adults. If convicted, they face incarceration in an adult prison.

Between 1985 and 1997 the number of juveniles in adult prisons increased each year, eventually reaching a peak of about 5,500. But since 1997, fewer juveniles were incarcerated in adult facilities (see Figure 15-1). Today, only about 2,300 persons under age 18 are in custody in adult prisons, with another 6,700 housed temporarily in adult jails. Juveniles account for slightly less than 0.2 percent of all inmates in state prisons.

Nearly 4,100 juveniles were admitted to adult prisons in 2002. Compared with young adult inmates ages 18 to 24, juvenile admissions involved youths with a greater proportion of violent offenses (primarily robbery and assault) and a smaller proportion of drug offenses. Nearly all (96 percent) of juvenile admissions were male, and most (79 percent) were age 17. African Americans

Juveniles convicted of serious crimes and sentenced to adult prisons experience more severe deprivations than youths in juvenile institutions. They are also more likely to be exploited or victimized while incarcerated. Should juvenile offenders always be separated from adult inmates?

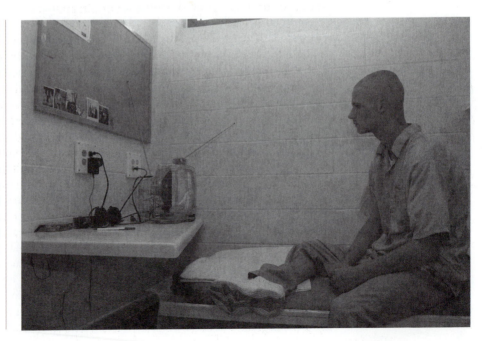

figure 15-1 One-Day Count of Juveniles in State Prisons

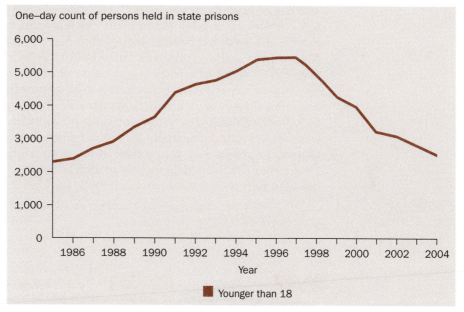

One–day count of persons held in state prisons

Source: Howard Snyder and Melissa Sickmund, *Juvenile Offenders and Victims: 2006 National Report* (Washington, DC: National Center for Juvenile Justice, 2006), p. 238.

accounted for 59 percent of new admissions; whites, 28 percent: and Hispanics, 11 percent. Youths of other race/ethnicity accounted for 2 percent of new admissions.[91]

One of the most serious dilemmas of incarcerating juvenile offenders in adult prisons is the issue of separating or integrating juvenile and adult inmates. Because juveniles are more vulnerable than older inmates and more likely to be victimized, should they be housed in separate facilities, segregated in special units within institutions, or placed in the general adult inmate population? States have responded very differently to this question. Most states allow juvenile inmates to be housed in state correctional facilities with other adult offenders as part of the general population. Only 13 percent of states with juvenile inmates maintain separate facilities or units for youthful offenders.[92] Six states (Arizona, Hawaii, Kentucky, Montana, Tennessee, and West Virginia) require all inmates under age 18 to be housed separately from adults. In North Dakota and California, no person under age 16 can be held in an adult prison. Graduated incarceration is employed in 12 states. In this system, inmates under age 18 begin their sentences in a juvenile facility until they reach a certain age (typically 18). The offender can then be transferred to an adult facility to serve the remainder of the sentence or, if the state chooses, released. Eight states use segregated incarceration in assigning certain underage offenders to specific facilities based on age and programming needs. For example, in Florida, juveniles convicted in criminal court can be sentenced to the youthful offender program that separates ages 14 to 18 from ages 19 to 24.[93]

Juveniles incarcerated in the general prison population in adult prisons are subject to a greater variety of risks and are more vulnerable to violent victimization

think
about it

Juveniles who commit serious crimes often face adult sanctions. Is this an appropriate response to youth crime? Does the criminal justice system effectively "wash its hands" of juvenile delinquents who engage in serious criminal offending?

than youths incarcerated in juvenile institutions. Among the greater risks for juveniles are an increased likelihood of suicide, risk of being sexually assaulted, and risk of being beaten by staff.[94] A 17-year-old boy incarcerated in the juvenile cellblock of an adult jail in Ohio was murdered by six adult prisoners. In Florida, a 17-year-old boy was strangled to death by his 20-year-old cellmate.[95] Martin Forst and his colleagues found that, whereas about half of the juvenile offenders assigned to a juvenile institution or adult prison reported being victims of property crime, juveniles in prison were more likely to be victims of violent crime than those in a juvenile institution: Only 37 percent of those assigned to juvenile facilities were victims of violence, compared with 46 percent of the juveniles in prison. In addition, they found that sexual assault of youths was five times more common in prison than in juvenile facilities and that youths were 50 percent more likely to be victims of attacks by other inmates involving weapons than were their counterparts in juvenile facilities.[96]

PAROLE

Parole, also referred to as *aftercare,* is the release and subsequent community supervision of an individual from an institution before the scheduled period of commitment has ended. Juvenile parole has its origins in the early house-of-refuge practice of requiring child inmates to work several years in private homes after their term of incarceration. It was the responsibility of the receiving family to feed and clothe the child, as well as to decide when he or she had earned complete freedom.[97]

Today, the decision to grant parole and the determination of conditions of parole are generally made at the discretion of state officials, often by a parole board or the staff of the institution where the juvenile is confined. However, entrusting the important decision of whether to grant parole to the discretion of institutional staff raises some serious concerns. When coupled with the traditional provision for indeterminate sentencing, allowing such discretion gives institutional officials great power over a juvenile's life for a long period of time. Juvenile codes that do not deal with parole typically require judicial review of any modifications of disposition. This approach seems better designed to protect juveniles' rights because the review gives them the opportunity to be heard in matters of vital concern to them.

Nearly 100,000 juveniles are paroled back into the community each year. These youths coming out of institutional placements often come from dysfunctional families or single-parent homes in which other relatives have been incarcerated. More than half have at least one family member who served time in jail or prison and nearly 20 percent had two or more such family members.[98] In addition, these youths tend to be seriously lagging behind educationally when compared with others in their age bracket (nearly 60 percent have not completed 8th grade, compared with only 24 percent in the general population). More than half report drinking alcohol on a regular basis prior to their commitment, and more than 60 percent report using drugs, excluding alcohol, on a regular basis. The majority of paroled youths are nonviolent offenders but have spent a large proportion of their adolescence in some form of institutional placement.[99]

Parole is similar to *probation* in that it is conditional and requires a youth to submit to supervision by a parole officer. Conditions of supervision are very similar to probation conditions—parolees are required to, among other things, obey all laws, observe curfews, attend school or maintain employment, report to their probation officers regularly, and often submit to random drug or alcohol tests. Parole revocation may result when a youth violates the law or one of the discretionary conditions of supervision. If revoked, the youth is returned to a correctional facility deemed appropriate. And while parole supervision and programming for aftercare treatment of juvenile offenders is one of the most important elements in juvenile corrections, it is also given relatively little attention by policy makers.[100]

Because a significant, although small, portion of youths released from correctional facilities are serious violent offenders, intensive aftercare programs (IAPs) have been developed to provide communities with greater protection through intensive supervision of these youths. Intensive aftercare program officers have very restricted caseloads and are required to have multiple face-to-face meetings with their parolees each week. Some IAPs, such as the Philadelphia program begun in 1988, restrict caseloads to only 12 youths, expect IAP officers to assume supervision of the youths immediately following disposition as the youths enter institutional placement, have monthly visits with the juvenile and his or her family in preparation for release, and have at least three face-to-face meetings per week with the youth during the first six weeks after release and then two meetings per week for the next six weeks. In addition, IAP officers are expected to establish and maintain contact with the juvenile's parents or guardians, school authorities, and/or employer at least once every other week.[101]

The recidivism rates of juvenile offenders released from out-of-home placement is very high. Over 90 percent of those released from California Youth Authority institutions were rearrested or had their parole revoked within three years.[102] Nearly 45 percent of youths released from secure facilities in Delaware had been rearrested for felonies within one year.[103] Finally, 60 percent of youths incarcerated for murder or attempted murder in Florida returned to prison, with the majority of those doing so within three years.[104]

A number of communities have developed aftercare wraparound programs to help reduce recidivism by juveniles. Wraparound programs are designed to build constructive relationships and support networks between delinquent youths and their families, teachers, and other caregivers and agencies in the community.[105] The main purpose of a wraparound program is to integrate service delivery for juveniles requiring services from multiple service providers through team-driven treatment planning that includes youths, caregivers, agencies, and community services. These programs often involve a coordination of services including clinical therapy, substance use treatment, special education, medication, caregiver support, medical health care, transportation, mentorship, and public assistance.[106]

Evaluations of wraparound programs are limited; however, a few have been conducted and generally report positive effects, including reduced recidivism, lower likelihood of recidivism or to recidivate with a felony, being less assaultive, serving less time in detention, and less likely to runaway from home or to be suspended from school.[107] An example of a successful wraparound program is Wraparound Milwaukee, begun in 1995 and currently serving more than 400 adjudicated delinquent youths. Wraparound Milwaukee is discussed in Box 15-3.

box 15-3   DELINQUENCY PREVENTION
Wraparound Milwaukee

Wraparound Milwaukee integrates or coordinates care services from eight lead agencies and a network of agencies representing mental health, child welfare, juvenile justice, and education services in the Milwaukee area. The major components of Wraparound Milwaukee include care coordinators, who assess the situation, put together a plan, and then coordinate needed services; child and family teams, composed of family members, other relatives, church members, and juvenile justice workers to form the core of the support system; mobile crisis teams, available to provide 24-hour crisis intervention; and a provider network of more than 170 service providing agencies.

The use of residential treatment has decreased by more than 60 percent since the start up of Wraparound Milwaukee program, inpatient psychiatric hospitalization has dropped by 80 percent, and average overall cost of care per child has dropped from more than $5,000 per month to less than $3,300 per month. Moreover, one-year recidivism rates have been cut in half.

Services in the Wraparound Milwaukee program include:

- Care coordination
- In-home therapy
- Medication management
- Outpatient–individual family therapy
- Alcohol and substance abuse counseling
- Psychiatric assessment

- Psychological evaluation
- Housing assistance
- Mental health assessment/evaluation
- Mentoring
- Parent aide
- Group home care
- Respite care
- Child care for parent
- Tutoring
- Specialized camps
- Emergency food pantry
- Residential treatment
- Foster care
- Day treatment or alternative school
- Nursing assessment and management
- Job development and placement
- Kinship care
- Transportation services
- Supervision and observation in home
- After-school programs
- Recreation and child-oriented activities
- Discretionary funds or flexible funds
- Housekeeping and chore services
- Independent living support
- Psychiatric inpatient hospital
- Crisis home care
- Treatment foster care

Source: Bruce Kamradt, "Wraparound Milwaukee: Aiding Youth with Mental Health Needs," *Juvenile Justice Journal* 7:14–23 (2000).

THE JUVENILE DEATH PENALTY

Although few juveniles have ever been executed in the United States, at least 366 were legally executed between 1642 and 2007. The first recorded execution of a juvenile took place in Plymouth Colony: Thomas Graunger, age 16, was executed for the crime of bestiality. James Arcene, only 10 years old when he committed his crime, was the youngest juvenile to be executed. Arcene, a Cherokee, was 22 when he was finally hanged at Fort Smith, Arkansas, for his participation in a murder. The last juvenile executed was Scott Hain, in Oklahoma, on April 3, 2003.

Since the 1890s, juveniles accounted for less than 2 percent of all persons executed. From the 1890s to 1930, fewer than 30 juveniles were executed in any given decade. However, in the decades of the 1930s and 1940s, there was an unusual increase in juvenile executions, with 40 and 50 such executions in the respective decades. Between 1965 and 1984, no juveniles were executed. With the execution of Charles Rumbaugh in Texas on September 11, 1985, juveniles once again faced execution.

Between 1985 and April 2003, 22 persons were executed who had been juveniles at the time they committed their crimes. Of these, 19 were executed in southern states, with 13 (68 percent) in Texas. All 22 were males, 10 were white, 11 were African American, and one was Hispanic. All but one were age 17 at the time of their crimes. On February 4, 1999, Sean Sellers was executed in Oklahoma for three murders he had committed when he was 16 years old. In 1985 Sellers killed Oklahoma City convenience store clerk Robert Bower, and then 6 months later, in 1986, he shot his mother and stepfather, Vonda and Paul Bellofatto. Prior to Sellers's execution, the last person to be executed for a crime committed at age 16 was Leonard Shockley, who was put to death in Maryland in 1959.[108]

Debate over the Juvenile Death Penalty

That the United States continued to sentence juveniles to death into the 21st century appears to be an anomaly within the context of the nation's traditional juvenile justice philosophy. In 1982 the Supreme Court heard the case of *Eddings v. Oklahoma*.[109] Monty Lee Eddings, a 16-year-old male, killed a highway patrol officer and was sentenced to death. Upon appeal, the Court overturned the lower court's sentence. However, the Court avoided dealing directly with the issue of whether it was constitutional to execute juveniles. Instead, it argued that the lower court had not taken into consideration all required mitigating circumstances. In the *Eddings* case, the sentencing judge had refused to review evidence of the boy's background, including beatings administered by his father and the child's severe emotional disturbance. In a 5-to-4 decision, the Court remanded the case, indicating that the Eighth Amendment requires consideration of a defendant's background and record in addition to the immediate circumstances of the offense. And even though the Court noted that youthfulness of the offender was one of the mitigating circumstances that must be considered in a capital case, it refused to rule that application of the death penalty for juveniles violates the Eighth Amendment. Eddings was resentenced to death but that sentence was then modified to life imprisonment.[110]

In 1988 the Supreme Court held in *Thompson v. Oklahoma* that the execution of a person who was under age 16 at the time of the commission of his or her crime was unconstitutional.[111] William Wayne Thompson was 15 years old when he premeditatedly murdered his former brother-in-law by beating him, shooting him twice, cutting his throat, and stabbing him in the chest and abdomen. Although only 15, Thompson was transferred to adult court for prosecution, where he was convicted and sentenced to death.

In the *Thompson* decision (see Box 15-4), the Court held what is a fundamental principle of our society that no one who is as little as one day short of

think
about it

What do we think of juveniles who commit violent murders? Are they more disturbed than adults who commit similar murders? Are they less able to control themselves than adults? Does this make them more dangerous than adult killers?

box 15-4   FROM THE BENCH

Thompson v. Oklahoma

William Wayne Thompson, a 15-year-old boy, together with three older persons, brutally murdered Thompson's former brother-in-law. However, Thompson was a "child" according to Oklahoma law. At the waiver hearing, the trial court concluded "that there are virtually no reasonable prospects for rehabilitation of William Wayne Thompson within the juvenile system." He was certified to stand trial as an adult, convicted, and sentenced to death.

A divided U.S. Supreme Court vacated the sentence, holding that no child under age 16 should be eligible for the death sentence. The Court argued that "the reasons why juveniles are not trusted with the privileges and responsibilities of an adult also explain why their irresponsible conduct is not as morally reprehensible as that of an adult," and that a "normal 15-year-old is not prepared to assume the full responsibilities of an adult." Moreover, the Court believed that "it would offend civilized standards of decency to execute a person who was less than 16 years old at the time of his or her offense," noting that the only executions of a person under age 16 in the United States in the 20th century occurred prior to 1949, that only a minority of the states provide for capital punishment in cases involving persons under age 16, and that the death penalty for juveniles has been abolished in nearly all other countries.

Source: Thompson v. Oklahoma, 487 U.S. 815 (1988).

his or her 16th birthday can have sufficient maturity and moral responsibility to be subjected to capital punishment for any crime.[112] Part of the reasoning by the Court in setting age 16 as the minimum was that it is generally recognized as the age separating childhood from adulthood. In most states, this is the age at which minors are legally allowed to take on some adult responsibilities, such as driving a car.[113]

The Supreme Court rejected appeals in a combination of two cases in 1989 (*Stanford v. Kentucky* and *Wilkins v. Missouri*) that could have prohibited execution of anyone younger than 18 at the time of commission of the crime (see Box 15-5).[114] Justice Antonin Scalia, writing the majority opinion in the combined cases, noted that even though Congress established 18 as the minimum age for the death penalty in drug-related murders, "this does not establish the degree of national consensus that this Court has previously thought sufficient to label a particular punishment cruel and unusual."[115]

In 2002 Kevin Stanford appealed his death sentence once more to the U.S. Supreme Court.[116] The Court, in a 5-to-4 decision, declined to hear the case. Stanford's appeal this time argued that the Supreme Court had just prohibited the death penalty for mentally retarded offenders in *Atkins v. Virginia* and that the reasoning was analogous to juvenile offenders.[117] In *Atkins* the Court had held that

> Those mentally retarded persons who meet the law's requirements for criminal responsibility should be tried and punished when they commit crimes. Because of their disabilities in areas of reasoning, judgment, and control of their impulses, however, they do not act with the level of moral culpability that characterizes the most serious adult criminal conduct.[118]

box 15-5   FROM THE BENCH

Stanford v. Kentucky

Kevin Stanford was 17 years and 4 months old at the time he raped and sodomized and then shot and killed 20-year-old Barbel Poore during an armed robbery. Heath Wilkins was 16 years and 6 months old when he stabbed to death Nancy Allen, a 26-year-old mother of two who was a sales clerk at a convenience store. Stanford was transferred to criminal court for trial and were convicted and sentenced to death. Both cases were appealed to the U.S. Supreme Court.

In a 5-to-4 opinion, the Court stated that the thrust of the petitioner's arguments is that the imposition of the death penalty on those who were juveniles when they committed their crimes falls under the Eighth Amendment's prohibition against "cruel and unusual punishments" and that the punishment is contrary to the "evolving standards of decency that mark the progress of a maturing society." However, the Court noted that the majority of the states that permit capital punishment authorize it for crimes committed at age 16 or above, and that between 1982 and 1988 a total of 15 death sentences were imposed on persons age 16 or under and 30 on individuals who were age 17 at the time of the crime. The Court concluded:

We discern neither a historical nor a modern societal consensus forbidding the imposition of capital punishment on any person who murders at 16 or 17 years of age. Accordingly, we conclude that such punishment does not offend the Eighth Amendment's prohibition against cruel and unusual punishment.

Source: Stanford v. Kentucky, 492 U.S. 361 (1989).

think about it

If a youth is considered criminally culpable and sufficiently morally responsible to be tried as an adult and face life in prison without possibility of parole, then why should the youth not be eligible for the death penalty?

Justice Stevens, in his dissent in the new *Stanford* case, recalled the dissenting opinion in the first *Stanford* case and argued that the reasons for not executing juvenile and mentally retarded offenders were essentially the same. In addition, he argued that the trend regarding the age for taking on legal responsibilities has moved toward requiring individuals to be older, rather than younger, noting that all states now require one to be at least 18 in order to marry without parental consent, and that the Court should "put an end to this shameful practice."[119] Although the Supreme Court declined further review of the *Stanford* case, the Kentucky governor granted clemency to Kevin Stanford, and now he is serving a sentence of life in prison without the possibility of parole.

Two states, Kansas and New York, reenacted their capital punishment laws in the mid-1990s and set age 18 as the minimum age for execution. Between 1999 and 2004, four states abolished their juvenile death penalty laws: Montana in 1999, Indiana in 2002, and South Dakota, and Wyoming in 2004.

State legislatures were clearly shifting away from the juvenile death penalty, although public support for applying the death penalty to juvenile offenders continued to be relatively high. Most surveys found very strong support for execution of "normal" adult offenders convicted of murder (around 68 percent) unless an alternative of life in prison without possibility of parole is provided, in which case support drops substantially. Surveys found lower support for execution of juvenile murderers, generally between 20 and 40 percent, but that also dropped when the prison-without-parole option was given.[120]

End of the Juvenile Death Penalty

Christopher Simmons was 17 years old when he told two friends (ages 15 and 16) that he wanted to kill someone. On several occasions, he discussed with his friends his plan to burglarize a house and to murder the victim by tying the victim up and pushing him from a bridge. Simmons said they could "get away with it" because they were minors. Following his plan, Simmons and a 15-year-old accomplice broke into Shirley Crook's home in the middle of the night, forced her from her bed and used duct tape to cover her eyes and mouth and to bind her hands. They then drove her to a state park, reinforced her bindings, and covered her head with a towel. They tied her hands and feet together with electrical wire, wrapped her whole face with duct tape and threw her from the bridge, drowning her in the waters below. The medical examiner reported that Crook died as a result of drowning and noted that she still was alive before being pushed from the bridge. On the same afternoon fishermen recovered the victim's body, Simmons was bragging about the killing, telling friends he had killed a woman "because the bitch seen my face." [121] Simmons was arrested the next day, waived his

The U.S. Supreme Court ruled in a case involving 17-year-old murderer Christopher Simmons that the execution of a person who was age 16 or 17 at the time of their crime constituted cruel and unusual punishment and was, therefore, unconstitutional.

| box 15-6 | **FROM THE BENCH** |

Roper v. Simmons

Christopher Simmons murdered Shirley Crook in a brutal manner and bragged about it to friends. He confessed and was sentenced to death; his case was eventually appealed to the U.S. Supreme Court. Why, after only 15 years since the Court had ruled in *Stanford* that the execution of 16- and 17-year-olds was constitutional, did the Court reverse itself and hold that such executions were a violation of the Eighth Amendment's prohibition against cruel and unusual punishment?

The majority opinion in this divided 5-to-4 decision argued that 16- and 17-year-old murderers must be categorically exempted from capital punishment because they "cannot with reliability be classified among the worst offenders." This conclusion was premised on three perceived differences between adults and juveniles. First, juveniles lack maturity and responsibility and are more reckless than adults. Second, juveniles are more vulnerable to outside influences because they have less control over their surroundings. And third, a juvenile's character is not as fully formed as that of an adult. According to the Court, "these differences render suspect any conclusion that a juvenile falls among the worst offenders" and that "from a moral standpoint it would be misguided to equate the failings of a minor with those of an adult." The Court also expressed its belief that juvenile murderers could be reformed: "Only a relatively small proportion of adolescents who experiment in risky or illegal activities develop entrenched patterns of problem behavior that persist into adulthood." Finally, the Court argued that the evolving standards of decency and a perceived reduction in support for the juvenile death penalty, combined with "the overwhelming weight of international opinion against the juvenile death penalty," led the Court to draw its own conclusions that the executions of juvenile offenders could no longer be considered constitutional.

Justice O'Connor and Justice Scalia (joined by Chief Justice Rehnquist and Justice Thomas) wrote separate, critical dissenting opinions. O'Connor argued the majority had provided "no evidence impeaching the seemingly reasonable conclusion reached by many state legislatures: that at least some 17-year-old murderers are sufficiently mature to deserve the death penalty in an appropriate case" and the majority's analysis "is premised on differences in the aggregate between juveniles and adults, which frequently do not hold true when comparing individuals." Scalia argued that no evidence of a national consensus opposing the juvenile death penalty was presented and that, indeed, "a number of legislatures and voters have expressly affirmed their support for capital punishment of 16- and 17-year-old offenders since *Stanford*." With regard to the role of international opinion in forming the Court's decision, Scalia wrote that "the basic premise of the Court's argument—that American law should conform to the laws of the rest of the world—ought to be rejected out of hand." Finally, both O'Connor and Scalia were critical in the Court's failing to "reprove, or even acknowledge, the Supreme Court of Missouri's unabashed refusal to follow our controlling decision in *Stanford*." O'Connor said it was "clear error," while Scalia wrote that "allowing lower courts to reinterpret the Eighth Amendment whenever they decide enough time has passed for a new snapshot leaves this Court's decisions without any force."

Source: Roper v. Simmons, 543 U.S. 551 (2005).

Source: Jeff Parker "Minors must be this tall to be lethally injected." © 2005 Florida Today.

constitutional rights to counsel, and confessed to the murder. At trial, Simmons was convicted and sentenced to death.

On May 3, 2002, Simmons filed a petition for *writ of habeas corpus* with the Supreme Court of Missouri. In 2003 that court held that contemporary standards of decency reject the death penalty for juveniles, that "a national consensus has developed against the execution of juvenile offenders," and that the U.S. Supreme Court's ruling in *Atkins* establishes a basis for finding the juvenile death penalty unconstitutional.[122] Simmons's death sentence was set aside, and he was resentenced to life in prison without the possibility of parole. The state of Missouri appealed the decision to the U.S. Supreme Court, arguing that *Stanford v. Kentucky* was the current law of the land and that it permits the execution of persons who were age 17 at the time of the crime and that a state court may not overrule a U.S. Supreme Court's ruling. On March 1, 2005, the Court handed down its 5-to-4 decision in **Roper v. Simmons,** holding that "the death penalty is disproportionate punishment for offenders under 18" and is therefore a violation of the Eighth Amendment's prohibition against cruel and unusual punishment.[123]Although the Court was divided with strongly worded dissents (see Box 15-6), the juvenile death penalty in America had come to an end.

Since 2000, only five countries in the world are known to have executed offenders who were under age 18 at the time of their crimes: China, Democratic Republic of Congo (DRC), Iran, Pakistan, and the United States. Although Pakistan and China have abolished the juvenile death penalty, nationwide compliance with their laws has been less than uniform, leading to the extralegal execution of some juveniles.[124]

conclusions

The need to preserve an orderly society has been a pervasive concern throughout our nation's history. From the beginning, correctional institutions for juveniles were quickly filled to overcrowding; staffs were largely untrained, poorly paid, and not up to the task of caring for sizable numbers of children. The institutions themselves were often inadequately built and financed. The incontrovertible evidence of institutional shortcomings and neglect and actual physical abuse of institutionalized children stands in stark contrast to the goodwill, enthusiasm, and energy of the reformers who conceived the new programs.

From both historical and contemporary perspectives, we have not obtained the knowledge we need to design, or even agree on, effective methods of reforming individuals. In addition, there has been an abysmal lack of experience and information regarding construction of institutions that would adequately house large populations. One prime factor in the perpetuation of existing programs has been the fear of alternatives. If difficult children were not institutionalized or placed under the wing of the juvenile court, where would they go? Many fear that such youths would be free to disrupt and damage the lives and homes of law-abiding citizens. In addition to developing a commitment to the ideals and dynamics of reform, we must rigorously strive to understand the realities and complexities of the challenges that face us.

key terms

Boot camps   Short-term confinement facilities where youths are exposed to a militaristic environment in which the emphasis is on physical conditioning, work, and education.

Decarceration   The policy, since the early 1970s, of removing status offenders from "secure" institutions.

Eddings v. Oklahoma   Courts must consider all mitigating circumstances before imposing the death penalty.

Electronic monitoring   An active or passive computer-based tracking system in which electronic signals are used to verify that the youth is where he or she is supposed to be.

Fine   A cash payment determined by the court and paid by the youth.

Home confinement   The intensive supervision and monitoring of an offending youth within his or her home environment.

Intensive aftercare programs (IAPs)   Programs that provide communities with greater protection through intensive supervision of paroled youths who had been convicted of violent offenses.

Parole   The release of an offender from a correctional institution before the scheduled period of confinement has ended. It typically involves supervision by a parole officer.

Parole revocation   If a youth violates the law or one of the discretionary conditions of parole, parole may be revoked and the youth returned to a correctional facility.

Probation   The conditional freedom granted by the court to an alleged or adjudicated offender, who must adhere to certain conditions and is generally supervised by a probation officer.

Pseudo families   Relationships established in correctional institutions for girls that are intended to substitute for those found on the outside.

Restitution   A court-ordered action in which an offender pays money or provides services to victims of the offense or to the community.

Roper v. Simmons   The death penalty for persons under the age of 18 is a violation of the Eighth Amendment's prohibition against cruel and unusual punishment.

Stanford v. Kentucky   The execution of a person who was age 16 or 17 at the time of his or her offense is not unconstitutional.

Thompson v. Oklahoma   The execution of a person under age 16 at the time of his or her crime is unconstitutional.

Wraparound programs   Programs designed to build constructive relationships and support networks between delinquent youths and their families, teachers, and other caregivers and agencies in the community.

SELECTED AMENDMENTS TO THE U.S. CONSTITUTION

FIRST AMENDMENT

Congress shall make no law respecting an establishment of religion, or prohibiting the free exercise thereof; or abridging the freedom of speech, or of the press; or the right of the people peaceably to assemble, and to petition the Government for a redress of grievances.

SECOND AMENDMENT

A well-regulated militia, being necessary to the security of a free State, the right of the people to keep and bear arms, shall not be infringed.

THIRD AMENDMENT

No soldier shall, in time of peace, be quartered in any house, without the consent of the owner, nor in time of war, but in a manner to be prescribed by law.

FOURTH AMENDMENT

The right of the people to be secure in their persons, houses, papers, and effects, against unreasonable searches and seizures, shall not be violated, and no warrants shall issue, but upon probable cause, supported by oath or affirmation, and particularly describing the place to be searched, and the person or things to be seized.

FIFTH AMENDMENT

No person shall be held to answer for a capital, or otherwise infamous crime, unless on a presentment or indictment of a Grand Jury, except in cases arising in the land or naval forces, or in the militia, when in actual service in time of war or public danger; nor shall any person be subject for the same offense to be twice put in jeopardy of life or limb; nor shall be compelled in any criminal case to be a witness against himself, nor be deprived of life, liberty, or property, without due process of law; nor shall private property be taken for public use, without just compensation.

SIXTH AMENDMENT

In all criminal prosecutions, the accused shall enjoy the right to a speedy and public trial, by an impartial jury of the State and district wherein the crime shall have been committed, which district shall have been previously ascertained by law, and to be informed of the nature and cause of the accusation; to be confronted with the witnesses against him; to have compulsory process for obtaining witnesses in his favor, and to have the assistance of counsel for his defense.

SEVENTH AMENDMENT

In suits at common law, where the value in controversy shall exceed twenty dollars, the right of trial by jury shall be preserved, and no fact tried by a jury shall be otherwise reexamined in any court of the United States, than according to the rules of the common law.

EIGHTH AMENDMENT

Excessive bail shall not be required, nor excessive fines imposed, nor cruel and unusual punishments inflicted.

NINTH AMENDMENT

The enumeration in the Constitution, of certain rights, shall not be construed to deny or disparage others retained by the people.

TENTH AMENDMENT

The powers not delegated to the United States by the Constitution, nor prohibited by it to the States, are reserved to the States respectively, or to the people.

FOURTEENTH AMENDMENT

Section 1. All persons born or naturalized in the United States, and subject to the jurisdiction thereof, are citizens of the United States and of the State wherein they reside. No State shall make or enforce any law which shall abridge the privileges or immunities of citizens of the United States; nor shall any State deprive any person of life, liberty, or property, without due process of law; nor deny to any person within its jurisdiction the equal protection of the laws.

HOW TO READ A CASE CITATION

Students unfamiliar with legal case citations may find them confusing. Citations are easy to understand, once you know what to look for. A case citation provides in shorthand form all the information necessary to find a copy of the report. A typical citation includes the volume number, the abbreviated name of the reporter or who compiled the record, the page number of the first page of the report, and the year the case was decided. For example, 421 U.S. 519 (1975), the citation for *Breed v. Jones,* will be found in volume 421 of the *United States Reports,* beginning on page 519. Many of the abbreviated forms and corresponding full names of the reporters cited in this index are shown in the following list. For additional information on identifying legal court citations see Mary Miles Prince, *Dictionary of Legal Citations,* 7th edition (Buffalo, NY: William S. Hein & Co., 2006). The information presented here identifies some of the more commonly referenced reporters by their abbreviations.

Cal. 2d	*California Reporter Second Series*
Cal. App. 3d	*California Appeals Third Series*
CrL.	*Criminal Law Reporter*
F. 2d	*Federal Reporter, Second series*
F. Supp.	*Federal Supplement*
Idaho	*Idaho Reporter*
Ill.	*Illinois Reporter*
L. Ed. 2d	*United States Reports, Lawyers Edition*
R.I.	*Rhode Island Reports*
S. Ct.	*Supreme Court Reporter*
U.S.	*United States Reports*
U.S.L.W.	*United States Law Week*
Wharton	*[Early Supreme Court Reporter]*

CASEST

Abington School District v. Schempp, 374 U.S. 203 (1963). A Pennsylvania law that permitted the reading of 10 verses from the Bible at the opening of each school day is overturned.

Atkins v. Virginia, 536 U.S. 304 (2002). Execution of a mentally retarded offender violates the prohibition against cruel and unusual punishment.

Baker v. Owen, 423 U.S. 907 (1975). Teachers can administer reasonable corporal punishment for disciplinary purposes.

Bethel School District No. 403 v. Fraser, 478 U.S. 675 (1986). A school may prohibit vulgar and offensive language.

Board of Education of Independent School District No. 92 of Pottawatomie County et al. v. Earls et al., 536 U.S. 822 (2002). A school can require students to submit to a urinaly-sis for illegal drugs prior to participating in *any* competitive extracurricular activity.

Breed v. Jones, 421 U.S. 519 (1975). A criminal prosecution of a child after he or she has had a juvenile court hearing on the same offense constitutes double jeopardy.

Brewer v. Williams, 430 U.S. 387 (1977). Once a suspect has requested an attorney, the police cannot make statements designed to elicit responses from him or her without legal counsel present.

Buck v. Bell, 274 U.S. 200 (1927). Sterilization laws are constitutional.

Chimel v. California, 395 U.S. 752 (1969). The one-arm's-length rule is established.

Commonwealth v. Fisher, 213 Penn State Reports 54 (1905). The state has the right to intervene in the lives of children without ensuring that their constitutional rights are protected.

Davis v. Alaska, 415 U.S. 308 (1974). A defendant's Sixth Amendment right to confront witnesses must prevail over the state's interest in protecting juveniles from adverse publicity.

Davis v. State, 422 S.E. 546 (Ga. 1992). A youth's competency to consent to a search is based on number of factors, such as the youth's age, mental maturity, totality of the circumstances, and ability to knowingly and willingly give consent.

Eddings v. Oklahoma, 455 U.S. 104 (1982). A lower court must consider a juvenile's age as a mitigating circumstance during a capital sentencing.

Engel v. Vitale, 370 U.S. 421 (1962). It is unconstitutional for a school to require students to recite school prayers.

Entertainment Software Association v. Foti, 3:06-CV-00431 (Louisiana) (2006). A preliminary injunction against makers of violent games is issued, while investigation into whether the games are protected by the First Amendment (free speech) is ongoing.

Epperson v. Arkansas, 393 U.S. 97 (1968). The Arkansas state law prohibiting the teaching of evolution is unconstitutional.

Escobedo v. Illinois, 378 U.S. 478 (1964). A criminal suspect has the right to have an attorney present during police questioning when the "finger of suspicion" points to the suspect.

Ex parte Crouse, 4 Wharton 9 (1838). A Pennsylvania court ruled in support of the doctrine of *parens patriae.*

Ex parte Sharpe, 15 Idaho 127 (1908). The state court ruling that upheld the right of the state to intervene in the lives of children without ensuring that their constitutional rights are protected.

Fare v. Michael C., 439 U.S. 1310 (1978). There is no need for courts to impose special protections for minors during interrogation.

(The chapter in which the term is used is shown in parentheses.)

30-day prevalence   The use of a drug at least once during the previous month. (4)

Achieved status   A status that is earned. (1)

Adjudication hearing   A hearing held to determine whether the child committed the offense of which he or she is accused. (14)

Adolescence-limited offenders   Juveniles whose delinquent behavior is confined to their teenage years. (2, 8)

Age-crime curve   The empirical trend that crime rates increase during preadolescence, peak in late adolescence, and steadily decline thereafter. (2, 8)

Aging-out phenomenon   The gradual decline of participation in crime after the teenage years. (2)

Annual prevalence   The use of a drug at least once during the prior year. (4)

Ascribed status   A status that is received at birth. (1)

Assortative mating   The concept that people tend to choose mates that are similar to themselves. (8)

Atavistic beings   The idea that criminals are a throwback to a more primitive stage of development. (5)

Attention Deficit/Hyperactivity Disorder (ADHD)   The most common neurobehavioral childhood disorder. (5)

Authoritarian parents   Parents who place a high value on obedience and conformity, tending to favor more punitive, absolute, and forceful disciplinary measures. (10)

Authoritative parents   Parents who are warm but firm; they set standards of behavior for their child and highly value the development of autonomy and self-direction. (10)

Baby boomers   Persons born between 1946 and 1964. (1)

Bail   A money or cash bond deposited with the court or bail bondsman allowing the person to be released on the assurance he or she will appear in court at the proper time. (14)

Baker v. Owen   Teachers can administer reasonable corporal punishment for disciplinary purposes. (11)

Bethel School District No. 403 v. Fraser   Schools may prohibit vulgar and offensive language. (11)

Blended sentencing   Juvenile courts may impose adult criminal sanctions on particular types of juvenile offenders. (14)

Board of Education of Independent School District No. 92 of Pottawatomie County et al. v. Earls et al.   Expanded *Acton;* schools may require students to submit to a urinalysis for illegal drugs prior to participating in *any* competitive extracurricular activities. (4, 11)

Bond   The glue that connects a child to society. (6)

Booking   The official recording of a person into detention after arrest. (13)

Boot camps   Short-term confinement facilities where youths are exposed to a militaristic environment in which the emphasis is on physical conditioning, work, and education. (15)

Brady Bill   Federal legislation that mandated a five-day waiting period for the purchase of handguns. (3)

Breed v. Jones   Criminal prosecution of a child following a juvenile court hearing is unconstitutional because it constitutes double jeopardy. (14)

Bullying   Negative acts by students carried out against other students repeatedly over time. (11)

Child Savers   The nineteenth century reformers who believed children were basically good and blamed delinquency on a bad environment. (1)

Chivalry hypothesis   Lower rates of crime among females reflect men's deference and protective attitude toward women whereby female offenses are generally overlooked or excused by males. (9)

Chronic offenders   Youths who continue to engage in law-breaking behavior as adults. They are responsible for the most serious forms of delinquency and violent crime. (2)

Chronic status offender   Children who continue to commit status offenses in spite of repeated interventions by family, school, social service, or law enforcement agencies. (1)

Classical School   A school of thought that blames delinquency on the choices people make. (5)

Coercive exchange   A test of wills, in which a child uses misbehavior to extort a desired outcome from his parents. (8)

Collective efficacy   Mutual trust among neighbors combined with willingness to intervene on behalf of the common good, specifically to supervise children and maintain public order. (6)

Communal school organization   Exists when teachers have shared values and expectations of student learning and appropriate student behavior. (11)

Community-oriented policing   Police officers and private citizens working together can help solve community problems related to crime, fear of crime, social and physical disorder, and neighborhood decay. (13)

Comorbidity   The overlapping behavioral problems that mutually reinforce one another but ultimately stem from some other cause. (4)

Compulsory school attendance law   A legislative act that requires students to attend school between specific ages, e.g., 6–16 years old. (11)

Concentrated disadvantage   Economically impoverished, racially segregated neighborhoods with high crime rates. (2)

531

Conduct norms   Rules that reflect the values, expectations, and actual behaviors of groups in everyday life. They are not necessarily the norms found in the criminal law. (7)

Conflict theory   Argues that society is held together by force, coercion, and intimidation and that the law represents the interests of those in power. (7)

Continuity of crime   The idea that chronic offenders are unlikely to age-out of crime and more likely to continue their law-violating behavior into their adult lives. (2)

Corporal punishment   The infliction of physical pain as a penalty for violating a school rule. (11)

Crime Index   A statistical indicator consisting of eight offenses used to gauge the amount of crime reported to the police. It was discontinued in 2004. (2)

Crime norms   Criminal laws that prohibit specific conduct and provide punishments for violations. (7)

Crimes of interest   The crimes that are the focus of the National Crime Victimization Survey. (2)

Cultural transmission   The process through which criminal values are transmitted from one generation to the next. (6)

Cumulative disadvantage   The process by which successive misbehavior leads to a serious detriment for an individual's life chances. (8)

Dark figure of crime   The gap between the actual amount of crime committed and crime reported to the police. (2)

Decarceration   The policy, since the early 1970s, of removing status offenders from "secure" institutions. (15)

Decriminalization   Relaxing of the enforcement of certain laws, for example, drug laws. (4)

Delinquent career   The pattern of delinquent behavior that an individual exhibits over the course of his or her life. (8)

Delinquent propensity   The likelihood of committing delinquency, and other antisocial acts; it is a trait that is largely set in early childhood. (8)

Demand waiver   A juvenile may request to have his or her case transferred from juvenile court to criminal court. (14)

Detention   The temporary confinement of children pending adjudication, disposition, or implementation of disposition. (14)

Determinate sentences   Prison sentences of a fixed amount of time, such as 5 years. (5)

Developmental theories   Theories that focus on an individual's entire life course, rather than one discrete point in time. (8)

Differential coercion theory   Children who are exposed to coercive environments are more likely to develop social-psychological deficits that increase the possibility of their committing crimes. (7)

Differential oppression theory   Delinquency is the culmination of a process that begins at conception and evolves through adolescence; the more a child is oppressed, the greater the likelihood he or she will become delinquent. (7, 9)

Differential social organization   Neighborhoods are differentially organized. (6)

Disintegrative shaming   A form of negative labeling by the juvenile justice system that stigmatizes and excludes targeted youths, tossing them into a class of outcasts. (7)

Disposition hearing   A juvenile court hearing in which the court determines what action will be in the youth's and community's best interests; the equivalent of the sentencing stage in the criminal court process. (14)

Dizygotic twins (DZ)   Fraternal twins who develop from two eggs fertilized at the same time. (5)

Double jeopardy   The prosecution of an individual a second time for the same offense. It is prohibited by the Fifth Amendment. (14)

Doubly oppressed   Adolescent girls are oppressed both as children and as females. (9)

Drug Abuse Resistance Education (D.A.R.E.)   A program aimed at children in kindergarten through twelfth grade, designed to equip students with appropriate skills to resist substance abuse and gangs. (4)

Drug courts   These are intensive treatment programs established within and supervised by juvenile courts to provide specialized services for eligible drug-involved youth and their families. (14)

Dualistic fallacy   This idea questions the notion that delinquents and nondelinquents are two fundamentally different types of people. (7)

Ecology fallacy   Occurs when neighborhood-level data are used to draw conclusions about individual residents. (2, 6)

Eddings v. Oklahoma   Courts must consider all mitigating circumstances before imposing the death penalty. (15)

Electronic monitoring   An active or passive computer-based tracking system in which electronic signals are used to verify that the youth is where he or she is supposed to be. (15)

Enhancement model   Adolescents who are already involved in delinquency are most apt to join a gang (selection) but, after joining, their delinquency is likely to increase significantly (facilitation). (12)

Etiological (etiology)   The scientific name for the cause of antisocial behavior, such as delinquency. (3)

Exclusionary rule   Evidence police produce illegally is not admissible in court. (13)

Facilitation model   A "kind of group" explanation which suggests that the normative structure of the gang along with group processes and dynamics increase delinquency among youth. (12)

Family Dependency Treatment Courts   Family courts that specifically adjudicate child welfare cases involving child abuse and neglect and parental substance abuse. (10)

Fine   A cash payment determined by the court and paid by the youth.

Focal concerns   The primary values that monopolize lower-class consciousness. (6)

Free will   The idea that people choose one course of action over another. (5)

Garcia v. Miera   School authorities that use excessive or extreme punishment against a child may be sued for damages suffered by the student and attorney fees. (11)

Gender-role identities   Individual identities based on sexual stereotypes. (9)

Genotype   A person's genetic composition. (5)

Goss v. Lopez   Students who may be suspended for 10 or more days must receive a hearing. (11)

Hall v. Tawney   Parents do not have a constitutional right to exempt their children from corporal punishment in public schools. (11)

Harm reduction   Using a public health model to reduce the risks and negative consequences of drug use. (4)

Hazelwood School District v. Kuhlmeier   School administrators can regulate the content of student publications in public schools for educational purposes. (11)

Hierarchy rule   In the *Uniform Crime Reports,* the police record only the most serious crime incident.

Home confinement   The intensive supervision and monitoring of an offending youth within his or her home environment. (15)

Homophily   Meaning "love of the same," it is the process of people selecting those who are most similar to them. (12)

In re Gault   Juveniles may not be denied basic due process rights in juvenile adjudicatory hearings. (14)

In re Winship   In delinquency cases, juveniles have the right to be convicted only if there is proof beyond a reasonable doubt. (14)

Incidence   The number of delinquent acts committed. (2)

Indeterminate sentences   Prison sentences of varying time lengths, such as 5 to 10 years. (5)

Indifferent parents   Parents who are unresponsive to their child and, in extreme cases, may be neglectful. (10)

Individual justice   The idea that criminal law must reflect differences among people and their circumstances. (5)

Individual theories   Theories that blame delinquency on personal traits such as temperament, genetics, and brain chemistry. (5)

Indulgent parents   Parents who are more responsive, accepting, benign, and passive in matters of discipline and place few demands on their child. (10)

Infanticide   Homicide in which recently born children are killed by relatives who do not want the children or who are suffering from childbirth-related psychiatric disturbances. (3)

Informal adjustment   Cases that are handled through discretionary nonjudicial dispositions. (14)

Informal probation   A case adjustment practice in which the child and family comply with requirements of probation personnel without a formal court order. (14)

Ingraham v. Wright   Corporal punishment does not violate the cruel and unusual punishment clause of the Eighth Amendment. (11)

Injunction or abatement   A civil process in which gang members are prohibited from engaging in mundane activities, such as loitering at schools or hanging out on street corners, or face arrest. (12)

Intake   The initial case-screening process in the juvenile court system. It is designed to screen out cases that do not warrant a formal court hearing. (14)

Integrated structural-Marxist theory   Serious delinquency is the result of the reproduction of coercive control patterns tied to the relationship between production and class structure in capitalist societies. (7)

Intelligence   The ability to learn, exercise judgment, and be imaginative. (5)

IQ   The ratio of one's mental age multiplied by 100 and divided by their chronological age. (5)

Judicial waiver   A method used for transferring youths to criminal court in which the juvenile court judge is the primary decision maker in determining whether the youth should be transferred. (14)

Justice model   A corrections philosophy that promotes flat or fixed-time sentences, abolishment of parole, and use of prison to punish offenders. (5)

Juvenile delinquency   Behavior committed by a minor that violates a state's penal code. (1)

Juvenile delinquent   A child with a long and problematic history of involvement in crime. (1)

Juveniles   Persons under age 18. (1, 2)

Kansas City Gun Experiment   An 1992 experiment in which the use of additional police to patrol in target areas for the exclusive purpose of gun detection significantly increased gun seizures and decreased gun crimes. (3)

Kent v. United States   A formal waiver hearing must take place before transfer of a juvenile to criminal court. (14)

Klikas   Age cohorts within Hispanic gangs. (12)

Labeling theory   Assumes that social control leads to deviance; how behavior is reacted to determines whether it is defined as deviant. (7)

Latchkey children   Children who regularly care for themselves without adult supervision after school or on weekends. (10)

Legalization   The elimination of many laws currently prohibiting drugs, but not necessarily eliminating all regulation. (4)

Liberation hypothesis   Changes brought about by the women's movement triggered a wave of female crime. (9)

Life-course persistent offenders   Individuals who suffer from a number of neuropsychological deficits that are likely to cause them to engage in delinquency throughout their lives. (8)

Lifetime prevalence   The use of a drug at least once during the respondent's lifetime. (4)

Maltreatment   Severe mistreatment of children, including physical and sexual abuse, physical neglect, lack of supervision, emotional maltreatment, educational maltreatment, and moral-legal maltreatment. (10)

Master status   Feature of a person that is most important to him or her as well as to others. (7)

McKeiver v. Pennsylvania   Juveniles do not have a constitutional right to a jury trial in juvenile court. (14)

Member-based definition   Defining a crime as gang-related when a gang member or members are either the perpetrators or the victims, regardless of the motive. (12)

Middle-class measuring rod   The standards used by teachers to assign status to students. (6)

Miranda v. Arizona   Established the right to protection from self-incrimination under the Fifth Amendment and the right to legal counsel under the Sixth Amendment. (13)

Mitigating circumstances   Factors that may be responsible for an individual's behavior, such as age, insanity, and incompetence. (5)

Monozygotic twins (MZ) Identical twins who develop from one fertilized egg. MZ twins have identical DNA. (5)

Motive-based definition Defining a crime as gang-related when committed by a gang member or members in which the underlying reason is to further the interests and activities of the gang. (12)

National Crime Victimization Survey An annual nationwide survey of criminal victimization conducted by the U.S. Bureau of Justice Statistics. (2)

National Opinion Research Center The first nationwide victimization survey. (2)

National Youth Survey The nationwide self-report survey of approximately 1,700 people who were between the ages of 11 and 17 in 1976. (2)

Neoclassical School A school of thought that considers mitigating circumstances when determining culpability for delinquency. (5)

New Jersey v. T.L.O. School officials can conduct warrantless searches of individuals at school on the basis of reasonable suspicion. (11)

Operation Ceasefire A gun prevention program in Boston involving direct law enforcement attack on illicit firearms traffickers supplying juveniles with guns. (3)

Parens patriae The doctrine that defines the state as the ultimate guardian of every child. (1)

Parole The release of an offender from a correctional institution before the scheduled period of confinement has ended. It typically involves supervision by a parole officer. (15)

Parole revocation If a youth violates the law or one of the discretionary conditions of parole, parole may be revoked and the youth is returned to a correctional facility. (15)

Part I crimes The eight offenses that form the Crime Index and are used to gauge the amount of crime reported to police; also referred to as Index crimes. (2)

Part II crimes These are the 21 less serious offenses included in the Uniform Crime Reports. (2)

Patriarchy A social system that enforces masculine control of the sexuality and labor power of women. (9)

Peer groups Groups of youths of similar ages and interests. (12)

Petition A document setting forth the specific charge against a juvenile. (14)

Police discretion The authority of police to choose one course of action over another. (13)

Positive School A school of thought that blames delinquency on factors that are in place before crime is committed. (5)

Power-control theory Emphasizes the consequences of the power relations of husbands and wives in the workplace on the lives of children. (9)

Precocious transitions An important life event (e.g., pregnancy) that is experienced too early in life. (8)

Prevalence The percentage of juveniles committing delinquency. (2)

Primary deviation Deviant behavior that everyone engages in occasionally. (7)

Probable cause A set of facts that would lead a reasonable person to believe a crime has been committed and the person to be arrested committed it. (13)

Probation The conditional freedom granted by the court to an alleged or adjudicated offender, who must adhere to certain conditions and is generally supervised by a probation officer. (15)

Prosecutorial waiver This allows the prosecutor to be the primary decision maker in determining whether a youth should be transferred to adult court. (14)

Protective factors Situations, settings, events, or characteristics that *decrease* the likelihood that one will be delinquent. (8)

Pseudo families Relationships established in correctional institutions for girls and intended to substitute for those found on the outside. (15)

Psychopathy A personality disorder that results in affective, interpersonal, and behavioral problems including violent criminal behavior that is committed without conscience. (2)

Racial profiling A practice where police use race as an explicit factor in "profiles" for guiding their decision-making. (2)

Radical nonintervention An approach to juvenile justice whereby police and the courts would, whenever possible, "leave kids alone." (7)

Rational choice theory Suggests that delinquents are rational people who make calculated choices regarding what they are going to do before they act. (5)

Reintegrative shaming The expression of community disapproval of delinquency, followed by indications of forgiveness and reacceptance into the community. (7)

Restitution A court-ordered action in which an offender pays money or provides services to victims of the offense or to the community. (15)

Restorative justice Designed to restore or repair relationships disrupted by crime, holding offenders accountable by requiring restitution to victims or the community harmed by the crime, promoting offender competency and responsibility, and balancing the needs of community, victim, and offender through involvement in the restorative process. (14)

Retribution A punishment philosophy based on society's moral outrage or disapproval of a crime. (5)

Reverse waiver A juvenile who is being prosecuted as an adult in criminal court may petition to have the case transferred to juvenile court for adjudication or disposition. (14)

Risk factors Situations, settings, events, or characteristics that *increase* the likelihood that one will be delinquent. (8)

Roper v. Simmons The Supreme Court held that the death penalty for persons under the age of 18 was a violation of the Eighth Amendment's prohibition against cruel and unusual punishment. (15)

Routine activities theory Argues that motivated offenders, suitable targets, and absence of capable guardians produce delinquency. (5)

Schall v. Martin Juveniles may be held in preventive detention while awaiting adjudication if they are determined to be "serious risks" to the community. (14)

School Resource Officer Program A control-based policy where a police officer works within the school to perform a variety of specialized duties. (11)

Seattle Social Development Project   A leading study in the creation and application of developmental theory. (8)

Secondary deviation   Deviant behavior based on the youth's taking on and accepting the deviant role as part of his or her identity. (7)

Selection model   A "kind of person" explanation of gang initiation which argues that adolescents with a strong propensity for delinquency seek out gangs. (12)

Self-report studies   Unofficial measures of crime in which juveniles are asked about their law-breaking behavior. (2)

Single-parent families   Families composed of children and one parent who is divorced or widowed or who was never married. (10)

Social support   The perceived and actual amount of instrumental and expressive or emotional supports that one receives from primary relationships, social networks, and communities. (7)

Socialization   The process through which children learn the norms and values of a particular society or social group so that they can function within it. (10)

Sociopathy (sociopath)   A form of psychopathy, sometimes referred to as secondary psychopathy, which is produced from early life environmental factors such as parental abuse and neglect. (3)

Somatotype   The idea that criminals can be identified by physical appearance. (5)

Stanford v. Kentucky   The Supreme Court held that the execution of a person who was age 16 or 17 at the time of his or her offense was not unconstitutional. (15)

Status   A socially defined position in a group. (1)

Status offense   Acts illegal only for children, such as truancy. (1, 2)

Statutory exclusion   A method used for transferring youths to criminal court, whereby the most serious or persistent offenders or those over a certain age are excluded from juvenile court jurisdiction and automatically prosecuted as adults. (14)

Stigmata   Distinctive physical features of born criminals. (5)

Stubborn Child Law   This law passed in 1641 stated that children who disobeyed their parents might be put to death. (1)

Suppression   A police response to gang and includes selective surveillance, arrest, and prosecution of gang members. (12)

Sweep search   A search of all lockers. (11)

Techniques of neutralization   Rationalizations used to engage in crime. (6)

Theories   Integrated sets of ideas that explain and predict phenomena. (5)

Thompson v. Carthage School District   School officials may legally search students and their lockers without consent. (11)

Thompson v. Oklahoma   Supreme Court ruled that the execution of a person under age 16 at the time of his or her crime was unconstitutional. (15)

Tinker v. Des Moines Independent Community School District   Students have the right of free expression as long as their behavior does not interrupt school activities or intrude in the school affairs or the lives of others. (11)

Token economy   A system of handing out points that can be exchanged for privileges such as watching TV and punishing behavior by taking those same privileges away. (5)

Turf   A gang's sense of territoriality. (12)

Turning points   Key life events that can either drive someone toward delinquent behavior or initiate the process of desisting from it. (8)

Uniform Crime Reports   The annual publication from the Federal Bureau of Investigation presenting data on crimes reported to the police, number of arrests, and number of persons arrested. (2)

United States v. Lopez   A U.S. Supreme Court case which held that the Gun Free School Zones Act of 1990 was unconstitutional. (3)

Utilitarian punishment model   The idea that offenders must be punished to protect society. (5)

Vernonia School District 47J v. Acton   Students participating in school athletic activities must submit upon request to an involuntary drug test (urinalysis). (11)

Victimization survey   A method of producing crime data in which people are asked about their experiences as crime victims. (2)

West Virginia State Board of Education v. Barnette   Students do not have to salute the flag while reciting the Pledge of Allegiance. (11)

Wraparound programs   Programs designed to build constructive relationships and support networks between delinquent youth and their families, teachers, and other caregivers and agencies in the community. (15)

Yarborough v. Alvarado   Police do not need to factor in the age and inexperience of a suspect in their decision of whether to read a juvenile his or her *Miranda* rights if the youth is not believed to be "in custody." (13)

Youth court   This is an alternative to the traditional juvenile court that allows young offenders to take responsibility for their acts, to be held accountable, and to receive appropriate dispositions imposed by their peers. (14)

Youth gang   A group of youths willing to use deadly violence to claim and protect territory, to attack rival gangs, or to engage in criminal activity. (12)

CHAPTER 1

1. Children's Defense Fund, *The State of America's Children, 2006* (Washington, DC: Children's Defense Fund, 2007).

2. "Teenage Murder Suspect's Journal Fixated on Violence," *Japan Times,* March 21, 2004:5; "Florida Boys Plead Guilty to Third-Degree Murder in Father's Slaying," online at: http://www.courttv.com/trials/king/111402_cnn.html, accessed February 2, 2004; Paul Bradley, "Who Pulled the Trigger?" online at: http://www.rickross.com/reference/malvo/malvo55.html, accessed January 31, 2004; "Sniper Reportedly Details 4 New Shootings," *Yahoo News,* June 16, 2006.

3. "Police: Teen Boy Dupes BMW Dealership," *USA TODAY,* February 13, 2004:3A.

4. Philippe Grandjean, Katsuyuki Murata, Esben Budtz-Jorgensen, and Pal Weihe, "Cardiac Autonomic Activity in Methylmercury Neurotoxicity: 14-Year Follow-Up of a Faroese Birth Cohort," *Journal of Pediatrics* 144:169–176 (2004); "Two Drinks Can Kill Brain Cells in a Fetus, Studies Suggest," *The New York Times,* February 15, 2004:A21.

5. Arloc Sherman, *Poverty Matters* (Washington, DC: Children's Defense Fund, 1997); Elena Lesley, "Expert Warns of Alcohol's Effect on Fetus," *St. Petersburg Times,* June 10, 2006; online at: http://www.sptimes.com, accessed June 11, 2006.

6. Alexander Liazos, "Class Oppression: The Functions of Juvenile Justice," *The Insurgent Sociologist* 5:2–23 (1974); "Colorado Student Assessment Program Results (CSAP)," online at: http://www.harrison.k12.co.us/curr-inst/assessment/results/resultsall/resultspage.html, accessed April 20, 2007.

7. Lisa Marshall, "Volume Control," *Boulder Daily Camera,* February 3, 2004:1D.

8. Charles Gill, "Essay on the Status of the American Child, 2000 A.D.," *Ohio Northern University Law Review* 17:543–579 (2000).

9. Stephen Lazoritz and Eric Shelman, "Before Mary Ellen," *Child Abuse and Neglect* 20:235–237 (1996).

10. Eric Shelman and Stephen Lazoritz, *Out of the Darkness* (Baltimore: Dolphin Moon Publishing, 2000), pp. 263–267.

11. Shelman and Lazoritz, note 10.

12. David Lohr, "Nicole Beecroft Murders Her Newborn Child, Stabbing Her 135 Times," online at: http://www.crimelibrary.com/news/original/0407/1601_nicole_beecroft.html, accessed April 18, 2007).

13. "Charged with Burning Daughter," online at: http://www.cnn.com/2004/US/Northeast/02/11/child.cellar.ap/index.html, accessed December 15, 2004.

14. John Jay College of Criminal Justice, *The Nature and Scope of the Problem of Sexual Abuse of Minors by Catholic Priests and Deacons in the United States 1950–2002* (New York: John Jay College of Criminal Justice, 2004); Rachel Zoll, "Report: 11,000 Clergy Abuse Claims Filed," *Guardian Unlimited,* February 16, 2004:1–3; Cathy Lynn Grossman, "Catholics Brace for Abuse Report," *USA TODAY,* February 23, 2004:6D.

15. Children's Defense Fund, note 1.

16. Cathy Widom and Michael Maxfield, *An Update on the Cycle of Violence* (Washington, DC: National Institute of Justice, 2001).

17. Richard Cherry, *Lectures: Growth of Criminal Law in Ancient Communities* (London: Macmillan and Company, 1890).

18. Robert Garland, "Juvenile Delinquency in the Graeco-Roman World," *History Today* 41:12–19 (1991).

19. Lloyd deMause, *The History of Childhood* (New York: Peter Bedrick, 1988).

20. Fredrick Ludwig, *Youth and the Law* (New York: Foundation Press, 1955), p. 12.

21. Mary Perry, *Crime and Society in Early Modern Seville* (Hanover, NH: University Press of New England, 1980), p. 195.

22. Perry, note 21.

23. Wiley Sanders, *Juvenile Offenders for a Thousand Years* (Chapel Hill: University of North Carolina Press, 1970).

24. Sanders, note 23.

25. Sanders, note 23.

26. Sanders, note 23, p. 135.

27. John Tobias, *Crime and Industrial Society in the 19th Century* (New York: Schocken Books, 1967).

28. David Walters, *The Physical and Sexual Abuse of Children* (Bloomington: Indiana University Press, 1975), pp. 17–18.

29. Stephen O'Conner, *Orphan Trains* (Boston: Houghton Mifflin, 2004).

30. David Rothman, *The Discovery of the Asylum* (Boston: Little, Brown, 1970).

31. Joseph Hawes, *Children in Urban Society* (New York: Oxford University Press, 1971), p. 19.

32. Hawes, note 31.

33. Edwin Powers, *Crime and Punishment in Early Massachusetts* (Boston: Beacon Press, 1966), p. 442.

34. LaMar Empey, *American Delinquency* (Homewood, IL: Dorsey Press, 1978).

35. George Haskins, *Law and Authority in Early Massachusetts* (New York: Archon Books, 1968).

36. Sanders, note 23.

37. Richard Johnson, *Juvenile Delinquency and its Origins* (Cambridge, England: Cambridge University Press, 1979), p. 83.

38. Anthony Platt, *The Child Savers* (Chicago: University of Chicago Press, 1969), p. 76.

39. Platt, note 38; O'Conner, note 29; Liazos, note 6.

40. Platt, note 38.

41. deMause, note 19.

42. *Ex parte Crouse,* 4 Warton 9 (1838).

43. New York State Board of Charities, *Report of the Secretary of State in 1824 on the Relief and Settlement of the Poor* (Albany, NY: State of New York, 1901), cited in Robert Bremner (ed.), *Children and Youth in America* (Cambridge: Harvard University Press, 1970).

44. Clifford Dorne, *Crimes against Children* (New York: Harrow and Heston Publishers, 1989).

45. Timothy Hurley, *Origin of the Illinois Juvenile Court Law* (New York: AMS Press, 1907/1977).

46. Grace Abbott, *The Child and the State* (Chicago: University of Chicago Press, 1938), pp. 392–401.

47. Hurley, note 45.

48. Hurley, note 45.

49. Robert Mennel, *Thorns and Thistles* (Hanover, NH: University Press of New England, 1973), p. 132.

50. Ellen Ryerson, *The Best Laid Plans* (New York: Hill and Wang, 1978), pp. 444–445.

51. Charles Hoffman, "The Fundamental Principles of the Juvenile Court and Its Part in Future Community Programs for Child Welfare," in U.S. Children's Bureau (ed.), *Proceedings of the Conference on Juvenile Court Standards* (Washington, DC: U.S. Government Printing Office, 1922), pp. 13–25.

52. Evelina Belden, *Courts in the United States Hearing Children's Cases* (Washington, DC: U.S. Government Printing Office, 1920).

53. Justine Polier, *A View from the Bench* (New York: National Council on Crime and Delinquency, 1964).

54. Paul Tappan, *Juvenile Delinquency* (New York: McGraw-Hill, 1949).

55. Liazos, note 6.

56. Hawes, note 31.

57. National Advisory Commission on Criminal Justice Standards and Goals, *Juvenile Justice and Delinquency Prevention* (Washington, DC: U.S. Government Printing Office, 1976), p. 312.

58. Barry Krisberg and James Austin, *The Children of Ishmael* (Palo Alto, CA: Mayfield, 1978), p. 63.

59. Bureau of Justice Statistics, *BJS Data Report, 1987* (Washington, DC: U.S. Government Printing Office, 1988).

60. Mary Twining, *Assessment of Model Programs for the Chronic Status Offenders and Their Families* (Washington, DC: U.S. Government Printing Office, 1987).

61. Norval Morris and Gordon Hawkins, *Report to the Congress on Juvenile Delinquency* (Washington, DC: U.S. Department of Health, Education and Welfare, 1960), p. 16.

62. Charles Dickens, *Oliver Twist* (New York: Oxford University Press, 1837/1949).

63. Stephen Crane, *Maggie* (New York: Norton, 1884/1977).

64. Mark Twain, *The Adventures of Tom Sawyer* (Garden City, NY: Doubleday, 1875/1985); Mark Twain, *The Adventures of Huckleberry Finn* (New York: 1884/1977).

65. David Sandberg, *The Child Abuse-Delinquency Connection* (Lexington, MA: Lexington Books, 1969).

66. Theodore Dreiser, *An American Tragedy* (New York: Sun Dial Press, 1926).

67. Richard Wright, *Black Boy* (New York: Harper, 1945).

68. Irving Shulman, *The Amboy Dukes* (New York: Doubleday, 1947); Hal Ellson, *The Golden Spike* (New York: Ballantine Books, 1952); Warren Miller, *The Cool World* (Boston: Little, Brown, 1959).

69. Evan Hunter, *The Blackboard Jungle* (New York: Simon & Schuster, 1954).

70. J. D. Salinger, *The Catcher in the Rye* (Boston: Little, Brown, 1951).

71. Michael Gordon, *Juvenile Delinquency in the American Novel, 1915–1965* (Bowling Green, OH: Bowling Green University Press, 1971).

72. Mark McGee and R. Robertson, *The J.D. Films* (Jefferson, NC: McFarland and Company, 1982), p. 6.

73. James Lull, "Listeners' Communicative Uses of Popular Music," pages 140–174 in James Lull (ed.), *Popular Music and Communication* (Newbury Park, CA: Sage, 1987).

74. Craig Anderson, Douglas Gentile, and Katherine Buckley, *Violent Video Game Effects on Children and Adolescents* (New York: Oxford University Press, 2007).

75. Anderson et al., note 74.

76. *Entertainment Software Association v. Foti,* Case 3:06-cv-00431—JJB-CN (Louisiana) (2006); "Preliminary Injunction Issued Against Louisiana Video Game Law," online at: http://gamepolitics.livejournal.com/347139.html, accessed December 31, 2006.

77. Terrie Moffitt, "'Life-Course Persistent' and 'Adolescence-Limited' Antisocial Behavior," *Psychological Review* 100:674–701 (1993).

CHAPTER 2

1. Sir Josiah Stamp, *Some Economic Matters in Modern Life* (London: King and Sons, 1929), pp. 258–259.

2. Edwin Sutherland, *Principles of Criminology,* 4th edition (Philadelphia: Lippincott, 1947), p. 29.

3. Albert Biderman and Albert Reiss, "On Exploring the 'Dark Figure' of Crime," *Annals of the American Academy of Political and Social Science* 374:1–15 (1967), p. 1.

4. Clayton Mosher, Terence Miethe, and Dretha Phillips, *The Mismeasure of Crime* (Thousand Oaks, CA: Sage, 2002), p. 6.

5. Federal Bureau of Investigation, *Uniform Crime Reporting Handbook, 2005* (Washington, DC: U.S. Department of Justice, 2006).

6. Federal Bureau of Investigation, *Developments in the National Incident-Based Reporting System* (Washington, DC: U.S. Department of Justice, 2004).

7. "Complying with Jeanne Clery Act," online at: http://www.securityoncampus.org/schools/cleryact/index.html, accessed April 21, 2007.

8. Walter Gove, Michael Hughes, and Michael Geerken, "Are *Uniform Crime Reports* a Valid Indicator of the Index Crimes?" *Criminology* 23:451–503 (1985).

9. Shannon Catalano, Criminal Victimization, 2005 (Washington, DC: U.S. Department of Justice, 2006).

10. Adolphe Quetelet, *Treatise on Man and the Development of His Faculties* (Edinburgh, Scotland: S. W. R. Chambers, 1842).

11. Edwin Sutherland, "White-Collar Criminality," *American Sociological Review* 5:1–12 (1940), p. 4.

12. Otto Pollack, *The Criminality of Women* (Philadelphia: University of Pennsylvania Press, 1951).

13. Ramona Rantala and Thomas Edwards, *Effects of NIBRS on Crime Statistics, Special Report* (Washington, DC: U.S. Department of Justice, 2000).

14. Robert O'Brien, *Crime and Victimization Data* (Beverly Hills, CA: Sage, 1985).

15. Philip Ennis, *Criminal Victimization in the United States* (Washington DC: U.S. Government Printing Office, 1967).

16. David Cantor and James Lynch, "Self-Report Measures of Crime and Criminal Victimization," pages 85–138 in U. S. Department of Justice *Criminal Justice 2000,* Volume 4 (Washington, DC: National Institute of Justice, 2000).

17. L. Edward Wells and Joseph Rankin, "Juvenile Victimization," *Journal of Research in Crime and Delinquency* 32:287–307 (1995).

18. Albert Biderman and James Lynch, *Understanding Crime Incidence Statistics* (New York: Springer-Verlag, 1991).

19. Janet Lauritsen and Robin Schaum, *Crime and Victimization in the Three Largest Metropolitan Areas, 1980–1998* (Washington, DC: U.S. Department of Justice, 2005).

20. Alfred Blumstein, Jacqueline Cohen, and Richard Rosenfeld, "Trend and Deviation in Crime Rates: A Comparison of *UCR* and NCS Data for Burglary and Robbery," *Criminology* 29:237–264 (1991); Michael Hindelang, "The *Uniform Crime Reports* Revisited," *Journal of Criminal Justice* 2:1–17 (1974); David MacDowall and Colin Loftin, "Comparing the *UCR* and NCS Over Time," *Criminology* 30:125–132 (1992); Steven Messner, "The 'Dark Figure' and Composite Indexes of Crime: Some Empirical Explorations of Alternative Data Sources," *Journal of Criminal Justice* 12:435–444 (1984).

21. Austin Porterfield, *Youth in Trouble* (Austin: Leo Potishman Foundation, 1946).

22. James Wallerstein and J. C. Wyle, "Our Law-Abiding Law-breakers," *Federal Probation* 25:107–112 (1947).

23. James Short, Jr., "A Report on the Incidence of Criminal Behavior, Arrests and Convictions in Selected Groups," *Research Studies of the State College of Washington* 22:110–118 (1954).

24. James Short, Jr., and F. Ivan Nye, "Extent of Unrecorded Juvenile Delinquency," *Journal of Criminal Law, Criminology, and Police Science* 49:296–302 (1958).

25. Maynard Erickson and LaMar Empey, "Court Records, Undetected Delinquency and Decision-Making," *Journal of Criminal Law, Criminology, and Police Science* 54:456–469 (1963).

26. Jay Williams and Martin Gold, "From Delinquent Behavior to Official Delinquency," *Social Problems* 20:209–229 (1972).

27. Suzanne Ageton and Delbert Elliott, *The Incidence of Delinquent Behavior in a National Probability Sample* (Boulder, CO: Behavioral Research Institute, 1978); Delbert Elliott and Suzanne Ageton, "Reconciling Race and Class Differences in Self-Reported and Official Estimates of Delinquency," *American Sociological Review* 45:95–110 (1980).

28. William Chambliss and Richard Nagasawa, "On the Validity of Official Statistics," *Journal of Research in Crime and Delinquency* 6:71–77 (1969); Leroy Gould, "Who Defines Delinquency," *Social Problems* 16:325–336 (1969); Michael Leiber, "Comparison of Juvenile Court Outcomes for Native Americans, African Americans, and Whites," *Justice Quarterly* 11:257–279 (1994).

29. John Blackmore, "The Relationship between Self-reported Delinquency and Official Convictions amongst Adolescent Boys," *British Journal of Criminology* 14:172–176 (1974).

30. Martin Gold, "Undetected Delinquent Behavior," *Journal of Research in Crime and Delinquency* 3:27–46 (1966); Robert Dentler and Lawrence Monroe, "Social Correlates of Early Adolescent Theft," *American Sociological Review* 26:733–743 (1961); John Clark and Larry Tifft, "Polygraph and Interview Validation of Self-reported Deviant Behavior," *American Sociological Review* 31:516–523 (1966).

31. Michael Hindelang, Travis Hirschi, and Joseph Weis, *Measuring Delinquency* (Beverly Hills, CA: Sage, 1981), p. 114.

32. Stephen Cernkovich, Peggy Giordano, and Meredith Pugh, "Chronic Offenders," *Journal of Criminal Law and Criminology* 76:705–732 (1985), p. 706.

33. U. S. Census Bureau, *Statistical Abstract of the United States, 2006,* 126th edition (Washington, DC: U. S. Census Bureau, 2007).

34. Federal Bureau of Investigation, *Crime in the United States, 2005* (Washington, DC: U.S. Department of Justice, 2006).

35. Howard Snyder and Melissa Sickmund, *Juvenile Offenders and Victims: 2006 National Report* (Washington, DC: Office of Juvenile Justice and Delinquency Prevention, 2006).

36. Catalano, note 9.

37. Richard Willing, "Violent Crime on the Rise, Summit Participants Say," *USA TODAY,* August 31, 2006:5A.

38. Jeffrey Butts and Howard Snyder, *Too Soon to Tell: Deciphering Recent Trends in Youth Violence* (Chicago: Chapin Hall Center for Children, 2006).

39. Steven Levitt, "Understanding Why Crime Rates Fell in the 1990s: Four Factors That Explain the Decline and Six That Do Not," *Journal of Economic Perspectives* 18:163–190 (2004).

40. Steven Messner and Richard Rosenfeld, *Crime and the American Dream,* 3rd edition (Belmont, CA: Wadsworth, 2001).

41. John Conklin, *Why Crime Rates Fell* (Boston: Allyn & Bacon, 2003); Thomas Bonczar and Allen Beck, *Lifetime Likelihood of Going to State or Federal Prison* (Washington, DC: U.S. Department of Justice, 1997).

42. James Q. Wilson and George Kelling, "Broken Windows," *Atlantic Monthly,* March:29–38 (1982).

43. James Alan Fox and Alex Piquero, "Deadly Demographics: Population Characteristics and Forecasting Homicide Trends," *Crime & Delinquency* 49:339–359 (2003).

44. Eric Baumer, Janet Lauritsen, Richard Rosenfeld, and Richard Wright, "The Influence of Crack Cocaine on Robbery, Burglary, and Homicide Rates: A Cross-City, Longitudinal Analysis," *Journal of Research in Crime and Delinquency* 35:316–340 (1998).

45. Meda Chesney-Lind and Randall Shelden, *Girls, Delinquency, and Juvenile Justice,* 3rd edition (Pacific Grove, CA: Brooks/Cole, 2004).

46. James Short, Jr., *Delinquency and Society* (Englewood Cliffs, NJ: Prentice Hall, 1990), p. 115.

47. Roy Austin, "Recent Trends in Official Male and Female Crime Rates," *Journal of Criminal Justice* 21:447–466 (1993).

48. Joycelyn Pollock and Sareta Davis, "The Continuing Myth of the Violent Female Offender," *Criminal Justice Review* 30:5–29 (2005).

49. Lori Dorfman, *Off Balance* (Berkeley, CA: Berkeley Media Studies Group, 2001).

50. William Helmreich, *The Things They Say behind Your Back,* 2nd edition (New Brunswick, NJ: Transaction Publishers, 1984).

51. Arloc Sherman, *Poverty Matters* (New York: Children's Defense Fund, 1997).

52. U.S. Census Bureau, note 33.

53. David Huizinga and Delbert Elliott, *Self-Reported Measure of Delinquency and Crime* (Boulder, CO: Behavioral Research Institute, 1984).

54. National Institute on Drug Abuse, *Monitoring the Future Report, 1975–1999* (Washington, DC: National Institute on Drug Abuse, 2000).

55. Williams and Gold, note 26.

56. Elliott and Ageton, note 27.

57. Delbert Elliott, David Huizinga, and Scott Menard, *Multiple Problem Youth* (New York: Springer-Verlag, 1989); Delbert Elliott, "Serious Violent Offenders: Onset, Developmental Course, and Termination," *Criminology* 32:1–21 (1994); David Farrington, Rolf Loeber, Magda Stouthamer-Loeber, W. B. Van Kammen, and Lisa Schmidt, "Self-Reported Delinquency and a Combined Delinquency Seriousness Scale Based on Boys, Mothers, and Teachers: Concurrent and Predictive Validity for African-Americans and Caucasians," *Criminology* 34:493–514 (1996).

58. Terence Thornberry and Marvin Krohn, "The Self-Report Method for Measuring Delinquency and Crime," pages 38–44 in David Duffee (ed.), *Measurement and Analysis of Crime and Justice,* volume 4 (Washington, DC: National Institute of Justice, 2000); Barbara Mensch and Denise Kandel, "Underreporting of Substance Use in a National Longitudinal Youth Cohort," *Public Opinion Quarterly* 52:100–124 (1988).

59. Callie Rennison, *Violent Victimization and Race* (Washington, DC: U.S. Department of Justice, 2001); Callie Rennison, *Hispanic Victims of Violent Crime* (Washington, DC: U.S. Department of Justice, 2002).

60. William Julius Wilson, *The Declining Significance of Race: Blacks and Changing American Institutions* (Chicago: University of Chicago Press, 1978); William Julius Wilson, *The Truly Disadvantaged: The Inner City, The Underclass, and Public Policy* (Chicago: University of Chicago Press, 1987); William Julius Wilson, *When Work Disappears: The World of the New Urban Poor* (New York: Vintage, 1997).

61. James Short, Jr., *Poverty, Ethnicity, and Violent Crime* (Boulder, CO: Westview Press, 1997); Douglas Massey and Nancy Denton, *American Apartheid: Segregation and the Making of the Underclass* (Cambridge, MA: Harvard University Press, 1993); Douglas Massey and Mitchell Eggers, "The Ecology of Inequality: Minorities and the Concentration of Poverty, 1970–1980," *American Journal of Sociology* 95:1153–1188 (1990).

62. John McWhorter, *Losing the Race: Self-Sabotage in Black America* (New York: HarperCollins, 2001).

63. James Unnever, Francis Cullen, and Robert Agnew, "Why is Bad Parenting Criminogenic? Implications from Rival Theories," *Youth Violence and Juvenile Justice* 4:3–33 (2006).

64. James Q. Wilson, *The Marriage Problem: How Our Culture Has Weakened Families* (New York: Harper Paperbacks, 2003).

65. Karen Parker and Tracy Johns, "Urban Disadvantage and Types of Race-Specific Homicide: Assessing the Diversity in Family Structures in the Urban Context," *Journal of Research in Crime and Delinquency* 39:277–303 (2002).

66. John MacDonald and Angela Gover, "Concentrated Disadvantage and Youth-on-Youth Homicide," *Homicide Studies* 9:30–54 (2005).

67. Paul Bellair, Vincent Roscigno, and Thomas McNulty, "Linking Local Labor Market Opportunity to Violent Adolescent Delinquency," *Journal of Research in Crime and Delinquency* 40:6–33 (2003); Charis Kubrin and Tim Wadsworth, "Identifying the Structural Correlates of African American Killings: What Can We Learn from Data Disaggregation?" *Homicide Studies* 7:3–35 (2003).

68. Elijah Anderson, *Code of the Street* (New York: Norton, 1999).

69. Timothy Brezina, Robert Agnew, Francis Cullen, and John Paul Wright, "The Code of the Street: A Quantitative Assessment of Elijah Anderson's Subculture of Violence Thesis and Its Contribution to Youth Violence Research," *Youth Violence and Juvenile Justice* 2:303–328 (2004); Eric Stewart and Ronald Simons, "Structure and Culture in African American Adolescent Violence: A Partial Test of the 'Code of the Street' Thesis," *Justice Quarterly* 23:1–33 (2006).

70. James Q. Wilson and Richard Herrnstein, *Crime and Human Nature* (New York: Simon and Schuster, 1987).

71. Wilson and Herrnstein, note 70, p. 471.

72. Francis Cullen, Paul Gendreau, Roger Jarjoura, and John Wright, "Crime and the Bell Curve: Lessons from Intelligent Criminology," *Crime & Delinquency* 43:387–411 (1997).

73. Deborah Ramirez, Jack McDevitt, and Amy Farrell, *A Resource Guide on Racial Profiling Data Collection Systems* (Washington, DC: U.S. Department of Justice, 2000).

74. Richard Lundman and Robert Kaufman, "Driving While Black," *Criminology* 41:195–220 (2002); Robin Engel,

Jennifer Calnon, and Thomas Bernard, "Theory and Racial Profiling," *Justice Quarterly* 19:249–273 (2002); David Harris, "The Reality of Racial Disparity in Criminal Justice," *Law and Contemporary Problems* 66:71–97 (2003).

75. Robert Sampson, "The Community," pages 193–216 in James Q. Wilson and Joan Petersilia (eds.), *Crime* (San Francisco: ICS Press, 1995).

76. Clifford Shaw and Henry McKay, *Juvenile Delinquency and Urban Areas,* revised edition (Chicago: University of Chicago Press, 1969).

77. Ronald Akers, "Socioeconomic Status and Delinquent Behavior," *Journal of Research in Crime and Delinquency* 1:38–46 (1964); LaMar Empey and Maynard Erickson, *The Provo Experiment* (Lexington, MA: D. C. Heath, 1972).

78. Charles Tittle and Robert Meier, "Specifying the SES/Delinquency Relationship," *Criminology* 28:271–299 (1990).

79. Charles Tittle, Wayne Villemez, and Douglas Smith, "The Myth of Social Class and Criminality," *American Sociological Review* 43:643–656 (1978).

80. Robert Sampson, "Effects of Socioeconomic Context on Official Reactions to Juvenile Delinquency," *American Sociological Review* 51:876–885 (1986).

81. John Hagan, *Crime and Disrepute* (Thousand Oaks, CA: Sage, 1994).

82. Douglas Smith, "The Neighborhood Context of Police Behavior," pages 313–341 in Albert Reiss and Michael Tonry (eds.), *Communities and Cities* (Chicago: University of Chicago Press, 1986), p. 316.

83. Michael Hindelang, Travis Hirschi, and Joseph Weis, "Correlates of Delinquency," *American Sociological Review* 44:995–1014 (1979).

84. John Braithwaite, "The Myth of Social Class and Criminality Reconsidered," *American Sociological Review* 46:36–57 (1981), p. 37.

85. John Braithwaite, *Crime, Shame, and Reintegration* (New York: Cambridge University Press, 1989).

86. Elliott and Ageton, note 27.

87. Gary Kleck, "On the Use of Self-report Data to Determine the Class Distribution of Criminal and Delinquent Behavior," *American Sociological Review* 47:427–433 (1982); Charles Tittle, Wayne Villemez, and Douglas Smith, "One Step Forward, Two Steps Back," *American Sociological Review* 47:433–438 (1982), p. 437.

88. Tittle and Meier, note 78.

89. Gregory Dunaway, Francis Cullen, Velmer Burton, and T. David Evans, "The Myth of Social Class and Crime Revisited," *Criminology* 38:589–632 (2000).

90. Adolphe Quetelet, *Research on the Propensity for Crime at Different Ages* (Cincinnati: Anderson, 1831/1984).

91. Daniel Nagin, David Farrington, and Terrie Moffitt, "Life-course Trajectories of Different Types of Offenders," *Criminology* 33:111–139 (1995); David Farrington, "Age and Crime," pages 189–250 in Michael Tonry and Norval Morris (eds.), *Crime and Justice,* Volume 7 (Chicago: University of Chicago Press, 1986); Travis Hirschi and Michael Gottfredson, "Age and the Explanation of Crime," *American Journal of Sociology* 89:552–584 (1983).

92. Terrie Moffitt, "Adolescence-Limited and Life-Course Persistent Antisocial Behavior: A Developmental Taxonomy," *Psychological Review* 100:674–701 (1993).

93. Delbert Elliott, "Serious Violent Offenders," *Criminology* 32:1–21 (1994).

94. Lawrence Cohen and Kenneth Land, "Age Structure and Crime," *American Sociological Review* 91:170–183 (1987).

95. Marc Le Blanc, "Late Adolescence Deceleration of Criminal Activity and Development of Self- and Social Control," *Studies on Crime and Crime Prevention* 2:51–68 (1993); John Laub and Robert Sampson, "Turning Points in the Life Course," *Criminology* 31:301–325 (1993); Mark Warr, "Life-Course Transitions and Desistance From Crime," *Criminology* 36:183–215 (1998); David Rowe, *Biology and Crime* (Los Angeles: Roxbury, 2002); Diana Fishbein, *Biobehavioral Perspectives in Criminology* (Belmont, CA: Wadsworth, 2001); Robert Agnew, "Delinquency and the Desire for Money," *Justice Quarterly* 11:411–427 (1994).

96. David Tanenhaus, "The Evolution of Transfer Out of the Juvenile Court," pages 13–44 in Jeffrey Fagan and Franklin Zimring (eds.), *The Changing Borders of Juvenile Justice: Transfer of Adolescents to the Criminal Court* (Chicago: University of Chicago Press, 2000).

97. Moffitt, note 92, p. 678.

98. Matt DeLisi, *Career Criminals in Society* (Thousand Oaks, CA: Sage, 2005).

99. Sheldon Glueck and Eleanor Glueck, *Unraveling Juvenile Delinquency* (New York: The Commonwealth Fund, 1950); John Laub and Robert Sampson, "Unraveling Families and Delinquency: A Reanalysis of the Gluecks' Data," *Criminology* 26:355–380 (1988); Robert Sampson and John Laub, "Urban Poverty and the Family Context of Delinquency: A New Look at Structure and Process in a Classic Study," *Child Development* 65:523–540 (1994).

100. Sheldon Glueck and Eleanor Glueck, *500 Criminal Careers* (New York: Knopf, 1930); Sheldon Glueck and Eleanor Glueck, *Criminal Careers in Retrospect* (New York: The Commonwealth Fund, 1943).

101. Marvin Wolfgang, Robert Figlio, and Thorsten Sellin, *Delinquency in a Birth Cohort* (Chicago: University of Chicago Press, 1972).

102. Paul Tracy, Marvin Wolfgang, and Robert Figlio, *Delinquency Careers in Two Birth Cohorts* (New York: Plenum, 1990).

103. Paul Tracy and Kimberly Kempf-Leonard, *Continuity and Discontinuity in Criminal Careers* (New York: Plenum, 1996).

104. Marvin Wolfgang, Terence Thornberry, and Robert Figlio, *From Boy to Man, From Delinquency to Crime* (Chicago: University of Chicago Press, 1987).

105. Kimberly Kempf-Leonard, Paul Tracy, and James Howell, "Serious, Violent, and Chronic Juvenile Offenders: The Relationship of Delinquency Career Types to Adult Criminality," *Justice Quarterly* 18:449–478 (2001).

106. Alex Piquero, David Farrington, and Alfred Blumstein, "The Criminal Career Paradigm: Background and Recent

Developments," pages 359–506 in Michael Tonry (ed.), *Crime and Justice,* Volume 30 (Chicago: University of Chicago Press, 2003); Alex Piquero, David Farrington, and Alfred Blumstein, *Key Issues in Criminal Career Research: New Analyses of the Cambridge Study in Delinquent Development* (New York: Cambridge University Press, 2007).

107. David Farrington and Donald West, "Criminal, Penal, and Life Histories of Chronic Offenders: Risk and Protective Factors and Early Identification," *Criminal Behavior and Mental Health* 3:492–523 (1993); David Farrington, "Psychosocial Predictors of Adult Antisocial Personality and Adult Convictions," *Behavioral Sciences & the Law* 18:605–622 (2000); David Farrington, "Explaining and Preventing Crime: The Globalization of Knowledge," *Criminology* 38:1–24 (2000).

108. David Farrington and Brandon Welsh, *Saving Children from a Life of Crime: Early Risk Factors and Effective Interventions* (New York: Oxford University Press, 2007).

109. Franklyn Dunford and Delbert Elliott, "Identifying Career Offenders Using Self-Reported Data," *Journal of Research in Crime and Delinquency* 21:57–86 (1984); Delbert Elliott, David Huizinga, and Barbara Morse, "Self-Reported Violent Offending: A Descriptive Analysis of Juvenile Violent Offenders and Their Offending Careers," *Journal of Interpersonal Violence* 1:472–514 (1986).

110. Terence Thornberry, David Huizinga, and Rolf Loeber, "The Prevention of Serious Delinquency and Violence: Implications from the Program of Research on the Causes and Correlates of Delinquency," pages 213–237 in James Howell (ed.), *Serious, Violent, and Chronic Juvenile Offenders* (Thousand Oaks, CA: Sage, 1995).

111. David Huizinga, Rolf Loeber, Terence Thornberry, and Lynn Cothern, *Co-occurrence of Serious and Violent Juvenile Offending and Other Problem Behaviors* (Washington, DC: U.S. Department of Justice, 2000); Rolf Loeber, David Farrington, Magda Stouthamer-Loeber, Terrie Moffitt, Avshalom Caspi, and Donald Lynam, "Male Mental Health Problems, Psychopathy, and Personality Traits: Key Findings from the First 14 Years of the Pittsburgh Youth Study," *Clinical Child and Family Psychology Review* 4:273–297 (2001).

112. Donna Hamparian, Richard Schuster, Simon Dinitz, and John Conrad, *The Violent Few: A Study of Dangerous Juvenile Offenders* (Lexington, MA: Lexington Books, 1978).

113. Joan McCord and William McCord, "The Effects of Parental Role Model on Criminality," *Journal of Social Issues* 14:66–75 (1958); Joan McCord and William McCord, "A Follow-Up Report on the Cambridge–Somerville Youth Study," *Annals of the American Academy of Political and Social Science* 322:89–96 (1959); Joan McCord, "A 30-Year Follow-Up of Treatment Effects," *American Psychologist* 32:284–289 (1978).

114. Lyle Shannon, *Criminal Career Continuity: Its Social Context* (New York: Human Services Press, 1988); Lyle Shannon, *Changing Patterns of Delinquency and Crime: A Longitudinal Study in Racine* (Boulder, CO: Westview Press, 1991).

115. James Howell, "Diffusing Research into Practice Using the Comprehensive Strategy for Serious, Violent, and Chronic Juvenile Offenders," *Youth Violence and Juvenile Justice* 1:219–245 (2003).

CHAPTER 3

1. Howard Snyder, *Juvenile Arrests, 2003* (Washington, DC: U.S. Department of Justice, 2005).

2. Federal Bureau of Investigation, *Crime in the United States 2005* (Washington, DC: U.S. Department of Justice, 2006).

3. Kevin Johnson, "Police Tie Jump in Crime to Juveniles," *USA TODAY,* July 13, 2006:1–3A.

4. Kevin Johnson, "Gang Activity Cited for Jump in U.S. Homicides," *USA TODAY,* June 14, 2006:1A.

5. Rick Hampson, "Some Cities See Resurgent Wave of Street Crime," *USA TODAY,* July 28, 2006:5A.

6. Associated Press, "Five Boys Charged with Murder of 11-Year Old," *Boulder Daily Camera,* July 28, 2006:20A.

7. Police Executive Research Forum, *Violent Crime in America: 24 Months of Alarming Trends* (Washington, DC: Police Executive Research Forum, 2007), p.1.

8. Federal Bureau of Investigation, note 2.

9. Shay Bilchik, *Violence after School* (Washington, DC: Office of Juvenile Justice and Delinquency Prevention, 1999).

10. Federal Bureau of Investigation, note 2; Federal Bureau of Investigation, *Crime in the United States, Preliminary Semiannual Uniform Crime Reports* (Washington, DC: U.S. Department of Justice, 2006).

11. Terance Miethe and Wendy Regoeczi, *Rethinking Homicide: Exploring the Structure and Process Underlying Deadly Situations* (New York: Cambridge University Press, 2004), p. 188.

12. Howard Snyder and Melissa Sickmund, *Juvenile Offenders and Victims: 2006 National Report* (Washington, DC: Office of Juvenile Justice and Delinquency Prevention, 2006).

13. Ann Burgess, Christina Garbarino, and Mary Carlson, "Pathological Teasing and Bullying Turned Deadly: Shooters and Suicide," *Violence & Offenders* 1:1–14 (2006).

14. Howard Snyder and Monica Swahn, *Juvenile Suicides, 1981–1998* (Washington, DC: Office of Juvenile Justice and Delinquency Prevention, 2004); Child Trends Data Bank, http://www.childtrendsdatabank.org/indicators/70ViolentDeath.cfm, accessed April 22, 2007.

15. Alex Piquero, Leah Daigle, Chris Gibson, Nicole Piquero, and Stephen Tibbetts, "Are Life-Course-Persistent Offenders at Risk for Adverse Health Outcomes?" *Journal of Research in Crime and Delinquency* 44:185–207 (2007).

16. Robert Regoli and John Hewitt, *Delinquency in Society*, 3rd edition (New York: McGraw-Hill, 1997).

17. Howard Snyder and Melissa Sickmund, *Juvenile Offenders and Victims: A Focus on Violence* (Washington, DC: Office of Juvenile Justice and Delinquency Prevention, 1995), p. 7.

18. Louis Freeh, quoted in "U.S. Crime Dipped in 1994, but Worse Days Seen Ahead," *The Arizona Republic,* November 19, 1995:A16.

19. Franklin Zimring, cited in John Conklin, *Why Crime Rates Fell* (Boston: Allyn and Bacon, 2003), p. 5.

20. Marc Ouimet, "Explaining the American and Canadian Crime Drop in the 1990s," *Canadian Journal of Criminology* 44:33–50 (2002).

21. Conklin, note 19, pp. 191–194.

22. Alfred Blumstein and Joel Wallman, *The Crime Drop in America,* revised edition (New York: Cambridge University Press, 2005).

23. Alfred Blumstein, "Youth, Guns, and Violent Crime," *Children, Youth, and Gun Violence* 12:39–53 (2002).

24. Callie Rennison and Mike Planty, "Reassessing Who Contributed Most to the Decline in Violence During the 1990s: A Reminder That Size Does Matter," *Violence and Victims* 21:23–47 (2006).

25. Franklin Zimring, *American Youth Violence* (New York: Oxford University Press, 1998).

26. Meda Chesney-Lind, "What about the Girls? Delinquency Programming as if Gender Mattered," *Corrections Today,* February 2001:39.

27. Wiley Hall, "Trends Show Growing Violence among Girls," *Boulder Daily Camera,* April 27, 2004:6B.

28. Darnell Hawkins, John Laub, Janet Lauritsen, and Lynn Cothern, *Race, Ethnicity, and Serious and Violent Juvenile Offending* (Washington, DC: Office of Juvenile Justice and Delinquency Prevention, 2000); Matt DeLisi and Bob Regoli, "Race, Conventional Crime, and Criminal Justice: The Declining Importance of Skin Color," *Journal of Criminal Justice* 27:549–557 (1999).

29. Delbert Elliott, "Serious Violent Offending: Onset, Developmental Course, and Termination," *Criminology* 32:1–21 (1994).

30. Carl Pope and Howard Snyder, *Race as a Factor in Juvenile Arrests* (Washington, DC: Office of Juvenile Justice and Delinquency Prevention, 2003).

31. Pope and Snyder, note 30, pp. 4–6.

32. Forum on Child and Family Statistics, *America's Children: Key National Indicators of Well-Being 2004* (Washington, DC: Federal Interagency Form on Child and Family Statistics, 2004).

33. Amy Waldman, "Brothers, 8 and 9, Charged in Fatal Stabbing of Boy, 4," *The New York Times,* September 8, 2001:12A.

34. Katrina Baum, *Juvenile Victimization and Offending, 1993–2003* (Washington, DC: U.S. Department of Justice, 2005).

35. Harry Moskowitz, John Griffith, Carla DiScala, and Robert Sege, "Serious Injuries and Deaths of Adolescent Girls Resulting from Interpersonal Violence," *Archive of Pediatric Adolescent Medicine* 155:905 (2001).

36. Callie Rennison, *Criminal Victimization 1999: Changes 1998–99 with Trends 1993–99* (Washington, DC: Bureau of Justice Statistics, 2000), p. 6.

37. David Finkelhor and Richard Ormrod, *Characteristics of Crimes against Juveniles* (Washington, DC: Office of Juvenile Justice and Delinquency Prevention, 2000), pp. 7, 12.

38. Carl McCurley and Howard Snyder, *Victims of Violent Juvenile Crime* (Washington, DC: Office of Juvenile Justice and Delinquency Prevention, 2004).

39. Murray Straus and Sarah Savage, "Neglectful Behavior by Parents in the Life History of University Students in 17 Countries and Its Relation to Violence among Dating Partners," *Child Maltreatment* 10:124–135 (2005).

40. David Wolfe, Katreena Scott, Christine Wekerle, and Anna-Lee Pittman, "Child Maltreatment: Risk of Adjustment Problems and Dating Violence in Adolescence," *Journal of the American Academy of Child and Adolescent Psychiatry* 40:282–289 (2001).

41. Maura O'Keefe, *Teen Dating Violence: A Review of Risk Factors and Prevention Efforts* (Harrisburg, PA: National Resource Center on Domestic Violence, 2005).

42. Attorney General Alberto Gonzalez, *"Attorney General Hails Passage of the Child Protection Act," and "Fact Sheet: Department of Justice Project Safe Childhood Initiative,"* Press Releases (Washington, DC; U.S. Department of Justice, February 15, 2006, and July 25, 2006).

43. See James Jacobs, *Can Gun Control Work?* (New York: Oxford University Press, 2002; John Lott, *More Guns, Less Crime: Understanding Crime and Gun Control Laws* (Chicago: University of Chicago Press, 1998).

44. Anthony Braga and David Kennedy, "Illicit Acquisition of Firearms by Youth and Juveniles," *Journal of Criminal Justice* 29:379–388 (2001); Anthony Braga and Glenn Pierce, "Disrupting Illegal Firearms Markets in Boston," *Criminology and Public Policy* 4:717–748 (2005).

45. Craig Perkins, *Weapon Use and Violent Crime* (Washington, DC: U.S. Department of Justice, 2003); Federal Bureau of Investigation, note 2.

46. Jill DeVoe, Katherin Peter, Margaret Noonan, Thomas Snyder, and Katrina Baum, *Indicators of School Crime and Safety: 2005* (Washington, DC: U.S. Department of Justice and U.S. Department of Education, 2005).

47. Centers for Disease Control and Prevention, *Youth Risk Behavior Surveillance—United States, 2005* (Atlanta: U.S. Department of Health and Human Services, 2006).

48. Pamela Wilcox and Richard Clayton, "A Multilevel Analysis of School-Based Weapon Possession," *Justice Quarterly* 18:509–541 (2001).

49. Joseph Sheley and James Wright, *In the Line of Fire: Youth, Guns, and Violence in Urban America* (New York: Aldine De Gruyter, 1995), p. 43.

50. Rick Ruddell and G. Larry Mays, "Examining the Arsenal of Juvenile Gunslingers: Trends and Policy Implications," *Crime & Delinquency* 49:231–252 (2003), p. 243.

51. 103rd Congress, HR 3355, *The Violent Crime Control and Law Enforcement Act of 1994,* Title XI, Sec. 110201 (Washington, DC: U.S. Government Printing Office, 1994).

52. M. Schuster, T. Franke, A. Bastian, S. Sor, N. Halfon, "Firearm Storage Patterns in U.S. Homes with Children," *American Journal of Public Health* 90:588–594 (2000).

53. Sheley and Wright, note 49, pp. 46–50.

54. Caroline Harlow, *Firearm Use by Offenders* (Washington, DC: Bureau of Justice Statistics, 2001), p. 9.

55. Sheley and Wright, note 49, pp. 27–29; Joseph Sheley and James Wright, *Gun Acquisition and Possession in Selected Juvenile Samples* (Washington, DC: U.S. Department of Justice, 1993), p. 4.

56. Philip Cook and Jens Ludwig, "Does Gun Prevalence Affect Teen Gun Carrying After All?" *Criminology* 42:27–54 (2004), p. 41.

57. Michael Vaughn and Matthew Howard, "The Construct of Psychopathy and Its Potential Contribution to the Study of Serious, Violent, and Chronic Juvenile Offending," *Youth Violence and Juvenile Justice* 3:235–252 (2005); Michael Vaughn and Matt DeLisi, "Were Wolfgang's Chronic Offenders Psychopaths? On the Convergent Validity between Psychopathy and Career Criminality," *Journal of Criminal Justice* 35:in press (2007).

58. Robert Hare, "Psychopathy: A Clinical Construct Whose Time Has Come," *Criminal Justice & Behavior* 23:25–54 (1996); Christopher Patrick, *Handbook of Psychopathy* (New York: The Guilford Press, 2006); Hughes Herve and John Yuille, *The Psychopath: Theory, Research, and Practice* (Mahwah, NJ: LEA Press, 2006).

59. Philippe Pinel, *A Treatise on Insanity* (New York: Hafner, 1962, Original work published in 1801).

60. James Pritchard, *A Treatise on Insanity and Other Disorders Affecting the Mind* (London: Sherwood, Gilbert, and Piper, 1835).

61. Hervey Cleckley, *The Mask of Sanity* (St. Louis: C. V. Mosby, 1941), p. 268.

62. William McCord and Joan McCord, *The Psychopath: An Essay on the Criminal Mind* (New York: Van Nostrand Reinhold, 1964).

63. Lee Robins, *Deviant Children Grown Up* (Baltimore: Williams and Wilkins, 1966), p. 157.

64. Donald Lynam, Avshalom Caspi, Terrie Moffitt, Adrian Raine, Rolf Loeber, and Magda Stouthamer-Loeber, "Adolescent Psychopathy and the Big Five: Results from Two Samples," *Journal of Abnormal Child Psychology* 33:431–443 (2005).

65. Paul Frick, Eva Kimonis, Danielle Dandreaux, and Jamie Farell, "The 4-Year Stability of Psychopathic Traits in Non-Referred Youth," *Behavioral Sciences and the Law* 21:713–736 (2003).

66. Mary Ann Campbell, Stephen Porter, and Darcy Santor, "Psychopathic Traits in Adolescent Offenders: An Evaluation of Criminal History, Clinical, and Psychosocial Correlates," *Behavioral Sciences and the Law* 22:23–47 (2004).

67. Michael Vitacco and Richard Rogers, "Predictors of Adolescent Psychopathy," *Journal of the American Academy of Psychiatry and the Law* 29:374–382 (2001); John Edens, Jennifer Skeem, Keith Cruise, and Elizabeth Cauffman, "Assessment of 'Juvenile Psychopathy' and It's Association with Violence: A Critical Review," *Behavioral Sciences and the Law* 19:53–80 (2001); Matthew Howard, James Williams, Michael Vaughn, and Tonya Edmond, "Promises and Perils of a Psychopathology of Crime: The Troubling Case of Juvenile Psychopathy," *Journal of Law and Policy* 13:441–483 (2004).

68. Robert Blair, "Responsiveness to Distress Cues in the Child with Psychopathic Tendencies," *Personality and Individual Differences* 27:135–145 (1999); Lisa Fisher and Robert Blair, "Cognitive Impairment and its Relationship to Psychopathic Tendencies in Children with Emotional and Behavioral Difficulties," *Journal of Abnormal Child Psychology* 26:787–805 (1998).

69. Michael Vaughn, Matthew Howard, and Matt DeLisi, "Psychopathic Personality Traits and Delinquent Careers: An Empirical Examination," Unpublished manuscript, 2007.

70. Vaughn and DeLisi, note 57.

71. Diana Falkenbach, Norman Poythress, and Kathleen Heide, "Psychopathic Features in a Juvenile Diversion Population," *Behavioral Sciences and the Law* 21:787–805 (2003).

72. Raymond Corrado, Gina Vincent, Stephen Hart, and Irwin Cohen, "Predictive Validity of the Psychopathy Checklist: Youth Version for General and Violent Recidivism," *Behavioral Sciences and the Law* 22:5–22 (2004); Heather Gretton, Michelle McBride, Robert Hare, Roy O'Shaughnessy, and Gary Kumka, "Psychopathy and Recidivism in Adolescent Sex Offenders," *Criminal Justice and Behavior* 28:427–449 (2001).

73. Daniel Murrie, Dewey Cornell, Sebastian Kaplan, David McConville, and Andrea Levy-Elkon, "Psychopathy Scores and Violence among Juvenile Offenders: A Multi-Measure Study," *Behavioral Sciences and the Law* 22:49–67 (2004).

74. Sarah Spain, Kevin Douglas, Norman Poythress, and Monica Epstein, "The Relationship between Psychopathic Features, Violence, and Treatment Outcome," *Behavioral Sciences and the Law* 22:85–102 (2004).

75. Benjamin Karpman, "Conscience in the Psychopath: Another Version," *American Journal of Orthopsychiatry* 18:455–491 (1948); David Lykken, "A Study of Anxiety in Sociopathic Personality," *Journal of Abnormal Psychology* 55:6–10 (1957).

76. James Blair, Derek Mitchell, and Katrina Blair, *The Psychopath: Emotion and the Brain* (Oxford: Blackwell Publishing, 2005).

77. Norman Poythress and Jennifer Skeem, "Disaggregating Psychopathy: Where and How to Look for Subtypes," pages 172–192 in Christopher Patrick (ed.), *Handbook of Psychopathy* (New York: The Guilford Press, 2006).

78. Donald Lynam, "Early Identification of Chronic Offenders: Who Is the Fledgling Psychopath?" *Psychological Bulletin* 120:209–234 (1996); Donald Lynam, "Pursuing the Psychopath: Capturing the Fledgling Psychopath in a Nomological Net," *Journal of Abnormal Psychology* 106:425–438 (1997); Donald Lynam and Lauren Gudonis, "The Development of Psychopathy," *Annual Review of Clinical Psychology* 1:31–407 (2005).

79. Marnie Rice, Grant Harris, and Catherine Cormier, "A Follow-Up of Rapists Assessed in a Maximum Security Psychiatric Facility," *Journal of Interpersonal Violence* 5:435–448 (1992).

80. Robert Hare, Danny Clark, Martin Grann, and David Thornton, "Psychopathy and the Predictive Validity of the PCL-R: An International Perspective," *Behavioral Sciences and the Law* 18:623–645 (2000).

81. Grant Harris and Marnie Rice, "Treatment of Psychopathy: A Review of Empirical Findings," pages 555–572 in Christopher Patrick (ed.), *Handbook of Psychopathy* (New York: The Guilford Press, 2006).

82. Keith Cruise, Lori Colwell, Phillip Lyons, and Michael Baker, "Prototypical Analysis of Adolescent Psychopathy: Investigating the Juvenile Justice Perspective," *Behavioral Sciences and the Law* 21:829–846 (2006).

83. Mark Cohen, *The Costs of Crime and Justice* (London: Routledge, 2005).

84. Michael Caldwell, Michael Vitacco, and Gregory Van Rybroek, "Are Violent Delinquents Worth Treating? A Cost–Benefit Analysis," *Journal of Research in Crime and Delinquency* 43:148–168 (2006).

85. Kathleen Heide and Eldra Solomon, "Treating Today's Juvenile Homicide Offenders," *Youth Violence and Juvenile Justice* 1:5–31 (2003); Kathleen Heide, "Youth Homicide: A Review of the Literature and a Blueprint for Action," *International Journal of Offender Therapy and Comparative Criminology* 47:6–36 (2003).

86. George Kelling and William Bratton, "Declining Crime Rates: Insiders' View of the New York City Story," *Journal of Criminal Law and Criminology* 88:1217–1232 (1998); Jeffrey Fagan, Franklin Zimring, and June Kim, "Declining Homicide in New York City: A Tale of Two Trends," *Journal of Criminal Law and Criminology* 88:1277–1323 (1998).

87. Bernard Harcourt, *Illusion of Order: The False Promise of Broken Windows Policing* (Cambridge, MA: Harvard University Press, 2001).

88. Richard Rosenfeld, Robert Fornango, and Eric Baumer, "Did *Ceasefire, Compstat,* and *Exile* Reduce Homicide?" *Criminology and Public Policy* 4:419–450 (2005).

89. Franklin Zimring, "Kids, Guns, and Homicide: Policy Notes on an Age-Specific Epidemic," *Law and Contemporary Problems* 59:34 (1996).

90. Marc Riedel and Wayne Welsh, *Criminal Violence: Patterns, Causes, and Prevention* (Los Angeles: Roxbury, 2002), p. 307.

91. Shay Bilchik, *Promising Strategies to Reduce Gun Violence* (Washington, DC: Office of Juvenile Justice and Delinquency Prevention, 1999); David Sheppard, Heath Grant, Wendy Rowe, and Nancy Jacobs, *Fighting Juvenile Gun Violence* (Washington, DC: Office of Juvenile Justice and Delinquency Prevention, 2000).

92. Kirsten Scharnberg and Eric Ferkenhoff, "Girl Died after Parents Hit Her 160 Times, Court Told," *Chicago Tribune,* November 14, 2001:1A.

93. Laurence Steinberg, "Youth Violence: Do Parents and Families Make a Difference," *National Institute of Justice Journal,* April: 31–38 (2000); John Wilson, *Safe from the Start: Taking Action on Children Exposed to Violence* (Washington, DC: Office of Juvenile Justice and Delinquency Prevention, 2000).

94. Stephen Baron and Timothy Hartnagel, "Street Youth and Criminal Violence," *Journal of Research in Crime and Delinquency* 35:184 (1998).

95. Sharon Mihalic, Abigail Fagan, Katherine Irwin, Diane Ballard, and Delbert Elliott, *Blueprints for Violence Prevention* (Washington, DC: Office of Juvenile Justice and Delinquency Prevention, 2004).

96. Scott Henggeler, Sharon Mihalic, Lee Rone, Christopher Thomas, and Jane Timmons-Mitchell, *Multisystemic Therapy: Blueprints for Violence Prevention, Book Six* (Boulder, CO: Center for the Study and Prevention of Violence, 1998).

97. For a comprehensive review of the program's history and treatment results, see Carolyn Webster-Stratton, *The Incredible Years Training Series* (Washington, DC: Office of Juvenile Justice and Delinquency Prevention, 2000).

98. Sharon Mihalic, Katy Irwin, Delbert Elliott, Abigail Fagan, and Diane Hansen, *Blueprints for Violence Prevention* (Washington, DC: Office of Juvenile Justice and Delinquency Prevention, 2001), pp. 5–6.

99. *United States v. Lopez,* 514 U.S. 549 (1995).

100. Devon Brewer, J. David Hawkins, Richard Catalano, and Holly Neckerman, "Preventing Serious, Violent, and Chronic Juvenile Delinquency," pages 90–95 in James Howell, Barry Krisberg, J. David Hawkins, and John Wilson (eds.), *A Sourcebook: Serious, Violent & Chronic Juvenile Offenders* (Thousand Oaks, CA: Sage, 1995).

101. Mark Greenberg, Carol Kusche, and Sharon Mihalic, "*Promoting Alternative Thinking Strategies (PATHS): Blueprints for Violence Prevention, Book Ten* (Boulder, CO: Center for the Study and Prevention of Violence, 1998).

102. Dagmar McGill, Sharon Mihalic, and Jennifer Grotpeter, *Big Brothers/Big Sisters of America: Blueprints for Violence Prevention, Book Two* (Boulder, CO: Center for the Study and Prevention of Violence, 1998).

103. Shawn Bauldry, *Positive Support: Mentoring and Depression among High-Risk Youth* (Washington, DC: U.S. Department of Justice, 2006).

104. Dan Olweus, Sue Limber, and Sharon Mihalic, *Bullying Prevention Program: Blueprints for Violence Prevention, Book Nine* (Boulder, CO: Center for the Study and Prevention of Violence, 1998).

105. Dewey Cornell, "Prior Adjustment of Violent Juvenile Offenders," *Law and Human Behavior* 14:575 (1990).

106. Matt DeLisi, *Career Criminals in Society* (Thousand Oaks, CA: Sage, 2005).

107. Mark Lipsey, "Can Intervention Rehabilitate Serious Delinquents?" *Annals of the American Academy of Political and Social Science, 564,* 142–166 (1999), p. 163.

108. John Wilson and James Howell, "Comprehensive Strategy for Serious, Violent, and Chronic Juvenile Offenders," pages 36–46 in Howell et al., note 100.

109. Barry Krisberg, Elliot Currie, David Onek, and Richard Wiebush, "Graduated Sanctions for Serious, Violent, and Chronic Juvenile Offenders," pages 142–170 in Howell et al., note 100.

CHAPTER 4

1. Liz Szabo, "Movies Inspire Children to Smoke," *USA TODAY,* November 7, 2005:7D.

2. Donna Leinwand, "Survey: Parents Clueless on Booze, Drugs at Teen Parties," *USA TODAY,* August 17, 2006:8A.

3. Wendy Koch, "Meth's Impact on Children Probed," *USA TODAY,* April 26, 2006:6A.

4. Donna Leinwand, "Many More Treated for Meth, Pot," *USA TODAY,* April 25, 2006:1A.

5. Donna Leinwand, "Prescription Drugs Find Place in Teen Culture," *USA TODAY*, June 13, 2006:1A.

6. Marilyn Elias, "More Kids Get Multiple Psychiatric Drugs," *USA TODAY*, August 2, 2005:6D.

7. Donna Leinwand, "Anti-Drug Advertising Campaign a Failure, GAO Report Says," *USA TODAY*, August 29, 2006:5A.

8. "Girl, 11, Arrested on Heroin-Dealing Charges," online at: http://www.local6.com/2743591/detail.html, accessed April 21, 2007.

9. Jeffrey Kluger, "Medicating Young Minds," *Time,* November 3, 2003:48–58; Marilyn Elias, "Prozac Linked to Child Suicide Risk," *USA TODAY*, September 14, 2004:1A.

10. U.S. Census Bureau, *Statistical Abstract of the United States, 2006* (Washington, DC: U.S. Bureau of the Census, 2007).

11. Center on Addiction and Substance Abuse at Columbia University, *Malignant Neglect: Substance Abuse and America's Schools* (New York: Center on Addiction and Substance Abuse at Columbia University, 2001), p 11.

12. Lloyd Johnston, Patrick O'Malley, Jerald Bachman, and John Schulenberg, *Monitoring the Future: National Results on Adolescent Drug Use: Overview of Key Findings, 2006* (Bethesda, MD: National Institute on Drug Abuse, 2007).

13. U.S. Department of Health and Human Services, *Results from the 2005 National Survey on Drug Use and Health: National Findings* (Washington, DC: U.S. Department of Health and Human Services, 2006).

14. Centers for Disease Control and Prevention, *Youth Risk Behavior Surveillance—United States, 2005* (Atlanta: U.S. Department of Health and Human Services, 2006).

15. Howard Snyder, *Juvenile Arrests, 2003* (Washington, DC: Office of Juvenile Justice and Delinquency Prevention, 2005).

16. Federal Bureau of Investigation, *Crime in the United States, 2005* (Washington, DC: U.S. Department of Justice, 2006).

17. Federal Bureau of Investigation, note 16.

18. Office of National Drug Control Policy, *The President's National Drug Control Strategy February 2006* (Washington, DC: Executive Office of the President of the United States, 2006); U.S. Department of Health and Human Services, note 13.

19. Martha Irvine, "Teens Try More Drugs in Summer," *The Boulder Daily Camera*, June 5, 2004:1B.

20. Office of Applied Studies, Substance Abuse and Mental Health Services Administration, "Substance Use Treatment Need among Adolescents: 2003–2004," *The NSDUH Report,* December 18, 2006.

21. Joan McCord, Cathy Widom, and Nancy Crowell, *Juvenile Crime, Juvenile Justice* (Washington, DC: National Academy Press, 2001).

22. Federal Bureau of Investigation, note 16.

23. Charles Puzzanchera, Anne Stahl, Terrence Finnegan, Nancy Tierney, and Howard Snyder, *Juvenile Court Statistics, 1999* (Pittsburgh: National Center for Juvenile Justice, 2003).

24. Jason Ziedenberg, *Drugs and Disparity: The Racial Impact of Illinois' Practice of Transferring Young Drug Offenders to Adult Court* (Washington, DC: Building Blocks for Youth, 2001).

25. Schneider Institute for Health Policy, *Substance Abuse: The Nation's Number One Health Problem* (Princeton, NJ: Robert Wood Johnson Foundation, 2001), pp. 36–37.

26. Johnston et al., note 12.

27. Johnston et al., note 12; for an overview of the Monitoring the Future Survey, see Jerald Bachman, Patrick O'Malley, John Schulenberg, Lloyd Johnston, Alison Bryant, and Alicia Merline, *The Decline of Substance Use in Young Adulthood: Changes in Social Activities, Roles, and Beliefs* (Mahway, NJ: Lawrence Erlbaum Associates, 2002).

28. Donna Leinwand, "Latest Trend in Drug Abuse: Youths Risk Death for Cough-Remedy High," *USA TODAY*, December 29, 2003:1A.

29. James Short, Jr., *Delinquency and Society* (Englewood Cliffs, NJ: Prentice Hall, 1990), p. 119.

30. Larry McShane, "Poll: Kids' Drug Use Underestimated," *The Washington Post*, April 13, 1998:2.

31. Johnston et al., note 12.

32. Office of Applied Studies, Substance Abuse and Mental Health Services Administration, "How Youths Obtain Marijuana," *The NSDUH Report*, March 12, 2004.

33. Robert Merton, *Social Theory and Social Structure,* revised edition (New York: Macmillan, 1968).

34. Richard Cloward and Lloyd Ohlin, *Delinquency and Opportunity* (New York: The Free Press, 1960).

35. Stephen Baron and Timothy Hartnagel, "Street Youth and Labor Market Strain," *Journal of Criminal Justice* 30:519–533 (2002).

36. Nicole Leeper Piquero and Miriam Sealock, "Generalizing General Strain Theory: An Examination of an Offending Population," *Justice Quarterly* 17:449–484 (2000); Nicole Leeper Piquero and Miriam Sealock, "Gender and General Strain Theory: A Preliminary Test of Broidy and Agnew's Gender/GST Hypotheses," *Justice Quarterly* 21:125–158 (2004).

37. John Hoffman and Susan Su, "The Conditional Effects of Stress on Delinquency and Drug Use: A Strain Theory Assessment of Sex Differences," *Journal of Research in Crime and Delinquency* 34:46–78 (1997).

38. Michael Agar, *Ripping and Running: A Formal Ethnography of Urban Heroin Addicts* (New York: Academic Press, 1973); Patrick Biernacki, "Junkie Work, 'Hustles' and Social Status Among Heroin Addicts," *Journal of Drug Issues* 9:535–551 (1979); Charles Faupel, *Shooting Dope: Career Patterns of Hard-Core Heroin Users* (Gainesville: University of Florida Press, 1991).

39. Charles Faupel, Alan Horowitz, and Greg Weaver, *The Sociology of American Drug Use* (New York: McGraw-Hill, 2004), p. 125.

40. Edwin Sutherland, *Principles of Criminology* (Philadelphia: JB Lippincott Co., 1947).

41. Erich Goode, *Drugs in American Society*, 6th edition (New York: McGraw-Hill, 2005).

42. Angela Gover, "Risky Lifestyles and Dating Violence: A Theoretical Test of Violent Victimization," *Journal of Criminal Justice* 32:171–180 (2004).

43. Ruth Triplett and Brian Payne, "Problem Solving as Reinforcement in Adolescent Drug Use: Implications for Theory and Policy," *Journal of Criminal Justice* 32:617–630 (2004); L. Thomas Winfree and Frances Bernat, "Social Learning, Self-Control, and Substance Abuse by Eighth Grade Students: A Tale of Two Cities," *Journal of Drug Issues* 28:539–558 (1998).

44. Jacquelyn Monroe, "Getting a Puff: A Social Learning Test of Adolescent Smoking," *Journal of Child and Adolescent Substance Abuse* 13:71–83 (2004).

45. Madeline Dalton, James Sargent, Michael Beach, Linda Titus-Ernstoff, Jennifer Gibson, Bridget Ahrens, Jennifer Tickle, and Todd Heatherton, "Effect of Viewing Smoking in Movies on Adolescent Smoking Initiation: A Cohort Study," *The Lancet* 362:284 (2003).

46. Howard Becker, *Outsiders: Studies in the Sociology of Deviance* (New York: The Free Press, 1963), p. 58.

47. Erich Goode, *The Marijuana Smokers* (New York: Basic Books, 1970).

48. Brian Kelly, "Bongs and Blunts: Notes from a Suburban Marijuana Subculture," *Journal of Ethnicity in Substance Abuse* 4:81–97 (2005).

49. Denise Kandel, "Drugs and Drinking Behavior Among Youth," *Annual Review of Sociology* 6:235–285 (1980); Denise Kandel, "Inter- and Intragenerational Influences on Adolescent Marijuana Use," *Journal of Social Issues* 30:107–135 (1974); Denise Kandel, "Adolescent Marijuana Use: Role of Parents and Peers," *Science* 181:1067–1070 (1973).

50. Andy Hochstetler, "Opportunities and Decision: Interactional Dynamics in Robbery and Burglary Groups," *Criminology* 39:737–764 (2001); Andy Hochstetler, "Sprees and Runs: Opportunity Construction and Criminal Episodes," *Deviant Behavior* 23:45–73 (2002).

51. Darrell Irwin, "Straight Edge Subculture: Examining the Youths' Drug-Free Way," *Journal of Drug Issues* 29:365–380 (1999); Ross Haenfler, *Straight Edge: Clean-Living Youth, Hardcore Punk, and Social Change* (New Brunswick, NJ: Rutgers University Press, 2006).

52. Travis Hirschi, *Causes of Delinquency* (Berkeley: University of California Press, 1969).

53. Michael Maume, Graham Ousey, and Kevin Beaver, "Cutting the Grass: A Re-Examination of the Link between Marital Attachment, Delinquent Peers and Desistance from Marijuana Use," *Journal of Quantitative Criminology* 21:27–53 (2005).

54. Office of Applied Studies, Substance Abuse and Mental Health Services Administration, "Participation in Youth Activities and Substance Use among Youth," *The NSDUH Report*, September 18, 2006.

55. Office of Applied Studies, Substance Abuse and Mental Health Services Administration, "Religious Beliefs and Substance Use Among Youths," *The NSDUH Report*, September 18, 2006.

56. Office of Applied Studies, Substance Abuse and Mental Health Services Administration "Substance Use among School Dropouts," *The NSDUH Report*, September 18, 2006.

57. Lisbeth Schorr, *Within Our Reach: Breaking the Cycle of Disadvantage* (New York: Anchor Books, 1989), p. 20.

58. Anthony Jurich, Cheryl Polson, Julie Jurich, and Rodney Bates, "Family Factors in the Lives of Drug Users and Abusers," *Adolescence* 20:143–159 (1985).

59. Alfred Friedman, "Family Factors and the Family Role in Treatment for Adolescent Drug Abuse," pages 13–30 in Alfred Friedman and George Beschner (eds.), *Treatment Services for Adolescent Substance Abusers* (Washington, DC: U.S. Government Printing Office, 1985); Joan Kelly, "Children's Adjustment in Conflicted Marriage and Divorce: A Decade Review of Research," *Journal of the American Academy of Child and Adolescent Psychiatry* 39:963–973 (2000).

60. Rafaela Robles, Ruth Martinez, and Margarita Moscoso, "Predictors of Adolescent Drug Behavior," *Youth & Society* 11:415–430 (1980).

61. Mark Halebsky, "Adolescent Alcohol and Substance Abuse: Parent and Peer Effects," *Adolescence* 22:961–967 (1987); Roberta Pandina and James Schuele, "Psychological Correlates of Alcohol and Drug Use of Adolescent Students and Adolescents in Treatment," *Journal of Studies on Alcohol* 44:950–973 (1985).

62. Rick Kosterman, J. David Hawkins, Jie Guo, Richard Catalano, and Robert Abbott, "The Dynamics of Alcohol and Marijuana Initiation: Patterns and Predictors of First Use in Adolescence," *American Journal of Public Health* 90:360–366 (2000).

63. Michelle Miller, Finn Esbensen, and Adrienne Freng, "Parental Attachment, Parental Supervision and Adolescent Deviance in Intact and Non-Intact Families," *Journal of Crime & Justice* 22:1–29 (1999); Jeffrey Cookston, "Parental Supervision and Family Structure: Effects on Adolescent Problem Behaviors," *Journal of Divorce & Remarriage* 32:107–122 (1999).

64. Stephan Quensel, Paul McArdle, Aoife Brinkley, and Auke Wiegersma, "Broken Home or Drug Using Peers: 'Significant Relations'?" *Journal of Drug Issues* 32:467–489 (2002).

65. Peter Mulhall, Donald Stone, and Brian Stone, "Home Alone: Is It a Risk Factor for Middle School Youth and Drug Use?" *Journal of Drug Education* 26:39–48 (1996).

66. Ann Burgess, Carol Hartman, and Arlene McCormack, "Abused to Abuser: Antecedents of Socially Deviant Behaviors," *American Journal of Psychiatry* 144:1431–1440 (1987).

67. Richard Dembo, Max Dertke, Lawrence Lavoie, and Scott Borders, "Physical Abuse, Sexual Victimization and Illicit Drug Use: A Structural Analysis among High Risk Adolescents," *Journal of Adolescence* 10:13–34 (1987).

68. Suman Kakar, *Child Abuse and Delinquency* (New York: University Press of America, 1996); John Lemmon, "How Child Maltreatment Affects Dimensions of Juvenile Delinquency in a Cohort of Low-Income Urban Youths," *Justice Quarterly* 16:357–376 (1999); Carolyn Smith and Terence Thornberry, "The Relationship Between Childhood Maltreatment and Adolescent Involvement in

Delinquency," *Criminology* 33:451–477 (1995); Matthew Zingraff, Jeffrey Leiter, Kristen Myers, and Matthew Johnson, "Child Maltreatment and Youthful Problem Behavior," *Criminology* 31:173–202 (1993).

69. Timothy Ireland, Carolyn Smith, and Terence Thornberry, "Developmental Issues in the Impact of Child Maltreatment on Later Delinquency and Drug Use," *Criminology* 40: 359–396 (2002).

70. Office of Applied Studies, "Children Living with Substance-Abusing or Substance-Dependent Parents," *The NHSDA Report*, June 2, 2003; Office of Applied Studies, "Alcohol Dependence or Abuse among Parents with Children Living in the Home," *The NSDUH Report*, February 13, 2004.

71. F. I. Fawzy, Robert Coombs, and Barry Gerber, "Generational Continuity in the Use of Substances: The Impact of Parental Substance Use on Adolescent Substance Use," *Addictive Behavior* 8:109–114 (1983).

72. Denise Kandel, Ronald Kessler, and Rebecca Margulies, "Antecedents of Adolescent Initiation into Stages of Drug Use: A Developmental Analysis," *Journal of Youth and Adolescence* 7:13–40 (1978); Denise Kandel, Pamela Griesler, Gang Lee, Mark Davis, and Christine Schaffran, *Parental Influences on Adolescent Marijuana Use and the Baby Boom Generation: Findings from the 1979–1996 National Household Surveys on Drug Abuse* (Washington, DC: Department of Health and Human Services, 2001).

73. David Huizinga, Rolf Loeber, and Terence Thornberry, *Urban Delinquency and Substance Abuse: Initial Findings* (Washington, DC: Office of Juvenile Justice and Delinquency Prevention, 1994); Delbert Elliott, David Huizinga, and Scott Menard, *Multiple Problem Youth* (New York: Springer-Verlag, 1989).

74. Scott Menard, Sharon Mihalic, and David Huizinga, "Drugs and Crime Revisited," *Justice Quarterly* 18:269–300 (2001), p. 295.

75. Cheryl Carpenter, Barry Glassner, Bruce Johnson, and Julia Loughlin, *Kids, Drugs, and Crime* (Lexington, MA: D. C. Heath, 1988); James Farrow and James French, "The Drug Abuse-Delinquency Connection Revisited," *Adolescence* 21:951–960 (1986); John Watters, Craig Reinarman, and Jeffrey Fagan, "Causality, Context, and Contingency: Relationships between Drug Abuse and Delinquency," *Contemporary Drug Problems* 12:351–373 (1985).

76. John Welte, Grace Barnes, and Joseph Hoffman, "Gambling, Substance Use, and Other Problem Behaviors among Youth: A Test of General Deviance Models," *Journal of Criminal Justice* 32:297–306 (2004).

77. Office of Applied Studies, Substance Abuse and Mental Health Services Administration, "Marijuana Use and Delinquent Behaviors among Youths," *The NSDUH Report*, September 18, 2006; Office of Applied Studies, Substance Abuse and Mental Health Services Administration "Substance Use among Youths Who Had Run Away from Home," *The NSDUH Report*, September 18, 2006.

78. David Altschuler and Paul Brounstein, "Patterns of Drug Use, Drug Trafficking, and Other Delinquency Among Inner-City Adolescent Males in Washington, DC," *Criminology* 29:589 (1991).

79. Colleen McLaughlin, Jack Daniel, and Timothy Joost, "The Relationship Between Substance Use, Drug Selling, and Lethal Violence in 25 Juvenile Murderers," *Journal of Forensic Sciences* 45:349–353 (2000).

80. David Huizinga, Rolf Loeber, Terence Thornberry, and Lynn Cothern, *Co-occurrence of Delinquency and Other Problem Behaviors* (Washington, DC: Office of Juvenile Justice and Delinquency Prevention, 2000), p. 3.

81. Delbert Elliott, David Huizinga, and Suzanne Ageton, *Explaining Delinquency and Drug Use* (Beverly Hills, CA: Sage, 1985); Delbert Elliott and Barbara Morse, "Delinquency and Drug Use as Risk Factors in Teenage Sexual Activity," *Youth & Society* 21:32–60 (1989).

82. Helen Garnier and Judith Stein, "An 18-Year Model of Family and Peer Effects on Adolescent Drug Use and Delinquency," *Journal of Youth and Adolescence* 31: 45–56 (2002).

83. Andrea Hussong, "Differentiating Peer Contexts and Risk for Adolescent Substance Use," *Journal of Youth and Adolescence* 31:207–220 (2002).

84. Jeffrey Fagan, "The Social Organization of Drug Use and Drug Dealing Among Urban Gangs," *Criminology* 27:633–667 (1989); Finn Esbensen, Dana Peterson, Adrienne Freng, and Terrance Taylor, "Initiation of Drug Use, Drug Sales, and Violent Offending Among a Sample of Gang and Non-Gang Youth," pages 37–50 in C. Ronald Huff (ed.), *Gangs in America III* (Thousand Oaks, CA: Sage, 2002); C. Ronald Huff, *Comparing the Criminal Behavior of Youth Gangs and At-Risk Youths* (Washington, DC: National Institute of Justice, 1998); James Howell and Debra Gleason, *Youth Gang Drug Trafficking* (Washington, DC: Office of Juvenile Justice and Delinquency Prevention, 1999); Avelardo Valdez and Stephen Sifaneck, " 'Getting High by Getting By': Dimensions of Drug Selling Behaviors Among American Mexican Gang Members in South Texas," *Journal of Research in Crime and Delinquency* 41:82–105 (2004).

85. Marvin Krohn, Alan Lizotte, and Cynthia Perez, "The Interrelationship between Substance Use and Precocious Transitions to Adult Statuses," *Journal of Health and Social Behavior* 38:87–103 (1997).

86. Terrie Moffitt, "Life-Course-Persistent and Adolescence-Limited Antisocial Behavior: A 10-Year Research Review and a Research Agenda," pages 49–75 in Benjamin Lahey, Terrie Moffitt, and Avshalom Caspi (eds.), *Causes of Conduct Disorder and Juvenile Delinquency* (New York: Guilford, 2003); Terrie Moffitt, "A Review of Research on the Taxonomy of Life-Course Persistent Versus Adolescence-Limited Antisocial Behavior," pages 277–312 in Francis Cullen, John Paul Wright, and Kristie Blevins (eds.), *Taking Stock: The Status of Criminological Theory, Advances in Criminological Theory*, Volume 15 (New Brunswick, NJ: Transaction, 2006).

87. Ralph Hingson, T. Heeren, and M. Winter, "Age at Drinking Onset and Alcohol Dependence," *Archives of Pediatrics and Adolescent Medicine* 160:739–746 (2006).

88. Grace Barnes, John Welte, and Joseph Hoffman, "The Relationship of Alcohol Use to Delinquency and Illicit Drug Use in Adolescents: Gender, Age, and Racial/Ethnic Differences," *Journal of Drug Issues* 32:153–178 (2001).

89. Robert Corwyn and Brent Benda, "The Relationship between Use of Alcohol, Other Drugs, and Crime among Adolescents: An Argument for a Delinquency Syndrome," *Alcoholism Treatment Quarterly* 20:35–49 (2002); Richard Dembo et al., "Testing a Longitudinal Model of the Relationships among High Risk Youth's Drug Sales, Drug Use and Participation in Index Crimes," *Journal of Child and Adolescent Substance Abuse* 11:37–61 (2002); Rolf Loeber, David Farrington, Magda Stouthamer-Loeber, and Welmoet Van Kammen, *Antisocial Behavior and Mental Health Problems* (Mahway, NJ: Lawrence Erlbaum Associates, 1998).

90. Richard Jessor, *New Perspectives on Adolescent Risk Behavior* (New York: Cambridge University Press, 1998).

91. Denis Ribeaud and Manuel Eisner, "The Drug-Crime Link from a Self-Control Perspective: An Empirical Test in a Swiss Youth Sample," *European Journal of Criminology* 3:33–67 (2006).

92. Laetitia Thompson, Elizabeth Whitmore, Kristen Raymond, and Thomas Crowley, "Measuring Impulsivity in Adolescents with Serious Substance and Conduct Problems," *Assessment* 13:3–15 (2006).

93. Gregory Rainone, James Schmeidler, Blanche Frank, and Robinson Smith, "Violent Behavior, Substance Use, and Other Delinquent Behaviors among Middle and High School Students," *Youth Violence and Juvenile Justice* 4:247–265 (2006).

94. Karen Parker and Scott Maggard, "Structural Theories and Race-Specific Drug Arrests: What Structural Factors Account for the Rise in Race-Specific Drug Arrests over Time?" *Crime & Delinquency* 51:521–547 (2005).

95. Elliott Currie, *Reckoning: Drugs, the Cities, and the American Future* (New York: Hill and Wang, 1993); Michael Tonry, *Malign Neglect: Race, Crime, and Punishment in America* (New York: Oxford University Press, 1995); Franklin Zimring and Gordon Hawkins, *The Search for Rational Drug Control* (New York: Cambridge University Press, 1992).

96. Office of National Drug Control Policy, note 18.

97. Office of National Drug Control Policy, *Executive Summary FY 2008 Budget* (Washington, DC: Executive Office of the President of the United States, 2007).

98. Steven Belenko, "Research on Drug Courts: A Critical Review," *National Drug Court Institute Review* 1: 1–43 (1998); Cassia Spohn, Erika Frenzel, Thomas Martin, and R. K. Piper, "Drug Courts and Recidivism: The Results of an Evaluation Using Two Comparison Groups and Multiple Indicators of Recidivism," *Journal of Drug Issues* 31:149–176 (2001); Caroline Cooper, *Juvenile Drug Court Programs* (Washington, DC: Office of Juvenile Justice and Delinquency Prevention, 2001).

99. Brandon Applegate and Shannon Santana, "Intervening with Youthful Substance Abusers: A Preliminary Analysis of a Juvenile Drug Court," *The Justice System Journal* 21:281–300 (2000); Michael Shaw and Kenneth Robinson, "Summary and Analysis of the First Juvenile Drug Court Evaluations: The Santa Clara County Drug Treatment Court and the Delaware Juvenile Drug Court Diversion Program," *National Drug Court Institute Review* 1:73–85 (1998).

100. Nancy Rodriguez and Vincent Webb, "Multiple Measures of Juvenile Drug Court Effectiveness: Results of a Quasi-Experimental Design," *Crime & Delinquency* 50:306 (2004).

101. Rodriguez and Webb, note 100.

101. *Vernonia School District 47J v. Acton*, 515 U.S. 646 (1995).

102. *Board of Education of Ind. School District No. 92 of Pottawatomie County v. Earls et al.*, 536 U.S. 822 (2002).

103. Ryoko Yamaguchi, Lloyd Johnston, and Patrick O'Malley, "The Relationship between Student Illicit Drug Use and School Drug-Testing Policies," *The Journal of School Health* 73:159–164 (2003).

104. James Simonson and Pat Maher, *Promising Practices: Drug-Free Communities Support Program* (Washington, DC: Office of Juvenile Justice and Delinquency Prevention, 2001).

105. Brian Lawton, Ralph Taylor, and Anthony Luongo, "Police Officers on Drug Corners in Philadelphia, Drug Crime, and Violent Crime: Intended, Diffusion, and Displacement Impacts," *Justice Quarterly* 22:427–451 (2005).

106. Samuel Nunn, Kenna Quinet, Kelley Rowe, and Donald Christ, "Interdiction Day: Covert Surveillance Operations, Drugs, and Serious Crime in an Inner-City Neighborhood," *Police Quarterly* 9:73–99 (2006).

107. Jerry Mandel and Harvey Feldman, "The Social History of Teenage Drug Use," pages 32–51 in George Beschner and Alfred Friedman (eds.), *Teen Drug Use* (Lexington, MA: Lexington Books, 1986).

108. Protecting You/Protecting Me Fact Sheet, online at http://www.pypm.org/about_us/index.cfm, accessed April 21, 2007.

109. Bureau of Justice Assistance, *Drug Abuse Resistance Education (D.A.R.E.)* (Washington, DC: U.S. Department of Justice, 1995), p. 1.

110. Office of National Drug Control Policy, note 18, p. 50.

111. Dennis Rosenbaum and Gordon Hanson, "Assessing the Effects of School-Based Drug Education: A Six-Year Multilevel Analysis of Project D.A.R.E.," *Journal of Research in Crime and Delinquency* 35:381–412 (1998).

112. Susan Ennett, Nancy Tobler, Christopher Ringwalt, and Robert Flewelling, "How Effective Is Drug Abuse Resistance Education? A Meta-Analysis of Project D.A.R.E. Outcome Evaluations," *American Journal of Public Health* 84: 1394–1401 (1994).

113. Richard Clayton, Anne Cattarello, and Bryan Johnstone, "The Effectiveness of Drug Abuse Resistance Education (Project D.A.R.E.): 5-Year Follow-Up Results," *Preventive Medicine* 25:307–318 (1996).

114. Donald Lynam, Michard Milich, Rick Zimmerman, Scott Novak, T.K. Logan, Catherine Martin, Carl Leukefeld, and Richard Clayton, "Project D.A.R.E.: No Effects at 10-Year Follow-Up," *Journal of Consulting and Clinical Psychology* 67: 590–593 (1999).

115. Yvonne Terry-McElrath and Duane McBride, "Local Implementation of Drug Policy and Access to Treatment Services for Juveniles," *Crime & Delinquency* 50:60–87 (2004).

116. National Research Council, *Losing Generations: Adolescents in High-Risk Settings* (Washington, DC: National Academy Press, 1993), p. 96.

117. Dagmar Bolvin, Sharon Mihalic, and Jennifer Grotpeter, *Life Skills Training: Blueprints for Violence Prevention, Book Five* (Boulder, CO: Center for the Study and Prevention of Violence, 1998).

118. Stanley Kusnetz, "Services for Adolescent Substance Abusers," pages 123–153 in George Beschner and Alfred Friedman (eds.), *Teen Drug Use* (Lexington, MA: Lexington Books, 1986).

119. Michael Pullmann, Jodi Krebs, Nancy Koroloff, Ernie Veach-White, Rita Gaylor, and Dede Sieler, "Juvenile Offenders with Mental Health Needs: Reducing Recidivism Using Wraparound," *Crime & Delinquency* 52:375–397 (2006); Christopher Lowenkamp, Edward Latessa, and Alexander Holsinger, "The Risk Principle In Action: What Have We Learned from 13,676 Offenders and 97 Correctional Programs?" *Crime & Delinquency* 52:77–93 (2006).

120. Lester Thurow, "U.S. Drug Policy: Colossal Ignorance," *The New York Times*, May 8, 1988:29A.

121. Erich Goode, *Between Politics and Reason: The Drug Legalization Debate* (New York: St. Martin's Press, 1997); Duane McBride, Yvonne Terry, and James Inciardi, "Alternative Perspectives on the Drug Policy Debate," pages 9–54 in James Inciardi (ed.), *The Drug Legalization Debate*, 2nd edition (Thousand Oaks, CA: Sage, 1999).

122. DrugPolicy.org, "Support for Legalizing Marijuana is at Its Highest Level Ever. *USA TODAY*/CNN/Gallup Poll, August 2001," online at: http://www.drugpolicy.org/library/publicopinio/legalmj.cfm, accessed April 21, 2007; PollingReport.com, "Illegal Drugs," Oct. 23, 2002, online at: http://www.pollingreport.com/drugs.htm, accessed October 23, 2002.

123. Goode, note 41.

124. James Inciardi and Duane McBride, "The Case against Legalization," pages 45–79 in James Inciardi (ed.), *The Drug Legalization Debate* (Newbury Park, CA: Sage, 1991).

125. James Inciardi, *The War on Drugs III* (Boston: Allyn and Bacon, 2002), pp. 297–299.

126. John Donovan and Richard Jessor, "Structure and Problem in Adolescence and Young Adulthood," *Journal of Consulting and Clinical Psychology* 53:890–904 (1985); D. Wayne Osgood, Lloyd Johnston, Patrick O'Malley, and Jerald Bachman, "The Generality of Deviance in Late Adolescence and Early Adulthood," *American Sociological Review* 53:81–93 (1988).

127. Schorr, note 57.

128. Curtis VanderWaal, Duane McBride, Yvonne Terry-McElrath, and Holly VanBuren, *Breaking the Juvenile Drug-Crime Cycle: A Guide for Practitioners and Policymakers* (Washington, DC: U.S. Department of Justice, 2001).

CHAPTER 5

1. Leon Radzinowicz, *Ideology and Crime* (New York: Columbia University Press, 1966).

2. Cesare Beccaria, *On Crimes and Punishments,* translated by Henry Paolucci (Indianapolis: Bobbs-Merrill, 1764/1963).

3. Michael Radelet, "More Trends Toward Moratoria on Executions," *Connecticut Law Review* 33:845–860 (2001).

4. Frank Miller, Robert Dawson, George Dix, and Raymond Parnas, *The Juvenile Justice Process,* 4th edition (Mineola, NY: The Foundation Press, 2000).

5. Robert Martinson, "What Works? Questions and Answers About Prison Reform," *The Public Interest* 35:22–54 (1974); Douglas Lipton, Robert Martinson, and Judith Wilks, *The Effectiveness of Correctional Treatment* (New York: Praeger, 1975); William Bailey, "Correctional Outcome: An Evaluation of 100 Reports," *Journal of Criminal Law, Criminology, and Police Science* 57:153–160 (1966); Hans Eysenck, "The Effects of Psychotherapy," *International Journal of Psychiatry* 1:99–144 (1965).

6. James Q. Wilson, *Thinking about Crime,* revised edition (New York: Basic Books, 1983), p. 128.

7. Ronald Clarke and Derek Cornish, "Modeling Offender's Decisions," pages 147–185 in Michael Tonry and Norval Morris (eds.), *Crime and Justice: An Annual Review of Research,* Volume 6 (Chicago: University of Chicago Press, 1986).

8. Bruce Jacobs, "Crack Dealers' Apprehension Avoidance Techniques," *Justice Quarterly* 13:359–381 (1996).

9. Matthew Robinson, "Lifestyles, Routine Activities, and Residential Burglary Victimization," *Journal of Criminal Justice* 22:27–52 (1999).

10. Bruce Jacobs and Jody Miller, "Crack Dealing, Gender, and Arrest," *Social Problems* 45:550–566 (1998).

11. Lawrence Cohen and Marcus Felson, "Social Change and Crime Rate Trends," *American Sociological Review* 44:588–608 (1979); also see Ronald Clarke and Marcus Felson, *Routine Activity and Rational Choice* (New Brunswick, NJ: Transaction Books, 1993); Marcus Felson, *Crime and Everyday Life,* 3rd edition (Thousand Oaks, CA: Pine Forge Press, 2002); Marcus Felson, *Crime and Nature* (Thousand Oaks, CA: Sage, 2006).

12. Kenneth Tunnell, *Living off Crime,* 2nd edition (Boston: Rowan & Littlefield, 2006); Andrew Buck, Simon Hakim, and George Rengert, "Burglar Alarms and the Choice Behavior of Burglars," *Journal of Criminal Justice* 21:497–507 (1993); Kenneth Tunnell, *Choosing Crime* (Chicago: Nelson-Hall, 1992).

13. Ronald Clarke and Derek Cornish, "Rational Choice," pages 23–42 in Raymond Paternoster and Ronet Bachman (eds.), *Explaining Criminals and Crime* (Los Angeles: Roxbury, 2001), Marcus Felson, "The Routine Activity Approach," pages 42–46 in Raymond Paternoster and Ronet Bachman (eds.), *Explaining Criminals and Crime* (Los Angeles: Roxbury, 2001).

14. Dick Foster, "Two Teens Charged in Triple Slaying in Guffey," *Rocky Mountain News*, March 10, 2001:5A; "British Hold 4 Youths in Killing of Boy," *The New York*

Times, June 26, 2001:A8; Debbie Howlett, "Chicago Tot's Young Killers Test System," *USA TODAY,* November 28, 1995:3A.

15. Lisa Maher, "Hidden in the Light," *Journal of Drug Issues* 26:143–173 (1996); Neal Shover, *Great Pretenders* (Boulder, CO: Westview Press, 1996); John Petraitis, Brian Flay, and Todd Miller, "Reviewing Theories of Adolescent Substance Use," *Psychological Bulletin* 117:67–86 (1995); Paul Cromwell, James Olson, and D'Aunn Avary, *Breaking and Entering* (Beverly Hills, CA: Sage,1991); Richard Wright and Scott Decker, *Burglars on the Job* (Boston: Northeastern University Press, 1994); Eric Hickey, *Serial Murderers and Their Victims,* 4th edition. (Belmont, CA: Wadsworth, 2005); Janet Warren, Roland Reboussin, Robert Hazlewood, Andrea Cummings, Natalie Gibbs, and Susan Trumbetta, "Crime Scene and Distant Correlates of Serial Rape," *Journal of Quantitative Criminology* 14:231–245 (1998).

16. Kenneth Tunnell, "Choosing Crime," *Justice Quarterly* 7:673–690 (1990).

17. Ronald Akers, "Rational Choice, Deterrence, and Social Learning Theory in Criminology," *Journal of Criminal Law and Criminology* 81:653–676 (1990).

18. James Tedeschi and Richard Felson, *Violence, Aggression and Coercive Actions* (Washington, DC: American Psychological Association, 1994).

19. James Q. Wilson, *The Moral Sense* (New York: The Free Press, 1993), p. 10; also see Matt DeLisi, "Conservatism and Common Sense: The Criminological Career of James Q. Wilson," *Justice Quarterly* 20:661–674 (2003).

20. Hans Eysenck, *Crime and Personality,* 4th edition (London: Routledge and Kegan Paul, 1977); Hans Eysenck and Gilsi Gudjonsson, *The Causes and Cures of Criminality* (New York: Plenum Press, 1989); Hans Eysenck, *The Biological Basis of Personality* (New Brunswick, NJ: Transaction, 2006).

21. David Fogel, *We Are the Living Proof* (Cincinnati: Anderson, 1975).

22. David Fogel and Joe Hudson, *Justice as Fairness: Perspectives on the Justice Model* (Cincinnati: Anderson, 1981); Todd Clear, John Hewitt, and Robert Regoli, "Discretion and the Determinant Sentence," *Crime & Delinquency* 24:428–445 (1978).

23. Ernest van den Haag, *Punishing Criminals* (New York: Basic Books, 1975), p. 59.

24. Paul Gendreau and Robert Ross, "Revivification of Rehabilitation," *Justice Quarterly* 4:349–408 (1987); James Finkenauer and Patricia Gavin, *Scared Straight: The Panacea Phenomenon Revisited* (Prospect Heights, IL: Waveland Press, 1999).

25. Anthony Petrosino, Carolyn Turpin-Petrosino, and John Buehler, "Scared Straight and Other Juvenile Awareness Programs for Preventing Juvenile Delinquency: A Systematic Review of the Randomized Experimental Evidence," *Annals of the American Academy of Political and Social Science* 589:41–62 (2003).

26. J. Richard Udry, "Sociology and Biology: What Biology Do Sociologists Need to Know?" *Social Forces* 73:1267–1278 (1995); Jeremy Freese, Jui-Chung Li, and Lisa Wade, "The Potential Relevance of Biology to Social Inquiry," *Annual Review of Sociology* 29:233–256 (2003); Anthony Walsh and Lee Ellis, "Ideology: Criminology's Achilles Heel?" *Quarterly Journal of Ideology* 27:1–25 (2004).

27. Douglas Massey, "A Brief History of Human Society: The Origin and Role of Emotion in Social Life," *American Sociological Review* 67:1–29 (2002), p. 1.

28. Charles Darwin, *On the Origin of Species* (London: John Murray, 1859); Charles Darwin, *The Descent of Man* (London: John Murray, 1871); Cesare Lombroso, *On Criminal Man* (Milan, Italy: Hoepli, 1876); Marvin Wolfgang, "Pioneers in Criminology: Cesare Lombroso," *Journal of Criminal Law, Criminology, and Police Science* 52:361–369 (1961).

29. Charles Goring, *The English Convict* (London: His Majesty's Stationary Office, 1913).

30. Earnest Hooton, *The American Criminal* (Westport, CT: Greenwood Press, 1939/1969).

31. Zeynep, Benderlioglu, Paul Sciulli, and Randy Nelson, "Fluctuating Asymmetry Predicts Human Reactive Aggression," *American Journal of Human Biology* 16:458–469 (2004).

32. William Sheldon, *Varieties of Delinquent Youth* (New York: Harper & Row, 1949).

33. Sheldon Glueck and Eleanor Glueck, *Physique and Delinquency* (New York: Harper & Row, 1956).

34. Juan Cortes and Florence Gatti, *Delinquency and Crime* (New York: Seminar Press, 1972).

35. Adrian Raine, Chandra Reynolds, Peter Venables, Sarnoff Mednick, and David Farrington, "Fearlessness, Stimulation-Seeking, and Large Body Size at Age 3 Years as Early Predispositions to Child Aggression at Age 11 Years," *Archives of General Psychiatry* 55:745–751 (1998).

36. Adrian Raine, "Annotation: The Role of Prefrontal Deficits, Low Autonomic Arousal, and Early Health Factors in the Development of Antisocial and Aggressive Behavior in Children," *Journal of Child Psychology and Psychiatry* 43:417–434 (2002).

37. David Farrington, "The Relationship between Low Resting Heart Rate and Violence," pages 89–106 in Adrian Raine, Patricia Brennan, David Farrington, and Sarnoff Mednick (eds.), *Biosocial Bases of Violence* (New York: Plenum, 1997).

38. Diana Fishbein, *Biobehavioral Perspectives in Criminology* (Belmont, CA: Wadsworth Publishing Co., 2001); Terrie Moffitt et al., "Whole Blood Serotonin Relates to Violence in an Epidemiological Study," *Biological Psychiatry* 43:446–457 (1998).

39. Terrie Moffitt, "The Neuropsychology of Conduct Disorder: A Critical Review," pages 99–169 in Michael Tonry (ed.), *Crime and Justice: An Annual Review of Research, Volume 15* (Chicago: University of Chicago Press, 1990); Terrie Moffitt, "Juvenile Delinquency and ADHD: Developmental Trajectories from Age Three to Fifteen," *Child Development* 61:893–910 (1990); David Rowe et al., "Dopamine DRD4 Receptor Polymorphism and Attention Deficit Hyperactivity Disorder," *Molecular Psychiatry*

3:419–426 (1998); American Psychiatric Association, *Diagnostic and Statistical Manual for Mental Disorders,* 4th edition (Washington, DC: American Psychiatric Association, 1994).

40. G. J. August et al., "Prevalence of ADHD and Comorbid Disorders Among Elementary School Children Screened for Disruptive Behavior," *Journal of Abnormal Child Psychiatry* 24:571–595 (1996).

41. Russell Barkley, *Taking Charge of ADHD: The Complete, Authoritative Guide for Parents* (New York: The Guilford Press, 2000); Ronald Brown et al., "Prevalence and Assessment of ADHD in Primary Care Settings," *Pediatrics* 107:1–11 (2001).

42. Ronald Kessler et al., "The Prevalence and Correlates of Adult ADHD in the United States: Results from the National Comorbidity Survey Replication," *American Journal of Psychiatry* 163:716–723 (2006).

43. Sandra Goodman, "Girls' ADHD Often Overlooked, Under-Treated," *Boulder Daily Camera,* July 18, 2006:7D.

44. Miranda Gaub and Caryn Carlson, "Gender Differences in ADHD: A Meta-Analysis and Critical Review," *Journal of the American Academy of Child and Adolescent Psychiatry* 36:1036–1046 (1997).

45. Teresa Nadder, Judy Silberg, Michael Rutter, Hermine Maes, and Lindon Eaves, "Comparison of Multiple Measures of ADHD Symptomatology: A Multivariate Genetic Analysis," *Journal of Child Psychology and Psychiatry and Allied Disciplines* 42:475–486 (2001).

46. Joseph Biederman, "ADHD: A Selective Overview," *Biological Psychiatry* 57:1215–1220 (2005); Marilyn Elias, "Teen Girls with ADHD at Higher Risk of Mental Illness," *USA TODAY,* May 25, 2005:6D.

47. Soo Rhee, Irwin Waldman, David Hay, and Florence Levy, "Sex Differences in Genetic and Environmental Influences on *DSM-III-R* ADHD," *Journal of Abnormal Psychology* 108:24–41 (1999); Soo Rhee and Irwin Waldman, "Genetic and Environmental Influences on Antisocial Behavior: A Meta-Analysis of Twin and Adoption Studies," *Psychological Bulletin* 128:490–529 (2002).

48. Marilyn Elias, "ADHD Haunts Children into Adulthood, Study Shows," *USA TODAY,* August 22, 2005:5D.

49. M. L. Wolraich, J. N. Hannah, T. Y. Pinnock, A. Baumgaetel, and J. Brown, "Comparison of Diagnostic Criteria for Attention Deficit Hyperactivity Disorder in a County-Wide Sample," *Journal of American Academy of Child and Adolescent Psychiatry* 35:319–324 (1996); M. L. Wolraich, J. N. Hannah, T. Y. Pinnock, A. Baumgaetel, and J. Brown, "Examination of *DSM-IV* Criteria for Attention Deficit Hyperactivity Disorder in a County-Wide Sample," *Journal of Developmental and Behavioral Pediatrics* 19:162–168 (1998); James Unnever and Dewey Cornell, "Bullying, Self-Control, and ADHD," *Journal of Interpersonal Violence* 18:129–147 (2003); James Unnever, Francis Cullen, and Travis Pratt, "Parental Management, ADHD, and Delinquent Involvement," *Justice Quarterly* 20:471–500 (2003).

50. James Satterfield, Christiane Hoppe, and Anne Schell, "A Prospective Study of Delinquency in 110 Adolescent Boys with ADD and 88 Normal Adolescent Boys,"

American Journal of Psychiatry 139:795–798 (1982); James Satterfield and Anne Schell, "A Prospective Study of Hyperactive Boys with Conduct Problems and Normal Boys: Adolescent and Adult Criminality," *Journal of the American Academy of Child and Adolescent Psychiatry* 36:1726–1735 (1997).

51. Travis Pratt, Francis Cullen, Kristie Blevins, Leah Daigle, and James Unnever, "The Relationship of ADHD to Crime and Delinquency: A Meta-Analysis," *International Journal of Police Science and Management* 4:344–360 (2002).

52. Rita Rubin, "Re: Labeling ADHD Drugs as Psychosis/Mania Risk," *USA TODAY,* March 21, 2006:6D.

53. Liz Szabo, "Mixed Messages on ADHD," *USA TODAY,* February 15, 2006:13B.

54. Matthew Hutson, "Bugging Out," *Psychology Today,* September/October 2006:33.

55. Associated Press, "Study Finds Ritalin May Stunt Growth," *USA TODAY,* April 5, 2004:5D; Howard Abikoff et al., "Symptomatic Improvement in Children with ADHD Treated with Long-Term Methylphenidate and Multimodal Psychosocial Treatment," *Journal of the American Academy of Child and Adolescent Psychiatry* 43:802–811 (2004).

56. Malcolm Macmillan, *An Odd Kind of Fame: Stories of Phineas Gage* (Cambridge, MA: MIT Press, 2002).

57. Elkhonon Goldberg, *The Executive Brain: Frontal Lobes and the Civilized Mind* (New York: Oxford University Press, 2001); Earl Miller and Jonathan Cohen, "An Integrative Theory of Prefrontal Cortex Function," *Annual Review of Neuroscience* 24:167–202 (2001).

58. Adrian Raine, *The Psychopathology of Crime: Criminal Behavior as a Clinical Disorder* (San Diego: Academic Press, 1993).

59. Sharon Ishikawa and Adrian Raine, "Prefrontal Deficits and Antisocial Behavior," pages 277–304 in Benjamin Lahey, Terrie Moffitt, and Avshalom Caspi (eds.), *Causes of Conduct Disorder and Juvenile Delinquency* (New York: The Guilford Press, 2003).

60. Terrie Moffitt, "The Neuropsychology of Juvenile Delinquency: A Critical Review," pages 99–169 in Michael Tonry and Norval Morris (eds.), *Crime and Justice: An Annual Review of Research, Volume 12* (Chicago: University of Chicago Press, 1990), p. 115.

61. Adrian Raine, Terrie Moffitt, Avshalom Caspi, Rolf Lober, Magda Stouthamer-Loeber, and Don Lynam, "Neurocognitive Impairments in Boys on the Life-Course Persistent Antisocial Path," *Journal of Abnormal Psychology* 114:38–49 (2005); Emily Grekin, Patricia Brennan, Sheilagh Hodgins, and Sarnoff Mednick, "Male Criminals with Organic Brain Syndrome: Two Distinct Types Based on Age at First Arrest," *American Journal of Psychiatry* 158:1099–1104 (2001); Kevin Beaver, John Paul Wright, and Matt DeLisi, "Self-Control as an Executive Function: Reformulating Gottfredson and Hirschi's Parental Socialization Thesis," *Criminal Justice and Behavior* 34:in press (2007).

62. James Blair, "Neurobiological Basis of Psychopathy" *British Journal of Psychiatry* 182:5–7 (2003); Heather Gordon, Abigail Baird, and Alison End, "Functional Differ-

ences among Those High and Low on a Trait Measure of Psychopathy," *Biological Psychiatry* 56:516–521 (2004).

63. Andreas Meyer-Lindenberg et al., "Neural Mechanisms of Genetic Risk for Impulsivity and Violence in Humans," *Proceedings of the National Academy of Sciences* 103: 6269–6274 (2006).

64. Kathleen Heide and Eldra Solomon, "Biology, Childhood Trauma, and Murder: Rethinking Justice," *International Journal of Law and Psychiatry* 29:220–233 (2006); Angela Scarpa and Adrian Raine, "The Psychophysiology of Child Misconduct," *Pediatric Annals* 35:297–304 (2004).

65. Sandra Scarr and Kathleen McCartney, "How People Make Their Own Environments: A Theory of Genotype → Environment Effects," *Child Development* 54:424–435 (1983); Sandra Scarr, "Developmental Theories for the 1990s: Development and Individual Differences," *Child Development* 63:1–19 (1992).

66. Terrie Moffitt, "The New Look of Behavioral Genetics in Developmental Psychopathology: Gene-Environment Interplay in Antisocial Behaviors," *Psychological Bulletin* 131:533–554 (2005); Michael Rutter, *Genes and Behavior: Nature–Nurture Interplay Explained* (Malden, MA: Blackwell, 2006).

67. Hugh Lytton, "Child and Parent Effects in Boys' Conduct Disorder: A Reinterpretation," *Developmental Psychology* 26:683–697 (1990).

68. Anthony Walsh, *Biosocial Criminology: Introduction and Integration* (Cincinnati: Anderson, 2002).

69. Kevin Beaver, John Wright, and Matt DeLisi, "Delinquent Peer Group Formation: Evidence of a Gene X Environment Correlation," paper presented at the Annual Meeting of the American Society of Criminology, November 2006; Lisabeth DiLalla, "Behavior Genetics of Aggression in Children: Review and Future Directions," *Developmental Review* 22:593–622 (2002).

70. Henry Goddard, *Feeblemindedness* (New York: Macmillan, 1914).

71. John Slawson, *The Delinquent Boys* (Boston: Budget Press, 1926).

72. Barbara Burks, "The Relative Influence of Nature and Nurture upon Mental Development," in *Yearbook,* Part 1 (Washington, DC: National Society for the Study of Education, 1928).

73. Edwin Sutherland, "Mental Deficiency and Crime," pages 357–375 in Kimball Young (ed.), *Social Attitudes* (New York: Henry Holt, 1931).

74. Travis Hirschi and Michael Hindelang, "Intelligence and Delinquency," *American Sociological Review* 42:571–586 (1977).

75. Donald Lynam, Terrie Moffitt, and Magda Stouthamer-Loeber, "Explaining the Relation between IQ and Delinquency: Class, Race, Test Motivation, School Failure, or Self-Control? *Journal of Abnormal Psychology* 102:187–196 (1993).

76. Leslie Leve and Patricia Chamberlain, "Female Juvenile Offenders: Defining an Early-Onset Pathway for Delinquency," *Journal of Child and Family Studies* 13:439–452 (2004).

77. Jean-Pierre Guay, Marc Ouimet, and Jean Proulx, "On Intelligence and Crime: A Comparison of Incarcerated Sex Offenders and Serious Non-Sexual Violent Criminals," *International Journal of Law and Psychiatry* 28:405–417 (2005).

78. Adrian Raine, *The Psychopathology of Crime: Criminal Behavior as a Clinical Disorder* (San Diego: Academic Press, 1993).

79. Adrian Raine, Patricia Brennan, and Sarnoff Mednick, "Birth Complications Combined with Early Maternal Rejection at Age 1 Year Predispose to Violent Crime at Age 18 Years," *Archives of General Psychiatry* 51:984–988 (1994).

80. Darrick Jolliffe and David Farrington, "Empathy and Offending: A Systematic Review and Meta-Analysis," *Aggression and Violent Behavior* 9:441–476 (2004).

81. Travis Hirschi, *Causes of Delinquency* (Berkeley: University of California Press, 1969).

82. Jean McGloin and Travis Pratt, "Cognitive Ability and Delinquent Behavior among Inner-City Youth: A Life-Course Analysis of Main, Mediating, and Interaction Effects," *International Journal of Offender Therapy and Comparative Criminology* 47:253–271 (2003); Jean McGloin, Travis Pratt, and Jeff Maahs, "Rethinking the IQ–Delinquency Relationship: A Longitudinal Analysis of Multiple Theoretical Models," *Justice Quarterly* 21:603–635 (2004).

83. Chris Gibson, Alex Piquero, and Stephen Tibbetts, "The Contribution of Family Adversity and Verbal IQ to Criminal Behavior," *International Journal of Offender Therapy and Comparative Criminology* 45:574–592 (2001).

84. Thomas Bouchard, David Lykken, Matt McGue, Nancy Segal, and Auke Tellegren, "Sources of Human Psychological Differencism" *Science* 250: 223–250 (1990).

85. Alan Booth, Douglas Granger, Allan Mazur, and Katie Kivlighan, "Testosterone and Social Behavior," *Social Forces* 85:167–191 (2006).

86. James Dabbs and Robin Morris, "Testosterone, Social Class, and Antisocial Behavior in a Sample of 4,463 Men," *Psychological Science* 1:209–211 (1990).

87. Alan Booth and D. Wayne Osgood, "The Influence of Testosterone on Deviance in Adulthood: Assessing and Explaining the Relationship," *Criminology* 31:93–117 (1993).

88. James Dabbs, Robert Frady, Timothy Carr, and N. F. Besch, "Saliva Testosterone and Criminal Violence in Young Adult Prison Inmates," *Psychosomatic Medicine* 49:174–182 (1987).

89. James Dabbs, Timothy Carr, Robert Frady, and Jasmin Riad, "Testosterone, Crime, and Misbehavior among 692 Male Prison Inmates," *Personality and Individual Differences* 18:627–633 (1995).

90. James Dabbs, Jasmin Riad, and Susan Chance, "Testosterone and Ruthless Homicide," *Personality and Individual Differences* 31:599–603 (2001).

91. Richard Felson and Dana Haynie, "Pubertal Development, Social Factors, and Delinquency among Adolescent Boys," *Criminology* 40:967–988 (2002).

92. Dana Haynie, "Context of Risk? Explaining the Link between Girls' Pubertal Development and Their Delinquency Involvement," *Social Forces* 82:355–397 (2003).

93. Dana Haynie and Alex Piquero, "Pubertal Development and Physical Victimization in Adolescence," *Journal of Research in Crime and Delinquency* 43:3–35 (2006).

94. Kevin Beaver and John Paul Wright, "Biosocial Development and Delinquent Involvement," *Youth Violence and Juvenile Justice* 3:168–192 (2005).

95. Sheldon Glueck and Eleanor Glueck, *500 Criminal Careers* (New York: Knopf, 1930).

96. Sheldon Glueck and Eleanor Glueck, *500 Delinquent Women* (New York: Knopf, 1934).

97. Samuel Guze, Edwin Wolfgram, Joe K. McKinney, and Dennis Cantwell, "Psychiatric Illness in the Families of Convicted Criminals: A Study of 519 First-Degree Relatives. *Diseases of the Nervous System* 28:651–659 (1967).

98. C. Robert Cloninger and Samuel Guze, "Psychiatric Illness in the Families of Female Criminals: A Study of 288 First-Degree Relatives," *British Journal of Psychiatry* 122:697–703 (1973).

99. C. Robert Cloninger, Theodore Reich, and Samuel Guze, "The Multifactorial Model of Disease Transmission: II. Sex Differences in the Familial Transmission of Sociopathy (Antisocial Personality)," *British Journal of Psychiatry* 127:11–22 (1975); "The Multifactorial Model of Disease Transmission: III. Familial Relationships between Sociopathy and Hysteria (Briquet's Syndrome)," *British Journal of Psychiatry* 127:23–32 (1975).

100. David Rowe and David Farrington, "The Familial Transmission of Criminal Convictions," *Criminology* 35:177–201 (1997), p. 199.

101. David Farrington, Darrick Jolliffe, Rolf Loeber, Magda Stouthamer-Loeber, and Larry Kalb, "The Concentration of Offenders in Families and Family Criminality in the Prediction of Boys' Delinquency," *Journal of Adolescence* 24:579–596 (2001).

102. Anu Putkonen et al., "The Quantitative Risk of Violent Crime and Criminal Offending: A Case-Control Study among the Offspring of Recidivistic Finnish Homicide Offenders," *Acta Psychiatrica Scandanavia* 106:54–57 (2002).

103. Johannes Lange, *Crime as Destiny* (London: Allen & Unwin, 1929).

104. Sarnoff Mednick and Karl Christiansen, *Biosocial Basis of Criminal Behavior* (New York: Gardner Press, 1977).

105. David Rowe and D. Wayne Osgood, "Heredity and Sociological Theories of Delinquency: A Re-consideration," *American Sociological Review* 49:526–540 (1984).

106. David Rowe, "Genetic and Environmental Components of Antisocial Behavior: A Study of 265 Twin Pairs," *Criminology* 24:513–532 (1986).

107. David Rowe, *Biology and Crime* (Los Angeles: Roxbury, 2002); David Rowe and Bill Gulley, "Sibling Effects on Substance Abuse and Delinquency," *Criminology* 30:217–223 (1992).

108. Barry Hutchings and Sarnoff Mednick, "Criminality in Adoptees and Their Adoptive and Biological Parents," pages 127–143 in Sarnoff Mednick and Karl Christiansen (eds.), *Biosocial Basis of Criminal Behavior* (New York: Gardner Press, 1977).

109. Sarnoff Mednick, William Gabrielli, and Barry Hutchings, "Genetic Factors in the Etiology of Criminal Behavior," pages 67–80 in Eugene McLaughlin, John Muncie, and Gordon Hughes (eds.), *Criminological Perspectives,* 2nd edition (Thousand Oaks, CA: Sage, 2003).

110. Michael Bohman, C. Robert Cloninger, Soren Siguardson, and Anne-Liss von Knorring, "Predisposition to Petty Criminalistics in Swedish Adoptees," *Archives of General Psychiatry* 39:1233–1241 (1982).

111. Raymond Crowe, "The Adopted Offspring of Women Criminal Offenders," *Archives of General Psychiatry* 27:600–603 (1972).

112. Raymond Crowe, "An Adoptive Study of Psychopathy," pages 95–103 in Ronald Fieve, David Rosenthal, and Henry Brill (eds.), *Genetic Research in Psychiatry* (Baltimore: Johns Hopkins University Press, 1975).

113. Greg Toppo, "Violent Play Rewires Brain," *USA TODAY,* November 30, 2006:10D.

114. Ronald Burns and Michael Lynch, *Environment Crime: A Sourcebook* (New York: LFB Scholarly Publishing, 2004).

115. Liz Szabo, "Secondhand Smoke Debate 'Over,'" *USA TODAY,* June 28, 2006:4A.

116. Liz Szabo, "Babies May Absorb Smoke Residue in Home," *USA TODAY,* August 7, 2006:7D.

117. Nancy Day, Gale Richardson, Lidush Goldschmidt, and Marie Cornelius, "Effects of Prenatal Tobacco Exposure on Preschoolers' Behavior," *Journal of Developmental and Behavioral Pediatrics* 21:180–188 (2000); Marie Cornelius, Christopher Ryan, Nancy Day, Lidush Goldschmidt, and Jennifer Willford, "Prenatal Tobacco Effects on Neuropsychological Outcomes among Preadolescents," *Journal of Developmental and Behavioral Pediatrics* 22:217–225 (2001).

118. Patricia Brennan, Emily Grekin, and Sarnoff Mednick, "Maternal Smoking during Pregnancy and Adult Male Criminal Outcomes," *Archives of General Psychiatry* 56:215–219 (1999).

119. Patricia Brennan, Emily Grekin, Erik Mortensen, and Sarnoff Mednick, "Relationship of Maternal Smoking during Pregnancy with Criminal Arrest and Hospitalization for Substance Abuse in Male and Female Offspring," *American Journal of Psychiatry* 159:48–54 (2002).

120. Chris Gibson and Stephen Tibbetts, "A Biosocial Interaction in Predicting Early Onset of Offending," *Psychological Reports* 86:509–518 (2000); Chris Gibson, Alex Piquero, and Stephen Tibbetts, "Assessing the Relationship between Maternal Cigarette Smoking During Pregnancy and Age at First Police Contact," *Justice Quarterly* 17:519–542 (2000).

121. Lauren Wakschlag, Kate Pickett, Edwin Cook, Neal Benowitz, and Bennett Leventhal, "Maternal Smoking during Pregnancy and Severe Antisocial Behavior in Offspring: A Review," *American Journal of Public Health* 92:966–974 (2002); Travis Pratt, Jean McGloin, and Noelle Fearn, "Maternal Cigarette Smoking During Pregnancy and Criminal/Deviant Behavior: A Meta-Analysis," *Interna-*

tional Journal of Offender Therapy and Comparative Criminology 50:672–690 (2006).

122. Christine Gorman, "What Alcohol Does to a Child," *Time,* June 5, 2006:74.

123. Leadership to Keep Children Alcohol Free, *How Does Alcohol Affect the World of a Child?* (Washington, DC: National Institute on Alcohol Abuse and Alcoholism, 2006).

124. Jason Ford, "The Connection between Heavy Drinking and Juvenile Delinquency during Adolescence," *Sociological Spectrum* 25:629–650 (2005).

125. Catherine Kaukinen, "Adolescent Victimization and Problem Drinking," *Violence and Victims* 17:669–689 (2002); Ingeborg Rossow, Hilde Pape, and Lars Wichstrom, "Young, Wet, and Wild? Associations between Alcohol Intoxication and Violent Behavior in Adolescence," *Addiction* 94:1017–1031 (1999); Bu Huang, Helene White, Rick Kosterman, Richard Catalano, and J. David Hawkins, "Developmental Associations between Alcohol and Interpersonal Aggression during Adolescence," *Journal of Research in Crime and Delinquency* 38:64–83 (2001).

126. Robin Hubbard, "Crack Down on Mercury Pollution," *Boulder Daily Camera,* April 11, 2004:3E.

127. Associated Press, "Lead Confirmed in Beethoven's Death," *USA TODAY,* December 7, 2005:7D.

128. Pamela Meyer, Timothy Pivetz, Timothy Digman, David Homa, Jaime Schoonover, and Debra Brody, "Surveillance for Elevated Blood Lead Levels among Children—United States, 1997–2001," *Morbidity and Mortality Weekly Report* 52:1–21 (2003); Child Trends, "Lead Poisoning," online at: http://www.childtrendsdatabank.org/, accessed April 20, 2007.

129. Mark Opler, Alan Brown, Joseph Grziano, Manisha Desal, Wei Zheng, Catherine Schaefer, Pamela Factor-Litvak, and Ezra Susser, "Prenatal Lead Exposure, Aminolevulinic Acid, and Schizophrenia," *Environmental Health Perspectives* 112: 548–552 (2004); "Report: CA Ignored Poison Candy," online at: CBSNews.com, accessed April 25, 2004; "Lead-wrapped Lollipop Poses Health Hazard," *Denver Post,* April 27, 2001:15A.

130. Karen Florini, George Krumbhaar, and Ellen Silbergeld, *Legacy of Lead* (Washington, DC: Environmental Defense Fund, 1990); Herbert Needleman, *Human Lead Exposure* (Boca Raton, FL: CRC Press, 1991).

131. Herbert Needleman, C. McFarland, R. B. Nes, S. E. Fienberg, M. J. Tobin, "Bone Lead Levels in Adjudicated Delinquents," *Neurotoxicology and Teratology* 24:711–717 (2002); Herbert Needleman, Julie Riess, Michael Tobin, Gretchen Biesecker, and Joel Greenhouse, "Bone Lead Levels and Delinquent Behavior," *Journal of American Medical Association* 275:363–369 (1996); Herbert Needleman, Alan Schell, David Bellinger, Alan Leviton, and Elizabeth Allred, "The Long-Term Effects of Exposure to Low Doses of Lead in Children," *New England Journal of Medicine* 322:83–88 (1990); Herbert Needleman and Constantine Gatsonis, "Low-Level Lead Exposure and the IQ of Children," *Journal of the American Medical Association* 263:673–678 (1990).

132. Deborah Denno, "Sociological and Human Developmental Explanations of Crime," *Criminology* 23:711–741 (1985).

133. Meyer et al., note 128.

134. Jeanette Ewin and David Horrobin, *Fine Wines and Fish Oil* (London: Oxford University Press, 2001).

135. Nanci Hellmich, "Junk Food is as Easy as ABC to Get," *USA TODAY,* August 2, 2005:7D.

136. Stephen Schoenthaler, Ian Bier, Kelly Young, Dennis Nichols, and Susan Jansenns, "The Effect of Vitamin–Mineral Supplementation on the Intelligence of American School Children," *Journal of Alternative and Complementary Medicine* 6:19–29 (2000); Stephen Schoenthaler and Ian Bier, "The Effect of Vitamin–Mineral Supplementation on Juvenile Delinquency Among American Schoolchildren," *Journal of Alternative and Complementary Medicine* 6:7–17 (2000); Stephen Schoenthaler, Stephen Amos, Walter Doraz, Mary Ann Kelly, George Muedeking, and James Wakefield, "The Effect of Randomized Vitamin–Mineral Supplementation on Violent and Non-Violent Antisocial Behavior Among Incarcerated Juveniles," *Journal of Nutritional and Environmental Medicine* 7:343–352 (1997).

137. C. Bernard Gesch, Sean Hammond, Sarah Hampson, Anita Eves, and Martin Crowder, "Influence of Supplementary Vitamins, Minerals and Essential Fatty Acids on the Antisocial Behavior of Young Adult Prisoners," *British Journal of Psychiatry* 181:22–28 (2002).

138. Richard Carlton, Gerald Ente, Lila Blum, Nadine Heyman, William Davis, and Sal Ambrosino, "Rational Dosages of Nutrients Have a Prolonged Effect on Learning Disabilities," *Alternative Therapies* 6: 85–91 (2000).

139. Jianghong Liu, Adrian Raine, Peter Venables, and Sarnoff Mednick, "Malnutrition at Age 3 Years and Externalizing Behavior Problems at Ages 8, 11, and 17 Years," *American Journal of Psychiatry* 161:2005–2013 (2004).

140. Sigmund Freud, *The Standard Edition of the Complete Psychological Works of Sigmund Freud* (London: Hogarth Press, 1925).

141. Franz Alexander and William Healy, *Roots of Crime* (New York: Knopf, 1935); August Aichhorn, *Wayward Youth* (New York: Viking Press, 1936); Fritz Redl and David Wineman, *Children Who Hate* (New York: The Free Press, 1951).

142. B.F. Skinner, *The Behavior of Organisms* (New York: Appleton, 1938); B.F. Skinner, "Are Theories of Learning Necessary?" *Psychological Review* 57:211–220 (1950); B.F. Skinner, *Science and Human Behavior* (New York: Macmillan, 1953).

143. Albert Bandura, *Social Learning Theory* (Englewood Cliffs, NJ: Prentice Hall, 1977).

144. Herbert Blumer, *Movies, Delinquency, and Crime* (New York: Macmillan, 1933).

145. Scott Snyder, "Movies and Juvenile Delinquency: An Overview," *Adolescence* 26:121–132 (1991).

146. Associated Press, "Premiere of 'Juice' Sparks Violence in at Least 8 States," *Rocky Mountain News,* January 19, 1992:3; Dick Foster, "Officials Fear Movie Inspired Kids' Crime," *Rocky Mountain News,* March 17, 1995:8A; As-

sociated Press, "Does Crime Imitate Art?" *Rocky Mountain News,* November 30, 1995:57A.

147. Associated Press, "Movie-obsessed Murderers Convicted," *Boulder Daily Camera,* July 12, 1999:11A.

148. Wiley Hall, "Ladylike Behavior Takes it on the Chin," *Rocky Mountain News,* April 27, 2004:36A; Matt Sebastian, "Panel Looks at Reality, TV," *Boulder Daily Camera,* April 8, 1998:8C.

149. Diane Eicher, "TV Tempest That Never Dies," *Denver Post,* June 10, 2001:1K, 12–13K.

150. Ann Oldenburg, "TV, Films Blamed for Child Violence," *USA TODAY,* July 26, 2000:9D.

151. Jonathan Freedman, "Effect of Television Violence and Aggression," *Psychological Bulletin* 96:227–246 (1984); Jonathan Freedman, "Television Violence and Aggression: A Rejoinder," *Psychological Bulletin* 100:372–378 (1986).

152. Lowell Huesmann, Jessica Moise-Titus, Cheryl-Lynn Podolski, and Leonard Eron, "Longitudinal Relations Between Children's Exposure to TV Violence and Their Aggressive and Violent Behavior in Young Adulthood," *Developmental Psychology* 39: 201–221 (2003).

153. Gina Wingood, Ralph Clemente, Jay Bernhardt, Kathy Hareton, Susan Davies, Alyssa Robillard, and Edward Hook, "A Prospective Study of Exposure to Rap Music Videos and African American Female Adolescents' Health," *American Journal of Public Health* 93: 437–439 (2003).

154. Diana Fishbein, "The Importance of Neurobiological Research to the Prevention of Psychopathology," *Prevention Science* 1:89–106 (2000), p. 102.

CHAPTER 6

1. Clifford Shaw and Henry McKay, *Juvenile Delinquency in Urban Areas* (Chicago: University of Chicago Press, 1942); Clifford Shaw and Henry McKay, *Juvenile Delinquency in Urban Areas,* revised edition (Chicago: University of Chicago Press, 1969).

2. Shaw and McKay, note 1.

3. Robert Sampson and W. Byron Groves, "Community Structure and Crime," *American Journal of Sociology* 94:774–802 (1989).

4. Robert Sampson and Lydia Bean, "Cultural Mechanisms and Killing Fields: A Revised Theory of Community-Level Racial Inequality," pages 8–36 in Ruth Peterson, Lauren Krivo, and John Hagan (eds.), *The Many Colors of Crime: Inequalities of Race, Ethnicity and Crime in America* (New York: New York University Press, 2006); Bonita Veysey and Steven Messner, "Further Testing of Social Disorganization Theory," *Journal of Research in Crime and Delinquency* 36:156–174 (1999); Paul Bellair, "Social Interaction and Community Crime," *Criminology* 35:677–703 (1997).

5. D. Wayne Osgood and Jeff Chambers, "Social Disorganization Outside the Metropolis," *Criminology* 38:81–115 (2000).

6. Christopher Lowenkamp, Francis Cullen, and Travis Pratt, "Replicating Sampson and Grove's Test of Social Disorganization Theory," *Journal of Research in Crime and Delinquency* 40:351–373 (2003).

7. Kraig Beyerlein and John Hipp, "Social Capital, Too Much of a Good Thing?," *Social Forces* 84:677–703 (2005); Bellair, note 4; Paul Bellair, "Informal Surveillance and Street Crime," *Criminology* 38:137–167 (2000); Charis Kubrin and Ronald Weitzer, "New Directions in Social Disorganization Theory," *Journal of Research in Crime and Delinquency* 40:374–402 (2003); Fred Markowitz, Paul Bellair, Allen Liska, and Jianhong Liu, "Extending Social Disorganization Theory," *Criminology* 39:293–319 (2001).

8. Kubrin and Weitzer, note 7.

9. Mary Pattillo, "Sweet Mothers and Gangbangers," *Social Forces* 76:747–774 (1998).

10. Robert Sampson, Jeffrey Morenoff, and Felton Earls, "Spatial Dynamics of Collective Efficacy for Children," *American Sociological Review* 64: 633–660 (1999); Robert Sampson, Stephen Raudenbush, and Felton Earls, *Neighborhood Collective Efficacy—Does It Help Reduce Violence?* (Washington, DC: National Institute of Justice, 1998), p. 13; Robert Sampson, Stephen Raudenbush, and Felton Earls, "Neighborhoods and Violent Crime," *Science* 277:918–924 (1997).

11. Ivan Sun, Ruth Triplett, and Randy Gainey, "Neighborhood Characteristics and Crime: A Test of Sampson and Groves' Model of Social Disorganization," *Western Criminology Review* 5:1–16 (2004); Barbara Warner, "The Role of Attenuated Culture in Social Disorganization Theory," *Criminology* 41:73–98 (2003); Barbara Warner and Pamela Rountree, "Implications of Ghetto-Related Behavior for a Community and Crime Model," *Sociology of Crime, Law and Deviance* 2:39–62 (2000); Barbara Warner and Pamela Rountree, "Local Social Ties in a Community and Crime Model," *Social Problems* 44:520–536 (1997).

12. Edwin Sutherland and Donald Cressey, *Principles of Criminology,* 10th edition (Philadelphia: Lippincott, 1978); Ross Matsueda, "Differential Social Organization, Collective Action, and Crime," *Crime, Law, and Social Change* 46:3–33 (2006).

13. Ruth Kornhauser, *Social Sources of Delinquency* (Chicago: University of Chicago Press, 1978).

14. Warner and Rountree, note 11.

15. Elijah Anderson, *Code of the Street* (New York: Norton, 1999).

16. Don Gibbons, *The Criminological Enterprise* (Englewood Cliffs, NJ: Prentice Hall, 1979).

17. Edwin Sutherland, *Principles of Criminology,* 4th edition (Philadelphia: Lippincott, 1947).

18. Andy Hochstetler, Heith Copes, and Matt DeLisi, "Differential Association in Group and Solo Offending," *Journal of Criminal Justice* 30:559–566 (2002).

19. John Paul Wright and Francis Cullen, "Employment, Peers, and Life-Course Transitions," *Justice Quarterly* 21:183–205 (2004); Janne Kivivuori and Venla Salmi, "The Association between Social Capital and Juvenile Crime: The Role of Individual and Structural Factors," *European Journal of Criminology* 3:123–148 (2006).

20. Mark Warr, *Companions in Crime* (Cambridge: Cambridge University Press, 2002), p. 40; Mark Warr and Mark Stafford, "The Influence of Delinquent Peers," *Criminology* 29:851–866 (1991).

21. Nicole Piquero, Angela Gover, John MacDonald, and Alex Piquero, "The Influence of Delinquent Peers on Delinquency," *Youth & Society* 35:251–276 (2005); Nicole Leeper Piquero, Angela Gover, John MacDonald, and Alex Piquero, "The Influence of Delinquent Peers on Delinquency: Does Gender Matter?" *Youth & Society* 36:251–275 (2005).

22. Mark Warr, "Age, Peers and Delinquency," *Criminology* 34:11–17 (1996).

23. Barbara Costello and Paul Vowell, "Testing Control Theory and Differential Association," *Criminology* 37:815–842 (1999).

24. Warr and Stafford, note 20.

25. Daniel Glaser, "Criminality Theories and Behavioral Images," *American Journal of Sociology* 61:433–444 (1956).

26. C. Ray Jeffery, "Criminal Behavior and Learning Theory," *Journal of Criminal Law, Criminology, and Police Science* 56:294–300 (1965).

27. Robert Burgess and Ronald Akers, "A Differential Association-Reinforcement Theory of Criminal Behavior," *Social Problems* 14:128–147 (1966).

28. Ronald Akers and Gary Jensen, *Social Learning Theory and the Explanation of Crime* (New Brunswick, NJ: Transaction Publishers, 2007); Ronald Akers, *Deviant Behavior,* 3rd edition (Belmont, CA: Wadsworth, 1985).

29. Walter Miller, "Lower-Class Culture as a Generating Milieu of Gang Delinquency," *Journal of Social Issues* 14:5–19 (1958).

30. Miller, note 29.

31. Oscar Lewis, *The Children of Sanchez* (New York: Random House, 1961).

32. William Julius Wilson, *The Truly Disadvantaged* (Chicago: University of Chicago Press, 1987).

33. Pamela Jackson, "Crime, Youth Gangs, and Urban Transition," *Justice Quarterly* 8:379–397 (1991).

34. Edward Banfield, *The Unheavenly City Revisited* (Boston: Little, Brown, 1974).

35. William Kornblum, *Sociology in a Changing World* (New York: Holt, Rinehart, and Winston, 1988), p. 277.

36. Herbert Gans, "The Uses of Poverty," pages 155–161 in William Feigelman (ed.), *Sociology: Full Circle,* 4th edition (New York: Holt, Rinehart and Winston, 1985).

37. Emile Durkheim, *The Division of Labor in Society* (New York: Macmillan, 1893/1933).

38. Robert Merton, "Social Structure and Anomie," *American Sociological Review* 3:672–682 (1938); Robert Merton, *Social Theory and Social Structure,* revised edition (New York: Macmillan, 1968).

39. Margaret Farnworth and Michael Leiber, "Strain Theory Revisited," *American Sociological Review* 54:263–274 (1989); Scott Menard, "A Developmental Test of Mertonian Anomie Theory," *Journal of Research in Crime and Delinquency* 32:136–174 (1995).

40. Albert Cohen, *Delinquent Boys* (New York: Free Press, 1955).

41. Delbert Elliott and Harwin Voss, *Delinquency and Dropout* (Lexington, MA: Lexington Books, 1974); Starke Hathaway, Phillis Reynolds, and Elio Monachesi, "Follow-up on the Later Careers and Lives of 1,000 Boys Who Dropped Out of High School," *Journal of Consulting and Clinical Psychology* 33:370–380 (1969); Kenneth Polk, *Becoming Adult* (Eugene, OR: University of Oregon, 1981); Terrence Thornberry, "The Effect of Dropping Out of High School on Subsequent Criminal Behavior," *Criminology* 23:3–18 (1985).

42. Lee Rainwater, "The Problem of Lower-Class Culture," *Journal of Social Issues* 26:133–148 (1970); David Downes, *The Delinquent Solution* (London: Hutchinson, 1966); Steven Box, *Deviance, Reality and Society* (London: Holt, Rinehart and Winston, 1981).

43. Richard Cloward and Lloyd Ohlin, *Delinquency and Opportunity* (New York: Free Press, 1960).

44. Stephen Cernkovich, "Value Orientations and Delinquency Involvement," *Criminology* 15:443–458 (1979); Susan Datesman, Frank Scarpitti, and R. Stephenson, "Female Delinquency," *Journal of Research in Crime and Delinquency* 12:107–123 (1975); Jeffery Seagrave and Douglas Hastad, "Evaluating Three Models of Delinquency Causation for Males and Females," *Sociological Focus* 18:1–17 (1985).

45. James Short, Jr., and Fred Strodtbeck, *Group Process and Gang Delinquency* (Chicago: University of Chicago Press, 1965).

46. Robert Agnew, "Foundation for a General Theory of Crime," *Criminology* 30:47–87 (1992); Robert Agnew, *Why Do Criminals Offend?* (Los Angeles, CA: Roxbury, 2005); Robert Agnew, Timothy Brezina, John Paul Wright, and Francis Cullen, "Strain, Personality Traits, and Delinquency," *Criminology* 40:43–71 (2002).

47. Bill McCarthy and John Hagan, "Mean Streets," *American Journal of Sociology* 98:597–627 (1992).

48. Raymond Paternoster and Paul Mazerolle, "General Strain Theory and Delinquency," *Journal of Research in Crime and Delinquency* 31:235–263 (1994).

49. Paul Mazerolle, "Gender, General Strain, and Delinquency," *Justice Quarterly* 15:65–91 (1998).

50. John Hoffman and S. Susan Su, "The Conditional Effects of Stress on Delinquency and Drug Use," *Journal of Research in Crime and Delinquency* 12:107–123 (1997).

51. Robert Agnew and Timothy Brezina, "Relational Problems with Peers, Gender, and Delinquency," *Youth & Society* 29:84–111 (1997).

52. Timothy Brezina, "Adapting to Strain," *Criminology* 34:39–60 (1996).

53. Timothy Brezina, "Adolescent Maltreatment and Delinquency," *Journal of Research in Crime and Delinquency* 35:71–99 (1998); Lisa Broidy, "A Test of General Strain Theory," *Criminology* 39:9–33 (2001); Paul Mazerolle and Alex Piquero, "Linking Exposure to Strain with Anger," *Journal of Criminal Justice* 26:195–211 (1998); Nicole Piquero and Miriam Sealock, "Generalizing General Strain Theory," *Justice Quarterly* 17:449–484 (2000); Jack Katz, *Seductions of Crime* (New York: Basic Books, 1990).

54. Ronald Simons, Chen Yi-Fu, Eric Stewart, and Gene Brody, "Longitudinal Test of Strain Theory with an Afri-

can American Sample," *Justice Quarterly* 20:827–856 (2003); Eric Stewart and Ronald Simons, "Structure and Culture in African American Adolescent Violence: A Partial Test of the 'Code of the Street' Thesis," *Justice Quarterly* 23:1–33 (2006).

55. Carter Hay and Michelle Evans, "Violent Victimization and Involvement in Delinquency," *Journal of Criminal Justice* 34:261–274 (2006).

56. Agnew et al., note 46; Liqun Cao, "Returning to Normality: Anomie and Crime in China," *International Journal of Offender Therapy and Comparative Criminology* 51:40–51 (2007).

57. Steven Messner and Richard Rosenfeld, *Crime and the American Dream,* 4th edition (Belmont, CA: Wadsworth, 2006).

58. Michael Maume and Matthew Lee, "Social Institutions and Violence: A Sub-national Test of Institutional Anomie Theory," *Criminology* 41:1137–1172 (2003); Alex Piquero and Nicole Leeper Piquero, "On Testing Institutional Anomie Theory with Varying Specifications," *Studies on Crime and Crime Prevention* 7:61–84 (1998); Mitchell Chamlin and John Cochran, "Assessing Messner and Rosenfeld's Institutional Anomie Theory: A Partial Test," *Criminology* 33:411–429 (1995); Mitchell Chamlin and John Cochran, "Social Altruism and Crime," *Criminology* 35:203–228 (1997).

59. Thomas Hobbes, *Leviathan* (London: Guernsey Press, 1651/1987).

60. Walter Reckless, Simon Dinitz, and Ellen Murray, "Self-Concept as an Insulator against Delinquency," *American Sociological Review* 21:744–756 (1956); Walter Reckless, Simon Dinitz, and Barbara Kay, "The Self Component in Potential Delinquency and Potential Nondelinquency," *American Sociological Review* 25:566–570 (1957); Walter Reckless, "A New Theory of Delinquency and Crime," *Federal Probation* 25:42–46 (1961).

61. Frank Scarpitti, Ellen Murray, Simon Dinitz, and Walter Reckless, "The Good Boy in a High Delinquency Area," *American Sociological Review* 23:555–558 (1960); Simon Dinitz, Frank Scarpitti, and Walter Reckless, "Delinquency Vulnerability," *American Sociological Review* 27:515–517 (1962).

62. David Matza, *Delinquency and Drift* (New York: The Free Press, 1964).

63. Gresham Sykes and David Matza, "Techniques of Neutralization," *American Sociological Review* 22:664–670 (1957).

64. Short and Strodtbeck, note 45.

65. John Hagan, "Destiny and Drift," *American Sociological Review* 56:567–582 (1991).

66. Travis Hirschi, *Causes of Delinquency* (Berkeley: University of California Press, 1969).

67. James Coleman, "Toward an Integrated Theory of White-Collar Crime," *American Journal of Sociology* 93:406–439 (1987).

68. Jim Mitchell and Richard Dodder, "Types of Neutralization and Types of Delinquency," *Journal of Youth and Adolescence* 12:307–318 (1983).

69. Shadd Maruna and Heith Copes, "What Have We Learned from Five Decades of Neutralization Research?" *Crime and Justice* 32:221–320 (2005).

70. Michael Hindelang, "Moral Evaluations and Illegal Behavior," *Social Problems* 21:370–385 (1974).

71. Peggy Giordano, "The Sense of Injustice?" *Criminology* 14:93–112 (1976).

72. Hirschi, note 66.

73. Stephen Demuth and Susan Brown, "Family Structure, Family Processes, and Adolescent Delinquency," *Journal of Research in Crime and Delinquency* 41:58–82 (2004); Frank Elgar, John Knight, Graham Worrall, and Gregory Sherman, "Attachment Characteristics and Behavioral Problems in Rural and Urban Juvenile Delinquents," *Child Psychiatry and Human Development* 34:35–49 (2003); Joseph Allen, Penny Marsh, Christy McFarland, Kathleen McElhaney, Deborah Land, Kathleen Jodl, and Sheryl Peck, "Attachment and Autonomy as Predictors of the Development of Social Skills and Delinquency During Midadolescence," *Journal of Consulting and Clinical Psychology* 70:56–66 (2002); John Paul Wright and Francis Cullen, "Parental Efficacy and Delinquent Behavior," *Criminology* 39:677–707 (2001); Velmer Burton, Francis Cullen, T. David Evans, R. Gregory Dunaway, Sesha Kethinene, and Gary Payne, "The Impact of Parental Control on Delinquency," *Journal of Criminal Justice* 23:111–126 (1995); Robert Agnew, "Social Control Theory and Delinquency," *Criminology* 23:47–61 (1985); Michael Hindelang, "Causes of Delinquency," *Social Problems* 20:471–487 (1973); Antonia Abbey, Angela Jacques, Lenwood Hayman, Jr., and Joanne Soback, "Predictors of Early Substance Abuse among African American and Caucasian Youth from Urban and Suburban Youth," *Merrill-Palmer Quarterly* 52:305–326 (2006).

74. Trina Hope, Esther Wilder, and Toni Watt, "The Relationships among Adolescent Pregnancy, Pregnancy Resolution, and Juvenile Delinquency," *Sociological Quarterly* 44:555–577 (2003).

75. Stephen Demuth, "Understanding the Delinquency and Social Relationships of Loners," *Youth & Society* 35:366–394 (2004).

76. John Hepburn, "Testing Alternative Models of Delinquency Causation," *Journal of Criminal Law and Criminology* 67:450–460 (1976); Matthew Silberman, "Toward a Theory of Criminal Behavior," *American Sociological Review* 41:442–461 (1976); Michael Wiatrowski, David Griswold, and Mary Roberts, "Curriculum Tracking and Delinquency," *American Sociological Review* 47:151–160 (1982); Michael Wiatrowski, David Griswold, and Mary Roberts, "Social Control Theory and Delinquency," *American Sociological Review* 46:525–541 (1981).

77. Eric Linden and James Hackler, "Affective Ties and Delinquency," *Pacific Sociological Review* 16: 27–46 (1973).

78. Hirschi, note 66.

79. Marvin Krohn and James Massey, "Social Control and Delinquent Behavior," *Sociological Quarterly* 21:529–543 (1980).

80. Krohn and Massey, note 79.

81. Randy Lagrange and Helen White, "Age Differences in Delinquency," *Criminology* 23: 9–45 (1985).

82. Agnew, note 46.

83. David Greenberg, "The Weak Strength of Social Control Theory," *Crime & Delinquency* 45:66–81 (1999).

84. Charles Tittle, *Control Balance* (Boulder, CO: Westview Press, 1995).

85. Nicole Piquero and Alex Piquero, "Control Balance and Exploitative Corporate Crime," *Criminology* 44:397–430 (2006).

86. Matt DeLisi and Andrew Hochstetler, "An Exploratory Assessment of Tittle's Control Balance Theory," *The Justice Professional* 15:261–272 (2002).

87. Michael Gottfredson and Travis Hirschi, *A General Theory of Crime* (Stanford: Stanford University Press, 1990).

88. Matt DeLisi, "Self-Control Pathology," pages 21–38 in Chester Britt and Michael Gottfredson (eds.), *Control Theories of Crime and Delinquency* (New Brunswick, NJ: Transaction Books, 2003).

89. Travis Pratt and Francis Cullen, "The Empirical Status of Gottfredson and Hirschi's General Theory of Crime," *Criminology* 38:931–964 (2000).

90. L. Thomas Winfree, Jr., Terrance Taylor, Ni He, and Finn-Aage Esbensen, "Self-Control and Variability Over Time: Multivariate Results Using a 5-Year, Multisite Panel of Youths," *Crime & Delinquency* 52:253–285 (2006); George Higgins, "Gender and Self-Control Theory," *Criminal Justice Studies* 17:33–55 (2004); Charles Tittle, David Ward, and Harold Grasmick "Gender, Age, and Crime/Deviance," *Journal of Research in Crime and Delinquency* 40:426–453 (2003); Carter Hay, "Parenting, Self-Control, and Delinquency," *Criminology* 39:707–737 (2001); Velmer Burton, T. David Evans, Francis Cullen, Kathleen Olivares, and R. Gregory Dunaway, "Age, Self-Control, and Adults' Offending Behaviors," *Journal of Criminal Justice* 27:45–54 (1999); John Gibbs, Dennis Giever, and Jamie Martin, "Parental Management and Self-Control," *Journal of Research in Crime and Delinquency* 35:40–70 (1998); Harold Grasmick, Charles Tittle, Robert Bursik, and Bruce Arneklev, "Testing the Core Empirical Implications of Gottfredson and Hirschi's General Theory of Crime," *Journal of Research in Crime and Delinquency* 30:5–29 (1993).

91. Callie Harbin Burt, Ronald Simons, and Leslie Simons, "A Longitudinal Test of the Effects of Parenting and the Stability of Self-Control: Negative Evidence for the General Theory of Crime," *Criminology* 44:353–397 (2006).

92. T. David Evans, Francis Cullen, Velmer Burton, R. Gregory Dunaway, and Michael Benson, "The Social Consequences of Self-Control," *Criminology* 35:475–501 (1997); pp. 490–491.

93. Travis Hirschi and Michael Gottfredson, "Substantive Positivism and the Idea of Crime," pages 253–270 in Travis Hirschi and Michael Gottfredson (eds.), *The Generality of Deviance* (New Brunswick, NJ: Transaction Publishers, 1994), p. 261.

94. Stephen Baron, "Self-Control, Social Consequences, and Criminal Behavior," *Journal of Research in Crime and Delinquency* 40: 403–425 (2003); Gilbert Geis, "On the Absence of Self-Control as the Basis for a General Theory of Crime," *Theoretical Criminology* 4:35–53 (2000); Tim Newburn and Michael Shiner, "Young People, Mentoring and Social Inclusion," *Youth Justice* 6: 23–41 (2006).

95. John Paul Wright and Kevin Beaver, "Do Parents Matter in Creating Self-Control in Their Children? A Generally Informed Test of Gottfredson and Hirschi's Theory of Low Self-Control," *Criminology* 43:1169–1198 (2005).

96. Constance Chapple, "Self-control, Peer Relations, and Delinquency," *Justice Quarterly* 22: 89–106 (2005).

97. Travis Pratt and Francis Cullen, "Assessing Macro-Level Predictors and Theories of Crime," *Crime and Justice* 32:373–450 (2005); Travis Pratt, Francis Cullen, Kristie Blevins, Leah Daigle, and Tamara Madensen, "The Empirical Status of Deterrence," pp. 367–395 in Francis Cullen, John Paul Wright, and Kristie Blevins (eds.), *Taking Stock* (New Brunswick, NJ: Transaction, 2005).

98. DeLisi, note 88.

99. Michael Arter, "Police Mentoring: Moving toward Police Legitimacy," *Criminal Justice Studies* 19:85–97 (2006); Richard Lundman, *Prevention and Control of Juvenile Delinquency,* 3rd edition (New York: Oxford University Press, 2001); Anthony Sorrentino and David Whittaker, "The Chicago Area Project—Addressing the Gang Problem," *FBI Law Enforcement Bulletin* 63:8–12 (1994); Solomon Kobrin, "The Chicago Area Project," *Annals of the American Academy of Political and Social Sciences* 332:19–29 (1959); Steven Schlossman, Gail Zellman, and Richard Shavelson, *Delinquency Prevention in South Chicago* (Santa Monica, CA: RAND, 1984).

100. "Study Shows Positive Results from Early Head Start Program," online at: http://www.hhs.gov/news/press/2002pres/20020603.html, accessed April 20, 2007. Information on Project Head Start is available online at: http://www.headstartinfo.org., accessed April 20, 2007.

101. Gary Sailes, "Basketball at Midnight," online at: http://www.unesco.org/courier/1999_04/uk/dossier/txt16.htm, accessed April 20, 2007.

102. Bureau of Justice Statistics, *Boys and Girls Clubs of America* (Washington, DC: U.S. Government Printing Office, 2006).

103. Britt and Gottfredson, note 88, p. 17.

104. Carolyn Webster-Stratton, *The Incredible Years Training Series* (Washington, DC: Office of Juvenile Justice and Delinquency Prevention, 2005).

CHAPTER 7

1. Frank Tannenbaum, *Crime and the Community* (New York: Columbia University Press, 1938), pp. 19–20.

2. Charles Horton Cooley, *Human Nature and the Social Order* (New York: Scribners and Sons, 1902); George Herbert Mead, *Mind, Self, and Society* (Chicago: University of Chicago Press, 1934); W. I. Thomas, *The Unadjusted Girl* (Boston: Little, Brown, 1923).

3. Donald Shoemaker, *Theories of Delinquency,* 4th edition (New York: Oxford University Press, 2000), p. 196.

4. Tannenbaum, note 1, pp. 17–18.

5. Edwin Lemert, *Social Pathology* (New York: McGraw-Hill, 1951), pp. 70–75.

6. Lemert, note 5, p. 318.

7. Howard Becker, *Outsiders* (New York: The Free Press, 1963); Howard Becker, *The Other Side* (New York: The Free Press, 1964).

8. Daniel Curran and Claire Renzetti, *Theories of Crime,* 2nd edition (Boston: Allyn and Bacon, 2001), p. 174.

9. Edwin Schur, *Radical Nonintervention* (Englewood Cliffs, NJ: Prentice Hall, 1973); Edwin Schur, *Labeling Deviant Behavior* (New York: Harper & Row, 1971).

10. Erving Goffman, *Asylums* (New York: Doubleday, 1961), p. 123.

11. Ronald Akers and Christine Sellers, *Criminological Theories,* 4th edition (New York: Oxford University Press, 2007).

12. John Braithwaite, *Crime, Shame and Reintegration* (Cambridge: Cambridge University Press, 1989), p. 55.

13. Toni Makkai and John Braithwaite, "Reintegrative Shaming and Compliance with Regulatory Standards," *Criminology* 32:361–386 (1994).

14. Carter Hay, "An Exploratory Test of Braithwaite's Reintegrative Shaming Theory," *Journal of Research in Crime and Delinquency* 38:132–153 (2001).

15. Jon Vagg, "Delinquency and Shame: Data from Hong Kong," *British Journal of Criminology* 38:247–264 (1998).

16. Eric Baumer, Richard Wright, Kristun Kristinsdottir, and Helgi Gunnlaugsson, "Crime, Shame, and Recidivism: The Case of Iceland," *British Journal of Criminology* 42:40–59 (2002).

17. Ekaterina Botchkovar and Charles Tittle, "Crime, Shame, and Reintegration in Russia," *Theoretical Criminology* 9:401–442 (2005).

18. Lening Zhang and Sheldon Zhang, "Reintegrative Shaming and Predatory Delinquency," *Journal of Research in Crime and Delinquency* 41:433–453 (2004).

19. Terance Miethe, Hong Lu, and Erin Reese, "Reintegrative Shaming and Recidivism Risks in Drug Court: Explanations for Some Unexpected Findings," *Crime & Delinquency* 46:522–541 (2000).

20. Lawrence Sherman, Heather Strange, and Daniel Woods, *Recidivism Patterns in the Canberra Reintegrative Shaming Experiments (RISE)* (Canberra: Australian National University Press, 2000); Lawrence Sherman, "Reason for Emotion: Reinventing Justice with Theories, Innovations, and Research—The American Society of Criminology 2002 Presidential Address," *Criminology* 41:1–38 (2003).

21. Kenneth Jensen and Stephen Gibbons, "Shame and Religion as Factors in the Rehabilitation of Serious Offenders," *Journal of Offender Rehabilitation* 35:215–230 (2002); Darrell Steffensmeier and Jeffery Ulmer, *Confessions of a Dying Thief: Understanding Criminal Careers and Illegal Enterprise* (New Brunswick, NJ: Transaction, 2005).

22. Francis Palamara, Francis Cullen, and Joanne Gersten, "The Effects of Police and Mental Health Intervention on Juvenile Deviance: Specifying Contingencies in the Impact of Formal Reaction," *Journal of Health and Social Behavior* 27:90–106 (1986); Charles Thomas and Donna Bishop, "The Effects of Formal and Informal Sanctions on Delinquency," *Journal of Criminal Law and Criminology* 75:1222–1245 (1984); David Myers, "Adult Crime, Adult Time: Punishing Violent Youth in the Adult Criminal Justice System," *Youth Violence and Juvenile Justice* 1:173–197 (2003).

23. Jon Bernburg, Marvin Krohn, and Craig Rivera, "Official Labeling, Criminal Embeddedness, and Subsequent Delinquency: A Longitudinal Test of Labeling Theory," *Journal of Research in Crime and Delinquency* 43:67–88 (2006).

24. Lee Johnson, Ronald Simons, and Rand Conger, "Criminal Justice System Involvement and Continuity of Youth Crime: A Longitudinal Analysis," *Youth & Society* 36:3–29 (2004); Eric Stewart, Ronald Simons, Rand Conger, and Laura Scaramella, "Beyond the Interactional Relationship between Delinquency and Parenting Practices: The Contribution of Legal Sanctions," *Journal of Research in Crime and Delinquency* 39:36–59 (2002).

25. David Myers, "The Recidivism of Violent Youths in Juvenile and Adult Court: A Consideration of Selection Bias," *Youth Violence and Juvenile Justice* 1:79–101 (2003).

26. David Ward and Charles Tittle, "Deterrence or Labeling: The Effects of Informal Sanctions," *Deviant Behavior* 14:43–64 (1993).

27. Karen Heimer and Ross Matsueda, "Role-Taking, Role Commitment, and Delinquency: A Theory of Differential Social Control," *American Sociological Review* 59:365–390 (1994); Ross Matsueda, "Reflected Appraisals, Parental Labeling, and Delinquency: Specifying a Symbolic Interactionist Theory," *American Journal of Sociology* 97:1577–1611 (1992).

28. Karen Heimer, "Gender, Race, and the Pathways to Delinquency: An Interactionist Explanation," pages 140–167 in John Hagan and Ruth Peterson (eds.), *Crime and Inequality* (Stanford, CA: Stanford University Press, 1995), p. 140.

29. Dawn Bartusch and Ross Matsueda, "Gender, Reflected Appraisals, and Labeling: A Cross Group Test of an Interactionist Theory of Delinquency," *Social Forces* 75:145–177 (1996).

30. Mike Adams, "Labeling and Differential Association: Towards a General Social Learning Theory of Crime and Deviance," *American Journal of Criminal Justice* 20:147–164 (1996); Mike Adams, Craig Robertson, Phyllis Gray-Ray, and Melvin Ray, "Labeling and Delinquency," *Adolescence* 38:171–184 (2003).

31. Gordon Bazemore, "Young People, Trouble, and Crime: Restorative Justice as a Normative Theory of Informal Social Control and Social Support," *Youth and Society* 33:199–226 (2001); Barbara Warner, "The Role of Attenuated Culture in Social Disorganization Theory," *Criminology* 41:73–98 (2003).

32. Charles Wellford, "Labeling Theory and Criminology," *Social Problems* 22:332–345 (1975).

33. Charles Thomas and Donna Bishop, "The Effect of Formal and Informal Sanctions on Delinquency," *Journal of Criminal Law and Criminology* 75:1222–1245 (1984).

34. Steven Burkett and Carol Hickman, "An Examination of the Impact of Legal Sanctions on Adolescent Marijuana Use: A Panel Analysis," *Journal of Drug Issues* 12:73–87 (1982).

35. Jack Foster, Simon Dinitz, and Walter Reckless, "Perceptions of Stigma Following Public Intervention for Delinquent Behavior," *Social Problems* 20:202–209 (1972).

36. John Hepburn, "The Impact of Police Intervention upon Juvenile Delinquents," *Criminology* 15:235–262 (1977).

37. Lawrence Sherman and Richard Berk, "The Specific Deterrent Effects of Arrest for Domestic Assault," *American Sociological Review* 49:261–271 (1984); Douglas Smith and Patrick Gartin, "Specifying Specific Deterrence," *American Sociological Review* 54:94–106 (1989).

38. Albert Roberts, "Wilderness Experiences: Camps and Outdoor Programs," pages 327–346 in Albert Roberts (ed.), *Juvenile Justice: Policies, Programs, and Services*, 2nd edition (Chicago: Nelson-Hall, 1998).

39. Margaret Jackson and Angela Henderson, "Restorative Justice or Restorative Health? Which Model Best Fits the Needs of Marginalized Girls in Canadian Society?" *Criminal Justice Policy Review* 17:234–251 (2006); Jeanne Stinchcomb, Gordon Bazemore, and Nancy Riestenberg, "Beyond Zero Tolerance: Restoring Justice in Secondary Schools," *Youth Violence and Juvenile Justice* 4:123–147 (2006); Gordon Bazemore, "Restorative Justice and Earned Redemption: Communities, Victims, and Offender Reintegration," *American Behavioral Scientist* 41:768–813 (1998); Nancy Rodriguez, "Restorative Justice, Communities, and Delinquency: Whom Do We Reintegrate?" *Criminology and Public Policy* 4:103–130 (2005).

40. Jeff Latimer, Craig Dowden, and Danielle Muise, *The Effectiveness of Restorative Justice Practices: A Meta-Analysis* (Ottawa: Canada Department of Justice, 2001).

41. Karl Marx and Friedrich Engels, *Capital* (New York: International Publishers 1867/1967).

42. Ian Taylor, Paul Walton, and Jock Young, *Critical Criminology* (London: Routledge & Kegan Paul, 1975).

43. Willem Bonger, *Criminality and Economic Conditions* (New York: Agathon Press, 1916/1967), pp. 396–397.

44. Bonger, note 43, p. 532.

45. Bonger, note 43, p. 407.

46. Bonger, note 43, p. 671.

47. Thorsten Sellin, *Culture and Conflict in Crime* (New York: Social Science Research Council, 1938), p. 21.

48. Sellin, note 47, p. 3.

49. George Vold, *Theoretical Criminology* (New York: Oxford University Press, 1958); George Vold, Thomas Bernard, and Jeffrey Snipes, *Theoretical Criminology*, 5th edition (New York: Oxford University Press, 2002), p. 229.

50. Richard Quinney, *Critique of Legal Order* (Boston: Little, Brown, 1974).

51. Richard Quinney, *Class, State, and Crime,* 2nd edition (New York: David McKay Publishers, 1980), p. 3.

52. Quinney, note 51, p. 204.

53. John Hagan, John Simpson, and A. Gillis, "Class in the Household," *American Journal of Sociology* 92:788–816 (1987), p. 812.

54. Simon Singer and Murray Levine, "Power-Control Theory, Gender, and Delinquency," *Criminology* 26:627–647 (1988).

55. Brenda Blackwell, Christine Sellers, and Sheila Schlaopitz, "A Power-Control Theory of Vulnerability to Crime and Adolescent Role Exits—Revisited," *Canadian Review of Sociology and Anthropology* 39:199–218 (2002).

56. Gary Jensen and Kevin Thompson, "What's Class Got to Do with It?" *American Journal of Sociology* 95:1009–1023 (1990).

57. Merry Morash and Meda Chesney-Lind, "A Reformulation and Partial Test of the Power Control Theory of Delinquency," *Justice Quarterly* 8:347–377 (1991), p. 371.

58. Curran and Renzetti, note 8, p. 274.

59. James Messerschmidt, *Masculinities and Crime* (Boston: Rowman and Littlefield, 1993).

60. Ronald Akers, *Criminological Theories* (Los Angeles, CA: Roxbury, 1994), p. 174.

61. Mark Colvin and John Pauly, "A Critique of Criminology," *American Journal of Sociology* 89:513–551 (1987), pp. 513–514.

62. Colvin and Pauly, note 61, p. 537.

63. Steven Messner and Marvin Krohn, "Class, Compliance Structures, and Delinquency, *American Journal of Sociology* 96:300–328 (1990); Sally Simpson and Lori Ellis, "Is Gender Subordinate to Class?" *Journal of Criminal Law and Criminology* 85:453–480 (1994).

64. Mark Colvin, *Crime and Coercion: An Integrated Theory of Chronic Criminality* (New York: St. Martin's Press, 2002).

65. Gerald Patterson, "Coercion as a Basis for Early Age Onset of Arrest," pages 81–105 in Joan McCord (ed.), *Coercion and Punishment in Long-Term Perspective* (New York: Cambridge University Press, 1995); Carolyn Smith and Terence Thornberry, "The Relationship Between Childhood Maltreatment and Adolescent Involvement in Delinquency," *Criminology* 33:451–481 (1995); David Farrington and Brandon Welsh, *Saving Children from a Life of Crime: Early Risk Factors and Effective Interventions* (New York: Oxford University Press, 2007).

66. Matt DeLisi, *Career Criminals in Society* (Thousand Oaks, CA: Sage, 2005).

67. John Hewitt and Bob Regoli, "Differential Oppression Theory and Female Delinquency," *Free Inquiry in Creative Sociology* 31:1–10 (2003).

68. Francis Cullen, "Social Support as an Organizing Concept for Criminology," *Justice Quarterly* 11:527–560 (1994).

69. Andy Hochstetler, Matt DeLisi, and Travis Pratt, "Social Support and Feelings of Hostility among Released Inmates," paper presented at the Annual Meeting of the Academy of Criminal Justice Sciences, March 2007, Seattle, Washington; Francis Cullen, John Paul Wright, and Mitchell Chamlin, "Social Support and Social Reform: A Progressive Crime Control Agenda," *Crime &*

Delinquency 45:188–207 (1999); Mitchell Chamlin and John Cochran, "Social Altruism and Crime," *Criminology* 35:203–227 (1997); Francis Cullen, John Paul Wright, Shayna Brown, Melissa Moon, Michael Blankenship, and Brandon Applegate, "Public Support for Early Intervention Programs: Implications for a Progressive Policy Agenda," *Crime & Delinquency* 44:187–204 (1998).

70. Mark Colvin, Francis Cullen, and Thomas Vander Ven, "Coercion, Social Support, and Crime: An Emerging Theoretical Consensus," *Criminology* 40:19–42 (2002).

71. John Paul Wright, Francis Cullen, and Jeremy Miller, "Family Social Capital and Delinquent Involvement," *Journal of Criminal Justice* 29:1–9 (2001).

72. Benjamin Cornwell, "The Dynamic Properties of Social Support," *Social Forces* 81:953–978 (2003).

73. Elise Peplin and Victoria Banyard, "Social Support: A Mediator between Child Maltreatment and Developmental Outcomes," *Journal of Youth and Adolescence* 35:617–630 (2006).

74. Melissa Moon, Francis Cullen, and John Paul Wright, "It Takes a Village: Public Willingness to Help Wayward Youths," *Youth Violence and Juvenile Justice* 1:32–45 (2003).

75. Travis Pratt and Timothy Godsey, "Social Support and Homicide: A Cross-National Test of an Emerging Criminological Theory," *Journal of Criminal Justice* 30:589–601 (2002); Travis Pratt and Timothy Godsey, "Social Support, Inequality, and Homicide: A Cross-National Test of an Integrated Theoretical Model," *Criminology* 41:611–643 (2003).

76. Beverly Kingston, Bob Regoli, and John Hewitt, "The Theory of Differential Oppression: A Developmental-Ecological Explanation of Adolescent Problem Behavior," *Critical Criminology* 11:237–260 (2003); Robert Regoli and John Hewitt, *Delinquency in Society,* 6th edition (New York: McGraw-Hill, 2006); Robert Regoli and John Hewitt, *Delinquency in Society,* 2nd edition (New York: McGraw-Hill, 1994); Robert Regoli and John Hewitt, *Delinquency in Society* (New York: McGraw-Hill, 1991).

77. David Finkelhor, "The Victimization of Children," *American Journal of Orthopsychiatry* 65:177–193 (1997).

78. Alice Miller, *For Your Own Good* (New York: Farrar, Straus, & Giroux, 1984).

79. U.S. Department of Health and Human Services, *Child Maltreatment 2005* (Washington, DC: U.S. Government Printing Office, 2007).

80. Yvonne Vissing, Murray Straus, Richard Gelles, and John Harrop, "Verbal Aggression by Parents and Psychosocial Problems of Children," *Child Abuse and Neglect* 15:223–228 (1991).

81. P. M. Taylor, *Parent-Infant Relationships* (New York: Grune & Stratton, 1980).

82. Murray Straus, Richard Gelles, and Suzanne Steinmetz, *Behind Closed Doors: Violence In the American Family* (New York: Doubleday, 1980); Murray Straus and Richard Gelles, "Societal Change and Change in Family Violence from 1975 to 1985 as Revealed by Two National Surveys," *Journal of Marriage and the Family* 48:465–479 (1986); Murray Straus and Richard Gelles, *Physical Violence In American Families: Risk Factors and Adaptations to Violence in 8,145 Families* (New Brunswick, NJ: Transaction, 1989).

83. W. I. Munkel, "Neglect and Abandonment," pages 105–118 in J. A. Monteleone (ed.), *Recognition of Child Abuse for the Mandated Reporter* (St. Louis: G. W. Medical Publishing, 1996).

84. Herbert Needleman, A. Schell, D. Bellinger, A. Leviton, and E. Allred, "The Long Term Effects of Low Doses of Lead in Childhood: An 11-year Follow-up Report," *New England Journal of Medicine* 322:83–88 (1990).

85. Nancy Dubrow and James Garbarino, "Living in the War Zone," *Child Welfare* 68:3–20 (1989).

86. Terry Williams and William Kornblum, *Growing Up Poor* (Lexington, MA: DC Heath, 1985).

87. William Julius Wilson, *The Truly Disadvantaged* (Chicago: University of Chicago Press, 1987).

88. Greg Duncan, Jeanne Brooks-Gunn, and Pamela Klebanov, "Economic Deprivation and Early Childhood Development," *Child Development* 65:296–318 (1994); Greg Duncan and Willard Rodgers, "Has Children's Poverty Become More Persistent?" *American Sociological Review* 56:538–550 (1991); Greg Duncan and Jeanne Brooks-Gunn, *Consequences of Growing Up Poor* (New York: Russell Sage Foundation, 1997); Greg Duncan and Willard Rodgers, "Longitudinal Aspects of Childhood Poverty," *Journal of Marriage and the Family* 50:1007–1021 (1988).

89. Thomas McNulty, "Assessing the Race-Violence Relationship at the Macro Level: The Assumption of Racial Invariance and the Problem of Restricted Distributions," *Criminology* 39:467–490 (2001); Thomas McNulty and Paul Bellair, "Explaining Racial and Ethnic Differences in Adolescent Violence: Structural Disadvantage, Family Well-Being, and Social Capital," *Justice Quarterly* 20:1–31 (2003); Thomas McNulty and Paul Bellair, "Explaining Racial and Ethnic Differences in Serious Adolescent Violent Behavior," *Criminology* 41:709–748 (2003).

90. James Q. Wilson, *The Marriage Problem* (New York: HarperCollins, 2002).

91. Ann Masten and J. Douglas Coatsworth, "The Development of Competence in Favorable and Unfavorable Environments," *American Psychologist* 53:205–220 (1998), p. 216.

92. Darrell Steffensmeier and Emilie Allen, "Gender and Crime: Toward a Gendered Theory of Female Offending," *Annual Review of Sociology* 22:459–487 (1996); Lance Hannon and Lynn Dufour, "Still Just the Study of Men and Crime?" *Sex Roles* 38:63–71 (1998); Joanne Belknap, *The Invisible Woman: Gender, Crime, and Justice,* 3rd edition (Belmont, CA: Thomson/Wadsworth, 2007).

93. Carol Tosone, "Revisiting the 'Myth' of Feminine Masochism," *Clinical Social Work Journal* 26:413–426 (1998); Viktor Gecas and Michael Schwalbe, "Parental Behavior and Adolescent Self-Esteem," *Journal of Marriage and the Family* 48:37–46 (1986).

94. David Matza, *Delinquency and Drift* (New York: John Wiley & Sons, 1964); Jack Katz, *Seductions of Crime* (New York: Basic Books, 1988).

95. Gerald Marwell, "Adolescent Powerlessness and Delinquent Behavior," *Social Problems* 14:35–47 (1966).

96. Francis Ianni, *The Search for Structure* (New York: Free Press, 1989); Joseph Chandy, Robert Blum, and Michael Resnick, "Gender-Specific Outcomes for Sexually Abused Adolescents," *Child Abuse and Neglect* 20:1219–1231 (1996); Peggy Plass, "African-American Family Homicide: Patterns in Partner, Parent, and Child Victimization, 1985–1987," *Journal of Black Studies* 23:515–538 (1993).

97. Jackson Toby, "The New Criminology is the Old Sentimentality," *Criminology* 16:515–526 (1979).

98. Francis Allen, *The Crimes of Politics* (Cambridge: Harvard University Press, 1974).

99. David Shichor, "The New Criminology: Some Critical Issues," *British Journal of Criminology* 20:1–19 (1980).

100. J.A. Sharpe, *Crime in Early Modern England, 1550–1750* (London: Longmans, 1984).

101. Akers, note 60, p. 162.

102. Shoemaker, note 3, p. 221.

103. Lisa McLewin and Robert Muller, "Attachment and Social Support in the prediction of Psychopathology among Young Adults with and without a History of Physical Maltreatment," *Child Abuse & Neglect* 30:171–191 (2006).

104. Travis Pratt and Christopher Lowenkamp, "Conflict Theory, Economic Conditions, and Homicide: A Time-Series Analysis," *Homicide Studies* 6:61–83 (2002).

105. Matthew Petrocelli, Alex Piquero, and Michael Smith, "Conflict Theory and Racial Profiling: An Empirical Analysis of Police Traffic Stop Data," *Journal of Criminal Justice* 31:1–11 (2003).

106. Lonn Lanza Kaduce and Richard Greenleaf, "Age and Race Deference Reversals: Extending Turk on Police-Citizen Conflict," *Journal of Research in Crime and Delinquency* 37:221–236 (2000); Robert Weidner and William Terrill, "A Test of Turk's Theory of Norm Resistance Using Observational Data on Police-Suspect Encounters," *Journal of Research in Crime and Delinquency* 42:84–109 (2005).

107. Shanhe Jiang, Marianne Fisher-Giolando, and Liping Mo, "Social Support and Inmate Rule Violations: A Multilevel Analysis," *American Journal of Criminal Justice* 30:71–86 (2005).

108. Shanhe Jiang and L. Thomas Winfree, "Social Support, Gender, and Inmate Adjustment to Prison Life: Insights from a National Sample," *Prison Journal* 86:32–55 (2006).

109. Michael Reisig, Kristy Holtfreter, and Merry Morash, "Social Capital among Women Offenders: Examining the Distribution of Social Networks and Resources," *Journal of Contemporary Criminal Justice* 18:167–187 (2002).

110. Cathy Spatz Widom, "Child Abuse, Neglect, and Violent Criminal Behavior," *Criminology* 27:251–271 (1989); Carolyn Smith and Terence Thornberry, "The Relationship between Childhood Maltreatment and Adolescent Involvement in Delinquency," *Criminology* 33:451–477 (1995); Barbara Kelly, Terence Thornberry, and Carolyn Smith, *In the Wake of Childhood Maltreatment* (Washington, DC: Office of Juvenile Justice and Delinquency Prevention, 1997); Timothy Brezina, "Adolescent Maltreatment and Delinquency," *Journal of Research in Crime and Delinquency* 35:71–99 (1998); Kevin Thompson and Rhonda Braaten-Antrim, "Youth Maltreatment and Gang Involvement," *Journal of Interpersonal Violence* 13:328–345 (1998); David Wolfe, Katreena Scott, Christine Wekerle, and Anna-Lee Pittman, "Child Maltreatment: Risk of Adjustment Problems and Dating Violence in Adolescence," *Journal of the American Academy of Child and Adolescent Psychiatry* 40:282–289 (2001).

111. Cathy Spatz Widom and Michael Maxfield, *Update on the "Cycle of Violence"* (Washington, DC: National Institute of Justice, 2001), p. 4.

112. James Unnever, Mark Colvin, and Francis Cullen, "Crime and Coercion," *Journal of Research in Crime and Delinquency* 40:1–25 (2003).

113. Stephen Baron, "Canadian Male Street Skinheads," *Canadian Review of Sociology and Anthropology* 34:125–154 (1997), p. 148.

114. Lisa Hutchinson and D. Mueller, "Stick and Stones and Broken Bones: The Influence of Parental Verbal Abuse on Peer Related Victimization," Unpublished manuscript, 2007.

115. Lisa Wallace, "Responding Through Retaliation," paper presented at the Academy of Criminal Justice Sciences meeting, Las Vegas, 2004; Lisa Wallace, "Looking Inward: An Examination of the Internal Manifestation of Oppression in Adolescents," paper presented at the American Society of Criminology meeting, Denver, 2003; Lisa Wallace, "Reports From Rural Mississippi: A Look at School Violence," *Journal of Security Administration* 24:15–32 (2001); Lisa Wallace and Stacy Moak, "Assessing the Role of Anger and Frustration in Self-Reported Drug and Alcohol Use in Students Grades 6th–12th," paper presented at the Academy of Criminal Justice Sciences meeting, Boston, 2003; Lisa Hutchinson Wallace, Justin Patchin, and Jeff May, "Reactions of Victimized Youths: Strain as an Explanation of School Delinquency," Western Criminological Review, online at: http://www.wcr.sonoma.edu/v6n1/wallace.htm (2005), accessed April 29, 2007; Lisa Wallace and Wes Pullman, "Socialization and Prisonization: Examining Deprivations in the School Setting," paper presented at the Academy of Criminal Justice Sciences meeting, Las Vegas, 2004; Lisa Wallace and Ruth Seydlitz, "Looking Inward: An Examination of the Internal Manifestation of Oppression in Adolescents," paper presented at the American Society of Criminology meeting, Denver, 2003.

116. Michael Lynch, Herman Schwendinger, and Julia Schwendinger, "The Status of Empirical Research in Radical Criminology," pages 191–215 in Francis Cullen, John Paul Wright, and Kristie Blevins (eds.), *Taking Stock: The Status of Criminological Theory, Advances in Criminological Theory Volume 15* (New Brunswick, NJ: Transaction, 2006); John Randolph Fuller and John Wozniak, "Peacemaking Criminology: Past, Present, and Future," pages 251–276 in Francis Cullen, John Paul Wright, and Kristie Blevins (eds.), *Taking Stock: The Status of Criminological Theory, Advances in Criminological Theory Volume 15* (New Brunswick, NJ: Transaction, 2006).

CHAPTER 8

1. Daniel Nagin and Raymond Paternoster, "Population Heterogeneity and State Dependence: State of Evidence and Directions for Future Research," *Journal of Quantitative Criminology* 16:117–144 (2000).

2. Terence Thornberry, "Introduction: Some Advantages of Developmental and Life-Course Perspectives for the Study of Crime and Delinquency," pages 1–10 in Terence Thornberry (ed.), *Developmental Theories of Crime and Delinquency, Advances in Criminological Theory,* Volume 7 (New Brunswick, NJ: Transaction Publishers, 1997); Terence Thornberry, "Toward an Interactional Theory of Delinquency," *Criminology* 25:863–891 (1987).

3. Avshalom Caspi, "The Child is Father of the Man: Personality Continuities from Childhood to Adulthood," *Journal of Personality and Social Psychology* 78:158–172 (2000).

4. Travis Hirschi and Michael Gottfredson, "Age and the Explanation of Crime," *American Journal of Sociology* 89:522–584 (1983); David Greenberg, "Age, Crime and Social Explanation," *American Journal of Sociology* 91:1–21 (1985).

5. David Farrington, "Age and Crime," pages 189–250 in Michael Tonry and Norval Morris (eds.), *Crime and Justice: An Annual Review of Research,* Volume 7 (Chicago: University of Chicago Press, 1986); Darnell Hawkins, John Laub, Janet Lauritsen, and Lynn Cothern, "Race, Ethnicity, and Serious and Violent Juvenile Offending," *Juvenile Justice Bulletin* (Washington, DC: Office of Juvenile Justice and Delinquency Prevention, 2000); Alex Piquero, David Farrington, and Alfred Blumstein, "The Criminal Career Paradigm: Background and Recent Developments," pages 359–506 in Michael Tonry (ed.), *Crime and Justice: An Annual Review of Research,* Volume 30 (Chicago: University of Chicago Press, 2003).

6. Sung Jang and Marvin Krohn, "Developmental Patterns of Sex Differences in Delinquency among African American Adolescents: A Test of the Sex-Invariance Hypothesis," *Journal of Quantitative Criminology* 11:195–222 (1995).

7. Persephanie Silverthorn and Paul Frick, "Developmental Pathways to Antisocial Behavior: The Delayed-Onset Pathway in Girls," *Development and Psychopathology* 11:101–126 (1999).

8. For empirical evidence, see Daniel Nagin and David Farrington, "The Stability of Criminal Potential from Childhood to Adulthood," *Criminology* 30:235–260 (1992); L. Rowell Huesmann, Leonard Eron, Monroe Lefkowtz, and Leopold Walder, "Stability of Aggression over Time and Generations," *Developmental Psychology* 20:1120–1134 (1984); Matt DeLisi, "Extreme Career Criminals," *American Journal of Criminal Justice* 25:239–252 (2001); Donald Lynam, "Early Identification of Chronic Offenders: Who is the Fledgling Psychopath?" *Psychological Bulletin* 120:209–234 (1996); Elizabeth Piper, "Violent Recidivism and Chronicity in the 1958 Philadelphia cohort," *Journal of Quantitative Criminology* 1:319–344 (1985); Alex Piquero, "Frequency, Specialization, and Violence in Offending Careers," *Journal of Research in Crime and Delinquency* 37:392–418 (2000).

9. Richard Herrnstein, "Criminogenic Traits," pages 39–64 in James Q. Wilson and Joan Petersilia (eds.), *Crime* (San Francisco: ICS Press, 1995).

10. Glen Elder, "Military Times and Turning Points in Men's Lives," *Developmental Psychology* 22:233–245 (1986); Glen Elder, "Time, Agency, and Change: Perspectives on the Life Course," *Social Psychology Quarterly* 57:5–15 (1994).

11. Carolyn Smith, Marvin Krohn, Alan Lizotte, Cynthia Perez-McCluskey, Magda Stouthamer-Loeber, and Anne Weiher, "The Effect of Early Delinquency and Substance Use on Precocious Transitions to Adulthood Among Adolescent Males," pages 233–253 in Greer Fox and Michael Benson (eds.), *Families, Crime and Criminal Justice* (New York: JAI Press, 2000).

12. Gerald Patterson, "Performance Models for Antisocial Boys," *American Psychologist* 41:432–444 (1986).

13. Cesar Rebellon, "Do Adolescents Engage in Delinquency to Attract the Social Attention of Peers?" *Journal of Research in Crime and Delinquency* 43:387–411 (2006).

14. Gerald Patterson, "Coercion as a Basis for Early Age of Onset for Arrest," pages 81–105 in Joan McCord (ed.), *Coercion and Punishment in Long-Term Perspectives* (New York: Cambridge University Press, 1995); Gerald Patterson and Magda Stouthamer-Loeber, "The Correlation of Family Management Practices and Delinquency," *Child Development* 55:1299–1307 (1984); Matt DeLisi, "Zeroing in on Early Arrest Onset," *Journal of Criminal Justice* 34:17–26 (2006).

15. Gerald Patterson and Tom Dishion, "Contributions of Families and Peers to Delinquency," *Criminology* 23:63–79 (1985); Gerald Patterson, Barbara DeBaryshe, and Elizabeth Ramsey, "A Developmental Perspective on Antisocial Behavior," *American Psychologist* 44:329–335 (1989); Gerald Patterson and Karen Yoerger, "Two Different Models for Adolescent Physical Trauma and for Early Arrest," *Criminal Behavior and Mental Health* 5:411–423 (1995).

16. Terrie Moffitt, "Life-Course Persistent and Adolescent-Limited Anti-social Behavior: A Developmental Taxonomy," *Psychological Review* 100:674–701 (1993).

17. Alex Piquero and Timothy Brezina, "Testing Moffitt's Account of Adolescence-Limited Delinquency," *Criminology* 39:353–370 (2001).

18. Seth Schwartz, James Cote, and Jeffrey Arnett, "Identity and Agency in the Individualization Process," *Youth & Society* 37:201–229 (2005).

19. Daniel Nagin, David Farrington, and Terrie Moffitt, "Life-Course Trajectories of Different Types of Offenders," *Criminology* 33:111–139 (1995); Kristen McCabe, Richard Hough, Patricia Wood, and May Yeh, "Childhood and Adolescent Onset Conduct Disorder: A Test of the Developmental Taxonomy," *Journal of Abnormal Child Psychology* 29:305–316 (2001); Benjamin Aguilar, Alan Sroufe, Byron Egeland, and Elizabeth Carlson, "Distinguishing the Early-Onset/Persistent and Adolescence-Onset Antisocial Behavior Types: From Birth to 16 Years," *Development and Psychopathology* 12:109–132 (2000); Robert Agnew, "An Integrated Theory of the Adolescent Peak in Offending," *Youth & Society* 34:263–299 (2003).

20. Terrie Moffitt, "Juvenile Delinquency and Attention Deficit Disorder: Boys' Development Trajectories from Age 3 to Age 15," *Child Development* 61:893–910 (1990).

21. Bradley Wright, Avshalom Caspi, Terrie Moffitt, and Paul Silva, "The Effects of Social Ties on Crime Vary by Criminal Propensity: A Life-Course Model of Interdependence," *Criminology* 39:321–351 (2001).

22. David Farrington, Gregory Barnes, and Sheila Lambert, "The Concentration of Offending in Families," *Legal and Criminological Psychology* 1:47–63 (1996); Bill Henry, Terrie Moffitt, Lee Robins, and Felton Earls, "Early Family Predictors of Child and Adolescent Antisocial Behavior: Who Are the Mothers of Delinquents?" *Criminal Behavior and Mental Health* 3:97–118 (1993); Bill Henry, Avshalom Caspi, Terrie Moffitt, and Phil Silva, "Temperamental and Familial Predictors of Violent and Nonviolent Criminal Convictions: Age 3 to Age 18," *Developmental Psychology* 32:614–623 (1996); Rolf Loeber and David Farrington, "Young Children Who Commit Crime: Epidemiology, Developmental Origins, Risk Factor, Early Interventions, and Policy Implications," *Developmental and Psychopathology* 12:737–762 (2000).

23. M. Douglas Ris, Kim Dietrich, Paul Succop, Omer Berger, and Robert Bornschein, "Early Exposure to Lead and Neuropsychological Outcome in Adolescence," *Journal of the International Neuropsychological Society* 10:261–270 (2004).

24. Bruce Lanphear, Robert Wright, and Kim Dietrich, "Environmental Neurotoxins," *Pediatrics in Review* 26:191–198 (2005).

25. Joe Braun, Robert Kahn, Tanya Froehlich, Peggy Auinger, and Bruce Lanphear, "Exposures to Environmental Toxicants and ADHD in U.S. Children," *Environmental Health Perspectives* September 2006, online at: http://www.ehponline.org/docs/2006/9478/abstract.html, accessed April 30, 2007.

26. For example, see Matt DeLisi, "Scaling Archetypal Criminals," *American Journal of Criminal Justice* 26:77–92 (2001); Chris Gibson, Alex Piquero, and Stephen Tibbetts, "The Contribution of Family Adversity and Verbal IQ to Criminal Behavior," *International Journal of Offender Therapy and Comparative Criminology* 45:574–592 (2001); Lynn Kratzer and Sheilagh Hodgins, "The Typology of Offenders: A Test of Moffitt's Theory among Males and Females from Childhood to Age 30," *Criminal Behavior and Mental Health* 9:57–73 (1999); Robert Krueger, Avshalom Caspi, and Terrie Moffitt, "Epidemiological Personology: The Unifying Role of Personality in Population-Based Research on Problem Behaviors," *Journal of Personality* 68:967–998 (2000); Terrie Moffitt, Donald Lynam, and Phil Silva, "Neuropsychological Tests Predict Persistent Male Delinquency" *Criminology* 32:277–300 (1994); Alex Piquero, "Testing Moffitt's Neuropsychological Variation Hypothesis for the Prediction of Life-Course Persistent Offending," *Psychology, Crime & Law* 7:193–215 (2001).

27. Robert Sampson and John Laub, *Crime in the Making: Pathways and Turning Points through Life* (Cambridge, MA: Harvard University Press, 1993); Robert Sampson and John Laub, "Life-Course Desisters? Trajectories of Crime among Delinquent Boys Followed to Age 70, *Criminology* 41:555–592 (2003), John Laub and Robert Sampson, *Shared Beginnings, Divergent Lives: Delinquent Boys to Age 70* (Cambridge, MA: Harvard University Press, 2003).

28. John Laub and Robert Sampson, "Unraveling Families and Delinquency: A Reanalysis of the Gluecks' Data," *Criminology* 26:355–380 (1988); Robert Sampson and John Laub, "Urban Poverty and the Family Context of Delinquency: A New Look at Structure and Process in a Classic Study," *Child Development* 65:523–540 (1994).

29. John Laub and Robert Sampson, "Turning Points in the Life Course: Why Change Matters to the Study of Crime," *Criminology* 31:301–326 (1993); p. 320; Robert Sampson and John Laub, "Crime and Deviance over the Life Course: The Salience of Adult Social Bonds," *American Sociological Review* 55:609–627 (1990).

30. Robert Sampson, John Laub, and Christopher Wimer, "Does Marriage Reduce Crime? A Counterfactual Approach to within-Individual Causal Effects," *Criminology* 44:465–508 (2006).

31. Terence Thornberry, "Toward an Interactional Theory of Delinquency," *Criminology* 25:863–892 (1987); Robert Brame, Shawn Bushway, Raymond Paternoster, and Terence Thornberry, "Temporal Linkages in Violent and Nonviolent Criminal Activity," *Journal of Quantitative Criminology* 21:149–174 (2005).

32. Terence Thornberry, Alan Lizotte, Marvin Krohn, Margaret Farnworth, and Sung Jang, "Testing Interactional Theory: An Examination of Reciprocal Causal Relationships among Family, School, and Delinquency," *Journal of Criminal Law and Criminology* 82:3–35 (1991).

33. Shawn Bushway, Terence Thornberry, and Marvin Krohn, "Desistance as a Developmental Process: A Comparison of Static and Dynamic Approaches," *Journal of Quantitative Criminology* 19:129–153 (2003); Sung Jang, "Age-Varying Effects of Family, School, and Peers on Delinquency: A Multilevel Modeling Test of Interactional Theory," *Criminology* 37:643–686 (1999); Timothy Ireland, Carolyn Smith, and Terence Thornberry, "Developmental Issues in the Impact of Child Maltreatment on Later Delinquency and Drug Use," *Criminology* 40:359–400 (2002); Terence Thornberry, Alan Lizotte, Marvin Krohn, Margaret Farnworth, and Sung Jang, "Delinquent Peers, Beliefs, and Delinquent Behavior: A Longitudinal Test of Interactional Theory," *Criminology* 32:47–83 (1994).

34. Terence Thornberry and Marvin Krohn, "Applying Interactional Theory to the Explanation of Continuity and Change in Antisocial Behavior," pages 183–209 in David Farrington (ed.), *Integrated Developmental and Life-Course Theories of Offending, Advances in Criminological Theory*, Volume 14 (New Brunswick, NJ: Transaction, 2005).

35. Richard Catalano and J. David Hawkins, "The Social Development Model: A Theory of Antisocial Behavior," pages 149–197 in J. David Hawkins (ed.), *Delinquency and Crime: Current Theories* (New York: Cambridge University Press, 1996); J. David Hawkins and Joseph Weis, "The

Social Development Model: An Integrated Approach to Delinquency Prevention," *Journal of Primary Prevention* 6:73–97 (1985).

36. Charles Fleming, Richard Catalano, Monica Oxford, and Tracy Harachi, "A Test of the Generalizability of the Social Development Model across Gender and Income Groups with Longitudinal Data from the Elementary School Developmental Periods," *Journal of Quantitative Criminology* 18:423–439 (2002).

37. Charles Ayers, James Williams, J. David Hawkins, Peggy Peterson, Richard Catalano, and Robert Abbott, "Assessing Correlates of Onset, Escalation, De-escalation, and Desistance of Delinquent Behavior," *Journal of Quantitative Criminology* 15:277–306 (1999); Stephanie Hartwell, "Juvenile Delinquency and the Social Development Model: The Retrospective Accounts of Homeless Substance Abusers," *Criminal Justice Policy Review* 11:217–233 (2000); Todd Herrenkohl, Bu Huang, Rick Kosterman, J. David Hawkins, Richard Catalano, and Brian Smith, "A Comparison of Social Development Processes Leading to Violent Behavior in Late Adolescence for Childhood Initiators and Adolescent Initiators of Violence," *Journal of Research in Crime and Delinquency* 38:45–63 (2001); Bu Huang, Rick Kosterman, Richard Catalano, J. David Hawkins, and Robert Abbott, "Modeling Mediation in the Etiology of Violent Behavior in Adolescence: A Test of the Social Development Model," *Criminology* 39:75–108 (2001).

38. Ronald Simons, Chyi-In Wu, Rand Conger, and Fred Lorenz, "Two Routes to Delinquency: Differences Between Early and Late Starters in the Impact of Parenting and Deviant Peers," *Criminology* 32:247–276 (1994), p. 269.

39. Ronald Simons, Christine Johnson, Rand Conger, and Glen Elder, "A Test of Latent Trait Versus Life-Course Perspectives on the Stability of Adolescent Antisocial Behavior," *Criminology* 36:901–927 (1998); Mark Warr, "Life-Course Transitions and Desistance from Crime," *Criminology* 36:183–216 (1998); Bradley Wright, Avshalom Caspi, Terrie Moffitt, and Phil Silva, "Low Self-Control, Social Bonds, and Crime: Social Causation, Social Selection, or Both?" *Criminology* 37:479–514 (1999); Marc Ouimet and Marc Le Blanc, "The Role of Life Experiences in the Continuation of the Adult Criminal Career," *Criminal Behavior and Mental Health* 6:73–97 (1996).

40. Ronald Simons, Eric Stewart, Leslie Gordon, Rand Conger, and Glen Elder, "A Test of Life-Course Explanations for Stability and Change in Antisocial Behavior from Adolescence to Young Adulthood," *Criminology* 40:401–434 (2002).

41. Dana Haynie, Peggy Giordano, Wendy Manning, and Monica Longmore, "Adolescent Romantic Relationships and Delinquency Involvement," *Criminology* 43:177–210 (2005).

42. Andrea Leverentz, "The Love of a Good Man? Romantic Relationships as a Source of Support or Hindrance for Female Ex-Offenders," *Journal of Research in Crime and Delinquency* 43:459–488 (2006).

43. David Farrington, *Integrated Developmental and Life-Course Theories of Offending, Advances in Criminological Theory,* Volume 14 (New Brunswick, NJ: Transaction, 2005); Marc Le Blanc and Rolf Loeber, "Developmental Criminology Updated," pages 115–198 in Michael Tonry (ed.), *Crime and Justice: A Review of Research,* Volume 23 (Chicago: University of Chicago Press, 1998).

44. Terrie Moffitt, "A Review of Research on the Taxonomy of Life-Course Persistent Versus Adolescence-Limited Antisocial Behavior," pages 277–312 in Francis Cullen, John Paul Wright, and Kristie Blevins (eds.), *Taking Stock: The Status of Delinquency Theory, Advances in Criminological Theory,* Volume 15 (New Brunswick, NJ: Transaction, 2006), p. 278.

45. Per-Olof Wikstrom and Robert Sampson, "Social Mechanisms of Community Influences on Crime and Pathways in Criminality," pages 118–152 in Benjamin Lahey, Terrie Moffitt, and Avshalom Caspi (eds.), *Causes of Conduct Disorder and Juvenile Delinquency* (New York: Guilford, 2003).

46. Michael Gottfredson, "Offender Classifications and Treatment Effects in Developmental Criminology: A Propensity/Event Consideration," *Annals of the American Academy of Political and Social Science* 602:46–56 (2005).

47. Janet Lauritsen, "Explaining Patterns of Offending Across the Life Course: Comments on Interactional Theory and Recent Tests on the RYDS-RIS Data," *Annals of the American Academy of Political and Social Science* 602:212–228 (2005).

48. Robert Regoli, John Hewitt, and Matt DeLisi, "The Socialization of Violent Criminal Offenders: Notes from the Theory of Differential Oppression," in Matt DeLisi and Peter Conis (eds.), *Violent Offenders: Theory, Research, Public Policy, and Practice* (Sudbury, MA: Jones & Bartlett, 2008).

49. Amy D'Ungar, Kenneth Land, Patricia McCall, and Daniel Nagin, "How Many Latent Classes of Delinquent/Criminal Careers? Results from Mixed Poisson Regression Analyses," *American Journal of Sociology* 103:1593–1630 (1998).

50. Margit Wiesner and Deborah Capaldi, "The Relations of Childhood and Adolescent Factors to Offending Trajectories of Young Men," *Journal of Research in Crime and Delinquency* 40:231–262 (2003).

51. Daniel Nagin and Richard Tremblay, "Developmental Trajectory Groups: Fact or a Useful Statistical Fiction?" *Criminology* 43:873–904 (2005); Robert Sampson and John Laub, "Seductions of Method: Rejoinder to Nagin and Tremblay," *Criminology* 43:905–914 (2005); Daniel Nagin and Richard Tremblay, "From Seduction to Passion: A Response to Sampson and Laub," *Criminology* 43:915–918 (2005).

52. Dawn Bartusch, Donald Lynam, Terrie Moffitt, and Phil Silva, "Is Age Important? Testing a General versus a Developmental Theory of Antisocial Behavior," *Criminology* 35:13–48 (1997); Joanne Klevens, Ofelia Restrepo, Juanita Roca, and Adriana Martinez, "Comparison of Offenders with Early-and Late-Starting Antisocial Behavior in Colombia," *International Journal of Offender Therapy and Comparative Criminology* 44:194–203 (2000);

David Farrington and Rolf Loeber, "Transatlantic Replicability of Risk Factors in the Development of Delinquency," pages 299–329 in Patricia Cohen and Cheryl Slomkowski (eds.), *Historical and Geographical Influences on Psychopathology* (Mahwah, NJ: Lawrence Erlbaum Associates Publishers, 1999); Joan McCord, "Developmental Trajectories and Intentional Actions," *Journal of Quantitative Criminology* 16:237–253 (2000); Arjan Blokland, Daniel Nagin, and Paul Nieuwbeerta, "Life Span Offending Trajectories of a Dutch Conviction Cohort," *Criminology* 43:919–954 (2005).

53. Terrie Moffitt, Avshalom Capsi, Michael Rutter, and Phil Silva, *Sex Differences in Antisocial Behavior* (London: Cambridge University Press, 2001).

54. David Farrington, "Building Developmental and Life-Course Theories of Offending," pages 335–366 in Francis Cullen, John Paul Wright, and Kristie Blevins (eds.), *Taking Stock: The Status of Delinquency Theory, Advances in Criminological Theory,* Volume 15 (New Brunswick, NJ: Transaction, 2006).

55. For a review of family interventions, see Gail Wasserman and Angela Seracini, "Family Risk Factors and Interventions," pages 165–190 in Rolf Loeber and David Farrington (eds.), *Child Delinquents: Development, Intervention, and Service Needs* (Thousand Oaks, CA: Sage, 2001).

56. For a review of peer interventions, see John Coie and Shari Miller-Johnson, "Peer Factors and Interventions," pages 191–210 in Rolf Loeber and David Farrington, note 55.

57. For a review of school interventions, see Todd Herrenkohl, J. David Hawkins, Ick-Joong Chung, Karl Hill, and Sara Battin-Pearson, "School and Community Risk Factors and Interventions," pages 211–246 in Rolf Loeber and David Farrington, note 55.

58. Victor Battistich, Eric Schaps, Marilyn Watson, and Daniel Solomon, "Prevention Effects of the Child Development Project: Early Findings from an Ongoing Multisite Demonstration Trial," *Journal of Adolescent Research* 11:12–35 (1996).

CHAPTER 9

1. Allison Morris, Women, *Crime and Criminal Justice* (Oxford: Basil Blackwell, 1987), p. 1.

2. Joanne Belknap, *The Invisible Woman: Gender, Crime, and Justice,* 3rd edition (Belmont, CA: Thomson/Wadsworth, 2007), p. 6.

3. Dana Hubbard and Travis Pratt, "A Meta-Analysis of the Predictors of Delinquency among Girls," *Journal of Offender Rehabilitation* 34:1–13 (2002).

4. Charlotte Bronte, *Jane Eyre* (New York: Norton, 1971), p. 96.

5. Jean Stafford, *The Mountain Lion* (New York: Harcourt, Brace & World, 1947), p. 30.

6. Jean Bottcher, "Gender as Social Control," *Justice Quarterly* 12:33–58 (1995); Jean Bottcher, "Social Practices of Gender: How Gender Relates to Delinquency in the Everyday Lives of High-Risk Youth," *Criminology* 39:893–931 (2001).

7. Jeffrey Rubin, Frank Provenzano, and Zella Luria, "The Eye of the Beholder: Parents' Views of Sex of Newborns," *American Journal of Orthopsychiatry* 44:512–519 (1974).

8. Marie Richmond-Abbot, *Masculine & Feminine: Gender Roles over the Life Cycle,* 2nd edition (New York: McGraw-Hill, 1992), p. 69.

9. Beverly Fagot, "The Child's Expectations of Differences in Adult Male and Female Interactions," *Sex Roles* 11:593–600 (1984); Bernice Lott, *Women's Lives: Themes and Variations in Gender Learning,* 2nd edition (Pacific Grove, CA: Brooks-Cole, 1993).

10. Mary DeGenova and F. Philip Rice, *Intimate Relationships, Marriages, and Families,* 6th edition (New York: McGraw-Hill, 2004), p. 58.

11. Doreen Kimura, "Sex Differences in the Brain," *Scientific American* Presents, Special Issue: "Men: The Scientific Truth about Their Work, Play, Health, and Passions" 10:26–31, Summer Quarterly (1999).

12. Myra Sadker and David Sadker, *Failing at Fairness: How America's Schools Cheat Girls* (New York: Scribners, 1994).

13. Peggy Orenstein, *School Girls Young Women, Self-Esteem, and the Confidence Gap* (New York: Doubleday, 1994).

14. Jeanne Block, *Sex Role Identity and Ego Development* (San Francisco: Jossey-Bass, 1984); Pamela Richards and Charles Tittle, "Gender and Perceived Chances of Arrest," *Social Forces* 51:1182–1199 (1981).

15. Merry Morash, "Gender, Peer Group Experiences, and Seriousness of Delinquency," *Journal of Research in Crime and Delinquency* 23:43–67 (1986).

16. Robert Bursik, Don Merten, and Gary Schwartz, "Appropriate Age-Related Behavior for Male and Female Adolescents: Adult Perceptions," *Youth & Society* 17:115–130 (1985).

17. Stephen Gavazzi, Courtney Yarcheck, and Meda Chesney-Lind, "Global Risk Indicators and the Role of Gender in a Juvenile Detention Sample," *Criminal Justice and Behavior* 33:597–612 (2006).

18. Teresa LaGrange and Robert Silverman, "Low Self-Control and Opportunity: Testing the General Theory of Crime as an Explanation for Gender Differences in Delinquency," *Criminology* 37:41–72 (1999).

19. Carol Gilligan, *In a Different Voice: Psychological Theory and Women's Development* (Cambridge, MA: Harvard University Press, 1983).

20. Carol Gilligan, Nona Lyons, and Trudy Hanmer, *Making Connections: The Relational Worlds in Adolescent Girls at Emma Willard School* (Cambridge, MA: Harvard University Press, 1990), p. 40.

21. Kimberly Kempf-Leonard, Meda Chesney-Lind, and Darnell Hawkins, "Ethnicity and Gender Issues," pages 247–272 in Rolf Loeber and David Farrington (eds.), *Child Delinquents: Development, Intervention, and Service Needs* (Thousand Oaks, CA: Sage, 2001).

22. Lisa Broidy, Elizabeth Cauffman, Dorothy Espelage, Paul Mazerolle, and Alex Piquero, "Sex Differences in Empathy and Its Relation to Juvenile Offending," *Violence and Victims* 18:503–516 (2003).

23. Nancy Chodorow, *The Reproduction of Mothering* (Berkeley: University of California Press, 1978).

24. Erik Erikson, *Identity, Youth and Crisis* (New York: Norton, 1968), p. 283.

25. Sue Lees, "Learning to Love: Sexual Reputation, Morality and the Social Control of Girls," pages 19–26 in Maureen Cain (ed.), *Growing Up Good: Policing the Behavior of Girls in Europe* (Newbury Park, CA: Sage, 1989) p. 19.

26. Lees, note 25, pp. 24–25.

27. Meda Chesney-Lind and Randall Shelden, *Girls, Delinquency, and Juvenile Justice,* 3rd edition (Belmont, CA: Wadsworth, 2004), p. 135.

28. Belknap, note 2, p. 68.

29. Marguerite Warren and Jill Rosenbaum, "Criminal Careers of Female Offenders," *Criminal Justice and Behavior* 13:393–418 (1986).

30. Sheila Maxwell and Christopher Maxwell, "Examining the 'Criminal Careers' of Prostitutes within the Nexus of Drug Use, Drug Selling, and Other Illicit Activities," *Criminology* 38:787–810 (2000); Irene Sommers, Deborah Baskin, and Jeff Fagan, "Getting Out of the Life: Crime Desistance by Female Street Offenders," *Deviant Behavior* 15:125–149 (1994); Jody Miller and Rod Brunson, "Gender Dynamics in Youth Gangs: A Comparison of Males' and Females' Accounts," *Justice Quarterly* 17:419–448 (2000); Christopher Uggen and Candice Kruttschnitt, "Crime in the Breaking: Gender Differences in Desistance," *Law and Society Review* 32:339–366 (1998).

31. Robert Regoli and John Hewitt, *Delinquency in Society*, 6th edition (New York: McGraw-Hill, 2006); David Finkelhor, Theodore Cross, and Elise Cantor, *How the Justice System Responds to Juvenile Victims: A Comprehensive Model* (Washington, DC: Office of Juvenile Justice and Delinquency Prevention, 2005); Christopher Sullivan, "Early Adolescent Delinquency: Assessing the Role of Childhood Problems, Family Environment, and Peer Pressure," *Youth Violence and Juvenile Justice* 4:291–313 (2006); Matthew Durose, Caroline Wolf Harlow, Patrick Langan, Mark Motivans, Ramona Rantala, and Erica Smith, *Family Violence Statistics* (Washington, DC: U.S. Department of Justice, 2005).

32. Ronald Mullis, Thomas Cornille, Ann Mullis, and Jessica Huber, "Female Juvenile Offending: A Review of Characteristics and Contexts," *Journal of Child and Family Studies* 13:205–218 (2004).

33. Matt DeLisi, "Not Just a Boy's Club: An Empirical Assessment of Female Career Criminals," *Women & Criminal Justice* 13:27–45 (2002).

34. Amie Schuck and Cathy Spatz Widom, "Childhood Victimization and Alcohol Symptoms in Females," *Child Abuse and Neglect* 25:1069–1092; Cathy Spatz Widom, "The Cycle of Violence," *Science* 244:160–166 (1989); Cathy Spatz Widom, "Childhood Victimization: Early Adversity, Later Psychopathology," *National Institute of Justice Journal* 1:2–9 (2000).

35. Abigail Fagan, "The Gender Cycle of Violence," *Violence and Victims* 16:457–474 (2001); Abigail Fagan, "The Relationship between Adolescent Physical Abuse and Criminal Offending: Support for an Enduring and Generalized Cycle of Violence," *Journal of Family Violence* 20:279–290 (2005).

36. Cesare Lombroso and William Ferrero, *The Female Offender* (New York: Appleton, 1899), pp. 150–152.

37. W.I. Thomas, *The Unadjusted Girl* (New York: Harper & Row, 1923), p. 109.

38. Otto Pollak, *The Criminality of Women* (New York: Barnes and Company, 1950), p. 10.

39. John Cowie, Valerie Cowie, and Eliot Slater, *Delinquency in Girls* (London: Heinemann, 1968), p. 45.

40. Clyde Vedder and Dora Somerville, *The Delinquent Girl,* 2nd edition (Springfield, IL: Charles C. Thomas, 1975).

41. James Dabbs, Robert Frady, Timothy Carr, and Norma Besch, "Saliva Testosterone and Criminal Violence in Young Prison Inmates," *Psychosomatic Medicine* 49:174–182 (1987); James Dabbs, Barry Ruback, Robert Frady, Charles Hooper, and David Sgoutas, "Saliva Testosterone and Criminal Violence among Women," *Personality and Individual Differences* 9:269–275 (1988).

42. See Desmond Ellis and Penelope Austin, "Menstruation and Aggressive Behavior in a Correctional Center for Women," *Journal of Criminal Law, Criminology, and Police Science* 62:388–395 (1971); E. A. Hardie, "Prevalence and Predictors of Cyclic and Noncyclic Affective Change," *Psychology of Women Quarterly* 21:299–314 (1997).

43. Dana Haynie, "Contexts of Risk? Explaining the Link Between Girls' Pubertal Development and Their Delinquency Involvement," *Social Forces* 82:355–397 (2003).

44. Terrie Moffitt, Avshalom Caspi, Michael Rutter, and Phil Silva, *Sex Differences in Antisocial Behavior: Conduct Disorder, Delinquency, and Violence in the Dunedin Longitudinal Study* (New York: Cambridge University Press, 2001), p. 223.

45. Lee Ellis, "A Theory Explaining Biological Correlates of Criminality," *European Journal of Criminology* 2:287–315 (2005).

46. Bruce DiCristina, "Durkheim's Latent Theory of Gender and Homicide," *British Journal of Criminology* 46:212–233 (2006).

47. Frederic Thrasher, *The Gang* (Chicago: University of Chicago Press, 1927), p. 228.

48. Clifford Shaw and Henry McKay, *Social Factors in Juvenile Delinquency* (Chicago: University of Chicago Press, 1931); Clifford Shaw and Henry McKay, *Juvenile Delinquency in Urban Areas* (Chicago: University of Chicago Press, 1942).

49. Barbara Warner, "The Role of Attenuated Culture in Social Disorganization Theory," *Criminology* 41:73–98 (2003).

50. Walter DeKeseredy, Martin Schwartz, Shahid Alvi, and Andreas Tomaszewski, "Perceived Collective Efficacy and Women's Victimization in Public Housing," *Criminal Justice* 3:5–27 (2003).

51. Robert Merton, "Social Structure and Anomie," *American Sociological Review* 3:672–682 (1938).

52. Ruth Morris, "Female Delinquencies and Relational Problems," *Social Problems* 43:82–88 (1964).

53. Ozden Ozbay and Yusuf Ziya Ozcan, "Classic Strain Theory and Gender: The Case of Turkey," *International Journal of Offender Therapy and Comparative Criminology* 50:21–38 (2006).

54. Lisa Broidy and Robert Agnew, "Gender and Crime: A General Strain Theory Perspective," *Journal of Research in Crime and Delinquency* 34:275–306 (1997); Robert Agnew, Timothy Brezina, John Paul Wright, and Francis Cullen, "Strain, Personality Traits, and Delinquency: Extending General Strain Theory," *Criminology* 40:43–71 (2002).

55. Nicole Piquero and Miriam Sealock, "Gender and General Strain Theory: A Preliminary Test of Broidy and Agnew's Gender/GST Hypotheses," *Justice Quarterly* 21:125–158 (2004), p. 145.

56. Walter Miller, "Lower-Class Culture as a Generating Milieu of Gang Delinquency," *Journal of Social Issues* 14:5–19 (1958).

57. Eileen Leonard, *Women, Crime, & Society* (New York: Longmans, 1982), p. 134.

58. Albert Cohen, *Delinquent Boys: The Subculture of the Gang* (New York: The Free Press, 1955), pp. 137–147.

59. Ngaire Naffine, *Female Crime: The Construction of Women in Criminology* (Sydney, Australia: Allen and Unwin, 1987), pp. 11–12.

60. Richard Cloward and Lloyd Ohlin, *Delinquency and Opportunity* (New York: The Free Press, 1960), p. 49.

61. Edwin Sutherland, "Prevention of Juvenile Delinquency," pages 131–140 in Albert Cohen, Alfred Lindesmith, and Karl Schuessler (eds.), *The Sutherland Papers* (Bloomington: Indiana University Press, 1956).

62. See for example, Jeanette Covington, "Self-Esteem and Deviance: The Effects of Race and Gender," *Criminology* 24:105–138 (1986); Karen Heimer, "Gender, Interaction, and Delinquency: Testing a Theory of Differential Social Control," *Social Psychology Quarterly* 59:39–61 (1997); Daniel Mears, Matthew Ploeger, and Mark Warr, "Explaining the Gender Gap in Delinquency: Peer Influence and Moral Evaluations of Behavior," *Journal of Research in Crime and Delinquency* 35:251–266 (1998); Robert Crosnoe, Kristan Erickson, and Sanford Dornbusch, "Protective Functions of Family Relationships and School Factors on the Deviant Behavior of Adolescent Boys and Girls: Reducing the Impact of Risky Friendships," *Youth & Society* 33:515–544 (2002).

63. Kristan Erickson, Robert Crosnoe, and Sanford Dornbusch, "A Social Process Model of Adolescent Deviance: Combining Social Control and Differential Association Perspectives," *Journal of Youth and Adolescence* 29:395–425 (2000).

64. Karen Heimer and Stacy De Coster, "The Gendering of Violent Delinquency," *Criminology* 37:277–312 (1999).

65. Xiaoru Liu and Howard Kaplan, "Explaining the Gender Difference in Adolescent Delinquent Behavior: A Longitudinal Test of Mediating Mechanisms," *Criminology* 37:195–215 (1999).

66. Lonn Lanza-Kaduce, Michael Capece, and Helena Alden, "Liquor is Quicker: Gender and Social Learning among College Students," *Criminal Justice Policy Review* 17:127–143 (2006).

67. Coramae Richey Mann, *Female Crime and Delinquency* (Montgomery: University of Alabama Press, 1984), p. 263.

68. Rachelle Canter, "Family Correlates of Male and Female Delinquency," *Criminology* 20:149–166 (1982).

69. See Delbert Elliott, David Huizinga, and Scott Menard, *Multiple Problem Youth: Delinquency, Substance Use, and Mental Health Problems* (New York: Springer-Verlag, 1989); Julie Wall, Thomas Power, and Consuelo Arbona, "Susceptibility to Antisocial Peer Pressure and its Relation to Acculturation in Mexican-American Adolescents," *Journal of Adolescent Research* 8:403–448 (1993); Mark Warr, *Companions in Crime: The Social Aspects of Criminal Conduct* (New York: Cambridge University Press, 2002).

70. Constance Chapple, Kurt Johnson, and Les Whitbeck, "Gender and Arrest among Homeless and Runaway Youth: An Analysis of Background, Family, and Situational Factors," *Youth Violence and Juvenile Justice* 2:129–147 (2004).

71. Bobbi Jo Anderson, Malcolm Holmes, and Erik Ostresh, "Male and Female Delinquents' Attachments and Effects of Attachments on Severity of Self-Reported Delinquency," *Criminal Justice and Behavior* 26:435–452 (1999); Angela Huebner and Sherry Betts, "Exploring the Utility of Social Control Theory for Youth Development: Issues of Attachment, Involvement, and Gender," *Youth & Society* 34:123–145 (2002).

72. Michael Gottfredson and Travis Hirschi, *A General Theory of Crime* (Stanford, CA: Stanford University Press, 1990), pp. 148–149.

73. Bradley Wright, Avshalom Caspi, Terrie Moffitt, and Phil Silva, "Low Self-Control, Social Bonds, and Crime: Social Causation, Social Selection, or Both?" *Criminology* 37:479–514 (1999).

74. Heimer and De Coster, note 64.

75. George Higgins and Richard Tewksbury, "Sex and Self-Control Theory: The Measures and Causal Model May Be Different," *Youth & Society* 37:479–503 (2006).

76. Teresa LaGrange and Robert Silverman, "Low Self-Control and Opportunity: Testing the General Theory of Crime as an Explanation for Gender Differences in Delinquency," *Criminology* 37:41–72 (1999).

77. Brenda Sims Blackwell and Alex Piquero, "The Relationships between Gender, Power Control, Self-Control, and Crime," *Journal of Criminal Justice* 33:1–27 (2005).

78. Charles Tittle, David Ward, and Harold Grasmick, "Gender, Age, and Crime/Deviance: A Challenge to Self-Control Theory," *Journal of Research in Crime and Delinquency* 40:426–453 (2003).

79. Eric Stewart, Kirk Elifson, and Claire Sterk, "Integrating the General Theory of Crime into an Explanation of Violent Victimization Among Female Offenders," *Justice Quarterly* 21:159–181 (2004).

80. Edwin Schur, *Labeling Women Deviant: Gender, Stigma, and Social Control* (New York: Random House, 1984), pp. 8–12.

81. Brenda Geiger and Michael Fischer, "Naming Oneself Criminal: Gender Differences in Offenders' Identity Negotiation," *International Journal of Offender Therapy and Comparative Criminology* 49:194–209 (2005).

82. George Vold, Thomas Bernard, and Jeffrey Snipes, *Theoretical Criminology*, 4th edition (New York: Oxford University Press, 1998), p. 278.

83. James Messerschmidt, *Capitalism, Patriarchy, and Crime: Toward a Socialist Feminist Criminology* (Totowa, NJ: Rowman & Littlefield, 1986).

84. Ronald Akers and Christine Sellers, *Criminological Theories,* 4th edition (Los Angeles: Roxbury, 2004), pp. 261–262.

85. Darrell Steffensmeier, Emilie Allan, and Cathy Streifel, "Development and Female Crime: A Cross-National Test of Alternative Explanations," *Social Forces* 68:262–283 (1989).

86. John Hagan, A.R. Gillis, and John Simpson, "The Class Structure of Gender and Delinquency: Toward a Power-Control Theory of Common Delinquent Behavior," *American Journal of Sociology* 90:1151–1178 (1985); John Hagan, A.R. Gillis, and John Simpson, "Clarifying and Extending a Power-Control Theory of Gender and Delinquency," *American Journal of Sociology* 95:1024–1037 (1990); Bill McCarthy, John Hagan, and Todd Woodward, "In the Company of Women: Structure and Agency in a Revised Power-Control Theory of Gender and Delinquency," *Criminology* 37:761–788 (1999).

87. Chesney-Lind and Shelden, note 27, p. 153.

88. Roy Austin, "Women's Liberation and Increases in Minor, Major, and Occupational Offenses," *Criminology* 20:407–430 (1982).

89. John Hagan, Bill McCarthy, and Holly Foster, "A Gendered Theory of Delinquency and Despair in the Life Course," *Acta Sociologica* 45:37–46 (2002), p. 44; John Hagan and Holly Foster, "S/He's a Rebel: Toward a Sequential Stress Theory of Delinquency and Gendered Pathways to Disadvantage in Emerging Adulthood," *Social Forces* 82:53–86 (2003).

90. Simon Singer and Murray Levine, "Power-Control Theory, Gender, and Delinquency: A Partial Replication with Additional Evidence on the Effects of Peers," *Criminology* 26:627–647 (1988).

91. Merry Morash and Meda Chesney-Lind, "A Reformulation and Partial Test of the Power Control Theory of Delinquency," *Justice Quarterly* 8:347–377 (1991).

92. Michael Leiber and Mary Ellen Wacker, "A Theoretical and Empirical Assessment of Power Control Theory and Single-Mother Families," *Youth & Society* 28:317–350 (1997).

93. Christopher Uggen, "Class, Gender, and Arrest: An Intergenerational Analysis of Workplace Power and Control," *Criminology* 38:835–862 (2000).

94. Kristin Mack and Michael Leiber, "Race, Gender, Single-Mother Households, and Delinquency: A Further Test of Power-Control Theory," *Youth & Society* 37:115–144 (2005).

95. Mears et al., note 62, p. 263.

96. Meda Chesney-Lind, "Girls' Crime and Woman's Place: Toward a Feminist Model of Female Delinquency," *Crime & Delinquency* 35:5–29 (1989).

97. Meda Chesney-Lind and Lisa Pasko, *The Female Offender: Girls, Women, and Crime,* 2nd edition (Thousand Oaks, CA: Sage, 2004).

98. Beverly Kingston, Bob Regoli, and John Hewitt, "The Theory of Differential Oppression: A Developmental–Ecological Explanation of Adolescent Problem Behavior," *Critical Criminology* 11:237–260 (2003).

99. John Hewitt and Bob Regoli, "Differential Oppression Theory and Female Delinquency," *Free Inquiry in Creative Sociology* 31:165–174 (2003).

100. Joseph Rogers and M. D. Buffalo, "Fighting Back: Nine Modes of Adaptation to a Deviant Label," *Social Problems* 22:101–118 (1974).

101. Mark Fleisher, *Dead End Kids* (Madison: University of Wisconsin Press, 1998).

102. Danice Eaton, Laura Kann, Steven Kinchen, James Ross, Joseph Hawkins, William Harris, Richard Lowry, Tim McManus, David Chyen, Shari Shanklin, Connie Lim, Jo Anne Grunbaum, and Howell Wechsler, *Youth Risk Behavior Surveillance—United States, 2005* (Atlanta: Centers for Disease Control and Prevention, 2006).

103. Meda Chesney-Lind, "What about the Girls? Delinquency Programming as if Gender Mattered," *Corrections Today,* February (2001), p. 44.

CHAPTER 10

1. Douglas Morrison, *Juvenile Offenders* (New York: Appleton and Co., 1915), p. 121.

2. Frederick Elkin and Gerald Handel, *The Child and Society: The Process of Socialization*, 4th edition (New York: Random House, 1984); Mary DeGenova and F. Philip Rice, *Intimate Relationships, Marriages, and Families*, 6th edition (New York: McGraw-Hill, 2004), pp. 325–333.

3. Craig Calhoun, Donald Light, and Suzanne Keller, *Sociology*, 7th edition (New York: McGraw-Hill, 1997), pp. 132–133.

4. Michael Gottfredson and Travis Hirschi, *A General Theory of Crime* (Stanford, CA: Stanford University Press, 1990), p. 97.

5. Laura Argys, Danile Rees, Susan Averett, and Benjama Witoonchart, "Birth Order and Risky Adolescent Behavior," *Economic Inquiry* 44:215–233 (2006).

6. William Bennett, *The Book of Virtues* (New York: Simon & Schuster, 1993), p. 11.

7. Jennifer Wyatt and Gustavo Carlo, "What Will My Parents Think? Relations among Adolescents' Expected Parental Reactions, Prosocial Moral Reasoning, and Prosocial and Antisocial Behaviors," *Journal of Adolescent Research* 17:646–666 (2002).

8. James Q. Wilson, *On Character* (Washington, DC: AEI Press, 1991), pp. 30, 108.

9. Robert Coles, *The Moral Intelligence of Children* (New York: Random House, 1997), p. 17.

10. The Children's Defense Fund, "Every Child Deserves a Moral Start" (Washington, DC: CDF Reports, 2006).

11. Bruce Chadwick and Brent Top, "Religiosity and Delinquency among LDS Adolescents," *Journal for the Scientific Study of Religion* 32:52 (1993).

12. Colin Baier and Bradley Wright, "'If You Love Me, Keep My Commandments': A Meta-Analysis of the Effect of Religion on Crime," *Journal of Research in Crime and Delinquency* 38:3–21 (2001), p. 14.

13. Byron Johnson, David Larson, Spencer Li, and Sung Jang, "Escaping from the Crime of Inner Cities: Church Attendance and Religious Salience among Disadvantaged Youth," *Justice Quarterly* 17:377–391 (2000).

14. Brent Benda and Robert Corwyn, "Are the Effects of Religion on Crime Mediated, Moderated, and Misrepresented by Inappropriate Measures?" *Journal of Social Service Research* 27:70–81 (2001), p. 80.

15. Travis Hirschi and Rodney Stark, "Hellfire and Delinquency," *Social Problems* 17:202–213 (1969).

16. Rodney Stark and William Bainbridge, *Religion, Deviance, and Social Control* (New York: Routledge, 1997), p. 69.

17. See Mark Harris, "Religiosity and Perceived Future Ascetic Deviance and Delinquency among Mormon Adolescents: Testing the 'This-Worldly' Supernatural Sanctions Thesis," *Sociological Inquiry* 73:28–51 (2003); Byron Johnson, Sung Jang, David Larson, and Spencer Li, "Does Adolescent Religious Commitment Matter? A Reexamination of the effects of Religiosity on Delinquency," *Journal of Research in Crime and Delinquency*, 38:22–43 (2001); Brent Benda, "An Examination of a Reciprocal Relationship Between Religiosity and Different Forms of Delinquency Within a Theoretical Model," *Journal of Research in Crime and Delinquency* 34:163–186 (1997); John Cochran, Peter Wood, and Bruce Arneklev, "Is the Religiosity-Delinquency Relationship Spurious? A Test of Arousal and Social Control Theories," *Journal of Research in Crime and Delinquency* 31:92–123 (1994); Paul Higgins and Gary Albrecht, "Hellfire and Delinquency Revisited," *Social Forces* 55:952–958 (1977).

18. Stark and Bainbridge, note 16, p. 7.

19. J. Ross Eshleman and Richard Bulcroft, *The Family*, 11th edition (Boston: Allyn and Bacon, 2005).

20. Travis Hirschi, "The Family," pages 128–129 in James Q. Wilson and Joan Petersilia (eds.), *Crime* (San Francisco: ICS Press, 1995).

21. Steven Levitt and Stephen Dubner, *Freakonomics: A Rogue Economist Explores the Hidden Side of Everything*, revised edition (New York: William Morrow, 2006); Stephen Dubner and Steven Levitt, "Do Parents Matter?" *USA TODAY*, May 4, 2005:13A.

22. U.S. Census Bureau, "Families and Living Arrangements, 2005" *Current Population Reports* (Washington, DC: U.S. Bureau of the Census, 2006).

23. Maxim Kniazkov, "For First Time, Unmarried Households Reign in U.S.," *USA TODAY*, October 15, 2006:1A.

24. Associated Press, "Nearly 4 in 10 U.S. Babies Born Out of Wedlock," online at: http://www.msnbc.msn.com/id/15835429/, accessed May 1, 2007.

25. James Q. Wilson, *The Moral Sense* (New York: Free Press, 1993), p. 176.

26. Jennifer Schwartz, "Family Structure as a Source of Female and Male Homicide in the United States," *Homicide Studies* 10:253–278 (2006).

27. Sharon Jayson, "Society Switches Focus Away From Children," *USA TODAY*, July 12, 2006:1D.

28. Suzanne Bianchi, John Robinson, and Melissa Milkie, *Changing Rhythms of American Family Life* (New York: Russell Sage Foundation, 2006).

29. Sharon Jayson, "Study: Family Ties 'As Strong As Ever' Technology Keeps People in Touch," *USA TODAY*, February 22, 2006:10B.

30. Sharon Jayson, "American Families are Envied, Disdained," *USA TODAY*, April 13, 2006:6D.

31. Linda Gordon and Sara McLanahan, "Single Parenthood in 1900," *Journal of Family History* 16:97, 100–101 (1991).

32. David Blankenhorn, *Fatherless America: Confronting Our Most Urgent Social Problem* (New York: Basic Books, 1995), pp. 23, 239.

33. Stephanie Ventura and Christine Bachrach, *Nonmarital Childbearing in the United States, 1940–99* (Washington, DC: U.S. Department of Health and Human Services, 2000); James Q. Wilson, *The Marriage Problem: How Our Culture Has Weakened Families* (New York: HarperCollins, 2003).

34. Annie Casey Foundation, *2004 Kids Count Data Book* (Baltimore: Annie Casey Foundation, 2006).

35. Sara Jaffee, Avshalom Caspi, Terrie Moffitt, Jay Belsky, and Phil Silva, "Why Are Children Born to Teen Mothers at Risk for Adverse Outcomes in Young Adulthood? Results from a 20-year Longitudinal Study," *Development and Psychopathology* 13:377–397 (2001).

36. Wilhelmina Leigh, *National Costs of Teen Pregnancy and Teen Pregnancy Prevention* (Washington, DC: The Joint Center for Political and Economic Studies, 2003).

37. Hirschi, note 20, p. 138.

38. Terence Thornberry, Evelyn Wei, Magda Stouthamer-Loeber, and Joyce Van Dyke, *Teenage Fatherhood and Delinquent Behavior* (Washington, DC: Office of Juvenile Justice and Delinquency Prevention, 2000).

39. Thornberry et al., note 38, pp. 5–7.

40. Evelyn Wei, Rolf Loeber, and Magda Stouthamer-Loeber, "How Many of the Offspring Born to Teenage Fathers Are Produced by Repeat Serious Offenders?" *Criminal Behavior and Mental Health* 12:83–98 (2002).

41. Maxine Seaborn Thompson and Margaret Ensminger, "Psychological Well-Being among Mothers with School Age Children," *Social Forces* 67:715–730 (1989); Alison Clarke-Stewart, Deborah Vandell, and Kathleen McCartney, "Effects of Parental Separation and Divorce on Very Young Children," *Journal of Family Psychology* 14:304–326 (2000).

42. Jeffrey Grogger, "Incarceration-Related Costs of Early Childbearing," in Rebecca Maynard (ed.), *Kids Having Kids: Economic Costs and Social Consequences of Teen Pregnancy* (Washington, DC: The Urban Institute Press, 1997), p. 253.

43. Ronald Simons, Leslie Simons, and Lora Wallace, *Families, Delinquency and Crime: Linking Society's Most*

Basic Institution to Antisocial Behavior (Los Angeles: Roxbury, 2004), p. 108.

44. Lisa Borrine, Paul Handa, and Nancy Brown, "Family Conflict and Adolescent Adjustment in Intact, Divorced, and Blended Families," *Journal of Consulting and Clinical Psychology* 59:753–755 (1991); Joan Kelly, "Children's Adjustment in Conflicted Marriage and Divorce: A Decade Review of Research," *Journal of the American Academy of Child and Adolescent Psychiatry* 39:963–973 (2000).

45. Frances Rice, Gordon Harold, Katherine Shelton, and Anita Thapar, "Family Conflict Interacts with Genetic Liability in Predicting Childhood and Adolescent Depression," *Journal of the American Academy of Child & Adolescent Psychiatry* 45:841–848 (2006).

46. Matthew Bramlett and William Mosher, *Cohabitation, Marriage, Divorce, and Remarriage in the United States* (Washington, DC: Department of Health and Human Services, 2002); Susan Stewart, *Brave New Stepfamilies: Diverse Steps toward Stepfamily Living* (Thousand Oaks, CA: Sage, 2007).

47. Frank Furstenberg and Andrew Cherlin, *Divided Families: What Happens to Children When Parents Part* (Cambridge, MA: Harvard University Press, 1991); Andrew Cherlin, *Marriage, Divorce, Remarriage* (Cambridge, MA: Harvard University Press, 1992).

48. See George Thomas, Michael Farrell, and Grace Barnes, "The Effects of Single-Mother Families and Nonresident Fathers on Delinquency and Substance Abuse in Black and White Adolescents," *Journal of Marriage and the Family* 58:884–894 (1996); Stephen Demuth and Susan Brown, "Family Structure, Family Processes, and Adolescent Delinquency: The Significance of Parental Absence Versus Parental Gender," *Journal of Research in Crime and Delinquency* 41:58–81 (2004); Jeffrey Cookston, "Parental Supervision and Family Structure: Effects on Adolescent Problem Behaviors," *Journal of Divorce and Remarriage* 32:107–122 (1999); Heather Juby and David Farrington, "Disentangling the Link Between Disrupted Families and Delinquency," *British Journal of Criminology* 41:22–40 (2001).

49. Ann Goetting, "Patterns of Homicide among Children," *Criminal Justice and Behavior* 16:63–80 (1989).

50. Edward Wells and Joseph Rankin, "Families and Delinquency: A Meta-Analysis of the Impact of Broken Homes," *Social Problems* 38:71–93 (1991).

51. Michelle Miller, Finn-Aage Esbensen, and Adrienne Freng, "Parental Attachment, Parental Supervision and Adolescent Deviance in Intact and Non-Intact Families," *Journal of Crime & Justice* 22:1–29 (1999).

52. William Comandor and Llad Phillips, "The Impact of Income and Family Structure on Delinquency," *Journal of Applied Economics* 5:220–230 (2002), p. 228.

53. Laurence Steinberg, "Single Parents, Stepparents, and the Susceptibility of Adolescents to Antisocial Peer Pressure," *Child Development* 58:269–275 (1987); Sadi Bayrakal and Teresa Kope, "Dysfunction in the Single-Parent and Only-Child Family," *Adolescence* 25:1–7

(1990); Jeffrey Cookston, "Parental Supervision and Family Structure: Effects on Adolescent Problem Behaviors," *Journal of Divorce & Remarriage* 32:107–122 (1999); Mallie Paschall, Christopher Ringwalt, and Robert Flewelling, "Effects of Parenting, Father Absence, and Affiliation with Delinquent Peers on Delinquent Behavior Among African-American Male Adolescents," *Adolescence* 38:15–34 (2003); Christopher Kierkus and Douglas Baer, "A Social Control Explanation of the Relationship between Family Structure and Delinquent Behavior," *Canadian Journal of Criminology* 44:450 (2002).

54. Simons et al., note 43, p. 106.

55. Mavis Hetherington, *Review of Child Development Research* (New York: Russell Sage Foundation, 1977); Mavis Hetherington and Ross Parke, *Contemporary Readings in Social Psychology* (New York: McGraw-Hill, 1981); Mavis Hetherington and Ross Parke, *Child Psychology* (New York: McGraw-Hill, 1979).

56. Nicholas Davidson, "Life without Father," *Policy Review* 51:40–44 (1990); Dinesh D'Souza, *The End of Racism* (New York: The Free Press, 1996); John McWhorter, *Authentically Black: Essays for the Black Silent Majority* (New York: Gotham Books, 2003).

57. Judith Wallerstein and Joan Berlin Kelly, *Surviving the Breakup* (New York: Basic Books, 1980).

58. Judith Wallerstein and Sandra Blakeslee, *Second Chances* (New York: Ticknor and Fields, 1989).

59. Constance Ahrons, *The Good Divorce* (New York: Harper, 1995).

60. Madlen Read, "Do-It-Yourself Divorces Get Easier With Online Service," *Boulder Daily Camera*, March 12, 2006:3F.

61. Elizabeth Marquardt, cited in Karen Peterson, "Children of Divorce Straddle a Divided World," *USA TODAY*, July 14, 2003:6D.

62. Simons et al., note 43, p. 114.

63. Cesar Rebellon, "Reconsidering the Broken Homes/Delinquency Relationship and Exploring its Mediating Mechanism(s)," *Criminology* 40:103–136 (2002).

64. U.S. Bureau of Census, *Statistical Abstract of the United States: 2006* (Washington, DC: U.S. Census Bureau, 2007).

65. Russell Hill and Frank Stafford, "Parental Care of Children," *Journal of Human Resources* 15:219–239 (1979).

66. Keith Melville, *Marriage and the Family Today*, 4th edition (New York: Random House, 1988), p. 352.

67. Matthijs Kalmijn, "Mother's Occupational Status and Children's Schooling," *American Sociological Review* 59:257–275 (1994).

68. Jay Belsky, "Parental and Nonparental Child Care and Children's Socioemotional Development: A Decade in Review," *Journal of Marriage and the Family* 52:885–903 (1990); Jay Belsky and David Eggebeen, "Early and Extensive Maternal Employment and Young Children's Socioemotional Development: Children of the National Longitudinal Survey of Youth," *Journal of Marriage and the Family* 53:1083–1110 (1991).

69. Travis Hirschi, *Causes of Delinquency* (Berkeley: University of California Press, 1969).

70. David Popenoe, *Life without Father: Compelling Evidence that Fatherhood and Marriage are Indispensable for the Good of Children and Society* (New York: The Free Press, 1996), p. 6.

71. April Brayfield, "Juggling Jobs and Kids: The Impact of Employment Schedules on Fathers' Caring for Children," *Journal of Marriage and the Family* 57:321–332 (1995).

72. Sharon Vandivere, Kathryn Tout, Jeffrey Capizzano, and Martha Zaslow, *Left Unsupervised: A Look at the Most Vulnerable Children* (Washington, DC: Child Trends Research Brief, 2003).

73. Laurence Steinberg, "Latchkey Children and Susceptibility to Peer Pressure," *Developmental Psychology* 22:433–439 (1986).

74. Susan Byrne, "Nobody Home," *Psychology Today* 10:40–47 (1977).

75. Lawrence Kutner, "Parents of Latchkey Children Need to Make the Most of an Undesired Situation," *The New York Times,* October 19, 1989:B6.

76. Michael Resnick, Peter Bearman, Robert Blum, Karl Bauman et al., "Protecting Adolescents from Harm: Findings from the National Longitudinal Study on Adolescent Health," *Journal of the American Medical Association* 278:823–865 (1997).

77. U.S. Census Bureau, *Who's Minding the Kids? Child Care Arrangements* (Washington, DC: U.S. Bureau of the Census, 2003).

78. Richard Lowry, "Nasty, Brutish, and Short: Children in Day Care—and the Mothers Who Put Them There," *National Review* May 28:36–42 (2001).

79. Claudia Wallis, "The Case for Staying Home: Caught Between the Pressures of the Workplace and the Demands of Being a Mom, More Women are Sticking with the Kids," *Time*, March 22: 52–52 (2004).

80. John Laub and Robert Sampson, "Unraveling Families and Delinquency," *Criminology* 26:355–380 (1988); Ross Matsueda, "Testing Control Theory and Differential Association," *American Sociological Review* 47:489–504 (1982).

81. Jan Sokol-Katz, Roger Dunham, and Rick Zimmerman, "Family Structure Versus Parental Attachment in Controlling Adolescent Deviant Behavior: A Social Control Model," *Adolescence* 32:199–215 (1997).

82. Marc Zimmerman, Deborah Salem, and Kenneth Maton, "Family Structure and Psychosocial Correlates among Urban African-American Adolescent Males," *Child Development* 55:1598–1613 (1995).

83. Sheldon Glueck and Eleanor Glueck, *Unraveling Juvenile Delinquency* (Cambridge: Harvard University Press, 1950; F. Ivan Nye, *Family Relationships and Delinquent Behavior* (New York: John Wiley & Sons, 1958); William McCord and Joan McCord, *Origins of Crime: A New Evaluation of the Cambridge-Somerville Study* (New York: Columbia University Press, 1959).

84. Gerald Patterson, "Children Who Steal," pages 73–90 in Travis Hirschi and Michael Gottfredson (eds.), *Understanding Crime* (Beverly Hills, CA: Sage, 1980).

85. James Snyder and Gerald Patterson, "Family Interaction and Delinquent Behavior," pages 216–243 in Herbert Quay (ed.), *Handbook of Juvenile Delinquency* (New York: John Wiley & Sons, 1987).

86. Travis Hirschi, "Crime and the Family," pages 53–68 in James Q. Wilson (ed.), *Crime and Public Policy* (San Francisco: Institute for Contemporary Studies Press, 1983).

87. Hirschi, note 86, p. 62.

88. Patterson, note 84, p. 227.

89. Grace Barnes and Michael Farrell, "Parental Support and Control as Predictors of Adolescent Drinking, Delinquency, and Related Problem Behaviors," *Journal of Marriage and the Family* 54:763–776 (1992).

90. Jaana Haapasalo and Richard Tremblay, "Physically Aggressive Boys from Ages 6 to 12: Family Background, Parenting Behavior, and Prediction of Delinquency," *Journal of Consulting and Clinical Psychology* 62:1044–1052 (1994).

91. See Robert Sampson and John Laub, "Urban Poverty and the Family Context of Delinquency: A New Look at Structure and Process in a Classic Study," *Child Development* 65:523–540 (1994); Patrick Heaven, "Family of Origin, Personality, and Self-Reported Delinquency," *Journal of Adolescence* 17:445–459 (1994).

92. Sung Jang and Carolyn Smith, "A Test of Reciprocal Causal Relationships among Parental Supervision, Affective Ties, and Delinquency," *Journal of Research in Crime and Delinquency* 34:307–336 (1997).

93. John Paul Wright and Francis Cullen, "Parental Efficacy and Delinquent Behavior: Do Control and Support Matter?" *Criminology* 39:677–706 (2001), pp. 691–693.

94. Diana Baumrind, "Parental Disciplinary Patterns and Social Competence in Children," *Youth and Society* 9:239–276 (1978); Diana Baumrind, "The Influence of Parenting Style on Adolescent Competence and Substance Use," *Journal of Early Adolescence* 11:56–95 (1991).

95. Richard Clark and Glenn Shields, "Family Communication and Delinquency," *Adolescence* 32:81–92 (1997); Karla Klein, Rex Forehand, Lisa Armistead, and Patricia Long, "Delinquency During the Transition to Early Adulthood: Family and Parenting Predictors from Early Adolescence," *Adolescence* 32:61–79 (1997); Bobbi Anderson, Malcolm Holmes, and Erik Ostresh, "Male and Female Delinquents' Attachments and Effects of Attachments on Severity of Self-Reported Delinquency," *Criminal Justice and Behavior* 26:435–452 (1999).

96. Randy LaGrange and Helen White, "Age Differences in Delinquency," *Criminology* 23:19–45 (1985).

97. Linda Weber, Andrew Miracle, and Tom Skehan, "Family Bonding and Delinquency: Racial and Ethnic Influences among U.S. Youth," *Human Organization* 54:363–372 (1995).

98. Angela Huebner and Sherry Betts, "Exploring the Utility of Social Control Theory for Youth Development: Issues of Attachment, Involvement, and Gender," *Youth & Society* 34:136 (2002).

99. Miller et al., note 51, p. 21.

100. Donald West and David Farrington, *Who Becomes Delinquent?* (London: Heinemann, 1973).

101. Laub and Sampson, note 80, p. 375.

102. Helen Garnier and Judith Stein, "An 18-Year Model of Family and Peer Effects on Adolescent Drug Use and Delinquency," *Journal of Youth and Adolescence* 31:45–56 (2002), p. 54.

103. David Farrington, Darrick Jolliffe, Rolf Loeber, Magda Stouthamer-Loeber, and Larry Kalb, "The Concentration of Offenders in Families and Family Criminality in the Prediction of Boys' Delinquency," *Journal of Adolescence* 24:579–596 (2001).

104. Ralph Welsh, "Spankings: A Grand Old American Tradition," *Children Today* 14:27 (1985).

105. Bridget Freisthler, Darcey Merritt, and Elizabeth LaScala, "Understanding the Ecology of Child Maltreatment: A Review of the Literature and Directions for Future Research," *Child Maltreatment* 11:263–280 (2006); Elise Pepin and Victoria Banyard, "Social Support: A Mediator between Child Maltreatment and Developmental Outcomes," *Journal of Youth and Adolescence* 35:617–630 (2006); Jeffrey Steuwig and Laura McCloskey, "The Relation of Child Maltreatment to Shame and Guilt among Adolescents: Psychological Routes to Depression and Delinquency," *Child Maltreatment* 10:324–336 (2005).

106. U.S. Department of Health and Human Services, *Child Maltreatment 2005* (Washington, DC: U.S. Government Printing Office, 2007).

107. Steven Swinford, Alfred DeMaris, Stephen Cernkovich, and Peggy Giordano, "Harsh Physical Discipline in Childhood and Violence in Later Romantic Involvements: The Mediating Role of Problem Behaviors," *Journal of Marriage and the Family* 62:508–519 (2000); Ronald Simons, Chyi-In Wu, Kuei-Hsiu Lin, Leslie Gordon, and Rand Conger, "A Cross-Cultural Examination of the Link between Corporal Punishment and Adolescent Antisocial Behavior," *Criminology* 47–79 (2000); Ronald Simons, Leslie Simons, Callie Burt, Gene Brody, and Carolyn Cutrona, "Collective Efficacy, Authoritative Parenting, and Delinquency," *Criminology* 43:989–1030 (2005).

108. Centers for Disease Control and Prevention, *Child Maltreatment Fact Sheet* (Atlanta: National Center for Injury Prevention and Control, 2006); U.S. Department of Health and Human Services, note 106.

109. Gail Wasserman and Angela Seracini, "Family Risk Factors and Interventions," pages 165–189 in Rolf Loeber and David Farrington (eds.), *Child Delinquents: Development, Intervention, and Service Needs* (Thousand Oaks, CA: Sage, 2001).

110. John Lemmon, "How Child Maltreatment Affects Dimensions of Juvenile Delinquency in a Cohort of Low-Income Urban Youths," *Justice Quarterly* 16:357–376 (1999).

111. Timothy Ireland, Carolyn Smith, and Terence Thornberry, "Developmental Issues in the Impact of Child Maltreatment on Later Delinquency and Drug Use," *Criminology* 40:359–396 (2002).

112. Jane Siegel and Linda Williams, "The Relationship between Child Sexual Abuse and Female Delinquency and Crime: A Prospective Study," *Journal of Research in Crime and Delinquency* 40:71–94 (2003).

113. Cathy Spatz Widom, "Understanding Child Maltreatment and Juvenile Delinquency: The Research," pages 1–10 in Janet Wiig, Cathy Spatz Widom, and John Tuell (eds.), *Understanding Child Maltreatment & Juvenile Delinquency* (Washington, DC: Child Welfare League of America, 2003).

114. Delores Smith and Gail Mosby, "Jamaican Child-Rearing Practices: The Role of Corporal Punishment," *Adolescence* 38:369–381 (2003).

115. Meghan Wheeler and Carson Fox, "Family Dependency Treatment Court: Applying the Drug Court Model in Child Maltreatment," *Drug Court Practitioner Fact Sheet* 5:1–8 (2006).

CHAPTER 11

1. Joel Spring, *American Education,* 11th edition (New York: McGraw-Hill, 2004); Steven Tozer, Paul Violas, and Guy Senese, *School and Society,* 4th edition (New York: McGraw-Hill, 2002).

2. U.S. Bureau of Census, *Statistical Abstract of the United States 2006,* 126th edition (Washington, DC: U.S. Bureau of Census, 2007).

3. Tracey Wong Briggs and Adrienne Lewis, "Home-Schooled, With Siblings," *USA TODAY,* September 7, 2006:10A.

4. David Stuckey and Frank Pompa, "Organized Trouble at School," *USA TODAY,* July 17, 2006:1A.

5. Wayne Welsh, Jack Greene, and Patricia Jenkins, "School Disorder: The Influence of Individual, Institutional, and Community Factors," *Criminology* 37:73–116 (1999).

6. Wayne Welsh, "The Effects of School Climate on School Disorder," *Annals of the American Academy of Political and Social Science* 567:88–107 (2000).

7. Graham Ousey and Pamela Wilcox, "Subcultural Values and Violent Delinquency: A Multilevel Analysis of Middle Schools," *Youth Violence and Juvenile Justice* 3:3–22 (2005).

8. Jonathan Kozol, *Savage Inequalities* (New York: Harper Perennial, 1992); Jonathan Kozol, *The Shame of the Nation: The Restoration of Apartheid Schooling in America* (New York: Three Rivers Press, 2006).

9. Deborah Meier, Alfie Kohn, Linda Darling-Hammond, Theodore Sizer, and George Wood, *Many Children Left Behind: How the No Child Left Behind Act is Damaging Our Children and Our Schools* (Boston: Beacon Books, 2004); Alex Kotlowitz, *There Are No Children Here: The Story of Two Boys Growing Up in the Other America* (New York: Anchor Books, 1992).

10. Associated Press, "Students Suspended for Rest of School Year," *Des Moines Register,* May 10, 2006:2A.

11. Christy McDonald and Chris Pavelich, "First-grader Shot Dead at School," March 8, 2000, online at: http://www.ABC-NEWS.com/2000/3/8, accessed May 3, 2007.

12. Matt DeLisi, "The Columbine High School Massacre and Criminal Justice System Response: An Exploratory Case Study," *The Social Science Journal* 39:19–29 (2002).

13. Rachel Dinkes, Emily Forrest Cataldi, Grace Kena, Katrina Baum, and Thomas Snyder, *Indicators of School Crime and Safety: 2006* (Washington, DC: U.S. Department of Justice, 2006).

14. S. P. Kachur, G. M. Stennies, K. E. Powell, W. Modzeleski, R. Stephens, R. Murphy, M. Kresnow, D. Sleet, and R. Lowry, "School-Associated Violent Deaths in the United States, 1992–1994," *Journal of the American Medical Association* 275:1729–1733 (1996).

15. Sarah Ingersoll and Donni LeBoeuf, *Reaching Out to Youth Out of the Education Mainstream* (Washington DC: U.S. Department of Justice, 1997); Richard Lawrence, *School Crime and Juvenile Justice,* 2nd edition (New York: Oxford University Press, 2007).

16. Centers for Disease Control and Prevention, *Special Analysis of 1999 YRBS Data* (Atlanta: Centers for Disease Control, 2000).

17. Gary Gottfredson, Denise Gottfredson, Ellen Czeh, David Cantor, Scott Crosse, and Irene Hantman, *Summary: National Study of Delinquency Prevention in Schools* (Ellicott, MD: Gottfredson Associates, 2000).

18. Nels Ericson, *Addressing the Problem of Juvenile Bullying* (Washington, DC: Office of Juvenile Justice and Delinquency Prevention, 2001); Valerie Besag, *Bullies and Victims in Schools* (Philadelphia: Open University Press, 1989); Daniel Olweus, *Bullying in School* (Oxford: Blackwell, 1993).

19. Rebecca Griffin and Alan Gross, "Childhood Bullying: Current Empirical Findings and Future Directions for Research," *Aggression and Violent Behavior* 9:379–400 (2004); Claire Fox and Michael Boulton, "Longitudinal Associations between Submissive/Nonassertive Social Behavior and Different Types of Peer Victimization," *Violence and Victims* 21:383–400 (2006); Ann Burgess, Christina Garbarino, and Mary Carlson, "Pathological Teasing and Bullying Turned Deadly: Shooters and Suicide," *Victims & Offenders* 1:1–14 (2006).

20. Tonja Nansel, Mary Overpeck, Ramani Pilla, June Ruan, Bruce Simons Morton, and Peter Scheidt, "Bullying Behaviors Among US Youth," *Journal of the American Medical Association* 289:2094–2100 (2001); Tonja Nansel, Mary Overpeck, Denise Haynie, June Ruan, and Peter Scheidt, "Relationship Between Bullying and Violence Among U.S. Youth," *Archives of Pediatric and Adolescent Medicine* 157:348–353 (2003).

21. Nansel et al., note 20; Dinkes et al., note 13.

22. Dan Olweus and Susan Limber, *Blueprints for Violence Prevention: Bullying Prevention Program* (Boulder, CO: University of Colorado, 1999).

23. Matt DeLisi, *Career Criminals in Society* (Thousand Oaks, CA: Sage, 2005).

24. Peter Gill and Max Stenlund, "Dealing with a Schoolyard Bully: A Case Study," *Journal of School Violence* 4:47–62 (2005).

25. Robert Geffner, Marti Loring, and Corinna Young, *Bullying Behavior* (Binghamton, NY: Haworth, 2002).

26. Dan Olweus, *Bullying at School: What We Know and What We Can Do* (London: Blackwell, 1993); Barbara Coloroso, *The Bully, The Bullied, and the Bystander: From Preschool to High School, How Parents and Teachers Can Help Break the Cycle of Violence* (New York: Harper-Collins, 2004).

27. Dinkes et al., note 13.

28. Centers for Disease Control and Prevention, "Violence-Related Behaviors among High School Students—United States, 1991–2003," *Morbidity and Mortality Weekly Report* 53:651–655 (2004).

29. Gallup Organization, *Parents of Children in K–12,* August 24–26 (Princeton, NJ: Gallup Organization, 1999); Gallup Organization, *1025 Adults,* May 7–9 (Princeton, NJ: Gallup Organization, 1999).

30. Pamela Wilcox, Michelle Campbell Augustine, Jon Bryan, and Staci Roberts, "The Reality of Middle-School Crime: Objective vs. Subjective Experiences among a Sample of Kentucky Youth," *Journal of School Violence* 4:3–28 (2005).

31. Nancy Brener, Thomas Simon, Etienne Krug, and Richard Lowry, "Recent Trends in Violence-Related Behaviors among High School Students in the United States," *Journal of the American Medical Association* 282: 440–446 (1999).

32. *Goss v. Lopez,* 419 U.S. 565 (1976).

33. Irwin Hyman, *Reading, Writing, and the Hickory Stick* (Lexington, MA: Lexington Books, 1991).

34. Philipe Aris, *Centuries of Childhood* (New York: Knopf, 1962), p. 190.

35. Proverbs 13:24, *New American Standard Bible* (New York: Cambridge, 1977).

36. Herbert Falk, *Corporal Punishment* (New York: Columbia Teachers College, 1941).

37. *Baker v. Owen,* 395 F. Supp. 294 (1975).

38. *Ingraham v. Wright,* 430 U.S. 651 (1977); *Garcia v. Miera,* 817 F.2nd 650 (10th Cir. 1987); *Hall v. Tawney,* 621 F.2nd 607 (4th Cir. 1980).

39. Jodi Wilgoren, "Paddling Opponents Get Change in Teacher Liability Amendment," *The New York Times,* May 11, 2001:A26; Mary Beth Marklein, "More Educators Sparing the Rod," *USA TODAY,* June 6, 1997:9D.

40. National Coalition to Abolish Corporal Punishment in Schools, "Number of Students Struck Each Year in School," online at: http://www.stophitting.com/disatschool/, accessed May 3, 2007; Associated Press, "Paddling Becoming Uncommon at School," *USA TODAY,* July 12, 2000:2D; Steven Shaw and Jeffery Braden, "Race and Gender Bias in the Administration of Corporal Punishment," *School Psychology Review* 19:378–383 (1990).

41. Murray Straus and Julie Stewart, "Corporal Punishment by American Parents," *Clinical Child and Family Psychology Review* 2:55–70 (1999); Murray Straus, David Sugarman, and Jean Giles-Sims, "Spanking by Parents and Subsequent Antisocial Behavior of Children," *Archives of Pediatric Adolescent Medicine* 151:761–767 (1997); Murray Straus, *Beating the Devil Out of Them* (San Francisco: Jossey-Bass, 1994).

42. Andrew Grogan-Kaylor, "Corporal Punishment and the Growth Trajectory of Children's Antisocial Behavior," *Child Maltreatment* 10:283–292 (2005).

43. Emily Douglas and Murray Straus, "Assault and Injury of Dating Partners by University Students in 19 Countries and Its Relation to Corporal Punishment Experienced as a Child," *European Journal of Criminology* 3:293–318 (2006).

44. Nat Hentoff, "U.S. Schools Still Legalize Abuse," *Rocky Mountain News,* August 7, 1995:29A; Murray Straus, Demie Kurtz, Donileen Loseske, and Joan McCord, "Discipline and Deviance," *Social Problems* 38:133–154 (1991); Rick Lyman, "In Many Public Schools, the Paddle is No Relic," *The New York Times,* October 2, 2006:18A.

45. Steven Anderson and Matthew Payne, "Corporal Punishment in Elementary Education," *Child Abuse and Neglect* 18:377–386 (1994); A. Shumba, "Epidemiology and Etiology of Reported Cases of Child Physical Abuse in Zimbabwean Primary Schools," *Child Abuse and Neglect* 25:265–277 (2001).

46. Ralph Welsh, "Delinquency, Corporal Punishment, and the Schools," *Crime & Delinquency* 24:336–354 (1978)

47. *Thompson v. Carthage School District,* 87 F3d 979 (1996).

48. *New Jersey v. T.L.O.,* 469 U.S. 325 (1985).

49. *Vernonia School District 47J v. Acton,* 515 U.S. 646 (1995); *Board of Education of Independent School District No. 92 of Pottawatomie County et al. v. Earls et al.,* 536 U.S. 827 (2002); Ryoko Yamaguchi, Lloyd Johnston, and Patrick O'Malley, "Relationship Between Student Illicit Drug Use and School Drug-Testing Policies," *Journal of School Health* 73:159–164 (2003); Donna Leinwand, "More Schools Test for Drugs," *USA TODAY,* July 12, 2006:1A..

50. *West Virginia State Board of Education v. Barnette,* 319 U.S. 624 (1943).

51. *Tinker v. Des Moines Independent Community School District,* 393 U.S. 503 (1969).

52. *Bethel School District No. 403 v. Fraser,* 478 U.S. 675 (1986); "Supreme Court Reverses Fraser," *SPLC Report,* Fall: 3–4 (1986), p. 3.

53. *Hazelwood School District v. Kuhlmeier,* 484 U.S. 260 (1988).

54. Jeffery Selingo, "Student Writers Try to Duck the Censors by Going Online," *The New York Times,* June 7, 2001:D6.

55. *Morse v. Frederick,* 06-278 (2007).

56. Paul Copperman, *The Literacy Hoax* (New York: Morrow, 1980); Dinesh D'Souza, *Illiberal Education: The Politics of Race and Sex on Campus* (New York: The Free Press, 1991).

57. Michael Turner, Alex Piquero, and Travis Pratt, "The School Context as a Source of Self-Control," *Journal of Criminal Justice* 33:327–339 (2005).

58. Gary Gottfredson, Denise Gottfredson, Allison Payne, and Nisha Gottfredson, "School Climate Predictors of School Disorder: Results from a National Study of Delinquency Prevention in Schools," *Journal of Research in Crime and Delinquency* 42:412–444 (2005); Allison Payne, Denise Gottfredson, and Gary Gottfredson, "Schools as Communities: The Relationships among Communal School Organization, Student Bonding, and School Disorder,"

Criminology 41:749–778 (2003); Denise Gottfredson, *Schools and Delinquency* (New York: Cambridge University Press, 2000).

59. James Coleman, *High School Achievement* (New York: Basic Books, 1982), p. 178.

60. Coleman, note 59, p. 111.

61. Greg Toppo, "Charter Schools Fail to Top Their Public Peers," *USA TODAY,* August 23, 206:4D; Diana Schemo, "Public Schools Perform Near Private Ones in Study," *The New York Times,* July 15, 2006:1E.

62. Michelle Campbell Augustine, Pamela Wilcox, Graham Ousey, and Richard Clayton, "Opportunity Theory and Adolescent-School-Based Victimization," *Violence and Victims* 17:233–253 (2002).

63. August Hollingshead, *Elmstown Youth* (New York: John Wiley, 1949).

64. Robert Rosenthal and Lenore Jacobson, *Pygmalion in the Classroom* (New York: Irvington, 1988).

65. Commission on Behavioral and Social Sciences and Education, *Losing Generations* (Washington, DC: National Academy Press, 1993).

66. Walter Schafer and Carol Olexa, *Tracking and Opportunity* (San Francisco: Chandler, 1971); Walter Schafer, Carol Olexa, and Kenneth Polk, "Programmed for Social Class," pages 34–54 in Kenneth Polk and Walter Schafer (eds.), *Schools and Delinquency* (Englewood Cliffs, NJ: Prentice Hall, 1972; Christine Eith, *Delinquency, Schools, and the Social Bond* (New York: LFB Scholarly Publishing, 2005).

67. Karen Randolph, Mark Fraser, and Dennis Orthner, "Educational Resilience among Youth at Risk," *Substance Use and Misuse* 39:747–767 (2004).

68. Delos Kelly, "Status Origins, Track Position, and Delinquent Involvement," *Sociological Quarterly* 16:264–271 (1975).

69. Adam Gamoran and Robert Mare, "Secondary School Tracking and Educational Inequality," *American Journal of Sociology* 94:1146–1183 (1989).

70. Eric Stewart, "School Social Bonds, School Climate, and School Behavior: A Multilevel Analysis," *Justice Quarterly* 20:575–604 (2003).

71. Richard Felson and Jeremy Staff, "Explaining the Academic Performance-Delinquency Relationship," *Criminology* 44:299–320 (2006).

72. Richard Rehberg and Evelyn Rosenthal, *Class and Merit in the American High School* (New York: Longmans, 1978).

73. Kenneth Polk, "Curriculum Tracking and Delinquency," *American Sociological Review* 48:282–284 (1983).

74. James Rosenbaum, *Making Inequality* (New York: John Wiley & Sons, 1980); Ernest Boyer, *High School* (New York: Harper & Row, 1980); John Goodlad, *A Place Called School* (New York: McGraw-Hill, 1984).

75. Michael Wiatrowski, David Griswold, and Mary Roberts, "Curriculum Tracking and Delinquency," *American Sociological Review* 47:151–160 (1982).

76. Polk, note 73.

77. Samuel Bowles and Herbert Gintis, *Schooling in Capitalist America* (New York: Basic Books, 1976).

78. Henry Giroux, *Theory of Resistance* (South Hadley, MA: Bergin and Garvey, 1983).

79. Jay MacLeod, *Ain't No Makin' It: Aspirations and Attainment in a Low-Income Neighborhood* (Boulder, CO: Westview Press, 1995).

80. Paul Willis, *Learning to Labour* (Lexington, MA: D. C. Heath, 1979).

81. Elizabeth Stearns and Elizabeth Glennie, "When and Why Dropouts Leave High School," *Youth & Society* 38:29–57 (2006).

82. Roslyn Caldwell, Richard Wiebe, and H. Harrington Cleveland, "The Influence of Future Certainty and Contextual Factors on Delinquent Behavior and School Adjustment among African American Adolescents," *Journal of Youth and Adolescence* 35:591–602 (2006); Alexander Vazsonyi, H. Harrington Cleveland, and Richard Wiebe, "Does the Effect of Impulsivity on Delinquency Vary of Level of Neighborhood Disadvantage?" *Criminal Justice & Behavior* 33:511–541 (2006).

83. Timothy Brezina, Alex Piquero, and Paul Mazerolle, "Student Anger and Aggressive Behavior in School," *Journal of Research in Crime and Delinquency* 38:362–386 (2001).

84. Derek Kreager, "Strangers in the Halls: Isolation and Delinquency in School Networks," *Social Forces* 83:351–390 (2004).

85. Priscilla Coleman and Caroline Byrd, "Interpersonal Correlates of Peer Victimization among Young Adolescents," *Journal of Youth and Adolescence* 32:301–314 (2003).

86. Marilyn Elias, "At Schools, Less Tolerance for 'Zero Tolerance,'" *USA TODAY,* August 10, 2006:6D.

87. Russell Skiba, *Zero Tolerance, Zero Effectiveness* (Bloomington: Indiana Education Policy Center, 2000); Russell Skiba, Robert Michael, Abra Nardo, *The Color of Discipline* (Bloomington: Indiana Education Policy Center, 2000).

88. Devon Brewer, J. David Hawkins, Richard Catalono, and Holly Neckerman, "Preventing Serious, Violent, and Chronic Juvenile Delinquency," pages 61–141 in James Howell, Barry Krisberg, J. David Hawkins, and John Wilson (eds.), *A Sourcebook: Serious, Violent & Chronic Juvenile Offenders* (Thousand Oaks, CA: Sage, 1995).

89. Cynthia McCluskey, Timothy Bynum, and Justin Patchin, "Reducing Chronic Absenteeism: An Assessment of an Early Truancy Initiative," *Crime & Delinquency* 50:214–234 (2004).

90. Michael White, James Fyfe, Suzanne Campbell, and John Goldkamp, "The School–Police Partnership: Identifying At-Risk Youth through a Truant Recovery Program," *Evaluation Review* 25:507–532 (2001).

91. Daniel Lockwood, *Violence among Middle School and High School Students* (Washington, DC: National Institute of Justice, 1997).

92. Ira Pollack and Carlos Sundermann, "Creating Safe Schools," *Juvenile Justice* 8:14 (2001).

93. C. Ronald Huff and Kenneth Trump, "Youth Violence and Gangs," *Education and Urban Society* 28:492–503 (1996); Randy Page and John Hammermeister, "Weapon-Carrying and Youth Violence," *Adolescence* 32:505–513 (1997).

94. Peter Finn, "School Resource Officer Programs: Finding the Funding, Reaping the Benefits," *FBI Law Enforcement Bulletin* 75:1–7 (2006).

95. Bryan Vossekuil, Marisa Reddy, Robert Fein, Randy Borum, and William Modzeleski, *Safe Schools Initiative* (Washington, DC: U.S. Secret Service National Threat Assessment Center, 2000).

96. Larry Copeland, "Students Paid for Tattling on Peers," *USA TODAY,* April 18, 2005:1A; Elaine Cloyd, "Tips Can Stop Crime," *USA TODAY,* April 26, 2005:12A.

97. Jackson Toby, "Crime in American Public Schools," *The Public Interest* 58:18–42 (1980).

98. Xia Wang, Thomas Blomberg, and Spencer Li, "Comparison of the Educational Deficiencies of Delinquent and Non-Delinquent Students," *Evaluation Review* 29:291–312 (2005).

99. Delbert Elliott, "Delinquency, School Attendance, and School Dropout," *Social Problems* 13:307–314 (1966); Delbert Elliott and Harwin Voss, *Delinquency and Dropout* (Lexington, MA: Lexington Books, 1974).

100. Terence Thornberry, Melanie Moore, and R. L. Christenson, "Dropping Out of High School on Subsequent Criminal Behavior," *Criminology* 23:3–18 (1985).

101. David Farrington, B. Gallagher, L. Morley, R. J. St. Ledger, and D. J. West, "Unemployment, School Leaving, and Crime," *British Journal of Criminology* 26:335–356 (1986).

102. Roger Jarjoura, "Does Dropping Out of School Enhance Delinquency Involvement?" *Criminology* 31:149–172 (1993).

103. Rolf Loeber and David Farrington, "Young Children Who Commit Crime," *Development and Psychopathology* 12:737–762 (2000).

104. Eileen Garry, *Truancy: First Step to a Lifetime of Problems* (Washington, DC: Office of Juvenile Justice and Delinquency Prevention, 1996).

105. Jane Sprott, Jennifer Jenkins, and Anthony Doob, "The Importance of School: Protecting At-Risk Youth From Early Offending," *Youth Violence and Juvenile Justice* 3:59–77 (2005).

CHAPTER 12

1. Malcolm Klein and Henry Pontell, *Chasing after Street Gangs: A 40-Year Journey* (Upper Saddle River, NJ: Prentice Hall, 2007).

2. Mark Fleisher, *Dead End Kids: Gang Girls and the Boys They Know* (Madison: University of Wisconsin Press, 1998); David Brotherton and Luis Barrios, *The Almighty Latin King and Queen Nation: Street Politics and the Transformation of a New York City Gang* (New York: Columbia University Press, 2004); James Short, Jr., and Lorine Hughes, *Studying Youth Gangs* (New York: AltaMira Press, 2006).

3. Mark Warr, *Companions in Crime: The Social Aspects of Criminal Conduct* (Cambridge: Cambridge University Press, 2002), p. 40.

4. Clifford Shaw and Henry McKay, *Social Factors in Juvenile Delinquency* (Washington, DC: U.S. Government Printing Office, 1931).

5. Sheldon Glueck and Eleanor Glueck, *Unraveling Juvenile Delinquency* (Cambridge: MA: Harvard University Press, 1950); Delbert Elliott and Scott Menard, "Delinquent Friends and Delinquent Behavior: Temporal and Developmental Patterns," pages 28–67 in J. David Hawkins (ed.), *Delinquency and Crime: Current Theories* (Cambridge: Cambridge University Press, 1996); Terence Thornberry, Alan Lizotte, Marvin Krohn, Margaret Farnworth, and Sung Joon Jang, "Delinquent Peers, Beliefs, and Delinquent Behavior: A Longitudinal Test of Interactional Theory," *Criminology* 32:47–84 (1994); David Fergusson, Nicola Swain-Campbell, and L. John Horwood, "Deviant Peer Affiliations, Crime and Substance Use: A Fixed Effects Regression Analysis," *Journal of Abnormal Psychology* 30:419–430 (2002).

6. Albert Reiss, "Co-Offender Influences on Criminal Careers," pages 121–160 in Alfred Blumstein, Jacqueline Cohen, Jeffrey Roth, and Christy Visher (eds.), *Criminal Careers and "Career Criminals"* (Washington, DC: National Academy Press, 1986), p. 128.

7. Michael Hindelang, "With a Little Help from Their Friends: Group Participation in Reported Delinquent Behavior," *British Journal of Criminology* 16:109–125 (1976).

8. Andy Hochstetler, Heith Copes, and Matt DeLisi, "Differential Association in Group and Solo Offending," *Journal of Criminal Justice* 30:559–566 (2002).

9. Helen Garnier and Judith Stein, "An 18-Year Model of Family and Peer Effects on Adolescent Drug Use and Delinquency," *Journal of Youth and Adolescence* 31:45–56 (2002).

10. Kimberly Maxwell, "Friends: The Role of Peer Influence Across Adolescent Risk Behaviors," *Journal of Youth and Adolescence* 31:274 (2002); Andrea Hussong, "Differentiating Peer Contexts and Risk for Adolescent Substance Use," *Journal of Youth and Adolescence* 31:207–220 (2002).

11. Travis Hirschi, *Causes of Delinquency* (Berkeley: University of California Press, 1969); Matthew Ploeger, "Youth Employment and Delinquency: Reconsidering a Problematic Relationship," *Criminology* 35:659–675 (1997).

12. Warr, note 3, p. 125.

13. Finn Esbensen, L. Thomas Winfree, Ni He, and Terrance Taylor, "Youth Gangs and Definitional Issues: When is a Gang a Gang, and Why Does it Matter?" *Crime & Delinquency* 47:105–130 (2001).

14. Frederic Thrasher, *The Gang* (Chicago: University of Chicago Press, 1927).

15. Joan Moore, "Gangs and the Underclass: A Comparative Perspective," in John Hagedorn (ed.), *People and Folks: Gangs, Crime and the Underclass in a Rustbelt City,* 2nd edition (Chicago: Lake View Press, 1998), p. 5.

16. Walter Miller, "Gangs, Groups, and Serious Youth Crime," in David Schicor and Delos Kelley (eds.), *Critical Issues in Juvenile Delinquency* (Lexington, MA: Lexington Books, 1980), p. 121.

17. Ruth Horowitz, "Sociological Perspectives on Gangs: Conflicting Definitions and Concepts," pages 37–54 in C. Ronald Huff (ed.), *Gangs in America* (Newbury Park, CA: Sage, 1990), p. 45.

18. California Penal Code, Section 186.32.

19. Arlen Egley, James Howell, and Aline Major, "Recent Patterns of Gang Problems in the United States: Results from the 1996–2002 National Youth Gang Survey," pages 90–108 in Finn Esbensen, Stephen Tibbetts, and Larry Gaines (eds.), *American Youth Gangs at the Millennium* (Long Grove, IL: Waveland Press, 2004), p. 95.

20. Charles Katz, "Issues in the Production and Dissemination of Gang Statistics: An Ethnographic Study of a Large Midwestern Police Gang Unit," *Crime & Delinquency* 49:485–516 (2003).

21. Malcolm Klein and Cheryl Maxson, *Street Gang Patterns and Policies* (New York: Oxford University Press, 2006).

22. Finn Esbensen and David Huizinga, "Gangs, Drugs, and Delinquency in a Survey of Urban Youth," *Criminology* 31:565–589 (1993); Finn Esbensen, David Huizinga, and Anne Weiher, "Gang and Non-Gang Youth: Differences in Explanatory Factors," *Journal of Contemporary Criminal Justice* 9:94–111 (1993).

23. Terence Thornberry, Marvin Krohn, Alan Lizotte, and Deborah Chard-Wierschem, "The Role of Juvenile Gangs in Facilitating Delinquent Behavior," *Journal of Research in Crime and Delinquency* 30:55–87 (1993).

24. Sara Battin, Karl Hill, Robert Abbott, Richard Catalano, and J. David Hawkins, "The Contribution of Gang Membership to Delinquency Beyond Delinquent Friends," *Criminology* 36:105–106 (1998).

25. Dana Peterson, Terrance Taylor, and Finn Esbensen, "Gang Membership and Violent Victimization," *Justice Quarterly* 21:793–815 (2004).

26. Terence Thornberry and James Burch, *Gang Members and Delinquent Behavior* (Washington, DC: Office of Juvenile Justice and Delinquency Prevention, 1997); Terence Thornberry, Marvin Krohn, Alan Lizotte, Carolyn Smith, and Kimberly Tobin, *Gangs and Delinquency in Developmental Perspective* (New York: Cambridge University Press, 2003).

27. Terence Thornberry, "Membership in Youth Gangs and Involvement in Serious and Violent Offending," pages 147–166 in Rolf Loeber and David Farrington (eds.), *Serious and Violent Juvenile Offenders: Risk Factors and Successful Interventions* (Thousand Oaks, CA: Sage, 1998); Uberto Gatti, Richard Tremblay, Frank Vitaro, and Pierre McDuff, "Youth Gangs, Delinquency and Drug Use: A Test of Selection, Facilitation, and Enhancement Hypotheses," *Journal of Child Psychology and Psychiatry* 46:1178–1190 (2005).

28. L. Thomas Winfree, Larry Mays, and Teresa Vigil-Backstrom, "Youth Gangs and Incarcerated Delinquents: Exploring the Ties between Gang Membership, Delinquency, and Social Learning Theory," *Justice Quarterly* 11:229–253 (1994); L. Thomas Winfree, Teresa Vigil Backstrom, and Larry Mays, "Social Learning Theory, Self-Reported Delinquency, and Youth Gangs," *Youth & Society* 26:147–177 (1994).

29. Scott Decker and Barrik Van Winkle, *Life in the Gang: Family, Friends, and Violence* (New York: Cambridge University Press, 1996); G. David Curry and Scott Decker, *Socialization to Gangs in St. Louis Project: Background and*

Executive Summary, Final Report (Washington, DC: Office of Juvenile Justice and Delinquency Prevention, 2000).

30. Rachel Gordon, Benjamin Lahey, Eriko Kawai, Rolf Loeber, Madga Stouthamer-Loeber, and David Farrington, "Antisocial Behavior and Youth Gang Membership: Selection and Socialization," *Criminology* 42:55–87 (2004).

31. David Eitle, Steven Gunkel, and Karen Van Gundy, "Cumulative Exposure to Stressful Life Events and Male Gang Membership," *Journal of Criminal Justice* 32:95–111 (2004).

32. James Howell and Arlen Egley, "Moving Risk Factors into Developmental Theories of Gang Membership," *Youth Violence and Juvenile Justice* 3:334–354 (2005).

33. Marvin Krohn and Terence Thornberry, *Longitudinal Perspectives on Adolescent Street Gangs* (Washington, DC: National Institute of Justice, 2006); Mons Bendixen, Inger Endresen, and Dan Olweus, "Joining and Leaving Gangs: Selection and Facilitation Effects on Self-Reported Antisocial Behavior in Early Adolescence," *European Journal of Criminology* 3:85–114 (2006); William Craig, Frank Vitaro, C. Gagnon, and Richard Tremblay, "The Road to Gang Membership: Characteristics of Male Gang and Non-Gang Members from ages 10–14," *Social Development* 11:53–68 (2002); Gina Hall, Terence Thornberry, and Alan Lizotte, "The Gang Facilitation Effect and Neighborhood Risk: Do Gangs Have a Stronger Influence on Delinquency in Disadvantaged Areas?" pages 47–61 in James Short, Jr., and Lorine Hughes (eds.), *Studying Youth Gangs* (New York: AltaMira Press, 2006); Karl Hill, James Howell, J. David Hawkins, and Sara Battin-Pearson, "Childhood Risk Factors for Adolescent Gang Membership: Results from the Seattle Social Development Project," *Journal of Research in Crime and Delinquency* 36:300–322 (1999).

34. Terence Thornberry, Marvin Krohn, Alan Lizotte, and Deborah Chard-Wierschem, "The Role of Juvenile Gangs in Facilitating Delinquent Behavior," *Journal of Research in Crime and Delinquency* 30:55–87 (1993).

35. Martín Sánchez-Jankowski, *Islands in the Street: Gangs and American Urban Society* (Berkeley: University of California Press, 1991), pp. 40–47.

36. Martín Sánchez-Jankowski, "Gangs and Social Change," *Theoretical Criminology* 7: 191–216 (2003).

37. Cheryl Maxson and Monica Whitlock, "Joining the Gang: Gender Differences in Risk Factors for Gang Membership," pages 30–49 in C. Ronald Huff (ed.), *Gangs in America III* (Thousand Oaks, CA: Sage, 2002), p. 32.

38. Jody Miller, *One of the Guys: Gangs, Girls, and Gender* (New York: Oxford University Press, 2001); Jenna St. Cyr and Scott Decker, "Girls, Guys, and Gangs: Convergence or Divergence in the Gendered Construction of Gangs and Groups," *Journal of Criminal Justice* 31:423–433 (2003).

39. Randall Shelden, Sharon Tracy, and William Brown, *Youth Gangs in American Society*, 3rd edition (Belmont, CA: Wadsworth, 2004).

40. Laura Caldwell and David Altschuler, "Adolescents Leaving Gangs: An Analysis of Risk and Protective Factors, Resiliency and Desistance in a Developmental Context,"

Journal of Gang Research 8: 21–34 (2001); Scott Decker and Janet Lauritsen, "Leaving the Gang," pages 51–67 in C. Ronald Huff (ed.), *Gangs in America III* (Thousand Oaks, CA: Sage, 2002).

41. Walter Miller, "American Youth Gangs," pages 291–320 in Abraham Blumberg (ed.), *Current Perspectives on Criminal Behavior* (New York: Knopf, 1981).

42. R. Lincoln Keiser, *The Vice Lords* (New York: Holt, Rinehart and Winston, 1969), p. 8.

43. James Short, Jr., "Collective Behavior, Crime, and Delinquency," pages 403–449 in Daniel Glaser (ed.), *Handbook of Criminology* (Chicago: Rand McNally, 1974).

44. Gene Muehlbauer and Laura Dodder, *The Losers: Gang Delinquency in an American Suburb* (New York: Praeger, 1983).

45. Robert Jackson and Wesley McBride, *Understanding Street Gangs* (Costa Mesa, CA: Custom, 1985).

46. Joan Moore, *Homeboys* (Philadelphia: Temple University Press, 1978).

47. Julie Amato and Dewey Cornell, "How Do Youth Claiming Gang Membership Differ from Youth Who Claim Membership in Another Group, Such as Crew, Clique, Posse, or Mob?" *Journal of Gang Research* 10:13–23 (2003).

48. Miller, note 41, p. 297.

49. Lewis Yablonsky, *The Violent Gang* (New York: Macmillan, 1962); Lewis Yablonsky, *Gangsters* (New York: New York University Press, 1997).

50. Barry Krisberg, *The Gang and the Community* (San Francisco: R&E Research Associates, 1975).

51. John Hagedorn, *People and Folks: Gangs, Crime and the Underclass in a Rustbelt City*, 2nd edition (Chicago: Lake View Press, 1998), p. 92.

52. Irving Spergel, "Youth Gangs: Continuity and Change," pages 171–276 in Michal Tonry and Norval Morris (eds.), *Crime and Justice: A Review of Research*, Volume 12 (Chicago: University of Chicago Press, 1990).

53. Sánchez-Jankowski, note 36, p. 199.

54. Thrasher, note 14.

55. Malcolm Klein, *Street Gangs and Street Workers* (Englewood Cliffs, NJ: Prentice Hall, 1971), p. 91.

56. James Short, Jr., and Fred Strodtbeck, *Group Process and Gang Delinquency* (Chicago: University of Chicago Press, 1965).

57. Scott Decker, "Collective and Normative Features of Gang Violence," *Justice Quarterly* 13:342–264 (1996); Klein and Pontell, note 1; Short and Hughes, note 2.

58. Jacqueline Schneider, "Niche Crime: The Columbus Gangs Study," *American Journal of Criminal Justice* 26:93–107 (2001).

59. Geoffrey Hunt, Karen Joe, and Dan Waldorf, "Drinking, Kicking Back and Gang Banging: Alcohol, Violence and Street Gangs," *Free Inquiry in Creative Sociology* 24:126 (1996).

60. Walter Miller, *The Growth of Youth Gang Problems in the United States: 1970–98* (Washington, DC: Office of Juvenile Justice and Delinquency Prevention, 2001).

61. Arlen Egley, James Howell, and Aline Major, *National Youth Gang Survey, 1999–2001* (Washington, DC: Office of Juvenile Justice and Delinquency Prevention, 2006).

62. Arlen Egley and Christina Ritz, *Highlights of the 2004 National Youth Gang Survey* (Washington, DC: Office of Juvenile Justice and Delinquency Prevention, 2006).

63. Shelden et al., note 39, pp. 30–31.

64. James Howell, *The Impact of Gangs on Communities, National Youth Gang Center Bulletin* (Washington, DC: Office of Juvenile Justice and Delinquency Prevention, 2006).

65. Miller, note 60.

66. Cheryl Maxson, *Gang Members on the Move* (Washington, DC: Office of Juvenile Justice and Delinquency Prevention, 1998).

67. Richard Zevitz and Susan Takata, "Metropolitan Gang Influence and the Emergence of Group Delinquency in a Regional Community," *Journal of Criminal Justice* 20:93–106 (1992).

68. Sanyika Shakur, *Monster: The Autobiography of an L.A. Gang Member* (New York: Penguin Books, 1993); James Short, Jr., *Poverty, Ethnicity, and Violent Crime* (Boulder, CO: Westview, 1997); Shaun Gabbidon, *Race, Crime, and Justice: A Reader* (London: Routledge, 2006).

69. James Alan Fox and Morris Zawitz, *Homicide Trends in the United States* (Washington, DC: U.S. Department of Justice, 2006).

70. Egley et al., note 61.

71. Alison Rhyne and Douglas Yearwood, "An Assessment of Hispanic/Latino Gangs in North Carolina: Findings from a General Law Enforcement Survey," *Journal of Gang Research* 13:1–14 (2006).

72. James Vigil, *Barrio Gangs: Street Life and Identity in Southern California* (Austin: University of Texas Press, 1988).

73. Avelardo Valdez and Stephen Sifaneck, "Getting High and Getting By: Dimensions of Drug Selling Behaviors among American Mexican Gang Members in South Texas," *Journal of Research in Crime and Delinquency* 41:82–105 (2004).

74. Alice Cepeda and Avelardo Valdez, "Risk Behaviors Among Young Mexican American Gang-Associated Females: Sexual Relations, Partying, Substance Use, and Crime," *Journal of Adolescent Research* 18:90–106 (2003), p. 98.

75. Ko-lin Chin, *Chinese Subculture and Criminality: Nontraditional Crime Groups in America* (Westport, CT: Greenwood Press, 1990).

76. Delbert Joe and Norman Robinson, "Chinatown's Immigrant Gangs: The New Young Warrior Class," *Criminology* 18:341–344 (1980).

77. James Vigil and Steve Yun, "Vietnamese Youth Gangs in Southern California," pages 146–162 in C. Ronald Huff (ed.), *Gangs in America* (Newbury Park, CA: Sage, 1990).

78. Yoko Baba, "Vietnamese Gangs, Cliques, and Delinquents," *Journal of Gang Research* 8:14 (2001).

79. Malcolm Klein, *The American Street Gang: Its Nature, Prevalence, and Control* (New York: Oxford University Press, 1995).

80. Geoffrey Hunt, Karen Joe, and Dan Waldorf, "Culture and Ethnic Identity among Southeast Asian Gang Members," *Free Inquiry in Creative Sociology* 25:9–21 (1997); Kay Kei-ho Pih and KuoRay Mao, "'Golden Parachutes' and Gangbanging: Taiwanese Gangs in Suburban Southern California," *Journal of Gang Research* 12:59–72 (2005); Glenn Tsunokai, "Beyond the Lenses of the 'Model' Minority Myth: A Descriptive Portrait of Asian Gang Members," *Journal of Gang Research* 12:37–58 (2005).

81. John Wang, "Bank Robberies by an Asian Gang: An Assessment of the Routine Activities Theory," *International Journal of Offender Therapy and Comparative Criminology* 46:555–568 (2002); D. A. Lopez, "Asian Gang Homicides and Weapons: Criminalistics and Criminology," *Journal of Gang Research* 13:15–29 (2006).

82. Janice Joseph and Dorothy Taylor, "Native-American Youths and Gangs," *Journal of Gang Research* 10:45–54 (2003).

83. Joseph Donnermeyer, R. Edwards, E. Chavez, and F. Beauvais, "Involvement of American Indian Youth in Gangs," *Free Inquiry in Creative Sociology* 24:167–174 (1996).

84. Les Whitbeck, Dan Hoyt, Xiaojin Chen, and Jerry Stubben, "Predictors of Gang Involvement among American Indian Adolescents," *Journal of Gang Research* 10:11–26 (2002).

85. Joseph and Taylor, note 82, p. 48.

86. Liz Martinez, "Gangs in Indian Country," *Law Enforcement Technology* 32:20–27 (2005).

87. Erika Harrell, *Violence of Gang Members, 1993–2003* (Washington, DC: U.S. Department of Justice, 2005).

88. Chip Yost, "Questions Raised about DPD Under-Reporting Gang Crime," online at: http://www.9news.com/acm_news.aspx/html, accessed May 1, 2007.

89. Andrew Glazer, "Black-Hispanic Gang Rivalries Hit Los Angeles," *Boulder Daily Camera,* August 13, 2006:6B.

90. Matt DeLisi, Mark Berg, and Andy Hochstetler, "Gang Members, Career Criminals, and Prison Violence: Further Specification of the Importation Model of Inmate Behavior," *Criminal Justice Studies* 17:369–383 (2004), p. 370.

91. James Howell, "Youth Gang Homicides: A Literature Review," *Crime & Delinquency* 45:208–241 (1999).

92. Tony Rackauckas, *2002 Annual Gang Cases Report* (Orange County, CA: Office of the Orange County District Attorney, 2003).

93. Egley et al., note 61.

94. Donna Leinwand, "Raids Target Gang behind Deadly Heroin Mix," *USA TODAY,* June 22, 2006:2A.

95. Arielle Baskin-Sommers and Ira Sommers, "Methamphetamine Use and Violence among Young Adults," *Journal of Criminal Justice* 34:661–674 (2006).

96. Jeffrey Fagan, "The Social Organization of Drug Use and Drug Dealing among Urban Gangs," *Criminology* 27:633–667 (1989).

97. Finn Esbensen, Dana Peterson, Adrienne Freng, and Terrance Taylor, "Initiation of Drug Use, Drug Sales, and Violent Offending among a Sample of Gang and Non-gang Youth," page 37–50 in C. Ronald Huff (ed.), *Gangs in America III* (Thousand Oaks, CA: Sage, 2002).

98. G. David Curry, Scott Decker, and Arlen Egley, "Gang Involvement and Delinquency in a Middle School Popu-

lation," *Justice Quarterly* 19:275–292 (2002); G. David Curry, "Self-reported Gang Involvement and Officially Recorded Delinquency," *Criminology* 38:1253–1274 (2000); Scott Decker and G. David Curry, "Gangs, Gang Homicides, and Gang Loyalty: Organized Crime or Disorganized Criminals," *Journal of Criminal Justice* 30:343–352 (2002).

99. H. Range Hutson, Deidre Anglin, D. Kyriacou, J. Hart, and K. Spears, "The Epidemic of Gang-Related Homicides in Los Angeles County from 1979 through 1994," *Journal of the American Medical Association* 274:1031–1036 (1995).

100. C. Ronald Huff, *Comparing the Criminal Behavior of Youth Gangs and At-Risk Youths* (Washington, DC: National Institute of Justice, 1998).

101. George Knox et al., *The Facts about Gang Life in America Today: A National Study of over 4,000 Gang Members* (Peotone, IL: National Gang Crime Research Center, 2004).

102. Cheryl Maxson, K. Woods, and Malcolm Klein, "Street Gang Migration: How Big a Threat?" *National Institute of Justice Journal* 230:26–31 (1996).

103. Jeffrey Fagan, "Gangs, Drugs, and Neighborhood Change," pages 39–74 in C. Ronald Huff (ed.), *Gangs in America,* 2nd edition (Thousand Oaks, CA: Sage, 1996).

104. James Howell and Debra Gleason, *Youth Gang Drug Trafficking* (Washington, DC: Office of Juvenile Justice and Delinquency Prevention, 1999).

105. Klein, note 79, pp. 41–42.

106. James Inciardi, Ruth Horowitz, and Anne Pottieger, *Street Kids, Street Drugs, Street Crime: An Examination of Drug Use and Serious Delinquency in Miami* (Belmont, CA: Wadsworth, 1993).

107. National Alliance of Gang Investigators Associations, *2005 National Gang Threat Assessment* (Washington, DC: Bureau of Justice Assistance, 2006).

108. Finn Esbensen and David Huizinga, "Gangs, Drugs, and Delinquency in a Survey of Urban Youth," *Criminology* 31:565–589 (1993); Finn Esbensen, Elizabeth Deschenes, and Thomas Winfree, "Differences Between Gang Girls and Gang Boys: Results from a Multisite Survey," *Youth & Society* 31:27–53 (1999); Dana Peterson, Jody Miller, and Finn Esbensen, "The Impact of Sex Composition on Gangs and Gang Member Delinquency," *Criminology* 39:411–440 (2001); Alan Turley, "Female Gangs and Patterns of Female Delinquency in Texas," *Journal of Gang Research* 10:1–10 (2003).

109. Beth Bjerregaard, "Operationalizing Gang Membership: The Impact Measurement on Gender Differences in Gang Self-Identification and Delinquent Involvement," *Women & Criminal Justice* 13:79–100 (2002).

110. Jody Miller and Rod Brunson, "Gender Dynamics in Youth Gangs: A Comparison of Males' and Females' Accounts," *Justice Quarterly* 17:419–448 (2000).

111. Joan Moore and John Hagedorn, *Female Gangs: A Focus on Research* (Washington, DC: Office of Juvenile Justice and Delinquency Prevention, 2001), p. 5.

112. Jody Miller and Scott Decker, "Young Women and Gang Violence: Gender, Street Offending, and Violent Victimization in Gangs," *Justice Quarterly* 18:115–140 (2001).

113. Esbensen et al., note 108, p. 41.

114. Geoffrey Hunt, Karen Joe-Laidler, and Kristy Evans, "The Meaning and Gendered Culture of Getting High: Gang Girls and Drug Use Issues," *Contemporary Drug Problems* 29:375–417 (2002); Kathleen MacKenzie, Geoffrey Hunt, and Karen Joe-Laidler, "Youth Gangs and Drugs: The Case of Marijuana," *Journal of Ethnicity in Substance Abuse* 4:99–134 (2005).

115. Miller, note 38.

116. Joan Moore and John Hagedorn, "What Happens to Girls in the Gang?" pages 205–218 in Huff, note 103, p. 207.

117. Miller, note 38, p. 37.

118. Anne Campbell, *The Girls in the Gang* (New York: Basil Blackwell, 1984), p. 266.

119. Geoffrey Hunt, Kathleen MacKenzie, and Karen Joe-Laidler, "'I'm Calling My Mom': The Meaning of Family and Kinship among Homegirls," *Justice Quarterly* 17:1–31 (2000).

120. Turley, note 108, p. 8.

121. Mary Harris, "Cholas, Mexican-American Girls, and Gangs," *Sex Roles* 30:289–301 (1994).

122. Scott Decker, *Policing Gangs and Youth Violence* (Belmont, CA: Wadsworth, 2003).

123. Charles Katz, "The Establishment of a Police Gang Unit: An Examination of Organizational and Environmental Factors," *Criminology* 39:37–74 (2001).

124. Egley and Ritz, note 62.

125. Bureau of Justice Assistance, *Urban Street Gang Enforcement* (Washington, DC: U.S. Department of Justice, 1997).

126. *Violent Crime Control and Law Enforcement Act of 1994, Title XV* (Washington, DC: U.S. Government Printing Office, 1994).

127. Eric Fritsch, Tory Caeti, and Robert Taylor, "Gang Suppression through Saturation Patrol and Aggressive Curfew and Truancy Enforcement: A Quasi-Experimental Test of the Dallas Anti-Gang Initiative," pages 267–284 in Scott Decker (ed.), *Policing Gangs and Youth Violence* (Belmont, CA: Wadsworth, 2003).

128. Edmund McGarrell, Steven Chermak, Jeremy Wilson, and Nicholas Corsaro, "Reducing Homicide through a 'Lever-Pulling' Strategy," *Justice Quarterly* 23:214–231 (2006).

129. Susan Popkin, Victoria Gwiasda, Dennis Rosenbaum, Jean Amendolia, Wendell Johnson, and Lynn Olson, "Combating Crime in Public Housing," *Justice Quarterly* 16:519–557 (1999).

130. Scott Decker and G. David Curry, "Suppression without Prevention, Prevention without Suppression: Gang Intervention in St. Louis," pages 191–213 in Scott Decker (ed.), *Policing Gangs and Youth Violence* (Belmont, CA: Wadsworth, 2003).

131. Anthony Braga, Jack McDevitt, and Glenn Pierce, "Understanding and Preventing Gang Violence: Problem Analysis and Response Development in Lowell, Massachusetts," *Police Quarterly* 9:20–46 (2006).

132. Michael Meyers, "Operation Clean Sweep: Curbing Street-Level Drug Trafficking," *FBI Law Enforcement Bulletin* 69:22–24 (2000).

133. Claire Johnson, Barbara Webster, and Edward Connors, *Prosecuting Gangs: A National Assessment* (Washington, DC: National Institute of Justice, 1995); Alan Jackson, *Prosecuting Gang Cases: What Local Prosecutors Need to Know* (Washington, DC: Bureau of Justice Assistance, 2004).

134. Brian Whitbread and Susan Mazza, "Gang Abatement: Utilizing Civil Laws to Combat Gangs, Part I," *Law Enforcement Quarterly* 28:28–31 (1999).

135. Egley et al., note 61.

136. George Knox and Curtis Robinson, "Trying to Live 'Gang Free' in Cicero, Illinois: A Study of Municipal Gang Abatement Efforts," *Journal of Gang Research* 6:57–70 (1999).

137. Cheryl Maxson, Karen Hennigan, and David Sloane, " 'It's Getting Crazy Out There': Can a Civil Gang Injunction Change a Community?" *Criminology & Public Policy* 4:577–606 (2005).

138. Jack Greene, "Gangs, Community Policing, and Problem Solving," pages 3–16 in Scott Decker (ed.), *Policing Gangs and Youth Violence* (Belmont, CA: Wadsworth, 2003).

139. John Hagedorn, "Homeboys, Dope Fiends, Legits, and New Jacks," *Criminology* 32:197–219 (1994); "Neighborhoods, Markets, and Gang Drug Organization," *Journal of Research in Crime and Delinquency* 31:264–294 (1994).

140. J. Robert Flores, *L.A.'s Homeboy Industries Intervenes with Gang-Involved Youth* (Washington, DC: Office of Juvenile Justice and Delinquency Prevention, 2006).

141. Huff, note 100, p. 326.

142. Finn Esbensen, Wayne Osgood, Terrance Taylor, Dana Peterson, and Adrienne Freng, "How Great is G.R.E.A.T.? Results from a Longitudinal Quasi-Experimental Design," *Criminology & Public Policy* 1:87–119 (2001).

CHAPTER 13

1. Egon Bittner, *The Functions of the Police in Modern Society* (Washington, DC: National Institute of Mental Health, 1970).

2. Robert Carter, "The Police View of the Justice System," pages 123–133 in Malcolm Klein (ed.), *The Juvenile Justice System* (Beverly Hills, CA: Sage, 1976), p. 131.

3. The discussion of police history draws from David Johnson, *American Law Enforcement* (St. Louis: Forum Press, 1981); James Richardson, *The New York Police* (New York: Oxford University Press, 1970); Samuel Walker and Charles Katz, *The Police in America,* 5th edition (New York: McGraw-Hill, 2006).

4. Arthur Cole, *The Irrepressible Conflict, 1850–1865* (New York: Macmillan, 1934).

5. Robert Fogelson, *Big-City Police* (Cambridge, MA: Harvard University Press, 1977).

6. David Wolcott, "The Cop Will Get You: The Police and Discretionary Juvenile Justice, 1890–1940," *Journal of Social History* 35:349–371 (2001).

7. David Wolcott, "Juvenile Justice before Juvenile Court: Cops, Courts, and Kids in Turn-of-the-Century Detroit," *Social Science History* 27:109–136 (2003).

8. David Tanenhaus, *Juvenile Justice in the Making* (New York: Oxford University Press, 2004).

9. Wolcott, note 7.

10. Wolcott, note 7.

11. *Pekin Police Department, Special Services Division,* October 21, 2006, online at: http://www.ci.pekin.il.us/policedept/investigation.asp, accessed May 3, 2007.

12. *Miranda v. Arizona,* 384 U.S. 436 (1966).

13. *Escobedo v. Illinois,* 378 U.S. 478 (1964).

14. *Miranda v. Arizona,* note 12.

15. *Payton v. New York,* 445 U.S. 573 (1980); *United States v. Mendenhall,* 466 U.S. 544 (1984); *Florida v. Bostick,* 489 U.S. 1021 (1991).

16. *Mapp v. Ohio,* 367 U.S. 643 (1961).

17. *U.S. v. Matlock,* 415 U.S. 164 (1974).

18. *In re Scott K.,* 595 P.2d 105 (1979).

19. *People v. Jacobs,* 729 P.2d 757 (Cal. 1987).

20. *Montana v. Schwarz,* No. 05–370 (2006).

21. *State v. Tomlinson,* 648 N.W.2d 367 (Wis. 2002); *State v. Kriegh,* 937 P.2d 453 (Kan. App. 1997); *State v. Will,* 885 P.2d 715 (Or. App. 1994); *Davis v. State,* 422 S.E.2d 546 (Ga. 1992).

22. Martin Gardner, *Understanding Juvenile Law,* 2nd edition (Newark, NJ: Matthew Bender & Co., 2003), p. 208.

23. *Ill. Ann. Stat.,* Ch. 705, para.405/5–401(1) (a) (Smith-Hurd 1999).

24. *New York Family Court Act 718* (McKinney Supp.1988).

25. *Michigan Rules of Court,* Rule 5.933 (West 1988).

26. *Gilbert v. California,* 388 U.S. 263 (1967); *United States v. Wade,* 388 U.S. 218 (1967); *United States v. Euge,* 444 U.S. 707 (1980).

27. *Ohio Revised Code* 2151.313 (1984).

28. *Sealing Juvenile Records,* online at: http://www.clcm.org/sealing_records.htm, accessed May 3, 2007.

29. *Sealing Juvenile Court Records in Washington State,* online at: http://www.lawhelp.org/documents/2168014902EN.pdf?stateabbrev=/WA/, accessed May 3, 2007.

30. *In re Carlo,* Supreme Court of New Jersey 48 N.J. 224 A.2d 110 (1966).

31. *In re Gault,* 387 U.S. 1 (1967).

32. *State v. McMillian* (Mo.), 514 S.W.2d 528 (1974).

33. *West v. United States,* 399 F.2d 467 (5th Cir. 1968).

34. *State v. Jerrell C. J.,* 269 Wis. 2d 442, 674 N.W. 2d 607 (2005).

35. *Fare v. Michael C.,* 439 U.S. 1310 (1978).

36. *State v. Javier M.,* 2001 NMSC 30, 131 N.M. 1,33 P.3d 1.

37. Maria Touchet, "Children's Law: Investigatory Detention of Juvenile in New Mexico: Providing Greater Protection than *Miranda* Rights for Children in the Area of Police Questioning—*State of New Mexico v. Javier M.,*" *New Mexico Law Review* 32:393–408 (2002).

38. *Tex. Fam. Code Ann.,* 51.09(b)(1) (Vernon Supp. 1989).

39. *Colo. Rev. Stat.,* 19-2-210(1) (Supp. 1996).

40. *Gilbert v. California,* note 26; *United States v. Wade,* note 26; *In re Holley,* 107 R.I. 615 (1970).

41. *Jackson v. State,* 300 A.2d. 430 (Md. Ct. Spec. App. 1973).

42. Mark Stafford, "Children's Legal Rights in the U.S.," *Marriage and the Family Review* 21:121–140 (1995).

43. Stephanie Myers, *Police Encounters with Juvenile Suspects: Explaining the Use of Authority and Provision of Support* (Washington, DC: National Institute of Justice, 1999).

44. Carl Werthman and Irving Piliavin, "Gang Members and the Police," pages 56–98 in David Bordua (ed.), *The Police: Six Sociological Essays* (New York: John Wiley & Sons, 1967).

45. Sandra Lee Browning, Francis Cullen, Liqun Cao, Renee Kopache, and Thomas Stevenson, "Race and Getting Hassled by the Police," *Police Studies* 17:1–11 (1994).

46. Douglas Smith, "The Neighborhood Context of Police Behavior," pages 313–341 in Albert Reiss and Michael Tonry (eds.), *Crime and Justice,* volume 8 (Chicago: University of Chicago Press, 1986).

47. Howard Snyder and Melissa Sickmund, *Juvenile Offenders and Victims: 2006 National Report* (Washington, DC: National Center for Juvenile Justice, 2006), p. 152.

48. Robert Terry, "Discrimination in the Handling of Juvenile Offenders by Social-Control Agencies," *Journal of Research in Crime and Delinquency* 4:218–230 (1967).

49. Donald Black and Albert Reiss, "Police Control of Juveniles," *American Sociological Review* 35:63–77 (1970).

50. Myers, note 43.

51. Nathan Goldman, *The Differential Selection of Juvenile Offenders for Court Appearance* (New York: National Council on Crime and Delinquency, 1963).

52. Terry, note 48.

53. Aaron Cicourel, *The Social Organization of Juvenile Justice* (New York: John Wiley & Sons, 1976), p. 119.

54. Black and Reiss, note 49; Irving Piliavin and Scott Briar, "Police Encounters with Juveniles," *American Journal of Sociology* 70:206–214 (1964).

55. Black and Reiss, note 49.

56. Kenneth Novak, James Frank, Brad Smith, and Robin Engel, "Revisiting the Decision to Arrest: Comparing Beat and Community Officers," *Crime & Delinquency* 48:70–98 (2002).

57. *Terry v. Ohio,* 392 U.S. 1 (1968).

58. Terrence Allen, "Taking a Juvenile into Custody: Situational Factors that Influence Police Officers' Decisions," *Journal of Sociology and Social Welfare* 32:121–129 (2005).

59. Geoffrey Alpert, John MacDonald, and Roger Dunham, "Police Suspicion and Discretionary Decision Making During Citizen Stops," *Criminology* 43:407–434 (2005).

60. Myers, note 43.

61. Douglas Smith and Christy Visher, "Street-Level Justice," *Social Problems* 29:167–177 (1981); Stephen Mastrofski, Robert Worden, and Jeffrey Snipes, "Law Enforcement in a Time of Community Policing," *Criminology* 33:539–563 (1995); Ronet Bachman, "Victim's Perceptions of Initial Police Responses to Robbery and Aggravated Assault," *Journal of Quantitative Criminology* 12:363–390 (1996); David Huizinga and Delbert Elliott, "Juvenile Offenders," *Crime & Delinquency* 33:206–223 (1987).

62. Federal Bureau of Investigation, *Crime in the United States, 2005* (Washington, DC: U.S. Department of Justice, 2006).

63. Samuel Walker, Cassia Spohn, and Miriam DeLone, *The Color of Justice,* 2nd edition (Belmont, CA: Wadsworth, 2000).

64. John Boydstun, *San Diego Field Interrogation* (Washington, DC: The Police Foundation, 1975).

65. Black and Reiss, note 49.

66. Robert Sampson, "Effects of Socioeconomic Context on Official Reaction to Juvenile Delinquency," *American Sociological Review* 51:876–885 (1986).

67. Joan McCord, Cathy Widom, and Nancy Crowell, *Juvenile Crime/Juvenile Justice* (Washington, DC: National Academy Press, 2001).

68. Werthman and Piliavin, note 44.

69. Robert Brown, "Black, White, and Unequal: Examining Situational Determinants of Arrest Decisions from Police-Suspect Encounters," *Criminal Justice Studies* 18:51–68 (2005).

70. Terrance Taylor, K. B. Turner, Finn Esbensen, and L. Thomas Winfree, "Coppin' an Attitude: Attitudinal Differences among Juveniles toward Police," *Journal of Criminal Justice* 29:295–305 (2001).

71. Piliavin and Briar, note 54, p. 210.

72. Cicourel, note 53.

73. Black and Reiss, note 49; Piliavin and Briar, note 54.

74. Richard Lundman, "Demeanor and Arrest: Additional Evidence from Previously Unpublished Data," *Journal of Research in Crime and Delinquency* 33:306–323 (1996); Robert Worden and Robin Shepard, "Demeanor, Crime, and Police Behavior: A Reexamination of the Police Services Study Data," *Criminology* 34:83–105 (1996); Robert Worden, Robin Shepard, and Stephen Mastrofski, "On the Meaning and Measurement of Suspects' Demeanor toward the Police: A Comment on 'Demeanor and Arrest,'" *Journal of Research in Crime and Delinquency* 33:324–332 (1996).

75. Novak et al., note 56.

76. David Klinger, "Demeanor or Crime?" *Criminology* 32:475–493 (1994); David Klinger, "More on Demeanor and Arrest in Dade County," *Criminology* 34:61–82 (1996); David Klinger, "Bringing Crime Back In," *Journal of Research in Crime and Delinquency* 33:333–336 (1996); David Klinger, "Quantifying Law in Police-Citizen Encounters," *Journal of Quantitative Criminology* 12:391–415 (1996).

77. Robin Engel, James Sobol, and Robert Worden, "Further Exploration of the Demeanor Hypothesis: The Interaction Effects of Suspects' Characteristics and Demeanor on Police Behavior," *Justice Quarterly* 17:249 (2000).

78. Stephen Mastrofski, Michael Reisig, and John McCluskey, "Police Disrespect toward the Public: An Encounter-Based Analysis," *Criminology* 40:519–551 (2002); Michael Reisig, John McCluskey, Stephen Mastrofski, and William Terrill, "Suspect Disrespect toward the Police," *Justice Quarterly* 21:241–268 (2004).

79. Mastrofski et al., note 78, p. 534.

80. George Bodine, "Factors Related to Police Dispositions of Juvenile Offenders," paper presented at the annual meeting of the American Sociological Association, 1964.

81. Terence Thornberry, "Race, Socioeconomic Status, and Sentencing in the Juvenile Justice System," *Journal of Criminal Law and Criminology* 64:90–98 (1973).

82. Cicourel, note 53.

83. Novak et al., note 56; Mastrofski et al., note 61; McCord et al., note 67, p. 245.

84. Thomas Monahan, "Police Dispositions of Juvenile Offenders," *Phylon* 31:91–107 (1970).

85. Delbert Elliott and Harwin Voss, *Delinquency and Dropout* (Lexington, MA: Lexington Books, 1974).

86. Gail Armstrong, "Females under the Law—Protected but Unequal," *Crime & Delinquency* 23:109–120 (1977); Meda Chesney-Lind, "Judicial Paternalism and the Female Status Offender," *Crime & Delinquency* 23:121–130 (1970).

87. Katherine Teilman and Pierre Landry, "Gender Bias in Juvenile Justice," *Journal of Research in Crime and Delinquency* 18: 47–80 (1981).

88. Ruth Horowitz and Ann Pottieger, "Gender Bias in Juvenile Justice Handling of Seriously Crime-Involved Youth," *Journal of Research in Crime and Delinquency* 28:75–100 (1991).

89. Christy Visher, "Gender, Police Arrest Decisions, and Notions of Chivalry," *Criminology* 21:15 (1983).

90. Visher, note 89, pp. 22–23.

91. Meda Chesney-Lind and Randall Shelden, *Girls, Delinquency, and Juvenile Justice,* 3rd edition (Pacific Grove, CA: Brooks/Cole, 2004).

92. Marvin Krohn, James Curry, and Shirley Nelson-Kilger, "Is Chivalry Dead? An Analysis of Changes in Police Dispositions of Males and Females," *Criminology* 21:417–437 (1983).

93. Teilman and Landry, note 87.

94. Goldman, note 51.

95. Alexander McEachern and Rita Bauzer, "Factors Related to Dispositions in Juvenile Police Contacts," pages 148–160 in Malcolm Klein (ed.), *Juvenile Gangs in Context* (Englewood Cliffs, NJ: Prentice Hall, 1967).

96. Bodine, note 80.

97. James Q. Wilson, *Varieties of Police Behavior* (Cambridge, MA: Harvard University Press, 1968).

98. Richard Sundeen, "A Study of Factors Related to Police Diversion of Departmental Policies and Structures, Community Attachment and Professionalization of the Police," doctoral dissertation, University of Southern California, 1972.

99. Robin Engel, "The Effects of Supervisory Styles on Patrol Officer Behavior," *Police Quarterly* 3:283 (2000).

100. James Baldwin, *Nobody Knows My Name* (New York: Dial Press, 1961).

101. Michelle Fine, Nick Freudenberg, Yasser Payne, Tiffany Perkins, Kersha Smith, and Katya Wanzer, "Anything Can Happen with Police Around: Urban Youth Evaluate Strategies of Surveillance in Public Places," *Journal of Social Issues* 59:141–168 (2003); Clive Norris, Nigel Fielding, Charles Kemp, and Jane Fielding, "Black and Blue: An Analysis of the Influence of Race on Being Stopped by the Police," *British Journal of Sociology* 43:207–224 (1992); Nancy Boyd-Franklin and A. J. Franklin, *Boys into Men* (New York: Dutton, 2000).

102. Delores Jones-Brown, "Debunking the Myth of Officer Friendly," *Journal of Contemporary Criminal Justice* 16:209 (2000).

103. Roger Parks, Stephen Mastrofski, Christina DeJong, and M. Kevin Gray, "How Officers Spend Their Time with the Community," *Justice Quarterly* 16:483–518 (1999); Marcia Chaiken, *Kids, COPS, and Communities* (Washington, DC: U.S. Department of Justice, 1998); Gerasimos Gianakis and G. John Davis, "Reinventing or Repackaging Public Services? The Case of Community-Oriented Policing," *Public Administration Review* 58:485–507 (1998); James Q. Wilson and George Kelling, "The Police and Neighborhood Safety: Broken Windows," *Atlantic Monthly* 127:29–38 (1982); Peter Manning, "Community Policing," *American Journal of Police* 3:205–227 (1984); Herman Goldstein, *Problem-Oriented Policing* (New York: McGraw-Hill, 1990); Wesley Skogan and Susan Hartnett, *Community Policing, Chicago Style* (New York: Oxford University Press, 1997).

104. Robert Trojanowicz and Bonnie Bucqueroux, *Community Policing: A Contemporary Perspective* (Cincinnati: Anderson, 1990), p. 5.

105. Walker and Katz, note 3; Robert Trojanowicz, Victor Kappeler, and Larry Gaines, *Community Policing: A Contemporary Perspective,* 3rd edition (Cincinnati: Anderson, 2002), p. 235.

106. Trojanowicz and Bucqueroux, note 104, p. 236.

107. Linda Miller and Karen Hess, *The Police in the Community: Strategies for the 21st Century,* 3rd edition (Belmont, CA: Wadsworth, 2002), pp. 403–404.

108. James Forman, "Community Policing and Youths as Assets," *Journal of Criminal Law and Criminology* 95:1–48 (2004).

109. Miller and Hess, note 107.

110. Snyder and Sickmund, note 47.

111. Walker and Katz, note 3.

112. Malcolm Klein, "Issues and Realities in Police Diversion Programs," *Crime & Delinquency* 22:421–427 (1976).

113. Klein, note 112.

CHAPTER 14

1. Robert Mennel, *Thorns and Thistles: Juvenile Delinquents in the United States* (Hanover, NH: University Press of New England, 1973), p. 132.

2. Mark Haller, "Urban Crime and Criminal Justice: The Chicago Case," *Journal of American History* 57:619–635 (1970).

3. Sanford Fox, "Juvenile Justice Reform: A Historical Perspective," *Stanford Law Review* 2:1187–1239 (1970).

4. Howard Snyder and Melissa Sickmund, *Juvenile Offenders and Victims: 2006 National Report* (Washington, DC: Office of Justice Programs, 2006), p, 103.

5. Frank Miller, Robert Dawson, George Dix, and Raymond Parnas, *The Juvenile Justice Process,* 4th edition (New York: Foundation Press, 2000), pp. 215–216.

6. Snyder and Sickmund, note 4, pp. 157–158.

7. Snyder and Sickmund, note 4, p. 177.

8. Martin Gardner, *Understanding Juvenile Law,* 2nd edition (New York: Matthew-Bender, 2003), p. 249.

9. Snyder and Sickmund, note 4, pp. 177–183.

10. Lisa Bond-Maupin, James Maupin, and Amy Leisenring, "Girls' Delinquency and the Justice Implications of Intake Workers' Perspectives," *Women and Criminal Justice* 13:51–77 (2002), p. 72.

11. Michael Leiber and Kristin Mack, "The Individual and Joint Effects of Race, Gender, and Family Status on Juvenile Justice Decision-Making," *Journal of Research in Crime and Delinquency* 40:34–70 (2003), p. 57.

12. James Austin, Kelly Johnson, and Ronald Weitzer, *Alternatives to the Secure Detention and Confinement of Juvenile Offenders* (Washington, DC: Office of Juvenile Justice and Delinquency Prevention, 2005).

13. Barry Feld, *Cases and Materials on Juvenile Justice Administration* (St. Paul, MN: West, 2000), p. 313.

14. *Ala. Code* 12-15-59(a) (1975).

15. Joan McCord, Cathy Widom, and Nancy Crowell, *Juvenile Crime, Juvenile Justice* (Washington, DC: National Academy Press, 2001), p. 177.

16. *Schall v. Martin,* 467 U.S. 253 (1984).

17. Charles Puzzanchera, Anne Stahl, Terrence Finnegan, Nancy Tierney, and Howard Snyder, *Juvenile Court Statistics, 1999* (Washington, DC: U.S. Department of Justice, 2003), p. 22.

18. Snyder and Sickmund, note 4, p. 168.

19. Eleanor Hoytt, Vincent Schiraldi, Brenda Smith, and Jason Ziedenberg, *Reducing Racial Disparities in Juvenile Justice* (Baltimore: Annie E. Casey Foundation, 2002), p. 11.

20. Gaylene Armstrong and Nancy Rodriguez, "Effects of Individual and Contextual Characteristics on Preadjudication Detention of Juvenile Delinquents," *Justice Quarterly* 22:521–539 (2005).

21. Snyder and Sickmund, note 4, p. 169.

22. Michael Leiber and Kristan Fox, "Race and the Impact of Detention on Juvenile Justice Decision Making," *Crime & Delinquency* 51:470–497 (2005).

23. American Bar Association and National Bar Association, *Justice by Gender: The Lack of Appropriate Prevention, Diversion and Treatment Alternatives for Girls in the Justice System* (Washington, DC: American Bar Association and National Bar Association, 2001) pp. 18–19.

24. Francine Sherman, *Detention Reform for Girls: Challenges and Solutions* (Baltimore: The Annie E. Casey Foundation, 2005).

25. Christy Sharp and Jessica Simon, *Girls in the Juvenile Justice System: The Need for More Gender-Responsive Services* (Washington, DC: Child Welfare League of America, 2004), p. 11.

26. Bond-Maupin et al., note 10, p. 73.

27. Barry Feld, *Bad Kids: Race and the Transformation of the Juvenile Court* (New York: Oxford University Press, 1999), p. 162.

28. Daniel Mears, "Sentencing Guidelines and the Transformation of Juvenile Justice in the 21st Century," *Journal of Contemporary Criminal Justice* 18:6–19 (2002).

29. See, Donna Bishop and Charles Frazier, "Gender Bias in Juvenile Justice Processing: The Implications of the JJDP Act," *Journal of Criminal Law and Criminology* 82:1162– 1186(1992); Kimberly Leonard, Carl Pope, and William Feyerherm, *Minorities in Juvenile Justice* (Thousand Oaks, CA: Sage, 1995); Edmund McGarrell, "Trends in Racial Disproportionality in Juvenile Court Processing: 1985–1989," *Crime & Delinquency* 39:29–48 (1993), John MacDonald and Meda Chesney-Lind, "Gender Bias and Juvenile Justice Revisited: A Multiyear Analysis," *Crime & Delinquency* 47:173–195 (2001).

30. MacDonald and Chesney-Lind, note 29, p. 189.

31. Snyder and Sickmund, note 4, pp. 177–179.

32. Snyder and Sickmund, note 4, pp. 174–175.

33. Michelle Heward, *An Update on Teen Court Legislation* (Lexington, KY: National Youth Court Center, 2006); Sarah Pearson and Sonia Jurich, *A National Update: Communities Embracing Youth Courts for At-Risk Youth* (Washington, DC: American Youth Policy Forum, 2005).

34. Jeffrey Butts and Janeen Buck, *Teen Courts: A Focus on Research* (Washington, DC: Office of Juvenile Justice and Delinquency Prevention, 2000).

35. Heward, note 33.

36. Steven Belenko, *Research on Drug Courts: A Critical Review 2001 Update* (New York: The National Center on Addiction and Substance Abuse at Columbia University, 2001); Glenn Schmidt, *Drug Courts: The Second Decade* (Washington, DC: U.S. Department of Justice, 2006).

37. Caroline Cooper, *Juvenile Drug Court Programs* (Washington, DC: Office of Juvenile Justice and Delinquency Prevention, 2001).

38. Shelly Listwan, Jody Sundt, Alexander Holsinger, and Edward Latessa, "The Effect of Drug Court Programming on Recidivism: The Cincinnati Experience," *Crime & Delinquency* 49:389–411 (2003); Robert Granfield, Cynthia Eby, and Thomas Brewster, "An Examination of the Denver Drug Court: The Impact of a Treatment-Oriented Drug-Offender System," *Law & Policy* 20:183–202 (1998); Gennaro Vito and Richard Tewksbury, "The Impact of Treatment: The Jefferson County (Kentucky) Drug Court Program," *Federal Probation* 62:46–52 (1998); Roger Peters, Amie Haas, and Mary Murrin, "Predictors of Retention and Arrest in Drug Courts," *National Drug Court Institute Review* 2:33–60 (1999).

39. Terance Miethe, Hong Lu, and Erin Reese, "Reintegrative Shaming and Recidivism Risks in Drug Court: Explanations for Some Unexpected Findings," *Crime & Delinquency* 46:522–541 (2000).

40. Brandon Applegate and Shannon Santana, "Intervening with Youthful Substance Abusers: A Preliminary Analysis of a Juvenile Drug Court," *The Justice System Journal* 21:281–300 (2000); Marsha Miller, Evelyn Scocas, and John O'Connell, *Evaluation of the Juvenile Drug Court Diversion Program* (Dover, DE: Statistical Analysis Center, 1998).

41. Nancy Rodriguez and Vincent Webb, "Multiple Measures of Juvenile Drug Court Effectiveness: Results of a Quasi-Experimental Design," *Crime & Delinquency* 50:292–314 (2004).

42. See, John Braithwaite, *Restorative Justice and Responsive Regulation* (New York: Oxford University Press, 2002); John Perry, *Repairing Communities through*

Restorative Justice (Lanham, MD: American Correctional Association, 2002); Gerry Johnstone, *Restorative Justice: Ideas, Values, Debates* (Portland, OR: Willan Publishing, 2002); Allison Morris and Gabrielle Maxwell, *Restorative Justice for Juveniles: Conferencing, Mediation, and Circles* (Oxford, England: Hart Publishing, 2001); Daniel Van Ness and Karen Strong, *Restoring Justice,* 2nd edition (Cincinnati: Anderson, 2001); Shay Bilchik, Gordon Bazemore, and Mark Umbreit, *Balanced and Restorative Justice for Juveniles: A Framework for Juvenile Justice in the 21st Century* (Washington, DC: Office of Juvenile Justice and Delinquency Prevention, 1997).

43. Lynn Urban, Jenna St. Cyr, and Scott Decker, "Goal Conflict in the Juvenile Court: The Evolution of Sentencing Practices in the United States," *Journal of Contemporary Criminal Justice* 19:454–479 (2003).

44. Urban et al., note 43, p. 467.

45. Braithwaite, note 42; Gordon Bazemore and Curt Griffiths, "Conferences, Circles, Boards, and Mediations: The 'New Wave' of Community Justice Decision-Making," *Federal Probation,* 61:25–37 (1997).

46. Mark Umbreit, Robert Coates, and Betty Voss, "The Impact of Victim-Offender Mediation: Two Decades of Research," *Federal Probation* 65:29–35 (2001).

47. Heather Strang, Lawrence Sherman, Caroline Angel, Daniel Woods, Sarah Bennett, Dorothy Newbury-Birch, and Nova Inkpen, "Victim Evaluations of Face-to-Face Restorative Justice Conferences: A Quasi-Experimental Analysis," *Journal of Social Issues* 62:281–306 (2006).

48. Sharon Levrant, Francis Cullen, Betsy Fulton, and John Wozniak, "Reconsidering Restorative Justice: The Corruption of Benevolence Revisited?" *Crime & Delinquency* 45:3–27 (1999).

49. Carol Gilligan, *In a Different Voice* (Cambridge, MA: Harvard University Press, 1982).

50. Lori Elis, "Restorative Justice Programs, Gender, and Recidivism," *Public Organization Review: A Global Journal* 5:375–389 (2005).

51. Adam Crawford and Todd Clear, "Community Justice: Transforming Communities through Restorative Justice?" pages 127–149 in Gordon Bazemore and Marie Schiff (eds.), *Restorative Community Justice* (Cincinnati: Anderson, 2001).

52. *Kent v. United States,* 383 U.S. 541 (1966).

53. *In re Gault,* 387 U.S. 1 (1967).

54. *In re Gault,* note 53.

55. *In re Gault,* note 53.

56. Feld, note 27, p. 125.

57. George Burruss and Kimberly Kempf-Leonard, "The Questionable Advantage of Defense Counsel in Juvenile Court," *Justice Quarterly* 19:37–68 (2002).

58. Janet Ainsworth, "Re-imagining Childhood and Reconstructing the Legal Order: The Case for Abolishing the Juvenile Court," *North Carolina Law Review* 69:1083–1133 (1991).

59. Judith Jones, *Access to Counsel* (Washington, DC: Office of Juvenile Justice and Delinquency Prevention, 2004).

60. Barry Feld, *Justice for Children: The Right to Counsel and the Juvenile Courts* (Boston: Northeastern University Press, 1993); Steven Clarke and Gary Koch, "Juvenile Court: Therapy or Crime Control, and Do Lawyers Make a Difference?" *Law and Society Review* 14:263–308 (1980); Burruss and Kempf-Leonard, note 57.

61. Lori Guevara, Cassia Spohn, and Denise Herz, "Race, Legal Representation, and Juvenile Justice: Issues and Concerns," *Crime & Delinquency* 50:344–371 (2004).

62. *In re Winship,* 397 U.S. 358 (1970).

63. *In re Winship,* note 62.

64. *In re Manuel L.,* 7 Cal.4th 229 (1994).

65. *McKeiver v. Pennsylvania,* 403 U.S. 528 (1971).

66. *McKeiver,* note 65.

67. Joseph Sanborn, "The Right to a Public Jury Trial: A Need for Today's Juvenile Court," *Judicature* 76:233 (1993).

68. *In the Interest of G.O.,* 304 Ill.App.3d 719 (1999).

69. *Breed v. Jones,* 421 U.S. 519 (1975).

70. Gardner, note 8, p. 238.

71. Miller et al., note 5, pp. 338–339.

72. *Schall,* note 16.

73. *Schall,* note 16.

74. *Breed,* note 69.

75. Snyder and Sickmund, note 4, p. 108.

76. *Davis v. Alaska,* 415 U.S. 308 (1974).

77. *Oklahoma Publishing Company v. District Court,* 430 U.S. 308 (1976).

78. *Smith v. Daily Mail Publishing Company,* 443 U.S. 97 (1979).

79. Snyder and Sickmund, note 4, p. 109.

80. Robert Shepherd, "The Rush to Waive Children to Adult Court," *Criminal Justice* 10:39–42 (1995); Patricia Torbet, Richard Gable, Hunter Hurst, Imogene Montgomery, Linda Szymanski, and Douglas Thomas, *State Responses to Serious and Violent Juvenile Crime* (Washington, DC: National Center for Juvenile Justice, 1996); Patricia Torbet, Patrick Griffin, Hunter Hurst, and Lynn MacKenzie, *Juveniles Facing Criminal Sanctions: Three States That Changed the Rules* (Washington, DC: Office of Juvenile Justice and Delinquency Prevention, 2000).

81. *Violent Crime Control and Law Enforcement Act of 1994,* Title XIV, Sec. 14000.1 (Washington, DC: U.S. Government Printing Office, 1994).

82. Feld, note 27.

83. *Kent,* note 52.

84. *Kent,* note 52.

85. Patrick Griffin, *Trying and Sentencing Juveniles as Adults: Analysis of State Transfer and Blended Sentencing Laws* (Pittsburgh: National Center for Juvenile Justice, 2003).

86. Francis McCarthy, "The Serious Offender and Juvenile Court Reform: The Case for Prosecutorial Waiver of Juvenile Court Jurisdiction," *Saint Louis University Law Journal* 38:654 (1994).

87. Simon Singer, *Recriminalizing Delinquency: Violent Juvenile Crime and Juvenile Justice Reform* (New York: Cambridge University Press, 1996).

88. Snyder and Sickmund, note 4, p. 186.

89. Lee Osbun and Peter Rode, "Prosecuting Juveniles as Adults," *Criminology* 22:195 (1984).

90. Snyder and Sickmund, note 4, p. 186.

91. Snyder and Sickmund, note 4, p. 187.

92. Sanjeev Sridharan, Lynette Greenfield, and Baron Blakley, "A Study of Prosecutorial Certification Practice in Virginia," *Criminology & Public Policy* 3:605–632 (2004).

93. Howard Snyder, Melissa Sickmund, Eileen Poe-Yamagata, and National Center for Juvenile Justice, *Juvenile Transfers to Criminal Court in the 1990's: Lessons Learned from Four Studies* (Washington, DC: Office of Juvenile Justice and Delinquency Prevention, 2000), pp. 14, 22.

94. Elizabeth Cauffman, Jennifer Woolard, and N. Dickon Reppucci, "Justice for Juveniles: New Perspectives on Adolescents' Competence and Culpability," *Quinnipiac College School of Law* 18:403–419 (1999); Thomas Grisso, Lawrence Woolard, Elizabeth Cauffman, Elizabeth Scott, and Sandra Graham, "Juveniles' Competence to Stand Trial: A Comparison of Adolescents' and Adults' Capacities as Trial Defendants," *Law and Human Behavior* 27:333–363 (2003); Janet Warren, Jeff Aaron, Eileen Ryan, Preeti Chauhan, and Jeanette DuVal, "Correlates of Adjudicative Competence Among Transfer Reforms," *Journal of the American Academy of Psychiatry and Law* 31:299–309 (2003).

95. Norman Poythress, Frances Lexcen, Thomas Grisso, and Laurence Steinberg, "The Competence-Related Abilities of Adolescent Defendants in Criminal Court," *Law and Human Behavior* 30:75–92 (2006).

96. Poythress et al., note 95.

97. Jodi Olson, "Waiver of Juveniles to Criminal Court: Judicial Discretion and Racial Disparity," *Justice Policy Journal* 2:1–20 (2005).

98. Jeffrey Fagan, Ellen Slaughter, and Eliot Hartstone, "Blind Justice? The Impact of Race on the Juvenile Justice Process," *Crime & Delinquency* 33:224–258 (1987).

99. Marcy Podkopacz and Barry Feld, "The End of the Line: An Empirical Study of Judicial Waiver," *Journal of Criminal Law and Criminology* 86:449–492 (1996).

100. Jolanta Juszkiewicz, *Youth Crime/Adult Time: Is Justice Served?* (Washington, DC: Building Blocks for Youth, 2001).

101. Mike Males and Dan Macallair, *The Color of Justice: An Analysis of Juvenile Adult Court Transfers in California* (Washington, DC: Youth Law Center, 2000).

102. Marilyn Houghtalin and Larry Mays, "Criminal Dispositions of New Mexico Juveniles Transferred to Adult Court," *Crime & Delinquency* 37:393–407 (1991); Podkopacz and Feld, note 99; "Kevin Strom, Steven Smith, and Howard Snyder, *State Court Processing Statistics, 1990–94: Juvenile Felony Defendants in Criminal Courts* (Washington, DC: U.S. Department of Justice, 1998).

103. Elizabeth Clarke, "A Case for Reinventing Juvenile Transfer," *Juvenile and Family Court Journal* 47:3–21 (1996); Kristine Kinder, Carol Veneziano, Michael Ficter, and Henry Azuma, "A Comparison of the Dispositions of Juvenile Offenders Certified as Adult with Juvenile Offenders not Certified," *Juvenile and Family Court Journal* 46:37–42 (1995).

104. Megan Kurlychek and Brian Johnson, "The Juvenile Penalty: A Comparison of Juvenile and Young Adult Sentencing Outcomes in Criminal Court," *Criminology* 42:485–517 (2004).

105. Randi-Lynn Smallheer, "Sentence Blending and the Promise of Rehabilitation: Bring the Juvenile Justice System Full Circle," *Hofstra Law Review* 28: 259–289 (1999).

106. Marcy Podkopacz and Barry Feld, "The Back-Door to Prison: Waiver Reform, 'Blended Sentencing,' and the Law of Unintended Consequences," *Journal of Criminal Law & Criminology* 91:997–1071 (2001).

107. Peter Benkos and Alida Merlo, *Controversies in Juvenile Justice and Delinquency* (Cincinnati: Lexis/Nexis, 2004), p. 113.

108. Snyder and Sickmund, note 4, p. 192.

109. Gardner, note 8.

CHAPTER 15

1. Barry Krisberg, "The Legacy of Juvenile Corrections," *Corrections Today,* August 1995, p. 122.

2. Krisberg, note 1, p. 124.

3. John Hewitt and Bob Regoli, "Holding Serious Juvenile Offenders Responsible: Applying Differential Oppression Theory," *Free Inquiry in Creative Sociology* 30:1–8 (2002).

4. Martin Gardner, *Understanding Juvenile Law* (New York: Matthew Bender, 1997), p. 293.

5. *Wash. Rev. Code Ann.* 13.40.010(2) [West Supp. 1996].

6. Brandon Applegate, Michael Turner, Joseph Sanborn, Edward Latessa, and Melissa Moon, "Individualization, Criminalization, or Problem Resolution: A Factorial Survey of Juvenile Court Judges' Decisions to Incarcerate Youthful Felony Offenders," *Justice Quarterly* 17:328 (2000).

7. Jamie Fader, Philip Harris, Peter Jones, and Mary Poulin, "Factors Involved in Decisions on Commitment to Delinquency Programs for First-Time Juvenile Offenders," *Justice Quarterly* 18:323–341 (2001).

8. Fader et al., note 7, pp. 336–337.

9. Charles Puzzanchera, Anne Stahl, Terrence Finnegan, Nancy Tierney, and Howard Snyder, *Juvenile Court Statistics, 1999* (Pittsburgh: National Center for Juvenile Justice, 2003).

10. Patricia Torbet, *Juvenile Probation: The Workhorse of the Juvenile Justice System* (Washington, DC: Office of Juvenile Justice and Delinquency Prevention, 1996).

11. Kimberly Fitzgerald, *Probation Conditions Imposed on Juveniles: What Types of Conditions Are Unreasonable and Unconstitutional?* (San Francisco: First District Appellate Project, 2004).

12. D. Evans, "Boston's Probation and Police Partnership," *Corrections Today* 59:126 (1997); Dale Parent and B. Snyder, *Police-Corrections Partnerships* (Washington, DC: U.S. Department of Justice, 1999).

13. Matthew Giblin, "Using Police Officers to Enhance the Supervision of Juvenile Probationers: An Evaluation of the Anchorage CAN Program," *Crime & Delinquency* 48:116–137 (2002).

14. Michael Tonry, "Intermediate Sanctions," pages 683–711 in Michael Tonry (ed.), *The Handbook of Crime and Punishment* (New York: Oxford, 1998).

15. Betsy Fulton, Edward Latessa, Amy Stichman, and Larry Travis, "The State of ISP: Research and Policy Impli-

cations," *Federal Probation* 61:65–76 (1997); Joan Petersilia and Susan Turner, "Intensive Probation and Parole," pages 281–336 in Michael Tonry (ed.) *Crime and Justice: A Review of Research,* volume 17 (Chicago: University of Chicago Press, 1993); Susan Turner and Joan Petersilia, "Focusing on High-Risk Parolees: An Experiment to Reduce Commitments to the Texas Department of Corrections," *Journal of Research in Crime and Delinquency* 29:34–62 (1992).

16. Susan Turner and Terry Fain, "Accomplishments in Juvenile Probation in California Over the Last Decade," *Federal Probation* 70:63–69 (2006).

17. Ronald Ball, Ronald Huff, and Robert Lilly, *House Arrest and Correctional Policy: Doing Time at Home* (Newbury Park, CA: Sage, 1988), pp. 46–47.

18. Bonnie Berry, "Electronic Jails," *Justice Quarterly* 2:1–22 (1985); Ronald Ball and Robert Lilly, "The Phenomenology of Privacy and the Power of Electronic Monitoring," pages 147–165 in Joseph Scott and Travis Hirschi (eds.), *Controversial Issues in Crime and Justice* (Newbury Park, CA: Sage, 1988).

19. Randall Chase, "State Expanding High-Tech Tracking Global Positioning Systems to Monitor Young Offenders with Greater Precision," *News Journal,* March 7, 2005: A3; Ellen Perlman, "Where Are They Now? States and Localities Are Using GPS to Put Moving Targets on the Map," *Governing Magazine* (October 2005), online at: http://66.23.131.98/archive/2005/oct/gps.txt, accessed May 4, 2007.

20. Gilbert Geis, "Foreword," pp. 10–13 in Ball et al., note 17.

21. William Staples, "Restitution as a Sanction in Juvenile Court," *Crime & Delinquency* 32:177–185 (1986).

22. Anne Schneider, *Guide to Juvenile Restitution* (Washington, DC: U.S. Government Printing Office, 1985).

23. Andrew Klein, *Alternative Sentencing* (Cincinnati: Anderson, 1988), pp. 156–157.

24. Doris MacKenzie, Angela Gover, Gaylene Armstrong, and Ojmarrh Mitchell, *A National Study Comparing the Environments of Boot Camps with Traditional Facilities for Juvenile Offenders* (Washington, DC: National Institute of Justice, 2001).

25. Office of Justice Programs, *Correctional Boot Camps: Lessons from a Decade of Research* (Washington, DC: U.S. Department of Justice, 2003).

26. Roberta Cronin, *Boot Camps for Adult and Juvenile Offenders: Overview and Update* (Washington, DC: National Institute of Justice, 1994), p. 36.

27. Michael Peters, David Thomas, Christopher Zamberlan, and Caliber Associates, *Boot Camps for Juvenile Offenders: Program Summary* (Washington, DC: Office of Juvenile Justice and Delinquency Prevention, 1997), p. 25.

28. Jerry Tyler, Ray Darville, and Kathi Stalnaker, "Juvenile Boot Camps: A Descriptive Analysis of Program Diversity and Effectiveness," *The Social Science Journal* 38:445–460 (2001).

29. MacKenzie et al., note 24.

30. Michael Peters, David Thomas, and Christopher Zamerlan, *Boot Camps for Juvenile Offenders: Program Summary* (Washington, DC: Office of Juvenile Justice

and Delinquency Prevention, 1997); Jeane Stinchcomb and W. Clinton Terry, "Predicting the Likelihood of Re-arrest among Shock Incarceration Graduates: Moving beyond Another Nail in the Boot Camp Coffin," *Crime & Delinquency* 47:221–242 (2001); Cynthia Kempinen and Megan Kurlychek, "An Outcome Evaluation of Pennsylvania's Boot Camp: Does Rehabilitative Programming within a Disciplinary Setting Reduce Recidivism?" *Crime & Delinquency* 49:581–602 (2003).

31. MacKenzie et al., note 24.

32. Howard Snyder and Melissa Sickmund, *Juvenile Offenders and Victims: 2006 National Report* (Washington, DC: National Center for Juvenile Justice, 2006), p. 237.

33. Snyder and Sickmund, note 32, p. 201.

34. Snyder and Sickmund, note 32, p. 198.

35. Arizona Department of Corrections, *Annual Report,* Phoenix, 2003; New Hampshire Department of Corrections, *Annual Report,* Manchester, NH, 2003; Minnesota Department of Corrections, Juvenile Community Services, online at: http://www.doc.state.mn.us/aboutdoc/supportservices/juvenile, accessed May 4, 2007; Texas Youth Commission, Juvenile Corrections System in Texas, online at: http://www.tyc.state.tx.us/about/overview.html, accessed May 4, 2007.

36. Federal Bureau of Investigation, *Crime in the United States, 2005,* Table 43 (Washington, DC: U.S. Department of Justice, 2006).

37. Snyder and Sickmund, note 32, p. 175.

38. Shay Bilchik, *Minorities in the Juvenile Justice System* (Washington, DC: Office of Juvenile Justice and Delinquency Prevention, 1999).

39. See, for example, Alfred Blumstein, "On the Racial Disproportionality of United States' Prison Populations," *Journal of Criminal Law and Criminology* 73:1259–1268 (1982); Patrick Langan, "Racism on Trial: New Evidence to Explain the Racial Composition of Prisons in the United States," *Journal of Criminal Law and Criminology* 76:666–683 (1985); Merry Morash, "Establishment of a Juvenile Record," *Criminology* 22:97–111 (1984); Paul Tracy, *Decision Making and Juvenile Justice: An Analysis of Bias in Case Processing* (Westport, CT: Praeger, 2002).

40. Carl Pope and Howard Snyder, *Race as a Factor in Juvenile Arrests* (Washington, DC: Office of Juvenile Justice and Delinquency Prevention, 2002).

41. See, for example, James Austin, "The Overrepresentation of Minority Youths in the California Juvenile Justice System," pages 153–178 in Kimberly Leonard, Carl Pope, and William Feyerherm (eds.), *Minorities in Juvenile Justice* (Thousand Oaks, CA: Sage, 1995); Barry Feld, *Bad Kids: Race and the Transformation of the Juvenile Court* (New York: Oxford, 1999).

42. David Hawkins, "The Nations Within: Race, Class, Region, and American Lethal Violence," *Colorado Law Review* 69:905–926 (1998).

43. George Bridges, Darlene Conley, Rodney Engen, and Townsand Price-Spratlen, "Racial Disparities in the Confinement of Juveniles: Effects of Crime and Community Social Structure on Punishment," pages 128–152 in Leonard et al., note 41; Eleanor Hoytt, Vincent Schiraldi,

Brenda Smith, and Jason Ziedenberg, *Reducing Racial Disparities in Juvenile Detention* (Baltimore: The Annie E. Casey Foundation, 2002).

44. Joan McCord, Cathy Widom, and Nancy Crowell, eds., *Juvenile Crime Juvenile Justice: Panel on Juvenile Crime: Prevention, Treatment, and Control* (Washington, DC: National Academy Press, 2001), p. 257.

45. Heidi Hsia and Donna Hamparian, *Disproportionate Minority Confinement: 1997 Update* (Washington, DC: Office of Juvenile Justice and Delinquency Prevention, 1998).

46. Michael Leiber, "Disproportionate Minority Confinement (DMC) of Youth: An Analysis of State and Federal Efforts to Address the Issue," *Crime & Delinquency* 48:3–45 (2002).

47. Joseph Moone, *Juveniles in Private Facilities, 1991–1995* (Washington, DC: Office of Juvenile Justice and Delinquency Prevention, 1997).

48. *Juvenile Justice and Delinquency Prevention Act of 2002,* 42 U.S.C. 5601 (2002).

49. Maggie Hughey, "Holding a Child in Contempt," *Duke Law Journal* 46:353–429 (1996).

50. Suzanne Hopf, "Detaining Status Offenders in Excess of Ten Days: A Practice that Violates Statutory Limits and Which is Contrary to the Department of Juvenile Justice Recommendations," *The Advocate* (March 2000), online at: http://e-archives.ky.gov/pubs/public_adv/mar00/status.html, accessed May 4, 2007.

51. Barbara Brenzel, *Daughters of the State* (Cambridge, MA: MIT Press, 1983).

52. Coramae Richey Mann, *Female Crime and Delinquency* (Tuscaloosa: University of Alabama Press, 1984).

53. Catherine Milton, *Female Offenders* (Washington, DC: U.S. Government Printing Office, 1976).

54. Snyder and Sickmund, note 32, p. 209.

55. John MacDonald and Meda Chesney-Lind, "Gender Bias and Juvenile Justice Revisited: A Multiyear Analysis," *Crime & Delinquency* 47:187 (2001).

56. MacDonald and Chesney-Lind, note 55, p. 188.

57. Donald Cressey, "Limitations on Organization of Treatment in the Modern Prison," pages 78–110 in George Grosser (ed.), *Theoretical Studies in Social Organization of the Prison* (New York: Social Science Research Council, 1960); Bernard Berk, "Organizational Goals and Inmate Organization," *American Journal of Sociology* 71:522–534 (1966); Rosemary Sarri and Robert Vinter, "Group Treatment Strategies in Juvenile Correctional Institutions," *Crime & Delinquency* 11:326–340 (1965); Mayer Zald, "Organizational Control Structures in Five Correctional Communities," *American Journal of Sociology* 68:335–345 (1962).

58. Berk, note 57.

59. Barry Feld, *Neutralizing Inmate Violence* (Cambridge, MA: Ballinger, 1977).

60. Tory Caeti, Craig Hemmens, Francis Cullen, and Velmer Burton, "Management of Juvenile Correctional Facilities," *The Prison Journal* 83:383–404 (2003).

61. Clemens Bartollas, *Juvenile Victimization* (New York: Halsted Press, 1976).

62. Eric Poole and Robert Regoli, "Violence in Juvenile Institutions," *Criminology* 21:213–232 (1983).

63. Human Rights Watch, *Children in Confinement in Louisiana* (New York: Human Rights Watch, 1995).

64. *State v. Werner,* 242 S.E.2d 907 (W. Va. 1978).

65. Terry Frieden, "Feds Sue Mississippi over Juvenile Facilities," online at: CNN.com, http://www.cnn.com/2003/LAW/12/18/miss.juvenile.abuse/index.html, accessed December 18, 2003.

66. Barbara Carter, "Reform School Families," pages 419–431 in Lee Bowker (ed.), *Women and Crime in America* (New York: Macmillan, 1973).

67. Carter, note 66; Rose Giallombardo, *The Social World of Imprisoned Girls* (New York: John Wiley & Sons, 1974).

68. Mann, note 52, pp. 188–189.

69. Neal Shover and Werner Einstadter, *Analyzing American Corrections* (Belmont, CA: Wadsworth, 1988).

70. Steven Pliszka, James Sherman, M. Virginia Barrow, and Shiela Irick, "Affective Disorder in Juvenile Offenders: A Preliminary Study," *American Journal of Psychiatry* 157:130–132 (2000).

71. Kathleen Skowyra and Joseph Cocozza, *A Blueprint for Change: Improving the System Response to Youth with Mental Health Needs Involved with the Juvenile Justice System* (Delmar, NY: National Center for Mental Health and Juvenile Justice, 2006).

72. B. F. Skinner, *Beyond Freedom and Dignity* (New York: Knopf, 1971); Bruno Bettelheim, *The Empty Fortress* (New York: Free Press, 1967); William Glasser, *Reality Therapy* (New York: Harper & Row, 1965).

73. Gary Gottfredson, "Peer Group Interventions to Reduce the Risk of Delinquent Behavior: A Selective Review and a New Evaluation," *Criminology* 25:671–714 (1987); Ronald Feldman, "The St. Louis Experiment: Effective Treatment of Antisocial Youths in Prosocial Peer Groups," pages 233–252 in Joan McCord and Richard Tremblay (eds.), *Preventing Antisocial Behavior: Interventions from Birth through Adolescence* (New York: Guilford, 1992); Clifford O'Donnell, "The Interplay of Theory and Practice in Delinquency Prevention: From Behavior Modification to Activity Settings," pages 209–232 in Joan McCord and Richard Tremblay (eds.), *Preventing Antisocial Behavior: Interventions from Birth through Adolescence* (New York: Guilford, 1992).

74. James Howell, *Preventing and Reducing Juvenile Delinquency: A Comprehensive Framework* (Thousand Oaks, CA: Sage, 2003), p. 138.

75. Thomas Dishion, Joan McCord, and Francois Poulin, "When Interventions Harm: Peer Groups and Problem Behavior," *American Psychologist* 54:755–764 (1999).

76. McCord et al., note 44.

77. The National Center on Education, Disability and Juvenile Justice, Juvenile Correctional Education Programs, online at: http://www.edjj.org/education.html, accessed May 4, 2007.

78. Dale Parent, Valerie Leiter, Stephen Kennedy, Lisa Livens, Danile Wentworth, and Sarah Wilcox, *Conditions of Confinement: Juvenile Detention and Corrections Facilities, Research Summary* (Washington, DC: U.S. Department of Justice, 1994).

79. Pamela Casey and Ingo Keilitz, "Estimating the Prevalence of Learning Disable and Mentally Retarded Juvenile Offenders: A Meta-Analysis," pages 82–101 in Peter

Leon (ed.) *Understanding Troubled and Troubling Youth* (Newbury Park, CA: Sage, 1990).

80. Brenda Robertson, "Leisure Education as a Rehabilitative Tool for Youth in Incarceration Settings," *Journal of Leisurability* 27:27–34 (2000).

81. Parent et al., note 78.

82. Jack Kresnak, "Juvenile Treatment Improves: Wayne County Helps More, for Less per Teen," *Detroit Free Press,* August 13, 2002:A3.

83. Aldis Putniņš, "Correlates and Predictors of Self-Reported Suicide Attempts Among Incarcerated Youths," *International Journal of Offender Therapy and Comparative Criminology* 49:143–157 (2005).

84. Lindsay Hayes, "Suicide Prevention in Juvenile Facilities," *Juvenile Justice* 7:24–32 (2000).

85. Joseph Penn, Christianne Esposito, L. A. R. Stein, Molly Lacher-Katz, and Anthony Spirito, "Juvenile Correctional Workers' Perceptions of Suicide Risk Factors and Mental Health Issues of Incarcerated Juveniles," *Journal of Correctional Health Care* 11:333–346 (2005).

86. Parent et al., note 78.

87. Rebecca Widom and Theodore Hammett, *HIV/AIDS and STDs in Juvenile Facilities* (Washington, DC: National Institute of Justice, 1996).

88. Linda Teplin, Amy Mericle, Gary McClelland, and Karen Abram, "HIV and AIDS Risk Behaviors in Juvenile Detainees: Implications for Public Health Policy," *American Journal of Mental Health* 93:906–912 (2003).

89. Linda Teplin, Katherine Elkington, Gary McCelland, Karen Abram, Amy Mericle, and Jason Washburn, "Major Mental Disorders, Substance Use Disorders, Comorbidity, and HIV-AIDS Risk Behaviors in Juvenile Detainees," *Psychiatric Services* 56:823–828 (2005).

90. Polly Cromwell, William Risser, and Jan Risser, "Prevalence and Incidence of Pelvic Inflammatory Disease in Incarcerated Adolescents," *Sexually Transmitted Diseases* 29:397–398 (2002); Karen Murray, Laura Richardson, Chihiro Morishima, James Owens, and David Gretch, "Prevalence of Hepatitis C Virus Infection and Risk Factors in an Incarcerated Juvenile Population: A Pilot Study," *Pediatrics* 111:153–157 (2003): Centers for Disease Control, "High Prevalence of Chlamydial and Gonococcal Infection in Women Entering Jails and Juvenile Detention Centers—Chicago, Birmingham, and San Francisco, 1998," *MMWR Weekly* 48:793–796 (1999).

91. Paige Harrison and Allen Beck, *Prison and Jail Inmates at Midyear 2005* (Washington, DC: U.S. Department of Justice, 2006); Snyder and Sickmund, note 32, p. 238.

92. James Austin, *Juveniles in Adult Prisons and Jails* (Washington, DC: Bureau of Justice Assistance, 2000), p. 43.

93. Melissa Sickmund, *Juveniles in Corrections* (Washington, DC: Office of Juvenile Justice and Delinquency Prevention, 2004), pp. 20–21.

94. Kimberly Burke, "All Grown Up: Juveniles Incarcerated in Adult Facilities," *Journal of Juvenile Law* 25:69–78 (2005).

95. Building Blocks for Youth, Children in Adult Jails, online at: http://www.buildingblocksforyouth.org/issues/adult-jails/factsheet.html, accessed May 4, 2007.

96. Martin Forst, Jeffrey Fagan, and T. Scott Vivona, "Youth in Prisons and Training Schools: Perceptions and Consequences of the Treatment-Custody Dichotomy," *Juvenile and Family Court Journal* 40:1–14 (1989).

97. Frederick Hussey, "Perspectives on Parole Decision-Making with Juveniles," *Criminology* 13:449–469 (1976).

98. Patrick Griffin, *Juvenile Court-Controlled Reentry: Three Practice Models* (Pittsburgh: National Center for Juvenile Justice, 2005).

99. Howard Snyder, "An Empirical Portrait of the Youth Reentry Population," *Youth Violence and Juvenile Justice* 2:39–55 (2004); Mercer Sullivan, "Youth Perspectives on the Experience of Reentry," *Youth Violence and Juvenile Justice* 2:56–71 (2004); Snyder and Sickmund, note 32, p. 233.

100. Richard Mendal, *Less Hype More Help: Reducing Juvenile Crime: What Works—and What Doesn't* (Washington, DC: American Youth Policy Forum, 2000), p. 57.

101. Lynn Goodstein and Henry Sontheimer, "The Implementation of an Intensive Aftercare Program for Serious Juvenile Offenders," *Criminal Justice and Behavior* 24:332–359 (1997).

102. Michele Byrnes, Daniel Macallair, and Andrea Shorter, *Aftercare as Afterthought: Reentry and the California Youth Authority* (San Francisco: Center on Juvenile and Criminal Justice, 2002).

103. Jorge Rodiguez-Labarca and John O'Connell, *Delaware Juvenile Recidivism: 1994–2004* (Dover, DE: State of Delaware, 2005).

104. Kathleen Heide, Erin Spencer, Andrea Thompson, and Eldra Solomon, "Who's In, Who's Out, and Who's Back: Follow-up Data on 59 Juveniles Incarcerated in Adult Prison for Murder or Attempted Murder in the Early 1080s," *Behavioral Sciences and the Law* 19:97–108 (2001).

105. Lucille Eber, George Sugai, Carl Smith, and Terrance Scott, "Wraparound and Positive Behavioral Interventions and Supports in the Schools," *Journal of Emotional and Behavioral Disorders* 10:171–186 (2002); John Franz, "'No More Clarences': Creating a Consistent and Functional Multisystem Resource for Children with Complex Needs and Their Families," *Journal of Disability Studies* 13:244–253 (2003); Jeffrey Anderson and Wanda Mohr, "A Developmental Ecological Perspective in Systems Care for Children with Emotional Disturbances and Their Families," *Education and Treatment of Children* 26:52–74 (2003).

106. Michale Pullmann, Jodi Kerbs, Nancy Koroloff, Ernie Veach-White, Rita Gaylor, and DeDe Sieler, "Juvenile Offenders with Mental Health Needs: Reducing Recidivism Using Wraparound," *Crime & Delinquency* 52:375–397 (2006).

107. Leonard Bickman, Catherine Smith, E. Warren Lambert, and Ana Andrade, "Evaluation of a Congressionally Mandated Wraparound Demonstration," *Journal of Child and Family Studies* 12:135–156 (2003); Michelle Carney and Frederick Buttell, "Reducing Juvenile Recidivism: Evaluating the Wraparound Services Model," *Research on Social Work Practice* 13:551–568 (2003); Pullman et al., note 106.

108. Victor Streib, "The Juvenile Death Penalty Today: Death Sentences and Executions for Juvenile Crimes," January 1, 1973–March 15, 2004," online at: http://law.onu.edu/faculty/streib, accessed June 1, 2004.

109. *Eddings v. Oklahoma,* 455 U.S. 104 (1982).
110. *Eddings v. State,* OK CR 79, 688 P.2d 342 (1984).
111. *Thompson v. Oklahoma,* 487 U.S. 815 (1988).
112. Streib, note 108.
113. Kenneth Gewerth and Clifford Dorne, "Imposing the Death Penalty on Juvenile Murderers," *Judicature* 75:11 (1991).
114. *Stanford v. Kentucky; Wilkins v. Missouri,* 492 U.S. 361 (1989).
115. *Stanford,* note 114.
116. *In re Kevin Nigel Stanford,* 537 U.S. 968 (2002).
117. *Atkins v. Virginia,* 536 U.S. 304 (2002).
118. *Atkins,* note 117.
119. *Atkins,* note 117.
120. Melissa Moon, John Paul Wright, Francis Cullen, and Jennifer Pealer, "Putting Kids to Death: Specifying Public Support for Juvenile Capital Punishment," *Justice Quarterly* 17:663–684 (2000); John Cochran, Denise Boots, and Kathleen Heide, "Attribution Styles and Attitudes toward Capital Punishment for Juveniles, the Mentally Incompetent, and the Mentally Retarded," *Justice Quarterly* 20:65–93 (2003); Stacy Mallicoat and Michael Radelet, "The Growing Significance of Public Opinion for Death Penalty Jurisprudence," *Journal of Crime and Justice* 27:119–130 (2004); *The Gallup Poll,* February 2006; *The Pew Forum on Religion and Public Life Survey,* August 3, 2005; *Angus Reid Global Scan: Polls & Research,* March 27, 2006; *CBS News Poll,* April 17, 2005.
121. *Roper v. Simmons,* 543 U.S. 551 (2005).
122. *Simmons v. Roper,* 112 S.W.3d 397 (Mo. 2003).
123. *Roper,* note 121.
124. "The Death Penalty Gives Up on Juvenile Offenders," *Amnesty International* (2006), online at: http://www.amnestyusa.org/abolish/juveniles.html, accessed May 4, 2007.

Italic page numbers refer to figures and tables.

Italic page numbers indicate material in tables or figures.